POWER AND RESISTANCE

POWER AND RESISTANCE

CRITICAL THINKING ABOUT CANADIAN SOCIAL ISSUES

Fifth Edition

edited by

LES SAMUELSON
WAYNE ANTONY

Fernwood Publishing • Halifax • Winnipeg

Editing: Eileen Young
Text design: Brenda Conroy
Cover design: John van der Woude
Printed and bound in Canada by Hignell Book Printing

Published in Canada by Fernwood Publishing
32 Oceanvista Lane, Black Point, Nova Scotia, B0J 1B0
and 748 Broadway Avenue, Winnipeg, Manitoba, R3G 0X3
www.fernwoodpublishing.ca

Fernwood Publishing Company Limited gratefully acknowledges the financial support of the Government of Canada
through the Canada Book Fund and the Canada Council for the Arts, the Nova Scotia Department of Communities,
Culture and Heritage, the Manitoba Department of Culture, Heritage and Tourism under the Manitoba Publishers
Marketing Assistance Program and the Province of Manitoba, through the Book Publishing Tax Credit,
for our publishing program.

Library and Archives Canada Cataloguing in Publication

Power and resistance: critical thinking about Canadian social issues /
Wayne Antony and Les Samuelson. -- 5th ed.

Includes bibliographical references and index.
ISBN 978-1-55266-483-4 (bound).--ISBN 978-1-55266-474-2 (pbk.)

1. Social problems--Canada. 2. Canada--Social conditions.
I. Antony, Wayne Andrew, 1950- II. Samuelson, Leslie, 1953-
III. Title.

HN103.5.P68 2012   305.0971   C2011-908426-0

Contents

Contents

ONLINE CASE STUDIES—ON TES (TEXT ENRICHMENT SITE)

Note: The following Case Studies can be found on the Text Enrichment Site that accompanies this text at **www.pearsoncanada.ca/fleras**.

Preface

Canada is a society of paradox. Paradoxes prevail in a Canada that is rapidly changing and increasingly diverse, yet seemingly gridlocked into preferences and perceptions from the past without a definitive blueprint for the future. Such an assessment is particularly relevant when applied to the politics of race, ethnic, and Aboriginal relations. Despite Canada's status as a rich and fertile ground for living together with differences, the challenges of a cooperative coexistence are proving more complex and contradictory than many had imagined. Every enlightened move forward is matched by a corresponding slip backward, with the result that engaging differences and diversity politics transcend the simplistic categories of "good" or "bad" but hover uneasily in between these oppositional poles.

Any introduction to the dynamics of race, ethnic, and Aboriginal relations must incorporate the inescapable: the politics of paradox. On one side, Canada remains a remarkably open society with a commitment to justice, inclusiveness, and tolerance that is widely admired and occasionally copied (Adams, 2007). No mean feat, of course, since no other country in the world must cope with such a dazzling array of conflicting demands, thanks to Canada's deeply divided and multilayered pluralism, including Aboriginal peoples, national-minorities, and racialized groups (Kymlicka, 2007). But rather than this ethnic tinderbox leading to an implosion from within, Canada's commitment to an inclusive multiculturalism is reaping society-building dividends. It may be a bit of a stretch to equate Canada's Multiculturalism with one of history's revolutionary ideals for organizing society (namely, the American, French, and Russian revolutions [Sandercock, 2006]). Nevertheless, Canada's success in integrating immigrants is virtually unparalleled by international standards, while Multiculturalism is seen as instrumental in facilitating successful newcomer outcomes (Kymlicka, 2010).

On the other side, however, racial politics and ethnic confrontations continue to perplex or provoke (Johnson & Enomoto, 2007). The prospect of an uncontested coexistence is compromised by the proliferation of faith-based communities and the politicization of ethno-cultural identity politics. Aboriginal peoples confront conditions that, frankly, are an embarrassment to Canada's lofty reputation as a beacon of enlightenment (see Long & Dickason, 2011). So-called visible (racialized) minorities continue to find themselves on the receiving end of discriminatory treatment, despite assurances and accommodations to the contrary (McDougall, 2009). Even the widely praised hallmarks of immigration and Multiculturalism have drawn criticism as "too much" or "not enough" (Grubel, 2009). Not surprisingly, paradoxes flourish precisely because of a growing reality gap, namely, government promises versus peoples' lived realities on one side; the way Canadians want to see themselves versus how others see them on the other side—as the following contradictions demonstrate:

- That race once mattered is beyond dispute. That race continues to matter at a time when most Canadians think it shouldn't or couldn't is proving a point of contention and confusion (Wallis & Fleras, 2008).

- Racism is widely perceived as a major problem in Canada. To the dismay of many, its existence has proven much more pervasive and tenacious than predicted, especially with the emergence of new and virulent forms of multiracisms that are increasingly difficult to detect or eradicate (Agnew, 2007; Bishop, 2005; Hier & Bolaria, 2007). And yet, paradoxically, few condone racism; even fewer Canadians admit to being a racist (Henry & Tator, 2010).

- References to ethnicity increasingly revolve around the dynamics of competition and conflicts rather than cuddly attachments for display in festivals and food courts. Moreover, as ethnic identities and differences deepen and become increasingly politicized, debates are mounting over ways of making Canada safe from ethnicity, yet safe for ethnicity.

- No amount of multicultural gloss can mask the obvious: Minority women and men continue to experience inequities in power, income, and privilege (Block, 2010; Galabuzi, 2006; Pendakur & Pendakur, 2010; Teelucksingh & Galabuzi, 2005). A growing legion of foreign-trained professionals who are driving taxis or delivering pizzas confirms the obvious: Canada is grossly mishandling its immigration "advantage" by transforming a potential "brain gain" into a "brain drain."

- Multiple narratives define the Aboriginal experience in Canada (Long & Dickason 2011). One situates Aboriginal peoples at the forefront of national political developments, including a right to confer with first ministers at constitutional talks (Belanger, 2008 Frideres, 2011). Another acknowledges how poverty and disempowerment of Aboriginal communities remain Canada's foremost human rights concern (Frideres & Gadacz, 2008). Still another points to a growing militancy among Aboriginal activists impatient with the snail-like progress over specific and comprehensive claim settlements. Another confirms an intermediate position: Many Aboriginal peoples live seemingly normal lives involving an interplay of success and disappointments, optimism and dismay, happiness and fear (Fleras, 2010b).

- The politics of Québécois nationalism are a constant reminder that Canada should never be taken for granted. Yes, Canada may be one of the world's oldest federal systems. Yet Canadian society is also politically fragile because of the French and English divide that it perpetually hovers on the brink of unravelling (Gagnon & Iacovino, 2007).

- Constitutional guarantees for gender equality are commendable, but minority women (including Aboriginal women, women of colour, and immigrant/refugee women) continue to experience concurrent patterns of exclusion and discrimination because of the way in which gender intersects with race, ethnicity, and class to amplify patterns of exploitation or exclusion (McMullin, 2010; Zawilski, 2010).

- Many regard Canada's immigration policy and programs as one of the world's more progressive models (Simmons, 2010). Yet the system is increasingly criticized as "broken" and in need of a major overhaul (Bissett, 2008; Hawthorne, 2008; Moens & Collacott, 2008). The emergence of new patterns of immigration ("transnationalism") and immigrants ("professional transients") puts pressure on us to address those issues that Canadians seem reluctant to debate. Of particular note is the challenge of devising a refugee determination process capable of fast-tracking those in need of Canada's protection while staunching the flow of those who manipulate the system for expedited entry.

- Canada may be the world's first and only robust example of official Multiculturalism; Nevertheless, Multiculturalism remains one of the more politically charged battlegrounds of our era, as demonstrated by debates over the politics of reasonable accommodation, especially of religious differences and faith-based communities (Fleras, 2009b; Stein et al., 2007). Concern is growing that in a globalizing age of transmigration and diaspora, the relevance of multiculturalism as a governance model is in doubt, when immigrant identities and belonging are no longer tied to place (Fleras, 2011c).

- A commitment to institutional inclusivity is widely proclaimed and actively pursued. But difficulties undercut this commitment to accommodate by way of workplaces that reflect, represent, and respond to difference, while providing services that are available, accessible, and appropriate. Particularly worrying are institutional structures and mindsets that remain unmistakably "pale male" in composition, process, and outcomes (Jiwani, 2006; Kobayashi, 2005).

- Canada's Difference Model is attracting attention as a principled blueprint for living together with differences. At the core of this model is the principle of differential accommodation, namely, accommodating different ways of accommodating diversity and difference (Fleras, 2009b; Jensen & Papillon, 2001). That these principles do not always match practice is the catalyst that drives the politics of race, ethnic, and Aboriginal relations.

- Debates over differences continue to question and contest. How much and what kind of differences can be tolerated before society explodes? Conversely, how much unity must be imposed before society implodes from within? Should differences because of race or ethnicity or aboriginality be ignored or incorporated in defining who gets what (Calder & Ceva, 2011)? Properly managed, a commitment to difference and diversity may enhance creativity and connections. Without an overarching vision, however, the clash of differences can undermine a commitment to community, cohesion, and identity—at least in the short run (see Putnam, 2007).

The evidence seems inescapable: Canada is, indeed, a paradox. The very dynamic that captures Canada's strength and pride—its management of diversities—may also prove its weakness. In theory, the health of Canada's race, ethnic, and Aboriginal relations should be getting better (whatever that might mean); in reality, it is not (however difficult that might be to measure). Instead of answers, Canadians are swamped with more questions. Rather than certainty and resolution, confusion prevails. Canadians express dismay over the proliferation of Aboriginal protests and occupations, legal challenges to the status quo, and the continued existence of a marginalized population. English-speaking Canadians are perplexed by Quebec's seemingly insatiable demands for special status, while the Québécois are equally puzzled by Anglo intransigence over letting go. No less confusing are the increasingly politicized challenges posed by multi-cultural minorities who want respect for their cultures (recognition) without sacrificing equality (redistribution). Despite the importance of these questions, nobody can claim to have all the answers. That shouldn't be a problem; after all, too much reliance on answers assumes a discoverable objective reality that unlocks its "truth" to the privileged observer. But in a mind-dependent world that denies the existence of objective truth except as discourses within contexts of power, the asking of questions may be just as important as the reassurances of answers.

To be sure, Canadians have become adept at "talking the walk" about race, ethnic, and Aboriginal relations. Canada's diversity landscape is peppered with sometimes sanctimonious bromides about "tolerance," "inclusion," or "celebrating." By clarifying and rethinking perennial debates in this field, *Unequal Relations* hopes to avoid the perils of sloppy reasoning, mindless clichés, lazy oversimplifications, and common-sense assumptions at odds with hard-hitting analysis. But because of costs or inconvenience, many Canadians are less enthralled with "walking the talk"—of putting principles into practice. Keywords from "inclusivity" to "racism" are stretched to mean everything yet nothing, without much concern for precision and clarity (Kymlicka, 2001). Concepts and theories intended to enlighten and clarify are ideologically loaded to the point of ambiguity and misuse, while the persistence of outdated frameworks bears mute testimony to an intellectual inertia best described as "paralysis by analysis." The prospects of navigating such a conceptual minefield are daunting as people end up "talking past each other," and this edition of *Unequal Relations* hopes to ground these free-floating concepts in ways that inform rather than inflame, enlighten rather than confuse, and empower rather than disengage.

The seventh edition of *Unequal Relations* is designed to confront these lacunae in our knowledge and analysis. It provides a sociologically informed introduction to the politics of race, ethnic, and Aboriginal relations as fundamentally unequal relations within a dynamic Canada that is both rapidly changing and increasingly diverse, yet more uncertain and confused. The book focuses on three dimensions of this dynamic: *constructed*, *contested*, and *community*.

1. A focus on the *constructed dimensions* reveals that race, ethnic, and Aboriginal relations neither originate in a social vacuum nor unfold outside a wider context. Nor is there anything natural or inevitable about the dynamics of intergroup relations in society. Rather, they constitute socially constructed relationships of inequality within contexts of power, privilege, and property relations. That makes it doubly important to deconstruct the processes by which these fundamentally unequal relations are created, expressed, and maintained, as well as challenged and transformed by way of minority protest, government policy, and institutional reform.

2. A focus on the *contested dimensions* envisages Canada as a conflicted site of competitively different groups in a competition for scarce resources. Attention is drawn to the competitive struggles of the three major ethnicities (Aboriginal peoples, French and English "charter" groups, and multicultural minorities) as they jockey to define priorities, secure interests, and impose agendas. The centrality of power is shown to be critical in driving the dynamics of diversity and the politics of difference. Certain groups dominate, not because of genetic superiority but because the

powerful can invariably define and control. Subdominant groups are subordinate, not because of racial inferiority but because they lack institutionalized power.

3. A focus on the *community dimension* addresses the challenges of constructing commitment, cohesion, and consensus across a multilayered and deeply divided Canada. Instead of diversities being simply reduced to the level of predominantly ahistorical tiles in Canada's multicultural mosaic, they are framed instead within the context of doing what is workable, necessary and fair, in establishing a principled framework for living together with differences, while advancing an inclusive Canada that is safe *for* differences, yet safe *from* differences.

The content and organization of *Unequal Relations* subscribe to the adage of "continuity in change." The first edition of the book was published in 1992 with the aim of providing an accessible introduction to the dynamics of race, ethnic, and Aboriginal relations in Canada. Rather than looking at race, ethnicity, or aboriginality as exotic cultures within Canada's multicultural mosaic, the book was designed to synthesize existing theoretical knowledge with current information about the politics of diversity and difference in an increasingly diverse and changing Canada. And while much has changed in the interim of two decades since the initial publication, the book's animating logic remains unchanged: that is, the importance of analyzing race, ethnic, and Aboriginal relations as essentially unequal relations with respect to how patterns of power, privilege, and property (wealth and income) are played out. And as long as these predominantly unequal intergroup relations continue to prevail and provoke, the politics of race, ethnicity, and aboriginality will remain a lively dynamic and contested domain. .

Much is retained in this seventh edition, including the basic chapter outline, . the content in terms of concepts and applications to Canadian society, and the framing of race, ethnic, and Aboriginal relations as socially constructed and fundamentally unequal. The book remains organized around three sections: theory, application, and practice. A certain logic underpins the rationale behind the sequence of topics: Concepts appear before application; theory before practice; abstractions before the concrete. Each section builds upon the other without necessarily precluding the possibility of alternative sequences. Every effort was made to smooth out the arguments, revise language, update the material, introduce new Case Studies, and keep the material fresh by synthesizing existing literature and sometimes obscure research that would otherwise be inaccessible to most readers. Finally, the core of the text remains as unwavering as ever; namely, to foster "diversity literacy." By diversity-proofing students in the same way that street-proofing provides navigational skills for negotiating the real world, the text encourages students to critically engage with the paradoxicality of diversity politics and the politics of difference—not by examining the issues and debates in the abstract, but by "painting oneself into the picture" (James 1998).

Of course, the seventh edition of this text is not without changes—as might be expected in a domain in which the mix of social patterns with conventional wisdom is rarely constant, often contested, and subject to changes. The usual amendments are in evidence, including revisions, updates, deletions, and additions where necessary. Additional tables and diagrams are introduced in hopes of facilitating the flow of information. Census data from 2006 with respect to racial, ethnic, and Aboriginal diversity in Canada are incorporated whenever possible. Many new Case Studies, Debate boxes, and Insight boxes have replaced those of earlier editions in the hope of keeping the material fresh and relevant to the lives of students. (Unlike previous editions, this supplementary material will be lodged online in a student-friendly website.) Newer concepts such as "racialization," "governance," "infrastructural racism," "transmigrants," and "reasonable accommodation" are incorporated, not because they are fashionable, but because they promote innovative ways of thinking. Newer material is incorporated as well, including a discussion of Canada's much acclaimed Difference Model in advancing the principles of "differential accommodation." Of particular note is the growing salience of religion and faith-based groups in challenging conventional notions for living together differently under a multicultural umbrella. Finally, Chapter 3, on racisms, has been expanded and revised to acknowledge the dynamics of a domain that never rests.

Despite its commitment to the theme of continuity-in-change, the book remains faithful to its core mission. *Unequal Relations* is neither a description of minority groups nor a catalogue of Canadian ethnic lifestyles as misleadingly conveyed by that quintessential of Canadian metaphors, "the multicultural mosaic." The book rarely provides a literary platform for minority "voices" or stories by minority authors, although there is much to gain from such an approach. To the extent that history is employed, it is history as it relates to the present not the past—about the "is" rather than the "was" (Walker, 2001b). Endorsed instead is the big picture, as might be expected of sociologically trained authorship. Priority is focused on a macro-sociological study of institutional dynamics, intergroup relations, and power politics rather than micro-models of individual behaviour, personal attitudes, or life experiences. References to diverse ethnocultural groups reflect a focus on relations—from accommodations to conflicts—within a context of inequality, thereby drawing attention to the centrality of power to complement that of identity and recognition (see also Winter, 2007, p. 491). Deconstructing the logic behind the politics of government policy, institutional reform, and minority resistance is evident throughout, yet the text tries to avoid regurgitating both blatant government propaganda, institutional spin, and ethnic posturing, without dismissing the rationale that propelled these dynamics in the first place.

The seventh edition of *Unequal Relations* comes at a critical juncture in Canadian history. Ours is the age of diversity and difference, not simply in the descriptive or celebratory sense, but because an increasingly politicized diversity is flexing its muscles in the competition for scarce resources. The boundaries of "being Canadian" are challenged by the deep differences and radical ethnicities of a society in the throes of transformative change. As a result, traditional images and conventional assumptions about Canada are no longer applicable. Such transformations do not come easily or without costs. Debates over difference and diversity—how much, what kind, who says so, and on what grounds—often pose a threat to people's sense of what it means to live in Canada or be a Canadian (see also Dion, 2005). After all, most of us have been taught to think of Canada as a kinder, gentler society of good and just people who disapprove of racism and racially based exploitation. Few, however, are equipped to grapple with the "myth-conceptions" of a Canada that conveniently cloaks a white supremacist history behind the soothing balm of "happy face" multiculturalism (Razack, 2004; Thobani, 2007; see also Leonardo, 2004). Fewer still are capable of seeing how the privileging of whiteness in defining who gets what contributes to the dis-privileging of Aboriginal peoples and the disempowering of racialized minorities.

The tone of this textbook is constructively critical, if only to counteract the prevailing discourses of race neutrality and colour-blindness. White-settler societies like Canada or Australia routinely rely on national mythologies (or narratives) to paper over ("whitewash") contradictions of origins and history (Razack, 2002). These self-serving narratives offer explanations that not only justify the colonial project but also rationalize its most destructive aspects, including the displacement and dispossession of Aboriginal peoples by European settlers and the subsequent importation of cheap migrant labour for Canada-building. Instead of "telling it like it is," namely, the colonization of Canada through conquest, expulsion, and exploitation of the inferiorized "other," Canada is portrayed as an empty land (*terra nullius* doctrine) that was peacefully settled in ways consistent with the rights of discovery, notions of Eurocentric progress, and the principles of Christian civilization. To the extent that these narratives focus on the innocence and heroism of Western settlement and white entitlement, they reflect a very one-sided view of what really happened (Schick, 2008). A commitment to unsettling these notions of Canada as privileged "white space" makes it doubly important to deconstruct the politics of power by incorporating the perspectives of those dispossessed and exploited.

To be sure, analyzing these highly politicized topics is neither for the timid nor the politically correct. The interplay of challenge with change invariably inflames passions by puncturing people's complacency over identity and self-esteem, core cultural values, the legitimacy of conventional authority, and taken-for-granted privileges. Nevertheless, a commitment to a critically informed analysis is crucial in adjusting to the realities of a post-9/11 world—with its warning to expect the unexpected, to think the unthinkable, and to cope with the uncontrollable. Moreover, it's not enough to simply understand the issues associated with the politics of diversity and difference, even when they are filtered through the prism (lens) of a diverse, changing, and unequal Canada. Emphasis must also focus on putting this knowledge into practice—either supporting and reinforcing a racialized status quo by doing nothing or, alternatively, of advancing a just and inclusive Canada through critically informed activism. To their credit, Canadians are slowly rising to the challenge of doing what is workable, necessary, and fair. Canada, in turn, is proving a pacesetter in balancing the concurrent demands and oppositional tensions of a multicultural governance that abides by the principles of multiculturalism. This *principled* approach for constructively governing race, ethnic, and Aboriginal relations not only elevates Canada to the forefront of countries in managing the diversity dividend but also secures the rationale for this and every new edition of *Unequal Relations*.

Pearson Canada would like to thank Fiona Angus of Grant MacEwan University and Nan McBlane of Thompson Rivers University for their feedback during the planning stages of this edition.

SUPPLEMENTS

Test Item File

This edition of *Unequal Relations* is accompanied by a Test Item File containing 25 multiple-choice questions, 15 fill-in-the-blank questions, and 1 essay question per chapter. The Test Item File is available for downloading from a password-protected section of Pearson Canada's online catalogue (**www.pearsoncanada.ca/highered**).

Navigate to your book's catalogue page to view a list of those supplements that are available. See your local sales representative for details and access.

Case Studies

Forty-seven Case Studies are also available with this edition of the text. They can be found at the Fleras Text Enrichment Site at **www.pearsoncanada.ca/fleras**. Featuring engaging subject matter such as the politics of the hijab, ethnicity and religion, genocide, and ethnic media, these supplementary Case Studies will challenge your students to apply the material they have learned in the text to contemporary issues of relevance to all Canadians.

CourseSmart for Instructors (ISBN 978-0-13-231080-2)

CourseSmart goes beyond traditional expectations—providing instant, online access to the textbooks and course materials you need at a lower cost for students. And even as students save money, you can save time and hassle with a digital eTextbook that allows you to search for the most relevant content at the very moment you need it. Whether it's evaluating textbooks or creating lecture notes to help students with difficult concepts, CourseSmart can make life a little easier. See how when you visit **www.coursesmart.com/instructors**.

CourseSmart for Students (ISBN 978-0-13-231080-2)

CourseSmart goes beyond traditional expectations—providing instant, online access to the textbooks and course materials you need at an average savings of 60 percent. With instant access from any computer and the ability to search your text, you'll find the content you need quickly, no matter where you are. And with online tools like highlighting and note-taking, you can save time and study efficiently. See all the benefits at **www.coursesmart.com/students**.

Technology Specialists

Pearson's Technology Specialists work with faculty and campus course designers to ensure that Pearson technology products, assessment tools, and online course materials are tailored to meet your specific needs. This highly qualified team is dedicated to helping schools take full advantage of a wide range of educational resources, by assisting in the integration of a variety of instructional materials and media formats. Your local Pearson Education sales representative can provide you with more details on this service program.

MySearchLab

MySearchLab offers extensive help to students with their writing and research project and provides round-the-clock access to credible and reliable source material.

Research Content on MySearchLab includes immediate access to thousands of full-text articles from leading Canadian and international academic journals, and daily news feeds from The Associated Press. Articles contain the full downloadable text—including abstract and citation information—and can be cut, pasted, emailed, or saved for later use.

Writing MySearchLab also includes a step-by-step tutorial on writing a research paper. Included are sections on planning a research assignment, finding a topic, creating effective notes, and finding source material. Our exclusive online handbook provides grammar and usage support. Pearson SourceCheck™ offers an easy way to detect accidental plagiarism issues, and our exclusive tutorials teach how to avoid them in the future. And MySearchLab also contains AutoCite, which helps to correctly cite sources using MLA, APA, CMS, and CBE documentation styles for both endnotes and bibliographies.

To order this book with MySearchLab access at no extra charge, use ISBN 978-0-13-282385-2.

Take a tour at **www.mysearchlab.com**.

Pearson Custom Library

For enrollments of at least 25 students, you can create your own textbook by choosing the chapters that best suit your own course needs. To begin building your custom text, visit **www.pearsoncustomlibrary.com**. You may also work with a dedicated Pearson Custom editor to create your ideal text—publishing your own original content or mixing and matching Pearson content. *Contact your local Pearson Representative to get started.*

The publisher would like to thank Fiona Angus, Grant MacEwan University, and Nan McBlanc, Thompson River University, for their feedback during the development of this textbook.

PART 1

Conceptualizing the Politics of Race, Ethnic, and Aboriginal Relations

It's been said that this "adventure" called Canada resembles an "enigma wrapped around a mystery inside a riddle." These seemingly mixed metaphors provide an intriguing twist to the turns in Canada's race, ethnic, and Aboriginal relations. Put bluntly, Canada has no business even existing, thanks to the implausibilities of its geography, history, and demographics. And yet it now stands as one of the world's oldest federal systems (alongside Switzerland and the United States). That assessment raises another question: How can a deeply divided and multilayered Canada continue to survive and flourish under conditions that would topple other societies? Answers vary, but all generally acknowledge a combination of good fortune and hard work with an astute management of diversity and difference. Its lofty status as a society-building success has elicited playful inversions about Canada as a "solution" in search of a "problem" (as a Mexican ambassador once aptly put it). Translation: Canada remains one of the world's best places to live—a society so blessed with physical resources and human resourcefulness that it must "invent" problems that less-advantaged countries might dismiss or ignore. That Canadians continue to dwell on the negative at the expense of the positive, even though they have much to be thankful for, may say more about being pampered than having problems.

The prospect of "living together with differences" remains a perplexing and provocative challenge. The world we inhabit is rapidly changing and sharply contested, with the result that confusion and uncertainty often prove the rule rather than the exception. Just as scholars have had to rethink those social moorings that conventionally secured

Canada, so too must Canadians grapple with a host of difference issues beyond their comprehension or control. Consider the following challenges:

1. Aboriginal peoples claim to be relatively autonomous political communities with collective and inherent rights to Aboriginal models of self-determining autonomy over land, identity, and political voice. Is it possible to construct a national governance framework to accommodate these **postcolonial** claims for a renewed relationship involving the principles of partnership, power sharing, and peoplehood (Belanger, 2008)? Or is such an arrangement likely to create a "Swiss cheese" Canada—so full of holes that there is nothing to keep it together?

2. National minorities like the Québécois are seeking to transform Canada's constitutional arrangements in hopes of constructing a new social compact based on the notion of Quebec as a nation rather than simply a province. The implications of this nationalism—with its projection of a multination society—underscore the challenges of forging unity from deep diversities.

3. Racialized minorities have become increasingly politicized in advancing a more inclusive Canada, one that is respectful of, reflective upon, and responsive to minority needs and demands. To the extent doubts remain over the quality of institutional responses to the inclusiveness challenge, the politics of reasonable accommodation are unlikely to subside.

The challenge of coping with each of these dynamics—and doing so in a principled way—poses a grave risk for Canadian society as we know it. But these challenges also represent a splendid opportunity for Canada-building along twenty-first-century lines. Part 1 of *Unequal Relations* addresses these challenges by providing a conceptual map for theorizing the politics of Canada's race, ethnic, and Aboriginal relations. Chapter 1 begins by exploring the concept of intergroup dynamics as they apply to race, ethnicity, and aboriginality. Chapter 2 addresses the politics of race in contemporary society. Chapter 3 is concerned with unmasking the many faces of racism in Canada. Chapter 4 examines ethnicity as a powerful force—both beneficial and costly—in Canadian society. Chapter 5 looks at social inequality as it affects racialized minorities. Chapter 6 focuses on the increasingly contested domain of gendered inequality as it applies to minority and migrant women. Together, these six chapters provide an introduction to key concepts and issues for understanding the complex and changing domain of race, ethnic, and Aboriginal relations.

CHAPTER 1

Race, Ethnic, and Aboriginal Relations: Patterns, Paradoxes, Perspectives

Framing Canada's Multiculturalism

To define Canada as multicultural is typically considered an understatement. References to **multiculturalism** in Canada range from the descriptive to the prescriptive, with the politics of policy in between. Canada's population is known to be multiculturally diverse; Canadians generally subscribe to the multicultural values of openness and tolerance; and both minority and political elites are known to play multicultural politics to advance vested interests (Lupul, 2005). Canada is also multicultural because of its commitment to an official Multiculturalism (note the use of an upper case "M" to denote official government policy; otherwise it is lower case). Entrenchment of Multiculturalism in the *Constitution Act* of 1982, followed by the passage of the world's first and only Multiculturalism Act in 1988, has further secured Canada's status as a trailblazer in multicultural governance (Fleras, 2009b).

Many support Multiculturalism as a principled approach for living together with **differences** (Adams 2007; Dasko, 2005; Fleras, 2002). Those familiar with the policy—and surveys suggest that the *majority* of Canadians are

unfamiliar with what Multiculturalism is doing—express pride in a home-grown initiative that many regard as Canada's foremost contribution to global harmony (Adams, 2007). Canada's official Multiculturalism is viewed as "quietly" revolutionary—comparable in stature to the animating ideals of the French, American, and Russian revolutions as a governance framework (Sandercock, 2006). Others are openly critical of its weaknesses or usefulness, and pounce on Multiculturalism as a good idea gone bad or, alternatively, a bad idea unfolding precisely to plan (Abu-Laban & Gabriel, 2002; Bannerji, 2000; Gregg, 2006; Mansur, 2010). Still others are unsure how to respond. Multiculturalism is "OK" in principle, but not if it (1) imposes inconveniences or costs, (2) makes excessive and illiberal demands, (3) unsettles Canada's social fabric, or (4) challenges core constitutional values. Yet others still acknowledge its paradoxical nature. On the one hand, Multiculturalism rarely means what it says or says what it means, with the result that it can mean everything—or nothing—depending on intentions

(Continued)

or context. On the other hand, Multiculturalism has a tendency to deny what it sets out to affirm—differences—while reinforcing what it hopes to eliminate—inequality—neither embracing differences for fear of disunity nor denying them because of political correctness (Kivisto & Ng, 2005).

Clearly, then, Canadians express a love–hate relationship with Multiculturalism. Those who embrace Multiculturalism as the solution to Canada's **diversity** challenges are themselves dismissive of those who dismiss it as more problem than solution. Conversely, those who denounce Multiculturalism as an evil incarnate are no less contemptuous of those who worship at its altar. In light of its paradoxical status, questions abound over the role of Multiculturalism in contributing to Canada-building. Is Multiculturalism a good thing or a bad thing for Canada? Hoax or help? Progress or regress? Benefit or cost? Living together or drifting apart? Responses to these questions are varied. Much depends on exploring the spaces that separate Multiculturalism from what it says it's doing with (1) what it intended to do, (2) what it's really doing, (3) what people think it's doing, (4) what the critics think it should be doing, and (5) what it realistically can do under the circumstances.

Different responses are possible because of the difficulties in formulating criteria for assessment. Consequently, any reference to the "good" or the "bad" may say more about the evaluator's agenda than anything about what is being evaluated or assessed. That is, any evaluation is contingent on the perceived role of Multiculturalism in advancing a particular vision of Canada as modern or postnational (see Chapter 12). Nor can debates over its "goodness" or "badness" be divorced from the central theme of this text: In that Canada's race, ethnic, and Aboriginal relations can be framed as unequal relations, what is the role of an official Multiculturalism in creating and sustaining patterns of inequality as well as challenging and changing them? The Debate Revisited box at the end of this chapter will explore how applying sociological models of society to Multiculturalism can provide principled responses to this complex question.

INTRODUCTION: THE GOOD, THE BAD, AND THE IN-BETWEEN

Canada is globally admired for its resources and resilience in securing a true north strong and free. Overseas observers are no less astonished by Canada's resourcefulness in weaving a remarkably cohesive society from the strands of diversity (Adams, 2007). How do Canadians manage to keep a lid on those ethnic tensions that have fractured other societies into warring factions? Why does the commitment to Multiculturalism persist in Canada, whereas it's experiencing a backlash in European countries and even Australia? Is there a principled rationale to account for the relatively smooth transformation of once-stodgy provincial capitals like Toronto and Vancouver into cosmopolitan complexes (Ibbitson, 2005b)? What is the secret behind Canada's ability to balance the often-competing demands of Aboriginal peoples with those of the Québécois and racialized minorities without experiencing paralyzing strife? To be sure, the potential for unravelling Canada's social fabric along ethnic lines is always present. But while other countries are groping for solutions to accommodate difference, Canada is embarking on a promising if unprecedented quest for cooperative coexistence along principled lines (Kymlicka, 2007). Or to put a slightly different spin to it, Canada constitutes a multicultural role model in the art of living together with differences equitably and in dignity (Fleras, 2009a).

How does this assessment stand up to scrutiny? Any response must begin with a sense of perspective. *First,* compared with its historical past, Canada's engagement with race, ethnicity, and aboriginality is showing signs of maturity. There is no shortage of cringe-inducing episodes and patterns that once scarred Canada's historical past. Canada originated in the dispossession of Aboriginal peoples and their lands, leaving behind a legacy that continues to diminish and demean. Canada-building was predicated on policies, programs, and practices that routinely exploited racialized minorities such as Chinese and East Indian immigrants (Li, 2003); the internment and dispossession of Japanese-Canadians during World War II (Kogawa, 1994); the enslavement of blacks and their segregation from mainstream institutions until the 1950s (Backhouse 1999; Walker, 1997); and the pervasive anti-Semitism of the 1920s and 1930s, which culminated in the rejection of Jewish emigrants from Nazi Germany (Penslar, 2005). The extent to which this exclusion went beyond the perversions of a few misguided bigots and pervaded both societal structures and government policies says a lot about the politics of power (Wallis & Fleras, 2008).

Times appear to have changed. Evidence of Canada's historical advancement can be gleaned from a list of global firsts in the diversity sweepstakes. Canada's ***Citizenship Act*** of 1947 ignored the distinction between **immigrants** and native-born persons as a basis for citizenship. The *Immigration Act* of 1967 was one of the first pieces of legislation to abolish all quotas or preferences on the basis of race or ethnicity, with the result that Canada's colour-blind immigration policies may well prove to be this country's proudest achievement (Ibbitson, 2005a). Canada is the only country in the world to have received the United Nations–sponsored Nansen Medal (awarded in 1986) for its humanitarian response to the global refugee problem. And with the provision of section 35 of the 1982 *Constitution Act*, Canada became the world's first and only country to constitutionally enshrine Aboriginal and treaty rights. Similarly, passage of the *Canadian Multiculturalism Act* in 1988 solidified Canada's status as the world's first country to institutionalize an official Multiculturalism as a principled framework for engaging difference. Its glowing reputation is further secured by Canada's consistent high placement in quality-of-life surveys—including its ranking for eight consecutive years (between 1993 and 2000) as the world's best place to live, according to a human development index.

Second, consider global comparisons. Compared with other societies that routinely violate **human rights**, with abuses ranging from ethnic cleansing and mass expulsion to forced exploitation and coercive assimilation, Canada possesses an enviable reputation as a paragon of virtue, tolerance, and compassion. Escalating numbers of mixed union couples from different ethnic and racialized backgrounds, including a 33 percent spurt between 2001 and 2006, attest to this openness (Agrell, 2010). Canada's commitment to the promotion of Aboriginal and minority rights is second to none, with both constitutional and statutory guarantees in place at the federal and provincial levels, although there is some evidence of backsliding at the global level (Maaka & Fleras, 2008). Endorsement of human rights protection, ranging from passage of the *Bill of Rights* in 1960 to the *Charter of Rights and Freedoms* that came into effect in 1985, further solidifies Canada's lofty status. Paradoxically, however, it's precisely this exalted status that exposes Canada to criticism. Even the smallest of infractions tend to be amplified in Canada because of its exacting standards, whereas they would receive barely a mention in many foreign countries (Levitt, 1997). Not surprisingly, Canadians appear perplexed and angry when international bodies chastise Canada for relatively "minor" human rights violations, including its use of the term "visible minorities" as a descriptive label for racialized minorities (Fleras, 2008), while rogue societies are allowed to get away with "bloody murder" without much condemnation.

Third, while Canada glitters in comparison to its past and with others, it also falls short of established benchmarks. Canadians are adept at "talking the walk" with respect to the ideals of tolerance, openness, and inclusiveness; however, they are less inclined to "walk the talk" by putting these ideas into practice. Relations between racialized minorities and the rest of Canada tend to waver uneasily between grudging acceptance and thinly veiled rejection with the spectre of public backlash ever present. For example, the UN Human Rights Committee has issued a stinging rebuke of Canada's treatment of vulnerable minorities, citing anti-terrorist legislation and safety certificates that are too broad and imprecise (Goar, 2005). Discrimination and racism are not simply relics from the past, but are so deeply ingrained and structurally embedded that any possibility of their disappearing is remote (Jiwani, 2006; Razack, 2004; Thobani, 2007). Nevertheless, while racism is no longer blatant, more subtle forms of racism exert an equally powerful negative impact. Anti-Semitism persists, albeit in different guises (Schoenfeld, 2004; Weinfeld, 2005); white supremacist groups are proliferating through digital technology; and racialized minorities continue to be marginalized, despite a commitment to inclusiveness, justice, and participation (Henry & Tator, 2006). The fact that highly skilled immigrants cannot secure appropriate employment prospects exposes a gap between the ideals of immigration and the realities of multiculturalism (Pendakur, 2005; Teelucksingh & Galabuzi, 2005). Of particular dismay is the country's most egregious human rights violation—the continued disengagement and disempowerment of many Aboriginal peoples (Belanger, 2008). That Aboriginal communities remain socio-economically depressed reflects poorly on Canada's much ballyhooed reputation as a beacon for enlightenment (Frideres & Gadacz, 2008).

This admittedly selective overview paints a discordant picture of Canadian race, Aboriginal, and ethnic relations. From a distance, Canada looks idyllic; up close the picture blurs, with little to boast about in the *mis*management of diversities and difference. That discord suggests the possibility of a *fourth* interpretation—that Canada is positioned somewhere in between the extremes of good and bad: Neither a paragon of virtue nor the fountainhead of all evils, Canada's record of managing diversity probably falls somewhere in the middle. In comparison to the past or to other countries, Canada soars; when compared to the ideals that many Canadians espouse, Canada misses the mark. Initiatives for "managing" race, ethnicity, and aboriginality are at times enlightened, at other times callously expedient in securing national and vested interests, and hopelessly muddled at still other times, especially as Canadians strive to balance "national interests" with minority rights.

This chapter conceptualizes the paradoxes and puzzles that inform Canada's race, ethnic, and Aboriginal relations. A conceptual map is proposed by cutting through the analytical clutter that conceals as much as it reveals, confuses as much as it clarifies, and distorts as much as it enlightens. This chapter also analyzes governance models of race, ethnic, and Aboriginal relations (namely, genocide, segregation, assimilation, integration, and pluralism); introduces sociological models of society (functionalism, conflict [Marxism and feminist theory], and symbolic interactionism) as explanatory frameworks in this field; and uses a Debate box to demonstrate how sociological models of society can cast light on Canada's official Multiculturalism. The theorizing of race, ethnic, and Aboriginal relations along these lines provides a conceptual underpinning for the remaining chapters.

First, the chapter begins with an overview of diversity in Canada based on 2006 Census data. The data in the box below have been broken down into ethnic categories— Aboriginal peoples, immigrants, and racialized ("visible") minorities—along national and urban lines.

Diversity in Canada: A Snapshot

Canada is widely proclaimed as a society of diversities. This claim has merit insofar as just over one in five Canadians is "non-white"—a figure that is likely to increase in light of Canada's immigration program and the relative youthfulness of the Aboriginal population. The following figures provide a breakdown:

Ethnicity in General

- Over 200 ethnic origins (including Aboriginal) were reported by the total population in the 2006 Census. In 1901, only 25 ethnic origins were reported.
- Canadian was the most frequently reported ethnic origin in 2006 with just over 10 million people reporting it, either alone or in combination with other ethnic origins (comprising 32 percent of the total responses, but a drop from 39 percent in 2001). Following behind Canadian were English (6.6 million), French, Scottish, Irish, German, Italian, Chinese, North American Indian, Ukrainian, and Dutch (1 million) (both single and multiple origins).
- The percentage of those reporting multiple origins continued to rise, from 35.8 percent in 1996 to 41.4 percent in 2006.

Aboriginal Peoples

- Based on the 2006 Census, 1 172 790 people self-identified as Aboriginal, including 698 025 North American Indians (or First Nations, including 564 870 as Status Indians who reported they were Registered Indians), 389 785 Métis, and 50 485 Inuit ("multiple" and "other" totalled 34 500).
- The proportion of Aboriginal peoples in Canada (3.8 percent) is second only to New Zealand, where the figure for Maori stands at about 15 percent of the population.

(Continued)

- Close to 1.7 million individuals (or 4.4 percent of Canada's population) report having Aboriginal ancestry in 2006; that is, an Aboriginal ancestor could be found in their genealogy. However, the respondent chose not to identify as Aboriginal.
- Increasingly, Aboriginal peoples are living off-reserve and in cities. Winnipeg had the largest urban Aboriginal population at 68 380 (the highest percentage per total population of major cities in Canada), while Toronto was fourth at 26 575 or 0.05 percent of its population.

Immigrants

- Nearly 21 percent of Canada's population is foreign born ("immigrants"). That figure puts Canada's immigrant population second to Australia's, which constitutes 24 percent of its total population.
- In contrast to a generation ago when most immigrants were from Europe and the United States, nearly 60 percent of newcomers to Canada arrive from East and South Asia. Less than 20 percent are from Europe and the United States.
- Over 40 percent of all immigrants to Canada live in Toronto.

Racialized (Visible) Minorities

- A total of 5 068 100 persons claimed to belong to the category of visible minority, accounting for 16.2 percent of Canada's population, up from 11.2 percent in 1996 and 4.1 percent in 1981.
- Canada's visible minority population increased by 27.1 percent between 2001 and 2006, compared with an increase of 5.4 percent for the total population.

- Seventy-five percent of all immigrants who arrived between 2001 and 2006 identified as visible minorities.
- South Asians surpassed Chinese as the largest visible minority group in 2006, with Blacks as the third-largest minority.
- Most South Asians reported ancestral backgrounds from the Indian subcontinent, with East India representing the largest number, followed by Pakistan and Sri Lanka.
- Nearly 96 percent of visible minorities lived in a metropolitan area, compared with 68.1 percent of the general population. If just Montreal, Toronto, and Vancouver are included, they are home to 75 percent of visible minorities.
- Not only does 42.9 percent of Canada's visible minority population live in Toronto, but about 42.9 percent of Toronto's population is from a visible minority category.
- The top ethnic origins reported in Toronto are (in descending order) English, Canadian, Scottish, Chinese, and Irish.
- Vancouver's visible minority population accounts for 41.7 percent of its total population; the figure for Montreal is 16.5 percent, with the vast majority living on the island rather than in the suburbs.
- Markham, Ontario (just north of Toronto) has the highest percentage of visible minorities at 65.4 percent of its population. Richmond, British Columbia, follows closely behind with about 64 percent.
- By contrast, cities such as Moncton, Trois-Rivières, and Saguenay reported statistically insignificant levels of visible minorities.

Source: See Citizenship and Immigration Canada, 2009; Statistics Canada, 2006a.)

While these diversity figures look impressive, a sense of perspective is helpful. First, compared with those of other countries, Canada's diversity figures pale. With increased immigration and refugee flows, together with expanded international commerce, many societies are increasingly diverse. For example, just over 30 percent of the population in the United States is non-white, namely, African American, Hispanic, Asian American, and Native American. The comparable figure for Canada is about 20 percent if both racialized minorities and Aboriginal peoples are included in the tally. Canada may be diverse, but much of this diversity is collapsed into four major regions—the 401 corridor from Windsor to Greater Toronto, Montreal, Calgary/Edmonton, and the Lower Mainland in British Columbia. With the exception of Aboriginal peoples, the rest of Canada is largely devoid of non-European diversities.

Second, Canadians are conflicted about the value of diversity. Some reject the principle of diversity and associated practices as inimical to Canada's interests and national identity. However, most Canadians endorse diversity's value and contribution, not only as a defining characteristic of Canada but also as a strength in improving our quality of life. In reality, diversity is double edged. On one side, it's a source of economic strength, social creativity and problem solving, cultural vitality, and national pride. On the other side, it's a recipe for social conflict, racial tension, political instability, and urban problems—from service demands and spiralling housing prices to the erosion of civic networks and interpersonal trust (also known as "social capital") (Boston, 2005; Putnam, 2007, but see Pendakur in Proudfoot, 2010). In other words, diversity may make human existence interesting because of the benefits it brings. At the same time, it can make life more challenging by imposing costs, especially when diversity becomes demanding.

Third, macro-sociological debates over diversity invariably raise questions about how much and what kind. How much diversity (and diversities within diversity) can Canada tolerate before it spins out of control, without a hub holding everything together? How much unity does Canada need to survive without stifling creativity and social change in the process? What kind of diversity is appropriate for Canada? Many Canadians like superficial expressions of diversity that do not entail costs or create inconveniences. However, anxiety levels mount over deep differences that not only challenge the legitimacy of Canada and Canadian values (as set out in the Charter) but also are intolerant of other differences (in effect, disagreeing with the liberal principle of agreeing to disagree) (Glazer, 2010). Where are the limits of Canada's multicultural tolerance? What principles or criteria should be employed in deciding which cultural and religious practices are unacceptable when they clash with Canada's multicultural commitments (see Boston, 2005)?

Clearly, then, the politics of diversity are more perplexing than implied by the mantra "celebrating differences." Without a powerful sense of national identity or well-defined dominant culture, Canadians are reluctant to impose their values and norms on others, in effect posing political paradoxes (Patrick Weil as cited in Allemang, 2005). How can we live together with our differences in dignity and equality without those differences and competing rights getting in the way of sharing and solidarity? How does a multicultural Canada accommodate differences without compromising the common values and the rule of law that holds it together? Answers are varied and problematic. Nevertheless, one thing is certain: The challenges of governing multiethnic, multireligious, multiracial, and multicultural Canada will prove difficult and demanding, and a defining characteristic of Canada (see Harell & Stolle, 2010).

MODELS OF RACE, ETHNIC, AND ABORIGINAL RELATIONS: INTERGROUP DYNAMICS AS GOVERNANCE PATTERNS

Canada is hardly alone in the diversity sweepstakes. The contemporary world is composed of many societies that are generally polyethnic or multinational in composition. In 2000, Walker Connor estimated that only seven countries in the world did not have significant minorities or divisions based on race or ethnicity, with the few exceptions including some Muslim countries from which long-established minorities had fled (Glazer, 2010). Patterns can be discerned from this diversity at large. In most ethnoracially diverse countries, one group tends to be dominant insofar as both national governance and social institutions are organized around its agenda and priorities. By contrast, **subdominant minority group** members are disadvantaged in the competition for power or privilege. The corresponding tension between competing interests can prove destabilizing: The dominant sector will do everything it can to preserve its lofty status, while subdominant minority groups demand a more equitable distribution of power and privilege. The ensuing interplay of interests reinforces a key theme of this text: race, ethnic, and Aboriginal dynamics as socially constructed relations within contexts of power and inequality.

What exactly is meant by the expression "race, ethnic, and Aboriginal relations"? What should be included in a study of race, ethnicity, and aboriginality (see Banton, 2005; Solomos & Bulmer, 2005)? Central to the study of race, ethnic, and Aboriginal relations are the dynamics of intergroup relations over time and across space (Marger, 2001). These intergroup relations exist because individuals with a shared culture and similar ancestral backgrounds continue to identify (or are identified by others) with each other and engage in behaviour that protects or promotes their interests at the expense of others (Kivisto & Ng, 2005). To be sure, pure racial, ethnic, and Aboriginal groups do not exist. Nor is it accurate to say that "races" interact with each other, although relationships may involve perceptions of race. But because a significant racial, ethnic, and Aboriginal component may inform the dynamics of intergroup relations, references to race or ethnicity may be invoked to (1) mobilize like-minded individuals into action; (2) justify patterns of action or inaction toward groups; and (3) provide a convenient label to simplify otherwise complex intergroup relations, resulting in patterns of interaction that become "raced" around power politics (Taras & Ganguly, 2002).

What produces the "relations" in race, ethnic, and Aboriginal relations? A series of prolonged contact situations may account for various intergroup relations in ethnically mixed societies. First, a **dominant group** incorporates or annexes a foreign territory by force or "rights of (European) discovery." The British conquest of the French on the Plains of Abraham in 1759 is an example of this, one that continues to rankle and provoke. The colonization of Turtle Island (North America) by French, British, and Spanish settlers and opportunists has proven no less provocative. Second, colonization and frontier expansion result in the acquisition of land or resources through diplomatic channels. Territories may be acquired by purchase or through treaties such as those between Canada's Aboriginal peoples and the Crown. Forced migration is a third possibility that involves a foreign population being forcibly brought into the country for essentially exploitative purposes. The importation of Africans for slave labour into the United States—and into Canada, albeit on a more limited basis—is a classic example. Fourth, voluntary migration from overseas entails some degree of choice in making the move. It stands to reason that the interests and aspirations of "voluntary migrants" will differ from the interests of those who have been forcibly incorporated through annexation or colonization.

Sustained contact between and among groups invariably leads to a patterned network of intergroup relations. Ranging in scope from hostility to acceptance, with varying levels of accommodation in between, the exact trajectory of these intergroup dynamics will vary with the nature of the contact situation—its duration, timing, conflicts of interest, magnitude, and intensity. In general, however, one group will dominate because of military might or technological prowess, while the others will comply and obey—sometimes voluntarily, sometimes by coercion. Interaction based on these dominant–subdominant relationships gives rise to a limited number of patterned responses that can be conceptualized along five models of intergroup governance, namely *genocide, assimilation, segregation, integration,* and *pluralism.* In theory, each of these governance models reflects a set of assumptions about the status of difference in society, the preferred relationship between dominant and subdomi- nant groups, prescriptions for "managing" race, ethnic, and Aboriginal relations, and proposed outcomes for society-building. In reality, however, these governance models are not strictly separate from each other. Overlap is the rule rather than the exception only because reality itself is contextual rather than categorical. Moreover, these models are not always explicitly articulated as governance or codified into law. But in many cases they are, even to the position of official policy status. That makes it doubly important to interpret these intergroup models for managing differences from a governance perspective.

Genocide

Genocide may be the most serious of punishable crimes under international law, and one of the few crimes for which UN military intervention supersedes the principle of state sover- eignty (Saunders, 2004). The concept of genocide encompasses a broad range of activities, according to the UN-based convention of 1948, including five classes of action: (1) members of a group are slaughtered with the intent of bringing about their disappearance as a people; (2) conditions are created that foster the dispersal of the group by destroying the essential foundations of community life, in the process pushing remnants of the population to an edge from which recovery is difficult; (3) intense psychological abuse or physical discomfort is inflicted, culminating in the dissolution of the group; (4) children are transferred from one group to another, thus bringing about the demise of the culture; and (5) births are prevented through involuntary sterilization, birth control, or abortion. Such a broad range of abusive activities complicates the search for a definition (Caplan, 2005).

Despite (or perhaps because of) its scope, genocide has proven difficult to define—a situation that *conveniently* impedes humanitarian assistance or UN-based intervention, even in contexts of extreme duress. Generally speaking, most definitions include the notion of deliberate and systematic mass killings of a despised domestic minority who live in a territory controlled by often government-backed killers (Taras & Ganguly, 2002). A state that openly condones violence against its own citizens furnishes the key criterion that distinguishes genocide from related crimes against humanity (Rummel, 2005). Others pre- fer a more expansive definition that includes the unintended yet fatal consequences of seemingly well-intentioned policy initiatives toward the minorities within (Deak, 2002).

For some, very few calamities meet UN criteria for genocide. The extermination of the German Jews (and other "undesirables" under Nazi Germany) and the Rwandan crisis in 1994 in which Tutsi (and moderate Hutu) were slaughtered by Hutu extremists are clear-cut examples of such catastrophes. For others, history is replete with genocidal-like purges of dehumanized minorities—whether deliberate or unintentional. In asserting colonial control over a land they saw as *terra nullius*, European settlers openly stalked and killed Australia's Aboriginal populations. Likewise, Aboriginal peoples such as the Beothuk in Newfoundland became extinct because of disruptive contact with early European colonialists. The twentieth-century killing fields were no less punitive: Ukrainians suffered massive losses in famines engineered by Stalinist purges; Armenians accused the Turkish regime of genocide during World War I; the blatant mistreatment of indigenous populations by Brazilian settlers and miners in the Amazonian rainforest appears no less genocidal. Even the proselytizing work of missionaries is deemed as genocidal in consequence because of the destruction wreaked on many indigenous people's communities. Also widely viewed as genocidal were the **ethnic cleansing** campaigns by Serbs against Albanians in Kosovo and Muslim populations in Bosnia (see Tatum, 2010).

Violence is endemic to genocides. As people are hacked, bludgeoned, raped, or shot to death, this violence often comes across as random and uncontrollable, involving high levels of testosterone-driven irrationality. But appearances can be deceiving. This mass liquidation process is neither an isolated act nor an unintentional one by poorly disciplined militia. The killing fields are neither an unfortunate byproduct of dormant tribal hatred nor a spontaneous spasm of uncontrolled primeval rage. To the contrary, genocide represents a calculated political decision to achieve political goals in a politically acceptable manner (Midlarsky, 2005). An orchestrated campaign of terror that sanctions the dehumanization and destruction of the "other" is activated to remove competitors or silence opponents. For example, the Darfuri conflict may be driven by a crude racist ideology of Arab supremacism for cleansing North Africa of African tribes, with Libya as its most ardent proponent (Petrou & Savage, 2006). Competition for scarce resources is no less critical, as African farmers and nomadic Arab herders compete for what little land there is in the face of creeping desertification, followed by a fierce government crackdown on Darfuri insurgents who attacked a government outpost (Wrzesnewskyj, 2005). What may look like mindless aggression is often a ruthless strategy to defend a sacred ideal, to destroy a group perceived as a threat to the ruling regime, to diminish those who are hated or envied, to eliminate foreign elements from society, to consolidate elite advantage, or to secure economic gain (Rummel, 2005; see also Koenigsberg, 2004) (see online Case Study 1.1).

In short, genocide does not necessarily erupt because of primitive urges, tribal hatred, or dormant hostilities. Outside of local outbursts that may spiral out of control, genocide involves the manipulation of racialized differences by cynical elites who will stop at nothing to retain power, achieve advantage, secure political support, conceal economic difficulties, and distract from internal squabbles (Ignatieff, 1995). Even the victims and victimizers fall into a gendered pattern, with young males often the perpetrators and victims, but increasingly women as targets for rape and the spread of infections. To be sure, not all genocides are blunt or direct. The process of genocide can encompass varying strategies: from those that explicitly seek to exterminate "troublesome minorities" to those well-intentioned initiatives that inadvertently have had the effect (rather than the intent) of eliminating the "other." Annihilation of this magnitude may be accomplished directly through military means, or indirectly through the spread of disease, loss of livelihood, compulsory sterilization, or forced re-socialization.

The resurgence of genocide in recent years is as disconcerting as it is disturbing—disconcerting because many thought we had put that part of history behind us; disturbing because of the intensity and savagery that accompany the killings (Caplan, 2005, 2007). Why have such crimes against humanity proven so common in recent years, despite seemingly severe sanctions and global outrage (Tatum, 2010)? How and why do neighbours who share social and cultural space suddenly turn into murderous enemies (Ward, 2004)? This lust for killing may compel a rethinking of human nature. That is: Are humans naturally good, but twisted by social circumstances beyond their control? Are genocides exceptions to the rule of natural goodness—even if many humans may be capable of unspeakable crimes against humanity under specific circumstances (Caplan, 2005)? Or, alternatively, are people naturally evil in the Hobbesian sense of living lives that are "nasty, brutish, and short," with the result that genocides reflect our hard-wiring as a flawed species? If this is true, should we be asking ourselves if, in fact, the rules of law and reason are contrary to human nature and secured only by an unremitting struggle that "goes against the grain" of doing what comes naturally (Ignatieff, 1994)? As John Maynard Keyes once said: "Civilisation is a thin and precarious crust, erected by the personality and will of the few, and only maintained by rules and conventions skillfully put across and guilefully preserved" (as cited in Skidelsky, 2004).

Assimilation

Generally speaking, **assimilation** has been referred to as a one-way process of absorption. The concept was borrowed from biology (absorption through digestion) and reflects a largely mistaken belief that social life could be better understood by drawing upon simplified analogies with the natural world (Jaret, 1995). But rather than something simple and straightforward, when applied to the human condition, assimilation represents a complex and multidimensional process that unscrolls at a varying pace, sometimes deliberately but often unconsciously, involves different intensities of absorption, ranges in scope from cultural to the social, and entails varying degrees of conformity (Zhou, 1997).

More specifically, assimilation involves a process whereby the dominant sector imposes its culture, authority, values, and institutions on subdominant sectors with a corresponding loss of their distinctiveness because of exposure to these conformity pressures. In the past, assimilation was endorsed as an official government policy in framing majority–minority relations. Under assimilation, all minorities would be expected to adopt the cultural values and social practices of the ruling majority, if only to secure the grounds for centralized control and smooth governance. Yet, assimilationist policies were rarely intended to transform minorities in their entirety. The complete absorption of everybody was neither easily attained nor always desired; after all, few majorities possessed either the resources or the political will to enforce wholesale conformity. Endorsed instead was a commitment to dominant-conformity (or **anglo-conformity** in areas under British control). A dominant-conformity model required outward compliance with dominant values and practices rather than actual incorporation or their absorption, especially if the minority in question was deemed incapable of such a move. To the extent that conformity not uniformity prevailed, select elements of a subdominant lifestyle could be tolerated as long as they (1) were restricted to the private or personal realm, (2) did not challenge prevailing patterns of authority, (3) conformed to majority notions of decency, and (4) did not violate moral principles or the law of the land.

Assimilation emerged as an "enlightened" social policy for its time, especially when compared with alternatives such as forced separation or genocide. A commitment to assimilation informed a government framework for managing **indigenous peoples** in settler societies (Pearson, 2001). At times this commitment was tacitly assumed as a guideline for government–indigenous people relations; at other times, it was explicitly articulated as official government policy. Through assimilation, the dominant element sought to (1) undermine the cultural basis of indigenous societies, (2) expose individuals to dominant norms as normal and acceptable, (3) convert them into patriotic, productive, and God-fearing citizens, and (4) facilitate their entry and transition into the mainstream. Dominant values, beliefs, and social patterns were valorized as inevitable or desirable; conversely, differences were demonized as inferior or irrelevant. Such Eurocentrism proved both paternalistic and patronizing. Those singled out for assimilation were often portrayed as children in need of discipline under the ever-vigilant eye of a judicious parent.

Assimilation no longer prevails as an explicit policy principle. There is little inclination to openly support an assimilationist agenda that once dismissed group differences as inferior, irrelevant, or a liability. Instead of a weakness to be denied or excluded, differences are now touted as a strength to be nurtured, especially as a gateway to global markets. Yet appearances can be deceiving: Although publicly scorned and officially rebuked as a model for managing diversity, assimilation as a process continues to play a prominent role in moulding immigrants into the mainstream, reasserting core values, and excluding those who don't fit. Even in Canada, where diversity under an official Multiculturalism is respected, conformity is mandatory if new Canadians hope to succeed (Li, 2003). Moreover, as racialized minorities become increasingly involved in the mainstream, assimilation is proving the rule rather than the exception—in large part because of the often unintended consequences of choices made by individuals who are looking to settle down, fit in, and move up. Assimilation may unfold informally as well: Consider how the offspring of immigrants intermarry, live in demographically diverse neighbourhoods, are employed in all economic sectors (including "white-collar" jobs), and share comparable levels of education and income with other groups (Denton & Tolnay, 2002). Finally, assimilation can also be inferred as the logic underlying all government actions. The logical consequences of even seemingly progressive initiatives to assist racialized minorities (for instance, employment equity initiatives) may have the effect of assimilating them deeper into the system.

Segregation/Separation

The concept of **segregation** provides another model of intergroup relations. Segregated societies are segmented into relatively autonomous dominant and subdominant groups who live apart because of perceived incompatibilities and power relations. When used as a policy model for managing difference within unequal contexts, the role of governments is critical. In cases of de jure segregation, the government deliberately keeps the races apart, thus stigmatizing and handicapping the vulnerable by confining them to inferior facilities. A de facto segregation results when the government tacitly condones a forced segregation by not actively intervening to dismantle the barriers that excludes and divides.

Segregation involves a forced and physical separation. Contact between the races is kept to an absolute minimum, except in contexts of obvious benefit to the controlling sector. What little interaction exists is conducted primarily in the marketplace ("selective incorporation"), where the dominant group exercises monopolistic control over the economy and distribution of wealth. Compliance in unequal contexts is rarely secured by voluntary consensus of cultural values or social norms. In the absence of any morally legitimate basis to govern, the dominant group must rely on physical threats to compel obedience. Moreover, segregation goes beyond a physical separation of unequal groups. Also implicated is a social relationship involving unequal patterns of power and domination (Jaret, 1995). The dominant group defines itself as superior because of technological prowess, military might, and moral superiority. "Others" are dismissed as inferior or irrelevant—or a threat—to the society-building process.

History is rife with patterns of interaction that segregate groups from one another. Few scenarios of segregation have been as highly profiled as that of apartheid in South Africa. A comprehensive set of segregation laws and practices compartmentalized blacks and whites into separate groups at social, economic, and political levels. No less segregationist was the colour bar that existed in both the United States and Canada (Horton & Horton, 2004). Whites were segregated from blacks at institutional, occupational, interactional, and residential levels, in large part because of the power of the Ku Klux Klan, which terrorized the American South. To the dismay of many Canadians, many parts of Canada were no less segregated, because of colour bars at schools, public institutions, and residential areas (Walker, 1997). Finally, the establishment of Canada's reserve system under the *Indian Act* of 1876 may also be interpreted as a version of segregation—at least in consequence if not intent—given the government's long-standing commitment to "no more Indians" as a solution to the so-called "Indian problem."

Segregation as a governance model is usually generated from the top down. As a governance model, however, segregation can also be generated from below by groups who prefer voluntary **separation** from a society for lifestyle or strategic purposes. Voluntary separation is not the same as segregation or apartheid, despite similarities in appearance and structure. Racialized minorities, indigenous peoples, and religious groups may prefer to isolate themselves from the mainstream to preserve their independence and identity (see online Insight 1.2). For example, the Hutterites of western Canada and other communal religious sects have voluntarily divorced themselves from the outside world through expressions of religion, language, communal lifestyle, dress, and social interaction. Aboriginal peoples in Canada are casting about for aboriginal models of self-determining autonomy as a basis for living *separately* together (Maaka & Fleras, 2005). Separatist ethnicities under a sovereign Québécois nationalism are also seeking to strategically "separate" from Canada without actually leaving it. Part 2 of this text will further explore the politics of separation in Canada.

Integration

Integration represents a fourth model of governance. It emerged as a preferred governance model after World War II, owing to a growing disillusionment with alternative models for living together. Resentment over segregation was particularly notable because of international conventions that sought to protect human rights through the removal of discriminatory barriers. Of particular note was the mounting assertiveness by blacks and Aboriginal peoples, who bristled over second-class treatment in a country that had gone to war to protect overseas freedom but denied it to their own citizens. The concept of integration stood in opposition to that of segregation—defined as the forced separation of people who live apart from each other, socially and geographically. **Integration**, by contrast, involved a process whereby individuals interact with each other at all institutional levels (Jaret, 1995). A distinction between desegregation and integration is also useful. Desegregation entails removing physical or social barriers to achieve formal equality; integration as the positive dimension involves unifying disparate parts into a cooperative and functioning whole.

The concept of integration may have originated to describe social patterns. References to integration now include a cultural dimension. Two variations underlie the integration-as-culture theme. First, integration represents a two-way process of adjustment by which the dominant and subdominant sectors are brought together in a single comprehensive lifestyle, without either losing its distinctiveness. Whereas assimilation endorses a one-way process of absorption in which minority identities are folded into the mainstream, integration upholds a reciprocating system of synthesis that proposes full and equal participation without forgoing cultural identity as the price of admission. A second variant involves a process by which the dominant and the subdominant groups merge together, like different colours of paint in a bucket. The result of this "blending" process is a new cultural entity, metaphorically captured by the concept of the **melting pot**. As an image that is often invoked to describe, and prescribe, American race and ethnic relations, all immigrants can be transformed into new Americans—a cultural alloy forged in the crucible of democracy, freedom, and civic responsibility (Glazer, 1997). To be sure, however popular and useful it may be, metaphors such as "melting pot" are problematic shorthands because they grossly distort reality by oversimplifying complex issues (Kivisto & Ng, 2005). Although immigrants to the United States are expected to create a new amalgam by melting into the American pot, this cauldron remains irrefutably "pale male" in composition and control. Any restructuring of American society is recast along the lines and priorities of the prevailing institutional framework, while the subdominant sector simply adds a "dash of spice" to an otherwise monocultural stew.

The concept of integration continues to attract growing attention. With an unprecedented movement of people across borders and continents, the adjustment of newcomers into society is increasingly focal to policy concerns, with an emphasis on finding interventions to facilitate the integration of immigrants (George, 2006). And with multiculturalism as governance in decline in many parts of the world, several European countries have shown a commitment to "civic integration" over multiculturalism as a preferred governance model for managing diversity. And yet despite (or perhaps because of) its popularity, the concept of integration remains poorly defined or theorized. Or as put by A. Sivanandan, director of Britain's Institute of Race Relations, "The problem of integration lies in the interpretation of integration itself" (as cited in Fekete, 2010). For some, integration falls somewhere in between multiculturalism and assimilation; for others, it's little more than a watered-down version of assimilation (Fekete, 2010). Terms such as "acculturation," "multiculturalism," "incorporation," and "adaptation" are used interchangeably with "integration," while the concept is often treated as a one-way process or a singular outcome. The outcomes of both integration and assimilation may be indistinguishable in practice, even though in theory they are meant to be different. Not surprisingly, while some associate integration with the attainment of equality and participation, others conjure up images of unwanted conformity, and still others wonder what all the fuss is about. In an effort to operationalize the concept, the Council of the European Union articulated the principles of integration that follow.

Common Basic Principles for Immigrant Integration Policy in the European Union

While there is little consensus regarding the meaning and scope of integration, the Council of the European Union adopted a commitment to common basic principles for immigrant integration policy in 2004 (Council of the European Union, 2004; for a critique, see Joppke, 2007; Fleras, 2009b). They are paraphrased below.

- Integration is a dynamic two-way process of mutual accommodation by immigrants and the host country.
- Integration implies respect for the basic values of the European Union.
- Employment is a key part of the integration process for immigrants and the host country.
- Basic knowledge of the host country's language, history, and institutions is indispensable to integration.
- Access to education is critical to the integration of immigrants.
- Immigrant integration requires full and non-discriminatory access to institutions, and public and private goods and services.
- Frequent encounters and creative interaction between immigrants and host-country citizens secures a successful integration.
- Integration is predicated on guaranteeing the practice of diverse cultures and religions, provided these practices do not conflict with rights or laws.
- Immigrant participation in the democratic process is critical, especially in the formulation of programs and policies that impact on their lives.
- Integration is contingent on mainstreaming (making more inclusive) polices and measures in all relevant portfolios and levels of government and public services.
- Clear goals, indicators, and evaluation mechanisms must be in place to adjust immigration policies and evaluate progress.
- A list of indicators for specifying the parameters of successful integration needs to be formulated but Reitz and Banerjee (2007) offer this Canadian list: a sense of belonging, trust in the other, identification with society at large, acquisition of citizenship, life satisfaction, a spirit of volunteerism, and exercise of voting rights).

These principles for immigrant integration policy—with their focus on a two-way process of accommodation—resemble those of Canada's inclusive Multiculturalism, most notably the *Canadian Multiculturalism Act* of 1988. As a result, it serves as a reminder that, while helpful, the distinction between integration and multiculturalism is potentially misleading since the goals of both are neither mutually exclusive nor necessarily at cross purposes (see Choudhry, 2007).

Source: http://europa.eu/rapid/pressReleasesAction.do?reference=MEMO/05/290&format=HTML&aged=0&language=EN&guiLanguage=en - fn3#fn3

Pluralism

Many countries are seeking to come to terms with difference and diversity (Rex, 2004). Yet governments of these countries find themselves in a governance dilemma. On the one hand, countries have historically been grounded on the attainment of a culturally and linguistically homogeneous population, resulting in a deliberate rejection of difference (Guibernau, 2007). On the other, government policies that once diminished the value of difference for society-building are now recognizing more inclusive models of race, ethnic, and Aboriginal relations. Acceptance of difference as a basis for governance within a national framework is called **pluralism**. Pluralism goes beyond a simple existence of racial or ethnic minorities in society, however. It also acknowledges the possibility of constructing a unified society from (or despite) difference as a desired and valued component of an egalitarian society. Not surprisingly, some degree of government intervention may be required to protect and promote minority needs, in part by reaffirming individual rights, rectifying past injustices, reducing social inequities by removing discriminatory barriers, providing positive actions through employment equity programs, and ensuring protection of traditional language and culture.

Both colour/culture-blind and colour/culture-conscious variants of pluralism can be discerned. For some, a pluralistic society is one that ignores differences as a basis for rewards and recognition, thereby ensuring that everyone is equal before the law regardless of race or ethnicity. In that no minority group receives special treatment, either positive or negative, a society of many cultures is possible as long as people's cultural differences do not preclude full and equal participation. For others, a pluralistic society is one that recognizes the centrality of differences. By incorporating diversity as a basis for **entitlement** and recognition, a culture-conscious model embraces a dual ideal: People must be treated equally ("similarly") as a matter of course, but must also be treated as equals ("differently") as situations arise. In other words, a society of many cultures is possible if people's cultural differences are taken into account when necessary to ensure equality and inclusiveness.

A commitment to pluralism can be expressed in diverse ways, including multiculturalism, biculturalism, and multinationalism. Canada's pluralistic commitments are enshrined in the concept of an official Multiculturalism. With Multiculturalism, Canada endorses the legitimacy of ethnic diversity as different yet equal by creating institutional space allowing all Canadians to interact without fear of ethnic entanglements. The United States has also experienced a multicultural turn in recent years (Glazer, 1997), including a critically insurgent style of multiculturalism that differs sharply from Canada's consensus-oriented **integrative multiculturalism** (Fleras, 2001; Goldberg, 1994a). Biculturalism resembles multiculturalism in many ways, but focuses on the relationship between two major groups or peoples, each of which stands in a partnership relation with the other. For example, biculturalism (or, more accurately, binationalism) describes the relationship between the indigenous Maori peoples and the non-Maori in New Zealand/Aotearoa (Fleras & Spoonley, 1999; Maaka & Fleras, 2008). To the extent that it persists, Canada's pluralistic commitment to biculturalism is expressed at the level of Quebec–Ottawa relations. Finally, multinationalism refers to the possibility of a society of multiple nations or many peoples who see themselves as political communities—autonomous (sovereign) in their own right, yet sharing in the sovereignty of society (Asch, 1997; Maaka & Fleras, 2005). Canada is increasingly described as a multinational

TABLE 1-1	**Race, Ethnic, and Aboriginal Relations as Governance Models**			
Model	**Objectives**	**Assumptions about diversity**	**Means**	**Outcomes**
Genocide	annihilation	despised	violence	racial purity
Assimilation	absorption	irrelevant	conformity	one people
Segregation	separation	isolated	force	colour bar
Integration	desegregation/ fusion/two-way	tolerant of	incorporation	formal equality
Pluralism	living together with differences	acceptance	inclusiveness	Multiculturalism, biculturalism, multinationalism

coalition comprising Aboriginal peoples, the Québécois, and the English-speaking sectors, including immigrants and descendants of immigrants.

To summarize, recurrent responses and patterned outcomes occur when competitively different groups come into sustained contact. A network of patterned relations is established, many of which become formalized into explicit governance policy for managing difference. Policy outcomes vary and may include those that deny differences (assimilation), reject minorities (segregation), and demonize out-groups (genocide), as well as those that espouse formal equality (integration) and positively engage diversity (pluralism). To be sure, some degree of overlap and duplication is inevitable in making the distinction; after all, social reality cannot possibly be squeezed into static and exclusive categories. Moreover, while definitions are critical for analysis and assessment, they do run the risk of simplifying, essentializing, or rigidifying what in reality is complex, shifting, and contextual. Table 1-1 highlights some of the key features of each model by comparing definitions, objectives, assumptions about diversity, means, and outcomes.

THEORIZING INTERGROUP RELATIONS: SOCIOLOGICAL MODELS AS EXPLANATORY FRAMEWORKS

Sociology as a discipline is often defined as the scientific study of social reality within a society. Society can be differently defined, but most profitably as a complex, contested, evolving, and unequal network of relations in the broadest sense of the term, ranging from the interpersonal to the international, with intergroup dynamics occupying an intermediate position. For sociologists, the centrality of social reality is critical to a study of society. What is the nature of this social reality? Is it prone to stability, order, and cooperation, or is the natural state inclined toward conflict, control, and disorder? How is it constructed, expressed, and sustained, as well as challenged, resisted, and transformed? To assist in answering these questions, different sociological models (perspectives or paradigms) are proposed. Each of the models, including **functionalism**, **conflict theory** (including feminist and Marxist streams), and **symbolic interactionism** differs from the others not only in how it analyzes and assesses social reality but also in how it explains the dynamics of intergroup relationships within society (see Banton, 2005).

Functionalism

Functionalist models of society provide a once-popular approach to the study of race, ethnic, and Aboriginal relations. For functionalists, society is viewed as a complex and integrated whole comprising interrelated parts that collectively contribute to maintenance and survival. Society is compared to a living organism; like any life form, it consists of parts that mesh for effective functioning, resists disruptive changes, and reacts to any invasion by isolating or removing the disruption to ensure stability and the status quo. Under optimal conditions, all elements of a society operate smoothly to enhance success. But tensions and conflicts associated with intrusive social change may unravel these relationships to a point of temporary disarray. Corrective measures are activated to remove potentially disruptive situations, thus restoring society to its natural state of equilibrium and order.

For functionalists, the combination of consensus, cooperation, and control are the keys to a successful society. To achieve this highly desirable state of unity and order, all members of society (but especially minorities) must internalize core beliefs and values. Not surprisingly, functionalists endorse assimilation (or integration) as the preferred model for race, ethnic, and Aboriginal relations. Failure to assimilate diversity is viewed as a potential threat to society. For example, the acceptance of immigrants to Canada has proven beneficial (functional) to its economic and cultural well-being. Immigrants often provide a valuable source of labour to meet the needs of an expanding economy, while also enriching Canadian society through the diversity of their cultural heritages. But for functionalists, immigrants' entry into Canada may be problematic because of settlement costs or disruptions to the status quo. To thwart any potential conflicts while facilitating the entry and settlement of new Canadians, measures are introduced for damage control and conflict management. On one side are assimilationist agencies, such as education and mass media; on the other side are initiatives such as official Multiculturalism for fostering consensus and shared values; on yet another side are employment equity programs calculated to improve the process of fitting in, settling down, and moving up. The anticipated result? A smoothly functioning Canada that defuses any disruptive potential for living together differently.

Conflict Theory: Feminist and Marxist

A conflict model of society differs sharply from a functionalist perspective. Whereas functionalists espouse a normative theory of society by emphasizing consensus and equilibrium, conflict perspectives prefer to emphasize control, contradiction, confrontation, and changes. A conflict perspective portrays society as a complex and unstable site of unequal yet competing groups in perpetual competition over scarce and valued resources. Dominant groups will rely on peaceful or violent methods to preserve privilege, property, and power. Subdominant sectors are more likely to challenge the status quo through different strategies of resistance, ranging from outright confrontation to passive resistance.

For conflict theorists, then, the normal state of society resonates with contradiction, conflict, and change. Instead of consensus or stability, society is held together by force or the threat of force because of disparities in power, privilege, and property (income and wealth). To be sure, a conflict perspective does not posit a perpetual state of conflict and confrontation. Of interest to conflict theorists is what happens in-between clashes. Certain **hegemonic** techniques are employed to maintain and legitimize a fundamentally unequal order without resorting to coercive tactics. At times, the dominant group is powerful enough to defuse the potential for overt conflict. At other times, even opposing groups find it mutually advantageous to put aside their differences in pursuit of common interests. This "double-edgedness" suggests that conflict and cooperation are strategically different dimensions of a single struggle.

With their focus on inequality and power, conflict models have proven valuable in explaining the politics of difference. One major variant (that many define as a distinct paradigm of society) is feminist theory. Like conflict models, a feminist perspective acknowledges the centrality of inequality and domination. Society is perceived as a site of domination in which institutions and values are designed and organized to reflect, reinforce, and advance male interests and priorities with respect to power, privilege, and property (Pateman, 1988). Unlike other conflict models, this perspective begins with the assumption that there is nothing natural or normal about patriarchal (male) domination. Rather, these patterns of domination, control, and inequality are socially constructed and culturally specific. And just as male-stream society tended to construct demeaning and debilitating images of women, so too are minority women (including Aboriginal women, immigrant and refugee women, and women of colour) defined and dismissed as irrelevant, inferior, or a threat. But, paradoxically, the social construction of this reality points to a solution: What has been socially constructed can also be deconstructed, then reconstructed to create societies where gender equality prevails.

Another variant of conflict theory incorporates **Marxist** approaches. Marxist conflict theory positions the concept of **class** at the heart of all exploitation and conflict. Marxists argue that the fundamental contradiction in any complex society entails two social classes: the working (subdominant) and the ruling (dominant) class. The ruling class profits by owning the means of production; members of the working class survive by selling their labour to the ruling class. The ruling class will do anything to facilitate the flow of profits, in part by shaving the costs of labour by creating split labour markets (paying some workers more than others), in part by fomenting internal divisions that pit worker against worker rather than against the true source of the exploitation. Over time, Marxist thinking has moved away from strict economic determinism, without discarding the importance of class relations to group dynamics. That is, intergroup relations may be shaped by economic forces in the first instance, thanks to the centrality of ideas in shaping outcomes, rather than in the final analysis. In short, minority women and men are seen as active subjects in solving problems, defending interests, and mobilizing into action groups—albeit in contexts and within structures beyond their control—rather than as passive objects victimized by impenetrable forces.

Symbolic Interactionism

Both functionalist and conflict models define society as taken-for-granted. Society is portrayed as durable and real, existing above and beyond the individual, yet exerting vast leverage over people's behaviour. By contrast, symbolic interactionist perspectives begin with the notion of society as an ongoing human accomplishment. Instead of something "out there" and determinative, society is perceived as socially constructed through meaningful interaction. According to this outlook, people do not live in a predetermined world of mechanistic outcomes. Rather, reality is constructed by applying provisional meanings to a variety of situations. Once a situation has been defined and redefined, jointly linked lines of action are developed. Society—as the sum total of these personal and group interactions at a given point in time and space—emerges from the interplay of these joint linkages. Not surprisingly, intergroup dynamics are couched in the framework of constant flux, dynamic tension, mutual adjustment, negotiated compromise, and ongoing movement.

A similar line of reasoning applies to race, ethnic, and Aboriginal relations. Intergroup relations are not defined by system needs, class conflict, or gender wars. On the contrary, they assume diverse forms as social constructions within specific contexts. Race, ethnicity, and aboriginality are treated as "factors" in defining situations, and action is taken on the basis of these definitions to create jointly linked patterns of interaction. In attempting to control or change the world they live in, minorities activate group-specific identities for advancing collective action, especially when there is a competitive advantage to group affiliation. Patterned interaction is thus generated and sustained by opposing elements that compete for definitional control of the situation to attract constituencies and promote interests. From a minority point of view, the question revolves around the benefits of working either within the system or outside of it. From a majority perspective the question is no less perplexing: Should minorities be allowed entry into the mainstream, or is it better to exclude them from meaningful involvement? These interactional styles and outcomes are not mutually exclusive, but intersect to create diverse group dynamics.

One variation of **interactionism** is known as **collective definition** (Blumer & Duster, 1980). A collective definition approach emphasizes the process by which intra- and intergroup relations are formulated and reformulated because of opposing dynamics (**dualisms**) that prevail within and between all groups. Both the dominant and subdominant groups may be internally divided into competing factions or dualisms. Within the dominant sector are at least two factions: On one side are those who support the inclusion (assimilation or integration) of minorities, especially if there is something to be gained by doing so; on the other side are those who prefer the status quo (and prevailing distribution of power, privilege, and property) by excluding minorities from full and equal participation. The subdominant sector is no less divided. On one side are those factions who insist on assimilation into the dominant sector as a solution to their problems; on the other are those who endorse separation through the creation of parallel institutions and independent power bases as the preferred option.

To sum up: Sociological models of society—functionalism, conflict theory, and symbolic interactionism—provide distinctly different ways of looking at social reality. These models differ from each other in defining (a) the nature of society, (b) the normal state of society, (c) the key question about society, (d) society's guiding metaphor, (e) what holds society together, and (f) an assessment of society (see Table 1-2). Each model should also be envisaged in ideal-typical terms. In drawing attention to some aspects of social reality but away from others, advocates of each model selectively emphasize those aspects of reality that enhance their respective standpoints, while downplaying those that are inconsistent with the model. For functionalists, society is seen as basically good; as a result, anything that contributes to this cohesion and consensus is deemed as functional, while anything that disrupts is dysfunctional and must be dislodged. Since society is fundamentally sound in functionalist models, any improvement must focus on changing the individual. By contrast, both variants of conflict theory see society as fundamentally exploitative and/or dominating. For conflict theorists,

TABLE 1-2	Sociological Models of Society			
	Functionalism	Conflict theory (class-based)	Conflict theory (feminist-based)	Symbolic interaction theory
The nature of society	Integrated whole of interrelated and functional parts	Site of class inequality	Site of male domination	Ongoing human accomplishment
The normal state of society	Stability, order, consensus, cooperation	Competition, conflict, control, change	Domination, conflict, control, change	Dynamic interactional process
The key question about society	How is order achieved?	How does inequality persist?	How is domination maintained?	How is reality socially constructed?
Society's guiding metaphor	Organic analogy	Combat zone	Gender wars	Unscripted reality show
What holds society together	Shared consensus	Hegemony + threat of force + power	Hegemony + threat of force + power	Negotiation, compromise, and self-interest
An assessment of society	Society is good.	Society is exploitative.	Society is dominating.	Society is just a blank slate.

anything that contributes to this control and inequality is negatively framed. Conversely, anything that challenges these unequal relations is defined as progressive. Inasmuch as individuals are basically good while society is evil, the social and structural must be the locus of transformative change. For social interactionists, society is neither good nor bad. It represents a contested site involving meaningful interaction; therefore, nothing should be prejudged but should be analyzed and assessed on the basis of context.

Each of these sociological models of society can also be applied to the diversity and difference domain of race, ethnic, and Aboriginal dynamics. For functionalists, diversity and difference pose a potential problem in need of solutions for the smooth functioning of society. For conflict theorists, diversity and difference may be manipulated by the ruling classes to advance interests or the status quo. However, the politicization of diversities can challenge and change the system toward more equitable outcomes. For symbolic interactionists, diversity and difference are neither good nor bad, but subject to negotiation and accommodation as the situation is defined. Moreover, as Henry and Tator (2003) point out, the field of race and ethnic relations has shifted its conceptual focus over time. Race and ethnic relations used to be conceptualized along the lines of a majority-minority approach or a race relations approach, with its emphasis on the success of minorities in integrating/assimilating into white society (functionalism). But in an effort to overcome limitations in uncritically applying a functionalist model of understanding to patterns of discrimination and racism (Dovidio et al., 2010a, 2010b), the conflict theories of the 1980s shifted attention to asymmetrical power relations. More recently, the focus on socially constructed approaches (symbolic interactionism) have shifted attention to more subtle and indirect forms of racism, acknowledging the centrality of symbols (especially media representations) in conceptualizing differences that normalize whiteness while problematizing minorityness.

To be sure, no sociological model of society or its application to race, ethnic, and Aboriginal relations is inherently more correct than the other. After all, social reality is experienced at times as stable, ordered, and cooperative. At other times, it is experienced as exploitative, domineering, and wildly out of control because of rapid social changes. Still at other times, it is experienced as open to negotiation and construction; that is, instead of viewing the world as something beyond one's control, people can define situations in ways that address their interests and act accordingly. In other words, social reality is experienced along the combined lines proposed by functionalism, conflict theorists, and social interactionism. One way of evaluating the analytical value of each sociological model of society is by analyzing Canada's official Multiculturalism along these lines (see the Debate Revisited box below).

DEBATE REVISITED

Canada's Official Multiculturalism: Problem or Solution?

At the beginning of the chapter, public and political reaction to Canada's Multiculturalism was shown to be extremely varied. For some, official Multiculturalism is perceived as a good thing in securing benefits; for others, multiculturalism is bad because of controlling properties; for still others, it is good *or* bad depending on the criteria; and for others yet, it is both good *and* bad because of the context (Fleras, 2002). Who is right, and on what grounds? How can sociological models of society provide a principled response?

A functionalist model of society acknowledges the contribution of Multiculturalism in creating a cohesive and consensual Canada. For functionalists, by positively contributing to Canada's shared consensus and cooperative coexistence, Multiculturalism is by definition "functional." Multiculturalism is perceived as an impression management device whose role (function) is to foster harmony by making both the majority and minority more comfortable with each other. The removal of prejudicial and discriminatory barriers further secures its status as a consensus-inducing strategy for living together with differences.

A conflict model of society disagrees with this positive spin. While functionalists point to the role of Multiculturalism in contributing to stability, cooperation, and order, conflict models emphasize its centrality in advancing a society's *vested interests*. According to conflict theorists, a top-down Multiculturalism is little more than a case of "ruling elites controlling unruly ethnics." It represents a calculated tactic employed by the ruling elites to secure consent in preserving the prevailing distribution of power, privilege, and property. As a conflict management device, a commitment to Multiculturalism tends to foster a false consciousness (hegemony). With Multiculturalism as a governance model, the real sources of exploitation in society are camouflaged by proposing cultural solutions to structural problems. Multiculturalism thus creates the "illusion of inclusion" by securing a smokescreen for control and exploitation.

The controlling dimensions of Multiculturalism are particularly evident when applied to women. With certain forms of multiculturalism, particularly those laissez-faire European models that tend to promote group rights over the individual rights of women (see Chapter 10), women are doubly penalized by society and by ethnic communities. According to feminist conflict theory, women may be victimized in those Multicultural contexts that promote cultural differences or religious beliefs at odds with women's opportunities and rights, in the process raising the question of whether discriminatory practices within faith-based groups constitute a reasonable limit on a woman's equality rights (Okin, 1999; Stein, 2007; Whyte, 2007). However, in both versions of conflict theory, a bottoms-up approach to multiculturalism that uses diversity and difference as a catalyst for challenge and change may prove liberating or empowering (see the discussion of "critical multiculturalism" in Chapter 10).

Interactionists differ in focus from functionalists or conflict theorists. Rather than assessing it on a scale of good or bad, they frame Multiculturalism as a negotiated site involving socially constructed and meaningful interaction. People define situations in terms of their perception of Multiculturalism and then respond on the basis of these definitions. Multiculturalism itself becomes a site in which different interests interact to impose their definition of the situation at the expense of others. Within the dominant sector, Multiculturalism may be endorsed by some as a basis for economic growth or cultural vitality. It may be rejected by others as a recipe for disaster that inadvertently reinforces ethnic divisions and intergroup conflicts. Conversely, the subdominant sector may support Multiculturalism as a window of opportunity in levelling the playing field or, alternatively, repudiate it as a hegemonic

device for co-opting minorities into the mainstream. The interplay of these factions contributes to the ongoing and socially constructed dynamic that animates the politics of Canada's official Multiculturalism.

Each sociological model of society casts a different spin on official Multiculturalism. Multiculturalism is seen as "functional" in bolstering the collective and moral sentiments upon which order and stability are conveyed; in "conflict" terms, Multiculturalism reflects, reinforces, and advances an unequal status quo either through domination or exploitation; and for social interactionists, Multiculturalism is part of a broader process in collectively and socially constructing reality.

None of the models describing the relationship of Multiculturalism to society is inherently superior to the other. Each paradigm reflects a particular vision of a changing and diverse society, together with the role of Multiculturalism in advancing this vision. Insofar as there is no consensus in assessing the value or priority of one model over another, it is the interplay of these models that provides a more complex and comprehensive view of what is going on (Gilroy, 2004). In the final analysis, preference for one perspective over another is rarely a case of right or wrong. Rather, the key lies in acknowledging the multidimensionality of Multiculturalism as positive yet negative, empowering yet disempowering, constraining yet constructed—depending on the criteria, context, and consequences. The push and pull of these multicultural paradoxes culminate in the sometimes fierce debates over the politics of governance in advancing a framework for living together with differences equitably and in dignity.

Chapter Highlights

- Sociological interest in race, ethnic, and Aboriginal relations focuses on the politics of intergroup dynamics within the contexts of power, privilege, and property. Race, Aboriginal, and ethnic relations as relationships of inequality related to power, privilege, and property are constructed, expressed, and supported, as well as challenged and transformed, by way of government practices, institutional reform, and minority resistance.
- Canada's race, ethnic, and Aboriginal relations record requires a working perspective. Compared with the past, Canada has come a long way in managing diversity more equitably. When the human rights violations in other countries are considered, Canada is indeed a beacon of enlightenment. However, compared with the ideals that Canadians espouse, we still have a long way to go.
- Canada is an extremely diverse society. However, it's not nearly as diverse as some other countries; its diversity comes with benefits and costs, and debates over how much and what kind of diversity persist.
- Governance models of race, ethnic, and Aboriginal relations that describe recurrent patterns of interaction—namely genocide, assimilation, segregation, integration, and pluralism—materialize when racially and culturally different groups come into sustained contact and compete over scarce resources. These models differ in terms of objectives, assumptions about diversity, means, and anticipated outcomes.
- Various sociological models or perspectives on society exist for the study of racial and ethnic relations. Functionalist models are concerned with demonstrating how diversities are managed to ensure stability and order. Conflict models envision society as a site of competition for scarce resources between ethnically different groups. Symbolic interactionist models emphasize the socially constructed nature of minority–majority relations.
- The contested notion of official Multiculturalism as good, bad, good or bad, or good and bad provides insights into a key sociological truism: How one interprets social reality depends on which sociological paradigm is applied as an explanatory framework for understanding the relationship of Multiculturalism to society.

For further study, you can access the Case Studies referenced in this chapter at **www.pearsoncanada.ca/fleras**.

Review Questions

1. What is meant by the concept of race, Aboriginal, and ethnic relations?
2. Briefly compare and contrast the concepts of genocide, assimilation, integration, segregation/separation, and pluralism as strategies for "managing" race, Aboriginal, and ethnic relations.
3. Compare the status of Canada's official Multiculturalism from the perspective of all three sociological models of social reality.

4. Select any issue or incident involving racial, ethnic, or Aboriginal groups. Analyze the issue or incident from the perspective(s) of one or all three sociological models of social reality.

5. Canada's record in engaging with racial, ethnic, and Aboriginal peoples can be summed up by the expression "the good, the bad, and the in-between." Indicate what is meant by this expression. Do you agree or disagree with this assessment? Why?

Endnotes

1. Racialized minorities and immigrants are not necessarily synonymous. Immigrants can be racialized (from Asia or Africa) or not (from Europe or the Antipodes), whereas racialized minorities can be foreign born (immigrants) or Canadian born.

Links and Recommendations

FILMS

Hotel Rwanda (2004)

Based on a true story of a hotelier who saved hundreds of people from the machetes of Hutu extremists, the first half of the film provides a chilling example of how hatred is mobilized to justify the genocidal killing of friends and neighbours. Also recommended are the equally powerful indictments of the Rwandan tragedy, *Sometimes in April* (2005) and *Shake Hands with the Devil* (2004).

The Devil Came on Horseback (2007)

No punches are pulled in this award-winning and searing documentary of the genocide in Darfur, Sudan, based on exclusive photographs and first-hand testimony from a military observer. The audience is taken on a harrowing nightmare across Darfur where the province is being purged of its black and largely animist or Christian population by the combination of an Arab/Muslim-run government in Khartoum, with the assistance of its unofficial militia (Janjaweed warriors). Be forewarned: This film is not for the squeamish.

Rabbit-Proof Fence (2002)

An Australian film that captures the notion of genocide in slow motion through forced assimilation. No one can be unmoved by the pluck of three young Aborigine children who travel over 2100 kilometres to escape boarding school and return to their community (twice, no less) by following a fence for keeping out rabbits.

BOOKS

A Companion to Racial and Ethnic Studies, edited by David Theo Goldberg and John Solomos (2002). A powerful collection of original articles that cover a broad spectrum of issues pertaining to race and ethnicity, with a slant toward Europe, but still applicable to Canada.

Race and Ethnicity in Canada: A Critical Introduction (2nd ed.), by Vic Satzewich and Nikolaos Liodakis (2010). An excellent introduction to a complex and highly charged field that challenges the reader to critically engage with and reflect upon the politics of difference in Canada.

Race and Ethnicity: Finding Identities and Inequalities (2nd ed.), by Leo Driedger (2003). By combining insights from a variety of disciplines, this book by one of the intellectual giants in the field provides a comprehensive survey of race and ethnic relations in Canada from a multiethnic and pluralistic perspective.

Understanding Diversity: Ethnicity and Race in the Canadian Context, by Wsevolod Isajiw (1999). Written by one of the leading lights in Canadian ethnicity studies, this book encourages Canadians to think about race and ethnicity in a more analytical manner if they want to better understand the role and status of ethnicity in Canada and abroad.

Identity and Belonging: Rethinking Race and Ethnicity in Canadian Society, by Sean P. Hier and B. Singh Bolaria (2007). This collection of previously published material should provide a critically informed selection of readings to supplement any introductory text on race, ethnic, and Aboriginal relations.

WEBSITES

Centre for Research–Action on Race Relations—One of Canada's leading non-profit race relations organizations, with a mandate to promote racial harmony and equality:
  www.media-awareness.ca/english/resources/profiles/advocacy/crarr_profile.cfm

Genocide Watch—Access to a clearinghouse of information on how to end the senseless slaughter of human beings:
  www.genocidewatch.org

Citizenship and Immigration Canada—An overview of multiculturalism in Canada is provided by this government site:
  www.cic.gc.ca/english/multiculturalism/index.asp

Race and Ethnicity Server—A wealth of general information on race and ethnic relations:
  http://race.eserver.org

CHAPTER 2

The Politics of Race

Police Racial Profiling: A Few Bad Apples or the Whole Rotten Barrel?

Both sociologists and filmmakers have long known what postmodernists claim to have popularized: People see the world differently because of who they think they are, what they own, how they work, and where they are socially located in society. The acclaimed Japanese film director Akira Kurosawa explored this perspectival theme in his brilliantly conceived film *Rashomon*. This 1951 epic pivots around competing versions of a brutal incident involving a woman, her samurai husband, a bandit, and a peasant woodcutter as eyewitness, each differently interpreting the death of the husband (murder or suicide?) and the bandit's sexual tryst with the samurai's wife (rape or seduction?), albeit in a self-serving manner, resulting in wildly divergent accounts (Heider, 1988). In presenting this multi-perspectival viewpoint in which there are no innocent perspectives or value-free perceptions, Kurosawa tapped into the postmodernist credo that neither absolute truth nor objective reality exist, only discourses about truth or reality whose "truthfulness" or objectivity are situationally constructed. The process by which divergent viewpoints interpret the same incident in mutually exclusive

ways based on their location in society has come to be known as the "Rashomon effect."

The cognitive relativism implicit in the Rashomon effect may help to untangle a paradox in race relations. That is, why do some believe that racism in Canada is under control while others think it is out of control? At one end of this debate are those who underplay the salience of racism in Canadian society. They prefer to see racism as an isolated and random act of a dysfunctional individual (a "few bad apples" thesis) whose aberrant actions violate the norms of a tolerant society. At the other end are those who emphasize the spiralling magnitude and corrosive effect of racism. Racism is deemed to be institutionalized, deeply embedded within the framework of a racialized society, resistant to change because of systemic barriers, and reflective of a system that is fundamentally rotten to the core, with the "bad apples" simply a manifestation of the creeping rot (Gosine, 2003). Or as Lincoln Alexander, former lieutenant-governor of Ontario once declared about the pervasive reality of racism in the daily lives of blacks: "Racism is everywhere.

(Continued)

There's racism all over the bloody place" (as cited in Duncanson, Freed, & Sorensen, 2003, p. A16).

This perceptual divide is largely racialized. Minority discourses criticize Canada for being a systemically racist society in need of transformation from the top down. For the mainstream, however, Canada is fundamentally tolerant, with a few untutored lumps to spoil an otherwise healthy brew. A similar perceptual divide prevails in the United States, where public attitudes toward the criminal justice system remain bifurcated along racialized lines: a number of whites see the system as colour-blind and fair (i.e., the "few bad apples" thesis), while a number of blacks see it as severely biased against them (i.e., the "whole rotten barrel" thesis) (Tator & Henry, 2006).

Nowhere is this polarization more contested than in the paradoxes that pervade the politics of police **racial profiling**. While evidence is overwhelming that police engage in some kind of racial profiling (Tator & Henry, 2006), the fact that denials persist (see Satzewich & Shaffir, 2007/2009) underscores the importance of analyzing what is going on and why? Analysis is question-driven: Do police engage in a criminal profiling based on unlawful behaviour? Or are police actions motivated by racialized stereotypes (Wortley, 2005)? Is a BMW stopped because its driver is speeding, or because the driver is a young black male? If the police do profile, what is the nature of this profiling—random/isolated ("few bad apples") or institutionalized/ routine (the "whole rotten barrel")? If they don't, why does it appear *as if* they do? What kind of database can assist in sorting through this thicket of accusations and denials?

The Kingston Police Services Data Collection Project: Putting Profiling to the Test

The highly contentious issue of police race profiling was put to the test when the Kingston Police Services released the results of a one-year study to determine if profiling existed (Closs & McKenna, 2006). The project was designed to gather information on the nature of non-casual contacts between Kingston police officers and the general public. To determine whether the exercise in police discretion results in discriminatory treatment, each police officer was instructed to fill out a "contact card" that indicated the "race" (i.e., as determined by police officers) as well as the gender and age of those individuals who were stopped on a non-casual basis. A total of 10 114 incidents were eventually tabulated, with traffic stops accounting for about one-third of the stops and pedestrian incidents the remainder.

The results of the report, entitled *Bias-Free Policing* and compiled by University of Toronto criminologist Scot Wortley, proved to be both interesting and provocative, yet somewhat misleading. According to a literal reading of the results, some racialized minorities are stopped more often than others. Blacks, who constitute 0.6 percent of Kingston's resident population, accounted for 2.2 percent of all stops, yielding a stop ratio of 3.67. Compare this figure to whites, who accounted for 92 percent of the stops, as well as 92 percent of the population, for a stop ratio of close to 1.0. Aboriginal peoples were also overrepresented in police stops; however, this overrepresentation was eliminated by controlling for the same individuals who were stopped on multiple occasions. South Asians, who comprise 2.5 percent of Kingston's population, accounted for 1.3 percent of the stops for a stop ratio of 0.5, while other Asians, who comprise 1.3 percent of Kingston's population, accounted for 0.9 percent of the stops for a stop ratio of about 0.8. Or consider the number of stops per 1000 persons of a race (keeping in mind that small population bases can grossly distort ratios): black males 213/1000; black females 74/1000; West Asian males 105/1000; West Asian females 23/1000; Hispanic males 83/1000; Hispanic females 10/1000; white males 75/1000; white females 29/1000; South Asian males 63/1000; South Asian females 19/1000; Aboriginal males 51/1000; Aboriginal females 35/1000; other Asian males 42/1000; Asian females 16/1000.

For some, the results of the Kingston Police Services study confirmed what they already suspected: Some racialized minorities (especially young black males) are unfairly stereotyped and routinely targeted by police. The fact that blacks are disproportionately stopped by the police is overwhelming proof of "anti-black racism." (It should be noted that of the 289 413 contact cards filled out by the Toronto police officers in 2008 when stopping and questioning people, 24.4 percent of the contacts were identified by the police as black, although blacks account for only 8.4 percent of the city's population [*Toronto Star*, Race Cards?, February 2, 2010]). According to Karen Mock of the Canadian Race Relations Foundation and the late Dudley Laws of Toronto's Black Action Defence Committee, police are clearly guilty of racial profiling because of who they stop rather than what they stop (as cited in Freeze, 2005) (see online Case Study 2.3). Both local and regional media headlines appeared to endorse this conclusion: "Kingston proves race bias," "Activists pounce on police race study," "Kingston police apologize after racial bias study." These headlines were consistent with statements in the *Report of the Commission of Inquiry into Systemic Racism in Ontario's Criminal Justice System* (1995) when it concluded that ". . . police stops for the purpose of control are racialized" (p. 8).

Other studies and surveys tend to reinforce this perception. The head of Quebec's Human Rights and Youth Commission has accused Montreal police services of systemic racial profiling, despite police denials that dismiss any complaint as an exception to standard procedures (Curran, 2010). This claim that young black men are stopped more frequently than young white men is based on an internal report prepared for the Montreal police in 2009, yet quietly shelved despite a database of 163 000 police files ("contact reports") from 2001 to 2007. Between 2006 and 2007, 40 percent of young black men in the communities of Montreal North and Saint Michel were stopped and asked for identification, compared with approximately 5 percent of young white men. About 40 percent of the young blacks who were pulled over were neither fined nor charged with any offence, while about two-thirds of those

(Continued)

questioned by police "fishing expedi-
tions" had no links to local street
gangs.

Montreal police dismissed the
validity of the findings, citing methodological flaws, while acknowledging
a program in place to educate police
officers about the perils of profiling
(Gordon, 2010). A similar reaction
greeted the Kingston Project report.
The president of the Toronto Police
Association was adamant that the
report "proves nothing," much less the
existence of systemic racism within
the police services (see Melchers, 2005,
on methodological problems with the
study. As far as the police are concerned, what critics claim is racial profiling constitutes instead a legitimate
exercise in crime prevention (see
Satzewich & Shaffir, 2007/2009). An
editorial in a major Toronto paper was
equally skeptical of unsubstantiated
claims: If racial profiling exists, why
do police not direct this bias at other
Asians? Perhaps an anti-white bias

could be inferred from the results, as
Asian and South Asian groups are
stopped less frequently per 1000 persons of a race than white people. Is
there a sexist bias (gender profiling) in
light of the three-to-one ratio of male
stops to female stops? Do the data
point to an anti-youth bias (age profiling)? After all, only 7 percent of stops
involved those aged 55 and over, compared with 35 percent of stops for those
between 15 and 24 years of age.

So what is going on, and who is
right (Wortley, 2005)? Do the data
point to an anti-black bias by police?
Or is it the case that young black males
are more likely to engage in unlawful
or suspicious behaviour? Or are blacks
more likely to attract police attention
because of their visibility and preference for public spaces? (See online
Insight 2.1.) How to explain the seemingly polarized reactions to charges of
police profiling? The Debate Revisited
box at the end of this chapter will
address these questions.

INTRODUCTION: PERCEPTIONS AS REALITY

Few will dispute the significance of **race** in shaping intergroup dynamics (Brace, 2005).
References to race not only rationalized nineteenth-century European colonization but
also conferred a pseudo-scientific legitimacy for arbitrarily pigeonholing people into
mutually exclusive categories. The classification of colonized peoples into racialized
"others" secured a simple yet self-serving explanation during the era of European exploration, capitalistic expansion, and imperialist adventures. Race "mattered" for various
reasons, but primarily as (1) a tool for justifying control and inequality, (2) an excuse for
doing the inexcusable, (3) a framework for explaining human differences, and (4) a
rationalization for salving guilty consciences. The race concept may have been little
more than a fiction—a socially constructed **discourse** in defence of white domination—
but its capacity to inflict injury was anything but fictitious.

That race mattered in the historical past is beyond doubt. In both the United States
and Canada, an essentialized vision of race as natural and universal was widely assumed
(Dalmage, 2004). But many are dismayed that race continues to matter in a time when
we should know better (Frederico & Luks, 2005). Perceptions of race exert a pervasive

influence at many different levels of reality—from where people live, to whom they hire, to what they can expect from life. Public participation and political decision making are influenced by prevailing stereotypes and racial prejudices. Social rewards are allocated on the basis of racial affiliation, with the result that race remains a key predictor of who gets what—not because it's real but because people believe it's real and respond accordingly (Galabuzi, 2006; Hier & Bolaria, 2007). Racialized minorities bear the brunt of negative treatment, ranging from polite snubs to blatant racism, resulting in class-action race-discrimination lawsuits against offending institutions (Dei, 2007). Race profiling remains a major problem in the policing of young males, both black and Aboriginal (Tanovich, 2006; Tator & Henry, 2006; Wortley, 2005).

The fact that race continues to matter for precisely the same reasons as in the past—to explain or to rationalize for purposes of control or exploitation—should be cause for concern. Instead of being banished to the dustbins of history, as might be expected of such an erroneous notion, the seemingly antiquated concept of race persists and provokes (Sarich & Miele, 2004). Race in a colour-conscious society represents a tainted status that is deeply discrediting and shameful—a stigma or badge of incompetence—that hinders and hurts. Race matters not because groups of people are biologically inferior, as proclaimed by the narrow-minded or politically incorrect. Rather, it matters because people *perceive* others to be racially distinct and rely on these perceptions to discriminate or differentiate. As a result, race matters because it's experienced as real and discriminatory by those racially coded (that is, "racialized") (Dei, 2005, 2006). And as long as racism and racialized inequality persist in societies that claim to be colour-blind, race will continue to matter in privileging some while disempowering others (Cose, 1997; Morris & Cowlishaw, 1997).

Such persistence raises a perplexing question: Why has a biological concept of minimal scientific worth exerted such a punishing impact in shaping the course of history? Why, indeed, does a largely discredited concept enjoy such enduring power in a multicultural Canada that aspires to colour-blind coexistence? For example, other pre-twentieth century concepts like the theory of phlogiston no longer carry any credibility. But references to race continue to flourish. Divergent opinions account for the persistence. Some believe race is real and must be taken into account in explaining social reality (see online Insight 2.2). Others believe race should never enter public discourse because races do not exist, only perceptions of differences that are elevated to objective status. Still others see race as a biologically based social construction that is politically significant in shaping identities and predicting success (Harding, 2002). In other words, the reality of race is rejected; however, because people perceive it to be real, it continues to matter, in effect reaffirming W.I. Thomas's prescient notion that "things do not have to be real to be real in their consequences."

Admittedly, Canadians appear to be deeply conflicted over the concept of race. In the merit-based and achievement-oriented society that Canada aspires to be, references to race are thought to be retrograde or offensive, especially when the value of a person is downgraded to the level of a stigma beyond one's control. A preoccupation with race compromises the so-called colour-blind principles of liberal universalism, which assert that what we have in common as rights-bearing and morally autonomous individuals is more important for purposes of recognition or reward than what divides us as members of racially distinct groups. And yet the paradoxes of race are all too real (Wallis &

Fleras, 2008). Canadians explicitly reject the race concept, yet unconsciously employ race to make sense of the world. Race may reflect an accident of birth, but it profoundly shapes a person's life or life chances. Race may be skin deep, but remains an infallible marker of a person's worth and predictor of success. Race should never justify differential treatment, either positive or negative, yet it is increasingly salient in reversing discrimination. Finally, reference to race is rejected in evaluating capacity and talents. Nevertheless, Canadians implicitly condone a race-based and unequal status quo that mocks Canada's Multiculturalism principles and inclusiveness commitments.

Not surprisingly, reactions to race invariably invite scorn or criticism, regardless of the position taken. Those who endorse the race concept tend to be dismissed as little more than "knuckle-dragging Neanderthals." Conversely, those who dismiss race as a fantasy are criticized for compromising a people's identity by trampling on social history, group solidarity, or cultural aspirations. Regardless of reactions, the politics are unmistakably real. Race remains a potent social dynamic and political category around which individuals and groups formulate identities or organize their resistance within the very context that denies or excludes (Goldberg & Solomos, 2002). The dangers of delving into a topic that, paradoxically, is real yet surreal are captured below:

> [race] . . . can be seen as nothing but a phantom invented to justify a myriad of power relationships but, on the other hand, is one of history's most instrumental agencies of social composition? How does one write about the most potent instrument of taxonomy ever imposed on humankind without giving added credence to the idea of race as a viable organizing tool? (Hall, 2000, p. 120)

The challenge is clearly before us: References to race must stay clear of dismissing it as purely an "illusion," without falling into the trap of **reifying** race as a definitive category. Race may not be real, but its perception and consequences are. Under these circumstances, we would do well to remember that, when it comes to race, perception *is* reality—even when largely unfounded by empirical evidence. After all, even if race is a socially constructed perception, it is a powerful perception that impacts profoundly on social reality. And yet Canadians appear reluctant to talk about race for fear it may provide more credence than the term deserves, while reflecting poorly on anyone who dares use the *r* word in public. George Sefa Dei (2004) nails it succinctly when he alludes to race as the elephant in the room that no one wants to talk about:

> Race has powerful material, political, and economic currency in our society. Rather than dismiss race, we ought to be honest about it and spend time reflecting on it through critical discussion, instead of sweeping it under the carpet and hope that this will settle everything. Racial categories such as "black," "white," and "brown," etc., no matter how imperfect, are not the problem in themselves. The reality is that these categories organize our society. Rather than deny them, we must challenge the interpretations attached to them.

In other words, race matters not because it is real, but because people tend to act *as if* it were real, with perversely real consequences. Race matters even though it should not, but because it constitutes a lived experience for many, the issue of race must be confronted squarely. Race matters because a person's (or group's) perceived racial location in society will influence identity, experiences, opportunities, and outcomes. And race matters because its presence is so deeply ingrained that dislodging it from people's mindsets will prove a tricky affair (see Foster, 2005). Ken Wiwa (2001) concedes as much when reviewing Lawrence Hill's book *Black Berry, Sweet Juice: On Being Black and White in Canada*:

> Race is just about the trickiest topic to write about with any measure of objectivity, and only brave men or fools should try. Anyone who wants to walk the minefield of race should invest in a thick skin with chameleon-like pigment . . . Because the trouble with race is that there are black and white and a kaleidoscope of shades in between.

Finally, race matters because of its embeddedness in settler societies. Rather than simply an error of perception or exercise in rationalization, as Goldberg (2002) and others note (Thobani, 2007), the race concept proved integral to the emergence of the modern nation-state, resulting in the formation of a caste-like state well into the middle of the twentieth century, with whites occupying what virtually amounted to a racial dictatorship. Even today, Canadian society is neither as colour-blind nor as race neutral as many claim. Instead, it is so profoundly racialized and Eurocentric in its foundational principles, constitutional order, and governance structures that dominant interests and agendas are invariably secured and advanced—sometimes deliberately, sometimes systemically (see Doane, 2007; Goldberg, 2002; Mills, 1997; Omi & Winant, 1994). The institutionalization of a racial(ized) and white supremacist Canada is conveyed by Constance Backhouse (1999) when chiding those commentators who want to eliminate race from consideration in the mistaken hope of smoothing out the past:

> But proponents of "race-neutrality" neglect to recognize that our society is not a race-neutral one. It is built upon centuries of racial division and discrimination. The legacy of such bigotry infects all of our institutions, relationships, and legal frameworks. To advocate "colour-blindness" as an ideal for the modern world is to adopt the false mythology of "racelessness" that has plagued the Canadian legal system . . . and serve[s] to condone the continuation of white supremacy across Canadian society. (p. 274)

The politics of race represent one of the most bewildering dilemmas in contemporary society. While the race concept marks relations of privilege and exploitation for some, it also serves as an indicator of identity, community, and history for others, even if identifying with racial categories as resistance may well intensify the injustice by reifying race (Goldberg & Solomos, 2002). Key questions provide coverage for this chapter: Why did this compulsion to pigeonhole people into predetermined categories arise in the first place (Gallagher, 2007)? Why does race-based thinking persist in the present? Is there any empirical justification for the race concept? How does race continue to justify rules of entitlement and patterns of engagement? Will race continue to matter in the future? Should whiteness be racialized as a (privileged) race? While questions are many, answers are few, and this chapter addresses this paradox by exploring the race concept with respect to (1) meaning and content, (2) genesis and rationale, (3) impact and implications, and (4) validity and value. The chapter reveals those historical and social forces that advanced the race concept as a misguided yet powerful explanatory tool. Emphasis throughout the chapter is on the politics of race in defining "who gets what, and why" rather than on an analysis of race traits per se. In acknowledging that the issue is not about race per se but about people's belief in the existence of something called "race," a shift in thinking is unmistakable—from race as a biological *thing* to race as socially constructed *process* (Blank, Dabady, & Citro, 2004; Wallis & Fleras, 2008).

ON THE ORIGINS OF RACE

> There is in the world a hierarchy of races . . . [Some] will direct and rule the others, and the lower work of the world will tend in the long run to be done by the lower breeds of men. This much we of the ruling colour will no doubt accept as obvious. (Murray, 1900, as cited in Banton, 1987, p. vii)

For many, the race concept has outlived its utility as an explanatory framework. The concept itself originated with European expansion, conquest, and settlement, including the expansion of the cross-Atlantic slave trade, crude evolutionary theories, the appearance of human and biological sciences (with their focus on comparative anatomy), and international competition (Brace, 2005). European expansion in regions with culturally diverse populations spawned a global division of labour in which "races" were assigned particular economic functions based on their physical appearance, local resources, power to resist, geographical location, and cultural proximity to Europe (Walker, 1997). European imaginations were piqued by sustained contact with highly diverse populations whose appearances and cultures stimulated amusement, fascination, and repulsion. Clearly, then, any theorizing of race must go beyond simple cultural politics or misaligned perceptions by acknowledging its structure and dynamics within the crucible of political and economic developments (Anderson, 2007).

Exploration and "Enlightenment"

Race thinking thrived in the intellectual climate of the Age of Enlightenment. Reference to race was consistent with Enlightenment philosophies that extolled the virtues of human progress and individual perfectibility. Enlightenment doctrines reflected the humanist thesis that sharply distinguished humans from animals, so that humanity entailed a progressive movement beyond nature by transcending its limitations (Anderson, 2007). Increasingly precise systems of classification were formulated and aligned hierarchically on the following assumptions: that each life form (1) occupied a distinctive and specific place within the natural order of things, (2) embodied a singular and defining essence that left no room for ambiguity, and (3) possessed a distinctive set of identifiable and fixed characteristics that distinguished it from others (Ewan & Ewan, 2006). The classification of diverse peoples into ranked race categories secured a "common-sense" framework for explaining human differences beyond simple references to climate or history. Far from being the product of irrationality or hate, the race concept bolstered an Enlightenment commitment to classifying the diversity of the world's plants, animals, and peoples into a single grand scheme (Goldberg, 1993).

To be sure, references to race prevailed prior to European exploration and expansion. Embryonic forms of race thinking existed among the Chinese and Arabs in the late Middle Ages (Goldberg, 1993). Ancient peoples possessed an intense aversion to those who were different. But this antipathy toward others was anchored in superstition or ignorance rather than in comprehensive theories rooted in a quasi-scientific commitment to quantification and measurement (Jaret, 1995). Europeans, too, had long relied on other criteria for demonizing those beyond the pale of Christianity. For instance, the world of the Middle Ages was divided into Christian and non-Christian sectors. Non-Christians were viewed as wild and untamed pagans who had crawled out from beneath the flat world to test Christian patience. Heathens were dispatched to the lower rungs of the ladder of creation—a stable and static hierarchy that relegated lesser beings to one end and Christians to the other. Primitives and savages were fortunate to have occupied the realms in between.

The dichotomy between believers and non-believers should not be underestimated. The intensity and cruelty of the violence espoused by the Crusades, the Inquisition, and the Protestant Reformation—all in the name of God—verify this. Still, these earlier patterns of exclusion were no match for the ruthlessness unleashed under the banner of race. Disparaging non-Westerners as worthless and unsalvageable except as beasts of burden was one thing. It was quite another to construct elaborate classificatory schemes that invoked crypto-scientific explanations to legitimize worldwide exploitation and domination. With the publication of Robert Knox's *The Races of Man* in 1850, relations of inferiority/superiority were no longer aligned along the religious plane, but fixed in the terrestiality of somatic hierarchies (Anderson, 2007). The European races self-anointed themselves as superior, while other so-called races were assigned an inferior status, with colour and character as badges of social inferiority. Of course, not all of Europe was awash with racists who relished every opportunity to disparage and exploit distant peoples (Biddiss, 1979). Concern and compassion surely existed. But Europeans were among the first to popularize the race concept as a quantifiable formula for explaining away human diversity in an expansionist era.

Justifying Colonial Exploitation

It has been suggested that Europeans manipulated the concept of race as one way of domesticating human diversity. The proliferation of racial doctrines or dogmas fed into the racial mindset. Racial doctrines originated to condone the negative treatment of non-Western populations who were perceived as irrelevant or inferior. Under the sway of these dogmas, Europeans embarked on so-called civilizing crusades that cloaked the exploitation of inhabitants, with an attendant disregard for their human rights (Hommel, 2001). The requirements of an expanding capitalist system were reflected in a need for new foreign markets, investment opportunities, cheap labour, and accessible resources. In addition, European imperialist expansion intensified an obsession with accumulating foreign territories for nationalistic, decorative, or strategic reasons. Admittedly, the race concept did not necessarily originate to justify European control or domination of others; nevertheless, the imposition and unintended impact of these demeaning doctrines had a controlling effect on indigenous populations. When sanctioned by human and biological sciences, these classifications made group differences appear more rigid, entrenched, comprehensive, and scientifically valid (Stepan, 1982; Stocking, 1968). When harnessed to military prowess and technological advances, the effects proved fatal.

This predatory approach toward global relations concealed a paradox. First, how could the so-called civilized and Christian nations rationalize and justify the blatant exploitation of others? Second, how could colonialist exploitation be sustained without contradicting the image of Europeans as a sophisticated and enlightened people with a moral duty to civilize and convert? Answers to these uncomfortable questions inspired an ideology that condoned the mistreatment of others as natural or normal—even necessary. The contradiction between Christian ideals and exploitative practices was masked and mediated by the racist conviction that lower-ranked races would accrue benefits from servitude, exposure, and close supervision (Lerner, 1997). This ideology not only rationalized the sorting of populations along racial lines but also set the tone for asserting absolute European supremacy at the expense of those most vulnerable. As Martin and Franklin (1973) write:

> [The] advent [of race] seemed to be due in large measure to the need for a rationalization of the exploitation of certain groups . . . This proposition was also advanced to justify the imperialism and colonialism that flourished . . . Racism became a convenient ideological defense for social practices which patently and flagrantly violated basic social and institutional principles. (p. 71)

Racial doctrines arose to "soften" the impact of imperialist encounters throughout Central and South America, the Caribbean, Africa, Australia, and New Zealand. By dismissing overseas races as inferior or subhuman, Europeans could exploit "inferior stocks" with impunity while oppressing them without remorse or guilt. And because racial differences were ingrained as fixed and immutable, Europeans were excused of any wrongdoing when improving the plight of the less fortunate in the name of Progress. With consciences salved, they were free to do whatever was expedient to conquer or colonize.

Clearly, references to race must go beyond its status as a folk theory. Rather, race reflects, reinforces, and advances the principle of white supremacy as a global system of domination for the last 500 years (Keevak, 2011). According to Mills (1997), race is the quintessential racism project that requires a global theoretical framework to explain the displacement of indigenous peoples and exploited minorities. Or as W.E.B. Du Bois (1940) wrote, the history of the modern world is ". . . epitomized in one word—Empire; the domination of white Europe over Black Africa and Yellow Asia through political power built on the economic control of labour, income, and ideas" (p. 96). To be sure, Mills writes, a cabal of whites did not conspire to dominate the world. Nevertheless, whites in positions of power embarked on a mission to expand their power and privilege through the exploitation of the global south. The conclusion seems inescapable: When race is framed as a global historical occurrence, neither racial harmony nor racial justice will materialize without acknowledgment of the broader context in which both whites and non-whites operate, the degree to which whiteness permeates every issue and institution in society, and the role of white privilege in defining who gets what and why (Thomas, 2007; see also Garvey & Ignatieff, 1996; McIntosh, 1988; Omi & Winant, 1994).

In other words, the modern state is a racial and racialized state. Not only is it implicated in the reproduction of local conditions of racist exclusion, but it has always conceived of itself as racially configured with respect to who gets what. While the apartheid regime in South Africa and the colour bar in the United States are the most egregious examples of race regimes on behalf of white interests, the settler societies of Canada and Australia were no less racialized, sometimes openly, but often more subtly and systemically (Fleras & Spoonley, 1999). Rather than something incidental to the functioning of the state both then and now, race is fundamental in establishing and maintaining a system of racial domination that espouses colour-blind principles but tolerates colour-conscious discrimination. Race underlies political systems of power and privilege, and that alone should disabuse any notions of simple or simplistic solutions (Vickers, 2002).

Doctrines of Racial Superiority

As noted by many, race emerged as an eighteenth-century concept to label, describe, and classify large groups of people by reference to immutable traits such as the colour of their skin. Doctrines of racial superiority began to appear once racial types were assigned a fixed moral value—that is, prescribed by nature as superior or inferior, and backed by the unquestioned authority of science. These hierarchies were intrinsically racist in that they employed the authority of science to confirm the superiority of some groups over others (Stepan, 1982). Despite the arbitrariness of the criteria or classification, their impact was devastating. In justifying inequality between races, the doctrines endorsed the commodi- fication of races as objects for exploitation or control, as targets of pity or contempt, and as victims of progress to be pushed around with impunity. The most egregious of these doctrines included *social Darwinism, eugenics,* and *scientific racism.*

Social Darwinism evolved into a widely acceptable doctrine of racial superiority toward the end of the nineteenth century. The doctrine borrowed a number of Darwin's biological propositions, then reworked them to further the aims of overseas exploitation. Foremost were the notions of a "struggle for survival" and "survival of the fittest" on a global scale. Social Darwinist philosophies provided a philosophical justification for Western **colonialism** by condoning the subjugation of colonized peoples on grounds consistent with the laws of nature. In the words of Nancy Stepan (1982):

> Evolutionism provided a new emotionally charged, yet ostensibly scientific language with which to express old prejudices . . . [T]he "lower races" were now races that had "evolved" least far up the evolutionary ladder, had lost out in the "struggle for survival" and were "unfit" for the competition between tribes. Or they represented the evolutionary "childhood" of the white man. (p. 83)

Social Darwinism portrayed the social world as a gladiatorial arena where popula- tions were locked in mortal combat over scarce and valuable resources. Those who were better adapted to compete in this ongoing struggle prospered and progressed to the apex of the evolutionary ladder. Those with less adaptive attributes were vanquished in the competitive struggle for evolutionary survival. A race-based pecking order was estab- lished that justified spoils to the victor; for the vanquished, a life of servitude and suffer- ing. These doctrines not only exonerated the colonialists of responsibility for colonizing the indigenes but also explained European superiority and justified out-group exploita- tion, while promulgating the virtues and inevitability of **capitalism** as the engine room of human progress and social enlightenment.

Eugenics With **eugenics**, racist doctrines assumed even more sinister proportions at the turn of the twentieth century. Countries like the United States, Britain, Russia, and Japan proposed the idea that the social, mental, and behavioural qualities of the human "race" could be improved by selective manipulation of its hereditary essence (Gillette, 2007). Fortified by the discovery of hereditary laws, the eugenics movement collectively advo- cated the improvement of human stock by purging undesirables through selective breed- ing procedures. Eugenics operated on the assumption that the genetically unfit were a threat to society. Defectives such as racial minorities, the congenitally deformed, and the "retarded" would be sterilized in hopes of curbing the further "bastardization" of the human species (Banton, 1987). By contrast, racially superior stocks were encouraged to freely propagate to ensure the proliferation of the "fittest" (Stepan, 1982).

Eugenicists in the United States were instrumental in restricting immigration from less "fit" countries in Eastern and Southern Europe. They promoted sterilization laws in 31 states that disproportionately targeted lower-income groups (Kevles, 1995). In Canada, the 1928 *Sexual Sterilization Act* in Alberta condoned the sterilization of nearly 3000 women, most of them poor or Aboriginal, before being repealed in 1972 (Caulfield & Robertson, 1996). Eugenics as an ideological movement culminated with the compulsory sterilization and mass destruction of millions of "undesirables" under Nazi genocide. In time, however, eugenics collapsed as a doctrine, largely because of the declining legitimacy of race as an explanatory framework. Nevertheless, the idea of eugenics has persisted into the present, albeit in diverse and somewhat more disguised forms, and without the backing of a receptive public.

Scientific Racism Racial dogmas under the umbrella of **scientific racism** became especially marked in the United States. The existence of an indigenous Native population, a more mobile black population, and the ongoing influx of European immigrants transformed the United States into a fiercely contested site. The movement of black Americans from the south to the north further intensified competition in urban areas, where blacks competed with white immigrants for jobs and housing (van den Berghe, 1967). In light of such social turmoil, American whites were clearly receptive to any scientific support for putting racialized minorities in their place. The most popular of these was the intelligence quotient (IQ) test, which continues to fascinate some, but repel others.

Scientific racism was predicated on the premise that racial capacities between populations could be measured and evaluated by statistical means. The introduction of the IQ test proved invaluable in supporting a link between race and intelligence. The IQ test (or the Stanford-Binet test) was designed at Stanford University by French psychologist Alfred Binet to assist in locating deficiencies in French pupils' cognitive skills. American interests co-opted the test—which had never been intended to measure an individual's level of intelligence—and applied it indiscriminately. A notable application took place during the latter stages of World War I: Since blacks were more likely than whites to perform poorly on these Eurocentric tests, the IQ test quickly established itself as a means of racializing recruits. Better-educated whites became officers, while blacks and poor whites were consigned to "cannon fodder" status.

Repeated tests revealed that blacks, on average, scored about 15 percentage points less than whites on the IQ test. This gap was taken as proof that blacks were inherently intellectually inferior. With few exceptions, many believed that this biogenetic gap could never be bridged, even with environmental improvements and enrichment programs. But in their hurry to promote white intellectual supremacy, the advocates of the IQ test took some unwarranted liberties with the results. For example, while blacks scored consistently lower than whites as a group, the range of variation between black and white scores was comparable. The highest and the lowest scores within each category were approximately the same. Also relevant but widely ignored were variations in group averages. Whereas blacks on average scored about 15 percent lower than whites, 15 percent of the blacks scored higher than the average score for whites—implying by inference that some blacks were intellectually superior to many whites. Furthermore, both the social environment and the test's cultural bias were ignored as possible explanations.

Debates persist about the relevance of race to explaining intellectual differences. For some, environments can strongly influence a person's intelligence, with the result that the interplay of genetic and environmental factors makes them impossible to separate (Sternberg & Grigorenko, 1997). Individual variation in intelligence is not the same as a race-based theory of fixed intelligence. Furthermore, low IQ scores or differences in cognitive ability do not create social problems or social inequality. On the contrary, they may originate from conditions of poverty and powerlessness, which are likely to foster lower IQ scores. For others, intelligence is largely inherent and inherited. According to the authors of *The Bell Curve: Intelligence and Class Structure in American Life*, Charles Murray and Richard J. Herrnstein (1994), the relatively low levels of intelligence exhibited by certain races such as blacks are (1) real, (2) measurable by IQ tests, (3) inherited, (4) predictive, and (5) resistant to modification. Low levels of intelligence, in turn, are responsible for social problems such as poverty, lawlessness, and dysfunctional families. And in a June 2005 issue of the journal *Psychology, Public Policy, and Law*, co-authors Philippe Rushton and Arthur Jensen continue to assert that genes explain 50 percent of the differences in IQ between different races, with Asians ranked higher than whites in intelligence, but whites higher than blacks.

Two reasons may account for the tenacity of scientific racism. First, if intelligence is biologically innate and largely impervious to environmental modification, then the mainstream cannot be held responsible for the plight of racialized **minority groups**. The results of these tests can be used to justify the negative treatment of minorities, ranging from segregated facilities to inferior programs. These results can also be employed to preempt progressive change, as there is little hope for improvement, despite evidence that group averages can rise over time (Flynn, 1984). Second, IQ tests are an effective device for explaining away differences through their logical presentation of "facts" and simple causal explanations. They possess an aura of scientific validity that is substantiated by the "hocus pocus" of quantification and measurement. The halo effect associated with science can also create the impression that race is a respectable intellectual position with a legitimate place in the national agenda.

RETHINKING THE RACE CONCEPT: FROM BIOLOGICAL REALITY TO SOCIAL CONSTRUCTION

The completion of the Human Genome Project in 2000 revealed what many had suspected: Human beings belong to a single biological species (*Homo sapiens*) within a larger grouping or genus (*Homo*). Humans as a species are 99.9 percent genetically identical, with just 0.1 percent of genetic material accounting for human diversity. The term "species" is used in the genetic sense of a breeding population whose members possess the capacity to naturally produce fertile offspring. Within the human species numerous populations exhibit genetically diverse frequencies. These gene frequencies are manifest in readily observable characteristics including skin colour (*phenotypes*) in addition to less discernible attributes such as blood types (*genotypes*). Biologically speaking, then, the race concept refers to this distribution of genes based on clusters of phenotypes or genotypes between populations. It may also refer to a subpopulation of the species in which certain hereditary features appear more frequently in some population pools than others because of relative reproductive isolation (Jaret, 1995).

On the surface, it might appear as if human diversity were too broad to incorporate humanity into a single species. But appearances can be deceiving. Judging by our capacity to propagate with each other, and produce fertile offspring, all individuals qualify as members of the human "race" (or, more accurately, human species). Human beings constitute a single intrabreeding species with phenotypic and genotypic variation, but this variation generally exists only at the most superficial level. In that sense, humans resemble other floral and faunal species that also exhibit varying gene frequencies and distributions. Anatomical differences exist, of course, and span the spectrum from phenotypical features such as skin colour and consistency of ear wax (moist or crumbly) to genotypical attributes such as blood chemistry (A, B, O, AB), metabolic rates, and physiological functions such as susceptibilities to disease (Jaret, 1995). Most differences reflect environmental adaptations in accordance with conventional evolutionary principles of mutation and natural selection. These differences presumably contributed to our collective survival as relatively distinct population clusters.

There was no dearth of initiatives to study human diversity within a race-based framework. This preoccupation with classifying humans into categories of race reflected an Enlightenment-era quest for unitary schemes to explain the totality of human experience (Goldberg, 1993). Just as early anthropologists devised a host of unilinear evolutionary schemes to explain the coexistence of civilization with barbarism and savagery, so too did social theorists resort to race as an all-encompassing framework for understanding human differences and group inequalities (Biddiss, 1979). With the race concept, the world was partitioned into a fixed and finite number of permanent categories, each with a distinctive assemblage of physical and behavioural characteristics, and ranked accordingly in descending and ascending orders of superiority and inferiority. On the strength of measurements as proof of fundamental differences, a slew of classificatory schemes (or **racial typologies**) evolved from the eighteenth century onward, with the most common and widely known system of classification consisting of a threefold division of humanity into "Caucasoid" (white), "Negroid" (black), and "Mongoloid" (Asian or Oriental) (see Brace, 2005). Each of these categories was distinguished from the others by common physical features such as skin colour, hair form (fuzzy, wavy, or straight), shape of the eyelid, and so on. Each was also thought to have evolved (or to have had divinely bestowed upon it) its own unique and fixed bundles of characteristics arranged hierarchically based on their cultural sophistication or biological proximity to European stock.

These typologies continue to elicit interest. A professor of psychology from the University of Western Ontario, Philippe Rushton, unleashed a storm of controversy when his 1994 book, *Race, Evolution, and Behavior: A Life History Perspective*, promoted a theory of racialized evolution to account for human differences across a broad range of domains. While few social scientists concurred with Rushton's claims, his ideas did resonate with that portion of the population that finds comfort in inferiorizing others. Rushton argued that separate races, namely, "Oriental," "Caucasoid," and "Negroid" (Rushton's terminology), evolved distinctive packages of physical, social, and mental characteristics because of different reproductive strategies in diverse environments. High reproductive strategies (many offspring, low nurturing) evolved in tropical climates; low reproductive strategies (few offspring, intense nurturing) in temperate climates. A racial pecking order resulted: "Orientals" (Rushton's terminology) are deemed superior to "Caucasoids" on a range of sociobiological factors. "Caucasoids" are in turn ranked superior to "Negroids" on the grounds of measurements involving skull size, intelligence, strength of sex drive and genital size, industriousness, sociability, and rule-following. For Rushton, "Orientals" as a group have the biggest brains, the smallest genitals, and the least promiscuity; they also are more intelligent, more family focused, and more law abiding than "Negroids," who have the smallest brains, the biggest genitals and the most testosterone, the lowest IQs, and the highest crime rates. "Caucasoids," Rushton concluded, fall in between.

How valid is the race concept as an explanatory tool? Most social scientists have rejected the validity of the race concept as germane to the understanding of human diversity (Brace, 2005; but see Sarich & Miele, 2004). Racial types and typologies have been discredited as pseudo-science and dangerous politics without any redeeming scientific value or empirical merit. Arguments against race thinking are numerous; the most common include the following:

1. Reference to race cannot explain reality because discrete and distinct categories of racially pure people do not exist. The intermingling effect of migration with intermarriage has made it impossible to draw a line around human populations with certain characteristics on one side, but not on the other (Martin & Franklin, 1973). According to the Human Genome Project, humans share 99.9 percent of the same genetic material; not surprisingly, genetic differences within the so-called races are larger than those between races (Gee, 2001). Explicit boundaries between racial groups are non-existent (unlike political boundaries, which are fixed at some point in time). Instead, populations with variable characteristics merge into one another, thus forming gradients (or clines). This makes any division between races a somewhat arbitrary exercise that reflects the whims of the investigator rather than anything intrinsic to reality itself. For example, picture the composition of populations from the north of Europe to the Mediterranean and across to Africa. Where do we draw the line between white, brown, and black populations? Any proposed demarcation is open to dispute as light-skinned northwestern Europeans merge into relatively darker Mediterranean populations and into progressively darker black-skinned populations in Africa. Ultimately, such a division is a subjective decision on the part of the investigator.

2. The integrity of racial typologies is open to question because of high rates of internal variation. Just as physical differences exist among persons who are categorized as Caucasoid ("Nordic, Alpine, Mediterranean, and Indo-Pakistani"), so too equally significant diversity exists within the Asian and black categories. Such internal diversity would appear to invalidate the credibility of any system of classification that strives for universality and consistency. The options are lose–lose: Either an awkwardly large number of distinct categories are created to account for this diversity, or a restricted number of classifications overlook the rich diversity within the human species. Yet no system of classification—expansive or restrictive—can possibly include those that invariably fall into the cracks.

3. There is a tendency to confuse the race concept with human variation. Social scientists do not reject the reality of biogenetic differences between individuals or among groups (populations). Anatomical variations do exist and may help to account for differences in human behaviour, such as sports ability. Nor do social scientists deny the validity of studying these differences in an objective and scholarly fashion. Specific patterns of traits can be classified, for example, but not races as clearly articulated groups since all populations represent bundles of different combinations of traits (Rensberger, 1994). Problems can arise when valid scholarly pursuits that seek to explore human differences harden into an obsession about racial classifications as an explanatory framework. In short, differences exist; what do *not* exist are races as distinct populations with fixed inventories of shared characteristics that can be ranked in ascending and descending orders of superiority.

4. Biological determinism links biology with culture and behaviour. There is no evidence to suggest that some groups (or races) are inherently smarter or faster or more criminal. Human behaviour is a complex, adaptive, and evolving process, involving an interplay of genes with culture and social structure.

5. References to a racial hierarchy represent one of the more odious consequences of the race concept. With race, a doctrine emerges that upholds the proposed superiority of one one over another. On the grounds that races do not exist, it becomes pointless to devote countless studies to the notions of "racial superiority" when reality fails to conform with perception, while perception becomes reality.

Racializing The Race Concept

The politics of race have proven both explosive and divisive in shaping the dynamics of intergroup relations. No matter how often discredited or dismissed as intellectually dead, race continues to bounce back as a politically charged marker of differences and discrimination. Often used unconsciously and without intentional malice, race remains a potent element in everyday life and social encounters, with untapped potential for conflict and misunderstanding (Holdaway, 1996). Even defining race has proven elusive (Biddiss, 1979). There is much value in Ellis Cose's (1997) reference to race ". . . as a strange and flexible concept, with an endless capacity to confound" (p. 1). Part of the problem reflects the multidimensionality of race as a concept in a constant state of flux, both fluid and malleable and sharply contested (Gallagher, 2007; Keevak, 2011). And because its meaning is socially constructed from an array of arbitrary characteristics that are deemed socially important, definitions tend to be highly politicized—dynamic and shifting as well as contradictory and ambiguous, but never far from the thrust and parry of privilege and power (Brace, 2005). In that perceptions of race have proven critical in how reality is defined, organized, and lived by both the dominant and subdominant sectors (James, 2005), the power of an illusion to move or motivate cannot be underestimated.

But the concept of race has shifted in recent years. Where once defined as a thing—a tangible object that could be measured as a fixed biological entity—race is now conceptualized as a process involving the construction and imposition of racially linked meanings. For Goldberg and Solomos (2002), race involves a process (both social and political) by which differences are represented so that attributes like skin colour serve as proxies for identifying, naming, and categorizing the "other." In shifting the focus from race as a thing (i.e., a naturally occurring category) to race as a socially constructed process, attention no longer dwells on the physical attributes of minority groups and their presumed inferiority. Emphasis instead focuses on the perceptions and motivations of those powerful enough to impose race labels that control or restrict opportunities (Chan & Mirchandani, 2002).

Racialization best describes this socially constructed process by which negative racial significance is imposed on groups of people or their activities. As a process by which groups come to be defined as ("racially") different and on that basis subject to negative treatment when, in fact, race is irrelevant, racialization incorporates race as a relevant factor in defining persons, situations, or activities as different, dangerous, and inferior (Bleich, 2006; Coates, 2008; Fleras, 2008; Henry & Tator, 2003). The implications of this shift are critical in rethinking the concept of race relations. Put simply, there is no such thing as race relations in the sense of a "race" of people who stand in a relationship to another "race." To the extent that the race concept has no empirical justification except in perceptual terms, it is more accurate to speak of relationships that have been "racialized" than race relations per se (Bonilla-Silva, 1996). Similarly, it is more accurate to say "racialized minorities" rather than "racial minorities," in part to avoid reifying a concept with no empirical value, in part to reject the **essentializing** of groups as uniform and determined, and in part to acknowledge how minorities are assigned these labels by those with the power to make them stick. Clearly, then, in reflecting, reinforcing, and advancing relationships of power and politics, reference to race says more about those constructing and imposing the labels than about those who are "raced."

To sum up, the concept of race has no biological validity or scientific justification (Brace, 2005). Rather, it represents a social construct that reflects human interests rather than anything inherent or self-evident within reality (Miles, 1982; see also Achenbach, 2004). The consequences of this shift in thinking are significant in rethinking intergroup relations. Race relations are not about relations between races, but rather about relations that have been infused with race overtones ("racialized") by those with power. Race relations are not biological relations, but constitute relations of inequality in which minorities are racialized as inferior or irrelevant. The racialization of relationships confirms the sociological axiom that socially constructed phenomena do not have to be real to be real in their consequences.

TAKING RACE SERIOUSLY: RACE MATTERS

Its entrenchment in Western thought and practice notwithstanding, the legitimacy of race as scientific orthodoxy began to erode shortly after World War I (Walker, 1997). The race concept lost its clout as an explanatory framework, at least among intellectuals, thanks to the pioneering efforts of American anthropologists Franz Boas and Margaret Mead, who proposed social and cultural alternatives; the American sociologist Robert Park, who argued that race was a ruse devised by the ruling class to preserve their privilege; the Swedish sociologist/economist Gunnar Myrdahl, who suggested there was nothing natural about distinctive racial characteristics except as the result of prolonged discrimination; and Sir Julian Huxley, who wrote in 1935 that references to race may have justified political ambitions, economic ends, social bitterness, and class prejudice, but "human races don't biologically exist" (as cited in Pascal, 2006). The UNESCO Statement on Racism in 1950 asserted what was increasingly self-evident: Race was not a biological phenomenon but a social myth that inflicted staggering human costs. Without the backing of the United Nations, the race concept gradually lapsed into disrepute at least in its most explicit form and within polite circles (Brattain, 2007). And yet a paradox prevails: Almost no one believes in race; nevertheless, race continues to be central yet submerged, unimportant yet all consuming, a social fabrication yet a material reality, and a familiar part of the social landscape yet conflicted in meanings and unrestrained by the demands of logic or proof (Pascale, 2007, p. 23).

Race in the United States

That race matters in the United States may be taken as self-evident. Critics point to a country riddled with a historical legacy of slavery and segregation as well as lynchings and the Ku Klux Klan. American racism was animated by a belief in the innate differences between people as a basis for justifying unequal treatment. Even today, the race subtext is unmistakable in public discourses about crime, poverty, and urban decay. Social problems are framed as black-or-white issues, with the result that everything from welfare to income is refracted through the prism of skin colour (Mitchell, 1998). Public debates take place in which welfare mothers, inner-city violence, urban decay, and hard drugs are essentially code terms for "blackness." (Clark-Avery, 2007; White, 2007). Statistical evidence confirms how race matters when it comes to distinguishing the "haves" from the "have-nots." To be sure, race appears to be less important to Americans born after 1960; for example, in a Gallup poll that asked if Americans would vote for a black president, only 5 percent said no compared with 41 percent in 1967 (Lewis, 2008). Nevertheless, the status for many black Americans continues to stagnate or even deteriorate in the aftermath of the civil rights revolution (Assante, 2003): The real median household income for blacks has declined, while an increasing number of black households and children hover below the federal poverty line. To date, the election of the first black president does not appear to have had an appreciable effect in shifting prevailing patterns of power, privilege, and income/wealth.

Not surprisingly, the politics of race continue to perplex and provoke. On one side, race-based distinctions that formerly stigmatized individuals as inferior or irrelevant now serve as a mark of distinction for oppressed groups who are transforming the stigma of oppression into a mark of pride, identity, or resistance (Lerner, 1997). On the other side, the so-called race card may be routinely invoked to instill public fears or to manipulate legal decisions that adversely affect minority women and men. "Black rage" defence strategies are predicated on the principle that the social context in which racialized minorities find themselves may reinforce a state of mind that induces criminal behaviour (Harris, 1997). On yet another side, references to race may be used to solve problems on the grounds that if race is the problem, it must be part of the solution. For example, public schools in the United States remain segregated, including Northeast public school districts, with 51 percent of black students attending schools in which students of colour comprise 90 percent of the student body. The Supreme Court has ruled that these districts can use race to remedy historic discrimination but must find alternative ways to sustain progress once they've corrected past wrongs (DiversityInc, 2008). (See online Debate 2.4 on black-focused schools in Canada.)

Race in Canada

Does race matter in Canada (Vickers, 2002)? Canadians and Americans are often perceived as poles apart when it comes to race relations. Compared with Americans, Canadians appear to reject the notion that race matters or that it should matter (Backhouse, 1999; James & Shadd, 1994, p. 47). Canada is widely applauded for emphasizing achievement and merit rather than skin colour as the basis for recognition, reward, and relationships. Canadians like to exult in the myth that they have a deep aversion to judging others by the colour of their skin. Discussions about race tend to be muted, often employing circumlocutions such as **visible minorities** or ethnicity for fear of inflaming public passions (Fleras, 2008; Li, 2003). A quick reality check suggests otherwise (see online Debate 2.4).

Canada's history was infused by a perception of Canada as a "white man's society"—a view reinforced by Prime Minister Robert Borden, who declared that the Conservative Party stood for a white Canada (as cited in Taylor et al., 2007; see also Razack, 2002; Thobani, 2007). In keeping with the notion of Canada as a white nation, the ideals of racial purity played a pivotal role in defining who got what and why (Agnew, 2007). Immigration programs capitalized on racial factors; immigrants with darker skins were less desirable than those with lighter skins, and considerable effort was expended to keep them out (Avery, 1995; Satzewich, 2007). Legislators and judges endlessly manipulated classifications of race into rigid definitions under Canadian law, erected racial hierarchies, justified racial discrimination, denied racial groups the right to vote, and segregated minorities according to race. For example, the paternalistic and archaic *Indian Act* of 1876, which remains in effect today, is possibly one of the few pieces of legislation in the world designed for a particular race of people. Perceptions of Aboriginal peoples as an inferior race simplified the task of divesting the original occupants of their land and resources.

Race continues to affect contemporary Canada. Racialized minorities bear the brunt of negative treatment, ranging from local snubs to half-hearted service delivery. Prevailing stereotypes and racial prejudices continue to influence people's level of involvement in society, whereas social rewards are allocated on the basis of racial affiliation. Foreign-born racialized minorities tend to earn less than whites, even when educational levels are held constant (Galabuzi, 2006; Pendakur, 2005), while minority women and men with professional degrees find it difficult to get jobs consistent with their credentials (Roscigno et al., 2007). Even the emergence of race-conscious state policies to ameliorate disadvantage, like the *Employment Equity Act*, have endured criticism as tokenistic or divisive (see the Debate box at the beginning of Chapter 5). **People of colour** continue to be employed as cheap and disposable labour in often menial tasks, with racialized minorities serving as the hewers of wood and drawers of water as part of a racialized division of labour (Galabuzi, 2006; Reitz & Banerjee, 2007). Clearly, race matters because minority experiences, identities, and opportunities continue to be racialized—often against their best interests (Fernando, 2006). As Kobayashi and Johnson (2007) put it:

> Canadian society is a landscape of negotiation, in which skin colour takes on multiple shades of meaning. As inhabitants of this landscape, we use culture, ethnicity and physical characteristics to assign places and positions to one another, to fix identities. We do so every day by a simple word or gesture, an exchange over a service counter, or a glance across the room, so that the racialized body is constantly marked and its meaning reinforced. Such assignments of place can deepen or reduce the racial divides created by the meanings we attribute to identity. (p. 1)

In short, race constitutes a moving target that twists and bends across space and time—shifting its shape from race as a biological classification to race as a social myth; from race as objectively real to the reality of race as a social construction; from race as a thing to race as a process; from race as determinative to race as discourse; from race as a personal flaw to the embeddedness of race within society (Backhouse, 1999; Blank, Dabady, & Citro, 2004; Guess, 2006). In such a dynamic and political framework, the following insights into "race matters" are increasingly self-evident:

- Race matters not because it is real ("out there") or because people are inherently inferior, but because people perceive it to be real ("in here") and respond by acting in a manner consistent with this perception, often with negative consequences for those who are "racialized" (Wallis & Fleras, 2008).
- Race matters because settler societies like Canada are designed, are organized, and operate on values, agendas, and standards that privilege the dominant group as normal and necessary, while "others" are dismissed as irrelevant, inferior, or a threat.
- Race matters not because of biological ("racial") differences, but because an exclusive preoccupation with biology detracts from scrutinizing those opportunity structures that may account for inequalities.
- Race matters because reference to race has a controlling effect on those who are racially devalued (or racialized).
- Race matters because whiteness matters, not in the sense of biological superiority, but because it is tacitly assumed to be normal and necessary in (1) defining who gets what, (2) establishing norms of right, acceptable, and desirable, and (3) providing a normative standard for judging and criticizing "others" in Canada. Not surprisingly, those with the most power and privilege are least aware of their privileged status because it all seems so normal—as the box that follows demonstrates.

Whiteness Matters: Racializing Whiteness as Race Privilege

Race Matters in a White-Dominated Society

There is a paradox at play in contemporary race debates. Many believe that race shouldn't matter for two reasons: First, the concept lacks empirical validity or biological reality; second, skin colour (shorthand for race) is irrelevant in an ostensibly merit-based and colour-blind society. And yet, in a white-dominated society, race matters. As Henry and Tator (1993) remind us,

people's skin colour may be the single most important factor in determining their dignity, identity, self-esteem, and opportunities. Or put in slightly more sociological terms, where one is socially located in society with respect to skin colour (or race) will profoundly influence a person's life (experiences), self-image (identity), and life chances (outcomes).

Most Canadians will admit that certain minorities are disadvantaged because of skin colour. Many may also concede that, because of colour-coded barriers, minority disadvantages have less to do with individual failure and more to do with restricted opportunity structures. But few Canadians are prepared to concede how "whiteness" plays a critical role in privileging some while disprivileging others (Wise, 2005). They are reluctant to acknowledge whiteness as a category of race, just as men are often excluded from the category of gender. As a result, whites will see "others" as "races," but view themselves as "raceless"—as a neutral and colourless norm that manages to be everything yet nothing, everywhere yet nowhere. Yet whites are "raced" just as men are "gendered," and failure to acknowledge this reality renders whites above the fray of racial politics.

Reference to whiteness is not intended as an attack on whites. Like the editors of *Race Traitor* magazine whose motto, "treason to whiteness is loyalty to humanity,"[1] advocates abolishing white privilege, the focus here is critically self-reflective: first, challenging whites to think of their social location, experience, and identities as racialized (Byrne, 2010); second, analyzing whiteness as a power relation structured in the service of privilege and domination (Garner, 2007; Kil, 2010); third, reflecting on how white skin preference has operated openly or unconsciously as an unmarked and unearned marker of privilege that permeates society (Henry & Tator, 2003); and fourth, acknowledging that a pattern of white privilege and advantage cannot exist outside the context of a white supremacist society and those acts, decisions, and policies that bolster a process of domination (Leonardo, 2004).

Moreover, just as whiteness as race is rendered invisible, so too are its privileges and benefits (McIntosh, 1988; Satzewich, 2007). Being white means one can purchase a home in any part of town without being "blacklisted" or "red-lined" by the local real estate market. Being white allows one to go strolling around shopping malls without the embarrassment of being "blackballed" (e.g., followed, frisked, monitored, or fingerprinted). Being white ensures one a freedom of movement without being pulled over by the police for "driving while black" ("DWB") or "flying while Arab" ("FWA"). Being white simplifies identity construction since whiteness is normal, whereas identity construction is a central and ongoing aspect of minority existence because people must define who they are in relationship to whiteness (see *Race Is a Four-Letter Word*, National Film Board of Canada, 2006). Finally, being white allows one to take credit for success without raising suspicion. Meanwhile, blame for failure is a white person's alone, without implicating the entire community in the process. In other words, being white excuses a person from having to feel guilty about, be judged by, or make excuses for the misdeeds of individuals from the group. Or, as an Australian Aboriginal woman once put it, "If a whitefella does something wrong, he's wrong; if a blackfella does something wrong, we're all wrong" (as cited in Morris & Cowlishaw, 1997).

Put bluntly, whiteness is a privilege that is largely unearned yet tacitly

(Continued)

accepted as representing normality, dominance, and control. Stamped into one's skin by an accident of birth (Garner, 2007), whiteness is a kind of "passport" that opens doors and unlocks opportunities, just as identity cards in South Africa once defined privilege by the lightness or darkness of one's skin colour. Not surprisingly, there is a booming market for skin whiteners in parts of the world where whiteness is equated with beauty, success, and popularity. The privileging of whiteness is neither openly articulated nor logically deserved, but assumed and universalized as normal and natural, transcending scrutiny or criticism. Whiteness is the "natural" way of being human: that is, whites are unaware of their whiteness and privilege in the same way that fish are unaware of their "wetness."

White Framing

In short, whites tend to see the world through a "white gaze" (Henry & Tator, 2003; see also the discussion of the "Rashomon effect" in the Debate box at the beginning of this chapter). With a white gaze, interpretations of the world and human experiences are framed and understood in a manner consistent with this privileged position of power. Attitudes, behaviours, and arrangements that appear normal and ordinary to a white gaze are, in fact, a racialized prism (or lens) through which racist stereotypes and discriminatory actions are sustained and rationalized. Three levels of white gaze ("white framing") can be discerned:

- At the most general level of conceptualization, white framing defines whites as superior in culture and accomplishment, while whiteness comes to symbolize certain values and status positions that signify intellectual, moral, and cultural advancement (Feagin, 2006; Feagin & Cobas, 2008; Picca & Feagin, 2007). Dimensions of a white racialized framing may include (1) a belief in liberal universalism (the rights and commonalities of individuals prevail over group differences); (2) the virtues of an ideology to justify colour-blind Canada (or America) as aspiration and description; (3) the centrality of morally autonomous and rights-bearing individuals; (4) the importance of reason and science in advancing both individual and collective progress; and (5) distinctive orientations to time and space, including its value and measurement. (In this sense, both a white gaze and white framing are similar to the concept of Eurocentrism which, too, reflects a tendency to see, interpret, and assess reality from a predominantly white point of view, a view seen as normal, desirable, and superior.)
- At a deeper conceptual level, whites tend to see the prevailing distribution of institutionalized white power and white-controlled institutions as not only unremarkable but also inevitable or deserved.
- At the deepest levels are stereotypes and prejudices toward racialized minorities that unconsciously reinforce their perceived inferiority, thus accentuating white (especially male) virtues, while privileging whites as masters of the social universe.

Whiteness: Everything yet Nothing

Herein, then, lies the "genius" of white privilege. Whiteness is *everything yet nothing*: *everything*, because whiteness is the normative but unmarked standard by which reality is judged or interpreted without much awareness of the process; *nothing*, because whiteness is perceived by whites to be inconsequential in privileging or disprivileging (Garner, 2007). And while whiteness (like power) is invisible to those who benefit from it, to those who don't, it is painfully obvious and blatantly ubiquitous (Applebaum, 2010). Whiteness shapes people's lives by symbolizing (1) dominance rather than subordination, (2) normativity rather than marginality, and (3) privilege rather than disadvantage. Conversely, those without the privilege of whiteness are stigmatized as the "other" and demonized accordingly. Otherness (for example, blackness) represents the antithesis of whiteness in terms of privilege or entitlement—a highly visible stigma (or marked category) that denies, excludes, or exploits. Unlike whites who rarely experience whiteness, people of colour have little choice except to confront blackness on a daily basis. Those in positions of disadvantage routinely experience the dynamics of being different, of having to defend these differences, and of being disadvantaged by them (Henry & Tator, 2003). No aspect of existence, no moment of the day, no contact, no relationship, no response is exempt from the stigma of otherness in a racialized society (Philip, 1996).

To be sure, not everyone views whiteness as an unmarked vehicle of privilege. White supremacist groups have cleverly transformed whiteness into victimhood—in much the same way as some men's movements have depicted males as victims of radical feminism and political correctness.

Whiteness is valorized as the hallmark of an endangered or persecuted race, according to supremacists, one under threat and challenge by minorities because of quotas or "reverse discrimination" (see Ferber, 1998). Yet these challenges to "whiteness" need to be put into context. True, whites no longer possess the exclusive power and the uncontested privilege of the past. But moving over and making space is not the same as transforming patterns of institutional power or white privilege (see also the discussion of "subliminal racism" in Chapter 3). Moreover, as the noted anti-racist scholar Tim Wise (2008) points out, if privilege is associated strictly with money issues, not all whites are economically privileged or able to get everything they want or win every competition. However, if privilege is to include psychological issues, then whites possess race privilege because they have the luxury of not worrying about their "race" as a negative marker in looking for work or housing, whereas even rich black and brown folks are subject to stereotyping and racial profiling.

To understand how white privilege works, Tim Wise (2008) provides an interesting analogy. Take able-bodied persons as opposed to individuals with disabilities. To say that able-bodied persons possess advantages ("privileges") over people with disabilities who confront numerous obstacles in everyday life is surely beyond debate. Although persons with disabilities may overcome these obstacles, that fact doesn't take away from the fact that these obstacles exist and that the able-bodied have an edge, in part because they have one less thing to worry about from entering a

(Continued)

building to crossing a street. Moreover, the fact that some able-bodied persons are poor, while some people with disabilities are rich and have power, doesn't alter the rule. That is, on balance it pays to be able-bodied—just as in general it's better to be a member of the dominant white group because of the general advantages.

Whites as Race, Whiteness as Racism?

Two final questions remain: First, are whites a race? Technically no, because there is no such thing as race per se. Yes, because in a world of perceptions where there is no position from nowhere, everybody is perceived to be racially located, whether they are aware of it or not. That alone makes it doubly important to racialize whiteness *as if* it were a "race" ("racialization")—not in the sense of biological superiority but as a socially constructed convention—if only to paint whites into the picture by recognizing whiteness as a manifestation of the human experience rather than assumed as a universal norm. Whiteness needs to be racialized in order to expose the dominant and hegemonic role that it plays in perpetrating exclusion and discrimination (Henry & Tator, 2003). After all, to exclude whiteness as an unmarked race category that stands outside history or convention is to redouble its

privilege and **hegemony** by naturalizing it as normal, inevitable, and superior (Fleras & Spoonley, 1999).

The second question is no less provocative: Is whiteness synonymous with racism? That is, to what extent are the *systemically privileged* complicit in perpetuating social injustice? In that whiteness is tied to structures of domination and oppression, does being white make it impossible to be a good person (see Applebaum, 2010)? No, not in the sense that being white automatically makes one a racist. But yes, if the largely unearned privileges of whiteness and the benefits of living in a white society are taken for granted rather than acknowledged (Frankenburg, 1993; Mackey, 1998). The racism in whiteness reflects the Eurocentric tendency to interpret reality from a white point of view ("white gaze") as natural and normal, while "othered" viewpoints are dismissed as irrelevant or inferior. Finally, whiteness may qualify as racism in that white privilege inheres within the foundational principles of Canada's constitutional governance in defining who gets what—without people's awareness of its presence or consequences. To be sure, whiteness may not set out to dominate and control; nevertheless, the interplay of white rules and "pale male" agendas may have a controlling effect in perpetuating a racialized status quo in defence of white privilege.

WILL RACE MATTER IN THE FUTURE?

The persistence of race raises a central question: Will race continue to matter in the future? Or will Canada (and the United States) endorse a race-neutral society in which race is irrelevant in defining who gets what and why? Some would argue that we are just about there (Foster, 2005; but see Doane, 2006, 2007). An ideology of colour-blindness (or race neutrality) has emerged that waxes optimistically about the current state of race relations in Canada and the United States. According to the tenets of colour-blind ideology and the principle of liberal universalism, race no longer matters because, fundamentally, we are all the same under our skin and equal before the law. The combination of civil rights, human rights safeguards, and a multicultural orthodoxy not only discredits racial prejudice and discriminatory barriers but also dislodges structural and ideological barriers that block success. To the extent that race-base perceptions persist, proponents of the colour-blind doctrine argue, it is largely a survival from the past, restricted to isolated hate crimes, and expressed by prejudicial individuals (Doane, 2007). To the extent that inequality in the United States persists—and it does, with the black median income at $30 939 in 2005, which represents just 61 percent of the white median income and is down from 63 percent in 2002 and up only 1 percent from 1968 (Millman, 2007a, 2007b; see also Pew Forum on Religion and Public Life, 2007)—the blame lies with dysfunctional individuals and social pathologies within minority communities.

The implications of this race denial are far reaching. In a so-called colour-blind society, where race allegedly no longer matters, taking race into consideration for policy making is problematic, even if the goal is to ameliorate inequality or redress past injustices (Bonilla-Silva, 1996; Doane, 2006). According to this line of thinking, race-differentiated policies for removing racial segregation and racial equality are themselves deemed racist, unfair to whites, and a violation of core values pertaining to liberal universalism. But are Canada and the United States as race neutral and colour-blind as advocates seem to say? If yes, is this neutrality reflective of reality or rhetoric? If no, is it possible to create a race neutral and colour-blind society?

Put bluntly, there is no such thing as a race-neutral society. Human societies are socially created constructions that deliberately or inadvertently ("systemically") reflect, reinforce, and advance the realities, experiences, and interests of the dominant sector. The values, ideals, and priorities of those who created or control society are so deeply embedded in the governance, institutions, and foundational principles of society that society is designed, organized, and operates accordingly. The result is a racialized society: that is, one in which ideas and ideals pertaining to race (in terms of what is acceptable or desirable) are structurally aligned in ways that promote mainstream white interests over those of other racialized groups without people's awareness of the biases at play. Clearly, then, since a colour-blind society is a contradiction in terms, at least in the foundational sense of the term, race will continue to matter for the foreseeable future, as the following demonstrates:

- Moves to create a more inclusive equitable society cannot paper over the inevitable. Race is deeply embedded in the core values, institutional arrangements, and Eurocentric principles of Canada's constitutional order. Reference to race neutrality cannot dislodge the centrality of a structural whiteness that continues to define, evaluate, and promote.

- Despite laws outlawing discrimination at individual and institutional levels, structural barriers and systemic biases remain that advance the interests of whites over those of non-whites (Fleras, 2007c). Moreover, laws cannot possibly eradicate deep-seated prejudices or subliminal biases that continue to influence people's identities, experiences, and outcomes. Not surprisingly, critics argue, by doing nothing and justifying it on principled grounds, a commitment to colour-blindness is little more than a thinly veiled exercise in subliminal racism (see Chapter 3).

- Formal equality before the law sounds good in theory. In practice, without special treatment, groups that are historically disadvantaged because of a late start will continue to falter. That is, in contexts of inequality, applying similar standards to unequal situations has the effect of freezing the status quo with its prevailing distribution of power and resources.

In short, the embeddedness of race in constructing a future society cannot be ignored or underestimated (Goldberg, 2002; Vickers, 2002). In creating a Canada that *is safe for race and safe from race*, the challenge is twofold. First is the problem of acknowledging the continuing salience of race in an ostensibly race-neutral society. As long as racism and racialized inequality persist in a society where people are rewarded or penalized without justifiable cause (Cose, 1997), race will matter in privileging some and disempowering others (Morris & Cowlishaw, 1997). The second challenge is to deconstruct the coded concepts and subtextual discourses by which people continue to attribute social significance to race in everyday life, despite laws and norms that discourage its use to differentiate, deny, or exclude (Li, 2007). In that structural bias and biased mindsets are unlikely to be dislodged in the foreseeable future, race will continue to matter whether we like it or not, approve or disapprove.

Clearly, then, rethinking the race concept as a frame of reference is critical. Race is not a thing out there—a kind of objective reality—but rather a socially constructed activity by which people are designated as (racially) different and subject to discriminatory treatment (racialization). Moreover, race is not simply a psychological disorder or a mindset that reflects flawed assumptions about human nature. Rather, as a political project it is fundamental to the origins, character, and functioning of modern states, including its manifestations in justice and law enforcement, politics, legislation, and bureaucracy (a racialized society). That this line of thinking can be applied to Canada-building in constructing a "white man's society" provides a unifying theme for Chapter 3.

DEBATE REVISITED

Reaction to the Kingston Police Services Data Collection Project: The Good, the Bad, and the Ugly

Strictly speaking, the data in the Kingston project cannot prove anything except group disparities in police stops; that is, young black males experience more stops than other demographic groups. Three interpretations are possible from the data: (1) blacks commit more crime; (2) they and their activities are more visible, thus more likely to attract attention; and (3) police do profile young black males. Not surprisingly, reactions to the politics of police racial profiling are varied: Some say no,

never; others say yes, always; and still others say maybe, but only occasionally. The police may deny that they racially profile, but racialized minorities believe that they do so on a regular basis. On the assumption that those with less power may read situations more "accurately" because their survival depends on it (Bishop, 2005), their personal experiences may carry more weight. Nevertheless, this perceptual gap was nicely captured by one senior police official who proclaimed,

"You think we profile, we think we don't" (as cited in Hurst, 2003). Kingston Police Chief William Closs acknowledged as much when, in responding to the report, he apologized for the disparities in stops, but fell short of admitting any racial profiling.

Police authorities at both local and provincial levels vehemently deny the existence of institutional (or systemic) racial profiling—either as principle or practice. Although conceding the possibility of a few rogue officers who slipped through the screening/training process, the police contend that only criminal behaviour is profiled, regardless of skin colour. If blacks are overrepresented in crime statistics, police argue, it's because they engage in unlawful actions that increase the risk of apprehension. Moreover, insofar as profiling persists, it represents a necessary if unfortunate byproduct of sensible policing. After all, all modern police work is predicated on the principle of preventing crime through proactive policing, including more extensive surveillance of people's movements in high-crime areas (Closs, 2003). Because police are trained to use their intuition and experience in performing their duties, they tend to be more attentive to danger signals, including a heightened suspicion toward those stereotyped as the "usual suspects" (Satzewich & Shaffir, 2007/2009).

This denial and corresponding rationales were sharply rejected by academics (Henry & Tator, 2002; Tanovich, 2006; Tator & Henry, 2006), anti-racist organizations, and members of the black community (Brown, 2004; Smith, 2004), including an ad hoc coalition of organizations and individuals named the African Canadian Community Coalition on Racial Profiling. Each supported the findings of the *Toronto Star* as consistent with what black male youth have long proclaimed: *Police tend to stop who they see rather than what they see* (Hurst, 2003). Studies also indicate that black youths are twice as likely to be arrested than young whites, according to Christopher McAll (as cited in Chung, 2010), particularly when doing or selling drugs in public places, while not a single white has ever been charged with a drug offence when spotted by police. In light of this close scrutiny and over-surveillance of black youths, parents in Montreal have complained that the police disproportionally and unfairly criminalize race, youth, and poverty because of a zero-tolerance policy against incivilities. In the words of one anguished and angry parent:

> There is no greater pain or anger than seeing your son being treated like an animal by the very people who are paid by your tax dollars to serve and protect you. (Mothers United Against Racism, 2005)

Regardless of right or wrong, how much or how little, the impact of racial profiling cannot be lightly dismissed. Dangers lurk when profiling goes beyond personal prejudice to solidify the basis for public policy that infringes on the civil rights of specific populations to patterns (Muharrar, 2005). Once a problem is racialized by profiling, it not only encourages a suspiciousness that typically stigmatizes an entire group for punitive treatment (reinforcing how the unlawful conduct

(Continued)

of a small number of wrongdoers who call attention to themselves glosses over the vast majority who conduct themselves lawfully). It also results in selective police stops and searches that can prove to be an embarrassing inconvenience for some or a humiliating experience for others (Tator & Henry, 2006). In further marginalizing underprivileged groups, this alienation generates mistrust in public institutions and diminishes people's sense of citizenship (Ontario Human Rights Commission, 2003). A climate of distrust toward police is fostered, with the result that minority communities become unpoliceable, in part because of depolicing (police refusing to respond to situations involving racialized minorities), thus amplifying those very conditions that justify an even more invasive police presence. And when taken to the extreme, the politics of profiling can culminate in violence (CBC News, 2010).

Deconstructing Police Profiling: the Rashomon Effect

Clearly, then, each racialized group assesses the situation differently. Whites acknowledge the possibility of a "few bad apples" in an essentially colour-blind and fair police services, whereas minorities define policing as "rotten to the core" with the bad apples a sign of the decay (Tator & Henry, 2006). Reference to the Rashomon effect may explain the disparity in police and black responses to the crisis. According to the Rashomon effect, where one stands in society will influence what one sees, thinks, or experiences. For example, senior police officials who rarely encounter any discrimination because of their whiteness, power, and affluence tend to underestimate the magnitude and scope of racism. Their privileged status diminishes the possibility of being victimized because of race or ethnicity. Moreover, because they believe the system is colour-blind and fair, racial disparities are attributed to greater black criminality rather than discriminatory police behaviour (Hurwitz & Peffley, 2010; Satzewich & Shaffir, 2007/9). To the extent that racial profiling is thought to exist within the police service, it's defined by a prevailing police culture in motivational terms (i.e., racism as individualistic, intentional and deliberate). In other words, those unlikely to be victims tend to underestimate the scope and pervasiveness of racism, restricting its presence to a "few bad apples" who can be rehabilitated through sensitivity training.

By contrast, the racialized and less privileged see it differently insofar as they are differently located in society. In light of their visibility, powerlessness, and poverty, blacks and other racialized minorities may emphasize the systemic extent and intensity of racism—largely because racism is not something abstract or arbitrary but a reality that is always potentially present. Police racism is seen as part of the institutional structure of the "whole rotten barrel." In that discrimination pervades every nook and cranny of the criminal justice system in general and policing specifically, whiteness/ Eurocentricity remains the institutional norm, resulting in bias and second-class treatment of racialized minorities because of ingrained institutional policies and practices (Hurwitz & Peffley, 2010). In generating arrests from random stops, strips, and searches, this racism amounts to little more than institutionalized harassment as police use their authority to "over-police" those street crimes where visibility becomes a factor.

What to do? The rightness or wrongness of each position is less relevant than the need to allay minority perceptions. If the police are to regain the trust of disaffected minority youth, they must acknowledge perceptual realities by going beyond denial or trivialization (Closs, 2003). After all, if members of racialized communities believe profiling is real and exists, that alone defines it as a serious problem that needs a solution—on the grounds that justice must not only be done, but also be seen to be done to make things right. A commitment to the principles of restorative justice is a good start. In contrast to criminal justice principles of what law was broken, who did it, and how much punishment is required, the principle of restorative justice works on asking how much harm was done, who was harmed, and what must be done to restore the balance/relationship. Or, as put by Kingston Police Chief Bill Closs (2003) in urging officers to better understand the implications of pulling over a person of colour:

> Visible minorities may have been victims of racism and discrimination in the past, so police training must foster an understanding that, when members of visible minorities are stopped and interrogated of crime they did not commit, the police should anticipate that police motives may be questioned.

Closs's message is clear: Because accusations of differential treatment arise in contexts where authorities exercise high levels of discretion, it becomes doubly important for police officers to clearly articulate the grounds for every stop.

For the police, the Rashomon effect is double-edged. The existence of profiling with the service does not necessarily imply police are racist in the conventional sense. Nevertheless, they must acknowledge that their actions may be interpreted as profiling and racist by those with different lived experiences. Furthermore, the perception that police do profile must be addressed since perceptions *are* reality when it comes to doing justice. But reference to a Rashomon effect does not exonerate police services of blame. Just because senior management rejects the practice of police profiling, there is no guarantee of rank-and-file compliance. Racism exists because race is frequently a factor in making discretionary judgments even if the motives behind the profiling may be largely unconscious (i.e., subliminal). In a country that prides itself on being a multicultural beacon of inclusiveness, the idea that authorities rely on skin colour as an investigative tool has racist consequences.

Analyzing the problem is one thing; doing something about it is a lot tougher. If the problem of profiling is the result of a few rogue officers, energies must focus on behavioural modification through attitude change and consciousness-raising (Editorial, 2010). If the problem is institutional, structural changes related to rules, priorities, and agendas are necessary. If the problem is a function of the job, the very

(Continued)

concept of policing in a twenty-first century multicultural society may have to be rethought, in part by rejecting a "thin blue line" (us versus them) mindset with its militaristic overtones. Perhaps the problem is societal? Race is not a direct factor in accounting for criminal activity. Rather, the real culprits are social problems beyond the scope of policing, including poverty, powerlessness, dysfunctional families, derelict housing, availability of guns and drugs, inadequate social supports, cultural values, lifestyle habits, and immigration patterns that separate parents from children over long periods of time (James, 2002). Until society begins to profile the social dimensions of crime and criminality, the police will continue to unfairly bear the brunt.

Chapter Highlights

- The politics of race are explored by looking at its value as an explanatory framework to account for human differences and disadvantages related to intelligence or crime, the role of racial doctrines as instruments of colonialist expansion and contemporary control, and the status of race in the construction of human reality.
- The key theme of this chapter is this: Human differences exist, and race does not, although people act as if it does.
- Race constitutes a political resource employed by both the dominant and subdominant sectors for legitimizing and advancing their identities, interests, claims, and power (Goldberg & Solomos, 2002).
- The race concept is a social construct, without any biological basis or scientific validity. As a social construct, the race concept implies not only a belief in innate differences as unequal, determinative of behaviour, and resistant to change, but also a division of humanity into discrete groups that can be hierarchically arranged.
- Race matters. Race may be a social construction, but it is a social fiction with material consequences—thus confirming that phenomena such as race do not have to be real to be real in their consequences.
- Technically speaking, whites are not a race, as there is no such thing as race. Nevertheless, the privileges that are associated with whiteness compel us to approach whites as if they are a race.

For further study, you can access the Case Studies referenced in this chapter at **www.pearsoncanada.ca/fleras**.

Review Questions

1. Race has little to do with genes or biological reality, but everything to do with perceptions about genes and biology. Explain this assertion that race is about society (a social construction), not about biology (a naturally occurring category).

2. Why did racial doctrines emerge in nineteenth-century Europe, and why do they persist into the twenty-first century?

3. What do we mean by the statement that there is no such thing as race relations, only relationships that have been "racialized"? Include reference to the concept of racialization as a process and a structure.

4. Race matters not because race is real, but because people believe it to be real and act according to this belief, with very real consequences. Explain what this means, and provide an example.

5. Discuss what it means to be white in Canada.

6. Is racial profiling a necessary evil in this era of terrorism? Or is it an unacceptable violation of an individual's civil rights?

Endnotes

1. *Race Traitor* is about abolishing white privilege rather than whites per se. The editors write in advocating dissolution of the "club": "The white race is a club, which enrols certain people at birth, without their consent, and brings them up according to its rules. For the most part the members go through life accepting the benefits of membership, without thinking about the costs. When individuals question the rules, the officers are quick to remind them of all they owe to the club, and warn them of the dangers they will face if they leave it." From *Race Traitor*, "Abolish the White Race—By Any Means Necessary." Available online at http://racetraitor.org/abolish.html.

Links and Recommendations

VIDEO

Talk: Tim Wise on White Privilege (2008)

A talk by Tim Wise—an essayist and polemicist, and one of America's most inspired anti-racists—on the privileges of whiteness. Available online by Googling "Tim Wise" and selecting the 58-minute YouTube version of his talk. You won't regret it.

FILMS

Race Is a Four-Letter Word (2006)

A useful documentary by the National Film Board about how race is played out in the lives of racialized Canadians, including what it means to be black in a multicultural Canada.

Crash (2005)

Directed by Paul Haggis, this Oscar-winning film by Lions Gate Entertainment (not to be confused with David Cronenberg's quirky film of the same title) consists of a series of vignettes that take place over two days in Los Angeles. The storyline follows a series of characters whose lives are informed by race and interconnected because of racism.

BOOKS

"Race" Is a Four-Letter Word: The Genesis of the Concept, by C. Loring Brace (2005). A well-written critique of the race construct as biological reality and explanatory framework.

Race: The Reality of Human Differences by Vincent Sarich and Frank Miele (2004). A defence of race as real in terms of description and explanation.

Race and Racialization: Essential Readings, edited by Tania Das Gupta et al. (2007). An excellent collection of previously published articles on the race construct.

Souled Out? How Blacks Are Winning and Losing Their Way in Sports, by Shaun Powell (2008). A provocative insight into black participation in American sports, resulting in success in some ways, failure in others, and misconceptions in many other ways.

Theorizing Race, by Maria Wallis and Augie Fleras (2008). An overview of race as a construct with respect to racialization, racism, and anti-racism, both in the past and the present.

WEBSITES

Canadian Race Relations Foundation—Canada's foremost site for issues pertaining to race and discrimination provides access to news, events, research, and publications:
    www.crr.ca

Urban Alliance on Race Relations—The organization produced Canada's only journal that deals exclusively with race-related articles and research:
    www.urbanalliance.ca

Race: The Power of an Illusion—An excellent companion site to a PBS series that explores the characteristics and consequences of race as a powerful illusion:
    www.pbs.org/race/000_General/000_00-Home.htm

About.com: Race Relations—A splendid clearinghouse of information pertaining to issues of race:
    http://racerelations.about.com

Project Implicit—So you think you haven't got a racist bone in your body? Take the Implicit Association Test to see if there are some racialized residues lurking in the recesses of your mind:
    https://implicit.harvard.edu/implicit/

CHAPTER 3

Racisms in Canada

DEBATE

Is Canada a Racist Society?

Is Canada a racist society? If the answer is no, why do some believe it is? If yes, who says so, why, and on what grounds? What exactly constitutes a racist society? Does the presence of racisms and racists equal a racist Canada? Are racisms under control (decreasing) or out of control (increasing)? Is Canada entering a post-racism era much like that of the United States under President Obama, suggesting the possibility of a colour-blind and race-neutral society? Why do Canadians remain conflicted and confused about racisms (see Lamoin & Dawes, 2010)? Answers to these questions are complex and problematic, yet pivotal in the struggle toward "erasing" racism. Moreover, analyzing the nature and magnitude of racism is hardly an idle intellectual exercise. In a society defined by its commitment to an **inclusive Multiculturalism**, many believe that the presence of racism is a blot on Canada.

A sense of perspective is critical. For some, Canada is inherently racist in design and outcomes, with a thin veneer of tolerance that camouflages a pervasive white superiority complex (Alfred, 1999; Henry & Tator, 2006; Lian & Matthews, 1998). A highly respected academic from Queen's

University has claimed that "we live in a racist society" (as cited in Kingston Whig-Herald, 2003), while a high-profile Aboriginal leader called Canadians "racist" (as cited in *The Globe and Mail,* 3 November 2001). In reaction to underemployment of visible minorities in government jobs (8.6 percent of the positions but 10.4 percent of the workforce), the vice-president of the Public Service Alliance of Canada exclaimed "we're a racist nation" (Butler, 2008).

For others, Canada is a fundamentally sound society—the "least racist society in the world," according to Raymond Chan, the former Minister of State for Multiculturalism (Canadian Press, 2005). Notwithstanding the presence of a few bad apples to spoil an otherwise wholesome batch, many like to think of Canada as largely colour-blind—a country where people are judged by what they do rather than who they are (Foster, 2005). For still others, perceptions of racism in Canada depend on where one stands in the wider scheme of things. Many whites are inclined to see racism as a random and irrational aberration from the normal functioning of society. For **racialized minorities**, however, racism is so hardwired into the very fabric of society that it's inextricably linked to Canada's emergence,

(Continued)

historical development, and institutional structure (Das Gupta, 2009; Thobani, 2007). Yet others still argue that references to racism in Canada depend on how broadly or narrowly the term is defined and conceptualized (Satzewich, 2011).

Is Canada a racist society or is it a society of racists? Responses are trickier than one might anticipate. First, what is meant by the word "racism" when applied to Canadian society? Racism is still understood by Canadians as a direct and overt act that is physically manifested in hostility or discrimination (Henry & Tator, 2006). Yet as the "Whiteness Matters: Racializing Whiteness as Race Privilege" box in Chapter 2 demonstrates, racism can be far more subtle—indirect, covert, and unconscious—with inadvertent and unintended discriminatory outcomes at individual or institutional levels. Canada is home to many different kinds of racism, with the result that different groups may experience racism differently at different times and places. For some, racism is about race and biology; for others, cultural differences are the new racism; for still others, racism is inextricably linked to structures. Such a contested domain raises additional questions: Is racism about prejudice or power? Is it about treating people differently because of their differences, or treating everyone the same regardless of their differences? Is a racist person someone who openly vilifies minorities, as opposed to one whose indifference and inactivity reinforce an unequal status quo? Is racism a "rational" response to competitive contexts, or should racism be relegated to the level of "knuckle-dragging" Neanderthals?

Second, how do we measure the concept of "a racist society" (Fleras & Spoonley, 1999)? Is a racist society based on a minimum number of racial incidents per year (whatever that may be)? Or should the focus be on those institutionalized biases that unintentionally perpetuate inequality? Too much of what constitutes a so-called racist society is based on surveys that measure racially related incidents. But survey-driven statistical measures have inherent drawbacks; for example, surveys cannot reveal the ratio of reported to unreported acts, with the result that what they conceal may be more important than what they reveal (Blank, Dabady, & Citro, 2004). Increases in the number of reported acts may not reflect more racism, but rather a greater public awareness of racism, together with an increased willingness to act on it by pressing charges or informing authorities. Lastly, statistical measures are a crude measure of public attitudes, not only because surveys tend to oversimplify complex problems, but also because they fail to distinguish between what people think and how they behave.

Third, what constitutes a "racist society"? Logic suggests that a racist society is one where racism is part of a broader state project that defines belonging and entitlement along exclusionary lines (Goldberg, 2002). Insofar as it's integral to the emergence and development of the modern state, racism is (1) deeply embedded in the design, organization, and operations of society; (2) reflected in and reinforced by official cultural values; (3) expressed through widely accepted social norms; (4) tacitly approved by the state or government; (5) codified into laws and policies that openly discriminate against minorities; (6) reflected in restrictive policies of membership and citizenship; and (7) inseparable from the normal functioning of society (Aguirre & Turner, 1995). In a racist society, prejudice toward others is institutionally entrenched as part of the normal functioning of society, while formal boundaries are drawn around racialized groups to separate them from the exalted mainstream (Thobani, 2007). The complicity of central authorities in solidifying racism is crucial: The government does little or nothing to prevent the outbreak of racist incidents at individual or institutional levels; even less is done to "arrest" these violations when they occur.

According to these criteria, South Africa would have qualified as a racist society.[1] Under an official apartheid, a system of race-based segregation was introduced that separated whites from blacks, including an archipelago of homelands that surrounded South Africa. Blacks were cruelly exploited as miners or domestics, thereby securing power and privilege for the white ruling class. Both the United States and Canada could also be defined as racist societies prior to the mid-1950s because of state-endorsed colour bars that segregated blacks from challenging white privilege (Horton & Horton, 2004). As well, racism was used to justify the conquest and colonialism of both these countries, resulting in persistent patterns of domination, intolerance, and violence (see Mills, 1997). But how valid is such an indictment of Canada at present? The Debate Revisited box at the end of this chapter will explore this question more thoroughly.

INTRODUCTION: THE TOXICITY OF RACISMS IN CANADA

From a distance, Canada strikes many as a paragon of racial tranquility. Racism may loom as the single most explosive and divisive force in other countries, including the United States, but surely not in Canada, where racism is publicly scorned and officially repudiated. In contrast to the United States, where racism continues to segregate or suppress, or the United Kingdom where, since 1993, an average of five people die each year because of racial violence (Institute of Race Relations, 2010), Canada's racism is perceived as relatively muted, isolated to fringe circles, a relic from the past, or the perversions of a twisted few. Laws are in place that criminalize racism; brazen racists and white supremacists are routinely charged for disseminating hate propaganda; race riots are virtually unheard of except in history books; and blatant forms of racial discrimination are vigorously challenged. Canada prides itself on being a society in which individuals are rewarded on the basis of merit, no group is singled out for negative treatment, and race is deemed to be irrelevant in determining a person's status or entitlements. Moreover, the popularity of terms such as "multiculturalism," "inclusiveness," and "equity" suggests that Canadians have learned to "talk the walk."

To their credit, Canadians are learning to "walk the talk" as well (United Nations, 2007). No longer are Aboriginal peoples excluded from Canada's political and constitutional affairs as was once the case (Ponting & Gibbins, 1980). As peoples with rights, they are clearly in ascendancy in reclaiming some degree of self-determining autonomy as the "nations within" (Fleras & Elliott, 1992; Maaka & Fleras, 2005). As proof, consider the "watershed" agreement in 2000 that finalized the Nisga'a settlement, thereby establishing a third tier of Aboriginal governance alongside the federal and provincial (see online case study 7.3). The situation is similar with the Québécois who, for all intents and purposes, function as a distinct society and as a "nation within" a united Canada, following federal recognition in 2006. Another positive indicator is the demographic revolution that has transformed once staunchly anglocentric cities such as Vancouver and Toronto into vibrant, cosmopolitan centres. Not surprisingly, Canada remains the destination of choice for would-be global immigrants because of its much touted commitment to freedom, democracy, quality of life, and tolerance for diversities (Historica-Dominion Institute, 2010). Finally, the institutionalization of Multiculturalism has catapulted Canada into the global spotlight as a blueprint for democratic governance. The fact that the United Nations had ranked Canada as the most livable country on the planet for eight consecutive years (in 2010 Canada sat fourth on the list) must surely say something about doing it right.

But what sparkles from a distance loses lustre up close. Canadians could be smug about their enlightened status if racism were a mere blip on Canada's race relations screen. This, sadly, is far from the truth. Not only was racism deeply embedded in Canada's history, culture, law, and institutions (see Backhouse, 1999; Satzewich, 1998; Walker, 1997). The extent to which racism remains a powerful force at present, albeit in more subtle and systemic ways, speaks volumes of its resilience and malleability (Das Gupta, James, Maaka, Galabuzi, & Andersen, 2007; Hier & Bolaria, 2007). Racism furnished the ideological life support for capitalism at large, for society-building in general, and for the exploitation of racialized minorities in particular (Bishop, 2005; Bolaria & Li, 1988). Canada was founded on the colonization of its indigenous peoples, the dispossession of their land and resources, the exploitation of immigrant labour for Canada-building purposes, and the preferential treatment of white European settlers (Thobani, 2007) (see online Case Study 3.1). Minority women and men were racialized as inferior or irrelevant, and then arranged into a hierarchy of acceptance or rejection based on their proximity to the French and English as primary reference groups. Even that most quintessential of American racist institutions, slavery, flourished in Canada (Cooper, 2006) as conveyed by this advertisement:

> TO BE SOLD, A BLACK WOMAN, named Peggy, aged about forty years; and a black boy her son, named JUPITER, aged about fifteen years, both of them the property of the subscriber. The woman is a tolerable Cook and washerwoman and perfectly understands making Soap and Candles. The Boy is tall and strong of his age, and has been employed in Country Business, but brought up principally as a House Servant—They are each of them Servants for life . . . PETER RUSSELL. York, Feb. 10th 1806. (adapted from Bristow et al., 1993)

Other minorities suffered as well. Migrants from Eastern European countries were vilified as a subterranean underclass to avoid at all costs. Paranoia and hate compelled authorities to intern thousands of minorities, including the placement of 5000 Ukrainians in concentration camps during World War I—at great personal cost to themselves and their families. An equally spiteful internment was inflicted on Japanese Canadians in British Columbia. Most were rounded up like Jews in Nazi Germany, their property confiscated and civil rights suspended, and were confined to labour internment camps. Restrictions were not lifted until 1949. Contrary to public opinion, the Ku Klux Klan flourished in Canada, assuming a major profile during the 1920s and 1930s in central and western Canada (Backhouse, 1999). The "Kanadian Klan" aimed its racist bile at Catholics, French-Canadians, Asians, and blacks, who routinely encountered exclusion because of segregation at schools, housing, and public venues like movie theatres.

Viola Desmond: A Posthumous Revolutionary

Unlike the United States, where there is at least an admission of the fact that racism exists and has a history, in this country one is faced with a stupefying innocence.

—*Dionne Brand*

On 14 April 2010, Nova Scotia apologized and granted a posthumous pardon to Viola Desmond, a black woman who was wrongfully convicted in 1946 for sitting in a whites-only section of a movie theatre. In the period after World War II, segregation of blacks from whites was still the norm in many parts of Nova Scotia (and Canada). Despite mounting sensitivity about the inappropriateness of racism for a country that had just fought for freedom overseas, popular attitudes did not translate into reforms. The postwar potential could not be transformed into genuine opportunities without dramatic incidents, carefully planned logistics, and the inspiration of dynamic personalities. Viola Desmond provided this spark.

As a 32-year-old Halifax-born, African Canadian beautician, Desmond was driving from Halifax to Sydney when her 1940 Dodge broke down in New Glasgow. While awaiting the car repairs, she decided to see a movie at the Roseland Theatre. Desmond paid for what she thought was a general admittance ticket and sat downstairs—unaware of the theatre's rules that blacks could sit only upstairs in the balcony seats. Once seated, she was asked to leave the "whites-only" house seats, but refused. Eventually the manager and a police officer forcibly removed her from the theatre and put her in jail overnight.

The next day, Desmond was charged and convicted of tax evasion. In her defence, Desmond argued that she had requested a ticket for the main floor, had paid for it, had no way of knowing that the balcony was the designated seating area for blacks because no one had posted signs to that effect, and had offered to pay for the difference when informed of the policy. To no avail: According to the prosecution, Desmond had committed a crime. She didn't pay the full amount for front seats (40 cents including 3 cents tax) since the theatre would sell only a cheaper balcony ticket (30 cents including 2 cents tax) to a black woman. In other words, Desmond had evaded paying the proper amusement tax for a pricier ticket on the white segregated floor—*a difference of one cent.* Interestingly, the prosecution made no mention of race, although the unspoken truth was clear: Desmond was charged and eventually convicted of being a black person who dared step outside her defined place in society. She was fined $20 (about $250 in 2010 dollars) and $6

(Continued)

court costs (the alternative was 30 days in jail) for defrauding the government.

Desmond paid the fine. But upon the advice of a doctor who examined bruises and injuries to her hip and knees, she decided to take legal action against the cinema and fight the case with the help of the newly created Nova Scotia Association for the Advancement of Coloured People (NSAACP). Although she lost the first appeal, Desmond won the second on a technicality, but few black Nova Scotians took comfort in this. As Walker (1997) notes, segregation was still legal according to the highest court of the province. Clearly, if transformative change toward equality was to be achieved, it had to begin with the law; after all, the problem of discrimination was systemic—rooted in society rather than a few overt racists. Under pressure from Labour, Church, and the NSAACP, the Nova Scotia government eventually dismantled and repealed its discriminatory laws by the mid-1950s (as did Ontario), thus making it illegal to discriminate on grounds of race in hiring or promotion or in serving customers in public institutions.

Desmond's conviction was never overturned by the higher courts.

Nevertheless, her ordeal earned her the unofficial recognition as Canada's Rosa Parks, who made history in the United States in 1955 for refusing to give up her seat to a white man on a Montgomery, Alabama, bus; Parks's arrest prompted a massive bus boycott that launched the civil rights movement, brought Martin Luther King into national prominence, and eventually led to a Supreme Court Ruling outlawing segregation on public transport.

After the trial, Desmond closed her business and moved to Montreal, then to New York, where she died in 1965 at the age of 51.

In an interesting twist of fate, Desmond's pardon was signed by Mayann Francis, Nova Scotia's first African Canadian and second female lieutenant-governor. Ironically, however, the timing of the pardon was marred by another incident in Nova Scotia in which a biracial family was victimized by racialized violence: first a cross burning on their lawn in winter, then a firebombing of their car in mid-April. The conclusion seems inescapable: plus ça change . . . (See CBC News, 2010; Editorial, 2010b; Rooney, 2008; Walker, 2001a;.)

The present may be equally racist, albeit more quietly and by consequence than loudly or by intent. Instead of improvement, as might be expected because of human rights legislation and an official Multiculturalism, indicators suggest the opposite—in the process reinforcing the profoundly historical character of racism as something that is always with us like a reservoir constantly tapped to bolster racist ideas or new modes of expression (Lee & Lutz, 2005). People of colour continue to be politely—and not so politely—denied equitable access to housing, employment, media, education, policing, and social services (Henry & Tator, 2006). The Ontario Human Rights Commission (2005) pulled no punches in pointing out the reality behind the facade:

> Racialized persons experience disproportionate poverty, over-representation in the prison population, under-representation in the middle and upper layers of political, administrative, economic, and media institutions, and barriers to accessing employment, housing, and health

care to name just a few. Courts have recognized that racism exists in Canada. It is all too easy for those who do not experience it to deny the reality of racism. This is counterproductive and damaging to our social fabric. Racial discrimination and racism must be acknowledged as a pervasive and continuing reality as a starting point . . . (p. 1)

Survey data support this conclusion. The 2002 Ethnic Diversity Survey and Statistics Canada census data reinforce the reality of racism and racial discrimination in Canada (Government of Canada, 2005). Over a third of those interviewed indicated that they had experienced discrimination because of their race or ethnicity, including 50 percent of black Canadians and 33 percent of South Asian and Chinese respondents. The Ethnic Diversity Survey also revealed that blacks in Canada were more likely to be targets of discrimination, with 32 percent indicating such experiences in the past five years, compared with 21 percent for South Asian Canadians and 18 percent for Chinese Canadians. Jewish Canadians remain targets of hate as well. According to B'nai B'rith, 1042 anti-Semitic incidents were reported in 2007—an increase of 11.4 percent over the 2006 totals, and the highest total in the audit's history. Two-thirds of the reported incidents were classified as harassment, about one-third as vandalism, and 3 percent involved outright violence, with 50 percent of the incidents occurring in Toronto and 25 percent in Montreal. Finally, a Sun Media report (2007), based on a Léger Marketing opinion sampling of just over 3000 Canadians, confirmed what other surveys implied or concluded: that 47 percent of the respondents admitted they were strongly (1 percent of the total), moderately, or slightly racist, while 66 percent of racialized minority respondents indicated they were victimized by racial discrimination.

In short, critics charge that racism is alive and well in Canada, with only its worst effects camouflaged by a Teflon veneer of tolerance and politeness (Henry & Tator, 2006). Yes, Canada may have been spared the stigma of institutionalized slavery or the ravages of American-style ghettos or race riots. Yet such a fortuitous state of affairs may reflect exceptional good fortune and a powerful myth-making machine instead of enlightened policies or public goodwill. Such an accusation may puzzle the reader; after all, at a cognitive level, many Canadians appear to have internalized the values of tolerance, equality, and justice, in addition to rejecting notions of racial inferiority. But while overt racism is strongly condemned, acts of blatant racism persist, in part because Canadians may react to racism with indifference (Kawakami, Dunn, Karmali, & Dovidio, 2009) (see online Case Study 3.7). Moreover, racism persists at subconscious levels of prejudice (Caines, 2004), while institutions continue to deny and exclude because of rules and protocols that inadvertently exert a discriminatory impact (Teelucksingh, 2006). Rather than disappearing or becoming marginalized, racism assumes many different permutations, ranging from spontaneous individual outbursts to systemic institutional biases (Agnew, 2007; Patriquin, 2007; Woodward, 2005). Even improvements can deceive: To the extent that institutions have become more accommodative, says Hamlin Grange, president of the Toronto-based consultancy group DiversiPro, this commitment may reflect expediency (in "staying one step ahead of the law") or appeasement (in "cooling out" troublesome constituents). In that Canadians are more tolerant than in the past, this trend may say less about injustice or conviction than it does about cowardice or political correctness.

The faces of racism are changing as well (see Satzewich, 2004). In line with its image as a defiantly white-man's country, Canada once possessed few qualms about defining itself as openly and proudly racist. Until the early 1950s, neither bigotry nor domination of racialized others was seen as racism in the sense of antipathy or inferiorization (according to the 2nd edition of the *Oxford English Dictionary*, the word "racism" did not appear in the English language until the mid-1930s). To the extent that minorities were segregated or excluded, their treatment as second-class citizens was rationalized as a natural reflection of divine will or the iron-clad laws of evolutionary progress. Over time, however, race-based exclusion was increasingly condemned as immoral, then unlawful, but above all, déclassé (Wallis & Fleras, 2008). Canada at present claims to be resolutely anti-racist and colour-blind, with a commitment to the principles of multiculturalism and inclusiveness. In reality, racism continues to persist, albeit in ways more polite than openly blunt, often coded in polite language, camouflaged behind principled grounds, and embedded within Canada's institutional structures and foundational principles. Such is the fear of being labelled racist, that Canadians may be reluctant to criticize migrants and minorities unless a higher principle can justify the criticism ("reverse discrimination," "jumping the queue," "equal opportunity"). Not surprisingly, racism is so tacitly assumed as part of the normal functioning of Canadian society that its detection is problematic, as described by Senator David Oliver:

> . . . not something readily discernable by the senses: you cannot see it, hear it, smell it, touch it, but it does exist. It is subtle, invisible, and ethereal. (as cited in a report by the Conference Board of Canada, 2004)

In that racism is in constant motion and continually morphing into new and insidious forms, it no longer means what it used to mean (Lee & Lutz, 2005). References to racism can span a spectrum, from the openly defamatory to those systemic patterns that unobtrusively confer institutional advantage to some but not to others. Persistent, complex, changing, and subtle, racism can also include those subliminal forms that generally escape detection except when experienced by victims (Berkeley, 2010; Solomos & Back, 1996). Certain types of racism are spontaneously expressed in isolated acts at irregular intervals because of individual impulse or insensitivity. Other expressions of racism are neither spontaneous nor sporadic, but institutional and structured, and are manifest through discriminatory outcomes that inadvertently exclude or exploit. Certain actions are unmistakably racist, others are labelled racist to shut down debate, and still others are defined as racist because of context or consequence. Some see racism as something that individuals do, while others claim racism involves what people don't do. Exaggerating people's difference when irrelevant is racist, yet ignoring their differences when necessary may prove equally racist. In that continuing discrimination against minorities stands in sharp contrast to the ideals of an inclusive Multiculturalism and the realities of a diverse demographic, there is talk of a distinctly Canadian brand of racism.

Racism discourses (i.e., distinctive ways of thinking and talking) have shifted as well (see Hier & Walby, 2006). Once thought of as bad people with bad attitudes doing bad things to those less fortunate, racism is now perceived as structural, unconscious, indirect, and systemic—from overt practices involving prejudice or antipathy to racism as a system in which the covert and the overt combine at societal, institutional, cultural, and individual levels to produce and reproduce racial injustice (Applebaum, 2010). Not surprisingly, racism is less likely to be defined as a thing that can be isolated and contained, but more as a floating signifier that can mean anything (from the institutional to the ideological to all points in between) depending on the context, criteria, and consequences.

References to racisms include the following points of emphasis: (1) the proliferation of multi-racisms depending on the context and the target group; (2) racism as a moving target rather than a stationary object; (3) racism as a process or activity (a verb) rather than a thing (a noun); (4) racism as an attribute applied after the fact (unintended consequences rather than deliberate intent); (5) racism as structural and systemic rather than individual and attitudinal; (6) racism as perspectival, depending on where one is racially located in society; (7) racism as institutional power rather than personal prejudice; (8) racism as integral to Canada-building; (9) racism as a majority problem rather than a minority flaw; and (10) the prevalence of covert racism (Wallis & Fleras, 2008). In other words, reference to racism as an easily identifiable "thing" "out there" no longer resonates with the same authority it once did. It has been displaced, as it were, by **discursive** frameworks that acknowledge racisms as a complex and contradictory dynamic (Banton, 2000). Table 3-1 provides a summary of the evolution of discourse on racisms.

Racist or non-racist? Racism or anti-racism? Out of control or under control? Perhaps racisms in Canada should be assessed and depicted as lying somewhere in between the naiveté of the optimists and the cynical pessimism of the skeptics. Canada is home to a baffling blend of hardcore racists and resolute anti-racists, with most individuals aligned along the continuum between these extremes. Accordingly, it makes no more sense to exaggerate the magnitude and scope of racisms in Canada than to underestimate

TABLE 3-1	Conceptualizing Racisms: Evolving Trends, Shifting Discourses	
From (the past)	**Toward (now)**
Overt	Covert
Deliberate intent	Unintended consequences
Sender initiated	Receiver dependent
Individual pathology	Business as usual: systemic + infrastructural
Doing something	Doing nothing
Focusing on differences	Ignoring differences
Minority problem (inferior)	Majority problem (whiteness)
Prejudice driven	Power driven
Singular	Plural: racisms
	• Specific group racisms
	• Intersectionality: race × gender × class × ethnicity (see Chapter 6)
Direct, active, systematic	Indirect, passive, systemic
Anomaly, problem	Integral to white Canada-building and white identity construction
Stationary object/easily defined	Moving target
	• Contextual
	• Perspectival (racial Rashomon)
Thing (racism as noun)	Process (racism as verb)

its impact and implications. In acknowledging the many faces of racism ("multi-racisms") as a moving target difficult either to pin down or to put away (Frederickson, 2002), this chapter will explore racisms in Canada as historically evolving, socially con-structed, situationally defined, and power driven. The different dimensions of racism are analyzed by reference to its many different definitions, namely as (1) biology, (2) ideol-ogy, (3) culture, (4) structure, and (5) power. Reference to racism is dissected into its component elements, that is, prejudice (including ethnocentrism and stereotyping) and discrimination (including harassment). The different levels of racism are also com-pared: from the interpersonal (including hate, polite, and subliminal) and the institutional (including the systematic and systemic) to the ideological (including everyday and nor-mative) and infrastructural (society). Also explored in this chapter are the historical origins of racism; its expression as social Darwinism, eugenics, and scientific racism; the reasons behind its persistence in the present against seeming odds; its impacts on minorities; and its costs to society. Finally, anti-racism strategies are addressed at vary-ing levels of problem definition and proposed solutions—individual, institutional, and inclusive.

PROBLEMATIZING RACISMS IN CANADA

Nowadays we seem to have a lot of racism but very few racists. How do you explain this paradox? What is the nature of this racism that dares not to be identified as such? (Blaut, 1992, p. 289)

Liberal racism, laissez-faire racism, modern racism (Barker, 1981), environmental racism, inferential racism, "soft" racism, new-age racism, aversive racism, "friendly" racism, transit racism, racism without race, neo-liberal and colour-blind racism (Giroux, 2008), experiential racism, integrative racism (Dei, 2000), masked racism (Davis, 1998), democratic racism, silent racism (Trepagnier, 2007), intellectual racism (Huston, 1995), closet racism (Gorski, 2004), Racism 1.0 and 2.0 (Wise, 2009), reverse racism, enlightened racism, cultural racism, the new racism, deliberative racism, anti-racism racism, genteel racism (Coates, 2008), masked racism (Davis, 1998), multicultural racism, imperial multiculturalism, feminist racism (Rodriguez, 2009), democratic racism, discursive racism (Henry & Tator, 2010), two-faced racism (Picca & Feagin, 2007), colonial racism, paternalistic racism (Halstead, 1988), Eurocentric racism, new racism (Sivanandan, 2009), Western racism, anti-Muslim racism, anti-immigrant/anti-asylum racism, elite racism (Bhavnani, Mirza, & Meetoo, 2005), anti-multicultural racism, subjective/objective racism (Mayer & Michelat, 2001), nice racism (Goldberg, 2006), white racism, anti-white racism, epistemological racism (Kuokkanen, 2007; Scheurich & Young, 2002), civilizational racism, intellectual racism (James & Shadd, 2001), pre-reflective/post-reflective gut racism (Halstead, 1988), global racism, state racism (Hesse, 2007), infrastructural racism (Sammel, 2009), xeno-racism (Fekete, 2009), neoracism (Cassin, Krawchenko, & VanderPlaat, 2007), digital racism (see online Insight 3.2). And, last but hardly least, Canadian racism (Canadian Race Relations Foundation, 2008).

Judging by the proliferation of terms and references, the profile of racism has expanded exponentially, reinforcing its status as the defining issue of contemporary times. References to racism consist of those ideologies that explicitly extol racial superiority, those beliefs or practices involving coded comments about inferiority, and those individuals and institutions without any clear racialized reference but whose actions may exert adverse consequences (Small, 2002). Such a range of references complicates any consensus over (1) defining racism, (2) determining its nature and magnitude, and (3) finding effective solutions. And yet prolonged exposure has not translated into consensus. Insofar as references to racism can mean everything yet nothing—a kind of floating signifier full of sound and sizzle but stripped of substance—efforts to problematize the different types of racism in Canada can prove tricky (see online Insight 3.5). Consider the following points of debate:

1. Are incidents of racism and racial conflict increasing across Canada? Or do numbers reflect both a growing public awareness of racism and a willingness to report violations to proper authorities?

2. How valid are all references to racism? Or are people prone to exaggerate racism as a scapegoat to justify failure or as a smokescreen to foreclose debate by diverting attention from the issues at hand? Is it racist to question the existence of racism or its relevance in defining who gets what (Henry & Tator, 2002; Satzewich & Shaffir, 2007/2009)?

3. To what extent is racism a case of individual ignorance or fear? Or should racism be interpreted as a complex system of practices and discourses that are historically defined, embedded within institutional structures, reflective of patterns of power, and woven into an ideological fabric?

4. Can racism be isolated and analyzed independently? Or must it be seen as constitutive of other forms of exclusion related to class, gender, ethnicity, or sexual preference in ways that intersect, interlock, and intensify? Are there materialist (class- based) or ideological explanations to account for racism and racial discrimination (Mac an Ghaill, 1999)?

5. Is there such a thing as a racist person? Or is it more accurate to say that individuals think and act in ways that can be defined as racist at certain times or in certain places?

6. In what way is racism a "thing" out there (see Hier & Walby, 2006)? Or is it a process that sustains relationships of inequality within contexts of power (Essed, 2002)? Or rather than something intentional, is racism receiver-dependent, that is, an attribute applied to an action after the fact, depending on the context, criteria, or consequence?

7. Is racism about treating people differently or the same? Is it possible to balance equal treatment regardless of difference with treatment as equals precisely because of differences that disadvantage?

8. Is there a distinctive Canadian form of racism, or should racism be framed in universalistic terms that apply to all times and all places (see Mac an Ghaill, 1999)? Or do we live in a world of multi-racisms whose permutations vary according to time and place (see Agnew, 2007; McVeigh & Lentin, 2006; Sinha, 2006).

9. Is it possible for individuals to be colour-blind yet stand accused of racism? For some, taking differences seriously is critical to challenging racism. For others, taking differences into account for any reason is fundamentally racist.

10. Is there a danger of overusing the word "racism"? Blaming racism for everything when race is irrelevant may be racist in its own right, in part because attention is deflected away from the root causes of minority problems. It also draws attention away from prejudice (stereotype and ethnocentrism) and discrimination as key factors.

11. Do whites who rarely experience racism because of their privileged status perceive it differently than racialized minorities do?

12. Is any criticism directed at people of colour a form of racism by definition? Or is a reluctance to criticize minorities a kind of racism in its own right by implying minority actions are beyond reproach or immune to criticism?

13. Is racism rational or irrational? Many regard racism as essentially irrational in that it discriminates against others on the basis of arbitrary characteristics; others frame it as a "rational" strategy employed by vested interests to secure advantage.

14. Do all racialized minorities experience racism in the same way? Or is racism differently understood and experienced by blacks (with its focus on their failures or acts of deviance), Muslims (with its focus on their differences or the dangers posed [Dunn, Klockerm, & Salabay, 2007]), Chinese (with its focus on their rate-busting successes), and Aboriginal peoples (with its focus on their militancy or unreasonable demands) (Banting, Courchene, & Seidle, 2007)?

The problematizing of racism reinforces what some suspect: First, racism refuses to go away even though we should know better or would like it to. Instead, racism has proven notoriously resistant and adaptive—intellectually dead, as many have noted, but ready to leap into action during times of danger or anxiety. For example, what was once seen in the civil rights era as helpful in eradicating racism—colour-blindness, formal and legal equality, and equal opportunity—are now seen as perpetuating new kinds of racism. That is, applying equal standards to unequal and racialized contexts tends to perpetuate patterns of inequality. In brief, racism is proving to be a "scavenger" ideology that parasitically pounces on the most unlikely of sources, bobbing and weaving to escape detection, and losing its precision when used loosely or analyzed too closely (Frederickson, 2002). Second, racisms exist, to be sure, but ambiguities prevail in unpacking (deconstructing) the "what," "why," "who," "where," and "when." Certain actions are unmistakably racist; others are labelled racist for political or social reasons; yet others still become defined as racist because of context, criterion, or consequences. Not surprisingly, racism has become so expansive in scope and application, with such an array of meanings from context to context, that it no longer conveys a meaning in the conventional sense of a single understood definition (Winant, 1998). Accordingly, racism can mean whatever people want it to mean and, while such expansiveness may prove helpful at times, it can also confuse and provoke.

DEFINING RACISM

Definitions of racism have varied and multiplied over time and place. They cover such an impossibly broad range of (in)activities that racism can mean everything, yet ends up meaning nothing. Or as Simon Holdaway (2003) writes, "Racism has been used in so many different ways that it has become a catch-all, sometimes referring to individual racists, sometimes to wholly reified institutions, and sometimes to whole societies, as if none of these phenomena have any relation to human action, other than one of straight-forward determinism" (p. 50). Older theories associated racism with a specific set of beliefs and actions, with clearly defined victims and perpetrators. To be a racist in the past meant believing certain groups of people to be racially inferior. The situation is much different today. In expanding its reference from doctrines to systems, (in)actions, consequences, and contexts, racism can refer to situations in which racialized minorities (a) feel uncomfortable in the presence of whites (Paikin, 2010), (b) believe that progress is too slow in bringing about equality and inclusiveness, (c) acknowledge racism's presence as so subtle that only victims can recognize and experience it, and (d) claim that any criticism toward them may reflect an unconscious racism.

References to racism are multidimensional rather than singular or monolithic (Winant, 1998), and this multidimensionality is captured by exploring the different ways that racism is defined. While numerous definitions exist—reviewing even a small portion would be exhausting—most definitions of racism fall into one of five ideal-typical categories, namely, racism as biology, ideology, culture, structure, and power. Phrased differently, definitions of racism have historically revolved around five major themes categorized accordingly: (1) dislike of others because of who they are (racism as biology); (2) disdain for others because of a particular world view (racism as ideology); (3) distrust of people for what they do (racism as culture); (4) exclusion of others that is institutionalized (racism as structure); and (5) domination over others (racism as power). To be sure, many definitions incorporate several of these dimensions; after all, references to reality are contextual rather than categorical. Nevertheless, these distinctions may be analytically separated for conceptual purposes.

Racism as Biology Many definitions of racism are anchored in the root, "race," with its attendant notion that biology is destiny. References to *racism as biology* entail a belief in innate differences as socially significant in two ways. First, racism is defined as any belief that links behaviour with biology (biological determinism). Racism involves a process by which individuals are reduced to their skin colour using group categories to make negative inferences about the person (see Paikin, 2010). Discriminatory treatment of others is then justified on the grounds of innate differences that are natural and fixed. Second, racism can be defined as any treatment—either negative or positive—directed at others solely because of race (or skin colour). To deny or exclude others because of race is clearly racism. To provide preferential assistance to others because of race is no less racist. In both cases, individuals are singled out for different treatment on the basis of who they are rather than what they need or are entitled to.

Racism as Ideology Strictly speaking, the concept of race is concerned with perceived differences. Racism, by contrast, transforms these differences into a relatively coherent ideology that justifies the racial superiority of one group over another. Ideologies in themselves are not necessarily evil or destructive; nevertheless, when wedded to institutionalized power relations, they can inflict devastation, including the purging of 6 million "undesirables" under a Nazi Germany. According to definitions of racism as ideology, humanity can be partitioned into a set of fixed and discrete categories of population known as race. Each of these racial categories embraces a distinctive and inherited assemblage of physical, cultural, and psychological characteristics that can be arranged in ascending or descending order of acceptance or desirability. From this emerges an ideology of intellectual or moral superiority—a hierarchy of superior and inferior races that unjustly diminishes others and justifies this denigration by reference to race. As a means for justifying national policies—whether expressed as civilizing, or as a Christianizing mission, or as reflecting the inherent right of superior peoples to rule and control, the concept of racism justified European imperialism and domination of others, although it was not until the late nineteenth century that arguments in support of racial inequality were articulated into official state ideology (Melle, 2009).

Racism as Culture In recent years, the definitional focus of racism has shifted from race-based racism to racism rooted in cultural differences (Dunn et al., 2007). Appeals to cultural inferiority and a dislike of others because of their differences are replacing a preoccupation with race (biology) as a basis for definition (Lamoin & Dawes, 2010). Racism is no longer defined as a universal discourse of dominance over racial inferiors as was the case with colonialism. The objective then was to destroy "the others" as an impediment, to exploit them for gain, or to absorb them in the name of progress. At present, however, the issue is about the danger that foreign cultural practices pose to national unity, identity, and citizenship (Fleras, 2004b). Dominant sectors are not defined as racially superior but as culturally normal and preferred. In turn, subdominant groups are dismissed as a culturally dangerous threat to a secular and liberal society rather than innately inferior. For example, while Islamophobia is widely acknowledged and pervasive, this fear of Muslims does not rely on perceptions of racial inferiority. Rather, Islam and Muslims are racialized as a threat to security, as barriers to integration and belonging, with differences inconsistent with mainstream values and beliefs (Dunn et al., 2007; Gottschalk & Greenberg, 2008). In that cultural differences are vilified as dangerous, irrelevant, or inferior, the racialization of others through claims of cultural superiority has proven as exclusionary in advancing structures of inferiority and differentiation as old-fashioned racial ideologies.

Racism as Structure Another set of definitions focuses on racism as structural. This broader definition goes beyond racism as a set of ideas or individual actions, despite the tendency for many to equate racism with extreme acts that incite prejudice, hatred, or violence. While such acts are common, ranging from racist graffiti to death threats (James, 2008), emphasis instead is on those structural biases within the broader context of social formation and institutional processes. Racism as structure is based on the idea that neither society nor institutions are neutral or value-free. To the contrary, their design, organization, assumptions, agendas, and operations reflect the foundational principles and deeply embedded values of the dominant sector that privileges some, while disadvantaging others (Editorial, 2005b; Teelucksingh, 2006). This racialized bias with respect to what is desirable and acceptable is woven into the very fabric of society, in effect becoming so normalized that people tend to think of it as natural (Kobayashi, 2001) or systemic (Kumi, 2008). In that societies are racialized in power and privilege, the system becomes self-perpetuating, while inequities are transmitted from one generation to the next without much disruption to the status quo. Or as critical race theorists like to remind us, the institutionalization of whiteness as an unmarked passport to privilege within the very structure of society is both a product and a producer of racisms (Schick & St. Denis, 2005).

Racism as Power Definitions of racism increasingly emphasize the concept of **power**. Racism as power consists of virtually any type of exploitation or exclusion by which the dominant group institutionalizes its privilege at the expense of others (Al-Krenawi & Graham, 2003). Power operates by fixing self-serving ideologies as common sense (Lee & Lutz, 2005), resulting in the dominance and control over another through a system of ideas, laws, and practices that regulates the aspirations, actions, and livelihood of racialized minorities (M. Brown, 2005). For example, the institutionalized power inherent within an old-white-boys' network effectively screens out minorities through discriminatory hiring and unintended promotional practices that deny or exclude. Or, as deftly phrased by Christine Silverberg (2004), former chief of the Calgary Police Services:

> [R]acism is not just an overt act of discrimination, or even a series of such incidents, but rather the use of institutional power to deny or grant whole groups of people rights, respect, and representation based on their skin colour.

Put bluntly, racism is about power, not pigmentation (Khayatt, 1994). Racism goes beyond individual prejudice, but focuses on those **institutional powers** to differentiate, categorize, and exclude. Racism is not about differences per se but about how those in positions of power racialize these differences to protect ruling-class privilege. Racism is not about treating others differently because they are different, but about their differential treatment within contexts of power that limit or oppress (Blauner, 1972). Finally, racism is not about people's attitudes, but about institutionalized power to establish agendas regarding what is normal, necessary, desirable, or acceptable, thus reinforcing the superiority of one group over another. bell hooks (1995) puts it into perspective by linking racism with power:

> Why is it so difficult for many white folks to understand that racism is oppressive not because white folks have prejudicial feelings about black people . . . but because it is a system that promotes domination and subjugation? (pp. 154–155)

To be sure, those with power are frequently least aware, yet most likely to acknowledge the centrality of power in intergroup dynamics (Scheurich & Young, 1997). Conversely, those with the least amount of power are most likely to be aware of its existence and potency. Moreover, the longer one group remains in power, the more their ways of thinking and acting about what is normal and necessary become normalized (socially correct and privileged) and universalized as measures of merit and predictors of success. In short, to act as if power does not exist ensures retention of the status quo with its prevailing distribution of privilege and resources.

A Working Definition of Racism

One thing is clear from this overview of definitions of racism: A working definition of racism must go beyond a personal ideology based on race prejudice. It must focus on a system of disadvantage founded on institutional power, anchored in values and beliefs, and predicated on a supremacist mindset. It must also incorporate actions that deny equality to minorities; institutional policies and practices that exclude, deny, or exploit others; and a set of generalized beliefs and actions that imply the superiority of one group over others. Mindful of these preconditions and multiplicities, **racism** can be defined as *those ideas and ideals (ideology) that assert or imply the assumed superiority of one social group over another, together with the institutional power to put these perceptions into practice in ways that control, exclude, or exploit those racialized as different or inferior.*

This working definition draws attention to key attributes of racism, namely, its status as an ideology either articulated or implied, a corresponding set of practices that involves deliberate intent or reflects inadvertent consequences, and an impact that embraces both personal and institutional dimensions. More importantly, it demonstrates how racism transcends simple expressions of individual prejudice. Rather, it entails a complex system of exclusionary conditions and dynamics, including ideologies, discourses, discursive practices, institutions, and values within a particular social, cultural, and historical context (Goldberg, 2002; Macedo & Gounari, 2006). Finally, the centrality of institutional power is duly acknowledged. In that racism is about power—and because those with power are rarely aware of it, yet disinclined to share it with others—any unmasking of racism is unlikely without a protracted struggle.

COMPONENTS OF RACISM

Racism does not reflect a monolithic reality. Rather, in a multicultural society, racism is a complex and multifaceted dynamic involving different components. Each of the components or building blocks of racism—namely, prejudice (including ethnocentrism and stereotypes), discrimination (including harassment), and power—contributes to the totality of racism as an ideology and practice.

Prejudice

The concept of **prejudice** refers to negative, often unconscious, and preconceived notions about others. Prejudice arises because of a very normal tendency to prejudge persons or situations (Bakanic, 2009). As a precondition for processing information about the world out there, there is nothing inherently racist about prejudice. Everyone makes prejudgments when defining situations or making sense of our fast-paced world. Prejudice becomes a problem only when people use these prejudgments to deny or exclude others.

In general, prejudice can be defined as any attitude or outlook toward members of a group that directly or indirectly implies negativity or hostility (Brown, 2010). More specifically, prejudice consists of *prejudgments* that are irrational and unfounded on grounds of existing or compelling evidence. A preconceived set of attitudes is embraced that mistakenly encourages people to see and judge others without taking into account internal differences (Holdaway, 1996). According to psychologist Frances Aboud, prejudice provides a very simple way of seeing the world, and this craving for simplicity may be transformed into a preference for in-group members (as cited in Abel, 2001). Such ignorance may persist into adulthood; unlike ignorance, however, prejudice is inflexible and characterized by a refusal to modify beliefs when presented with contrary evidence. At times, expressions of prejudice are conscious but politely worded to avoid open offence. At other times, individuals may not be aware of their prejudice except in those split-second situations that expose dormant dislikes. Tests, such as the Implicit Association Test at **www.tolerance.org/hidden_bias/index.html**, suggest that the vast majority of people have hidden and unconscious prejudices that stand in sharp contrast to explicitly egalitarian values (Banaji, 2003; Dow, 2003). Just as people don't always "speak their minds," so too do they rarely "know their minds," culminating in a disconnect between conscious and unconscious, belief and behaviour (also known as subliminal racism). This notion of prejudice as implicit (Bakanic, 2009; Caines, 2004)—a kind of "mental residue"—should not be discounted as trivial or inconsequential. In that people are a lot more prejudiced than they think they are, no one should underestimate the potential of prejudice to harm (Blank et al., 2004; *Economist*, 2009).

Prejudice is widely regarded as a psychological phenomenon with a corresponding set of rigid or authoritarian personality traits (Adorno et al., 1950; Allport, 1954). Negative attitudes toward others are seen in part as normal psychological processes, such as dividing the world into in-groups (that we favour) and out-groups (that we dislike). Others link these prejudgments with a visceral and deep-seated fear of those whose appearances or practices threaten the prevailing status quo. People who feel irrationally threatened by a particular group justify inflicting harm on "others" as acts of self-preservation (Schaller, 2004). In that prejudice may involve a projection of fear or displacement of anxieties upon others, such beliefs may say more about the perpetrator than the perpetrated upon (Curtis, 1997). Still others define prejudice as unmistakably social (or focus on its social dimensions). It neither materializes out of unresolved psychological issues nor necessarily reflects a warped personality. Rather, prejudice arises from group interaction within unequal contexts, namely, to control others in the competition for scarce resources. In that prejudice is more the result of competition than its cause, a racialized system is perpetuated that privileges some and disprivileges others.

Ethnocentrism can be defined as a belief in the superiority of one culture over another. Like prejudice, ethnocentrism is a normal and universal process, reflecting patterns of socialization that focus on generating in-group loyalty. In some cases, a belief in cultural superiority is openly articulated, for example, by comparing other cultures or cultural practices with one's own standards of right, acceptable, or desirable. In other cases, ethnocentrism involves the universal tendency to interpret reality from one's cultural perspective as natural and normal—and assume that others are doing so as well—while dismissing other perspectives as inferior, irrelevant, or threatening. To be sure, there is nothing intrinsically wrong with endorsing one's cultural values as self-evident and preferable. Difficulties arise when these standards become a frame of reference for negatively evaluating others as backward, immoral, or irrational. Further problems appear when these ethnocentric judgments are manipulated to condone the mistreatment of others. In other words, ethnocentrism is two-edged: Favouritism toward one's group may forge in-group cohesion and morale; it can also foster out-group tension and hostility. And when those in positions of power put their ethnocentrism into practice, the results can get discriminatory.

Ethnocentrism often leads to a proliferation of stereotypes about out-group members. **Stereotypes** are essentially generalizations about others, both unwarranted and unfounded on the basis of available evidence (Kashima, Fiedler, & Freytag, 2008). Stereotyping reinforces a universal tendency to reduce a complex phenomenon to simple (or simplistic) explanations that can be generalized to a whole category. It reflects an essentialized notion that all individuals within a certain category will act uniformly and predictably because of this membership (Essed, 1991). Those who are stereotyped often live up to them, or down to them in the case of underperforming racialized minorities (Steele, 2006). Evidence also suggests that people tend to view out-groups as uniformly homogeneous and an undifferentiated mass rather than as individuals with skills and talents.

Like ethnocentrism, stereotypes in themselves are harmless. But problems arise when these preconceived mental images give way to discriminatory practices or generate self-fulfilling prophecies. And like prejudice, stereotypes are social. Stereotypes do not necessarily represent an error in perception, at least no more so than prejudice is a case of erroneously processing information. More accurately, stereotyping is yet another instrument of social control. Consider how the dispossession of Aboriginal peoples' lands was facilitated through negative images of them as savages, cannibals, and brutes. A pervasive "anti-orientalism" in British Columbia fostered hatred against Asian populations, thereby simplifying the task of expelling 22 000 Japanese Canadians from the West Coast in 1942. And hostility toward Islam continues to fester in the light of demeaning media stereotypes that portray Arab-Muslim Canadians as (1) members of a devalued and backward minority, (2) colonized peoples without democratic traditions, and (3) a ragtag collection of terrorists and religious fanatics (Goldberg, 2005; Karim, 2002).

All negative stereotypes are hurtful; nevertheless, not all negative portrayals have an equivalent impact. Context and consequence are critical in shaping different outcomes and responses. For example, members of a dominant group need not be unduly concerned with negative stereotyping about themselves. As a group, they have control over a wide range of representations that flatter or empower. Negative stereotypes might cause discomfort for "pale males"; nevertheless, men as a group possess both the political authority and economic clout to neutralize or deflect negative portrayals. In that power and privilege provide a protective buffer, even a constant barrage of negativity can be absorbed without harm or damage. But for minorities with specific vulnerabilities, stereotyping is a problem, thanks to their lack of institutional power and resources (Elmasry, 1999). Each negative image or unflattering representation reinforces their peripheral status as not quite Canadian.

Discrimination

The word "discrimination" can be employed in different ways. Non-evaluative meanings indicate a capacity to distinguish (e.g., a colour-blind person may not be able to discriminate [distinguish] between blue and green). Evaluative meanings of discrimination can be used positively (a discriminating palate) or negatively (indicating narrow-mindedness). Section 15 of the *Canadian Charter of Rights and Freedoms* prohibits discrimination on the basis of race, ethnicity, or origins. Yet the Charter concedes the possibility of seemingly "discriminatory" measures, like employment equity, to assist historically disadvantaged minorities.

Distinctions are not discriminatory, in other words, if they have a demonstrably justified and legitimate goal of reversing discrimination by levelling the playing field (see the Chapter 5 Debate box on employment equity). Discrimination is also permissible if demonstrated to be a bona fide occupational requirement. In brief, some forms of discrimination are acceptable—even essential—to the functioning of a complex and democratic society (MacQueen, 1994). But in situations where racism is framed as a form of social exclusion, discrimination is defined as the process for putting this exclusivity into practice (Saloojee, 2005).

Patterns of discrimination may be differently expressed—blatant or oblique, individualized or institutionalized, deliberate or unintended—with the result that the motivation behind an act is secondary to its effect on the victim (Rusk, 2005). Discrimination itself has shifted its focus: From a predominantly individual problem reflecting prejudicial attitudes and based on the occasional differential treatment, discrimination is increasingly perceived as largely systemic and embedded in a complex interplay of institutional relations and practices whose negative consequences reflect the differential effects of apparently neutral policies and similar treatment (Henry & Tator, 2006). This indirect discrimination arises when the outcomes of rules or procedures that apply equally to everybody have the unintended effect of denying, controlling, or excluding others through no fault of their own. The applying of similar rules to unequal contexts may inadvertently perpetuate discrimination by failing to take differences and disadvantages into account (see also the discussion of systemic racism later in this chapter). Finally, the fact that discrimination is no longer socially or legally acceptable makes it less likely to occur unless it can be explained away on grounds other than prejudice (Dovidio et al., 2010a). For example, discounting the skills or credentials of foreignborn workers comes across as a legitimate criticism rather than prejudicial expression. And while direct discrimination aimed at an entire group is no longer legal or acceptable, it's permissible if directed at members of devalued groups who refuse to play by the rules (Yoshino, 2006). Combining these components—that is, differential treatment and differential effects because of race—produces a working definition along the lines proposed by the United Nations (see Blank et al., 2004; Editorial, 2005b): **Discrimination** *can be defined as any restrictive act, whether deliberate or not, that has the intent or the effect of adversely affecting ("denying" or "excluding") others on grounds other than merit or ability.*

Is there a relationship between prejudice and discrimination? Often there is: Whereas prejudice refers to attitudes and beliefs, *discrimination* entails putting these prejudgments into practice. A vicious cycle can be discerned: Prejudice toward groups creates a discriminatory effect resulting in marginalization and failure that then reinforces the original prejudice. And so the cycle continues, thus reinforcing the popular equation: Racism = Prejudice + Discrimination. But a distinction or relationship is neither clear-cut nor causal. Discrimination can exist without prejudice, especially when negative treatment of racialized minorities is deeply and systemically embedded. Thus, institutions can operate on discriminatory grounds even if the individuals themselves are free of prejudice (what is called systemic bias). Conversely, prejudice may flourish without its expression in discrimination. Individuals may be prejudiced, and yet compartmentalize these attitudes by refusing to act in a discriminatory manner for fear of losing face or facing retaliation. In brief, prejudice and discrimination are analytically distinct, if mutually related, concepts that can vary independently under certain conditions.

Harassment is commonly appraised as a type of discrimination. According to the Ontario Human Rights Commission, harassment means that someone is bothering you, threatening you, or treating you unfairly because of race or ethnicity. It consists of persistent and unwelcome actions of a racially oriented nature (from racial jokes to degrading pictures to insults and name-calling) by those who ought to reasonably know better. In the words of Monique Shebbeare (McGill University, 1994), harassment involves:

> [t]he abusive, unfair, or demeaning treatment of a person or group of persons that has the effect or purpose of unreasonably interfering with a person's or group's status or performance or creating a hostile or intimidating working or educational environment . . . (p. 6)

Like discrimination, harassment constitutes an abuse of institutional power. Seemingly minor and isolated incidents may amount to harassment when viewed over time or within an institutionalized context. The creation of a chilly climate or "poisoned environment" because of harassment can also have an adverse effect on work, study, involvement, or well-being. For some, harassment is ultimately defined from the perspective of the victim who determines what distinguishes offence from harassment, or consensual conduct from an abuse of power. Others disagree, and insist on making a principled distinction between harassment and causing offence. The definition of "harassment" should be restricted to speech or behaviour that habitually targets a particular individual or group in a way that prevents full and equal participation. To include merely offending someone through random ethnic jokes or thoughtless remarks may have the perverse effect of expanding harassment to include everything, yet nothing.

SECTORS OF RACISM

That racism in one form or another exists in Canada is surely beyond debate at this point in our history. With the benefit of some prodding and sharp reminders, Canadians are increasingly facing up to our checkered past, with its bewildering mixture of tolerance and repression. Canada was founded on racist principles, despite a tendency toward collective denial and historical amnesia (Henry & Tator, 2006; Razack, 2004), and it continues to be racialized because of foundational principles and fundamental values. Some forms of racism are now widely condemned and detested; other strands continue to be endemic to Canada, with few signs of disappearing. To complicate the issue further, the threat of social sanctions may have propelled racism to go underground or to redefine itself in seemingly more innocuous ways.

Clearly, then, racism is not a uniform concept that reflects a singular experience or common reality. On the contrary, different types of racism can be discerned that vary in intent, levels of awareness, magnitude and scope, depth of intensity, and consequences. These variations have led to the creation of a racism typology: (1) interpersonal racism (including hate, polite, and subliminal); (2) institutional racism (including systematic and systemic); (3) ideological racism (including normative and everyday); and (4) infrastructural racism (society) (see Table 3-2). Unmasking each of these ideal types will expose the complex and multidimensional nature of racism as theory and practice (see online Insight 3.8). Envisaging racism as multifaceted also underscores the complexity of matching solutions to problems.

Interpersonal

Interpersonal racism entails a pattern of dislike that occurs at the level of individual and group relations. This dislike is directed at the "other" because of who he is or what she stands for. Three types of interpersonal racism can be discerned: hate, polite, and subliminal.

Hate Racism The kind of racism that most commonly comes to mind is **hate racism**. It refers to the old-fashioned, in-your-face hatred of the racialized "other" that once prevailed in the past and continues to exist in the present among a handful of the reactionary or defiant. Intrinsic to hate racism is its explicit and highly personalized character. Hate racism is expressed through sharply personal attacks on those who are perceived as culturally or biologically inferior. These personalized attacks often consist of derogatory slurs and minority name-calling—but physical abuse may also be involved as well as destruction of property through vandalism.

Even a cursory glance over Canada's past exposes the stain of hate racism (Walker, 1997; Wallis & Fleras, 2008). This may come as a shock to many readers. Certain myths are deeply entrenched in our collective memories, especially those that extol Canada's progressive status, the absence of American-style race riots and prolonged slavery, and the entrenchment of multicultural and human rights principles. Close scrutiny suggests otherwise. Since Confederation, Canada's treatment of racial, Aboriginal, and **ethnic** minorities has left much to be desired (Backhouse, 1999). Chinese, Japanese, Indo-Pakistanis, First Nations, Jews, and blacks have been and continue to be the object of dislike or aversion. Laws and practices were invoked that segregated people of colour, especially blacks, from full and equal participation in Canadian societies until the 1950s and 1960s (Walker, 1997). Racist groups like the Ku Klux Klan have also relied on violence to cultivate an environment of fear and hatred against minorities throughout the United States and Canada (Barrett, 1987).

As noted throughout this text, hate racism persists at present (see online Insight 3.6). Anti-Semitism remains an ongoing problem in Canada, while anti-black racism is routinely encountered by young males within the criminal justice system. Of particular concern—especially since 9/11 and the spread of jihadist terrorism in the name of Islam—is mounting hatred toward anyone perceived as Middle Eastern. This **Islamophobia** reflects deeply ingrained and largely unexamined anxieties, fears, and distrust of Islam and Muslim cultures (Gottschalk & Greenberg, 2008). With Islamophobia, the isolated acts of a small number of extremists tend to be amplified out of proportion by the media, thereby reinforcing people's worst expectations and darkest concerns; providing proof that perpetuates prejudicial stereotyping of Muslim men as violent tyrants and Muslim women as

TABLE 3-2	Sectors of Racism		
Interpersonal	Institutional	Ideological	Infrastructural
hate	systematic	everyday	society
polite	systemic	normative	
subliminal			

helplessly oppressed; and convincing many of the irreconcilable differences between the West and Islamic "otherness." The end result of this rising tide of Islamophobia is a fundamental distrust that borders on hate, thus reinforcing the status of Arab Canadians as the "enemy within."

Of course, hate racism is no stranger to the United States. According to the Southern Poverty Law Center, the number of hate groups has jumped from 602 in 2000 to 888 in 2007 (DiversityInc, 2008). Canada is also a site for hate groups, including white supremacist groups from the Aryan Nation and Western Guard movements to neo-Nazi skinheads in urban areas (Barkun, 1994; Kinsella, 1994). These groups are committed to an ideology of racial supremacy that asserts the superiority of whites and the hatred of non-whites. On the surface, white supremacists may not be explicitly anti-minority preferring, instead, to see themselves as white Christians, fusing race and religion in a single nationalist crusade against the forces of evil (Jaret, 1995). The trauma of 9/11 reinforces a renewed conviction of a pending global racial war (Barrett, 2007), prompting the racist right to actively seeking out converts to its cause. Disaffected youth are an obvious target because of perceived government indifference to their plight in a changing and diverse world (Li, 1995). The combination of music, pamphlets, disinformation by telephone hotlines, and the Internet—from chat rooms to websites that offer unique ways of spreading hate (Back, 2002; Rajagopal, 2006)—concocts an appealing mishmash of neo-Nazi philosophies, KKK folklore, pseudo-Nordic mythology, and anti-government slogans (O'Hara, 2005). Admittedly, there is no way of gauging the number of hardcore supremacists in Canada; nonetheless, even a small number of racist ideologues can destabilize a society, especially when the economy is sputtering.

Polite Racism Few people at present will tolerate the open expression of racism. Compare this with the past, when racism was openly articulated and socially acceptable. There was no need for pretence or politeness; everything was upfront and proudly so. The passage of constitutional guarantees such as the *Canadian Charter of Rights and Freedoms* and human rights codes, however, has eroded the legitimacy of hate racism from public discourse. But while blatant forms of racism have dissipated to some extent, less candid expressions of bigotry and stereotyping remain in force. Instead of disappearing in the face of social reprisals and legal sanctions, as might have been expected, racism is increasingly couched in a way that allows people to conceal their dislike of others by way of coded language (Wetherell & Potter, 1993). According to Peter Li (2007), Canadians assign social significance to race, despite its social and legal sanctions, in large part by relying on euphemisms to express racial views without appearing racist (see also Berry & Bonilla-Silva, 2007; Kobayashi & Johnson, 2007). In that this polite racism tends to be banal rather than blatant, obliquely couched in the language of political correctness rather than obtrusive, and sugar "coded" with higher principles to confuse or deflect, its detection is rendered more difficult (Coates, 2008).

Polite racism can be defined as a disguised dislike of others manifested through behaviour that outwardly is non-prejudicial in appearance. These politely aversive feelings are not expressed through outright hostility or hate, but often through patterns of avoidance or rejection. Polite racism may consist of the "look" that "otherizes" racialized minorities as different and inferior and out of place in Canadian society. It often manifests itself in the use of coded or euphemistic language ("those people") to mask inner feelings behind a facade of gentility (Blauner, 1994). This politeness is especially evident when racialized minorities are ignored or turned down for jobs, promotions, or accommodation. For example, when approached by an inappropriate applicant, an employer may claim a job is filled rather than admit "no blacks need apply." "Sorry, the apartment is rented," is another polite way of rejecting undesirable tenants when the unit in question is, in truth, still vacant. Polite racism would appear to be less hurtful than its hate equivalent; nevertheless, the effect on the victims is no less debilitating.

Finally, consider anti-Semitism as polite racism. Jewish people have long been targets of hate. But a new strain of anti-Semitism is increasingly directed not at Jews per se or their wealth—given the social unacceptability of such blatant dislike—but at Israel's relationship with Palestinians in the "occupied" or "reclaimed" lands. The acceptable face of anti-Semitism challenges Israel's right to exist as an equal member of the family of nations, its right to defend borders against enemies, and its human rights record in comparison to other countries (Cotler, 2007). As put by the Friends of the Simon Wiesenthal Center for Holocaust Studies (2008) in a letter to the president of the University of Toronto:

> Criticism of Israel is not of itself anti-Semitic. However, the specific targeting of Israel alone is anti-Semitic. Denying the Jewish people their right to self-determination by claiming that the existence of Israel is a racist endeavor is anti-Semitic. Applying a double standard by requiring of Israel behaviour not demanded of any of its neighbors is anti-Semitic.

No one is suggesting that Israel is above the law or unaccountable for human rights violations. However, unduly harsh and one-sided criticism of Israel may reflect a politely articulated dislike of Jews (Bunzl, 2005; Cotler, 2007; Endelman, 2005; Weinfeld, 2005).

Subliminal Racism A third type of interpersonal racism—**subliminal racism**—operates at an unconscious level. At its root, subliminal racism constitutes a deeply buried dislike of others beyond the awareness of the perpetrator in question. If activated or exposed to the surface, this unconscious dislike of others hides behind principled statements, in effect reflecting a willingness to criticize minorities or diversity by disguising the dislike on loftier grounds. The end result is a gap between what people say and what they do— between what values they profess to endorse and those they prefer to practise. Not surprisingly, subliminal racism is found among that class of persons who openly abhor discriminatory treatment of minorities, yet appear incapable or unwilling to do something about it. When asked to justify this disconnect, they rely on rationalizations to oppose measures for remedying the problem of inequality (Augoustinos & Reynolds, 2001; see also Henry & Tator, 2006). In that a general principle is invoked to deny the legitimacy of specific instances, this opposition or criticism is coded in principled terms that politely skirt the issue by appealing to a higher sense of fair play or procedural justice.

There is no shortage of examples of subliminal racism—a racism that reflects a disconnect between conscious and unconscious beliefs, between thought and behaviour, and between principle and practice. Canadians generally are sympathetic toward refugees in distress, but less enamoured with those who are seen as breaking the rules (Angus Reid, 2010). So-called bogus refugee claimants are condemned not in blunt racist terminology; rather, their landed entry into Canada is criticized on principled grounds ranging from unfairness ("jumping the queue") and illegality of entry to posing the threat of terrorism and criminality. Employment equity initiatives may be endorsed in principle but rejected in practice as unfair to the majority or inconsistent with the principles of a colour-blind society. Individuals may support a commitment to inclusiveness as a matter of principle, yet disapprove of equity measures to achieve that goal. Support for the principle of equality for minorities may be widely endorsed, but individuals balk at the prospect of moving over and making space, especially if costs or inconvenience are incurred (see Berry & Bonilla-Silva, 2007).

In other words, those who profess egalitarian attitudes yet refuse to act on this conviction because of principled excuses may be exhibiting subliminal racism. How, then, do we explain the subliminality of this "love–hate" relation toward minorities? Cynics might argue that Canadians are hypocrites whose racism is candy-coated by platitudinous pieties. In a Canada where open racism is socially unacceptable, coded opposition to multiculturalism or immigration is more acceptable than brazen expressions of intolerance (Li, 2007; Palmer, 1996). But unlike the deliberate euphemisms of polite racism, a subliminal racism reflects a largely unconscious dislike of others behind a folksy veneer of respectability. Not surprisingly, Canadians appear reluctant to criticize minorities or government minority policies unless the criticism can be rephrased and conveyed along principled grounds. To be sure, criticism of racialized minority actions or demands is not necessarily racist, and it would be unfair to uniformly label critics as such. Nevertheless, principled opposition may well conceal a deeply seated racism. Even the unintended consequences of such opposition or criticism may be racist when reinforcing those very inequities that need to be eradicated (Hochschild, 2002; hooks, 1995). After all, the act of doing nothing to bring about progressive change is not neutrality but a tacit acceptance of an unequal and racialized status quo (see online Insight 3.3).

Institutional

Other types of racism go beyond the interpersonal in terms of scope, style, and impact. Racism at the institutional level represents such a shift, one that sees the problem of racism as embedded within the institutions of society rather than in individualized expression. It is predicated on the assumption that institutions are neither neutral sites nor passively devoid of agendas or consequences. Rather, institutions consist of values, structures, and practices infused with cultural assumptions that explicitly or inadvertently favour some at the expense of others. **Institutional racism** refers to the process by which organizational practices and procedures adversely penalize minority women and men through those rules, procedures, rewards, and practices that have the intent (systematic) or effect (systemic) of excluding or exploiting.

Systematic Racism A racism that directly and deliberately prevents minorities from full and equal institutional involvement is known as **systematic racism**. This institutionalized racism appears when discriminatory practices are legally sanctioned by the institution (or the state) and carried out by employees who act on its behalf and with its approval (Milloy, 2001). Systematic institutional racism flourished in societies that endorsed racial segregation. The regime of apartheid in South Africa is a classic example, as was the pre–civil rights United States. Canada was also tarnished by institutionally racist practices that directly and deliberately denied or excluded. Institutions at present can no longer openly discriminate against minorities, lest they attract negative publicity, encounter legal action, or incite consumer resistance. Nevertheless, systematic institutional racism continues to exist through discriminatory actions that the institutional culture discreetly endorses. For example, both Texaco and Dennys were hit with billion-dollar lawsuits in the 1990s for systematically discriminating against minorities. More recently, the US government paid out a $1.25 billion settlement to black farmers who had lodged a complaint of discrimination against the Department of Agriculture for refusing them loans and assistance (Christchurch Press, 2010).

Systemic Racism There is another type of institutional racism that is impersonal and unconscious, without much awareness of its presence or consequences except by those victimized. **Systemic racism** is predicated on the belief that institutional rules and procedures can be racist in design, by practice, or in their effects, even if the actors are themselves free of prejudicial discrimination (Canadian Race Relations Foundation, 2003). Unlike other forms of racism whose existence can be criticized as departures from the norm, systemic racism involves normal institutional functions that, paradoxically, exert negative consequences for some. Institutional rules, expectations, and rewards may appear to be universally applicable and ostensibly colour-blind. However, a commitment to a one-size-fits-all standardization (i.e., "we treat everyone the same around here") may discriminate against those who are disadvantaged through no fault of their own. Treating everyone the same when people's differences and disadvantages need to be recognized may exert a systemically biasing effect, that is, an unintended effect of inadvertently excluding those with different needs, goals, and values. In short, systemic racism embodies a bias that is normalized (inherent or institutionalized) within institutional structures, processes, and outcomes, primarily because of a pervasive Eurocentrism that defines conventions and standards by which others are judged or serviced, with the result that the application of these rules or norms can exert unequal or harmful consequences for vulnerable minorities.

With systemic racism, neither intent nor awareness count. (In this sense, systemic racism resembles the institutional equivalent of subliminal racism.) The context and the consequences are critical, since even seemingly neutral policies and programs, when applied evenly and equally, can exert an exclusionary effect on those whose differences are disadvantaging. Institutional rules, priorities, and practices may not be inherently racist or deliberately discriminatory; that is, institutions do not go out of their way to exclude or deprive minorities. But once entrenched within institutions, racism is no longer intent driven but is perpetuated by seemingly benign practices and programs (ERASE Racism, 2005). In that disadvantages are inherent within the system because the system itself is socially constructed by, for, and about the powerful and privileged, institutional rules that apply equally to all may have a discriminatory effect by ignoring how organizational practices reflect and reinforce white experiences as normal and necessary. Finally, systemic bias may arise because of the logical consequences of well-intentioned policies and initiatives that are based on faulty assumptions, ignore cultural differences, or fail to take context into account (Shkilnyk, 1985). Admittedly, references to systemic racism have proliferated in recent years across a bewildering range of domains (see Kumi, 2008), in the process suggesting a tendency toward misuse, as John Fraser (2006) writes:

> . . . whenever there is a battle royal on campus over race, creed, or gender, and there is no hard evidence of discrimination, the word "systemic" is sure to be wheeled into the fray. Once "systemic" is deployed, all counterarguments are automatically trumped. The more you argue against the point, the more you are thought to expose your pre-conscious intolerance.

Nevertheless, whether overused or not, systemic racism exists. In a one-size-fits-all world where people's differences can prove disadvantaging, failure to take differences into account creates consequences that are systemically biasing. In other words, the challenge is not to discard the concept but to employ it more judiciously.

How do mainstream institutions exert a systemic bias against minority women and men? For years, a number of occupations such as police officers, firefighters, and mass-transit drivers imposed minimum weight, height, and educational requirements for job applicants. In retrospect, while not openly racist, these criteria proved systemically discriminatory because they favoured males over females and white applicants over people of colour. No deliberate attempt was made to exclude anyone; after all, equal standards were uniformly applied. Valid reasons may have existed to justify these restrictions; nevertheless, the imposition of these qualifications inflicted a set of unfair entry restrictions, regardless of intent or rationale. And these criteria have had the controlling effect of excluding racialized minorities who, as a group, lacked the criteria for entry or success *through no fault of their own*.

Or consider the systemic bias experienced by migrant agricultural workers from Mexico and the Caribbean who qualify under Canada's Seasonal Agricultural Workers Program (Fleras, 2010c). Like all Canadian workers, migrant workers must pay premiums under the *Employment Insurance Act*. But unlike Canadian workers who don't have to leave the country upon completion of their authorized work terms, migrant workers cannot claim unemployment benefits or sick-leave benefits, because the Act stipulates that a claimant must be physically in Canada and available for work to receive benefits. In other words, the established rules of the *Employment Insurance Act*, when evenly applied to both categories of workers, have the effect of excluding migrant workers or because of circumstances beyond their control. Other examples of systemic racism may include the following: an insistence on Canadian-only experience for job placement; the devaluation of minority experiences and credentials as a precondition for professional employment; unnecessarily high educational standards for entry into certain occupations; entry exams that do not take a candidate's cultural or racial background into account; and other demanding qualifications that discourage membership in professional bodies. Finally, even academia is not exempt from the tarnish of systemic racism (Fleras, 1996; Samuel & Burney, 2003; Schick, 2008). As Henry and Tator point out (2006, 2009), universities perpetuate a culture of whiteness as the unquestioned norm, resulting in the privileging of white interpretations of standards, teaching evaluations, criteria for tenure and promotion, measurements of teaching and research, and legitimate forms of publication.

Ideological

Ideological racism constitutes that level of racism that pervades the general functioning of society. Ideological racism points to the prevalence of cultural values and communication patterns in advancing dominant interests as natural and normal at the expense of those who are defined as irrelevant and inferior. A distinction between the normative and everyday components of ideological racism is useful. **Everyday racism** consists of unconscious speech habits and everyday actions that have the cumulative effect of demeaning minority women and men. Normative racism, in turn, reflects a largely unconscious bias toward others because of prevailing societal values.

Everyday Racism Contemporary racism is no longer directly expressed. Instead, more culturally acceptable ways that achieve the same effect without attracting negative attention are preferred (Sirna, 1996; see also Jonas, 2006). Everyday racism consists of those racist practices that infiltrate the routines of everyday life by becoming a normal part of what is accepted by society (Essed, 1991, 2002). With everyday racism, a dislike of others is created and reconstructed through daily actions that are repetitive or routine. The role of language in perpetuating everyday racism is widely recognized (Blauner, 1994; Essed, 1991; Wetherell & Potter, 1993). Many think of language as equivalent to a postal system, namely, a relatively neutral system of exchange between sender and receiver for the transmission of messages created independently through a process called thinking. In reality, language is intimately bound up with our experiences of the world, followed by our efforts to convey that experience to others. Rather than a passive or mechanical transmitter of information, words are "loaded" with values and preferences that define some aspects of reality as normal and acceptable while drawing attention away from other aspects (see online Case Study 3.4). Words are not neutral; rather, they have a political dimension by virtue of conveying negative images beyond what is intended. Ideas and ideals are "trapped inside" language, in effect influencing patterns of thought and behaviour without our awareness. The two-edged nature of language is unmistakable. On the one hand, language can be used to enlighten and inform; on the other hand, as a discourse it can be employed to control, conceal, evade issues, draw attention, or dictate agendas.

Language can be readily manipulated to express intolerance toward the other (see online Case Study 3.4). In reflecting and recreating processes that include or exclude others as proper members of a community (Modan, 2007), language possesses the potency to socially construct reality by highlighting differences, enlarging distance, and sanctioning normalcy (Sirna, 1996). As Michael Pickering (2001) writes in *Stereotypes*, the boundaries between normal and deviant are constructed by language that defines the other as an object but also confirms the privileged position of the normal and natural subject. In doing so, the language of intolerance and stereotyping says more about who does the "othering." Language may be used to demonize minorities, as Robert Moore (1992) demonstrates in his oft-quoted article on racism in the English language, by way of obvious bigotry, colour symbolism ("black" = bad), loaded terms ("Indian massacres"), and seemingly neutral phrases that are infused with hidden anxieties ("waves of immigrants"). Negative meanings may infiltrate everyday speech, as the following passage from Moore (1992) demonstrates:

> Some may blackly (angrily) accuse me of trying to blacken (defame) the English language, to give it a black eye (mark of shame) by writing such black words (hostile) . . . by accusing me of being black-hearted (malevolent), of having a black outlook (pessimistic; dismal) on life, of being a blackguard (scoundrel) which would certainly be a black mark (detrimental fact) against me.

To be sure, the racism implicit in words and metaphors may not be intentional or deliberate. Nor will the occasional use of derogatory words transform into full-blown racism. But while it is inaccurate to say that language determines our reality, it provides a cultural frame of reference for defining what is desirable and important. Language, in short, represents an ideal vehicle for expressing intolerance by highlighting differences or sanctioning inequality through invisible yet real boundaries (Sirna, 1996).

Normative Racism   Reference to **normative racism** involves the perpetuation of racism by way of prevailing norms, values, standards, and beliefs. Certain ideas and ideals within a dominant culture are widely circulated that explicitly or implicitly assert the superiority of some people at the expense of others. Or, alternatively, dominant cultural beliefs, values, and norms tend to privilege mainstream patterns as the norm, while other cultural systems are devalued as irrelevant or inferior. In reflecting an ethnocentric tendency to see and interpret "others" through a conventional cultural lens, "they" come across as abnormal or unacceptable. To be sure, it's rarely the case that mainstream cultural values explicitly reject or demonize the "other" as racially inferior. Rather, "others" are defined as culturally inferior because of their incompatibility with conventional norms, values, and standards (Berry & Bonilla-Silva, 2007; Li, 2007). Take liberal universalism with its endorsement of universal humanity: Our commonalities as morally autonomous individuals are much more important for purposes of recognition or reward than those things that divide us as members of racially different groups. While commendable, this commitment to pretend pluralism does an injustice to those minorities whose differences matter, are deep, and must be taken seriously.

Normative racism contributed to Canada-building by facilitating expansion and exploitation. Historically, racism in Canada was normatively entrenched within those policies and programs that justified the invasion and continuing occupation of someone else's land (Turtle Island, for example). Racism was normatively reflected in Canada's treatment of immigrants and racialized minorities in domesticating the resource-rich expanses of Canada. A normative racism is embedded in a Canada that sometimes exploits immigrant labour for bolstering Canada's standard of living. Finally, racism plays out in a Canada whose normative principles continue to govern Canada's Eurocentric constitutional order—even while asserting cultural neutrality under the guise of universalism (Maaka & Fleras, 2005). In that these normative standards continue to reflect and reinforce patterns of white privilege and supremacy, racism is embedded in the very notion of "what Canada is for."

Infrastructural

There is yet another expression of racism that is deeply entrenched yet difficult to fathom. An infrastructural racism is predicated on the premise that the very foundations of society are neither neutral nor value-free. On the contrary, this foundational framework is infused with a tacitly assumed set of **Eurocentric**-based values and beliefs that advantage some, disadvantage others. Inasmuch as the Eurocentric foundational principles of a racialized constitutional order continue to be organized in ways that advance white interests at the expense of minorities, infrastructural racism is real and powerful, yet difficult to detect let alone to eradicate.

All complex societies are raced (or racialized). Inasmuch as societies conceive of themselves as racially configured with respect to emergence, formation, and development (Goldberg, 2002; Lentin, 2004), they make a distinction between superior and inferior groups (either racially or culturally defined); assign a corresponding division of power, privilege, and resources; and imbed these distinctions of inequality and inferiority within the foundational structures and cultural values of society. In some cases, a racist state/society explicitly endorses a racist ideology (like apartheid) by erecting a set of laws or initiatives for formalizing separate classes of citizenship and compromising civil rights. In other cases, open racism is rejected in favour of more inclusive language and the illusion of inclusion. Nevertheless, the tacitly assumed principles of white supremacy and white privilege continue to justify the racialized distribution of power and wealth (Leonardo, 2004). Rather than something incidental to the functioning of the state both then and now, infrastructural racism establishes a system of racialized domination that espouses colour-blind principles, yet tolerates colour-conscious discrimination and racism. The end result? Just as societies are gendered by virtue of androcentric mindsets and patriarchal structures, so too are they racialized insofar as society is infrastructurally *by, for*, and *about* "pale male" interests, experiences, and priorities.

According to dictionary sources, "infrastructure" (the Latin prefix *infra* means "below, beneath, underneath, invisible") can be loosely defined as those deeply embedded and tacitly assumed values, agendas, and priorities that underpin society's constitutional order—in the same way that infrastructures (i.e., basic installations and facilities from roads to power plants) contribute to the continuance, operation, and growth of communities. In the broadest sense of the term, a constitutional order can be defined as a governance involving a combination of foundational principles, fundamental rules, and normative understandings that collectively establish a functioning social order by regulating relations between citizens and a country's governing institutions (Fleras, 2009b; Fox & Ward, 2008). Or phrased alternatively, a constitutional order consists of a relatively stable set of foundational principles that foster decision making and political debate over a sustained period of time. Admittedly, these foundational principles are neither fixed nor final: Rather, they are fluid, evolving, and open to dispute and debates; they provide a framework for the expression of ordinary political debates and are not necessarily predictive of behaviour (Turton, 2007).

For example, the Canadian Constitution espouses a foundational commitment to colour-blind equality. But there is ample evidence that it continues to uphold a hierarchy of difference that seemingly endorses the principle of "white is right" (Alfred, 2005; Henry & Tator, 2006; Maaka & Fleras, 2005). While the principle of individual rights, fundamental freedoms, and guarantees of equality are explicitly expressed by the Constitution, what is not expressly articulated, but inferred from reading between the constitutional lines, are those hidden assumptions that privilege some, penalize others. True, all Canadians have the constitutional right to equal opportunity and freedom from discrimination; however, minorities find that they must exercise these rights in a racialized system neither designed with them in mind nor reflective of their experiences. Consider the principle of universal liberalism, which includes a commitment to our commonalities as individuals; an emphasis on doing rather than being; and a preference for reason rather than emotion as a way of getting things done. Similarly, notions of progress (movement upward and forward) at individual and societal levels qualify as a foundational if unstated principle of Canada's constitutional order.

Clearly, then, neither foundational principles nor the constitutional order can be defined as ideologically neutral, despite the appearances of neutrality. Rather, both are ideologically infused with values and beliefs in a way that racializes society (the state) along Eurocentric lines of what is good, right, and normal. The persistence of these deep biases reinforces the status of societies as racialized social systems whose design, organization, and operations are profoundly informed, influenced, and supported by socially defined race categories, racial ideologies, and racist language (Doane, 2006;

Wise, 2010). A mistaken belief in infrastructural neutrality is not inconsequential. Such a lapse in judgment not only bolsters the widely accepted claim that Canada is a colour-blind society, it also conceals how the foundational principles of Canada's constitutional order are racialized to protect and promote prevailing patterns of power and privilege. This deeply embedded notion of Eurocentric foundational principles and a racialized constitutional order informs the concept of infrastructural racism (see online Insight 3.8).

EXPLAINING RACISM: COSTS AND CAUSES

Costs

Racism costs all Canadians. But the costs of racism are absorbed unevenly across Canada, with some capitalizing on racism as a basis for preserving privilege or power while others suffer the consequences (Bonnett, 2000). The perpetuation of racism is nothing less than a blot upon Canadian society, with untold capacity to squander Canada's potential and reputation as a progressive and prosperous country. A toxic environment is created where existing prejudices are articulated, legitimized, and defended as a basis for white privilege (McKenna, 1994). Mixed messages are conveyed that often contradict the ideals of a socially progressive society, despite Canada's constitutionally protected human rights code and commitment to the principles of multiculturalism. As well, racism diminishes the number of people who can contribute to Canada, whilst useless energy is expended that otherwise could be funnelled into more productive channels. Racialized minorities live in perpetual fear of physical retaliation; they experience a loss of personal security that, in turn, intensifies isolation and self-defensive behaviours; and their self-worth plummets accordingly. Finally, institutions that cannot capitalize on a diverse workforce are destined to lose their competitive edge in the global marketplace.

How is racism a problem? Those whose lives are generally untouched by racism may wonder what all the fuss is about. Sure, blatant expressions of racism or racial discrimination are painful, but what's the big deal about ethnic jokes or racial slurs, especially when celebrities like Borat or Sarah Silverman achieve popularity and generate income by parodying others through racial stereotypes (but see Wright, 2007). In reality, racism inflicts a cost on all Canadians, but especially on racialized minorities. Racism not only perpetuates patterns of inequality and violates the rights of minority Canadians but also robs minorities of their self-esteem, sense of belonging, and contribution to Canada. It boxes one in; as one person put it in a Dalhousie University study (RVH Project, 2002/03), "Racism determines who you are. You want to be who you are but people won't let you. We suppress ourselves to fit into dominant society" (p. 11).

Exposure to racism may contribute to the poor health of minority women and men—with corresponding pressure on Canada's much beleaguered healthcare system (Hyman, 2009; Maioni, 2003; Picard, 2005). Similarly, in the United States, the stress, physical illnesses, and other injuries associated with racism constitute a serious public health problem for blacks, whose life expectancy remains up to seven years less than that of American-born whites (Feagin, 2005; Millman, 2007a, 2007b). According to Dalhousie University's Racism, Violence, and Health (RVH) Project (2002/03), racism is a disease that can make people sick (physically, emotionally, and psychologically). Studies routinely indicate that repeated exposure to discrimination and racism typically generate high levels of stress which, in turn, induce health problems such as diabetes, hypertension, and strokes (Kim, 2006). This excerpt from the Dalhousie study concurs:

> Participants identified the physical, emotional, and spiritual costs of being the only Black person in a workplace. When you have to be better to be considered equal, you can never allow yourself to stop measuring yourself against others. When you can't afford to make a mistake, you "can't come to a point of relaxation" and simply take your own competence for granted. The constant questioning erodes your confidence and increases an existing sense of isolation . . . (RVH Project, 2002/03, p. 14)

Or as the study stated, "Always having to prove how smart you are takes its toll." In the end, there is only so much negativity and self-hatred bred by racism that the body and mind can take before the onset of health problems, self-destruction, or the perpetuation of violence.

Causes

Why, then, does racism exist if it comes with such high costs? What are its causes? Do we look to biology, culture, social structure, or personality as the major sources? Should it be defined as a sickness, a bad habit, a conspiratorial plot, a cultural blind spot, a structural flaw, a historical act, or a relic from the past? Why does it persist despite its disapproval as a practice inimical to the realities of a modern society? How can its persistence in the face of government initiatives to condemn, curb, and control it be explained? Is it because of fear, greed, ignorance, or arrogance? Is it because of societal inertia or public disinterest, irrespective of its dysfunctional effects on society? (See online Case Study 3.7.) Or is it because racism is so embedded within the institutional structures of society that trying to eradicate it is unlikely to succeed?

Some attribute its pervasiveness to our biogenetic hardwiring from an evolutionary past. A fear of outsiders may have elicited a flee-or-fight response that remains in effect, so that recoiling from what is different seems only natural. This visceral dislike of out-groups may explain the universality of racism. Others see racism as the byproduct of ignorance or fear of the unknown. In that improper socialization is perceived as a cause, improving people's knowledge about diversity will gradually diminish the spectre of racism. Still others believe that racism persists because of its psychological benefits. While no demographic is exempt as perpetrators of racism, racial discrimination and prejudicial attitudes toward minority out-groups tend to be expressed by those with low education, income, and employment levels, as well as by males, older persons, and those with strong religious or conservative convictions (Semyonov, Raijman, & Gorodzeisky, 2008). Racism has a way of making a threatened mainstream feel good about itself in part by bolstering a collective self-image of superiority. This notion of racism as "functional" for white folk is captured in these words by Julian Bond of the National Association for the Advancement of Colored People (NAACP) when referring to the tenacity of white supremacist racism (as cited in White, 1999):

> It's still white supremacy. It still means so much to those who practice it. It defines who they are. It makes them feel that they are better than others. It ensures them positions in employment and college admissions they otherwise might not have. It still puts a lid on the dreams of black people. (p. 25)

In other words, and to paraphrase Derrick A. Bell of New York University (2006), racism is of such value to the mainstream that, if minorities didn't exist, whites would have to invent them. Every society needs its scapegoats whose presence presents the majority with a target for projecting fantasies, fears, and frustrations. Without racism to bond all whites into an unspoken alliance, inter-white fighting would be endemic and anarchy an ever-present reality (Mills, 1997; see also Le Guin, 1975).

Each of these explanations of racism bears merit. But reference to racism as a function of biology or psychology (either individually or collectively) cannot be divorced from its social dimensions. With the possible exception of sociobiologists (see van den Berghe, 1981), most sociologists would argue that individuals are not biologically programmed to act in a racist manner. There are no genes that express themselves in racial discrimination. No compelling reason exists to believe that people are genetically hardwired with a propensity to hate. Nor does racism exist solely in the minds of poorly socialized individuals. Rather than an error of perception or belief, people are conditioned to be racist by environments that foster ethnocentrism, out-group antipathy, and hate. They are conditioned to be racist as part of a broader process of social control for preserving the status quo in complex societies. Simply put, those in positions of power will do anything to preserve privilege in the competition for scarce resources—including sowing the seeds of racism—without drawing unnecessary attention to the contradictions and dysfunctions within the system (Galabuzi, 2006).

For many, racism is rooted in the material conditions of social life (Bolaria & Li, 1988; Satzewich, 1998). Neither a transient phenomenon nor an anomalous and unpredictable feature, racism is pivotal to Canada's historical and economic development, embedded within the institutional structures of an unequal society, endemic to core Canadian values, and integral to Canada-building. Like race, racism arose to explain and justify patterns of conquest, settlement, land appropriation, and economic domination (Macedo & Gounari, 2006). Canada's economic prosperity and standard of living were fostered by a racism that facilitated the building of the railways, the settlement of the west, the extraction of timber and mineral resources, and work on the assembly lines. The quality of life for most Canadians continues to be supported by racialized minorities who toil in low-paying and dangerous jobs to underwrite the costs of cheaper goods and services (Bishop, 2005). Racist ideologies were and continue to be employed for securing ready access to a cheap and disposable labour supply; to destabilize labour movements by undermining any potential show of unity or strength; to justify intrusive devices for controlling troublesome minorities; and to secure controlling functions in support of ruling-class interests. In short, racism originated and continues to persist within a capitalist Canada because of its usefulness in advancing class interests (Bolaria & Li, 1988).

The evidence is compelling: Racism cannot be reduced to individual attitudes born of prejudice and ignorance. Rather, racism as a political project emerged within the context of European colonialism (see Lentin, 2004; Mills, 1997). Racism persists not because it constitutes a set of fallacious beliefs or personality flaws, but because it involves patterns of (in)difference, privilege, and power that continue to promote Canada's vested and national interests (Macedo & Gounari, 2006; Paolucci, 2006). Nor is racism an anomaly in society and its ideals—a kind of irrational or dysfunctional feature of an otherwise rational and sound system—but a true expression of "what society is for." Rather than an unfortunate aberration from the norm of what constitutes Canada, racism *is* the logic behind a system constructed by, for, and about whites. The rephrasing of racism as perversely "logical" confirms its centrality within the broader context in which it is embedded, expressed, and nourished. Solutions to the problem of racism will vary accordingly.

ANTI-RACISM: INDIVIDUAL, INSTITUTIONAL, INCLUSIVE

Most Canadians are no longer racists in the classic sense of blatantly vilifying minority women and men. The "bad old days" of openly denying and excluding others because of appearances are long gone and unlikely to return in light of numerous checks and balances to prevent a repeat occurrence. Yet, as we have seen, racism continues to flourish in unobtrusive ways, deliberately or unconsciously, by way of action or inaction. Racism is rarely directly experienced, but rather endured through the cumulative impact of demeaning incidents that quietly accumulate day by day into a "tonne of feathers." Recognition of racism as a major social problem puts the onus on Canadians to do something about it (Bishop, 2005). As Tim Wise (1999), a renowned American anti-racism educator, puts it:

> [T]hose persons called "white" have a particular obligation to fight racism because it's *ours* [emphasis added], created in its modern form by us, for the purpose of commanding power over resources and opportunities at the expense of people of color. Furthermore all whites . . . have to address the internalized beliefs about white supremacy from which we all suffer. No one is unaffected by the daily socialization to which we are all subjected—specifically with regard to the way we are taught to think about persons of color in this society. (p. 17)

Clearly, a mindset shift is required for any progress to be made on the racism front. Most of us would agree that to do something to someone because of their skin colour is racism and something should be done about it. But doing nothing to confront racial discrimination may be no less racist; after all, fence-sitting (through inactivity or silence) is not impartiality or neutrality but tacit acceptance of a racialized and unequal status quo. The only option is to take a stand if only to be part of the solution rather than part of the problem.

The range of activities that directly challenge racism and racial discrimination is known as anti-racism. Yet the concept of anti-racism is not necessarily self-evident: Just as racism is multi-faceted and dynamic, so too is anti-racism. If racism is primarily about attitudes (racism as race) or beliefs (racism as ideology), then individual-based strategies are in order. But institutional models are required if racism entails patterns of power and structures (both systemic and systematic). And if racism reflects ideology (including norms and culture), the onus shifts to more comprehensive ideological changes. Mindful of this definitional span, **anti-racism** can be defined as the process that challenges racism through direct action at different levels. By contesting white privilege and eradicating structural barriers to full participation and equal citizenship rights (Dei, 2005), a commitment to anti-racism is all-consuming. Active involvement is necessary to dislodge the cultural values, personal prejudices, discriminatory behaviours, and institutional structures of society that perpetuate racism. Two general anti-racism strategies can be discerned: individual and institutional. One is concerned with modifying individual attitudes and behaviour through law, education, or interaction, the other with changing the institutional roots of racism through removal of discriminatory barriers. Combining both creates the possibility of an inclusive anti-racism.

Individual Anti-Racism

Taken at its most obvious level, racism is normally envisaged as a personal problem of hatred, fear, or ignorance. There is an element of truth to this assertion. Racism is often expressed through the thoughts and actions of individuals who dislike others because they perceive them as different or threatening. Thus, anti-racism strategies tend to focus on modifying defective attitudes related to prejudice, ethnocentrism, and stereotyping. Three of the more common personal anti-racism strategies for improvement are *interaction*, *education*, and *law*.

Interaction Learning through contact and interaction represents one technique for individual anti-racism change. Interaction with others is proposed for removing barriers that stem from a knowledge gap and replacing it with insight and sensitivity. But interaction in its own right is not necessarily beneficial (Harell & Stolle, 2010). It is doubtful whether the escape of thousands of tourists to the Caribbean each winter reduces racism. Improvement is unlikely in contexts in which interactional patterns tend to reinforce the gap between the haves and have-nots. Under these potentially degrading circumstances, the degree of resentment and contempt escalates in tune with the reconstituting of colonialist patterns of servitude and deference.

Reducing racism through interaction varies with the quality of interaction. Cooperative models of interaction may result in less fear of the other, whereas conflict models involving culturally different groups may intensify tension and the potential for confrontation. For any positive effect, interaction must be conducted between individuals who are relatively equal in status, who collaborate on a common endeavour in a spirit of trust and respect, whose interaction receives some degree of institutional and societal support, and who derive mutual benefit from cooperation of sufficient frequency and duration to foster a working relationship (Jaret, 1995). Interaction between unequals outside a supportive context simply upholds the status quo by perpetuating stereotypes in a negatively charged environment.

How Should You Respond to a Racist Joke?

What should you do if a colleague makes a racist joke? Do you ignore it? Refuse to laugh? Walk away? Bristle with indignation? Openly criticize the joke as offensive and racist? Regardless of your actions, there is a cost. Doing nothing implies a condoning of the behaviour. Doing something may elicit a range of defensive responses from hostility and aggression to a breach in your working relationship.

The best response should achieve three goals: (1) communicate that this behaviour is unacceptable; (2) indicate that the joke is racist; and (3) inflict as little damage as possible to the relationship. An interesting and recommended strategy is to *play dumb*. Put on a bewildered expression and ask the joker to explain the joke because you don't understand. The joker cannot explain the joke without invoking a racist stereotype. You can then question the validity of the stereotype, in the process pointing out the racism in the joke without being confrontational or humiliating your colleague.

Why does this approach work? Racist jokes rely on a shared knowledge of stereotypes. Without stereotypes, there is no humour. Thus, when you play dumb and ask someone to explain the joke, the racist stereotype is drawn out into the open, where its absurd and offensive nature can be openly dissected. And because you are feigning ignorance, the lesson/message can be conveyed without sabotaging your relationship with the joker (based on van Kerckhove, 2009).

Education It is widely assumed that education (or training) can reduce racism (Government of Canada, 2005). According to this line of thinking, racism arises when individuals are locked into ignorance or irrational beliefs. Therein lies the cure—educating people to realize the errors of their ways. People are deemed sufficiently rational to make the appropriate adjustments, once aware of their mistakes. This notion of enlightenment through anti-racism learning puts a premium on educational institutions. Milder versions of multicultural education propose modifying individual attitudes through exposure to diversity. Yet there are difficulties in defending the transformative properties of education and training in challenging racism (see the discussion on multicultural and anti-racist education in Chapter 11). According to Ontario's Human Rights Commission (2005), success or change are unlikely if the training is isolated from other initiatives; if it emphasizes cultural sensitivity or the celebrating of cultures; and if it ignores the dynamics of racism by reducing discrimination to cultural misunderstandings. Gloria Yamato (2001) captures the futility of quick-fix solutions to a complex problem that has taken centuries to grow, take root, invade space, and morph into variations:

> Many believe that racism can be dealt with effectively in one hellifying workshop, or one hour long heated discussion . . . I've run into folks who really think that we can beat this devil, kick this habit, be healed of this disease in a snap. In a sincere blink of a well-intentioned eye, pres-to—poof—racism disappears. "I've dealt with my racism . . . (envision a laying on of hands) . . . Hallelujah! Now I can go to the beach." Well fine, go to the beach. (p. 152)

Stronger versions of multicultural education encourage individuals to look inside themselves, to examine their own racism and privileged positions, to see how the dominant sector exercises power over racialized minorities, and to take responsibility for the disempowerment of others (McIntosh, 1988). Admittedly, while most white people can see and sympathize with victims of racism, fewer are capable of seeing the benefits and advantages that flow from whiteness. Many are equally reluctant to see how their privilege is directly connected with the disempowerment and exploitation of those at the wrong end of racism (Bishop, 2005). In other words, people need to be educated about whiteness by painting themselves into the picture of racism.

Law Recourse to law is sometimes upheld as an effective personal deterrent. Laws exist in Canada that prohibit the expression of racial discrimination against vulnerable minorities. The scope of these laws is broad. Some legal measures consist of protection for identifiable minorities through restrictions on majority behaviour. For example, the Supreme

Court of Canada has ruled repeatedly that prohibiting hate literature is a justifiable and reasonable limitation on the freedom of speech. Other measures are aimed at removing discriminatory barriers that preclude minority participation within society. On the assumption that most individuals are law abiding because of the threat of punishment or social ostracism, passage of anti-racist laws focuses on outward compliance with the letter of the law. Passage of these and related laws is not intended to alter people's attitudes or conviction, at least not in the short run. A democratic society such as Canada entitles people to their own private thoughts, even if they are repugnant or anti-social. But behaviour can be monitored and modified. Over time, moreover, people may realign their beliefs to match behaviour in hopes of reducing the dissonance between thought and action.

Institutional Anti-Racism

There is room for cautious optimism when discussing the effectiveness of individually tailored anti-racist programs. But are these initiatives of sufficient scope to remove racism? Racism may be expressed in and through people (who may be regarded as precipitating causes), but individuals are merely the conduits of racial antipathy. With individual anti-racism, the symptoms are addressed, not the cause or source. Worse still, an individual anti-racism tends to rely on multicultural platforms or attitude modification to ideologically cloak the structural supports of institutional racism (Scheurich & Young, 1997). Not surprisingly, personal solutions such as anti-racist training are criticized as the equivalent of applying a bandage to a gaping wound—compassionate and well-meaning to be sure, but ultimately inadequate to staunch the bleeding.

An institutional anti-racism approach draws attention to structural determinants of racism (see also the discussion on institutional inclusiveness in Chapter 11). According to this line of thinking, racism can be resolved only by attacking it at its source, namely, within the institutional structures that support patterns of power and inequality (Zine, 2002). Put bluntly, racism is not just about individuals with regressive beliefs or dormant prejudices. Rather, it is sourced in institutional structures that provide justifying ideologies and practices in those contexts organized (racialized) around the placement of minorities in racial categories (Bonilla-Silva, 1996; Lopes & Thomas, 2006). The problem of racism must be addressed within the wider confines of political domination and economic control, in large part by focusing on the systemic and institutional dimensions of white power, privilege, and the rationales for justifying domination, exclusion, and denial (Dei, 2005). Not surprisingly, with its commitment to changing behaviour and contesting structures instead of modifying individual attitudes, an institutional approach requires a different set of assumptions and tactics than those focusing on personal initiatives. Tactics may include fighting racist hate groups, direct action through protest, or civil disobedience, boycotts, and litigation (Jaret, 1995).

Toward an Inclusive Anti-Racism

It is relatively easy to reduce racism to a personal problem. Common sense dictates that people are the cause of racism. As individuals, people must reflect critically upon their degree of complicity in perpetuating racism through daily actions. But it is equally tempting to situate racism within a system of vast and impersonal institutional forces that are largely beyond individual control. However valid, such an approach runs the risk of absolving individuals of any responsibility. Neither of these positions is entirely correct. Individuals are not necessarily the cause of racism; nevertheless, racism is located within and carried by the person. Institutions may generate root causes; nonetheless, they do not exist apart from individuals who interact to create, support, maintain, and transform patterns of racism. The tension between agency and structure is palpable: Each of us must be held accountable for our actions, despite the presence of a broader social context over which we have less control.

Only an inclusive (or integrative) anti-racism approach can deliver the goods with any hope of success (Samuel, 2006). Integrative strategies acknowledge as source and solution the interplay of social forces and individual experiences. In rejecting an either/or approach for a both/and perspective with its embrace of contextuality, connectedness, and simultaneity of unequal relations, an inclusive anti-racism acknowledges the interplay of structure with agency (Dei, 2005). The personal may be political but in need of an institutional focus, while the institutional is structural but demands a sense of individual agency. The interlocking nature of racism must also be acknowledged (Bishop, 2005). Racialized minorities do not find themselves excluded because of race or class or gender. Rather, each of these inequities intersects with the other to amplify overlapping patterns of exclusion and denial within the broader context of globalization and global capitalism (see the discussion on intersectional analysis in Chapter 6). What can we conclude? The interdependence of race, class, and gender as intertwined strands of a wider, more complex, and self-perpetuating system of privilege and power makes it abundantly clear: The purging of racism must be confronted comprehensively in advancing an inclusive society based on the principle of treating people equally yet as equals.

DEBATE REVISITED

Deep Racism in a Racialized Canada

Is Canada as racist to the core as critics say? Or is Canada essentially an open and tolerant society, with only isolated and random acts of racism? Or does Canada prefer to mask its many racisms behind a myth of racelessness and under a blanket of whiteness (Backhouse, 1999; Das Gupta et al., 2007; Kobayashi, 2003; Razack, 2002; see also Michael Brown, 2005)? On one side are those who believe that, to the extent they exist, racism and racial discrimination are relics from the past, so that any inequalities that exist must

be attributable to minority failures. On the other side are those who contend that racism remains a key discriminatory barrier. For example, according to a Greater Toronto Area study that sent out 6000 mock resumés to local businesses, those with English-sounding last names were much more likely to land a job interview than those with foreign-sounding surnames, even with the same levels of education and work experience (Jimenez, 2009). Who is right?

True, Canadians may not be racists in the blatant sense of unfurling swastikas

(Continued)

and burning crosses. Nor is Canada racist in reflecting an indifferent government or apathetic public. Rather, racism in Canadian society is increasingly covert, embedded in normal operations of institutions, and beyond the direct discourse of racial terminology (Li, 2007). Despite perceptions to the contrary, the language, values, and institutions that predominate in Canada are neither neutral nor universal. Insofar as Canada is racialized as a society, distinctly racial connotations permeate instead, thus privileging whiteness and Eurocentricity as natural, normal, and superior (see Gilroy, 2004). David Gillborn (2006) deftly explains how white standards and Eurocentric norms masquerade as colour-blind principles:

> Most white people would probably be surprised by the idea of "White World"; they see only the "world," its whiteness is invisible to them because the racialized nature of politics, policing, education and every other sphere of public life is so deeply ingrained that it has become normalized— unremarked, and taken for granted. This is an exercise of power that goes beyond notions of "white *privilege*" . . . it is about *supremacy.* (p. 319)

In other words, Canada may be defined as a racist society not because there are a lot of racists or racisms. More accurately, Canada is racist because of a white supremacy rooted in a political, cultural, and economic system whose foundations are overwhelmingly controlled by white power,

resources, and a sense of entitlement, then routinely reenacted across a broad array of institutions and social settings (Ansley, 2004; Gillborn, 2006). Canada is racist because racism is deeply embedded in Canada's colonial history, institutionalized in those rules and practices that normalize "pale male" privilege, and embodied in the language, laws, and rules of Canadian society that are rendered largely invisible because of their normalcy. Canada is racist because differences are disadvantaging. Just as female differences are transformed into female disadvantages in a male-centred world, to rephrase Sandra Lipsitz Bem (1994), so too are minority differences defined (or racialized) as disadvantageous in a world designed and organized to reflect, reinforce, and advance "white-stream" interests. Finally, Canada is a racist society because Canada-building continues to be grounded on exploiting those perceived as racially inferior and culturally different. Consider how temporary foreign workers and irregular migrants are rendered expendable because of their precarious status, and subject to dismissal or removal for reasons often beyond their control. And references to Canada as a racist society will continue to resonate as long as the principles of Canada's constitutional order reflect, reinforce, and advance the interests of some but not others in a Canada that is structurally organized by, for, and about a Eurocentric whiteness as normal, necessary, and superior.

Chapter Highlights

- Racism exists and has always existed in Canada, although its magnitude and scope as well as depth and intensity have varied over time. Unmasking the many faces of racism, both past and present, is the central theme of this chapter.
- Racism is more than a simple expression of individual prejudice; it is a complex system of structures, ideologies, discourses, and vocabularies in which power, privilege, and resources are distributed unequally among socially different groups.
- Definitions of racism fall into five main categories: racism as biology, racism as ideology, racism as culture, racism as structure, and racism as power.
- In addition to prejudice, racism includes a behavioural component involving discriminatory practices that deny or exclude. Power underpins all forms of racism: without it, racism is indistinguishable from a host of negative attitudes and practices.
- The sectors of racism comprise (1) interpersonal racism (hate, polite, and subliminal); (2) institutional racism (systematic, systemic); (3) ideological racism (normative, everyday); and (4) infrastructural racism (society). The different types of racism can be compared on the basis of intent, awareness, and intensity.
- A variety of social and psychological explanations may account for the pervasiveness of racism in Canada. Racism persists because it provides "positive" functions for some in a society organized around the principles of profit and white privilege.
- Anti-racism is concerned with the elimination of racism through direct action at personal and institutional levels. An inclusive anti-racism promises a more comprehensive attack on the racism problem.

For further study, you can access the Case Studies referenced in this chapter at **www.pearsoncanada.ca/fleras**.

Review Questions

1. Compare and contrast the different types of racism that have been discussed in terms of degree of intent, level of awareness, and style of expression.
2. Discuss whether Canada is or is not a racist society. Use specific examples to support your answer.
3. It has been said that all white people are racists. Moreover, if you are white and living in Canada or the United States, odds are that you are a racist regardless of your socio-economic status (Sue, 2003). Explain the thinking behind this line of argument (include references to whiteness studies). Do you agree or disagree? Why?
4. How do we explain the persistence of racism? Be sure to emphasize the social dimensions of racism in your answer.

5. Compare the strategies of anti-racism at the individual level with those at the institutional level in terms of underlying assumptions, means, and anticipated outcomes.

6. Demonstrate how thinking about racism has moved beyond the classic sense of something that is open, direct, deliberate, and individual.

Endnotes

1. An ideal–typical distinction between racial(ized) and racist states is advised. In contrast to a racial(ized) state, in which race and nation are mutually constitutive of each other, a racist society explicitly endorses a state ideology (such as apartheid) to establish a set of laws or initiatives for formalizing separate classes of citizenship and compromising civil rights based on racial criteria. By contrast, the modern state is tantamount to a racial(ized) state because it is racially configured with respect to emergence, formation, and development. The racial(ized) state is implicated in the reproduction of local conditions of racist exclusion through its manifestations in justice and law enforcement, and politics, legislation, and bureaucracy. A range of strategies is employed to foster inclusion and exclusion, including tactics involving laws, technologies, or census, whose combined purpose is the assertion of white paramountcy and the control of those racialized as inferior (Goldberg, 2002).

Links and Recommendations

FILMS

The Birth of a Nation (1915)

A classic in filmmaking by D.W. Griffith, but disturbing in its content because it reflects prevailing perceptions about race and racism during this era. The demeaning portrayal of black people is reinforced by the triumphalist view of the Ku Klux Klan in rescuing the post–Civil War South from carpetbaggers and freed slaves.

American History X (1998)

A chilling look at urban racism and hate through the life of a person who drops in and drops out of a white supremacist movement in the United States.

Paperclips (2005)

A documentary based on the anti-racist activities of a middle school in small-town Tennessee. To get some idea of the millions who died during the Nazi Holocaust, students collected paperclips as a tangible expression of the needless deaths.

The "N" Word (2006)

Provides a wide-ranging discussion of the politics surrounding the word "nigger."

Reel Injuns (2009)

Cree filmmaker Neil Diamond provides a biting yet sometimes hilarious look at the often racist film depictions of Aboriginal peoples in Canada and the United States.

BOOKS

The Colour of Democracy: Racism in Canadian Society (4th ed.), by Frances Henry and Carol Tator (2009). This book is pretty much the standard in the field. Highly recommended.

Interrogating Race and Racism, edited by Vijay Agnew (2007). An excellent reminder that the reality of multi-racisms needs to be examined from a multidisciplinary perspective.

Hatreds: Racialized and Sexualized Conflicts in the Twenty-first Century, by Zillah Eisenstein (1996). For an insightful and provocative look at racism and sexism, check out this book.

WEBSITES

Work for All: Films against Racism in the Workplace—The National Film Board and Human Resources and Skills Development Canada teamed up to produce a series of short but informative films about racism at work. These consciousness-raising films can be viewed at:
http://workforall.nfb.ca/

The Canadian Ethnic Studies Association—The association publishes a journal and news items pertaining to (among other related issues) race and racism:
http://cesa.uwinnipeg.ca

Ipsos-Reid/Dominion Institute survey—A 2005 survey of Canadians on their attitudes about discrimination and racism in Canada:
www.dominion.ca/Downloads/IRracismSurvey.pdf

Global Issues: Racism—For a general overview of racism at different levels and in different parts of the world:
www.globalissues.org/HumanRights/Racism.asp

Debwewin—Another valuable site that includes numerous references to articles on racism:
www.debwewin.ca/racism.htm

CHAPTER 4

Ethnicity Experiences: Politics, Identity, and Power

Problematizing Ethnic Conflict: Real, Imagined, or Constructed?

If there is an iron law of ethnicity, it is that when ethnic groups are found in a hierarchy of wealth, power, and status, then conflict is inescapable. (Steinberg, 1989, p. 170)

If the postwar era could be described as the age of ideology involving capitalist and communist superpowers, the last decade of the twentieth century exposed yet another epoch in the making—the era of ethnic conflict. While wars between countries (interstate) had declined, internal (or intrastate) ethnic conflicts had leapt into prominence (Crawford, 2006). From the Congo to Chechnya, from Somalia to Sri Lanka, from Rwanda to Darfur, and from Bosnia to Burnt Church, the proliferation of ethnically driven civil wars, genocides, sectarian violence, and secessionist movements during the 1990s proved dismaying and destructive. Millions were displaced or killed—mostly civilians rather than soldiers, and mainly from starvation or disease rather than from bullets or landmines (Crawford & Lipschutz, 1998). Clearly, the ascendancy of ethnic conflicts is no longer an international exception. Ethnic conflicts as clashes between culturally different groups appear to have evolved into a global norm. And although ethnic differences per se do not necessarily culminate in large-scale violence and pitched battles (Habyarimana et al., 2008), conflict and confrontation are waged over a host of factors including social identity, territory, natural resources, self-determination, holy places, economic gains, cultural values, and personal and collective security (Ward, 2004).

The prognosis for the twenty-first century is not much better (Taras & Ganguly, 2009). The catastrophes in the Darfur region in Sudan (see online Case Study 1.1) and, more recently, inter-ethnic clashes in Krygystan attest to that, while US-led invasions of Afghanistan and Iraq have unleashed ethnic conflicts that may prove more debilitating in the long run than the bloodbath that accompanied the occupations. Instead of diminishing as might be expected because of an increasingly globalized world, ethnic conflicts have escalated into a dangerous dynamic with the potential to partition or pulverize. But a problem of analysis persists: However disruptive to the governance process or deadly in its consequences, the meaning of ethnic conflict is not readily transparent, largely because many violent conflicts are framed along ethnic lines (Taras & Ganguly, 2009). For some, the term "ethnic conflict" conjures up images of violent confrontations between tribes over pent-up hatreds. For others, it entails a clash of interests (both political and economic) involving cleavages and competition among and between major ethno-religious clusters (Caselli & Coleman, 2006, 2010). For still others, ethnic conflict is synonymous with any expression of violence between non-Western groups; as a result, the coalition forces (NATO/USA) and their "peacekeeping missions" in Iraq or Afghanistan are never framed as ethnic conflicts. Even reference to "ethnic conflict" is problematic: Does the "conflict" in "ethnic conflict" refer only to armed confrontations between ethnically different groups, or can it be applied to any low-intensity competition between different groups over valued resources (Steinberg, 1989)? What about the "ethnic" in "ethnic conflict"

as an explanatory framework? Is ethnicity a primary cause of hostilities? Or is it better framed as a trigger? How about as a variable? a symptom? a smokescreen? a default option?

Answers to these questions are critical: The persistence, salience, and intensity of ethnic conflict should be an anomaly in this era of globalization and global citizenship ("transnationalism"). Nevertheless ethnic conflicts remain a major player on the planetary stage, second only to international terrorism as a global security problem (Pieterse, 2007). They constitute a grave danger to the global order since ethnic conflicts threaten social cohesion, endanger public order, disrupt peaceful relations, and violate human rights and fundamental freedoms. Clearly, then, the quintessential twenty-first century challenge is now before us: How to make society safe for ethnicity, yet safe from ethnic conflict, without succumbing to stifling conformity or freewheeling chaos. That alone makes it doubly important to deconstruct the "ethnic" in ethnic conflicts to unravel what is going on and why.

INTRODUCTION: GLOBAL IMPLOSION/ETHNICITY EXPLOSION

Two distinct but seemingly contradictory dynamics are in play at present. The interplay of these ostensibly opposing trends has proven perplexing and provocative, both conceptually and politically. On the one hand are the imploding forces of globalization: Nation-states are inexorably drawn into the vortex of a single global economy, with its diversity-dampening commitment to rationality and universalism, conformity and consumerism. The local and the national are conflated into a single world system that compresses and homogenizes, thanks to the existence of mass communication, mass travel, mass consumerism, and mass education. But fears are mounting over a pending "McDonaldization" of societies—a kind of one-size-fits-all standardization in which differences are commodified as "ethnic chic"—little more than a residual category to fall back on as a default option (Hutchinson & Smith, 1996).

On the other hand is an equally robust dynamic. The centripetal (the inward-leaning and pulling in) forces of globalization are in conflict with the centrifugal (outward-leaning and pushing out) dynamics of ethnicity. A powerful dynamic has evolved that transforms ethnicity into a cutting edge for collectively challenging the status quo (Nagel & Olzak, 1982; See & Wilson, 1988). Minority women and men have become increasingly assertive in capitalizing on ancestral differences for expressive and instrumental purposes. The proliferation of ethnicity-based identity groups has proved no less disruptive in challenging the prospect of living together with ethnic differences. The **politicization** of ethnicity has not only redefined conventional intergroup relations; it has also eroded the rhythms of an established global order. Where certainty and consensus once prevailed, the new global order is pervaded by uncertainty and confusion because of politicized ethnicities whose past clashes with the present, with no foreseeable resolution in the future (Castles & Miller, 2009).

Paradoxically, the surge in ethnicity may be directly related to the dynamics of globalization. That is, the greater the pressure for conformity because of standardization, the greater the incentive for promulgating ethnic differences (Behrens, 1994; Fukuyama, 1994). The very globalization that threatens to dilute distinctiveness may also spark a renewed interest in ethnic attachments in two ways: first, by creating new hybrid identities that oscillate between the "here" and the "there" by way of the "in-between" (Gillespie, 1996; Hall, 1996; Wiwa, 2003); second, by uncoupling ethnicity from place because of global population movements, resulting in vastly more fluid identities that are increasingly transnational in scope and definition (Simmons, 2010). The corresponding diaspora is hardly inconsequential. A new set of "transnational" identities increasingly contests conventional notions of being and belonging, as do new ways of thinking and talking about immigration (Satzewich & Wong, 2006).

Its centrality in shaping human behaviour and intergroup dynamics notwithstanding, the politics of ethnicity has elicited mixed reaction (Yinger, 1994). For some, ethnic experiences are dismissed as "regressive" because of their capacity to unleash dormant hatreds for settling old scores. The cult of ethnicity is demonized as an inexcusable reversion to "tribalism" that panders to humanity's basest instincts. The "ethnification" (fragmentation) of society into squabbling ethnic communities also clashes with society-building imperatives, prompting some central authorities to dispose of this disruption by expulsion, extermination, cleansing, forced assimilation, or segregation (Taras & Ganguly, 2009). For others, ethnicity can be "progressive" in providing a community of like-minded individuals with a lifeline to continuity, commitment, and connections in a changing, confusing, and competitive world. Still others are resigned to ethnicity as a persistent presence in human affairs, with the potential to harm or help, depending on the circumstances. Societies that historically have championed ethnicity as an asset will flourish; conversely, those in arrears for managing ethnicity will struggle in balancing the particular with the universal without spiralling into chaos. In that the preferred option lies in putting ethnicity to good use, without capitulating to a worst-case scenario of division or destruction, the challenge is deceptively simple: Making society safe *for* ethnicity, as well as safe *from* ethnicity (Schlesinger, 1992).

Scholarly perceptions of ethnicity are also undergoing a conceptual shift (Simmons, 2010, p. 201). Ethnicity was once perceived as a relatively static and bounded category of ancestrally linked people whose shared distinctiveness isolated them from others. Classifying people into ethnic groups tended to "essentialize" minorities into fixed ethnocultural categories that not only determined how all members should think and act but also ignored the intersectional and fluid nature of people's identities. Metaphorical references to the Canadian multicultural mosaic captured this line of thinking. But because of social and ideological changes, ethnicity is less frequently framed along these essentialized lines. On the contrary, ethnicity is increasingly defined in non-essentialist terms as a fluid and flexible resource instead of a separate state of being into which differences are slotted into pre-existing categories. Rather than a stable point of reference that determines how everyone will think and act, ethnicity is perceived as a contextual process constructed and reconstructed through interaction and adjustment. And instead of treating ethnicity as insulated and isolated social phenemona rooted in a single place, the focus is increasingly contextual in framing ethnicity within transnational and global contexts. Not surprisingly, static and homogeneous models of ethnicity (ethnicity as a thing or noun) are ceding ground to more dynamic and hybridic discourses for framing the ethnic experience (ethnicity as a process or verb) (see Simmons, 2010). As Rogers Brubaker points out:

> Ethnicity, race, and nation should be conceptualized not as substances or things or entities or organisms or collective individuals . . . but rather in relational, processual, dynamic, eventful, and disaggregated terms. This means thinking of ethnicity not in terms of substantial groups or entities but in terms of practical categories, situated actions, cultural idioms, cognitive schemas, discursive frames . . . contingent events. It means thinking of ethnization, racialization, and nationalization as political, social, cultural, and psychological processes . . . taking as a basic analytical category not the "group" as an entity but groupness as a contextually fluctuating conceptual variable. (as cited in Da Costa, 2007, p. 6)

Table 4-1 contrasts (albeit in ideal-typical terms) conventional and new models of ethnicity.

TABLE 4-1	Rethinking Ethnicity: Conventional and New Models
Conventional (mosaic) models	**New (kaleidoscope) models**
• Ethnicity as a thing or noun	• Ethnicity as a process or verb
• Situated in a fixed site or location	• Situated in a fluid field of flows and connections involving many actors at different levels and across numerous contexts
• Tied to a particular geographic location or cultural homeland	• De-linked from specific locations, labels, expectations
• Singular and exclusive identities:	• Multiple/hyphenated/fractured identities:
— Determinant of behaviour (essentializing)	— Flexible resource
— Stable point of reference	— Situational, constructed, contested
	— Intersects with gender and class to amplify
• Objective reality:	• Subjective experiences:
— Separate states of being	— Relations in constant state of becoming
— Static and bounded categories of discrete groups	— Porous and overlapping boundaries
• Rooted in modernity	• Rooted in postmodernity
• Integrity/borders of the group	• Hybridity and sense of "groupness"
• Canada as ethnic mosaic	• Canada as kaleidoscope of ethnicities

As well, ethnicity is no longer framed as a cuddly nostalgic blanket or an irrational and embarrassing relic from the past that—like religion—is largely incommensurable with the modernist project. On the contrary: Far from drifting into oblivion, ethnicity has catapulted to the forefront of intergroup dynamics and **identity politics**. The so-called end of history (or ideology) unleashed an era of explosive ethnic revivals across the globe that are proving disruptive at best, destructive at worst (Hutchinson & Smith, 1996). With domestic ethnic conflicts displacing external state conflicts as the most destabilizing source of global disorder (see Huntington, 1993), ethnicity is now positioned as a potentially powerful if enigmatic social dynamic capable of transformative changes that perplex yet illuminate, unite yet divide, empower yet enfeeble.

Canada is no exception to this global dynamic. Recent years have witnessed a convergence of controversies and challenges associated with ethnicity. The politics of Aboriginal ethnicity have challenged the very foundational principles that govern Canada's constitutional order. The open conflicts at Ipperwash and Caledonia, Gustafsen Lake and Burnt Church have seen to that. Québécois ethnicity continues to provoke English-speaking Canadians, many of whom are perplexed or apoplectic over Quebec's political posturing. **Multicultural minorities** have been no less adamant in politicizing their ethnicity in the competition for scarce resources (Mendelsohn, 2003). The interplay of these intergroup dynamics prompts a series of questions: Why do individuals and groups turn to ethnicity for expressive or instrumental goals? What is it about this powerful force that threatens to dismantle the conventional in exchange for the unorthodox? Why has ethnicity assumed such salience in shaping Canada's destiny? And how do the politics of ethnicity address the challenge of Canada-building? Answers to these questions are complex and contested; nevertheless, the quality of our responses will determine how adroitly Canadians can finesse the politics of ethnicity to advance toward living together with differences, equitably and in dignity.

This chapter explores the concept of "ethnicity experiences" as a formidable dynamic in shaping communities, identities, and actions. The chapter is organized around the theme that ethnicity once mattered, continues to matter even if many believed it wouldn't or shouldn't, and will continue to matter in the foreseeable future (albeit in forms that differ from the present). Ethnicity matters in two ways: First, as a key variable in influencing both individual and group behaviour, ethnicity makes something happen; second, it provides an explanatory framework for understanding behaviour, predicting success or failure (or justifying who gets what), mobilizing people into action groups, and legitimizing claims-making activities (Karner, 2007). More specifically, the chapter focuses on the politics of ethnicity when applied to a changing and diverse Canada. In that Canada's ethnic relations are predominantly relations of inequality, this chapter focuses on how ethnicity contributes to the creation and maintenance of inequities as well as to challenging and changing them. To address the issue of the ethnicity experience as power, identity, and politics, the chapter is organized accordingly: (1) What is ethnicity? (2) Why does it exist? (3) How is it expressed? (4) What is its relation to inequality? (5) What are its impacts on and implications for Canada-building? Particular attention is devoted to different expressions of ethnicity: (1) ethnicity as *community*, (2) ethnicity as *identity*, including lived, situational/symbolic, hybridic, transnational, and insurgent, and (3) ethnicity as *activity*, including social movements such as ethnic nationalism. The chapter concludes with a discussion of how the depoliticizing of ethnicity under Canada's Multiculturalism banner serves to make Canada safe from ethnicity, yet safe for ethnicity.

DEFINING ETHNICITY

Most societies are composed of racially and ethnically diverse groups (Isajiw, 1999). The range of variation is almost limitless. Some societies are relatively homogeneous in terms of ethnic composition (Japan and Korea); others have a single dominant majority with numerous minorities in different stages of assimilation (United Kingdom); others consist of dominant and subdominant groups that are locked in competition for power (Fiji); still others, including Australia and New Zealand, are constitutive of white settler colonies with immigrant populations superimposed on increasingly powerful indigenous nations (Fleras & Spoonley, 1999).

On the surface it might appear hopeless to extract a pattern from this seeming disarray. Nevertheless, two patterns can be discerned across societies. First, a dominant ethnic group prevails whose culture, language, values, and social patterns are privileged as normal and desirable. Those in control possess the power and resources to establish institutional arrangements and ideological systems consistent with their interests. Ethnocultural minorities have suffered as a result of this mistreatment, and many have reacted accordingly. A second pattern involves the proliferation of ethnically diverse groups who are increasingly restive because of their marginal status. Options open to these subdominant groups may be limited and limiting. Many endure constant pressure to conform to prevailing values, norms, and institutions. Others are kept securely in place to ensure a reserve pool of largely exploited labour. And still others are encouraged to retain diversity, but find themselves penalized or ostracized as a result.

Ethnic Diversity in Canada

Canada is unique in the ethnicity sweepstakes because of its unique combination of immigrant populations, including over 200 different ethnic groups, Aboriginal peoples, and a national minority of Quebec peoples. A generalized breakdown reflects the following trends based on the Ethnic Diversity Study (Statistics Canada, 2002) involving 45 000 respondents, aged 15 years and over (comprising 22.4 million of Canada's 31 million population).

1. 46 percent or 10.3 million = British, French, Canadian:
   - 21 percent = British only (includes English, Scottish, Irish, Welsh)
   - 10 percent = French only
   - 8 percent = Canadian only
   - 7 percent = mixed
2. 19 percent = descendents of other Europeans:
   - German, Italian, and Ukrainian = most common
3. 13 percent = non-European :
   - Chinese, East Indian = most common

4. 15 percent = mixed

5. 7 percent = unknown

To be sure, ethnic diversity is not only about numbers. Equally important are peoples' subjective feelings as they relate to ethnicity. In terms of importance, the Centre for Research and Information on Canada (2006) found that 59 percent of all respondents in a study claimed that ethnicity was important or very important to personal identity. Another 28 percent acknowledged the importance of ethnicity when selecting a spouse. Among racialized minorities, 75 percent said that ethnicity was important or very important for personal identity, while 37 percent said that ethnic background was important or very important in choosing a spouse. As well, a sense of ethnic attachment and its importance to people's identity varies with length of time in Canada. Specifically, 71 percent of those who arrived in Canada after 1991 said it was important; as did 65 percent of those who arrived prior to 1991; 57 percent of those defined as second generation; and 44 percent of those defined as third generation (both parents born in Canada) (Statistics Canada, 2007). Clearly, then, reactions to ethnicity vary: Some want to preserve or promote their ethnicity at all costs; others can't wait to discard their ethnic "straightjacket"; and still others want to fully participate in society without rejecting what makes them distinctive.

References to the term "ethnicity" continue to baffle and confuse as well as to infuriate and inflame. Ethnicity has evolved into an imprecise mélange of contested meanings that can be stretched to mean everything yet nothing, in the process acquiring the status of a cliché without much analytical clout. The term itself seems immune to rational analysis, thanks to its sprawling scope: How can a single term encompass everything from ethno-cide in the Darfur region of Sudan, to Québécois ethnic nationalism, to the contrived ethnicity of Kitchener-Waterloo's annual Oktoberfest celebration? What can be done with a word that people often use as a more polite euphemism for "race"? Or how does one cope with a term that is increasingly restricted to those of European origins, while non-European immigrants are framed as races and racialized accordingly? Finally, the term is subject to additional overuse. For example, consider how reference to ethnic con-flict is routinely employed to describe intergroup hostilities in Africa, but never applied to American militarism in Iraq or Afghanistan—even though ethnicity may well prove as pivotal a factor as political, religious, and economic factors.

Still, any definition must reflect certain prerequisites. A working definition must be sufficiently broad to capture the politics of ethnicity as principle and practice, yet not so sprawling as to lose this focus. A distinction between race and ethnicity provides a use-ful starting point. Whereas race connotes biological variation, genetic determinism, and imposed classifications, ethnicity differs in emphasizing self-generated cultural differ-ences related to values, lifestyle, and world view (Durie, 2005). Definitions must also acknowledge both subjective and objective dimensions at either individual or group levels. Or as Yinger (1994) notes, three components must prevail: (1) members of a so-called ethnicity see themselves as different; (2) others see them as different; and (3) people participate in shared activities with the intent of affirming their distinctiveness. With ethnicity, individuals experience a sense of belonging to a community of like-minded individuals who share a common attachment to identity markers such as language, history, birthright, kinship, and homeland. Broadly speaking, then, **ethnicity** can be defined as a principle and process in which a *shared awareness of a people's* *ancestral linkages and perceived commonalities serves as a basis for community, iden-tity, and activity.* This definition captures the multidimensionality of ethnicity as (1) embodying a consciousness of being different because of tradition and transmission, (2) an awareness of differences as socially constructed yet grounded in historical and structural realities, (3) a recognition that people perceive themselves as different and are seen by others as being different, and (4) an acknowledgment that ethnicity matters in securing recognition (identities), rewards (entitlements), or relationships (engagements).

There is some value in distinguishing ethnicity from ethnic groups and ethnic minorities. Ethnicity consists of those distinctive attributes that distinguish members of one category from another because of beliefs, values, emotions, and practices. In the case of ethnicity, persons who are related by birth, loyalty, culture, or homeland have the "option" of joining goal-directed action groups in pursuit of instrumental or expres-sive ends. **Ethnic groups**, by contrast, refer to actual communities of people who are socially and culturally distinct, who see themselves and are seen by others as distinct from other communities, and who are separated from others because of ancestries and boundaries. As widely noted, ethnic groups constitute a form of social organization with boundaries, a shared and transmitted culture and a sense of identity that fosters a sense of belonging among members. The extent to which ethnic groups maintain a strong con-sciousness among members will fluctuate, too; that is, some ethnic groups seek rapid assimilation and are quickly accepted by the mainstream, while others may stoutly defend their identity because of mainstream rejection or desire for distinctiveness (Cornell & Hartmann, 1998). Finally, the concept of "ethnic minority" refers to a group of culturally distinct people who occupy (or are seen to occupy) a marginal status in society, even though they may outnumber those of the dominant sector. In other words, references to minority versus majority—as well as dominant versus subdominant—are about power and differences, not about ratios.

COMPONENTS OF ETHNICITY

Canadian society was once envisioned as a mosaic of relatively durable and distinct ethnic entities whose totality was greater than the sum of its parts. Ethnicity embraced an objective and fixed compendium of cultural traits that identified a person as belonging to "x" rather than "y." As a key variable in explaining thought and behaviour, ethnicity was thought to profoundly influence a population's perception and response to the world, their personal and social identity, their norms and values for appropriate behaviour, and their limits to choices and opportunities (Gibb & Huang, 2003). A set of appropriate symbols and artifacts was attached to a particular community of people. Other groups were defined and distinguished by a different catalogue of qualities. Explicit and unbending boundaries were drawn around designated ethnic groups, reflecting an inven-tory of values, language, religion, and culture. This focus on the objective dimension of ethnicity culminated in a "cookie-cutter" approach to the study of ethnicity.

To ensure ethnic distinctiveness, boundaries are required. Ethnic boundaries can be defined as socially constructed barriers that provide a protective buffer by regulating of movement between ethnic groups (Barth, 1969). Neither totally impenetrable nor excessively permeable, these boundaries can be likened to "membranes" that simultane-ously inhibit yet permit the interflow of particles. In some cases, these boundaries are vigorously maintained for keeping some people in and others out. This boundary main-tenance is especially true when group members consider themselves under threat because of racist legislation, restricted economic opportunity, restrained cultural expression, or social rejection. In other cases, boundaries between these identities are fluid, contested, context dependent, and increasingly complex (Cornell & Hartmann, 1998). But difficulties arise in maintaining a degree of bounded distinctiveness. In countries like Canada, with its highly democratic and multicultural outlook, it is particularly hard to maintain ethnic boundaries. Under multiculturalism, paradoxically, the absence of official assimilationist pressure or out-group hostility increases the difficulty of preserving ethnic distinctiveness unless constant vigilance is exercised (Weinfeld, 2001).

This emphasis on objective ethnic content has waned in recent years. In its place has emerged an interest in the subjective experiences that embrace and the symbolic boundaries that encircle. A subjectivist orientation rejects the notion of ethnicity as a clearly articulated cultural category with an easily defined set of objective features. Ethnicity instead is informed by a shared "we feeling" that infuses the members of a particular group with a sense of who they are, where they originated from, and where they are headed. Emphasis is focused on ethnicity as an intersubjective activity, that is, a largely fluid and flexible resource for crafting patterns of meaningful interaction (Barth, 1969; Isajiw, 1999). In acknowledging that people may manipulate ethnicity to adapt, gain, or play, there is an unmistakable shift away from conventional notions that embrace static and homogeneous models.

But just as a laundry-list approach to ethnicity has proven inadequate, so too has an overemphasis on subjective experience. Ethnicity is more than a feeling of apartness or a sense of shared awareness; it is also grounded around those visible cultural symbols deemed essential to group survival. Select tangible markers such as patterns of kinship, descent, and obligations are required to validate a sense of continuity, collectivity, and commitment. Of those characteristics that shine as indices of ethnicity, from appearances to dietary habits, the most prominent are birthright, homeland, and language. Birthright is critical: Only persons with proven (or perceived) descent from a common source can claim membership to a particular ethnicity. No less crucial is a powerful attachment to a territory or homeland that may have been lost or left behind. Ethnic homelands are valorized as an embodiment of the past whose value must be defended at all costs. Language often represents the quintessential component of group distinctiveness. As a powerful symbol of distinctiveness, cohesion, and integrity, language requires little additional value in performing its integrative and identifying functions. (Chapter 8 will pursue this argument more fully.)

WHY ETHNICITY?

Ethnicity is evolving into one of the world's most powerful dynamics. Its salience in defining, shaping, and advancing group relations within multicultural contexts like those found in Canada is beyond doubt. Not surprisingly, many regard as a major challenge the construction of a society that is safe for ethnicity, yet safe from ethnicity. But such a concern was not always the case. The inevitable dissolution of ethnicity was widely predicted and anticipated as recently as a generation ago. Both socialism and liberalism attacked the particularist attachments associated with ethnicity as atavistic survivals at odds with universal progress and modernization. Ancient tribal hatreds would melt into memory because of a modernist belief in liberal universalism, with its attendant notion that, for purposes of reward and recognition, what people have in common as individuals is more important than what divides them because of membership in racial or ethnically distinct groups (Maaka & Fleras, 2005).

Ideological considerations were no less dismissive of ethnicity. Capitalism rejected ethnicity as anathema to progress or prosperity. With its backward-looking attachments to tribes and traditions, ethnicity would imperil the unfettered flow of labour, capital, and markets. A Marxist perspective was equally dismissive. If class relations constituted the fundamental dynamic in society, everything else, including ethnicity, was deemed to be derivative or residual. To think or to act otherwise, namely, in terms of ethnicity, would not only perpetuate false consciousness but also postpone the inevitable demise of capitalism. In short, both functionalism/capitalism and conflict/Marxist theorists pounced on ethnicity as inferior, irrelevant, doomed to obscurity, and an obstacle to progress and prosperity.

Predictions of its demise have been premature to say the least. Ethnicity has proven both resilient and tenacious, with no signs of diminishing or disappearing, despite powerful pressures to the contrary. Perpetuated at times by individuals as genuine culture (i.e., enjoyed for its own right); as an impetus for mobilizing people into goal-directed action (i.e., employed as a means to an end); and as a source of meaning, identity, and solidarity (Karner, 2007), the ethnicity "revolution" has profoundly redefined the notion of what society is for. People have turned to ethnicity as a means of protecting their immediate interests, especially when central authorities are unable or unwilling to regulate or control. No longer are ethnic attachments dismissed as archaic survivals from the past—quaint and colourful, perhaps, but irrelevant to contemporary realities. On the contrary, ethnicity matters, and this renewal of ethnic pride and identity has revealed a double-edged capacity not only to enhance or empower but also to destroy or dispossess.

The rejuvenation of ethnicity in Canada and elsewhere raises many questions: How do we account for the popularity and proliferation of ethnicity in contemporary societies? Why might people prefer to affiliate along ethnic lines rather than associate with political parties or trade unions? How can the visceral appeal of an inward-looking ethnicity possibly supersede the cosmopolitan lure of a modern society? Or rephrased along more grounded lines: Why would anyone want to be thought of as a Québécois or Aboriginal or Lithuanian-Canadian when they have the opportunity to identify solely as non-hyphenated Canadians? Three explanatory frameworks help to isolate the factors that underscore the popularity and persistence of the ethnicity experience, namely: the *primordial*, the *constructivist*, and the *instrumentalist*.

Primordial Explanation

The **primordial explanation** argues that the boom in ethnicity is essentially an extension of powerful and immutable instincts that cannot be indefinitely suppressed. People appear to have a genuine preference for aligning themselves with closely related blood kin; as a result, ethnicity represents an ancient and deep-rooted impulse for being with your "own kind." Suppression of these instinctive impulses for belonging with similar others doesn't make ethnicity go away, but forces it underground, only to have it re-emerge in an often explosive rage when the lid is lifted. These bonds are primordial because they appear to have been hardwired by evolution into the human species for survival purposes. This intrinsic dimension may help to explain the intensity of passions and emotions associated with the ethnic experience. Consider this statement by a Serbian-Canadian in rationalizing his loyalties during the 1999 NATO-led bombings of Serbia: "I'm a Canadian by birth and a Serbian by blood. I think family values come ahead of values or loyalties to your country . . . It's not a question of loyalty to Canada or Serbia" (as cited in Sarick, 1999). The primordiality of ethnic attachments may also explain the popularity of staunchly ethnic social movements in advancing collective interests (Bell-Fialkoff, 1993).

Within the primordialist camp are various biologically informed theories of ethnic bonding, the most popular of which is sociobiology. According to this slant, ethnicity is biogenetically "wired" into the human species as a mechanism for maximizing the transmission of genes from one generation to the next. Pierre van den Berghe (1981), for example, traces the origins of ethnic bonding to an extension of kinship group solidarity. Any kinship group tends to act in a self-preservative manner by providing mutual aid and cooperation for those related because of a common ancestor. Involvement with related others ensures the long-term survival of the kin groups—albeit at some expense to any specific individual. It follows from this that even ostensibly altruistic actions have the effect of protecting and promoting the evolutionary survival of one's own ethnic kin.

There is something of value in sociobiological explanations of ethnicity. By situating ethnic experiences within our genetic and evolutionary past, reference to sociobiology conveys the tenacity and the intensely emotional appeal of ethnicity (Brown, 1989). But sociologists are divided over the merits of sociobiology as an explanatory framework, especially as many reject any minimizing of the social as the preferred causal framework. Many are unsettled by the political implications of reductionist arguments that link biology with culture. True, we may be genetically "hardwired" to identify with our "own kind"; nevertheless, definitions of what constitutes our "own kind" will vary over time and across space. The fact that people are also free to choose otherwise, and that many have done so by repudiating their ethnic heritage, should caution against too uncritical an acceptance of primordiality.

Constructivist Explanation

In contrast to the primordial explanation, which sees ethnicity as natural and inevitable, a **constructivist explanation** focuses on the creation of ethnicity through meaningful interaction. The constructivist approach tends to see ethnic identity and affiliation as a complex and contested process whose construction cannot be understood outside the broader social, political, and historical context (Binder, 1999; Koenig & de Guchteneire, 2007). The "construction" in a social constructivist position confirms that there is nothing natural or normal about the world we live in, despite continued efforts by vested interests to make it seem so. Social conventions that guide or organize are continually constructed and reconstructed through a process of meaningful human interaction. Similarly, ethnicity is not a natural feature of society but a constructed response to material exclusion, a search for social meaning, a quest for identity, and a struggle for creating culturally safe spaces. Inasmuch as ethnicity represents a social construct, it is "imagined." But its effects on the lives and life chances of minority women and men are far from imaginary.

The identity thesis represents a variant of a constructivist explanation. According to the **identity thesis**, ethnicity persists because it provides a coping mechanism for addressing the globalizing demands of contemporary urban society. An identity perspective points to ethnicity as a buffer for insulating individuals from the pressures of an impersonal and competitive world. A commitment to ethnicity secures a source of stability in a world of diversity, uncertainty, and change; as an oasis of tranquility, it restores a measure of meaning in an increasingly meaningless world. Appeals to ethnicity foster a sense of relief, continuity, belonging, importance, and security—especially for those at the margins of society without alternative channels for coping with societal stress caused by intense global competition, radicalized individualism, a disintegrating civil society, increasingly porous territorial borders, the erosion of the nation-state as the primary source of legitimacy, and cultural upheavals created by the proliferation of digital technologies. The dissolution of the familiar and reassuring has undermined people's sense of social belonging, including a rootedness in traditional collectivities such as kinship or community. The confluence of uncertainty and change induces individuals to withdraw into ethnic enclaves that are familiar and emotionally satisfying (Littleton, 1996). As Manuel Castells (1997) writes:

> When the world becomes too large to be controlled, social actors aim at shrinking it back to their size and reach. When networks dissolve time and space, people anchor themselves in places, and recall their historic memory. (p. 66)

Ethnic involvements, in other words, permit meaningful identity to be crafted when meanings are in short supply. A "quasi-kinship" community is sustained that provides a buffer against the backdrop of unremitting rationality, standardization, and central control (Scott, 1998). This binding and bonding dimension also helps to explain the universal appeal of such affiliation for people confronting the relentless pressures for conformity and consensus.

Instrumentalist Explanation

An **instrumentalist explanation** views ethnicity as a resource for the pursuit of diverse goals (Hutchinson & Smith, 1996). One version refers to elite competition for scarce resources, in which ethnic symbols are manipulated to secure mass support. A second version refers to a process by which both leaders and followers maximize preferences, since pooled resources provide a competitive advantage in advancing vested interests. An instrumentalist approach is firmly grounded in a sociological understanding of group competition and rational choice theory; that is, ethnicity is designed to maximize in-group advantage by excluding others (Castles & Miller, 2003). The drawing power of ethnicity provides a competitive edge in the struggle for scarce and valued resources as groups rely on their ethnic attachments to mobilize, challenge, and change. Especially in contexts in which an ethnic division of labour persists (Gross, 1996; Hechter, 1975), dominant sectors tend to monopolize wealth and power at the expense of ethnically different subdominant groups, many of whom are locked into a position of inferiority because of their unskilled status. Resentment over this differential treatment boils over when expectations soar but the means to achievement are blocked, resulting in escalating ethnic activism (Nagel & Olzak, 1982; See & Wilson, 1988). Ethnic activism is further bolstered by the actions of opportunistic elites who often cloak personal interests behind a facade of altruism.

Two questions arise from an instrumentalist approach to ethnicity: First, why do ethnically like-minded persons prefer to act collectively to achieve their goals rather than as individuals? Put simply, a collective basis is superior for coping with the demands of a complex and bureaucratized society. According to **resource mobilization theory**, large-scale social movements possess the human resources and critical mass to compete effectively in the competition for scarce resources. Second, why are ethnic attachments important in securing the loyalty and commitment of members? What is the tactical advantage of relying on ethnicity as a basis for mobilizing people into groups? The best answer may be the most obvious. Recruitment by appealing to ethnicity is perceived as more natural and durable than the "artificial" linkages associated with political or economic ties. Ethnic bonds are consolidated by emotional involvement with persons of one's own kind, a kind of quasi-kinship that needs no justification beyond its own existence. These quasi-kinship ties also infuse the movement with the commitment for waging a protracted struggle against even seemingly insurmountable odds.

To sum up: Three theoretical approaches account for the popularity and persistence of ethnicity. By providing insights into aspects of the ethnic experience that others prefer to ignore, each of these approaches may be partially correct as far as explanatory frameworks go, including (1) ethnicity as an inherent affiliation that reflects an intrinsic need for belonging to one's own kind (primordial), (2) ethnicity as a constructed framework of social organization for securing meaning and continuity in a changing and uncertain world (constructivist), and (3) ethnicity as a tool for rational attainment of goals (instrumentalist). That said, there is no reason why primordial explanations cannot be incorporated into a broader explanatory framework (including the constructivist and instrumentalist explanations) in securing a multi-textured insight into the ethnicity experience.

EXPRESSING ETHNICITY: COMMUNITY, IDENTITY, ACTIVITY

Ethnicity can be expressed at different levels of reality. At one level, ethnicity is manifested in ethnic groups who live together in relatively self-sufficient communities. At another level, ethnicity manifests itself through different expressions of identity, including lived, symbolic and situational, hybridic, insurgent, and transnational. At a third level, ethnicity reflects activity best expressed through social movements with nationalistic overtones. These different expressions of the ethnic experience—*community*, *identity*, and *activity* (see Table 4-2)—may be analyzed separately; in reality, however, they tend to coexist, overlap, and intersect in complex ways.

TABLE 4-2	Expressing Ethnicity: Community, Identity, and Activity	
Ethnicity as community	**Ethnicity as identity**	**Ethnicity as activity**
Enclaves or "ghettos"	Lived	Nationalistic movements
	Situational/symbolic	Ethnic nationalism
	Hybridic	Civic nationalism
	Transnational	
	Insurgent	

Ethnicity as Community

Ethnicity refers to a principle of potential group/community formation. Persons with shared and felt identification may be classified into a category that mobilizes ancestrally related persons into action groups to advance individual or collective claims. Ethnicity also provides a basis for relatively permanent communities with clearly defined rules for living together. Preference for being with one's own kind may foster a commitment to community. Or pressures from the outside may also compel a closing of the ranks along community lines. The host society may impose a demeaning ethnic label on migrants who then capitalize on community bonds to cope with unfriendly environments.

Parts of urban Canada are composed of a mosaic of ethnic communities, including the widely celebrated Chinatowns in Vancouver and Toronto, South Asian communities in Brampton, and the relatively self-sufficient Hasidic Jews in Montreal. Or consider the town of Markham, located just north of Toronto, where nearly 65 percent of the population, according to the 2006 Census, identified themselves as ethnic—including one ward where 95 percent of the population self-identified as ethnic. According to Qadeer, Agrawal, and Lovell (2009), the percentage of South Asians residing in their respective ethnic enclaves in Toronto's Census Metropolitan Area in 2006 was 49.6 percent, followed by Chinese at 48.2 percent and Jewish at 40.6 percent. These ethnic communities can be conceptualized in different ways—either as segregated ghettos that intensify downward spirals or as vibrant ethnic enclaves that express community identity (Qadeer & Agrawal, 2009) (see online Case Study 4.3).

Ethnic communities can also be seen as a complex matrix of intergroup relations and intragroup dynamics. They consist of communities that offer emotional and material support for facilitating the transition from the society of origin to urban Canada. Recent immigrants may find economic and cultural refuge in ethnic communities because of organizations that assist in the preservation of language and transmission of culture. In providing a framework for collective activities, they also establish a power base for advancing political consciousness and action. These communities may attract resources and influence if local leaders can command community loyalty and deliver this "commodity" as electoral support for government initiatives. Still, internal tensions may threaten community solidarity or consensus on issues. Despite a constructed facade of wholesome unity, social fissures are readily apparent as people jockey for position, with a high potential for factional infighting and political cleavages because of politicized differences in age, sex, income, education, and length of residence.

Ethnicity as Identity

One of the identities open to Canadians is that of ethnicity. In a multicultural society like Canada, many individuals regard their ethnicity as important in defining their self-identity (see Cornell & Hartmann, 2007; Liu et al., 2006; Muir & Wetherell, 2010). Identity entails how a person defines who he or she is by seeking a degree of consistency in responding to questions such as these: How do I see myself? How would I like to see myself? How do I think others see me? How would I like others to see me? (As we shall see in the next chapter, ethnicity also serves as a critical determinant of "who gets what.") Ethnic identities can also be broadly defined as personal attachments involving a subjective sense of belonging to or identification with a group or tradition over time, based on commonalities with similar others (Driedger, 1989; Satzewich & Liodakis, 2010). In certain cases, ethnic identities are imposed by outside sources; in others, they are voluntarily adopted on the basis of how individuals or groups feel about themselves. Some identities, such as "white ethnicity," are somewhat muted since whites rarely express a conscious awareness of their whiteness unless challenged to do so (see online Debate 4.2). Other identities may be active in that individuals are conscious of them and act accordingly to protect or promote them. Still other identities are politicized in securing the basis for collective action to achieve goals. In all cases, identities are relational in that they are constructed through meaningful interaction—in effect rejecting the psychologizing of identities as inherent or maturational.

Expressions of ethnic identities can be varied (Simmons, 2010). Some Canadians reject their ethnic background except for special occasions, preferring instead to be identified only as Canadians for purposes of recognition, relationships, and rewards. Others maintain a dual (or "transnational") identity without much difficulty: Modern communication and transport technologies allow ethnic minorities to transcend national borders by participating in the internal affairs of the homeland without relinquishing a commitment to Canada. Such a dynamic makes it difficult to think of Canada as a collection of self-contained localities. Rather, the intensified transnational exchanges between localities and the homeland have altered how people think about identity, place, and borders (Papillon, 2002). Still others thrive on multiple identities. They flit in and out of different ethnic identities without undergoing a crisis of confusion. Their identities are fluid and contextual—even contradictory—in coping with the many opportunities that a postmodern society has to offer, especially as individuals and groups are drawn into an ever-expanding nexus of networks and linkages (Handa, 2003). And yet still others remain locked into an "old country" identity with neither the intent nor energy to change in defining who they are. Five expressions of ethnic identity can be discerned, at least for purposes of analysis, namely *lived, situational/symbolic, hybridic, transnational*, and *insurgent*.

Lived Ethnic Identity Individuals with common cultural values or religious beliefs may strongly identify with a particular ethnic group. Under a **lived ethnic identity**, individuals are born into these primary groups, membership is irrevocably assigned at birth, and the group remains a virtually exclusive source of identity throughout an entire lifetime. An attachment to the norms, values, and institutions of the group constitutes a serious statement about personal affiliation. Anabaptist sects such as the Hutterites are ethnic communities governed by rules, values, and sanctions. Here, the principle of ethnicity reflects and reinforces the organization of viable groups, with a corresponding powerful influence in shaping members' lives. These individuals admit that their identification with the cultural past makes a difference in how they think and behave. Involvement at this level presupposes a framework of constraints, demands, and responsibilities that cannot be casually discarded as moods shift or personalities change.

A lived ethnicity represents a difference that makes a difference in defining "who we are." There is no option or choice; either people conform or they are shunned or expelled. Not surprisingly, this "old-fashioned" style of ethnicity is disappearing, although there are signs of a renewal in larger urban centres. Restricted largely to rural areas and certain urban enclaves of Canada, conventional ethnic groups have lost much of their moral authority as arbiters of correct human behaviour. Many of these groups can no longer supply a common set of shared values, enforce mutual obligations or responsibilities, offer incentives or impose sanctions, or secure compliance from members. A lived ethnicity no longer appeals to those who are anxious to fully participate in an achievement-oriented society. A more flexible arrangement has appeared instead.

Situational/Symbolic Ethnic Identity Ethnicity in a multicultural society takes on a different dynamic. Ethnic identities are often part-time, focused on symbols rather than substance, and situation specific. The obligations of a lived ethnic identity are discarded in exchange for the flexibility associated with symbolic commitments and situational adjustments. This situationally specific and symbolically loaded identity often takes the form of a strategic personal resource that allows individuals to improve their life chances without rejecting their life sources. References to ethnic identities as situational or symbolic are not intended to trivialize or demean the ethnic experience as inauthentic or contrived. Emphasis instead is on its adaptiveness and resilience across time and place.

An ethnic identity based on situation and symbols reflects a uniquely distinct process of immigrant adaptation. Through involvement in their adopted country, incoming immigrants may become increasingly estranged from their cultural heritage—especially in terms of language use, friendship circles, and residential patterns—preferring instead to identify with the values and lifestyle of the host society. Ethnic attachments to the homeland culture begin to dissipate in light of host-country pressures to adapt and integrate. Involvement in ethnic organizations declines (except on isolated occasions or in favourable circumstances) to the point of insignificance—if measured by the frequency or intensity of institutional participation. Yet there is a reluctance to casually discard tradition, given its former importance as a blueprint for identity and relationships, with the result that many new Canadians may retain a strong emotional connection to the symbolic aspects of their cultural past. In resisting the lure of wholesale assimilation, they reveal an affective attachment to the community as a reference group, but reject as unacceptable both the restrictions and responsibilities of a lived ethnicity (Roberts & Clifton, 1990).

The emergence of this "part-time" ethnicity is known as **situational/symbolic ethnic identity**—situational, because its expression is context dependent rather than constant across time and space; symbolic, because identity is informed by an attachment to symbols rather than the substance of ethnicity. Ethnic salience is not measured by a person's degree of participation in ethnic clubs, knowledge of ethnic language, circle of friends, place of residence, or marital patterns. Importance instead is attached to identifying with the symbols of that ethnicity, with a willingness to activate those symbols when appropriate or for advantage. Individuals do not so much belong to an ethnic group as they voluntarily affiliate with relevant cultural symbols as preferences dictate and situations demand (Amarasingam, 2008). Admittedly, not everyone possesses a choice of options. The centrality of racialized visibility make this option less applicable to people of colour, who may find ethnic identities imposed on them against their will, rather than something they can opt into or out of when they please.

The situational and symbolic nature of ethnic identity provides insights into the ethnicity experience. First, can distinct ethnic identities survive in situations where the traditional culture has disappeared? Second, can individuals continue to identify themselves as "ethnics" long after abandoning all involvement in group activities? According to the logic of situational and symbolic ethnicity, the answer to both questions is yes. The decline of a particular lifestyle will not necessarily diminish the validity of the ethnic experience. What is critical for ethnic identity is the identification with select aspects of that cultural lifestyle—not the scope or intensity of affiliation. Needless to say, this style of identity is relatively painless and voluntary; moreover, its abstract and effortless style makes it well suited to the needs of an upwardly mobile society.

A third question is also of interest: Is a hyphenated Canadian a contradiction in terms? Is it possible to identify and participate as a Canadian, yet retain an affiliation with a certain ethnic heritage, such as Lithuanian (or New Zealander or German)? Again, the answer is in the affirmative. A hyphenated identity entitles people to compartmentalize their identities, then activate the appropriate identity according to the demands of a particular context. Dual (even multiple) identities are not mutually exclusive; rather, they may complement each other in fulfilling diverse personal needs and goals. Nor does identification with select symbolic elements necessarily interfere with the business of making a living. As long as identification is restricted to the cognitive rather than the behavioural level, everyone can regard themselves as an "ethnic" without relinquishing a commitment to Canada.

Hybridic Ethnic Identity Most perspectives on ethnicity reflect a modernist or "structuralist" approach. Structuralists tend to see social groups or institutional arrangements as the fundamental building blocks of society, a primary source of human identity, a critical factor in shaping behaviour, and the key determinant of intergroup relations. According to structuralist thought, for each identifiable group there is a single ethnoculture with a unique and unchanging essence that can be categorically grasped independently of context (McHugh, 1998). Ethnicities are envisioned as reflecting separate and fixed states of being into which individuals are slotted, with an attendant belief that everyone in this ethnic group will think and act in the same way.

But the seemingly locked-in identities of the modern era are eroding, giving way to the emergence of the **postmodern** self as relatively free-floating and detached from conventional structures of identity (Paradies, 2006). Individuals move into and out of so many different contexts and identities that it no longer makes sense to categorize people into stable ethnic groups (Uitermark, Rossi, & van Houtum, 2005). People are known to define themselves in terms of multiple national attachments involving identities that are both contested and contextual as well as fluid and flexible (Castells, 1997; May, 2002; Parekh, 2000). As personal resources for coping with diverse realities, ethnicities are increasingly evolving as hybrid identities that oscillate between the past and present, involving a multiplicity of crossovers and contingencies in a world where people live their paradoxes without fears of contradiction (Handa, 2003; Wiwa, 2003). (See online Case Study 4.1.)

Hybridic (or postmodern) ethnic identities reflect the predicaments and opportunities of a contemporary era. The postmodern world we live in is a diasporic reality where (1) immigrants mingle with national minorities and indigenous peoples; (2) increasingly porous cultural boundaries are constantly being invented or renegotiated; and (3) people politics assert multiple and hybridic patterns of belonging based on intersecting lines of gender, sexual preferences, homeland, and ethnicity. Rather than stable points of reference in which people are preslotted, ethnic identities are relational dynamics that come into being through interaction—continually changing and reinventing themselves by fusing the old with the new alongside other ethnicities, to create new and provisional hybrids that are neither stable nor coherent. Instead of being fixed in some kind of essentialized past, they are evolving, highly adaptive, involve crossings and connections, and are subject to the continuous play of context (Hall, 1996).

Transnational Ethnic Identity Both symbolic/situational and hybridic ethnicities reinforce the constructed nature of ethnic identities. References to **transnational ethnic identities** also follow this path. The concept itself acknowledges an emergent and fundamental reality: Globalization has challenged the conventional notions of belonging that linked a person's identity with a particular place (Cheng, 2005). Rather than treating homeland and host country as an either–or dichotomy in winning an immigrant's sense of identity and belonging, new notions of multiple homelands and multiple attachments in light of diasporic movements of people are emerging, with a corresponding fresh perspective on how ethnic identities can be imagined and constructed across national borders (Simmons, 2010; Fleras 2011b).

Reaction to transnational identities is understandably varied. For some, this multilocal identity may prove beneficial for society by providing linkages of value that span the borders of a global market economy. For others, however, these seemingly divided identities conjure up images of split loyalties, thus compromising the potential for political governance, societal integration, and assumption of citizenship responsibilities (Duncan, 2006). For example, creating a sense of belonging and attachment beyond Canada's borders may well undermine what it means to be Canadian. For still others, benefits come with costs, making it doubly important to understand how and why diasporic populations maintain ties with real and imagined homelands, what this means at the personal and community levels, and what kind of impact this has on society and culture (Satzewich & Wong, 2006; Vertovec, 2006).

The mixed reaction to transnational identities makes one thing abundantly clear: There is a growing acknowledgment of ethnic identities as a process or verb rather than a thing or a noun. Ethnic identities are no longer defined as rigid or fixed, especially as ethnicities from around the world regroup into new points of being and becoming. Because of transnational mobility, these diasporic experiences are not defined by essences or purity, but by the dynamics of hybridity and heterogeneity that define both the construction and negotiation of identities as well as how they are practised and experienced (Braziel & Mannur, 2003; Vertovec 2006).

Insurgent Ethnic Identity Both lived and situational/symbolic ethnic identities appear to be relatively innocuous. Hybridic identities are equally "harmless" because of their preoccupation with the discourses of authenticity rather than the politics of power. With few exceptions, by abiding by the liberal slogan of "agreeing to disagree," each of these identities upholds the multicultural axiom of "live and let live." But not all ethnic identities are so accommodating. **Insurgent ethnic identities** are much more assertive about what they believe is right or wrong, are highly politicized in terms of what they want, and appear more aggressive in achieving their goals. In transcending mere identification or celebration, an insurgent ethnicity reflects an exaggerated notion of a shared and conscious attachment to a people, tradition, or territory. Cooperative coexistence is replaced by a politicized assertion of peoplehood that establishes a new political order reflecting and reinforcing their superiority. An intense dislike of others may be actively fostered, especially when issues pertaining to religion, language, or homelands are factored into the competition. Such collectivities are willing to take whatever measures necessary to achieve their goals, including the revival of dormant grievances and recourse to violent measures (Taras & Ganguly, 2002).

Ethnicity as Activity: Nationalist Movements

Ethnicity as activity involves the process by which ideas and ideals are put into practice for goal attainment. Nowhere is this more evident than in the reality of ethnically related peoples engaging in organized action to achieve the political goals of identity, voice, or land. Appeals to ethnicity provide a basis for mobilizing individuals into collective action; they also furnish the motivation and rationale to achieve ethnically defined goals. This surge of ethnic-based movements has come about for various reasons. The UN-based principle of national self-determination articulated a normative basis for making ethnically based political claims against the state. The collapse of superpower colonialism has also given rise to social formations that emphasized ethnic loyalties rather than the abstractions of statehood (Ignatieff, 1994). Inter-tribal hatreds, once suppressed by colonialist control or Cold War politics, have created fertile conditions for ethnic conflict to flourish (Snyder, 2000). Or as Michael Ignatieff wrote in 1994, the "key narrative of the new world order is the disintegration of nation states into warring factions. The key architects of that order are warlords; and the key language of our age is *ethnic nationalism* (emphasis added)."

Nationalism constitutes the political expression of a **nation** whose peoples claim a common ancestry and shared destiny to govern themselves in a place they call a homeland. The nineteenth century gave rise to nationalism in Europe, resulting in the birth of modern Germany, with its rallying cry of "Germany for the Germans," but dismissiveness of Slavs, Jews, and Gypsies as unwelcome residue from past empires (Guibernau, 2007). In that the nation-state was defined by a shared language, culture, and identity (Smith, 1999), all expressions of nationalism remain grounded in a simple ideal: namely, the idea of group exclusiveness, cultural superiority, and collective loyalty against outside threats. As an ideological movement, the concept of nationalism asserts the divisibility of the world into fundamentally autonomous political communities by peoples who define themselves as a nation. They claim the status of an actual or potential nation, with corresponding rights to self-determination over homeland, identity, and political voice, either as independent entities (nation-states or countries) in their own right or as subunits within society (nations) by vesting political sovereignty in a people's right to self-rule (see Pearson, 2001). In making this claim for self-determining autonomy, unity, and identity, nations are seeking to establish jurisdictional control over a defined homeland, in addition to reclaiming the sovereignty denied to them as a subject people.

Nationalisms can be classified by who is entitled to join and belong. Two patterns of belonging are discernible—ethnic and civic—based largely on divergent patterns of belonging as criteria for group membership (Medrano & Koenig, 2005). **Ethnic nationalism** bases its notion of a nation on largely ascriptive characteristics such as kinship ties and blood lines to include or exclude. It is aimed at building nationhood by strengthening a "people" (or nation) at the expense of others if necessary. With its focus on ascription, bloodlines, and descent, membership in the nationhood is restricted to those who can demonstrate common roots rather than shared attachments to key institutions and central values. A moral community is proposed in which members express an emotional commitment to each other with a passionate attachment to a homeland as the site of preexisting ethnic entitlements (Mead, 1993). Membership is defined on the basis of birthright and descent from a common ancestry, with loyalty to the group or the homeland as paramount over any commitment to the **state** or to social classes. The territorial rights, distinctive language, and shared ethnicity of this imagined political community must be defended from hostile interlopers, both internal and external, by whatever means necessary.

White Nationalism: Separation or Supremacy?

Nationalist movements are difficult to evaluate. Are they "pro" their own kind or "anti" the other? Does living with your own kind really create a better society with less conflict and more consensus? A white racial advocacy movement has emerged in recent years that puts these questions to the test (Swain, 2002). Cultured and mannered, with impressive credentials from American universities, in contrast to the hooded Klansmen of the past, the new white nationalists rely on the language of nationhood and national self-determination as well as the discourses of civil rights and ethnic identity politics to advance a God-given right to a distinct white European society. Former white supremacists such as David Duke have reinvented themselves as white civil-rights crusaders whose rhetoric taps into people's fears of an America swamped by supposedly inferior black and brown people with potentially catastrophic consequences in diluting the culture and bloodlines that built America's greatness. As well, people's identities as whites are gravely threatened by the emergence of multiculturalism, affirmative action programs, identity politics, racial intermarriage, and large-scale migration from non-white societies (see Ferber, 1998).

White nationalists endorse a racialized view of the world. Although they dismiss charges of being racists or white supremacists, white nationalists believe that race is a legitimate criterion for inclusion and entitlement within a community; after all, those societies that are dominated by a single race tend to be the least faction ridden and conflict prone (Rushton, 1995). Toward the creation of a neo-apartheid system of governance, American white nationalists want to reclaim a part of the country in which whites would be able to freely develop their culture and pursue their identities without hindrance from members of other racial groups—in a manner envisaged by the original Founding Fathers such as George Washington and Thomas Jefferson. The Pacific Northwest is touted as an ideal site for a white nation because of the current small numbers of migrants and minorities. Ironically, white nationalists have joined forces with black nationalists who also reject integration and propose that racial separatism is the only solution for living together with differences (see Swain, 2002).

By contrast, **civic nationalism** bases its appeal on loyalty to a set of political ideals, rule of law, the principle of inclusiveness, and institutions that are perceived as just and effective (Heath & Tilley, 2005; Snyder, 2000). Civic nationalism is concerned with society-building by strengthening the organization of the state. It maintains that society should be composed of all individuals, regardless of race or ethnicity, as long as they subscribe to the norms of this constructed community. This nationalism is usually called civic because it envisages society as a constructed community of equal rights-bearing citizens organized around a commitment to the rule of law (although some civic nation-alisms have proven more ruthless than ethnic nationalism in advancing their goals). Ethnicity is largely irrelevant in determining belonging or inclusion, as membership is open to anyone who abides by core values and constitutional principles.

To be sure, the distinction between these nationalisms is problematic. Few if any nationalisms qualify as purely ethnic or civic: Ethnic nationalisms have proven more civic oriented than theory suggests; civic nationalisms, in turn, have proven more ethnically grounded than many give credit for (Kymlicka, 2001; Resnick, 2001; Vickers & de Seve, 2000). The case of Quebec is instructive where debate persists about the definition of nation: Does it include all Quebecers or only those of French-Canadian descent? On one side, Quebec's political aspirations were equated with ethnic nationalism because of a his-torical tendency to exclude non-white francophones (Ignatieff, 1994). On the other side, Quebec's drive for autonomy within the Canadian state is defended as civic nationalism, that is, broad, tolerant, and inclusive of all who make the commitment to construct a mod-ern political community without compromising its distinctiveness. The emergence of a hybrid nationalism such as Quebec's points to a conceptual framework for a postethnic and non-racialized nationalism that is neither a defensive reaction nor an inclusive embrace.

DEPOLITICIZING ETHNICITY: MAKING CANADA SAFE *FOR* ETHNICITY, SAFE *FROM* ETHNICITY

Ethnicity can no longer be dismissed as some primitive relic or primordial rage. Ethnicity goes beyond an obsessive craving to discover "roots" in the hopes of uncovering the past or collecting compensation. Nor should it be trivialized as a transient whimsy or a cultural backwater on the path to rational progress and democratic governance. Rather, ethnicity matters—for better or worse—in making things happen in advancing collective interests and maximizing social advantages (Gross, 1996). Recourse to ethnicity pro-vides a modicum of security in a highly impersonal and mechanized society by buffering the old from the new, the individual from society, and the familiar from the strange.

Ethnicity's potential for greatness or depravity is further magnified when coupled with the conflicting demands of a new global order. The new millennium is proving to be a bewildering place (Taras & Ganguly, 2009). Gone are the global certainties of the past: The relatively simple verities of an established order have been superseded by a complex and multipolar world of moral ambivalence and political ambiguity. With the obvious exception of the United States, no comparable political or military power has reclaimed the political vacuum created by the disintegration of the USSR, thus encour-aging both intermediate powers and ethnic nationalisms to compete for vacated space. Not surprisingly, the very forces that many thought would reduce the risk of group conflicts have, paradoxically, increased inter-ethnic strife (Snyder, 2000). The politics of ethnicity are here to stay, whether we like it or not. And as postmodernity "bites" deeper, more ethnic conflicts are inevitable (Smith, 1996).

Canada is not unaffected by these political and cultural upheavals. Just as international relations are animated by a clash of competing and often incommensurable world views, so too does Canada's ethnicity agenda reflect both conflict and confusion (Kymlicka, 2001). Rules that formerly defined right from wrong are openly challenged or dismissed as irrelevant. What once were defined as virtues are now vices, and vice versa. Aboriginal peoples are no longer willing to abide by colonial paradigms (Alfred, 2005); the Québécois are looking for a foundationally different kind of partnership with the rest of Canada (Gibbins & Laforest, 1998); and multicultural minorities want to re-contour Canada along inclusive lines (Fleras, 2009b). The politics of ethnicity are proving double-edged: Canada may be enriched by weaving national unity from the strands of diversity. Alternatively, ethnic forces may ignite a chain reaction that could derail Canada's society-building aspirations. This paradox—how to make Canada safe from ethnicity, yet safe for ethnicity— raises the question of Canada's resolve in the face of potentially divisive forces.

An official Multiculturalism represents Canada's answer to the politics of ethnicity. In advancing the unorthodox notion that Canadians from all cultural backgrounds could fully contribute to building a united Canada, official Multiculturalism pivots on the premise that a Canada of many different cultures and diverse peoples is possible, provided that ethnic differences don't get in the way of living together with differences. With Multiculturalism, this seemingly implausible balancing act is possible, in part by transcending the specifics of cultures to ensure that no one is excluded from full and equal participation in society for reasons beyond their control (namely, their ethnicity); in part by acknowledging the legitimacy of ethnic differences as long as they stay within limits (thus reinforcing the governance principle of *separating state from ethnicity*); and in part by taking these differences into account when necessary to ensure full participation and equal citizenship rights.

But respect for ethnocultural diversity as grounds for living differently together comes with a qualifier. Canada's multiculturalism is constructed around a narrow reading of ethnicity. Put bluntly, an official Multiculturalism is not concerned with promoting ethnic diversity or ethnic communities. Few societies could survive the strain of multiple competing groups, with clearly demarcated political boundaries, separate power bases, and parallel institutions. Even fewer are equipped to address the society-busting demands of ethnic nationalism. This aversion to a politicized ethnicity is evident in Canada, where the politics of ethnicity threaten to dismember or dissolve. To neutralize its immediacy and impact, ethnicity under Canada's multicultural commitments is justified only when stripped of its potency to divide or incite. Instead of politicized ethnicities in the competition for scarce resources, Multiculturalism endorses the symbols of differences at personal or private levels. Rather than taking differences seriously, the "pretend pluralism" endorsed by an official Multiculturalism accommodates the appearance of ethnicity rather than its substance.

In other words, an official Multiculturalism is not about promoting ethnic cultures as distinct and coherent lifestyles (Modood, 2007). More accurately, it promotes a depoliticizing ("neutering") of ethnicity by removing its potency to challenge or change. Under an official Multiculturalism, ethnicity is rendered tolerable to the extent that (1) people identify only with the symbols of their difference; (2) this identification is restricted to the personal and private rather than public realm; (3) this affiliation does not violate the laws of the land, interfere with the rights of others, or contravene core Canadian values and constitutional principles, and (4) people use their ethnicity as a way of belonging to Canada rather than for erecting inward-looking communities. Put bluntly, then, Canada's official Multiculturalism does not exist to "celebrate" ethnicity. More to the point, official Multiculturalism is concerned with neutering ethnicity as a framework for living together with what's left of our differences. Or to put it more finely, under Multiculturalism, all Canadians can belong to Canada through their ethnicity.

Herein, then, lies the appeal of hybridic, transnational, and situational/symbolic ethnic identities within a multicultural society. In contrast to insurgent or lived ethnicities, they (a) do not directly challenge the status quo, (b) are more concerned with the symbols of attachment, and (c) are more diffuse because of their potential to combine identities. In that people can and do have multiple and complementary identities, multicultural policies that allow these identities to flourish are likely to foster a cohesive and cooperative society-building (United Nations Development Programme, 2004). Promotion of ethnic identity at these levels comes across as relatively innocuous, since the recognition of multiple and complementary identities does not fundamentally alter the political landscape and economic status quo. In neutering the potential of ethnicity as a force for resistance and transformation, official Multiculturalism represents Canada's much-debated response to the challenges of *making society safe for ethnicity, as well as safe from ethnicity*. In a Canadian society of many cultures, no one should be denied or excluded because of their ethnic origins. By the same token, according to Canada's inclusive multiculturalism, no one should be given special treatment because of their ethnicity. Time will tell whether Canada's multicultural response for engaging ethnicity will be sufficient for those politicized ethnicities who want to reverse the governance formula by *making ethnicity safe from Canada, yet safe for Canada.*

DEBATE REVISITED

Ethnic Conflicts or Conflicts That Are Ethnicized?

The dismantling of the Berlin Wall in 1989 was widely heralded as a defining moment in global history. Many saw the Wall's destruction as a triumph of universalism and reason over the irrationalities of ideologues, rampant prejudices, and petty hostilities. But the promise proved short-lived; emergent instead was an intensely parochial era. With several exceptions, virtually all conflicts since 1990 have involved confrontations between ethnic groups within existing borders, largely because of the political vacuum created by collapsed states and stagnant economies (Gurr, 2001; Taras & Ganguly, 2009).

Ancient animosities and dormant hatreds have proliferated because of these ethno-chauvinisms. Incorporate religious intolerance, and these hostilities often invoke a passion and fury that has rattled an abiding faith in the decency of human nature (Behrens, 1994; Tishkov, 2004). Nevertheless, it is still important to ask the questions: Are ethnic conflicts really about ethnicities? Or is there more to them than meets the ethnic eye? Consider the possibilities:

- In some cases, the conflict that erupts between mutually antagonistic groups is motivated by historically deep-seated hatreds (Crawford, 2006). Tribal- or clan-based impulses that once were dormant or suppressed may be activated when the grip of central control is relaxed. Once unleashed and whipped into a frenzy by manipulative leaders, these primordial forces are difficult to stop, especially in clan- or tribal-based societies (since people trust only their own kind), while collective interests are defined in opposition to other group interests. In other words, the tribe (or clan) is everything—mutual aid, protection, source of trust—while outside the tribe is danger (Clarfield, 2007; Kay, 2007).

- In other cases, ethnicity is but one of many variables driving the dynamics of intergroup competition for scarce resources. Consider Africa, where states and boundaries between states were created for political, military, economic, and diplomatic reasons, with little regard for ethnic differences and tribal borders. With decolonization, these artificially constructed and politically expedient nation-states proved brittle and prone to fracture from within by tribal groups who sought a degree of autonomy or advantage at the expense of others (but see Bass, 2006). And when governments collapse and there is no state capable of guaranteeing personal security, the risk of ethnic conflict increases. Patterns of intergroup inequality (including poverty, corruption, and tribalism [Perry & Blue, 2008]) can also generate ethnic conflict, especially in those contexts where globalization unsettled an established **social contract**

that once normalized access to scarce resources or power relations along ethnic lines. When these social contracts are disrupted with a corresponding shift in power, ethnic patterns of discrimination and exclusion appear. The appearance of new resentments provides fertile ground for opportunistic leaders to mobilize public support around ethnic identities for advancing vested interests (Crawford, 2006).

- In still other cases, ethnicity is not a direct factor in the conflict; nevertheless, it may be invoked to impart a sheen of legitimacy, thus concealing political motives and economic interests. Most ethnic conflicts are not about ethnicity per se. In contexts involving sharp inequalities in power and wealth, coalitions form along ethnic lines in the competition for scarce resources, with the result that ethnicity serves as an identity marker in sorting out the winners (Caselli & Coleman, 2006/2010). Conflicts in this competitive context often become "ethnicized" through political elites, who capitalize on ethnicity as a propaganda tool for self-serving reasons (Collier, 2007; Marger, 1997). By taking advantage of the uncertainty to recruit or consolidate, power-hungry elites will readily exploit ethnic tension during times of political and social upheaval, such as the wave of democratization and institutional change that swept through Asia and Africa during the 1990s (Carment, 2007). In short, ethnic conflicts do not just erupt; they are constructed (Bass, 2006).

(Continued)

- In yet other cases, references to ethnic conflict are largely "fictional." In the absence of first-hand accounts, people's knowledge about ethnic conflict is conveyed by mainstream media, who perhaps unwittingly impose an ethnic-conflict spin in defining situations that may have little to do with ethnicity or conflict. Complex issues are framed into simple—even simplistic—formats that intensify North American stereotypes of tribal life as nasty, brutish, and short (Taras & Ganguly, 2002). The tendency to frame conflicts in ethnic terms—to ethnicize conflict by casting it as a conflict between ethnic groups—is not without consequences. Labelling these disputes as ethnic may legitimize and amplify the claims of ethnic militants by playing into the hands of those who have ethnicized the conflict in the first place. In other words, a heightened ethnicity may not cause conflict, but likely reflects its consequences (Taras & Ganguly, 2009).

Let's put all this into perspective: The phrase "ethnic conflict" is generally deployed in a descriptive and explanatory sense (Collier, 2007). As a description, it is unexceptional; as an explanation, it leaves much to be desired. Caution must be exercised in assuming that ethnic conflicts consist of "tribal" groups with uncontrollable instincts and insatiable urges to slaughter the demonized "other." Rather than spontaneous or irrational outbursts, although localized eruptions cannot be dismissed, ethnic conflicts often involve a calculated mayhem in the competition over identity, autonomy, or resources. Moreover, references to ethnic conflict may be misleading in yet another way: Instead of an entire ethnic group declaring a war against all, as implied by the term "ethnic conflict," hatred and conflict reflect the manipulations of a small cadre of calculating militants who claim to act on the group's behalf (Crawford, 2006).

The debunking of myths about ethnic(ized) conflict cannot come too soon if there is any hope of solving problems that many perceive as quintessential challenges to our existence. Ethnic conflicts are real enough; nevertheless, most conflicts involve an ethnic dimension that may camouflage broader issues pertaining to power and inequality. The question, then, is how and why do conflicts become ethnicized, especially in contexts involving competing yet legitimate claims to the same territory or valued resources? In that conflict appears to be an inescapable feature of the human species, particularly in those societies marked by shifting patterns of power and privilege, the challenge is before us. The solution is not in eliminating the "ethnicity" in ethnic conflict. The key to success is in guiding the "conflict" part into more constructive channels (Marger, 1997).

Chapter Highlights

- Ethnicity matters because it causes something to happen. Ethnicity represents a key variable in shaping people's identities, experiences, and outcomes. It also provides a framework that helps explain patterns of behaviour at individual and group levels.

- Ethnically diverse countries confront a challenge with respect to national identity and unity. Initiatives such as Canada's official Multiculturalism are best seen as moves to depoliticize ethnicity as a precondition for Canada-building.
- Ethnicity can be defined as a shared awareness of ancestral differences as a basis for community, identity, and activity. Both subjective experiences and objective properties are integral for mobilizing individuals into action groups.
- The surge in ethnicity can be explained by reference to primordial, constructivist, and instrumentalist approaches.
- Ethnicity is manifested in three ways: communities, identities, and activities.
- Ethnic identities can be expressed at the levels of lived, situational/symbolic, hybridic, transnational, and insurgent.
- In looking to make Canada safe *from* ethnicity and yet safe *for* ethnicity, official Multiculturalism provides a framework for depoliticizing ethnicity as a basis for living together with ethnic differences.
- Ethnic conflicts are often less about ethnicity and more about competition between leaders and groups over scarce resources in which ethnicity is manipulated to justify or mobilize.

For further study, you can access the Case Studies referenced in this chapter at **www.pearsoncanada.ca/fleras**.

Review Questions

1. Define ethnicity and demonstrate how and why both subjective and objective attributes should be part of the definition.
2. Two major approaches—primordial and constructivist—have historically been used to explain the ethnic surge. Compare how each frames the nature and extent of the ethnic experience.
3. Compare ethnic nationalism and civic nationalism as ideal types with respect to their underlying logic in creating a new society.
4. How is ethnicity expressed? Focus on the notions of community, identity, and activity.
5. What are the impact and implications for ethnicity in Canada's continuing efforts to make the country safe for ethnicity as well as safe from ethnicity?
6. Ethnicity is seen by sociologists as a key variable that accounts for patterns of human behaviour. Explain, with examples.

Links and Recommendations

FILMS

Israel and Palestine: 60 Years After on *The Agenda* with *Steve Paikin* (2007)

A four-part examination of the Israeli-Palestinian conflict that explores different perspectives on and dimensions of one of the world's most fiercely contested nationalisms, including both Palestinian and Israeli narratives.

Bollywood/Hollywood (2002), *Bend It Like Beckham (2002), and Monsoon Wedding* (2001)

These films, among others, capture some of the intergenerational ethnic tensions between children and parents.

The Point (2006)

A compelling National Film Board production that focuses on ethnically and racially diverse young adults as they try to make sense of one another and the sometimes chaotic and dangerous part of Montreal they inhabit. Think *Degrassi High* but outside the classroom.

BOOKS

The Chinese in Canada (2nd ed.), by Peter Li (1998). A useful overview of an ethnic minority that has experienced considerable hostility because of its racialized ethnicity.

Like Everyone Else . . . but Different: The Paradoxical Success of Canadian Jews, by Morton Weinfeld (2001). Weinfeld argues that the stealthy assimilation under an official Multiculturalism poses as grave a danger to Jewish ethnicity as blatant racial discrimination in the past.

The following books provide excellent insights into the micro-politics of identity that exist when young people need to walk the tightrope between "being here" and "over there":

Managing Two Worlds: The Experiences and Concerns of Immigrant Youth in Ontario, edited by Paul Anisef and Kenise Murphy Kilbride (2003).

Of Silk Saris and Mini Skirts: South Asian Girls Walk the Tightrope of Culture, by Amita Handa (2003).

JOURNAL

The fall 2005 issue of *Canadian Diversity* (vol. 4, no. 3) is devoted to *Negotiating Religious Pluralism: International Approaches*.

WEBSITES

Documentary videos of ethnic conflict in Sri Lanka, Darfur, Krygyzstan, Kenya, and other locations:

www.videosurf.com/videos/Ethnic+conflict

Canadian Ethnocultural Council:

www.ethnocultural.ca

Association for Canadian Studies—This site has numerous articles and research reports on ethnicity in Canada:

www.acs-aec.ca

Metropolis Canada—The Metropolis project is a global research "team" that explores issues of ethnicity and urbanization:

www.metropolis.net

CHAPTER 5

Racialized Inequality

Employment Equity: Less of a Solution or More of a Problem?

Canada is widely acclaimed as an egalitarian society whose commitment to inclusiveness is globally admired and occasionally emulated (Grabb & Guppy, 2010; McMullin, 2010). Yet Canada has proven a paradox in engaging diversity. Most major institutions are likely to have policies and programs in place to create a more inclusive environment. Both the federal public service and federally regulated institutions from banks to Crown corporations and telecommunications firms have incorporated inclusivity principles for doing business in the twenty-first century. Banks such as BMO, RBC, and CIBC have actively attracted and promoted a growing number of women and racialized minorities. Even the private sector is banking on inclusivity as a platform for attracting new talent and tapping into new markets.

But there is a less flattering narrative as well. However well intentioned, the results of this inclusivity push are modest at best, with many minorities continuing to experience workplace discrimination in terms of access, representation, and equity (Galabuzi, 2006; Toronto Board of Trade, 2010).

Both Aboriginal peoples and racialized minorities (including new Canadians) as a group tend to earn less, are underrepresented in higher management, gravitate toward the dirty, dull, and dangerous jobs ("precarious employment"), and experience an undervaluation of skills and credentials. To overcome this potentially embarrassing situation within the federal public service, the federal government's "Embracing Change" policy in 2002 stipulated a 20 percent target in the hiring, training, and promotion of racialized minorities. But as conveyed by the annual conference of the National Council of Visible Minorities in the Federal Public Service in 2009, modest improvements in the proportional representation of visible minorities does not match the rapid demographic changes in Canada (Xu, 2009).

In light of such discrepancies, several questions should immediately come to mind. How do we account for these disparities in a Canada committed to the principle of inclusivity? Is it because of personal failure by racialized minorities to take advantage of opportunities? Or is failure the result of opportunity structures that remain

(Continued)

closed to minority women and men—sometimes deliberately, other times systemically? What should be done to achieve a critical mass of minorities within the workforce?

The principles and practices of **employment equity** constitute Canada's response to this iniquitous state of affairs. With its commitment to improve minority access and representation at all levels, employment equity should be a proven winner in the accommodation sweepstakes. Yet few issues have elicited as much admiration or hostility. For some, this exercise in preferential hiring is nothing less than "reverse" discrimination against white males, creating more problems than it solves; for others, it is seen as a bold venture in **"reversing" discrimination**; for still others, it can take on different meanings—"reverse" or "reversing"—depending, of course, on the frame of reference. For still others, the true meaning of employment equity is not about placement or promotion. Rather, it symbolizes a litmus test for projecting onto the wider screen both the aspirations and anxieties of Canadians over core values and societal priorities under challenge in a changing world (see Harding, 2002).

Employment Equity as Philosophy

One way of cutting through this conceptual impasse is by making a key distinction: employment equity as a philosophy versus employment equity as official policy. Philosophically speaking, the concept of employment equity represents a commitment to equality through institutional inclusiveness. Even though workplace discrimination has been illegal since the early 1950s, the philosophy of employment equity is proactively aimed at assisting those historically disadvantaged minorities who find themselves excluded or underemployed through no fault of their own. According to the guiding principles of this philosophy, everybody should be treated equally and equitably, regardless of race, gender, ability, or ethnicity. Each person should be recruited, hired, promoted, trained, and rewarded on the basis of merit and credentials—assuming that the person is qualified for the available position. As a philosophy, then, employment equity embraces the following priorities:

• Ensure proportional representation of designated groups throughout all occupational and income levels at numbers consistent with their percentage in the regional workforce (Jain & Hackett, 1989). If discriminatory employment barriers did not exist, the argument goes, minority women and men would be evenly distributed along all occupational and income levels in accordance with their numbers in the population (allowing, of course, for individual choice and cultural differences, which may restrict occupational choices).

• Identify and remove employment practices that systematically or systemically discriminate against identifiable and devalued groups. Employment equity is premised on the belief that, left to their own, institutions will tend to reproduce discriminatory patterns unless an outside force is applied to break the circularity. Otherwise, like (males) will hire like (males) largely because it is easier and safer. Such institutional nepotism puts the onus on changing the hiring mindset to ensure that everyone is taken seriously as a candidate. But racially discriminatory barriers do not always arise from personal fear, ignorance, or self-interest. The hidden agendas and systemic biases within institutional structures are prime causes that may inadvertently distort the fairness of the recruitment, retention, and reward process.

- Acknowledge that true equality involves treating persons in the same way as a matter of course, but also differently through special measures when the situation arises. Employment equity is predicated on the premise that minorities suffer from a strict commitment to equal opportunity. The universality implicit in merit-based hiring penalizes minority women and men; after all, treating everyone the same when differences need to be taken into account penalizes those whose experiences, interests, and concerns fall outside the "white stream." Treating people alike in situations of inequality also has the negative effect of freezing the racialized status quo—in effect confirming the equity motto that treating people as equals may require treating them differently.

- Remedy adverse effects of past discrimination through positive programs that facilitate the entry, selection, promotion, and training of minorities. Race-conscious initiatives may be required on the assumption that racial problems respond

only to racial solutions, structural-problems to structural solutions, and institutional problems to institutional solutions.

- Ensure reasonable progress in meeting numerical targets and timetables as proof of a more inclusive workplace (Jain, 1988). The goal is to achieve a workplace environment where differences are seen as a natural and normal aspect as well as a legitimate and valued component of "how we do things around here."

Employment Equity as Policy

It is not that individuals in the designated groups are inherently unable to achieve equality on their own. It is that obstacles in their way are so formidable and self-perpetuating that they cannot be overcome without intervention. It is both intolerable and insensitive if we simply wait and hope that the barriers will disappear over time. Equality in employment will not happen unless we make it happen. (Judge Rosalie Silberman Abella, as cited in Abella, 1984)

It is generally accepted that most Canadians endorse the principle of inclusivity. To the extent that employment equity promotes inclusion to ensure that no one is excluded or denied because of who they are, it too is widely endorsed as part of Canada's multicultural commitments. Much more controversial is employment equity as policy or law. That is, while Canadians may be supportive of employment equity as a philosophy, they are much more agitated over employment equity as formal government intervention that many believe creates more harm than

(Continued)

benefits. Employment equity represents an official government policy with a corresponding set of programs for improving institutional accommodation of targeted minorities. In place since 1986 for the federally regulated private sector and updated in 1996 to include the federal public service, the *Employment Equity Act* was designed to achieve equality in the workplace by increasing the representation of members from the following designated groups: Aboriginal peoples, racialized (or "visible") minorities, persons with disabilities, and women (Statistical Analysis Unit, 2010). More specifically, the objective and mandate of the *Employment Equity Act* was highlighted in a background issues paper for reviewing the Act:

> The Act's original and continuing purpose is to achieve equality in federally regulated workplaces so that no person is denied employment opportunities for reasons other than their ability to do the job . . . to correct the conditions of disadvantage in employment experienced by visible minorities . . . [and] to develop an employment equity plan that would ensure reasonable progress toward full representation of these four groups. (Human Resources and Skills Development Canada, 2006, p. 2)

Terms of the Act apply to all federally regulated private-sector employers with 100 or more employees (banking), federal public services (Health Canada), public-sector companies (the RCMP), and Crown corporations. These companies are obligated to file and submit annual reports on the composition of their workforce to ensure appropriate levels of workplace representation, with particular reference to overall numbers and the type of work performed

by members from the four targeted groups. Federal contractors with at least 100 employees also fall under employment equity provisions. Each contractor must sign a certificate of compliance in accord with **equity** provisions if they intend to bid on government goods or services contracts worth $200 000 or more.

To put these objectives into practice, the Act instructs all employers to address four core obligations: (1) survey the workforce in terms of hires, occupation, salaries, promotion, retention; (2) analyze the under-representation of targeted minorities in each occupational group; (3) identify and remove employment barriers; and (4) introduce positive policies and programs to improve representation (hiring, training, promotion, retention) through reasonable accommodation. In contrast to America's Affirmative Action program, Canada's *Employment Equity Act* rejects the idea of government-mandated quotas and deadlines, including the idea of a rigid and externally imposed system of fixed percentages to be achieved within a certain timeframe to avoid penalty. Under Affirmative Action, American companies felt compelled to hire even unqualified personnel, if only to comply with the letter of the law, in order to circumvent penalties for compliance failure, or to secure government contracts. By contrast, goals under Canada's employment equity program are much more flexible as planning and evaluation tools, involving "reasonable expectations" about hiring and promotion of individuals from qualified groups when available for employment. In short, goals are preferred over quotas, timetables over deadlines, and reasonableness over ultimatums.

How should employment equity be assessed—as less of a solution or more of a problem? Just as Affirmative Action in the United States is subject to widespread controversy and backlash—many see it as unjustified and feel that it penalizes deserving whites (Sowell, 2004; Webb, 2010)—so too the *Employment Equity Act* in Canada triggers an avalanche of reactions, both supportive and dismissive. For supporters, employment equity is a first step in remedying past discrimination, eliminating discriminatory preferences and favouritism in hiring, and improving employment levels for the historically disadvantaged in the federal system (Public Service Alliance of Canada, 2010). For critics, employment equity is primarily a euphemism for reverse discrimination against white males that ultimately undermines the principle of meritocratic decision making (Loney, 1998).

Negative reaction to employment equity appears to vary along political lines. On the right, employment equity is criticized as a violation of (1) the principle of equality and **merit**, (2) principles of liberal universalism, and (3) the right of corporations to conduct business as they see fit. On the left, critics attack employment equity as a Band-Aid strategy that cannot address the root causes of unequal distribution. Passage of the Act may have sought to end workplace discrimination by improving minority recruitment and representation. Nevertheless, racialized groups and immigrants continue to confront numerous obstacles, including

a "revolving door" that makes entry and access difficult, a "sticky floor" that limits opportunities for initial advancement, and a "glass ceiling" that precludes achievement of senior positions (Conference Board of Canada, 2004).

In-between the "yeas" and the "nays" are those who agree with the intent of employment equity but express fears over backlash or unintended consequences, viewing it as a blunt instrument that homogenizes (essentializes) entire groups for policy purposes (Hum & Simpson, 2005). Many are puzzled by inherent inconsistencies as articulated below:

• Is employment equity about giving preferential treatment to minorities? Or is it about redesigning institutional criteria to provide minority women and men with the same opportunities as all Canadians?

• Is employment equity about changing the composition of the workforce by switching white incumbents for black and brown, or is it aimed at transforming the "business as usual" mindset to ensure the widest pool of applicants?

• Should employment equity be restricted only to the historically disadvantaged who have suffered decades of deprivation or exclusion? Or should it be directed at anyone who is poor or marginalized for reasons largely beyond their control?

• To what extent does employment equity help to right historical wrongs by "reversing" discrimination? Or is it really an exercise in political

(Continued)

correctness that—despite good intentions—discriminates against white males (reverse discrimination)?

- Does employment equity involve upholding the merit principle by ensuring the selection of qualified candidates regardless of race or ethnicity? Or does it violate the equality and fairness principle by privileging group entitlement and racial considerations over individual merit (Reyna, Korfmacher, & Henry, 2005; see also Calder & Ceva, 2011)? What exactly constitutes the concept of merit in the twenty-first century?

- Is it possible to create a better *Employment Equity Act* than the one in place? Can hiring exclusively on race grounds be eliminated by having employers acknowledge and take into account a person's race and ethnicity as a partial consideration in the hiring process (Jason Kenney, as cited in Friesen, 2010b).

The Debate Revisited box at the end of this chapter will address some of these issues by asking two questions: Is employment equity working? To what extent is it a form of reverse discrimination against white males?

INTRODUCTION: CANADA'S "RACIALIZED MOSAIC"

Canada cherishes its image as a fundamentally egalitarian society. Canadians like to see themselves as a predominantly "raceless" society that disdains the evils of prejudice, discrimination, and racism. There is some truth to this collective self-perception. Although it has yet to come to grips with its racist and exclusionary past, Canada has evolved into a mature and tolerant society with a powerful commitment to equality before the law, regardless of a person's background or beliefs. As aptly put by Irwin Cotler (2004):

> The test of a just society, a society organized around the principles of equality and human dignity, is how it treats the most vulnerable of its members—children, women, the elderly, the sick, refugees, minorities, and Aboriginals. We must aspire for a society in which no one is left behind, in which equality is not only an ideal but a constitutional norm, in which we extend a hand to those disadvantaged and discriminated against, in which we build bridges rather than erect walls in our multicultural mosaic.

Ideally, all the diversity tiles in Canada's multicultural "mosaic" are envisaged as contributing equally to the whole. Each component is also viewed as deserving of a fair share of the entitlements and rewards.

This bucolic portrayal is arguably true in a relative sense as well. But appearances are deceiving, despite the scale of inequities and exploitation elsewhere. Canada is more accurately portrayed as an unequal and stratified society—a racialized and "sticky" mosaic—with wealth concentrated in the hands of the few (Kunz, Milan, & Schetagne, 2001; Teelucksingh & Galabuzi, 2005). Income and opportunity gaps that privilege some while disempowering others have reinforced a pattern of racialized stratification that says a lot about the powers of self-deception. Racialized minorities continue to be stratified unequally against a vertical mosaic of raised (dominant) and lowered (subordinate) tiles (Porter, 1965; Public Service Alliance of Canada, 2010; Senate Standing Committee on Human Rights, 2010; Tepper, 1988). Pyramids of privilege exist that elevate the white "male stream" to the top of the heap and the racialized others to the bottom—often through no fault of their own. Neither Canada's official Multiculturalism nor its Employment Equity program have appreciably altered this arrangement, with some measures having had the somewhat perverse effect of perpetuating inequality. After all, as Canada becomes increasingly diverse, mainstream institutions are under increased pressure to standardize by adopting universal (that is, colour- and culture-blind) standards that transcend the claims of any one constituent group except, of course, that of the dominant group (Sowell, 2004).

In other words, all the deeply ingrained myths in the country cannot disguise the obvious: Canada remains a racially stratified society where differences because of race and ethnicity continue to make a difference in who gets what and how much (Block & Galabuzi, 2011; Nakhaie, 2007; Pendakur, 2005). Racism is a deeply embedded and defining characteristic of Canadian history despite a whitewashing over the stain (Backhouse, 1999). Some minorities do well because of, or in spite of, their race or ethnicity; others suffer and may never recover; and still others do not appear adversely affected one way or the other (Breton, Isajiw, Kalbach, & Reitz, 1990). This observation raises a number of questions for discussion and debate: What causes **racialized inequality**? Who is responsible—the victims or the system? Is it because of racism and racial discrimination, a lack of human capital (from education to work experience to language competence), or the play of market forces that limits economic opportunities (Reitz & Banerjee, 2007)? Is the problem attributable to minority cultures and values that discourage coping and success? Or should the finger be pointed at mainstream structures from social class to economic restructuring that, willfully or unintentionally, compromise minority life chances to the detriment of social justice and economic efficiency (Heath & Cheung, 2007; Yu & Heath, 2007)? Answers to these questions remain at the forefront of vigorous debate, with varied and contradictory responses reflecting different visions of race relations as fundamentally unequal relations (see online Case Study 5.1).

This chapter is predicated on the assumption that racialized inequalities are neither "natural" nor "healthy." On the contrary, they are highly toxic because of their corrosive effect in fraying the social fabric of society (Wilkinson, 2005). The devaluations and put-downs associated with low social status, dominance hierarchies, and dysfunctional communities can prove dangerously stressful, with devastating impacts on people's health and life chances. No less an indictment of inequality and its potentially negative effect on society is captured in this excerpt from a keynote address delivered by Kay McConney, Consul General of Barbados, at the recent Harry Jerome Awards in Toronto:

> The prosperity of Canada, this province, this city, are inextricably bound to the prosperity of its constituent communities. Should communities . . . be left behind in the margins of Canada's economic prosperity, then that prosperity that enfranchises only a few will not withstand the explosive anger of upheaval by the discontented masses. (cited in Editorial, 2005a)

This chapter draws on these themes by looking at the politics of racialized inequality in Canada. By exploring the inequitable relationship of racialized minorities to the distribution of valued resources, we see that inequality in Canada is not randomly distributed but shown to be stratified along racial lines (racialized stratification) and embedded within the broader institutional framework of society. These disparities are not simply the result of negative mindsets that are not amenable to reform; on the contrary, they are deeply embedded within the foundational principles of Canadian society (Galabuzi, 2006). Such a macro-perspective puts the onus on us to analyze how racialized inequities are created, expressed, and sustained, as well as challenged and transformed by way of government initiative, institutional reform, and minority assertiveness. Issues discussed include (1) the conceptualized racialized inequality, from a sociological perspective, (2) how this inequality is expressed within the contexts of power, politics, and structures, (3) why patterns of inequality persist, and (4) what can be done to reduce inequality to acceptable proportions.

The chapter begins by looking at the magnitude and scope of racialized inequality with respect to income, unemployment, and poverty. In exploring the causes, characteristics, and consequences of racialized stratification, the chapter demonstrates how discourses about inequality and equality are undergoing revision in response to social, political, and demographic changes. The chapter concludes by asking the inescapable question: What constitutes a just and equitable society—is it one that treats everyone the same regardless of differences? Or is it one that takes differences into account to ensure equality? Equal treatment or treatment as equals? Debates over employment equity as a philosophy and employment equity as a government program put these discursive dynamics to the test.

CONCEPTUALIZING ETHNIC INEQUALITY AS RACIALIZED STRATIFICATION

Canada's role in advancing multiculturalism and human rights deserves commendation. But national studies reinforce what many "intuitively" know: Not all Canadians are created equal when it comes to distributing the "goodies," with the result that Canada is characterized by layers of racialized inequality (Galabuzi, 2006). Race has long proven a key variable (predictor) in shaping unequal outcomes. First, racialized groups may be singled out as inferior or irrelevant, and dismissed accordingly. Second, racialized groups are criticized for embracing social patterns and cultural values that many see as disadvantaging in the competition for scarce resources. Finally, a racialized inequality acknowledges how inequities go beyond individual prejudice. They instead are embedded within the foundational principles and structures of society, including institutional levels, where hidden agendas and systemic biases are at play.

What is meant by inequality? What is the relation of inequality to stratification? Answers to these questions are critical; after all, the major theme that this book addresses is the notion that race relations are unequal relations, and that there is a corresponding need to understand their origins, expression, and maintenance, in addition to challenges and changes. At its simplest, inequality can be defined as a differential access to scarce resources, namely, power, privilege, and property, resulting in the uneven distribution of these valued resources across society. To the extent that sociologists are interested in inequality as a pattern of entitlement in defining who gets what and why, certain preconditions must apply. Sociological interest prevails when inequities are (1) pervasive and persistent, (2) patterned or clustered around certain groups, (3) harmful or exploitative, and (4) resistant to reform (Fleras, 2005).

The concept of stratification, with its notion of layers and strata, builds upon this idea of inequality. In general, stratification can be defined as a hierarchical ranking of groups of individuals in ascending and descending order, based on similar family background (the amount of power, privilege, and property, including income and assets) or similar relation to the means of production (class location as worker or manager or owner). These ranked differences in occupation or valued resources are not randomly distributed across the population. Nor are they of a transitory nature, that is, reflecting the "costs" of initial adjustment. These differences are patterned and pervasive insofar as they are socially significant, deeply embedded, and have proven difficult to dislodge. In terms of expression, stratification is most commonly manifested through social class, race and ethnicity, and gender, in addition to age and sexual preference. In acknowledging that society is stratified along racial (and ethnic) lines, the term **racialized stratification** is instructive in two ways: first, to hierarchical systems in which scarce resources are unequally distributed among diverse minority groups, who are disproportionately under-represented in terms of the "good things in life"; and second, to highly segmented systems involving minority groups' occupation of occupational statuses that reflect a racial(ized) division of labour (See & Wilson, 1988).

Sociological perspectives on racialized stratification vary widely. For some, inequality is a regrettable component of a modern complex system; for others, inequality is inevitable, but particularly in regimes that pivot around profit and private property. Many see inequality as the culmination of individual shortcomings; others blame inequality on structural barriers embedded in society. To what extent are ethnic inequities or intergroup tensions the result of race or class? For example, did nineteenth-century Chinese immigrants to Canada experience discriminatory exploitation because of pervasive "anti-Orientalism" (race)? Or did the mistreatment of the Chinese reflect their occupational status as essentially disposable and exploited labour for Canada-building purposes? Answers to these questions may be couched within the framework of two sociological theories of society, namely, *functionalism* and *conflict*, which offer differing analyses of the causes of racialized inequality.

Functionalist Perspectives

The existence of an economic division of labour is a starting point for functionalist models. For society to operate smoothly, functionalists argue, positions in the economic structure must be appropriately filled with suitable personnel. As these jobs differ in skill level and importance, people need to be rewarded appropriately for doing tasks of differing complexity. The occupational prestige hierarchy is the result of these differential rewards. Many accept as "natural" that physicians are compensated more for their services than plumbers, even though, arguably, both are crucial for our well-being (Davis & Moore, 1945). Leading sports figures are paid more than common labourers (in the United States, the average major league baseball player earned about US$3.3 million annually at the start of the 2010 season), while the average childcare worker earns minimum wage. This discrepancy arises not because one is more important to society. Salary and status gaps exist because certain skills are in short supply compared with the demand. Those high-powered skills that can generate more wealth for their owners are in shorter supply still, and, therefore, rewarded handsomely.

Functionalists distinguish "good" (functional) inequality from "bad" (dysfunctional) inequality. Inequality is "good" when achieved by the rules, that is, on the basis of merit, credentials, and equal opportunities; it is "bad" if unfairly acquired by excluding others because of irrelevant ascriptive attributes (such as race) outside a person's control. A commitment to "colour-blindness" is critical to the bottom line, as such a commitment can capitalize on the entire spectrum of brainpower for competing in a global market economy. To be sure, a degree of inequality is inevitable; after all, people are not equally endowed in the competition for scarce resources. Functionalists may accept the inevitability of innate differences, not necessarily in a racial way, but in terms of the skills an individual brings to the marketplace. For functionalists, then, inequality is necessary and desirable in a complex, merit-based, and openly competitive society.

Conflict Perspectives

Conflict theorists share with functionalists the view that complex societies are differentiated by inequality. They differ in their assessment of inequality as process and outcome. The inevitability of inequality—a basic tenet of functionalism—is anathema to conflict theory. For conflict theorists, society is envisaged as a site of inequality involving competitively different groups in a struggle for valued resources like power, privilege, and property. Society (including institutions, values, and relations) is designed and organized in a way that reflects, reinforces, and advances the interests and experiences of the rich and the powerful. Patterns of inequality are neither natural nor normal, but rather "naturalized" or "normalized" in those societies organized around the rational pursuit of profit. Inequities stem from the different class locations occupied by groups of people—owners versus workers—in relationship to the means of production. The ruling class does everything in its power to secure its power and privilege, including sowing the seeds of dissension to destabilize the working classes. The working classes, in turn, struggle to redefine the status quo with the resources at their disposal.

Class relations inform conflict theories of racialized inequality (Velez, 1998). The primacy of class is anchored in Marxist analysis of capitalist relations. Shared experiences notwithstanding, the working class is neither homogeneous in composition nor uniform in outlook. It is internally divided inasmuch as some workers are more exploited than others because of gender or race. White male workers are often better paid than non-white workers, while males in general earn more than females from all racialized groups. In addition to income differentials, males generally have access to more secure types of employment with greater opportunities for promotion and power. These class factions can also be manipulated to foster what Marx termed "false consciousness": Instead of directing their hostility at the source of their exploitation and domination (i.e., the capitalists), workers misplace their antagonism by scapegoating minorities. In other words, intergroup hostility is fostered by the ruling class to distract oppressed classes, mask the underlying relations of production, and conceal or mystify the primary source of exploitation. Fomenting racial prejudice and out-group hostility helps to perpetuate the status quo, prevents the formation of worker solidarity, improves capital formation, destabilizes countermovements, militates against the development of class consciousness, and justifies the exploitation of a cheap and disposable labour force by stigmatizing groups as inferior (Velez, 1998).

Under conflict models, the salience of race and ethnicity reflects their importance for capitalist relations of production. But the true source of racialized inequality is *not* race or ethnicity; rather, it's the logic of capitalist systems. Racial differences and confrontations are simply aspects of the wider struggle between classes. Minority concerns merely complicate the issue by distorting the reality of domination and cause of exploitation.

Thus, conflicts between racial groups are ultimately conflicts within and between classes—whether people are aware of it or not (see Farley, 2005). In that this text begins with the premise that race, ethnic, and Aboriginal relations are essentially unequal relations, a conflict perspective provides a richer insight into how these racialized inequalities are constructed and maintained or challenged and changed. Moreover, in contrast to functionalist models of social reality that tend to blame the victim (racialized minorities) for their difficulties, a conflict perspective puts the onus on the system. The debate over functionalism versus conflict theories will be further explored in later in the chapter, in the section "Explaining the Disparities."

RACIALIZED INEQUALITY IN CANADA

Canada takes pride in its reputation as a colour-blind society in which no one is denied or excluded because of race or ethnicity. As a society that endorses a merit-based system of rewards, Canada likes to consider itself open and tolerant, with equal opportunity for all regardless of who they are. But repeated references to Canada as multicultural and egalitarian have not translated into equal outcomes across the board when measured by statistical indicators such as income, unemployment, or poverty rates (Block & Galabuzi, 2011). Canada remains highly stratified along racial(ized) lines, with race continuing to matter, even though Canadians should know better. Moreover, despite claims to the contrary, the gap between the haves and have-nots is widening, becoming increasingly racialized and gendered, and appears more impervious to reform because of its embeddedness in society (Block, 2010; Pendakur & Pendakur, 2010; Teelucksingh & Galabuzi, 2005;). Nowhere is this more evident than at the level of income, employment/ unemployment, and poverty.

Income Differences

Inequality remains a fact of life in Canadian society when assessed by income differences (Pendakur & Pendakur, 2010). Income measures have historically been used to gauge inequality between groups—that is, to determine if there is labour market discrimination—by comparing the annual earnings of racialized minorities with those of white Canadians. Admittedly, income as a measure of inequality may conceal as much as it reveals (Hum & Simpson, 2000). Internal variations within the category of racialized minorities are glossed over (Pendakur, 2005). Averages don't tell the story of the range of disparities between the richest and the poorest. Nor does reference to annual wages provide insight into the number of hours that people have worked over the year. Inequities pertaining to power and privilege are ignored, as are those pertaining to ownership of wealth or assets in breaking the cycle of poverty (Shapiro, 2004). Important variables that account for the disparities may be excluded as well, including gender, place of birth, length of stay in Canada, levels of work experience, educational levels, language competence, and sample size (see Statistics Canada, 2007). Still, in the absence of more measurable indicators, income differences remain the index of choice for measuring inequality.

Consider the results of a recent Statistics Canada study, presented in Table 5-1, that looks at average employment income, visibility of Canadians (racialized versus all Canadians), and gender and age.

TABLE 5-1	Income, Visibility, Gender, and Age, 2000			
	Racialized minorities		All Canadians	
Age of persons*	Men	Women	Men	Women
15–24	$22 394	$20 707	$23 696	$19 634
25–44	$41 638	$32 462	$47 611	$35 048
45–64	$46 626	$33 664	$55 754	$37 407
65 and over	$41 568	$23 663	$44 661	$28 171
All over 14	$42 377	$32 143	$49 224	$34 892

*Includes only those in full-time, full-year employment
Source: Statistics Canada (2003).

According to the data in Table 5-1 (Statistics Canada, 2003), generalized patterns can be detected. Racialized women do more poorly than women in general and racialized men; racialized men do less well than men at all age levels; and older males and females, except for those in the retirement bracket, generally outperform younger men and women. Other studies indicate that race matters: Canadian-born blacks face a statistically significant wage gap, once other variables such as education are controlled (Hum & Simpson, 2000; Jedwab, 2004), earning about 69 percent of what whites earn, compared with blacks in the United States, who earn about 60 percent of white wages. And in a 2007 essay by Jeffrey Reitz and Rupa Banerjee, it was reported that the wage gap between whites and visible minorities was $9581 (whites were $1895 above the local average, whereas visible minorities were $7686 below the local average). House-hold incomes for most racialized groups were substantially below that of white households (see online Case Study 5.2).

Yet there are dangers in making such simple income comparisons. Such studies are incomplete—perhaps even misleading—because they lump all racialized minorities into a single category without distinguishing those born in Canada from those who are foreign-born (Hum & Simpson, 2000). Consider how an important study by Jean Lock Kunz and associates (2001) for the Canadian Race Relations Foundation focused on the earning disparities between white people (or non-racialized groups) and visible minorities (racialized groups) with regard to average annual income, gender, and immigrant status (foreign-born), as set out in Table 5-2. While this is more helpful, a failure to distinguish between recent immigrants (those here less than five years) and more established immigrants underscores the limitations of the study.

The table clearly demonstrates how labour market disadvantages exist for racialized immigrants (see also Alboim & McIsaac, 2007; Hum & Simpson, 2000). Canadian-born men, both racialized and non-racialized, outperform foreign-born racialized males but not foreign-born whites. Men across all categories do better than women, regardless of visibility and place of birth, whereas Aboriginal peoples rank at the bottom for both genders. With few exceptions, foreign-born visible minorities and Aboriginal peoples are underperforming in relation to the other categories—in the process reinforcing refer-ences to Canada as a racialized mosaic. Paradoxically, higher education levels may not improve income levels. Racialized immigrants have generally higher levels of education

TABLE 5-2	**Earnings* by Gender, Racialization, and Place of Birth**		
	Male	Female	Average
Racialized minority (CB)	$42 433	$33 519	$38 582
Racialized minority (FB)	$35 329	$27 075	$31 829
Whites (CB)	$43 456	$31 150	$38 529
Whites (FB)	$46 457	$31 627	$40 854
Aboriginal peoples	$32 369	$26 361	$29 290

* Full-time, full-year earnings for those aged 25 to 64.

CB = Canadian born

FB = Foreign born

Sources: Adapted from Kunz et al. (2001); 1996 Census, Public Use Microdata File.

than whites or Aboriginal peoples (but a larger percentage also possess less than a Grade 8 education), yet they tend to trail behind Canadian-born white people and minorities with regard to employment, income, and access to professional/managerial jobs (Kunz et al., 2001; Picot & Coulombe, 2007).

Among immigrants, there is an unexplained wage gap (Statistics Canada, 2007; Walters, Phythian, & Anisef, 2006). Immigrants appear to be losing ground in the income-earning sweepstakes both in initial income and income earnings over time. In 1980, according to Statistics Canada data, male and female immigrants who had lived in Canada for ten years earned about the same as Canadian-born workers. In 2000, immigrants who had resided in Canada for ten years were making much less than Canadian-born workers. A male immigrant's earnings as a percentage of earnings of a Canadian-born male had dropped to 79.8 percent, while a female immigrant's earnings fell to 87.3 percent. Recent data seem to support these figures, especially if distinguishing recent immigrants (in Canada for less than five years) from more established immigrants. According to the 2006 Census data issued by Statistics Canada (2008), in 1980, recent immigrant males with some employment income earned 85 percent of what their Canadian-born counterparts earned; by 2005, that figure had dropped to 63 percent. For recent immigrant women, the figures are even more pronounced, plummeting from 85 percent in 1980 to 56 percent in 2005. Nor does possessing a university degree make much difference: As shown in Table 5-3, in 2005 recent immigrant men with degrees earned 48 percent of their educated Canadian-born counterparts, whereas recent immigrant women with degrees earned 42 percent of what was earned by Canadian-born women with degrees (Perkel, 2008).

Finally, gender matters as well. As Tables 5-1 to 5-3 indicate, minority women (including racialized women, immigrant women, and Aboriginal women) earn significantly less than all men and white women. But a 2007 Statistics Canada study uncovered income disparities that shifted over time. Canadian-born daughters of visible minority immigrants performed better than daughters of Canadian-born parents. By contrast, Canadian-born males of visible minority immigrant parents earned 38 percent less in their first working years than all other young men. According to a *Toronto Star* editorial (Editorial, 2008), this earning gap cannot be attributed to language differences or

TABLE 5-3 **Earnings by Place of Birth, Education**		
	1980	**2005**
Recent immigrant males with university degrees	$48 581	$30 332
Canadian-born males with university degrees	$63 040	$62 556
Recent immigrant females with university degrees	$24 317	$18 969
Canadian-born females with university degrees	$41 241	$44 545
Source: Statistics Canada (2008). Median Earnings, using 2005 constant dollars for full-time wage earners (self-employed individuals excluded).		

unrecognized credentials since all males were born and raised in Canada (see also Halli-Vedanand, 2007).

In short, racialized immigrants start with a distinct earning disadvantage relative to the Canadian-born, a gap that admittedly narrows over time. But in recent years this initial earning gap has widened and the catch-up rate is slower. How do we account for this growing disparity? Barriers persist in converting international credentials and expertise into comparable occupational status and compensation in Canada (Teelucksingh & Galabuzi, 2005). Human capital skills do not transfer well and are discounted once in Canada, with the result that one year of overseas experience is deemed equivalent to one-third of a year of domestic experience, while foreign education is worth about 75 percent of a comparable education for a Canadian-born person (Finnie & Meng, 2002). Others suggest a three-fold factor in the earning gaps: (1) a shift in source countries since the 1960s that has enhanced the potential for prejudicial discrimination and concerns over language competence; (2) declining returns to foreign work experiences and educational levels among non-European immigrants; and (3) a general dip in labour market outcomes for new labour entrants, whereby immigrants are treated as new entrants in competition with a growing pool of Canadian graduates (Aydemir & Skuterud, 2004; Statistics Canada, 2006).

Employment/Unemployment

Another key indicator of racialized stratification entails levels of unemployment. Generally speaking, both racialized and recently arrived immigrants tend to be more unemployed than non-racialized immigrants who have been here longer. Consider the results from a recent Statistics Canada study, presented in Table 5-4.

The figures nearly speak for themselves. Compared to others, immigrants from Europe and the United States are less likely to be unemployed. According to Queen's University professor Charles Beach (2008), European immigrants are less likely to be subject to discrimination, whereas immigrants from "non-conventional sources" are perceived to lack the education, workplace experience, and language skills to mesh

TABLE 5-4	Unemployment Rates for Immigrants Aged 25 to 54 by Region of Birth and Landing Period, 2006	
Average unemployment rate for Canadian-born persons		4.9%
Average unemployment rate for Latin Americans:		
	Those who arrived between 2001 and 2006	10.5%
	1996 and 2005	6.5%
	Before 1996	6.1%
Average unemployment rate for African immigrants:		
	2001–2006	20.8%
	1996–2006	13.6%
	Before 1996	7.6%
Average unemployment rate for Asian immigrants:		
	2001–2006	11.1%
	1996–2001	7.3%
	Before 1996	5.5%
Average unemployment rate for European immigrants:		
	2001–2006	8.4%
	1996–2001	5.1%
	Before 1996	4.0%
Average unemployment rate for North American immigrants:		
	Before 1996	2.8%
	(other figures not available)	
Source: Statistics Canada (2008).		

smoothly into the labour market. Europeans who arrived before 1996 are also less unemployed than the national average, reflecting a pattern of greater adaptability as time goes on. Interestingly, immigrants born in Southeast Asia—particularly those from the Philippines—had the strongest labour market performance of all immigrants to Canada, regardless of when they landed, including rates comparable to Canadian-born workers (Keung, 2008; Statistics Canada, 2008). Their extended exposure to colonial domination may have predisposed them to Western language and culture (Beach, 2008).

Patterns of employment are no less ambiguous. Many university-educated immigrants fail to land employment consistent with their credentials or expertise, although 80 percent of new Canadians between the ages of 25 and 44 had found at least one job within two years of arrival in Canada. Among those that do, however, 60 percent end up working in areas other than those in which they are qualified (Statistics Canada, 2008). Failure to translate overseas work experience and educational qualifications into Canadian equivalents reflects bottlenecks in the licensing and accreditation process, a resistance to hiring those with international credentials, and an insistence on Canadian experience even when not job related (Galabuzi, 2006).

Racializing Poverty

Poverty in Canada is becoming increasingly racialized (Wallis & Kwok, 2008). That is, patterns of poverty are neither colour-blind nor randomly distributed across all Canadians, but clustered around certain historically disadvantaged minorities (Galabuzi, 2006; Picot & Coulombe, 2007). A study by Statistics Canada demonstrated how in 2000 the low-income cut-off line (poverty rate) for new Canadians stood at 35.8 percent, an increase from 24.6 percent in 1980, and more than twice the average for Canadian-born families (Dunphy, 2003). According to Statistics Canada (2003), immigrants' experience with low-income rates ("poverty") correlates with the number of years in Canada. In 2001, the low-income rate for Canadian-born persons was 16 percent: for those in Canada for 0–5 years, 37 percent; 6–10 years, 30 percent; and 11–15 years, 24 percent. Reinforcing this trajectory was a Statistics Canada (2007) study: In 2004, low-income rates for immigrants during their first year in Canada were 3.2 times higher than for Canadian-born persons—despite increased levels of education attainment among immigrants and a shift toward increasingly skilled immigration (Picot & Coulombe, 2007). Not surprisingly, concluded the Ontario Hunger Report by the province's food bank association, new Canadians accounted for nearly one-third of the 320 000 Ontario residents who depended on food banks every month—an increase of 14 percent since 2001—many of whom could not find affordable housing or access to well-paying jobs, despite the province's then booming economy (Canadian Press, 2007b).

These results are dismaying against the backdrop of Canada's commitment to an egalitarian society. According to the Colour of Poverty Campaign (2007), racialized minorities are experiencing disproportionately high levels of poverty, including 43 percent of children in Ontario living in poverty, in part because of racial barriers in finding and keeping jobs. Another study by Michael Ornstein (2006), based on racial and ethnic groups in Toronto, found that the 20 poorest groups were non-Europeans, with Somali, Afghan, and Ethiopian groups displaying poverty rates of over 50 percent. No less disturbing is the feminization of poverty. The 2005 Statistics Canada report "Women in Canada" indicated that poverty informed the lives of 28.8 percent of visible minority women in Canada, including those under the age of 15 at 33.8 percent living in poverty, compared with women in the general population at 15.9 percent. The poverty gap can be attributed to various reasons, including (1) racial discrimination; (2) discounting of education credentials and overseas experience; (3) increased competition with the educational credentials of the Canadian-born; (4) the shift in immigration sources; (5) a generally tightened labour market, especially for entry-level jobs; and (6) an immigration system that permits many to bypass the point system for identifying applicants with job-related skills (Grubel, 2005).

EXPLAINING THE DISPARITIES

Two theoretical perspectives provide an explanatory framework for ethnic inequality and racialized stratification. Whereas functionalists tend to blame inequality on ethnicity and individual shortcomings (the ethnicity paradigm), conflict models see the problem as more deeply embedded within institutional and opportunity structures (the equity paradigm).

Ethnicity Paradigm

A generation ago, references to racial(ized) stratification were couched within the discursive framework of an ethnicity paradigm (Fleras, 1993). Canadian society was envisaged as an open and competitive marketplace in which individuals competed as equals and were rewarded because of their skills or production. Individual success or failure reflected a person's level of human capital: Those with training, skills, and education succeeded; those without, did not. Ethnic differences were pivotal. On one side, ethnic minorities had to discard the debilitating aspects of their ethnicity that precluded participation. On the other side, those in charge also had to discard those prejudgments that precluded inclusiveness. Inception of a Multiculturalism policy in 1971 sought to diversify the workplace by ensuring that people's differences did not get in the way of who got what. It also sought to depoliticize ethnicity by eliminating its salience as a basis for public recognition and reward.

According to functionalist perspectives, the failure of minorities to penetrate the market may reflect a lack of expertise or credentials. Efforts to boost their "human capital" would focus on improving minority "skills" consistent with competitive labour force needs. Ethno-cultural deficits are no less a deterrent to minority success. As John Porter argued in his landmark book, *The Vertical Mosaic*, in 1965, ethnicity represented a key variable in predicting patterns of success, with non-British and non-French ethnic groups at the bottom of a vertical ranking (see also Breton et al., 1990; Helmes-Hayes & Curtis, 1998). Of particular relevance for Porter were those cultural values—from a lack of work ethic to kinship obligations—at odds with upward mobility and occupational performance. Clearly, becoming modern was key. To secure success, racialized minorities had to discard their unmodern ethnicity and assimilate by embracing modernist values, even if doing so could risk alienation from a supportive community of like-minded kin (Porter called this dilemma the *ethnic mobility trap*).

The Equity Paradigm

The concept of inequality underwent a shift in emphasis from the 1980s onward (Agocs & Boyd, 1993). It had become evident that the attainment of formal equality rights failed to generate an increased equality of outcome that many had anticipated (see also Squires, 2007a). Awareness also shifted from a focus on individual attributes such as prejudice and ethnicity as the source of the problem to a growing concern with discriminatory barriers and racism. This cognitive shift was driven by a concomitant increase in immigrants from developing countries. Multicultural commitments that focused on ethnicity no longer resonated with the language of relevance. Proposed instead were new equity discourses based on the principle of institutional inclusion, removal of discriminatory barriers at structural levels, and eradication of racism that precluded full and equal participation. (See also Chapter 10 on ethnicity versus equity multiculturalism.) References to inequality shifted accordingly in their focus—from individuals to structure, from ethnicity to race, from equality of opportunity to equal outcomes, and from a commitment to formal (abstract) equality to that of **substantive equality (equity)**—as shown below in Table 5-5.

TABLE 5-5	Explaining Racialized Inequality: Ethnicity versus Equity Paradigms	
	The ethnicity paradigm	**The equity paradigm**
Problem	Individuals "blaming the victim"	Institutional structures "blaming the system"
Root cause	Ethnicity	Discriminatory barriers
Focus of solution	Increase human capital	Improve institutional inclusiveness
Means of solution	Market forces	Government intervention
Sociological perspective	Functionalism	Conflict perspectives

In contrast to the once-dominant ethnicity paradigm, the equity paradigm emphasizes the bigger picture. According to an equity paradigm as an explanatory framework, the problem is not about individuals or attitudes per se. Rather, the source of the problem is embedded in the institutional *structures* of society. Inequality and barriers to advancement reflect structural constraints that were largely systemic in advancing "pale male" interests. That is, while the system pretends to be value-neutral under the guise of universality and colour-blindness, the very notion of a level playing field is discriminatory, because it puts racialized minorities at a structural disadvantage by treating them the same as dominant group members. In applying the metaphor of a competitive footrace with staggered starting blocks, it was obvious that not all contestants were equally positioned to compete in the labour market. The race was rigged because of ascribed characteristics that handicapped some because of skin colour or gender, while privileging others for precisely the same reasons. In short, the onus lay on the government to remove discriminatory barriers through legislation to create a more level playing field.

TOWARD EQUALITY

That most minorities aspire to social and economic equality is surely beyond dispute or debate. Many Canadians would also agree that equality is to be preferred over an inequality that is unfairly achieved. But the concept of "equality" is itself subject to diverse interpretations: as sameness, as proportional equivalence, and as equity (or substantive). For some, equality is synonymous with sameness—everyone is treated the same regardless of background or circumstances, because true equality is based on acknowledging our common humanity. No one is explicitly accorded special privileges in a market system designed around the principles of equal opportunity, equality before the law, and credential-based merit. For others, equality is used in the sense of numerical, or "proportional," equivalence. Under systems of preferential hiring and promotion, each group is allocated positions according to their numbers in society or the workforce. For yet others, the concept of equality is aimed at the principle of equity. References to equality as equity acknowledge the need to take seriously difference-based disadvantages. The unique circumstances of a person or group are taken into account to ensure "customized" treatment by way of institutional adjustments. Emphasis is on the attainment of equal outcomes (or conditions) rather than the abstract principle of equal opportunity.

Consider, for example, the so-called special treatment accorded to individuals with disabilities. Concessions such as wheelchair ramps, closed-caption TV, and designated parking spots can hardly be thought of as special or preferential. On the contrary, removing disability barriers ensures equality of opportunity by providing reasonable accommodation. Likewise, historically disadvantaged minorities with racially prescribed characteristics will encounter barriers as real and as debilitating as physical impediments. But just as building ramps for the wheelchair bound creates a more level playing field, so too does a similar logic apply to racialized minorities. In both cases, those with socially defined disabilities require different treatment, if only to ensure their right to equality of opportunity. A commitment to "reversing" discrimination by way of "customized" treatment makes it doubly important to treat unequals differently. To do otherwise, that is, treat everyone the same in contexts of inequality, perpetuates the prevailing distribution of power, privilege, and resources.

Each of these perspectives on equality differs from the other in terms of objectives and scope. **Formal equality** is concerned with mathematical equivalence and a market-driven means for establishing who gets what. Any criterion that rewards individuals on grounds other than merit or competition is criticized as unfair or counterproductive. More substantive versions of equality (or equity) disagree. Equity-based equality argues that seemingly neutral rules applied evenly and equally may exert an adverse, if unintended, impact on certain minority groups. A one-size-fits-all mentality can produce unequal results and perpetuate group-based inequities, according to the Ontario Human Rights Commission annual reports, especially when everyone is treated as asexual, deracialized, and classless, without a history or context for purposes of reward (McIntyre, 1993). Strict and equal application of a seemingly neutral rule or standard (which in fact reflects and reinforces deeply embedded majority worldviews and values) may infringe on a person's right to true equality. Insofar as treating everyone the same regardless of circumstances is not equality but the privileging of a racialized and unequal status quo, social policies must be judged by the actual effect they exert rather than by strict adherence to abstract legal principles (Cohen, 1999).

The distinction between equality and equity is captured by the debate over equivalence-based equality versus equity-based equality (see Table 5-6). An equivalence equality focuses on the rights of individuals to be free from discrimination when competing for the good things in life. By contrast, an equity equality concentrates on the rights of historically disadvantaged individuals to a fair and equitable share of the goods

TABLE 5-6	Comparing Equality Paradigms	
Equivalence-based equality	**Equity-based equality**
Formal (abstract and mathematical equivalent)	Substantive (context and consequences)
Everyone should be treated equally (the same)	People should be treated as equals (differently)
Pretend pluralism	Taking differences seriously/into account
Same treatment as a matter of course	Customized treatment when situation arises
Equal opportunity	Equitable outcomes
Discipline of the market	Government intervention

and services. While a commitment to equivalence equality openly advocates competition, inequality, and hierarchy as a natural and healthy way of allocating rewards and entitlements, an equity equality is concerned with controlled distribution and egalitarian outcomes for members of disadvantaged groups. This perspective recognizes the need for collective considerations over individual rights when the situation demands it. It also endorses the principle of social intervention for true equality, as equal outcomes are unlikely under competitive market forces. Finally, it embraces the inclusionary principle of a liberal universalism: that people should be treated the same ("equally"), despite their differences, as a matter of course, yet be treated as equals ("differently"), through accommodation of their differences, when the situation demands it.

Which version of equality should prevail? Is one more important than the other, or is it a case of one serving as a necessary, if insufficient, precondition for the other? By itself, the principle of equal opportunity structures cannot overcome the debilitating effects of systemic discrimination and institutional racism. For true equality to take root, additional measures are required over and above those available to the general population. Context and consequences are as important as abstract principles in righting the wrongs. Taking context into consideration may justify differential treatment in some cases, to achieve an equality of outcome. Taking consequences into account suggests that focusing on the effects of even well-intentioned programs in fostering equality is more important than their intent or awareness. The unintended consequences of even seemingly neutral practices may lead to the exclusion of qualified personnel, regardless of motive or consciousness.

In short, equity-based equality hinges on a key principle: Treating everyone the same is not equality or justice. References to equal opportunity may sound good in theory but rarely stand up to scrutiny when the playing field is tilted, the game is rigged, and the rules are always changing. What is required is a commitment to an equity-based equality, one that recognizes the need to take differences seriously. To be sure, an equity equality is not opposed to equal opportunities in defining equality. On the contrary, it acknowledges a commitment to the principle of equal opportunity as a preliminary step in overcoming entrenched racism and discrimination. But ultimately such a commitment cannot achieve a fair and just equality in deeply racialized contexts. Only a dual commitment to equitable outcomes and equal opportunities can create a substantive equality. To what extent, then, does employment equity help or hinder the achievement of equality and equity?

DEBATE REVISITED

Is Employment Equity Working?

Canada's Employment Equity program is predicated on a singular principle: to create institutional inclusiveness and equality by removing discriminatory barriers that impede the recruitment and representation of racialized minorities and Aboriginal peoples at all organizational levels.

The numbers suggest that employment equity is working. In the federally regulated private sector, the representation of racialized employees exceeds labour market availability, although gaps persist for Aboriginal peoples. Based on percentage representation in the workforce, the percentage of Aboriginal peoples in the federally regulated private sector increased from 1.6 percent in 2001 to 1.9 percent in 2007. In 1987, the figure stood at 0.7 percent. Employment of visible minorities grew from 11.8 percent in 2001 to 15.9 percent in 2007, compared with a base of 5 percent in 1987. Conversely, in the federal public service, the percentage of Aboriginal peoples exceeds labour market availability, in contrast to the under-representation of visible minorities (Public Service Alliance of Canada, 2010).

In the federal public sector, racialized minorities made up 10.8 percent of all personnel in 2007, compared with 2.8 percent in 1987. Aboriginal peoples represented 3.7 percent of the federal public service in 2007. When figures for the federally regulated private sector and the federal public sector are combined, racialized minorities account for 13.1 percent of the workforce, while Aboriginal peoples account for 2.6 percent (Public Service Alliance of Canada, 2010). The most recent data show a slight decrease in the number of racialized minorities in federal public service, in contrast to a slight increase in Aboriginal representation in this area (Canadian Press, 2010; Treasury Board of Canada, 2010). Nevertheless, the numbers can be misleading. Despite their seeming over-representation in the federal public service, Aboriginal peoples tended to be excluded at the executive and higher management levels; they tended to be clustered in certain jobs (technical and operational categories) and in four departments; their salaries on average were lower than those for the entire public service; and their rate of job separation is higher than their hiring rate (Public Service Alliance of Canada, 2010; Senate Standing Committee on Human Rights, 2010).

The gap in the representation of Aboriginal peoples and visible minorities in the workforce has narrowed over the last 20 years, so that both groups are better represented in the labour market than in the past (Statistical Analysis Unit, 2010). But critics counterargue that the numbers are deceiving, because advances for some have come at the expense of others. In replacing one form of discrimination with another, employment equity initiatives are less about removing discriminatory barriers than about displacing white men with quotas of racialized minorities and Aboriginal peoples (Loney, 1998). By encouraging a so-called reverse discrimination, employment equity programs come under criticism for discriminating against white, able-bodied males—either deliberately or through the unintended consequences of initiatives whose inadvertent effect is to exclude whiteness and maleness from the exercising of rights. It is unfair to discriminate against minorities, critics say, but it is just as wrong to give preference to minorities by unfairly penalizing whites. All distinctions based on race, gender, or ethnicity are discriminatory and wrong, according to this line of thinking, especially when this exercise in social engineering is little more than government-endorsed discrimination under the guise of fairness or equity.

(Continued)

Others disagree: Reference to context and consequences is important in evaluating employment equity. In opposition to those who believe that no Canadian should be barred from employment because of race or ethnicity, others argue that those who once were excluded because of race require a race-based solution to level the playing field (Stockwell Day in Friesen, 2010b). Admittedly, equity measures that seemingly privilege race over merit may appear like reverse discrimination; they seem to discriminate against whites, while securing preference for equity target groups. In reality, however, employment equity is aimed at "reversing" discrimination through the removal of discriminatory barriers, thereby expanding the pool of formerly excluded but qualified applicants. Instead of explicitly excluding "pale males" from the competition—although the unintended consequences (or collateral damage) of doing so are inevitable when someone has to move over and make space—a commitment to "reversing" discrimination fosters a workplace dynamic that is both inclusive and equitable, as well as progressive and productive. In other words, appearances are deceiving because words like "discrimination" do not always mean what they seem to. In the final analysis, a discrimination aimed at removing (or reversing) exclusion in order to foster inclusiveness differs sharply from a discrimination that

excludes by reinforcing a racialized status quo.

Regardless, employment equity remains a highly contested site. A clash of values is inescapable: On one side, employment equity appears to be consistent with core Canadian values related to justice, equity, and inclusiveness as this applies to the needs of historically disadvantaged minorities. On the other side, however, Canadians also put a premium on the principles of merit, formal equality before the law, and individualism. Thus, references to employment equity that assign a value to colour, race, or gender as grounds for entitlement are likely to elicit strong reaction from those who dismiss the relevance of race and gender in determining who gets what in a merit-driven, colour-blind society (Jason Kenney as cited in Friesen, 2010b). Not surprisingly, employment equity has evolved into a kind of litmus test for debating the kind of Canada Canadians want to see: namely, one that treats everyone equally (or the same) regardless of who they are (equality principle) or one that treats people as equals (equity principle) by taking into account their disadvantages and differences (see Harding, 2002). This "culture" clash may also explain why employment equity is seen by some as a solution to a problem (reversing discrimination) yet rejected by others as creating more problems (reverse discrimination) than it's worth.

Chapter Highlights

- The relationship between inequality and racialized minority groups is a complex and evolving one, but generally speaking, Canada remains stratified by race and ethnicity, judging by persistent gaps in income, employment, and poverty levels.

- Functionalists tend to see ethnic inequality as necessary and normal in a complex society. Conflict theorists prefer to think of inequality as inevitable only in securing the foundations of exploitative societies.
- The notion of racialized inequality is currently under reconsideration. The emphasis on ethnocultural differences and individual attitudes as the source of the problem (the ethnicity paradigm) is shifting toward structural factors as they relate to institutional rules, processes, and outcomes (the equity paradigm). With the emergence of the equity paradigm, the focus on structures as the problem has altered government solutions, with growing emphasis on institutional inclusion through removal of discriminatory barriers. The concept of equality has shifted as well, resulting in two competing models, namely, equivalence-based equality (treating everyone the same) and equity-based equality (treating people as equals by taking differences and context into account).
- Employment equity can be interpreted as a solution to the structural problem of inequality. A distinction needs to be made between employment equity as a principle (which many accept) and its application as a government program (which many reject).

For further study, you can access the Case Studies referenced in this chapter at **www.pearsoncanada.ca/fleras**.

Review Questions

1. How would you explain the kinds of income differences that characterize race and ethnic minorities in Canada? Compare and contrast the approaches of conflict versus functionalist theory as a means for explaining inequality and social stratification.

2. How would functionalists and conflict theorists align themselves in defending or criticizing Canada's *Employment Equity Act*?

3. Our thinking on inequality has evolved in recent years. The equity paradigm is replacing the ethnicity paradigm as an explanatory model. Explain how and why.

4. The concept of equality can mean different things. Discuss the different meanings of equality as they pertain to race and ethnicity.

5. An American literary critic has posed an interesting question: White people once set themselves apart from minorities and claimed privileges while denying them to others because of race or colour. Now, on the basis of race and employment equity, people of colour are claiming special status and reserving for themselves privileges that they deny to others. Not surprisingly, employment equity has been described as both "reverse" discrimination as well as a case of "reversing" discrimination. Expand on this idea by focusing on whether employment equity promotes racial equality through increased minority representation (reversing discrimination) or promotes artificial quotas and political correctness at the expense of merit, fairness, and qualifications (reverse discrimination).

Links and Recommendations

BOOKS

Theories of Social Inequality (5th ed.), by Edward Grab (2007). A useful introduction to classic theories of social inequality.

Social Inequality in Canada. Problems, Perspectives, by Edward Grab and Neil Guppy (2009). A reader with many useful articles written expressly for this volume and covering a broad range of topics.

Race, Class, and Gender (6th ed.), by Margaret Andersen and Patricia Collins (2006). An insightful anthology of key writings on the relationship of race and class (and gender) (mostly American sources).

Race and Ethnic Relations in Canada (2nd ed.), by Peter Li (1999). Contains many excellent articles on inequality and race.

WEBSITES

Metropolis Canada—The Metropolis site is excellent and covers material on immigration and inequality:
www.metropolis.net

The Fraser Institute—The Institute provides an often different slant on economic inequality and diversity in Canada:
www.fraserinstitute.org

The Canadian Centre for Policy Alternatives—It publishes numerous reports that analyze patterns of inequality in Canada:
www.policyalternatives.ca

Each of the following websites produces reports of value for information about ethnicity and inequality in Canada.

Canadian Council on Social Development:
www.ccsd.ca

Centre for Social Justice:
www.socialjustice.org

The Conference Board of Canada:
www.conferenceboard.ca

Gender Difference/Gendered Inequality

Violence and Minority Women's Lived Experience

Violence against women remains a persistent and pervasive problem both in Canada and abroad (Statistics Canada, 2006b; United Nations, 2010).[1] Violence limits the liberty of women and girls, exploits the unequal status of women and girls in society, and results in devastating harm to lives and life chances (Canadian Feminist Alliance for International Action [CFAFIA], 2008). Minority women in Canada (including Aboriginal, immigrant and refugee, and racialized women of colour) are particularly vulnerable to violence in their lives (Department of Justice, 2009; Jiwani, 2006). They are victimized by violence for many reasons, ranging from (a) a devalued status that leads to personalized violence within the community (including exposure to rape and domestic abuse); (b) institutionalized state violence (such as policing) directed at communities; and (c) racism within society at large that not only interlocks with other systems of exclusion, but also constitutes a form of violence in its own right (INCITE, 2006; Jiwani, 2001, 2010). In addition to concerns shared by all victimized women, immigrant and racialized women must endure the prospect of violence because of their immigrant status. The threat of violence is intensified by a lethal combination of restrictions—financial, legal, language, and cultural—because of discrimination and marginalization (Smith, 2004). As well, racialized minority women continually confront racial stereotypes that often punish immigrant women and racialized women of colour as less than human and undeserving of respect.

Sadly, there is no shortage of narratives to underscore this violence. A young Aboriginal woman, Helen Betty Osborne, was abducted by four white men in The Pas, Manitoba, in 1971, sexually assaulted and brutally stabbed to death. The police investigation took nearly 15 years to bring one of the four men to justice. Felicia Solomon was also a young Aboriginal woman who disappeared while attending school in Winnipeg. Three months later, a police river patrol found parts of her dismembered body. The crime remains unsolved (Khan, 2005). These tragedies and injustices are only a few of those inflicted on the nearly 600 Aboriginal women who have vanished or were murdered over the past 30 years, according to the Amnesty International Report *Stolen Sisters*. Canada's Aboriginal women confront racial and sexual violence by strangers and by (ex-)partners, in homes and in back

(Continued)

alleys, in remote locales and in urban areas (see online Case Study 6.2). Compared with Canadian women as a whole, Aboriginal women are three times more likely to report violence perpetrated by a current partner; they also run eight times the risk of death at the hands of an ex-partner after separation (Mann, 2005; Statistics Canada, 2006b).[2] To add insult to injury, the pursuit of justice is delayed or denied by official indifference and police apathy toward Aboriginal women, especially those who ply the sex trade (Amnesty International, 2004; Native Women's Association, 2004).

Racialized minority communities are no less afflicted. In October 2006, Canada's South Asian community was rocked to its foundation by reports of six violent incidents in British Columbia and Ontario that left five women dead and another in critical condition (Leong & Mapp, 2006). In some cases, daughters, sisters, and partners were killed for dishonouring the family, community, or religion; in other cases, women were murdered for daring to exercise choices or engage in actions beyond the acceptable range of permissible behaviour. These grotesquely misnamed "honour" killings are anything but honourable. More accurately, these "dishonourable killings" involve the murder of girls or women for daring to "defile" the family's honour through sexual infidelity or refusal to comply with an arranged marriage (Deveaux, 2006). The murder of women also reflects impulses of control and male domination, an obsession with ethnic or religious purity at any cost, and a slavish commitment to outdated templates of gender relations that

commodified women as property to be pushed around with relative impunity (Caplan, 2010; Khoday, 2007; Papp, 2010).

In a tragedy that shocked Canadians, Aqsa Parvez, a 16-year-young Muslim woman from Brampton, Ontario, was killed just before Christmas in 2007; her father was charged with murder. The two had repeatedly clashed over curfews and clothing (especially Aqsa's refusal to wear a traditional headscarf known as a hijab [Wente, 2007a]). Reaction to the Aqsa's being murdered for wanting to be normal and fitting in prompted fierce debates over root causes: For some, the young woman's death could be attributed to a *culture clash* between Western and Islamic cultures, with multiculturalism shouldering some of the blame for tolerating such intolerance (hence, criticism of multiculturalism as bad for women [Papp, 2010]). Others preferred to frame it as a *religious issue* involving strict Islamic rules at odds with Canada's liberal and secular values (interestingly, many of the debates over the limits of religious accommodation revolve around the rights and regulation of women [Shachar, 2005], suggesting that a commitment to gender equality may be manipulated as an excuse (smokescreen) to criticize minorities such as Muslims rather than out of any sense of outrage or commitment to justice). For others, it was best interpreted as an *intergenerational conflict*, often exacerbated within immigrant contexts between rebellious teens and "skittish" parents. For still others, it was about *peer pressure* to conform versus parental pressure to comply (e.g., young South Asian women routinely find themselves living double lives because of the double standards imposed on them by their father, brothers, or partners (Handa, 2003). And yet others saw the issue as one of domestic violence within the context of a patriarchal framework without necessarily excluding the aforementioned factors (see Alcoba, 2007). Is there a pattern to the indiscriminate killing of Aboriginal, racialized, and immigrant women? Do we explain its prevalence and pervasiveness by reference to **misogyny** (hatred of women [Sheehy, 2010]), or **sexism** (belief in the inferiority of women), or **androcentrism** (a tendency to see the world from a male normative standard), or **patriarchy** (a system designed by, prioritized for, and organized around male interests)? Is the source of the problem rooted in culture-based identity groups and a multicultural commitment to cultural differences whose relativist stance rejects the universality of women's human rights, especially in regard to women's equality (Papp, 2010; United Nations, 2010)? Do women suffer abuse because of the additive effects associated with gender

(sexism), or because they are powerless and poor (class), or because of race (racism), or because of cultural values (ethnicity) within their communities? Or instead of treating these variables independently, should studies focus on how they intersect in interlocking ways to *exponentially* intensify ("multiplier effect") the vulnerability of minority women to violence and victimization? Rajiva and Batacharya (2010) frame the murder of 14-year-old Reena Virk, from Saanich, British Columbia, accordingly:

> As a young South Asian woman, Reena was on the losing end of many of the binaries that secure social hierarchies. She was not just "different" but, rather, inferiorized according to hierarchies that privilege white skin and hairless thin bodies that are unequivocally middle class, heterosexual, and able-bodied; bodies that, in short, conform to the hegemonic definitions of gender and respectability. (p. 10)

The value of employing intersectionality as an explanatory framework for understanding violence against minority women will continue at the end of this chapter.

INTRODUCTION: GENDER RELATIONS IN A GENDERED CANADA

It is commonly acknowledged that all human societies are gendered. Four dimensions account for a **gendered society**. First, all societies make a distinction between male and female (although some societies have more fluid notions of gender, including intersexed and transgendered persons). Second, societies tend to endorse a division of labour, with men monopolizing the public domain of politics (from diplomacy to armed conflict), while women tend to gravitate toward the private realm of the maternal and domestic. Third, male public-domain activities are usually valued as superior, whereas the private (maternal, domestic) world of women is devalued (paradoxically) as inferior or irrelevant, or even dangerous. Fourth, this devaluation eventually becomes deeply embedded within the framework of society (patriarchy) by way of values and structures that appear to be normal, necessary, and neutral (rather than constructed, contingent, and gender based) in defining notions of what is right, acceptable, and desirable.

To be sure, there is little agreement on whether these male–female differences are fundamental and innate or superficial and situational. For some, gender differences are maximal, inherited, and difficult to dislodge or alter; for others, gender differences are contextual, reflecting specific socio-historical circumstances (Nelson, 2009). Nevertheless, most sociologists acknowledge the socially constructed nature of gender and gender relations. That is, there is nothing natural, inevitable, or normal about masculinity or femininity. These constructs reflect how those in positions of power can parlay their influence into defining gender and gender relations. As a result, what constitutes maleness and femaleness in any given society must be seen as relative, evolving, contested—and unequal.

Gender relations are invariably unequal relations because gender remains a key variable in shaping negative outcomes (Jiwani, 2006). This gendered inequality may be neither deliberate nor conspiratorial; rather it may reflect the logical consequences of well-meaning initiatives or ostensibly neutral ground rules that remain grounded on "androcentric" assumptions. Or gendered inequality may reflect the systemic biases inherent in the constitutional principles of a patriarchal order. Patriarchy refers to a society that is organized by, for, and around men. Under patriarchy, male interests, priorities, and experiences are reflected, reinforced, and advanced by a system in which (1) the social, political, economic, and cultural domains are controlled by men; (2) masculinity is more highly valued than feminine values; and (3) males have preferential access to power and privilege because of their gender. Patterns of gender stratification are established that perpetuate patterns of "pale male" power and privilege over females and children while reinforcing a gendered status quo (Boyd & Pikkov, 2008). The cumulative effect of such a patricentric bias is punitive. In rephrasing Sandra Bem's (1994) classic title, in a male-centred and male-dominated world, female differences are often transformed into female disadvantages, and dismissed or disparaged accordingly.

Few sociologists would deny the asymmetry of gender relations in Canada (Nelson, 2009). Women continue to be "put down" because of institutional and systemic bias, "put in their place" by way of outright violence or harassment, or "put out of sight" as inferior or irrelevant. Many are denied equality in the workplace or deprived of the human capital to compete equitably with men in the corporate boardroom. For example, the Canadian Labour Congress (2008) indicates that in 2005, women working full time in full-year employment earned an average of $39 200, or 70.5 percent of what men earned on average ($55 700)—despite the fact that women are more educated, are working in greater numbers and for longer hours, and having fewer children with less time away from work. The pay gap is even greater for university-educated women, who earned just 68 percent of what men earned in 2005, down from 75 percent in 1995. At times this gap is deliberate (systematic); examples include occupational segregation; the undervaluing of women's work and their status as the principal caregivers for children and the elderly; the restructuring of women's work because of privatization and outsourcing; and a lack of access to affordable public childcare. At other times, inequities are systemic, that is, they stem from a system designed around foundational principles that promote "pale male" interests at the expense of those of others (CFAFIA, 2008). Or as Susan Pinker argues in her 2008 book *The Sexual Paradox*, women are unfairly penalized because ". . . they're expected to play by the same testosterone-charged rules men do, rules that men made up decades ago while women were kept barefoot, pregnant and even illiterate" (as cited in Zerbisias, 2008).

Minorities within Minorities

Gendered biases remain a major problem for minority women. Racialized women of colour, immigrant and refugee women, and Aboriginal women continue to be denied or exploited because of their location within a predominantly "white man's" world. As a group, they confront denial and experience exclusion with respect to power, privilege, and property (income + assets) because of gender stereotypes, double standards, glass ceilings, and sticky floors. Table 5-2 in Chapter 5 clearly demonstrates how both for-eign- and Canadian-born racialized minority women in full-year, full-time employment earn on average about 70 percent of what is earned by racialized males (Block, 2010). Onsite discrimination may account for the gendered income disparities within the work-place. However, a more plausible reason is likely the much narrower range of occupa-tions open to minority women, most of whom are lower paid and offered fewer chances for promotion. Even those with credentials may default into low-paying employment when lacking the requisite amount of Canadian experience or expertise. This situation is compounded by the marginality of class status. After all, to be poor in a society that values wealth is marginalizing. To be poor and different—and a woman—intensifies the marginalization.

That racialized minorities experience exclusion and endure exploitation because of race, ethnicity, and social class is widely acknowledged (Henry & Tator, 2006; Satzewich, 1998). But minority women (including women of colour, immigrant women, and Aboriginal women) are additionally disadvantaged by discriminatory barriers that are uniquely related to their circumstances and experiences. As a group, they tend to earn less, experience discrimination and harassment at work, shoulder domestic respon-sibilities, and they are largely excluded from the corridors of power (CFAFIA, 2008; Wallis & Kwok, 2008). And yet, in the past, the literature on the inequality of minority women was neither well established nor taken seriously. Academics often tripped over the trap of approaching minorities as if they were a homogeneous category of people—regardless of age, socioeconomic status, origins, or gender (see Tastsoglou & Preston, 2006). Rather than being recognized as having a diversity of identities and experiences, all minority women were indiscriminately lumped together into an all-consuming category. Such reductionism had a controlling effect by reinforcing the invisibility of minority women at the expense of their realities and aspirations (Zinn, Hondagneu-Sotelo & Messner, 2011). Studies were further marred by a dearth of analytical sophisti-cation. Instead of situating gender within the context of race, ethnicity, and class, each of these indicators of inequality was separately analyzed in a mechanical and additive manner (see Stasiulis, 1990, 1999). Such an approach made it difficult to appreciate how the interlocking nature of gendered inequality intersected with other indicators of ine-quality to amplify exclusion or exploitation (Jiwani, 2006; see also McMullin, 2010; Zawilski, 2010).

The invisibility of gender in the study of race, ethnic, and Aboriginal relations is no longer the case. Awareness is growing that women are minorities as well as minorities within minorities. Excluding minority women from analysis diminishes a comprehensive understanding of social inequality—in the same way that excluding men from gender studies does society a disservice. This chapter takes advantage of this conceptual shift by exploring the politics of **gendered inequality** in terms of what, why, and how. A simple but profound premise predominates: Race, ethnic, and Aboriginal relations are neither gender neutral nor gender passive. On the contrary, assumptions and principles that inform and underpin society (Abraham, Chow, Maratou-Alipranti, & Tastsoglou, 2010) are fundamentally gendered and deeply stratified by way of asymmetrical relations of power, privilege, and resources (Boyd & Pikkov, 2008). Inasmuch as the gendered basis of female–male relations reflects a separate dynamic, with a distinctive history, rationale, and expression, minority women perceive reality differently than minority men do. But minority women experience reality differently than white women do because they are differently located with respect to the devalued and interrelated statuses of race, class, and ethnicity. As well, the category of minority women needs to be disassembled: Aboriginal women, immigrant and refugee women, and racialized women of colour also differ experientially from each other because of differing social locations.

The objectives of this chapter are doubly articulated: (1) to examine the politics of race, ethnic, and Aboriginal relations through the conceptual framework of gender; conversely, to examine the politics of gender by filtering it through the lens of race, ethnicity, and aboriginality; and (2) to explore how gender intersects with race, ethnicity, and class to create interlocking systems of inequality; conversely, to explore how race, class, and ethnicity intersect with gender to intensify unequal relations. The chapter begins by conceptualizing gender diversity as a framework for analyzing gendered inequality. Gender is shown to be differently organized, experienced, and expressed, when refracted through the prism of minority women's lived realities (Zinn, Hondagneu-Sotelo, & Messner, 2011). The impact of gendered inequality on minority women's lives and life chances demands an understanding of how and why these gendered inequalities are constructed, expressed, and maintained as well as challenged and transformed. The chapter concludes by demonstrating how gender is superimposed on and intersects with race, class, and ethnicity to differentially shape realities and outcomes for minority women in general, but for racialized, immigrant/refugee, and Aboriginal women in particular. Conceptualizing violence along intersectional lines provides a fitting if unhappy application (Rajiva & Batacharya, 2010).

A word of caution: A chapter on gendered inequality tends to be long on problems and short on optimism. Emphasis is on the "bad" things that are done to minority women, either by misogynist/sexist males or by systemically biased institutions within a patriarchal regime. But there is another narrative that warrants attention: Contrary to popular belief, Aboriginal women have displayed a tenacious resilience and remarkable pragmatism not only in response to multiple burdens and challenges (Aboriginal women with university degrees earn more than non-Aboriginal women with the same level of education [Friesen, 2010a]), but also as guardians of tradition in protecting their cultures while promoting their communities (Anderson, 2009; Castellano, 2009; Valaskakis, Dion Stout, & Guimond, 2009; Wesley-Esquimaux, 2009). Minority women's histories and contemporary realities incorporate narratives of contestation, resistance, struggle, and triumph in defending women's rights, equality, independence, job marketability, and socioeconomic conditions (Cummings, 2007; Hassan, 2008). (Online Case Study 6.1 on the politics of veiling demonstrates how women actively co-opt and transform potentially oppressive symbols into sites of personal liberation, individual empowerment, and political engagement; see also online Case Study 6.2.) In short, minority women cannot be reduced to the level of a dependent variable or a control group; instead, they are active agents in constructing their world—subjects rather than objects—coping with the sometimes competing demands of community and Canada on one side, and a commitment to gender and minority equality on the other.

GENDER DIFFERENCES AS GENDERED INEQUALITY

The concerns of racialized minority women and men often converge. Both are looking to forge productive and satisfying lives, to settle into Canada without forsaking their distinctiveness; desiring an end to discrimination in housing, employment, education, and delivery of social services; looking for protection of their fundamental human rights without having to put up with excessive bureaucratic interference; and wanting the best for their children without loss of their cultural heritage. But for racialized minorities, aspirations are one thing—reality may be quite another. They routinely endure denial or exclusion because their race, ethnicity, and social class are obstacles to equality (Galabuzi, 2006). Visibility continues to compromise their hopes of full and equal participation: Discrimination remains a factor in controlling minority lives, albeit more covertly than in the past. The lives and life chances of minorities are also controlled by a pervasive Eurocentrism that imposes restrictions in defining what is acceptable and desirable. Pressures to succeed are formidable, yet opportunities—from jobs to training—may be lacking. Even those with overseas credentials, foreign experience, and professional status may be consigned to menial and demeaning jobs. With such pressures, some individuals see little option except to reject the system by withdrawing into their ethnic enclaves or resorting to criminal lifestyles.

Minority Women, Minority Men

Both minority women and men suffer exclusion and exploitation because of factors beyond their control. For men, including fathers and husbands, coping with cultural differences can prove a jolting experience (Gordon, 2008). Males may have been raised in cultures in which their roles were largely authoritarian and centred on being the breadwinner and decision maker. In Canada, however, they are expected to assume the role of nurturer and equal partner, while trying to find work and secure settlement within a context of discrimination, and diminished social and economic status. As wives expand their social circles and children effortlessly soak up the language and culture, fathers begin to lose their confidence as positive role models, with a corresponding loss of face. For immigrant males who are unemployed or underemployed, the effect is even more debilitating, according to David Este (2008), a lead researcher for the Father Involvement Initiative, a cross-Canada research project on immigrant dads. Not only does marginalization undermine self-esteem while instilling a sense of hopelessness, but anxieties over procuring the family's needs are intensified as well. When men are humiliated, isolated, and outraged, the potential to lash out at daughters or wives is all too real.

Minority males may confront many challenges. But minority women are doubly jeopardized because of their membership in yet another historically devalued category, namely, female. Racialized women of colour, immigrant and refugee women, and Aboriginal women confront the same problems as minority men, but they are additionally disadvantaged because of their gender status in a patriarchal society. And yet patriarchy does not exert a similar impact on all women. Aboriginal women, racialized minority women, and immigrant and refugee women experience it differently because of differing histories, social locations, and legal statuses (Zinn, Hondagneu-Sotelo, & Messner, 2011). As a result, conclude Vickers and de Seve (2000), the unique yet unequal experiences of minority women because of gender may outweigh the commonalities they share with minority males. The conclusion seems inescapable: Just as racialized differences must be taken into account in crafting a multicultural Canada, so too must the different experiences of minority women be taken seriously in a gendered society. A Canada committed to the principle of inclusiveness cannot settle for anything less.

White Women, Minority Women

Women as a group may share common experiences of disadvantage because of male dominance. Yet not all women are equally disadvantaged at work or in the public domain. Nor do women represent a homogeneous group whose experiences are universally filtered through patriarchy. Minority women endure different patterns of control and domination because of race, ethnicity, class, and gender, reflecting their uniquely different status and social location as Aboriginal women, women of colour, and immigrant and refugee women (Gillespie, 1996). Aida Hurtado (1996) describes how gender disparities are experienced differently. Whereas white women are increasingly striding the corridors of power, minority women continue to mop the floors. White women are largely concerned with projecting private-sphere issues (such as accessible daycare for women in management positions) into the public realm. By contrast, minority women tend to focus on bread-and-butter issues related to discrimination, healthy children, and daily survival.

A conflict of interest is inevitable. Racialized women of colour, Aboriginal women, and immigrant and refugee women may confront similar issues as white women. Nevertheless, they experience them differently because of realities refracted through the prism of racism and ethnocentrism. Minority women experience difficulty in identifying with white **feminist** theories that ignore racial hierarchies, discrimination within the workplace, and oppressive patterns within their own ethnic communities. Moreover, the interlocking of gender with race, ethnicity, and class generates such a different set of outcomes that references to "sisterhood" as an all-encompassing category are both unrealistic and reductionist. As Stasiulis (1999) says,

> [T]o speak about or for "women" was no longer a liberating politics but a homogenizing gesture that masked the race privilege of racially dominant women and the racial oppression and marginalization of women of colour. (p. 355)

Even strategies for change differ. In contrast to white women, minority women are rarely in a position to divorce themselves from their male partners, since neither can exist without the other in the struggle against oppression (hooks, 1994, 1995). Nor are they in a position to compartmentalize their politics from broader struggles for inclusion and equality. Racialized minority women are caught in a double bind. They may be tempted to identify with white women with whom they share sexist discrimination; yet they may have little choice except to affiliate with their sometimes sexist menfolk, with whom they share a common experience of racism, ethnocentrism, and classism. To the extent that white women do not experience race and racism, they are free to focus on sexism. To the degree that minority women must confront racism, ethnocentrism, and classism in addition to sexism, they cannot afford to privilege the politics of gender over race, class, and ethnicity as the primary site of struggle.

Racialized Women of Colour

Racialized women of colour have long endured discrimination and exclusion in Canada. Numerous studies using different measures and samples appear to converge and confirm that racialized women of colour confront discrimination, both systematic and systemic (Satzewich, 2000). Black women were excluded from nursing in Canada before the 1940s, and continue to experience racism and discrimination in Canadian hospitals, often at the hands of white female nurses who collaborate with management to monitor, control, and harass them (Das Gupta, 2009; Hagey, 2004). Muslim women in Quebec who insist on wearing a niqab will find that under Bill 94 they can no longer receive government services, public employment, educational opportunities and even most medical care (Orwin, 2010; Perreaux, 2010). Outside of Quebec, women from racialized minority groups say they have difficulty in finding a doctor, getting appointments, or accessing specialists (Ubelacker, 2010). Racialized migrant women, such as Filipina and Caribbean women, continue to be exploited as cheap domestic labour under Canada's Live-In Caregiver Program (Henry & Tator, 2006). Moreover, both Canadian-born and foreign-born visible minority women earn less than minority men or white women (Kunz, Milan, & Schetagne, 2001). (See also Table 5-1 in Chapter 5, which demonstrates how racialized women in full-time, full-year employment earn on average about 70 percent of average male earnings)

To be sure, earning differences can measure only the tip of the discriminatory iceberg. After all, earnings are conditioned by many factors, including qualifications, experience, seniority, and number of hours, all of which need to be statistically controlled if labour market discrimination is to be proven (Hum & Simpson, 2000). Nevertheless, racialized women of colour find themselves ghettoized in occupations that are dangerous or unprotected; they experience the trauma of role overload because of both paid and unpaid labour; and they must endure both racism and sexism in the workplace, with a corresponding devaluation of their value and contributions. Access to opportunities and outcomes remains limited for racialized women of colour. As well, human rights laws have proven somewhat ineffective in eliminating systemic discrimination, resulting in the under-representation of racialized women of colour in political office; academia; corporate management; and the media, which continue to reproduce dominant and distorted images (CFAFIA, 2008; Littlefield, 2008). Finally, racialized women of colour experience racism differently from racialized men of colour, and differently among themselves, depending on age, class, ability, sexual preference, and place of residence.

They also experience gender discrimination differently from white women because of racism (see online Case Study 6.1).

Aboriginal Women

It's tragic but true: Indigenous peoples who have experienced colonialism and exploitation may internalize that hatred, then project it outward by inflicting violence and abuse on those most vulnerable among them (Deveaux, 2006). For example, the colonialism of the residential school system not only disrupted traditional family life but also initiated a cycle of domestic abuse that continues to haunt Aboriginal communities into the present (Pauktuutit, 2006). Aboriginal (indigenous) women in Canada are particularly vulnerable to colonialism and its legacy, from a diminuation of status and power to a loss of culture and language (Statistics Canada, 2006b; Valaskakis et al., 2009).

For Aboriginal peoples, the intersection of gender with colonialism has proved both complex and destructive (Green, 2007; Leigh, 2009). Aboriginal gender relations and family organization underwent major changes with the imposition of racist and sexist laws and legislation (i.e., the *Indian Act* of 1876). In contrast to the more fluid and open precontact gender roles in Aboriginal societies, which authorities and agents may have perceived as impediments to the colonizing project, the imposition of colonization and settler values reinforced European gender norms along Victorian lines. Under the *Indian Act* of 1876, which infantilized Aboriginal peoples in general, Aboriginal women were further marginalized when their legal status was linked to that of men and marriage. Put bluntly, under colonization, Aboriginal societies were reorganized along patriarchal lines, in the process displacing Aboriginal women from government and power, while aligning the interests of Aboriginal families with those of colonial powers (Leigh, 2009).

Aboriginal women's vulnerability to exploitation and victimization both within and outside their communities is reinforced by several factors. Of particular salience is their socioeconomic marginalization; a coercive assimilation, including that imposed by residential schools, that disrupted gender relations and cultural identity; and a perception of them as easy targets because of their over-involvement in the sex trade. The interplay of racism and discrimination with inequality and a generally precarious status in society compromises the safety and security of Aboriginal women (Green, 2008; Mann, 2005). The internalization of these pressures results in depression and self-hatred among Aboriginal women which, in turn, is reflected in high rates of suicide, alcohol dependency, and neglect of children. Compounding this volatile mixture is the pressure of derogatory stereotypes that reinforce their marginalization (Witt, 1984).

Historical and social factors also militate against the adequate recognition and rightful status of Aboriginal women. Those who married non-Aboriginal males were penalized through a loss of status and corresponding benefits (Aboriginal men who married non-Aboriginal women retained their status). Even the repeal of the offending passage (section 12(1)(b) of the 1985 *Indian Act*) by Bill C-31 did not remove all barriers. Although women who had lost their status and that of their children under section 12(1)(b) of the 1985 *Indian Act* were reinstated, resource-strapped bands have refused them membership and residence for political and economic reasons. Moreover, despite reinstatement, C-31 women could not pass on full status to their children; as a result, if the offspring of a C-31 woman married a non-status person, the status of any resulting children would lapse because of successive out-marriage (Mann, 2005). (An amendment to Section 6 of the 2009 *Indian Act* overturned this discriminatory bias.) The effects of this loss of status and lack of rights are incalculable.

> Aboriginal women do not enjoy the same rights as Aboriginal men with respect to passing their Indian status to their children and grandchildren. Nor do Aboriginal women living on reserves enjoy the same rights to the division of matrimonial property as their Aboriginal and non-Aboriginal counterparts who live off reserve. This discriminatory treatment of Aboriginal women at law affects their enjoyment—and the enjoyment of their children and grandchildren—of their right to culture, ancestral lands, the benefits of land claims, and other social and economic benefits provided to Indians. (CFAFIA, 2008, p. 10)

And yet, efforts by Aboriginal women to remove blatant forms of discrimination encounter resistance on the grounds that tampering with the status quo is both disruptive and disloyal (Weaver, 1993a). Not surprisingly, then, Aboriginal women have expressed grave concerns over the proposed entrenchment of those Aboriginal models of self-government at odds with women's equality provisions as set out in the *Constitution Act* and the *Charter of Rights and Freedoms* (Deveaux, 2006).

Both formal studies and personal testimonies indicate that Aboriginal women rank among the most severely disadvantaged people in Canada (Mann, 2005; Native Women's Association, 2004). Aboriginal women are known to experience a double oppression: As Aboriginal people who happen to be women, they must confront the foundational bias that governs the constitutional order of a capitalist and patriarchal society. As women who happen to be Aboriginal, they suffer from repressive practices, because of the colonial structures imposed by the *Indian Act*. Economically, in terms of income levels and employment options, they are worse off than both non-Aboriginal women and Aboriginal men; as a result, the feminization of poverty bites deeply, especially for lone-parent women in cities (Monture, 2004; Wallis & Kwok, 2008). Social hardships for these women are numerous, with reports of abusive male family members, sexual assaults and rapes, inadequate and overcrowded housing, squalid living conditions, unhealthy child-raising environments, and alcohol and drug abuse. Levels of violence directed against Aboriginal women and children are soaring, as explained by the Native Women's Association of Canada in a 1991 brief (as cited in Razack, 1994):

> We have a disproportionately high rate of child sexual abuse and incest. We have wife battering, gang rapes, drug and alcohol abuse, and every kind of perversion imaginable has been imported into our lives . . . (p. 910)

In that violence against Aboriginal women remains a persistent and pervasive problem, the prospect of gender equality does not look promising.

Immigrant and Refugee Women

Gender is a key variable in analyzing international migration (Piper, 2008). Immigration laws and policies affect women and men differently, resulting in both gendered patterns of immigration and gendered outcomes. Modes of entry into Canada are bimodal in pattern (Boyd & Pikkov, 2008). Women often enter Canada as wives or dependants of men who sponsor them; they also arrive as autonomous labour migrants, highly skilled professionals, and the undocumented (Khoo, Ho, & Voigt-Graf, 2008). Settlement programs for integrating immigrants into society also affect men and women differently, with corresponding diverse implications for livelihood, rights, and entitlements. Female immigrants encounter a gender-stratified labour market that ignores their credentials and expertise by slotting them into "women's work" (Khoo et al., 2008). In that gender intersects with other social relations, such as class and race, to create complex systems of stratification with their own power dynamics and patterns of exclusion in both origin (leaving) and destination (entry) societies, a gender lens is inestimable for understanding the politics, policies, and practices of immigration (Piper, 2008).

Nevertheless, too much of what passes for theorizing regarding immigration and immigrants tends to ignore gender as a key variable (Vickers & de Seve, 2000; Willis & Yeoh, 2000; but see Piper, 2008). In the past, immigrants were assumed to be gender-neutral beings with similar immigration experiences. But recent research has highlighted the gendered basis of Canada's immigration policy with respect to entry requirements, access to skills training and employment, and definitions of family and sponsorship (Boyd, 2006; Citizenship and Immigration Canada, 2010; see also Hyndman, 1999). Immigrant women routinely experience a more sexist reality than their fathers, partners, brothers, and sons. The pervasiveness of sexism in the lives of immigrant women is graphically captured in this excerpt from Himani Bannerji (2000) in depicting the fear, anxiety, humiliation, and anger that accompanied her transition into Canada. In the final immigration interview, she faced a white and balding elderly male:

> . . . [H]e asked me—"Do you speak Hindi?" I replied that I understood it very well and spoke it with mistakes. "Can you translate this sentence for me?" he asked, and proceeded to say in Hindi what in English amounts to "Do you want to fuck with me?" . . . I gripped the edge of my chair and stared at him—silently. His hand was on my passport, the pink slip of my "landing" document lay next to it. Steadying my voice I said "I don't know Hindi that well." . . . My interview continued.

Immigrant women encounter additional problems because of social class (Bannerji, 2000). They often find themselves restricted to the lower echelons of the Canadian labour force, including low-paying job ghettos such as manufacturing, service industries, and domestic work. According to Debbie Douglas (2005), executive director of the Ontario Council of Agencies Serving Immigrants and winner of the Social Action and Justice Award, many immigrant women in Toronto work in modern-day equivalents of nineteenth-century sweatshops, including 38 percent of women of colour who earn slightly more than minimum wage in jobs without union protection, benefits, or security. If undervalued and underpaid work isn't stressful enough, tradition may dictate double duty for women, with outside employment superimposed on maternal and domestic responsibilities that may go underappreciated and unrewarded. Or as sharply put by the *Report of the Ontario Joint Task Force on Immigration and Women*, a Canadian-born woman may have difficulty reconciling the conflicting demands of homemaking and motherhood with paid employment. But immigrant women must face these same problems, in addition to learning a new language and adjusting to a different culture, often while coping with the sometimes contradictory demands of rebellious teenagers and angry husbands.

For immigrant women, Canada is proving a gilded cage, as Melody Neufeld-Rocheleau and Judith Friesen (1987) write. Promises and opportunities notwithstanding, they must endure loneliness stemming from isolation (limited language, lack of training opportunities, child-rearing and school-related problems, racial prejudice, underemployment, lack of "Canadian" experience, and limited services to cater to their unique situations). Women are expected to know their place: Actions by women that do not conform to conventional norms or male privileges—although consistent with Canadian normative standards—may be criticized as betrayal or irresponsibility. For the sake of appearances, women are expected to defer to male authority, even if such deference may inhibit the acquisition of skills for societal success. For those who defy convention or authority, the consequences may prove costly. The family, the community, and the culture are often regarded as bastions of privacy from prying eyes, so that those women who go public to authorities with damning information may be shunned, ostracized, or physically punished.

Consider the case of temporary foreign workers in Canada, among the most vulnerable. Migrant labour has became a structural necessity, so that Canada is increasingly reliant on temporary workers as a form of cheap and subservient labour (Fleras, 2010a). The exploitation of migrants as cheap labour to do Canada's "dirty work" applies to men and women; nevertheless, only women are deliberately imported for gender-specific jobs pertaining to the sex trade, child rearing, and domestic labour (Macklin, 1999). The combination of temporary work permits and the program's "live-in" requirements strips domestic workers of the power to complain about punishing work schedules, unpaid wages (especially for overtime work), and unlawful confinement at the hands of their employers (Diocson, 2005; Stasiulis & Bakan, 1997). Three phases can be discerned in the development of the domestic worker program:

- First, in 1955, Canada established a foreign domestic-worker policy. Caribbean women were designated as live-in domestics to provide affluent Canadian families with cheap home childcare services and domestic labour. As migrant labour, live-in domestics were granted the right to stay in Canada, provided they stayed in domestic employment for at least one year after arrival (Satzewich, 2000). An initial quota of 200 domestics per year eventually grew to 1000 annual arrivals by the mid-1960s.

- Second, recruitment of Caribbean women as domestic servants was gradually displaced by increased recruitment from the Philippines, despite a historical bias against Asian immigration. As well, the 1992 Live-In Caregiver Program was tightened by the imposition of tougher barriers, such as stricter education and training eligibility criteria (12 years of schooling and six months of training) for all domestic workers, regardless of their country of origin.

- Third, by the early 1980s, domestic workers on temporary work visas, who would otherwise be ineligible to apply for landed immigrant status, were accorded the right to apply for permanent residency from within Canada. Under the terms of this agreement, foreign caregiver workers are obligated by law to live in their employers' homes for at least two years of a three-year period. As live-in nannies, they are legally classified as temporary workers and subject to deportation upon termination of their contract, unless they apply for landed immigrant status. Upon completion of their residency requirement, they can then sponsor children and partners to come to Canada. In 2005, according to the Immigration and Citizenship Department, 6200 caregiver visas were issued (the vast majority consisting of trained nurses from the Philippines), while 3700 domestic workers were granted permanent resident status.

To be sure, there are labour laws in place for the protection of live-in workers. But their vulnerable status as "foreign" and "domestic" workers creates an institutionalized power imbalance whereby they face the risk of overwork and underpay, the possibility of sexual assault, and the threat of deportation. Moreover, labour laws are of marginal value if live-in workers are unable to understand and exercise their rights or to seek redress. Of course, not all domestic workers are exploited; nevertheless, as Audrey Macklin (1999) concludes, the potential for exploitation is bolstered by the combination of unregulated work environments, the constant spectre of expulsion and deportation if they complain, and a perception among employers that they "own" these "indentured" workers.

Refugee women are no less vulnerable. The 1951 Convention on the Status of Refugees clearly defined a refugee as a person who is outside his or her country, who has a well-founded fear of persecution for reasons of race, religion, nationality, political opinion, or group membership, and whom the state is unwilling or unable to protect. Definitions of persecution were typically based on male experiences: A focus on the violation of fundamental freedoms pertaining to expression, association, or conscience emphasized the public domain as the site of persecution. Predictably, then, a refugee was typified as a male political dissident who was jailed or harassed for espousing anti-government views of a repressive regime (Ramirez, 2001). The definition historically has been interpreted in a way that ignores women's experiences that fall outside conventional (i.e., male) definitions of persecution—even though women and children account for about 80 percent of the world's refugees (Canadian Council for Refugees, 2001). Minimal attention was directed at the fact that refugee women faced not only the risks and dangers that men confronted in flight, resettlement, and exile, but also threats of sexual assault and exploitation (Matsuoka & Sorenson, 1999).

In short, the dangers of flight experienced by women differ from those of men (Status of Women Canada, 2007). Women's experiences of refugee persecution often take place in the "private sphere" of home and community, and may include rape, infanticide, genital mutilation, forced abortion, compulsory sterilization, sexual slavery, trafficking in women, and domestic violence (Ramirez, 2001). The evidence that women use in support of their refugee claims may be more difficult to validate or quantify. To its credit, Canada in 1993 became the first country to issue guidelines on female refugee claimants fleeing gender-related persecution, including female genital mutilation. The recognition of gender-based violence is now well established within Canada's refugee determination system.

Finally, "trafficking" in women remains big business (Macklin, 1999). Human trafficking is defined as the use of coercion or deception to recruit a person in order to exploit them against their will for sexual purposes or forced labour. The US Department of State's *Trafficking in Persons Report* estimated that up to 800 000 persons were trafficked across borders, with women and girls constituting about 80 percent and many destined for commercial sexual exploitation (as cited in Statistics Canada, 2006b). (In 2010, the US Department of State, in their 10th *Trafficking in Persons Report* estimated that there were 12.3 million trafficked adults and children around the world, with most in forced labour, bonded labour, or forced prostitution (Bureau of Public Affairs, 2010].) Not surprisingly, female domestic migrants and sex-trade workers are regarded by the United Nations as the most widely exploited and abused of migrant workers (Stasiulis & Bakan, 1997).

EXPLAINING GENDERED INEQUALITY: OVERLAPPING, INTERSECTING, AND INTERLOCKING

How do we account for gendered inequalities? Are they the result of innate differences or social conditioning? Does the blame lie with the structures of society or with the discipline of the market? Blame the victim or blame the system? Sociological theories emphasize the social and the structural as key explanatory variables. Of those social variables most responsible for gendered inequality, the most relevant hierarchies of exclusion are race, ethnicity, class, and gender. In the cold analytical language of sociologists, the concepts of race, ethnicity, gender, and class constitute "variables" that impact differently on minority women. To be sure, race, gender, ethnicity, and class may be treated as analytically distinct dimensions of inequality; nevertheless, their conceptualization as interlocking and mutually reinforcing categories is increasingly central to social analysis (Jiwani, 2006). Each operates in conjunction with the others to construct a complex set of interlocking and overlapping patterns of domination and control (Devine, Savage, Scott, & Crompton, 2005). In short, intersectionality is key: Taken alone or additionally, each of these barriers hinders; taken together and compounded, they create a multiplier effect by amplifying the exclusion or exploitation. As Pragna Patel notes,

> The idea of "intersectionality" seeks to capture both the structural and dynamic consequences of the interaction between two or more forms of discrimination or systems of subordination. It specifically addresses the manner in which racism, patriarchy, economic disadvantages and other discriminatory systems contribute to create layers of inequality that structures the relative positions of women and men, races and other groups. Moreover, it addresses the way that specific acts and policies create burdens that flow along these intersecting axes contributing actively to create a dynamic of disempowerment. (as cited in United Nations, 2010, p. 42)

Theoretical efforts to understand race, ethnic, and Aboriginal relations increasingly accept the intersectionality of social relations involving race, class, gender, and ethnicity (Andersen & Collins, 1998; Rothenberg, 2001; Zinn, Hondagneu-Sotelo, & Messner, 2011). According to Daiva Stasiulis (1999), feminist intersectional analysis approaches the social reality and broader contexts of women and men ". . . to be *multiply, simultaneously, and interactively* determined by various significant *axes of social organization*" (p. 347). An **intersectional analysis** goes beyond an additive model approach that (a) sees race and ethnicity as fixed and static, (b) ignores diversity within groups, and (c) glosses over the interactive elements of social location. A theoretical framework is proposed that incorporates the inseparability and simultaneity of race, ethnicity, class, and gender as interlocking and overlapping expressions of inequality, while acknowledging how the impact of one particular source of subordination will vary, depending on its combination with other sources of subordination (Denis, 2008). An intersectional analysis thus provides an alternative analysis to (1) the reductionist tendencies that characterize Marxist/socialist thought (which emphasizes the centrality of class relations in shaping dynamics and outcomes); (2) feminist thought that posits the "categorical hegemony" of gender as pivotal in explaining patterns of power and privilege over time and across space; and (3) anti-racist thought that "privileges" race and racism as the bane of minority women's existence (Stasiulis, 1999).

Clearly, then, there is much value in promoting the multiple, interactive, and simultaneous experiences of race, class, and gender as intersecting systems of privilege or inequality rather than as discrete categories that stand in a mechanistic and additive form

(United Nations, 2010). The centrality of social location is unmistakable to an intersectional analysis (Rajiva & Batacharya, 2010): That is, where minority women are socially located in society with respect to race, ethnicity, history, and class will profoundly influence their identities and experiences, opportunities and outcomes. As a result, minority women experience reality differently from white women, because they are differently located in terms of how race intersects with gender, ethnicity, and class (also age and sexual orientation) to create interlocking and overlapping hierarchies of inequality that intensify patterns of exclusion or exploitation. Within immigrant, racialized, and Aboriginal communities, for example, female demands for freedom or equality can prove disruptive by provoking vested interests (El-Tablawy, 2005). Similarly, minority women experience reality differently from minority men, because they are differently located in terms of how gender intersects with race, ethnicity, and class to create overlapping and interlocking hierarchies of inequality that intensify exploitation and marginalization.

Finally, there is also intersectionality within the intersections. That is, rather than treating gendered and minorities as a singular category, we should place our emphasis on acknowledging differences within differences. Aboriginal women, immigrant and refugee women, and racialized women of colour experience reality differently because *each* is differently located with respect to how race, ethnicity, and class intersect with gender to deny and exclude. For example, Muslim women confront dilemmas that other minority women do not, because of their appearance and their placement as the "other" caught between suspicions of the West and oppression of extremists. Aboriginal women confront a legacy of colonialism as a major barrier within both their communities and Canadian society at large. In short, there is much value in acknowledging the complexity of social realities for minority women—especially when it comes to violence—as demonstrated below in the Debate Revisited box.

DEBATE REVISITED

Intersecting Causes, Interlocking Outcomes

Many social and structural factors make women vulnerable to violence. At particular risk are minority women, but especially immigrant and refugee women, Aboriginal women, and racialized women of colour (CFAFIA, 2008). Why do minority women appear to be more vulnerable to violence? Is it because of gender or race or ethnicity or class? Or is it because gender intersects with race and ethnicity and class to amplify the danger? For Aboriginal women, gender intersects race, class, and colonization to produce distinctive patterns of and outcomes to violence. For racialized women of colour, their gender intersects differently with race, ethnicity, and class to generate different patterns of violence (Rajiva & Batacharya, 2010). And for immigrants and refugees, gender intersects still differently with race, ethnicity, and class to create a distinctive pattern of violence.

Take immigrant women: Upwardly mobile immigrant women may be targets of domestic violence by those tradition-bound males who expect servitude, deference, and submissiveness. This violence results from cultural traditions that (1) normalize male abuse of women, (2) naturalize abuse as a male entitlement to dominate and apply discipline when necessary, and (3) discourage public disclosure because of family honour or community pride. To be sure, references to "tradition" or "culture" to explain violence against immigrant and racialized women is problematic (United Nations, 2010). Too often, this pattern of violence is blamed on some cultural defect in need of intervention by the superior West. By contrast, the problem of violence against mainstream women is attributed to a disturbed and/or controlling individual rather than structurally embedded (Deckha, 2010). As a result, according to Maneesha Deckha, associate professor at University of Victoria, we tend to define minority cultures as patriarchical and its practices as violent, yet routinely dismiss the applicability of these labels to mainstream society. Consequently, non-Western cultures are framed in deterministic and essentialized terms by reducing the problem of violence to a simplistic and singular explanation (i.e., "patriarchal culture") (United Nations, 2010).

And yet immigrant and racialized women remain the "hushed-over" victims of violence. They may know neither that spousal abuse is a crime in Canada, nor where they can go for help (if you can't speak English, how can you dial 911?), or they may fear deportation if they complain (United Nations, 2010). The experience of domestic abuse may be further intensified because of loneliness, dependency, homesickness, lack of knowledge of English or access to services, and the threat of social ostracism. As Ekuwa Smith (2004) writes:

These women can be incredibly isolated in an unfamiliar environment where there seems to be no safe place, not even at home. The loss of traditional supports of extended family, friends, advisors from their home country of origin weighs heavily on some of these women and compounds their isolation. Some wives have never experienced abuse until they come here, when the trauma of adjusting economically and socially to the new country disrupts family life.

The fact that many women's shelters are neither equipped nor prepared to provide culturally sensitive services is problematic as well (Statistics Canada, 2006b). No less daunting is a wariness toward a criminal justice system that may prove as traumatizing as what triggered the response in the first place, so that women may be re-victimized by the very system they turn to for help. Finally, even escaping from abusive relations may not prove a panacea. The dearth of job prospects, because of prejudicial attitudes and institutional barriers, further intensifies the spectre of poverty and yet more isolation.

No one is suggesting that domestic violence is more prevalent in immigrant communities. Abuse is about power, and the abuse of power is displayed in all cultures and groups, regardless of ethnicity, race, or class (Paradkar, 2000). But domestic abuse impacts minority women differently because of the unique circumstances associated with immigrant status in a foreign country (United Nations, 2010). Without access to knowledge or resources, few options for escape exist, and those that do often lead to more

(Continued)

shame, physical retaliation, and isolation (Easteal, 1996; Leckie, 1995). Foreign-born women are told to "learn to deal with it and make sacrifices" (Etherington, 2001). When friends, relatives, priests/ministers, and others exert additional pressure to stay put, it becomes even more stressful to leave an abusive relationship.

Class matters, too: Minority women tend to occupy a class status below that of their mainstream sisters. Lower class status is not necessarily indicative of greater victimization. Nevertheless, minority women confront a doubly articulated class hierarchy—one based on their subordinate status within their communities, in addition to their subdominant position within society at large (see Jiwani, 2006). Thus, violence against minority women reflects their unequal status in society, together with the abuse of power within a context of inequality (Jiwani, 2001). Their ghettoization in dangerous and low-paying jobs—including that of prostitution and other sex-trade jobs—may expose them to greater danger in the workplace. Certain occupations are also more vulnerable to violence, including foreign domestic workers secluded in private homes and threatened with deportation if they complain of abuse (Statistics Canada, 2006b).

Paradoxically, what is most "striking" may be the class status of those who perpetuate the violence. While males who migrate to Canada may come from areas where abuse of women is tolerated, the stress of settling in and making a living may intensify conditions that incite yet more violence. Males who once wielded economic power and political clout now find

themselves marginalized and ignored. Making matters worse are humiliations and disappointments from underemployment or loss of domestic authority (Wente, 2007a). That makes it imperative to understand that eradication of violence must begin by understanding the logic behind the deeply felt beliefs and constraints of those who practise it (see African Canadian Legal Clinic, 2006).

In short, the gender-based violence experienced by minority women within their communities is compounded by the institutionalized racism and sexism they encounter on a daily basis (Jiwani, 2006). Just as none of the variables in isolation (gender, race, class, age, or ethnicity) can explain what happened to Aqsa Parvez or Reena Virk or Helen Betty Osborne, so too is it impossible to isolate a single factor that accounts for the pervasiveness and patterns of violence toward minority women. Violence against minority women involves multiple oppressions sustained by gendered power relations in addition to other axes of social difference (United Nations, 2010). Gender intersects with the variables of class, ethnicity, and race to create complex and interlocking systems of stratification that amplify patterns of in/exclusion both within the community as well as within society at large (Piper, 2008). Minority women must endure pressures within their own communities because of cultural values that undermine their lives and life chances. A commitment to culturalism—a belief that the integrity of cultural beliefs and values must be protected and promoted at all costs if multiculturalism and relativism are to mean anything—plays havoc with the realities, rights, and experiences of minority women (Phillips, 2007; United Nations, 2010).[3] In terms of race, women of colour and Aboriginal women are targets of violence by virtue of their visibility. Finally, the often impoverished and disempowered class status of minority women works against them by drawing them into high-risk occupations.

The interplay of these factors reinforces the necessity to contextualize violence in structural and situational terms rather than as individual pathologies. Attention must be focused on those factors (variables) that not only expose the vulnerability of minority women to different forms of violence (physical, spiritual, sexual, psychological, financial, and racial), but also serve to render invisible and to normalize the violence implicit in racism and sexism (Jiwani, 2006). This interplay also underscores the value of an intersectional analysis in demonstrating the interlocking dynamics of violence and oppression toward minority women. In addition, reference to gender may need to be disassembled, if only to acknowledge how the realities of Aboriginal women, racialized women of colour, and immigrant and refugee women differently intersect with race, ethnicity, class, and gender to institutionalize violence against them.

Chapter Highlights

- Both minority women and men tend to be exploited or excluded because of race, ethnicity, or class. Minority women are additionally handicapped because of gender discrimination.

- Two principles underpin this chapter on gendered diversity: First, race, ethnic, and Aboriginal relations are ultimately gendered relations; second, gendered relations are relationships of inequality.

- Aboriginal women, racialized women of colour, and immigrant and refugee women face similar issues, but the particular ways in which these issues are refracted through the prism of race, ethnicity, and class tend to amplify their effects.

- Gendered inequality is experienced differently by Aboriginal women, racialized women of colour, and immigrant and refugee women because of the different demands imposed by their specific location in society.

- Intersectional analysis involves the notion that gender is superimposed on and intersects with race, ethnicity, and class to create interlocking and overlapping hierarchies of privilege/disprivilege.

- Minority women experience violence differently because gender for Aboriginal women, racialized women of colour, and immigrant and refugee women intersects differently with race, class, and ethnicity to create different patterns and outcomes.

For further study, you can access the Case Studies referenced in this chapter at **www.pearsoncanada.ca/fleras**.

Review Questions

1. The concept of minority women includes Aboriginal women, racialized women of colour, and immigrant and refugee women. Compare the different experiences, concerns, and aspirations of each of these differently located women.

2. The concepts of race, ethnicity, gender, and class are widely perceived as having a differential impact on minority women. Each of these variables is determining in its own right, yet each intersects with the others to create interlocking patterns of inequality. Taken together, they create systems of gender inequality that have proven difficult to dismantle. Explain.

3. Compare the concepts of misogyny, sexism, androcentrism, and patriarchy as the basis for the unequal treatment of minority women in Canada.

Endnotes

1. Violence is defined as encompassing physical, sexual, and psychological dimensions within the family, the community, at work, in institutions, or within the context of the State (Statistics Canada, 2006b). Violence reflects abuses of power and is structural in relations of dominance that are pervasive and endemic (Jiwani, 2010).

2. This comparison is not intended to diminish non-Aboriginal deaths. More than 60 women in Canada are killed each year by their partners (Cross, 2007). Nor should a sense of perspective be ignored. Compare the 12 honour killings across Canada since 2002 with the 212 women in Ontario killed by their partners between 2002 and 2007 (Caplan, 2010). Although the Ontario killings are framed by the media (if, in fact, they report on them at all) as domestic suicides rather than the grotesquely phrased "honour killings," the same twisted rational underpins both: to control women as chattel by aggrieved men with a pathologically inflated sense of entitlement, due deference, and reputation (Khan, 2010).

3. Intersectional analysis tends to reject conventional views of culture as an explanatory variable. A refusal to acknowledge its dynamic, social, economic, gender, and historical context reifies the concept of culture into a rigid, homogeneous, and constraining force that mechanically determines people's behaviour ("essentialism"—i.e., fixing people into immutable categories that ignore the dynamic and shifting nature of people's identities and commitments). Instead, as James Nazroo, Saffron Karlsen, and many others have noted, culture should be framed as a fluid and flexible resource that is always changing and contested; open to diverse interpretation; intersecting with and structured by gender, race, or class; and modulated by previous experiences and relationships in providing guidelines for understanding and action.

Links and Recommendations

VIDEO

Me and the Mosque (2005)

An NFB look at how Muslim women continue to be victims of discrimination by Islamic religion.

FILMS

The New World (2005)

An interesting film in the tradition of *Dances with Wolves*. But while some stereotypes are reversed or toppled, Pocahontas continues to be exoticized as a "Barbie in buckskins."

Finding Dawn (2006)

A moving National Film Board feature by Métis director Christine Welsh goes beyond the tragedies of nearly 600 murdered or missing Aboriginal women. Importantly, it focuses on the empowerment of individuals and communities in taking control of the situation.

Backyard (El Traspatio) (2009)

A Mexican film that is much more harrowing than *Finding Dawn* in exposing the indifference and complicity of Mexican authorities toward the unexplained deaths of thousands of murdered women (femicide) in the city of Ciudad Juarez.

TV

Little Mosque on the Prairie

This CBC sitcom explores the often humorous, if misunderstood, interactions between Muslims and non-Muslim townspeople of "Mercy," Saskatchewan.

ARTICLE/REPORT

For an extremely useful application of intersectional analysis, see "Intersecting Inequalities: Immigrant Women of Colour, Violence, and Health Care," by Yasmin Jiwani (2001). Available online at **www.harbour.sfu.ca/freda/articles/hlth04.htm**.

BOOKS

Reena Virk: Critical Perspectives on a Canadian Murder, by Mythili Rajiva and Sheila Batacharya (2010). This book argues that while race and racism intersect with relations of power (including gender, class, age, sexuality) in explaining the murder of a young South Asian woman, the media's persistent denial of race and its spotlight on "girl violence" exposes fissures in Canada's imagined multicultural society.

Race, Class, and Gender: An Anthology (6th ed.), by Margaret L. Andersen and Patricia Hill Collins (2007). This book covers a lot of territory related to gender and diversity.

Gender Through the Prism of Difference (4th ed.), by Maxine Baca Zinn, Pierette Hondagneu-Sotelo, & Michael A Messner. (eds.) (2011). This excellent collection of readings applies both an intersectional analysis approach and an international focus.

Theorizing Empowerment: Canadian Perspectives on Black Feminist Thought, by Notisha Massaquoi and Njoki Nathani Wane (2007). This powerful and provocative set of essays points to the promise of empowering black women in Canada by transforming their lives at personal and institutional levels. The essays also reinforce the diversity of black women's experiences, realities, and identities with respect to personal resistance and political engagement.

Restoring the Balance: First Nations Women, Community and Culture, by Gail Valaskakis, Madeleine Dion Stout, and Eric Guimond (eds.) (2009). Fifteen Aboriginal scholars, activists, and community leaders focus on the challenges and successes of Aboriginal women in advancing cultural continuity and community development.

WEBSITES

PovNET—This site provides useful information of the status and experiences of minority women in Canada:
   www.povnet.org/node/806

The National Action Committee on the Status of Women—This is Canada's largest feminist organization:
   http://orgs.tigweb.org/national-action-committee-on-the-status-of-women-nac

NOIVMWC: A Global Effort to Bring Equality to All Women—This website draws attention to the concerns and activities of visible minority and immigrant women in Canada:
   www.noivmwc.org

Native Women's Association of Canada—This is the official site for Aboriginal women in Canada and has numerous links to issues involving identity, experiences, and opportunities:
   www.nwac.ca

University of Iowa's Communication Studies: Gender, Race, and Ethnicity in Media—A useful clearinghouse of information related to gender, race, ethnicity, and the media:
   www.uiowa.edu/~commstud/resources/GenderMedia/

PART 2

Diversities and Difference in Canada: Peoples, Nations, and Minorities[1]

> . . . Canada is a world leader in three of the most important areas of ethnocultural relations: immigration, indigenous peoples, and the accommodation of minority nationalisms . . . That we have managed to cope with all these forms of diversity simultaneously while still managing to live together in peace and civility is, by any objective standard, a remarkable achievement. (Kymlicka, 1998a, p. 3)

Canada encompasses a rich complexity of diversities. Over 200 racial and ethnic groups can be identified in Canada, including descendents of the British and French settlers, while Aboriginal peoples are no less internally diverse, including 50 different tribal groups (Haida, Mohawk, etc.) with over 50 different languages (INAC, 2003). Efforts to classify this astonishing array of diversities and difference into a coherent framework have proven perplexing. What to include and why? Should the focus of any typology be based on commonalities of colour (race) or culture (ethnicity) of minorities? Should it focus on shared features reflecting national origins or migration status? Or should emphasis be on how different groups see their collective status in society, in addition to their relationship to the Canadian state and other groups in Canada? Is it best to focus on

---

1   This section acknowledges a distinction between diversity and difference. "Diversity" is a largely descriptive term for describing differences in a heterogeneous society. "Difference," by contrast, is a more politicized term. It invokes the notion of power relations between, within, and among diverse racial, ethnic, and Aboriginal groups, together with the politicization of these differences as a basis for challenge and transformation.

shared group similarities with respect to who is entitled to what and why? What about focusing on that which groups share in terms of major challenges and proposed solutions?

Of the many proposals for solving this conceptual impasse, few have met with as much success as a typology that divides Canada's multilayered diversities and deep differences into a limited number of categories based on structural commonalities and relational status (Elliott, 1983). *Unequal Relations* follows this format. Canada's racial, ethnic, and Aboriginal composition is partitioned into three major "Ethnicities"— Aboriginal peoples (indigenous peoples), charter groups (national minorities, that is, French- and English-speaking), and multicultural minorities (immigrants and descendants of immigrants who are racialized as visible minorities). Each of these major Ethnicities is associated with a distinctive yet shared set of attributes; each also confronts a host of unique problems because of its constitutional and sociological status in Canadian society; and each is likely to espouse solutions and anticipate outcomes commensurate with its priorities (see also Jenson & Papillon, 2001; Kymlicka, 2001; Roth, 1998). As a result, these ethnicity categories can be compared on the basis of the following criteria: (1) constitutional status in society, (2) major problems, (3) proposed solutions, (4) anticipated outcomes, and (5) sociological framework.

The table below provides an overview of Canada's Difference Model by comparing the Ethnicities along the aforementioned lines. The table clearly demonstrates how Canada's major Ethnicities differ in terms of who they are, what they want, why they want it, how they propose to get it, and where they hope to end up.

- The politics of aboriginality are inseparable from Aboriginal peoples' constitutional status as the "first peoples" whose occupation on Turtle Island (North America) preceded European colonization. In contrast to immigrant minorities, who voluntarily migrated to Canada and are thus anxious to "get in," Aboriginal peoples were forcibly incorporated into the Canada-building project. Accordingly, they are anxious to "get out," primarily by decolonizing their relational status around a postcolonial social contract based on Aboriginal models of **self-determining autonomy** over land, identity, and political voice.

CANADA'S DIFFERENCE MODEL: THE THREE MAJOR ETHNICITIES

	Aboriginal Peoples	Charter Groups (Quebec*)	Multicultural Minorities
Sociological framework	Forcibly incorporated (colonized)	Forcibly incorporated (by conquest)	Voluntary minorities (by migration)
Constitutional status	Original occupants	Founding nations	Citizens
Core problem	Internal colonialism	Federalism	Discrimination
Proposed solution	Postcolonial social contract	Asymmetrical federalism	Equity programs/ Multiculturalism
Anticipated outcome	Self-determining autonomy	Nationhood/ distinct society	Inclusive society

*Although both French and English constitute Charter groups, the focus here is on Quebec as a national minority.

- Ottawa–Quebec relations pivot around the constitutional status of French and English (or more accurately, French- and English-speaking) as founding members of Canadian society. Conflicts involving Canadians/Canadien(ne)s who claim sovereign rights as national societies/communities reflect a failure to craft an innovative federal structure that formally acknowledges Quebec's status as a distinct society.

- Finally, multicultural minorities confront a different set of challenges in staking out a place in Canada. Instead of demands for revamping the foundational principles of Canada's constitutional order, the concerns of minority women and men are directed at institutional inclusion through removal of discriminatory barriers.

In short, each major Ethnicity differs in terms of agendas, priorities, and discourses. For Aboriginal peoples, prevailing discourses pertain to treaty rights, inherent Aboriginal rights, land title, self-governance, and self-determining autonomy; for Quebecers, the discursive framework includes duality, **bilingualism**, federalism, a distinct society, and nationhood; and for immigrant minorities, the central focus is diversity, multiculturalism, tolerance, citizenship, and integration (Banting, Courchene, & Seidle, 2007).

These broad sets of ethnicity claims provide a framework for analyzing race, ethnic, and Aboriginal relations as unequal relations. They secure a blueprint for fundamentally different governance structures that not only construct a "complex architecture for Canada-building" (Banting et al., 2007, p. 650), but also transform Canada into a contested site of competing interests over valued resources. Exceptions abound in this kind of ideal-typical typology, including anomalous status minorities such as Hutterites and francophones outside of Quebec. However, the goal of any typology is not to replicate reality in its exactitude—after all, the very nature of "ideal types" is prone to simplification or reductionism—but to render it intelligible for purposes of description or analysis. The classification of Canada's difference and diversities into three major Ethnicities solves several problems in one swoop. Recurrent themes and prevailing patterns in group behaviour can be foregrounded without lapsing into a welter of detail. Specifics are sacrificed along the way; still, much can be gleaned from exploring the inner logic behind the "bigger picture" instead of getting lost in the minutiae. This "big picture" approach also reinforces a macro-sociological view of society as a dynamic of competitively different groups in ongoing struggles over power, privilege, and property. Finally, acknowledging the different sociological and constitutional status of each major ethnicity helps to explain why some ethnicities are more entitled than others in terms of who gets what and why.

Part 2 is organized around this macro-level analysis of Canada as a multilayered and deeply divided society of competing groups, opposing agendas, and contested models for living together differently. Chapter 7 explores the politics of Aboriginal peoples–state relations within the context of Aboriginal peoples, who claim status as political communities with an inherent right to self-determining autonomy—albeit within the framework of Canadian society. Chapter 8 analyzes the politics of English–French (charter member) relations against the backdrop of an increasingly antiquated federalist structure. Quebec's nationalism is shown to be driven by claims to peoplehood, an aversion to being ruled by others, a commonality as a national community ("nationhood") with a shared language and customs, and a qualified form of sovereignty within an asymmetrical federalism. Chapter 9 looks at a variety of concerns that confront multicultural minorities as they cope with the challenges of "getting in," "settling down," "fitting in," and "moving up." Primary attention is given to various issues pertaining to immigration, including an overview of immigration policies, immigration patterns in the past and at present, debates over the pros/benefits and cons/costs of immigration, and insights into the immigrants' experiences in Canada, both positive and negative. Part 3, on multiculturalism and inclusiveness, will deal more specifically with the politics of institutional inclusion in addressing the needs and demands of new and racialized Canadians.

CHAPTER 7

Aboriginal Peoples in Canada: Repairing the Relationship

Disparities, Disempowerment, and Destructiveness: Canada's "Indian Problem" or the Indians' "Canada Problem"?

No matter how evaluated or assessed, Aboriginal peoples as a group remain at the bottom of the socioeconomic heap (Cooke & McWhirter, 2010; Frideres, 2011). Housing is inadequate or overcrowded on many reserves and fails to meet basic standards of amenities and structure, including proper sewer and water connections. The awkward location of many reserves and their limited resources undercut employment and development goals. Nevertheless, many residents are reluctant to abandon reserves for fear of losing band entitlements, resulting in what critics call "subsidies-to-stay," whose perverse effects have proven just as distorting for status Indians as they have for non-Aboriginal residents of Atlantic Canada (Fiss, 2004; Flanagan, 2001). Those off-reserve in towns and cities also encounter problems in terms of access to housing and employment, as well as discriminatory encounters with the criminal justice system. Of particular concern are Aboriginal peoples in prisons: Aboriginal offenders across Canada account for 19 percent of provincial admissions to custody

and 17 percent of federal admissions, including a whopping 80 percent of admissions in Saskatchewan—despite the fact that Aboriginal peoples comprise only 11 percent of the province's population (Roberts & Melchers, 2003).

A Misery Index: Social, Economic, Demographic Indicators

Equally worrying is the demographic time bomb that is ticking away in many Aboriginal communities. The combination of a relatively high birth rate with an extremely young population is exerting even greater pressure on limited reserve resources such as housing (Winsor, 2001). The fact that the Aboriginal identity population (persons who identify as Aboriginal) is relatively young, with less labour market experience (and less education as pointed out below), makes this demographic much more vulnerable during periods of economic slowdown and layoffs (Delic & Abele, 2010). Unemployment is a major cause of poverty and powerlessness. For example, while the jobless rate of non-Aboriginals was 5.2 percent in 2006, the Aboriginal

(Continued)

unemployment rate stood at 13.2 percent, down from 16.7 percent in 2001 (Environics Institute, 2010b). Employment rates for Aboriginal peoples of working age (25–54) stood at 65.8 percent in 2006 (61.2 percent in 2001), compared with 81.6 percent for non-Aboriginal workers (Delic & Abele, 2010). Even these figures can be misleading: On some reserves, up to 95 percent of the population are un- or underemployed and subsist almost entirely on government transfers.

Income inequality is no less a problem (Wilson & Macdonald, 2010). According to 2006 Census data, the median income for Aboriginal peoples was $18 962, or 30 percent less than the $27 097 median income for the rest of Canadians. The difference of $8135 in 2006 was marginally less than the difference of $9045 in 2001 or $9428 in 1996. Let's put this assessment into a global context. Canada may be perennially ranked by the United Nations as one of the world's best places to live, according to a human development index. However, if Canada's on-reserve Aboriginal peoples were disaggregated from the population and assessed independently, they would rank somewhere in the 60th to 70th range. That Aboriginal peoples live shorter lives in often substandard conditions puts Aboriginal reserves on the same par as medium-developed countries such as Mexico and Thailand. Such statistics are a stunning indictment of Canada's inability to address the so-called Indian problem (or, perhaps more accurately, the Indians' "Canada problem"). The fact that the community of Kasechewan First Nations along the Hudson Bay coast

has been evacuated four times since 2004 (most recently in the spring of 2008) for water-related problems (from contamination to flooding) speaks volumes about the indifference and expediency (see online Case Study 7.2). To Canada's embarrassment, various UN human rights committees have repeatedly criticized Canada's mistreatment of Aboriginal peoples as a hidden shame, contrary to international law, and its most egregious violation of human rights (as cited in Schlein, 2005, p. A11; see also CBC News, 2010).

To add insult to injury, Aboriginal peoples are increasingly pitted against one another. Disparities in wealth and power within communities may be as gaping as the gulf between Aboriginal peoples and non-Aboriginal Canadians. Internal class divisions prevail as well. A new class of senior managers and business elites has emerged, who reward their own, control a powerful network of patronage or nepotism, or divert cash into their own pockets. Those on the wrong side of the political tracks do without (see Blackduck, 2001; Fontaine, 2003). To be sure, the degree of fiscal mismanagement may be exaggerated by critics. According to the Auditor General, as reported in John Ibbitson, *The Globe and Mail* (2 February 2005), of the 557 bands audited in 2002–03, only 16 required remedial action. Still, the lack of transparency in and accountability for decision making cannot be lightly brushed off (Fiss, 2004).

The Marginalizing Effects of the Colonial Project

The demise of Aboriginal cultural values has compounded the difficulties of identity and adjustment. Numerous

Aboriginal languages are on the brink of extinction because of pressure from English (and French) in the schools and media, with only three (Ojibwa, Cree, and Inuktitut) on a relatively solid footing (Fleras, 1987). The damaging effects of the colonial project (from residential schools to forced location), including the experience of powerlessness, alienation, and irrelevance, have been no less detrimental (Environics, 2010b). As noted by David Courchene, former president of the Manitoba Indian Brotherhood, over a century of patronizing submission and paternalistic servitude has instilled psychological barriers that amplify material poverty (Buckley, 1992; see also Adams, 1999; Alfred, 2005). No more so than with the legacy of the residential school system (see online Case Study 7.1), which induced in many students a loss of language and culture, an inability to parent, inexplicable anger and aggression, and generations of silence (Rolfsen, 2008).

This interplay of powerlessness and poverty stimulates expressions of inner- and outer-directed violence, including violent death rates at four times the national average. Domestic abuse is so endemic within Aboriginal communities—21 percent of the population experiences spousal violence compared with 6 percent of the non-Aboriginal population—that few Aboriginal children grow into adulthood without first-hand experience of interpersonal violence (Drost, Crowley, & Schwindt, 1995; Government of Canada, 2010). With a suicide rate six to eight times the national average for certain age-specific groups, Aboriginal peoples represent

one of the most self-destructive groups in the world at present. According to Health Canada (2006), suicide rates for Aboriginal youth are five to seven times higher than for non-Aboriginal youth. Inuit youth suicide rates are eleven times higher than Canada's national average. Small, remote communities are also plagued by exorbitant patterns that indicate a great deal about the power of poverty and powerlessness. Consider Pikangikum—a small reserve with just over 2000 residents about 300 kilometres northeast of Winnipeg. In the year 2000, nine people committed suicide, some as young as 13 years old. According to British suicide expert Colin Sampson, at a rate of 450 per 100 000 of an admittedly small population base, Pikangikum is routinely crowned as Canada's (or even the world's) suicide capital

Suicide does not simply affect the immediate family. The entire community is impacted by the trauma because of the ripple effect in small and closely knit groups, perhaps accounting for suicide clusters (Health Canada, 2006). Dysfunctional communities are often the root cause of youth suicides. Studies indicate that certain protective factors seem to inhibit suicide rates (Chandler & Lalonde, 1998); Communities with some form of self government had the lowest rates, followed by communities with settled land claims and educational services. The lack of effective parenting has contributed to this breakdown in community life. But "bad" parenting itself may reflect earlier negative experiences, including the suicide of loved ones or the legacy of residential schools. And when combined

(Continued)

with contributing factors such as a lack of opportunity, boredom and despair, drug and alcohol abuse, positive identity, and an absence of positive role models to assist in meeting life's challenges, the conclusion is inescapable: Communities that fail to provide boundaries and coping skills are ticking time bombs. Not surprisingly, Aboriginal youth become impulsive, desperate, in pain, exposed to a culture of violence and despair—and, like all kids, want to imitate their friends ("Hope or Heartbreak," 2008). And so the wheel goes round and round as part of "the circle game"—as sadly acknowledged in a song with the same name, albeit in a different context, by legendary Aboriginal recording artist Buffy Sainte-Marie (the song was written by Joni Mitchell).

Health indicators continue to spiral downward—a scandalous state of affairs for a country that trumpets its much-vaunted healthcare system (Cooke et al., 2007). Aboriginal peoples experience heart problems at twice the rate of non-Aboriginals, are twice as likely to have cancer, and are five times more likely to have diabetes. Infectious diseases like tuberculosis are prevalent, and an AIDS epidemic is worrying (Brady, 2001). Infant mortality rates are about 60 percent higher than the national average. Alcohol and substance abuse are widely regarded as the foremost problems on most reserves, with alcohol-related deaths accounting for up to 80 percent of the fatalities on some reserves (Buckley, 1992). Violent crime victimization is a problem of epidemic proportions. Aboriginal peoples are victimized at a rate of 319 per 1000 population, including

461 per 1000 of those aged 15 to 34 years, compared with 101 per 1000 for non-Aboriginal Canadians (Government of Canada, 2010).

A Sense of Perspective and Hope

Despite the bad news, a sense of perspective is critical (Cannon & Sunseri, 2011; Newhouse, Voyageur, & Beavon, 2007). Both individual and community levels are showing signs of improvement, including patterns of increased life expectancy. In 1975, the life expectancy for a Canadian male was 11.1 years higher than for a status-Indian male. This gap had closed to 6.3 years in 2000, and is expected to drop to 5.3 years by 2020. Figures for Aboriginal women are also encouraging (INAC, 2003). In addition, not all Aboriginal peoples are synonymous with failure—even when measured by mainstream standards. Thanks to substantial sums of money and resources from successful land claims settlements, Aboriginal communities are riding the crest of an entrepreneurial wave by cashing in on developments in energy, forestry, and mining resources, in addition to earnings as landlords of on-reserve condos and luxury golf resorts (Curry, 2010). From airline companies and construction firms to wineries and technology consulting firms, Aboriginal entrepreneurship is thriving like never before, according to Roberta Jamieson, CEO of the National Aboriginal Achievement Foundation (Freeland, 2010): for example, there are 20 000 Aboriginal-owned businesses (about half on reserves), 50 Aboriginal financial institutions, and an Aboriginal trust company and bank.

Moreover, success should not be evaluated exclusively along mainstream lines. There are individuals who possess secure and satisfying prospects and exceptionally enriched lives without rejecting either cultures. Not all communities should be seen as dysfunctional, despite media coverage to this effect (Strauss, 2005). While many communities experience punishing rates of suicide, other groups seem relatively immune to the scourge, especially those with a solid governance structure in place (Chandler & Lalonde, 1998). In general, however, an unacceptable number of Aboriginal peoples endure punitive conditions that evoke images of grinding developing-world poverty and powerlessness.

Problematizing the So-called Indian Problem

In sum, the impoverishment that confronts Aboriginal peoples is a scathing indictment of the status quo. Aboriginal peoples tend to score poorly on those indicators that count, but soar on those that don't, with few indications of immediate improvements. To be sure, there are risks in focusing on Aboriginal peoples only as "problem people" who have or create problems. Framing Aboriginal peoples as "troublesome constituents" tends to gloss over the broader context of colonization and its legacy as contributing factors. Nevertheless, this Debate box raises questions that "problematizes" the so-called Indian problem:

1. What is the root cause of problems within Aboriginal communities—individuals (blaming the victim) or society (blaming the system)? Too much external pressure (assimilation) or not enough of it (too much separation or special treatment)?

2. Who is ultimately responsible for solving these problems? If it's an "Indian problem," should responsibility rest with Aboriginal peoples and communities? If it's a "Canada problem, " is Canada responsible for taking charge?

3. Should solutions focus on modernizing Aboriginal communities by discarding practices inconsistent with contemporary realities ("more like us")? Or must modernization-induced patterns of dependency and underdevelopment be discarded for more indigenous-controlled levels of self-determining autonomy ("less like you")?

4. Should solutions to problems of poverty, ill health, educational failure, and family violence proceed on a piecemeal basis? Or should solutions recognize how these problems reinforce one another, so that breaking the circle of disadvantage—in which family violence leads to educational failures leads to poverty leads to ill health and back again—means tackling them together (Centre for Social Justice, 2010)?

5. How pivotal is the role of education and improved educational outcomes in alleviating poverty and marginalization in Aboriginal communities (Richards & Scott, 2009)? True, increasing educational levels increases socioeconomic status, but it's precisely those in the lowest socioeconomic bracket who are least likely to become more educated (Mendelson, 2006).

(Continued)

The challenge is clearly before us: How can these disparities be explained? For some, Aboriginal peoples are widely thought to have brought inequality on themselves by choosing to live in regions of little employment or on reserves whose traditional economies have been decimated by remoteness and relocation. For others, the legacy and impact of colonialism is the prime culprit (Wilson & Macdonald, 2010). The Debate Revisited box provides responses to these complex and vexing questions.

INTRODUCTION: CONTESTING THE "SOCIAL CONTRACT"

Nearly 400 years of colonial contact has plunged many Aboriginal peoples into disarray and despair. The largely dysfunctional relationship between the colonizers and the colonized can be crudely captured by this blunt aphorism: "you the indigenous inhabitants got it [i.e., the land and resources], we the colonizers want it, and we are going to get it by hook, crook, or the book" (see also Adams, 1999). The colonizers sought to subordinate and eliminate Aboriginal peoples through a process of assimilation into "civilization"—resulting in the "taming" and "caging" of the indigenes that proved every bit as restraining as physical constraints (Churchill, 2004; Porter, 2005). In some cases, government policies deliberately destroyed the viability of Aboriginal communities in the relentless quest to divest them of their land, culture, and tribal authority. In other cases, the demise of Aboriginal peoples came about through unobtrusive but equally powerful assimilationist measures, such as education and missionization. In still other cases, the often unintended consequences of possibly well-intentioned, but ultimately destructive, government policies and programs such as reserve relocation or the residential school system have proven equally marginalizing (Miller, 1999; Shkilnyk, 1985). (See online Case Study 7.1.)

But times are changing. As recently as 1969, Canada's Aboriginal peoples were poised on the brink of legal extinction because of the assimilationist intent of the government's draft **White Paper**, under then Indian Affairs Minister, Jean Chrétien. Aboriginal concerns had focused largely on basic survival strategies, in response to the government's long-standing assimilationist commitments, with most seemingly resigned to life under powerful outside forces beyond their control. But Aboriginal protest mobilized over perceptions of the White Paper as predominantly a pretext for cultural genocide. By the late 1970s, a palpable sense of revolt was mounting because of government waffling over Aboriginal issues, a crisis that nearly derailed Trudeau's efforts at repatriating the Constitution. The constitutional entrenchment of Aboriginal and treaty rights in 1982 clearly confirmed the ascendant political clout of Aboriginal peoples. By the late 1980s and with Aboriginal nationalism firmly in place, Aboriginal leaders convened with First Ministers from Meech Lake to Charlottetown to construct a workable post-Oka social contract. Despite failure to advance the constitutional yardsticks, a new era dawned when, in 1995, the Liberal government acknowledged the "inherent right" of Canada's Aboriginal peoples to **self-government**. Ratification of the Nisga'a Final Agreement confirmed what some had suspected, but others feared: Aboriginal peoples were a force to be reckoned with in shaping Canada-building (Murphy, 2005).

One of the major themes in this chapter is the distance travelled by Aboriginal peoples in reclaiming legal and constitutional space (Belanger, 2008; Bird, Land, & Macadam, 2002; Long & Dickason, 2011). In a relatively short period of time, the status of Aboriginal peoples has leapt from that of wards of the state to self-determining peoples, from a minority group with needs to a people with rights, and from passive observers on the margins of Canada to robust actors on Canada's political stage. But another theme in this chapter is less hopeful, namely, the enormity of the distance that has yet to be traversed before Aboriginal peoples assume their rightful place in Canada. Canadians have been slow in addressing Aboriginal demands; even slower in acknowledging Aboriginal realities as a basis for "living together separately"; and slower still in recognizing the transformative dynamic of aboriginality. The relationship between Canada and Aboriginal peoples continues to be predicated on colonial foundational principles[1] that reflect a predominantly Eurocentric constitutional order. Canadians also appear reluctant to recognize the central reality that governs Aboriginal peoples–Canada relations: Aboriginal difference (Macklem, 2001). Aboriginal peoples possess inherent and collective rights that not only set them apart from the mainstream in terms of entitlements but also articulate a framework for re-priming their relationship to Canada.

It is not coincidental that Part 2 begins with an analysis of Canada's First Peoples. The term "first" in First Peoples is not to be taken lightly. The term "Aboriginal" itself refers to the original or "first" occupants of this country (or at least those immediately prior to European contact and conquest [Waldron, 2002]). Their status as original occupants (or more accurately, descendants of the original occupants) secures a moral legitimacy as first among equals in defining who gets what. The term "first" can also be used in a less flattering way. **Aboriginal peoples** are "first" in those social areas that count least (unemployment, undereducation, suicide, and morbidity rates), but rarely first in realms that matter most, including wealth, power, and privilege. They may be first as Canada's largest landowners, yet they are last in measures of prosperity (Flanagan, Alcantara, & Le Dressay, 2010). The colonialist structures that thwart Aboriginal aspirations have succeeded only too well in ensuring that the "first" are often the "last."

However badly treated and maligned, Aboriginal peoples have not stood by as passive and powerless victims (Ashini, 2002; Belanger, 2008; Long & Dickason, 2011; Maaka & Anderson, 2007; Ominayak & Bianchi, 2002; Samson, 2003). Many have taken the initiative in recalibrating their relationship to society, and the content of this chapter is anchored in these "initiatives" for moving forward rather than on the "inertia" of looking back. To be sure, the foundational principles that govern Canada's **constitutional order** are resistant to change because of vested interests and systemic bias, with the result that *conventions that refer to the rules may change, but rules that inform the conventions rarely do*. Nevertheless, the awareness that change is overdue but undervalued redoubles the need to focus on Aboriginal peoples–Canada relations in terms of underlying logic, hidden agendas, competing interests, and future outcomes. This chapter neither unfolds as a history nor reads as a description. Nor is it intended to obsess over social problems in Aboriginal communities, as if Aboriginal peoples were the sole architects of their misfortune. Rather, the chapter addresses the politics of "**aboriginality**" (being Aboriginal as the rationale for political challenge and transformative change) by analyzing the evolving and contested relationship of Aboriginal peoples to Canadian society. Also addressed are the politics of repairing a broken relationship. Time will tell if the current (neo-)colonial infrastructure can transition into a postcolonial social contract for living together separately.

Two narratives capture the reality of Aboriginal peoples in Canada at present (Fraser, 2004). One tells of the growing recognition of Aboriginal rights, court decisions that uphold Aboriginal peoples' claims to self-determining autonomy, and constitutional changes to the political architecture for framing the relationship (see Abele, 2004). The other narrative speaks of dispossession, disempowerment, degradation, and despair at individual and community levels. In acknowledging the concurrent reality of both narratives, this chapter begins with a brief overview of Aboriginal peoples with respect to their legal and socioeconomic status. This is followed by an examination of policy changes that have historically shaped the fortunes of the **"nations within."** Aboriginal policy is shown to have generated as many problems as it set out to solve, partly because of faulty premises that have induced negative outcomes and partly from privileging "national interests" over Aboriginal concerns (Shkilnyk, 1985). Not unexpectedly, there is mounting concern over Canada's governance model for relations with Aboriginal peoples: Is it working or is it beyond repair (Strauss, 2006)? Aboriginal proposals for renewing the relationship are discussed at three levels of engagement: (1) taking Aboriginal difference seriously, (2) recognizing Aboriginal title and treaty rights, and (3) promoting Aboriginal models of self-determining autonomy. The chapter concludes by exploring the politics of constructing a new relationship based on the postcolonial principles of power sharing, partnership, and participation.

A few words of warning to the reader: First, neither of the original authors (Augie Fleras and Jean Leonard Elliott) is of Aboriginal ancestry, so we cannot speak from an Aboriginal perspective by tapping into Aboriginal experiences. Such an outsider status can be a strength or a weakness, but invariably necessitates a certain deftness in approach—if only to avoid the trap of treacly sentimentality, overgeneralization, indignation, or defensiveness (see also Weisberger, 1999). Second, limitations of space cannot be ignored. With over 600 First Nations comprising 60–80 nation groups and more than 50 languages, it is impossible to compress into a single chapter the entirety of knowledge about Aboriginal peoples, either in the past or at present. Nor can the diverse concerns of Aboriginal peoples be squeezed into a singular position, especially when differences within Aboriginal communities may be as striking as differences with non-Aboriginal Canadians. Priorities vary widely. The political aspirations of Aboriginal "elites" may be widely endorsed in principle within Aboriginal communities, but their concerns do not always resonate with more pragmatic local concerns for healthy children and indoor plumbing (EKOS, 2004). On one side are those willing to work within the system without sacrificing their identity in the process; on the other side are those committed to more "radical" indigenism, who seek to work outside the system or want to fundamentally transform it along postcolonial lines (Alfred, 2005). Some Aboriginal leaders prefer the language of victimization by focusing on accusations and grievances; others reject this discourse because they don't consider themselves oppressed or victimized (Wente, 2008). The necessity to be selective reduces our options to a focus on the macro-dimension of Aboriginal realities, namely, the evolving political relationship of Aboriginal peoples with Canada through the prism of official government policy and Aboriginal assertiveness.

In short, references to Aboriginal peoples are confined to general terms. Such a level of generality increases the risk of glossing over the historical and cultural specifics of different Aboriginal communities. Aboriginal peoples constitute an extremely diverse constituency, with numerous tribes of varying size, access to resources, development levels, ecological adaptations, and social health. Politically speaking, Aboriginal peoples are legally divided into status, non-status, Métis, and Inuit, each with a specific set of priorities and aspirations. The diversity is amplified by ecological adaptations to unique physical environments, in addition to individual differences based on age, education levels, location, and socioeconomic status (Monture-Angus, 2002). Clearly, then, numerous traps await any discussion dealing with Aboriginal peoples as if they were a relatively homogeneous entity with a shared sense of community and commitment. (For some, even the term "Aboriginal" is a misnomer that should be banned because it's too homogenizing of differences [Alfred, 2008].) Common sense will dictate that they are as heterogeneous as non-Aboriginal Canadians in political outlook, socioeconomic status, and personality types. To admit this internal diversity is not to diminish the value of broad brushstrokes. Nevertheless, readers must be insulated against the temptation of imposing a uniform explanatory framework on a domain of astonishing complexity.

CANADA'S ABORIGINAL PEOPLES: DIVERSITY IN DISTRESS

Indian, Native, Status Indian, Aboriginal, Treaty Indian, Non-treaty Indian, Registered Indian, C-31s, Non-status Indian, Inuit, Métis—about all these different terms have in common is the unilateral manner in which they were imposed on the original inhabitants of Turtle Island, resulting in one of the most arbitrary yet oppressive classifications ever devised by a government to categorize and control (Sawchuk, 1998). Rather than reflecting cultural or historical distinctions, each of these terms describes a legality for political and bureaucratic reasons. Political authorities have reacted accordingly. While the Inuit and First Nations on reserves possess entitlements and rights, those who live off reserves and the Métis were perceived—until recently—as having needs. While the Métis are served by the healthcare system, like other Canadians, Health Canada oversees an annual expenditure of $1.1 billion for providing customized care for First Nations and Inuit communities (Abele, 2004). These divisions not only make it difficult for Aboriginal peoples to speak with one voice; they are also likely to lead to legal challenges, internal conflicts, intergovernmental disputes, and administrative snafus. Not surprisingly, perhaps, different national organizations have been established that promote the interests of specific Aboriginal peoples, reflect their distinctive world views, and reinforce their historical experiences.

Demographic Status

The term "Aboriginal peoples" in the Constitution describes the descendants of the original occupants. Their constitutional status can be further subdivided into the categories of Status Indians, Métis, and Inuit. According to Statistics Canada's 2006 Census, 1, 172, 790 people self-identified as Aboriginal, which includes 698 025 North American Indians (First Nations) (of which 564 870 are Status Indians; the rest are non-Status Indians), 389 785 Métis, and 50 485 Inuit. In other words, about two-thirds of Canada's entire Aboriginal population are Status or non-Status Indians, just under one-third are Métis, and about 5 percent are Inuit (Environics Institute, 2010b). Regional differences are noticeable, with the highest concentrations of First Nations and Métis in Ontario

(21 percent of Canada's Aboriginal population) and the western provinces. It should be noted that 22 reserves did not participate in the 2006 Census, including the 22 000 members of the Six Nations Confederacy near Brantford.

Those who identify as Aboriginal peoples comprise 3.8 percent of Canada's population. The increase from 2.8 percent in 1996 is due in part to higher fertility rates and a greater willingness to select aboriginality as an identity marker. This striking increase in Aboriginal identity population between 1996 and 2006 can be broken down accordingly, with Métis reflecting a 91 percent increase during this time span, followed by First Nations at 29 percent and Inuit at 26 percent. But while identity is one thing, ancestry (or origins) is another. Close to 1.7 million individuals in 2006 (or 4.4 percent of Canada's population) reported having Aboriginal ancestry, that is, an Aboriginal ancestor could be found in their genealogy, but the respondent chose not to identify as Aboriginal—thus accounting for the discrepancy between identity and origins. This overall total also reflects an increase from 1.2 million in 2001. As a result of this demographic boom, the proportion of Aboriginal peoples to non-Aboriginals in Canada is second only to New Zealand, where indigenous Maori tribes comprise about 15 percent of the population.

Constitutional Status/Legal Distinctions

The *Indian Act* of 1876 established the criterion for defining an Indian. This criterion did not reflect the realities of race or culture as much as the principle of patrilineal (on the male side) descent (Sawchuk, 1998). Not until 1951 did the *Indian Act* define an Indian as "a person who, pursuant to the *Indian Act,* is registered as an Indian or entitled to be registered as an Indian." The current definition of "Indian" embraces the rank of "status" or "registered" Indian. The federal government acknowledges responsibility for providing services and programs, but only for registered (status) Indians and the Inuit (Peters, 2001). Status Indians are further divided into treaty versus non-treaty Indians, depending on whether their ancestors signed a treaty with the federal government. Entitlements by status could be offset by loss of status for different reasons. Prior to 1985, Aboriginal women who married non-Aboriginal men lost their status. With reinstatement of status on the basis of of Bill C-31, many have returned to their reserve communities, with full access to housing and services; others, however, have been less fortunate. In that the Bill C-31 amendment to the *Indian Act* also redefined membership codes (i.e., transmission of status from one generation to the next), several classes of Indians now exist, including (1) those with registered Indian status and band membership, (2) those with registered status but no band membership, (3) those without status but with band membership, and (4) descendants of registered Indians but who are entitled to neither status nor membership (INAC 2004).

With some exceptions, membership as status Indians is defined by (1) registration in a general registry in Ottawa, (2) affiliation with one of 633 bands, (3) entitlement to residence on band reserve lands, and (4) jurisdiction under the *Indian Act* (Frideres & Gadacz, 2008). Status Indians are associated with one of 2567 reserves across Canada, ranging in population size from less than a dozen to over 22 000 at the Six Nations Reserve near Brantford, Ontario. But while status Indians may be entitled to live on reserves because of treaties signed with the Crown, the number of those who stay is slipping, despite incentives to remain. Finally, responsibility for status Indians rests with the federal government, which allocates around $9 billion per year for programs and administration. However, the national interests of status Indians are represented by the band chiefs who collectively comprise membership in the Assembly of First Nations.

Non-status Indians constitute a quasi-official category of Aboriginal peoples. Persons of Aboriginal ancestry are classified as non-status if their ancestors failed to register under the *Indian Act*, never signed a treaty with federal authorities, or lost their Indian status in exchange for the right to vote, drink alcohol off the reserve, or (in the case of Aboriginal women prior to 1985) marry a non-Indian. Unlike status Indians, non-status Indians do not qualify for recognition or rights under the *Indian Act*; rather, their status as Indian is defined by the *Constitution Act*. The exact number of non-status Indians is unknown, but estimates range from 75 000 to 125 000. Non-status Indians do not live on reserves (only status Indians are entitled to reserve life and band entitlements), but are scattered in small towns and large cities across Canada. Despite this formal estrangement from their roots, many non-status Indians continue to self-identify as Aboriginal peoples because of shared affinities. Nevertheless, relationships between non-status and status Indians remain fraught with tension because of competition over limited federal resources. Currently, non-status Indians are represented by the Congress of Aboriginal Peoples.

The second class of Aboriginal peoples, the Métis, constitutes a contested category. Comprising the descendants of mixed European–Aboriginal unions, the Métis peoples initially were defined as those inhabitants of the Red River Settlements in Manitoba who identified with the Métis nation. But reference to the Métis now includes anyone of mixed heritage who is recognized as such or who lives in Métis communities, in effect connoting a hybrid culture that cannot be associated with a particular culture or language but a "cultural, linguistic, and territorial mosaic" with which a population has identified and continues to evolve (Guimond, Kerr, & Beaujot, 2004; see also Sawchuk, 1998). Without much land base for developmental growth, the Métis remain hampered by their "Métis-ness." Even if they are officially regarded as a distinct Aboriginal people with constitutional protection and corresponding guarantees, lack of judicial recognition placing them on par with status Indians has undermined their legal authority to negotiate claims over traditional lands. The assumption was that Aboriginal constitutional rights of 1982 belonged to those who could prove original occupancy and claim an exclusive relationship to the land, possessed an authentic culture, and exercised Aboriginal title rights (Chartrand & Peeling, 2004). But the Ontario provincial court has ruled that Métis have the same right as status Indians to hunt and fish for food without a licence (Blackwell, 2000). The ruling also confirmed the Métis as full-fledged Aboriginal peoples with constitutionally protected rights to self-determining autonomy because of a shared culture, collective identity, and communal life (Harty & Murphy, 2005). The Métis National Council provides national representation and a lobby voice for Métis at the federal level.

The Inuit constitute the final category of Aboriginal peoples. They enjoy a special status and relationship with the federal government, despite never having signed any treaty arrangements or registered under the *Indian Act*. A Supreme Court ruling in 1939 defined the Inuit as Indians for purposes of federal jurisdiction and entitlements, although the federal government subsequently revised the *Indian Act* to exclude the Inuit (Cudmore, 2001). At local levels, the Inuit are governed by municipal councils, with various committees to discharge responsibilities for health and education. Inuit interests at national levels are represented by the Inuit Tapirisat (an association of various Inuit leaders) of Canada. The Inuit have concluded successful land claims settlements with Ottawa for control over their homeland in the Eastern Arctic. The territory of Nunavut, which came into being in 1999, shows great promise in self-determining growth, but confronts numerous problems, ranging from punishing rates of suicide to a dearth of employment opportunities outside the government sector.

Socioeconomic Status

Aboriginal peoples are disproportionately ranked among the poorest people in Canada based on disparities in income inequality (Wilson & Macdonald, 2010). As noted in the Debate box at the outset of this chapter, in 2006 the median income for Aboriginal peoples was 30 percent less than the median income for the rest of Canadians. Although this gap has been closing slowly, it persists regardless of location: In urban settings, the income gap between Aboriginal peoples and the rest of Canadians is $7083, while in rural settings it reaches $11 575. Even higher levels of education do not entirely eliminate these disparities (Wilson & Macdonald, 2010). In 2006, a gap of only $648 separated Aboriginal peoples with university degrees from the rest of Canadians with a B.A. (Admittedly, far fewer Aboriginal peoples have degrees; in 2006, according to Delic and Abele [2010], 43.6 percent of the total Aboriginal identity population had less than high school education, while 5.6 percent possessed a university degree or certificate; by contrast, the comparable figures for the non-Aboriginal population stood at 23.5 percent and 18 percent, respectively.) A Catch-22 is at play, according to Mendelson (2006): While higher education provides an escape from low socioeconomic status, it is precisely this depressed state of affairs that undermines the likelihood of higher education.

Gender income differences are apparent as well, but in surprising ways. Despite their status as the poorest of the poor, whose lives are blighted by the colonial legacy of violence and victimization, not all Aboriginal women are marginalized. As Wilson and Macdonald (2010) point out, Aboriginal women are obtaining university degrees at a higher rate than Aboriginal men; they are earning median incomes closer to that of Aboriginal men than is the case of non-Aboriginal women relative to non-Aboriginal men (this trend may reflect a depression of male wages rather than a strength in female earnings [Mendelson, 2006]); and Aboriginal women with degrees are earning more than non-Aboriginal women with equivalent education.

Not surprisingly, federal government programs have concentrated on narrowing these income and labour market gaps (Graham & Levesque, 2010). In recent years, the government has moved toward well-capitalized and partnership-oriented programs to foster economic development by encouraging a robust Aboriginal business sector, while bringing Aboriginal workers into the labour market (Delic & Abele, 2010). In 2009, the Federal Framework for Aboriginal Economic Development was released, with its focus on the following priorities: (1) supporting skills and training; (2) leveraging investments and promoting partnerships; and (3) removing barriers to Aboriginal entrepreneurship, including improving access to capital for Aboriginal businesses. With the 2009 budget allocation for Aboriginal-specific commitments estimated at up to $3.6 billion (Delic & Abele, 2010), it remains to be seen whether a business model of development (with its focus on jobs, income, and start-ups) will prove more sustainable than a political model based on nation-building (Graham & Levesque, 2010; see also Cornell & Kalt, 2003).

Urban Aboriginal Peoples: Despair or Enrichment?

Contrary to widespread perception, Aboriginal peoples are increasingly city folk. According to Richards and Scott (2009), nearly one half of those who identify as Aboriginal (49.5 percent) live off-reserve, with 29.1 percent in cities with populations of over 100 000, and 20.4 percent in cities with populations of under 100 000. Another 19.1 percent live in rural off-reserve regions; as a result, only 31.4 percent of the Aboriginal population remain on reserves. Statistics Canada (2008) indicates a slightly higher percentage (54 percent) of the Aboriginal population in urban centres, with First Nations (Native American Indian) accounting for 50 percent of the city population and Métis at 43 percent). In 2006, about one-quarter of urban Aboriginal peoples lived in seven census metropolitan areas: Winnipeg (68 385, or 10 percent of the city's population), Edmonton (52 100), Vancouver (40 310), Calgary (26 575), Toronto (26 575, or 0.5 percent of the census metropolitan area population), Saskatoon (21 535, or 9 percent of the population), and Ottawa/Gatineau (20 590) (Environics Institute, 2010b). The growing critical mass of Aboriginal peoples in cities is not just about numbers. It's also about the distinctive and enduring realities that Aboriginal peoples are constructing social patterns and cultural forms just as authentic and valid as traditional forms—as aptly phrased by David Newhouse and Evelyn Peters (2003):

> Relationships with urban landlords, searching for employment in urban economies, making spaces for Aboriginal cultures and languages in city places, interacting with neighbours from different cultures and building urban Aboriginal programs and institutions is as much part of Aboriginal realities as are land claims, conflicts over logging, hunting, and Treaty rights, and rural economic development. (p. 5)

Reasons for migrating to cities are numerous. Normally, they reflect a combination of "push" factors (lack of resources, opportunity, or excitement) and "pull" forces related to family, employment, education, lifestyle, and availability of services and amenities (Environics Institute, 2010b). Structural (band size, proximity to urban centres), social (poor housing, unemployment), and cultural (socialization) factors influence the decision to leave—or return. People leave because of misguided reserve policies; fiscal mismanagement involving ruling factions who dole out favours to relatives and supporters; and a lack of transparency and accountability for reserve decision making. Although reserves continue to be stigmatized as sinkholes of poverty and despair, with punishing levels of unemployment and dilapidated living conditions, they are also endorsed as life-affirming enclaves of Aboriginal identity, locales for cultural protection, catalysts for self-government, buffers against a hostile world, refuges for personal renewal, and engines of development. To be sure, Aboriginal patterns of migration to cities may be more circular than linear (Peters, 2004; see also Dosman, 1972). Except for the very young or very old, the link between reserve and city is increasingly fluid, flexible, and circular, with the promise of urban potential offset by a powerful sense of connection and commitment to communities of origin (Monture-Angus, 2002). Nevertheless, according to an Environics Institute (2010b) study, only 2 in 10 have ever returned to their community of origin or plan to return permanently—thus reinforcing the fact that Aboriginal peoples' sense of place (home) is defined as much by their city of residence as by their community of origin.

For many Aboriginal peoples, the move to cities is positive. Studies indicate that cities are increasingly sites of connection, prosperity, cultural vitality, creativity, and participation (Environics Institute, 2010b). Instead of framing urban Aboriginal peoples through a problem lens, cities need to be reframed as spaces replete with Aboriginal lawyers, teachers, nurses, and successful entrepreneurs who earn high incomes, have the respect of peers, and are actively involved in the community. This cohort neither ekes out lives in impoverished ghettos in inner cities nor faces insurmountable challenges in building culture and community. On the contrary, they are quite capable of balancing mainstream success and strong Aboriginal culture with pride in identifying as Canadian and Aboriginal (Environics Institute, 2010b; Peters, 2004). Or as expressed by the project manager for the 2010 Environics Institute study in a news release on the publication:

> When urban Aboriginal peoples are researched, it's often about problems like homelessness and sexual exploitation. There are hundreds and thousands of us living in cities, and there are a lot of interesting things happening in our communities; it's not all crises (Environics Institute, 2010a)

For others, however, the demands of a large urban centre are daunting and life destroying. Off-reserve life is beset with missed economic opportunities, abysmal living conditions and homelessness, exposure to substance abuse, discrimination and lack of cultural awareness, and repeated brushes with the law. For still others, the urban Aboriginal experience is one of loss and opportunity: loss, as in culture and sense of community; opportunity, as in employment and education (Newhouse & Peters, 2003; Royal Commission on Aboriginal Peoples, 1996b).

Too often, Aboriginal peoples in cities are ignored in debates over "who gets what" (Cairns, 2003; Dinsdale, 2009). Reserve communities continue to receive a disproportionate share of the federal funding, despite a rapidly growing urban Aboriginal population (Murphy, 2005). The implications of a reserve-o-centric focus of government spending are significant. The resultant policy void at the centre of Canadian politics (Dinsdale, 2009) ensures that government institutions are poorly equipped (both in terms of resources and needs assessments) to offer culturally sensitive services to Aboriginal clients. As a result, Aboriginal-run voluntary agencies and friendship centres have been established in urban centres to address a wide range of issues related to healthcare, traditional healing, shelter, education and training, and criminal justice (Abele, 2004; Warry, 2007). These programs incorporate a strong cultural dimension; they also range widely in funding and outreach, from Aboriginal head-start incentives to assistance for Aboriginal mothers. But jurisdictional wrangles are inevitable: The federal government disclaims any responsibility for the provision of services to off-reserve Aboriginal peoples, citing jurisdictional problems with the provinces as a stumbling block. (The federal government has jurisdiction and responsibility for "Indians and Lands reserved for Indians," while the *Constitution Act* of 1982 allocates responsibility for the provision of social services to the provinces [Dinsdale, 2009].) The spiralling costs of servicing a rapidly growing Aboriginal population exerts additional pressure on the federal government to look for ways of capping spending—despite the fact that the federal government's inability to address the depressed conditions on reserves may have precipitated the urbanization of Aboriginal peoples in the first place (Stokes, Peach, & Blake, 2004).

CANADA'S ABORIGINAL POLICY: FROM "NO MORE INDIANS" TO THE NATIONS' WITHIN

Do government Aboriginal policies promote Aboriginal interests? Or are they more likely to undermine Aboriginal efforts at self-determining autonomy over land, identity, and political voice? Can even seemingly progressive policy initiatives produce a marginalizing or controlling effect on Aboriginal communities (Abele, LaPointe, & Prince, 2005)? History has not been kind in exonerating the politics of policy. Many have amply documented both government policy and its (mis)administration by state bureaucracy in marginalizing Aboriginal peoples (Adams, 1999; Alfred, 2005; Cannon & Sunseri, 2011). Little more can be gleaned by rehashing the negative consequences of even well-intentioned actions by government officials more interested in careerism and empire-building than in doing their job (Ponting & Gibbins, 1980; Shkilnyk, 1985). What more can be added to the sorry legacy of official Aboriginal policy that advanced "national interests" at the expense of Aboriginal identity and empowerment? Harold Cardinal (1969) captured a sense of outrage in his book *The Unjust Society*:

> Generations of Indians have grown up behind a buckskin curtain of indifference, ignorance, and, all too often, plain bigotry. The history of Canada's Indians is a shameful chronicle of the white man's disinterest, his deliberate trampling of Indian rights.

The fact that aspects of this mindset prevail at present is unconscionable. For example, consider how the government's attempt to compensate residential school victims of physical and sexual abuse has induced a nightmare of Orwellian proportions. The survivors are dying at a much faster rate than rates of compensation (50 settled claims out of 12 000 between 2003 and 2006, yet Aboriginal claimants may be dying at the rate of five per week). To add insult to injury, the government spends $4 on administration for every $1 paid to victims in an atmosphere that many see as adversarial, litigious, and bereft of any compassion or healing (Travers, 2005). Recent moves have expedited the compensation process by establishing a proposed lump-sum payment to individuals depending on the length of residential stay and the level of abuse endured. In June 2008, the Canadian government also issued a formal apology on behalf of all Canadians for the damage inflicted by the residential school system.

Still, the verdict in assessing state performance and government actions is proving ambivalent. Both the government and the state are capable of progressive policies that enhance **indigenous rights**; they are equally capable of regressive measures that may exclude, deny, or exploit (Spoonley, 1993; Belanger, 2008; Long & Dickason, 2011). Policies of disempowerment tend to control the actions and options of indigenous peoples, whereas enabling policies provide a window of opportunity for empowerment (Hinton, Johnston, & Rigney, 1997). Policies have proven double-edged regardless of intent or impact. Thus the policy domain underpinning relations between Aboriginal peoples and the state is properly viewed as a contested and highly politicized domain of competing agendas, endless tensions, and contradictory dynamics (Maaka & Fleras, 2005).

Not surprisingly, Aboriginal relations with Canada have been mediated by progressive-sounding rhetoric, yet marred by duplicity and expediency. The Aboriginal affairs policy may have evolved through a series of overlapping stages, but has never wavered from its central mission: that is, to solve the "Indian problem" by ensuring that, through absorption into the system, there are "no more Indians." An initial period of cooperation and accommodation morphed into a paternalistic policy of assimilation, with its underlying racist assumptions of white superiority as a basis for control and coercion. A shift from assimilation to integration and "ordinary citizenship" gathered momentum after the late 1940s. But federal moves toward integration by "normalizing" its relations with Aboriginal peoples had the perverse effect of galvanizing Aboriginal peoples into protest and politics. Federal policy discourses shifted accordingly. A commitment to principles of **devolution** emerged, in part to defuse both mounting Aboriginal resentment and growing international disapproval over Canada's treatment of Aboriginal peoples. Recent policy initiatives revolve around the policy principles of a **conditional autonomy** model, including a collective and inherent right to self-governance within the constitutional framework of Canadian society.

The message is mixed. In theory, the policy dimension of Aboriginal peoples–Canada relations has evolved from a patron–client relationship to one more consistent with the principles of a government-to-government relationship. Prevailing images of Aboriginal peoples have evolved, as well, from one of allies to that of threats, then to children, to citizens, to minorities, and finally to peoples (nations). In reality, this evolutionary process is interrupted by detours and double-dealing that say more about hidden agendas and vested interests than about the principles that Canada aspires to. This disconnect between ideals and reality speaks volumes about how far Aboriginal peoples–Canada relations have progressed. It also acknowledges the distance left to travel before partnership and power-sharing are a reality rather than a platitude.

Accommodation

Aboriginal policy in the broadest sense began with the Royal Proclamation of 1763. The Proclamation sought to establish the principle of Crown sovereignty over the unexplored interior of Turtle Island. It also acknowledged that, rather than a Crown bestowal, Aboriginal interest in land was a pre-existing sovereign right because of traditional use and ancestral occupancy (Slattery, 1997):

> And whereas it is just and reasonable, and essential to our interests, and the security of our Colonies, that the several Nations of Tribes of Indians with whom We are connected, and who live under our protection, should not be molested or disturbed in the Possession of such Parts of Our Dominions and Territories as, not having been ceded to or purchased by Us, are reserved to them or any of them, as their Hunting Grounds (Royal Proclamation, 1763).

Those vast tracts of land encircled by the Thirteen Colonies, Rupert's Land, and the Mississippi River were subsequently designated as Aboriginal hunting grounds off limits to European trespass. The Proclamation prohibited individual purchase of these lands without the express approval of the authorities, so that only the Crown could purchase Aboriginal land—primarily as revenue for underwriting the costs of colonizing Canada (Rotman, 1996). In acknowledging that Aboriginal peoples could not be unilaterally dispossessed of their lands, and including their right to control the westward expansion of whites into their ancestral territories, the Royal Proclamation bore resemblance to treaties of peace and friendship in other parts of the British empire (such as New Zealand's Treaty of Waitangi in 1840) (Fleras & Spoonley, 1999).

The Royal Proclamation is widely seen as a blueprint for framing Aboriginal peoples–Crown relations (Hall, 2000, p. 130). But interpretations are rarely consistent. Some have argued that the Proclamation acknowledged Aboriginal tribes as "sovereign nations" under Crown protection with jurisdictional rights over land and resources (Clark, 1990). According to the Proclamation, the principles of partnership, mutual recognition, and non-interference would inform the Crown's relationship with Aboriginal peoples (Breton, 2001). The Supreme Court of Canada has ruled to this effect, arguing that British protectorate status did not extinguish Aboriginal orders of government, but reinforced their status as distinct political communities with exclusive authority over internal jurisdictions. Others disagree with that assessment. Under the Proclamation, according to them, the British Crown asserted its sovereignty over the people and the land, with proprietary rights to Aboriginal land by virtue of the prevailing doctrines of the time: "*terra nullius*" and "first discovery" (Boldt, 1993). Crown objectives were purely pragmatic in establishing control over settlers and property interests. The Proclamation hoped to enlist Aboriginal nations as allies to curb American territorial expansion, minimize the outbreak of costly Indian wars, and establish paramountcy over the newly acquired colony of Quebec (Rotman, 1996). To the extent that the Royal Proclamation contained a bracing mix of ideals with pragmatism as well as progress and stalemate, its ambiguity cannot be discounted. Such ambiguities and conflicting perspectives continue to haunt the policy paradoxes involving Canada and its Aboriginal peoples.

Assimilation

Our objective is to continue until there is not a single Indian in Canada that has not been absorbed into the body politic, and there is no Indian question, and no Indian department. (Duncan Campbell Scott, Deputy Superintendent of Indian Affairs, 1920, as cited in Royal Commission on Aboriginal Peoples, 1996a)

An initial period of cooperation characterized post-Proclamation relationships. Encounters involving Aboriginal peoples, French and British explorers, missionaries, and traders revolved around the goals of mutual coexistence, involving reciprocal trade and practical accommodation. Expediency prevailed: The British in North America were few in number and militarily weak, thus reinforcing their dependency on Aboriginal allies for survival in a harsh land (Rotman, 1996). Imperial interests were advanced by the forging of military alliances with powerful tribes. From 1755 to 1812, the British Indian Department (forerunner of the Department of Indian Affairs, and now Indian and Northern Affairs Canada) implemented the key tenet of British policy, namely, to blunt American and French imperial aspirations by forging alliances with Aboriginal tribes (Allen, 1993).

Once the British assumed control as the premier European power in Canada, this symbiosis unravelled (Purich, 1986). The end of the War of 1812 with the United States eliminated the need for Aboriginal allies, thus rendering them immaterial and expendable. Crown interests in land, minerals, and settlement at the expense of Aboriginal peoples displaced treaty commitments and trust responsibilities. To achieve these objectives, the Crown unilaterally asserted sovereignty over people and lands. Aboriginal consent was simply assumed or deemed irrelevant (Jhappan, 1995). Aboriginal tribes may have had "natural title" to land by virtue of prior occupancy; however, their seemingly uncivilized status allowed the British to rationalize acquisition in the name of civilization and Christianity (Allen, 1993). The post-1815 era was dominated by a commitment to pacify Aboriginal tribes through acculturation or, alternatively, their removal into remote and often inhabitable locales.

Passage of the *British North America Act* (or *Constitution Act*) of 1867 transferred duties of the British Colonial Office over to the Dominion of Canada. The 1867 Act enshrined state responsibility for Aboriginal peoples by establishing federal jurisdiction over Aboriginal lands and affairs (Kulchyski, 1994; Ponting & Gibbins, 1980). In keeping with the colonialist spirit of the times but inconsistent with earlier commitments to Aboriginal peoples as "nations within," the federal government approached them as hapless wards of the state with limited civil rights but fully entitled to federal custodial care (this trust relationship was subsequently transformed into a fiduciary responsibility) (Jhappan, 1995). The theme of assimilation defined a framework for solving the "Indian problem." In the pithy phrasing of Sir John A. Macdonald, in espousing a "no more Indians" national policy: "The great aim of our civilization has been to do away with the tribal system and assimilate the Indian people in all respects with the inhabitants of the Dominion, as speedily as they are fit for the change" (as cited in Miller, 1989).

Government integrity left much to be desired in light of racist and evolutionary philosophies that disparaged Aboriginal peoples as inferior impediments to progress (Weaver, 1984). The concept of guardianship reinforced the stereotype of Aboriginal peoples as childlike and unfit to look after themselves except under the stern but watchful eye of Crown-appointed guardians (Ponting, 1986; Ponting & Gibbins, 1980). Aboriginal languages, cultures, and identity were suppressed—ruthlessly at times—while band communities were locked into patterns of dependency and despondency that aborted any local development. Legislation served as an assimilationist tool in controlling Aboriginal peoples (Rotman, 1996). For example, one of the earliest directives aimed at the Aboriginal peoples, the *Gradual Enfranchisement Act* of 1869, sought to eliminate "Indian" status through enfranchisement and exposure to the ". . . white race in the ordinary avocations of life" (as cited in Allen, 1993, p. 202). Or consider the Indian Act:

The *Indian Act* of 1876: Micro-Managing "Indians"

Of particular note in hastening the goal of "no more Indians" was the *Indian Act*. The passage of the *Indian Act* in 1876 may have sought to protect and civilize Aboriginal peoples. Nevertheless, it had an eviscerating—rather than an empowering—effect in gouging out Aboriginal realities. The *Act* reflected the government's preoccupation with land management consistent with the 1867 *Constitution Act*, which conferred federal authority over (a) "Indians and lands reserved for Indians"; (b) First Nations members and local government; and (c) any initiatives leading to the eventual enfranchisement (assimilation) of "Indians." Despite numerous changes, most notably, in 1951 and 1985, the 1876 framework has remained fundamentally intact as a roadmap for exercising federal jurisdiction over status Indians. And while both Aboriginal leaders and political authorities have long criticized its paternalism and limitations as a framework for addressing their needs and relations, the Act does offer protections and entitlements—thus fostering a perverse appeal for retention (Hurley, 2009).

To say that the *Indian Act* represented an exercise in micro-management is an understatement. As federal legislation that secured the basic legal status and entitlements of Aboriginal peoples, the Act defined who came under its provisions (who could legally claim Indian status), what benefits status Indians could expect under the government's fiduciary obligations, who could qualify for disenfranchisement, what to do with reserve lands and trust funds, and how local communities were to be governed and administered, taxation, and money management (Hurley, 2009). Traditional leadership was stripped of its authority as a legitimate political voice (Dickason, 1992), while local **governance** took the form of elected band councils, many of which were perceived as little more than federal proxies with limited powers of administration rather than self-rule (Webber, 1994). Even economic opportunities were curtailed. Under the *Indian Act*, Aboriginal peoples could not possess direct title to land or private property. They were also denied access to revenue from the sale or lease of band property. Punitive restrictions not only foreclosed Aboriginal property improvements; they also forestalled the accumulation of development capital for investment or growth (Aboriginal land held in Crown trust could not be mortgaged or used as collateral because it was immune to legal seizure). And because the land was held in trust, approval from the federal government was mandatory for any development. Finally, those who wanted to work off-reserve needed a permit from the resident Indian agent.

The imposition of the *Indian Act* bestowed sweeping state powers to regulate every aspect of reserve life (Morse, 1985). Not surprisingly, the Act has been criticized for giving the chief and band council too little power to make decisions, with nearly 90 provisions in place that empower the minister of Indian Affairs over the band and band council. In that the *Indian Act* was an essentially repressive instrument of containment and control, its role in usurping Aboriginal authority could not have been more forcefully articulated. And yet, paradoxically, the Act gives the chief and band council too much power to make decisions over allocation of reserve land and housing, without much accountability to members of the community. According to Imai (2007), a contradictory state of affairs exists in which the federal government can manage band affairs by overturning decisions of the band council and chief, while the band council and chief have powers that can be exercised without input from the community. Not surprisingly, given the underlying logic of the *Indian Act*, the relational status of Aboriginal peoples fluctuated wildly—at times protected, at times ignored, and at times actively oppressed, but never fully embraced as equal members of Canadian society (Abele, 2004).

Integration

Neither assimilation as policy nor the reserve system as practice brought about the policy goal of "no more Indians" (Smith, 1993), although it proved menacing in that it disrupted the social and cultural foundations of Aboriginal society (Aboriginal Institutes' Consortium, 2005; Frideres & Gadacz, 2008). Failure of policies to bring about the intended results exerted additional pressure on government to rethink the Aboriginal affairs policy agenda, especially after World War II, when the concept of fighting for freedom overseas stood in contradiction to the denial of basic human rights at home. An official embrace of assimilation evolved into a commitment to integration as a blueprint for rethinking the relation. Strategies to desegregate once-isolated Aboriginal enclaves for re-entry into the mainstream proved increasingly attractive. Aboriginal services were costly to maintain, their effectiveness was questionable, and they caused international embarrassment. Besides, the isolation of Aboriginal peoples caused by reserves and legislation contributed to inequality, exacerbated negative social conditions, and pre-empted Aboriginal participation in society.

A discussion paper to solve the "Indian problem" was tabled by then minister of Indian Affairs Jean Chrétien. The White Paper proposed to terminate the special relationship between Aboriginal peoples and the Crown, thus eliminating the status of Aboriginal peoples as a legal entity (Weaver, 1981). By the simple expedient of doing away with Aboriginal peoples as a legal construct, there would be "no more Indians"; better still, no more "Indian problem." The key planks of the White Paper were unmistakably assimilationist, despite a discursive nod toward integration. Federal responsibility over Aboriginal peoples would be transferred to the provinces; the *Indian Act* was to be revoked and the Department of Indian Affairs dismantled; Aboriginal assets (including lands) would be liquidated, then divided on a per-capita basis for individual owners to do with as they saw fit; and the eventual abolition of Aboriginal treaty privileges and special status would facilitate the "normalizing" (transformation) of Aboriginal individuals into Canadian citizens. With integration, then, the solution to the "Indian problem" focused on modernizing Aboriginal peoples by making them more like "us."

But the government badly miscalculated Aboriginal aspirations. Reaction to the White Paper reflected competing visions of Aboriginal peoples and their relational status in Canadian society. On the government side, Aboriginal peoples were perceived as Canadian citizens whose progress into the future was shackled by tradition and the past. Salvation lay in removing these barriers, elimination of Indians as Indians, and their normalization as Canadian citizens. By contrast, Aboriginal peoples envisioned themselves as self-governing political nations with collective and inherent rights to self-determining autonomy (Brooks, 1998). What the government endorsed as progressive and inevitable was roundly condemned as regressive and expedient by Aboriginal elites and leaders. The White Paper was accused of everything from cultural genocide to callous expediency in offloading federal costs while reneging on Crown responsibilities. Taiaiake Alfred (1999) writes about the government's hidden agenda:

> Let us understand that it is Canada's goal, advanced through policy and the co-optation of our people, to undermine the strength and the very existence of our nations by taking away . . . everything that makes us unique and powerful . . . Historically, and into the present day, it's clear the Canadian government believes that by forcing us or enticing us into the legal, political, and cultural mainstream, every bit of distinction between us and them will disappear.

In that central authorities were chastened by a collective show of resistance to the White Paper, especially with the establishment of the National Indian Brotherhood (now the Assembly of First Nations), a rethinking of Aboriginal policy was in order—if only to reclaim control of the agenda.

Devolution

A general commitment to the principles of devolution gradually replaced the policy void vacated by assimilation. This shift was preceded by a period of impasse—even paralysis—as government responses lurched from crisis to crisis without any idea of how to bridge the divide. Developments hastened the shift: With its qualified support for the idea of Aboriginal land title, a 1973 Supreme Court ruling (the Calder decision) proved a catalyst in reassessing the plausibility of Aboriginal rights. The *Constitution Act* of 1982 parlayed Canada into the world's first country to constitutionally entrench Aboriginal and treaty rights. Constitutional enshrinement of Aboriginal rights established a blueprint for potentially innovative arrangements—albeit within a Eurocentric framework that superimposed the legitimacy of Canadian jurisdiction over all people and lands (Bell, 1997). Additional developments underscored the political shift. A series of First Ministers Conferences between 1983 and 1987 may have yielded few concrete results; nevertheless, they did sensitize decision makers to Aboriginal demands for **self-determination** through self-government as part of a new social contract (Brock, 1991).

Many applauded government initiatives to expand Aboriginal jurisdictions over matters of local relevance. A shift toward devolution increased Aboriginal input over local affairs, including greater control over service delivery, administration of departmental programs, and localized decision making. A devolutionary framework secured some impressive gains on the political front as well. In 1986, the government announced a devolutionary program of community-based, municipal-style self-government, to be pursued on a band-to-band basis and outside any federally imposed blueprint. The Sechelt of British Columbia capitalized on this federal legislation by establishing municipal-level self-governance structures that transcended the provisions of the *Indian Act*. A commitment to devolution proved productive: Aboriginal peoples received all the social provisions available to non-Aboriginal Canadians—albeit through Aboriginal-specific institutions—while those on reserves assumed local responsibilities over the design and delivery of health, education, and social services (Abele, 2004).

Developments within the Indian Affairs Department dovetailed with the shift toward devolution. The department had moved away from the control-and-deliver mentality that had prevailed since the nineteenth century. Reorganization of the federal department into a decentralized service delivery through direct band involvement drew its inspiration from three assumptions: (1) the need to establish Aboriginal rather than federal control over community affairs; (2) a perception that properly resourced and self-sufficient communities were better equipped to solve local problems; and (3) a suspicion that centralized structures were ineffective for problem solving across a geographically dispersed and culturally diverse people. The Department repositioned itself as a developmental and advisory agency that would transfer federal funds to community-based self-government structures in the same way that federal block funding for programs and services was disbursed to the provinces (Fleras, 1996). Service delivery on a program-by-program basis was replaced by more flexible funding arrangements to improve the quality of service delivery, develop long-term expenditure plans, reduce administrative burdens, emphasize local accountability in spending, and foster transparency in decision making. By the early 1980s, over 80 percent of the Department's program expenditure was administered by Aboriginal governments under comprehensive funding arrangements—even if some of the Aboriginal communities were poorly prepared to assume such responsibility.

But policy advances were offset by political stagnation. Impressive gains in establishing jurisdiction over land, identity, and political voice could not disguise the fact that aboriginality as a principle continued to be undefined and excluded from the national agenda. Devolution as a strategy for decentralizing service delivery along community development lines was a step in the right direction, but it could hardly address the increasingly politicized demands for restructuring the relationship. If anything, by transferring the administration of state services to Aboriginal communities, a commitment to devolution could be interpreted as a form of indirect rule to off-load government responsibility. Nor was there any urgency on the part of government to restore Aboriginal rights by crafting a new social contract for living together differently. That indifference was abruptly shattered by the 78-day Oka crisis (involving a protracted stalemate over use and ownership of disputed land along the Ottawa River), a wake-up call whose impact continues to reverberate at policy levels.

Conditional Autonomy

Recent developments have redefined the constitutional place of Aboriginal peoples. A shift toward the principles of conditional autonomy flowed from the aftermath of the Oka crisis. Four policy pillars were established, namely, accelerated land claims settlement, improved socioeconomic status on reserves, reconstruction of Aboriginal peoples–government relations, and fulfillment of Aboriginal concerns. A continuing commitment to explore Aboriginal people–state relations was further anchored around four general themes—renewing the partnership, strengthening Aboriginal governance, improving the quality of life, and supporting strong communities through sustainable development at varying levels (see INAC, 2004). Ottawa officially endorsed a parallel Aboriginal constitutional process that culminated in full assurances of their historic right to negotiate on a government-to-government basis.

The status of Aboriginal peoples as First Nations with a corresponding right to self-government was approved in 1995 when the government recognized ". . . an inherent right of self government as an existing Aboriginal right under section 35 of the *Constitution Act, 1982*"—including ". . . a right to govern themselves in relation to matters that are internal to their communities, integral to their unique cultures, identities, traditions, languages, and institutions, and with respect to their special relationship to their land and resources" (Indian and Northern Affairs Canada, 1995, p. 5). To be sure, any references to inherent self-government acknowledged a "strings attached" commitment. Any **Aboriginal self-governance** arrangement had to operate within the Canadian federal system, neither declare independence nor challenge Canada's territorial integrity, be in harmony with other governments, be consistent with the *Canadian Charter of Rights and Freedoms*, and enhance the participation of Aboriginal peoples in Canadian society. Still, the significance was unmistakable: In the space of a generation, the government shifted from policy proposals to terminate the special status of Aboriginal peoples to acknowledging their constitutional right to govern themselves over matters of internal interest.

The *Report of the Royal Commission on Aboriginal Peoples* in 1996 reflected and rein-forced the principles of a conditional autonomy (see below). The report contained a heady brew of progressive and controversial ideas about the place ("relational status") of Aboriginal peoples within a re-constitutionalized Canada. Compared with those contained in the White Paper, the conclusions and recommendations of the Royal Commission could not be more different (Brooks, 1998). While the White Paper had rejected any notion of Aboriginal difference as a basis for solving the "Indian problem," the Royal Commission concluded that Aboriginal peoples were First Nations, whose sovereignty must be respected and restored. The report called for the establishment of an Aboriginal order of governance that acknowledged an inherent right to self-government as a treaty right under Canada's Constitution. Also proposed was the concept of dual citizenship for Aboriginal peoples as Canadian citizens by way of membership in First Nations communities.

The Royal Commission on Aboriginal Peoples: A Blueprint for the Future

In 1990, a 78-day armed standoff between Canada and Aboriginal peoples at Oka proved a wake-up call for Canadians. The conflict not only tarnished Canada's reputation abroad but also alerted Canadians to the prospect of more Aboriginal militancy. In order to stave off a crisis of legitimacy while proposing solutions to stubborn problems and patterns of injustice, a Royal Commission on Aboriginal Peoples (RCAP) was established in 1991. It consisted of seven commissioners whose goals were to investigate issues through public hearings and publish a report on their findings that included advice for the government. For five years, RCAP engaged, analyzed, and considered a balanced strategy to move forward, with one paramount question prevailing: *In reaction to 150 years of failed policy direction, what constitutes a fair and honourable relationship between Aboriginal peoples and Canadian society?* To bring about change, RCAP argued, Aboriginal peoples had to be seen as nations—as political and cultural groups with values and lifeways distinct from other Canadians. Only as restored and autonomous nations in control of their lives could Aboriginal peoples repair the damage, structure their solutions, and create relations for improving their potential as contributors to Canada.

RCAP proposed a number of recommendations for creating the foundations of a just and equitable relationship between Aboriginal and non-Aboriginal peoples:

1. Recognize that Aboriginal individuals and communities continue to face many problems. These problems are largely the result of colonialism and the ongoing legacy of the *Indian Act*, including loss of land and resources; destruction of economies, social institutions, and cultures; and denial of their nationhood.

(Continued)

2. Establish a renewed relationship based on the following four principles: mutual recognition (acknowledge Aboriginal peoples as original occupants with a corresponding set of rights); mutual respect (as a bulwark against domination by one partner); sharing (giving and receiving benefits in fair measure); and mutual responsibility (accountability for promises and actions).

3. Acknowledge Aboriginal peoples as nations and partners in Canada-building, including the recognition of Aboriginal government as a third order of governance in Canada.

4. Recognize Aboriginal peoples as sovereign in their own right over their own affairs, yet sharing in the sovereignty of Canada as a whole.

5. Ensure the restoration of land and resources that rightfully belong to Aboriginal peoples to consolidate the transformation: Improve the comprehensive land claims process; foster economic development (from employment to education) on reserves; and renew a treaty-based relationship with Aboriginal peoples for resolving disputes.

6. Break the cycle of disadvantage—family violence leads to educational failure leads to poverty leads to disempowerment leads to ill health leads to violence—by way of holistic approaches rather than piecemeal reforms.

7. Undertake immediate action toward building capacity and gathering strength in four areas: health and healing, economic development, human resource development and education, and Aboriginal-focused institution building.

8. Embark on a plan to close the economic gap between Aboriginal peoples and non-Aboriginal peoples by 50 percent and improve social conditions in the next 20 years.

9. Recognize that positive outcomes in socioeconomic fields are contingent on restructuring the relationship, which would entail a new Royal Proclamation for the twenty-first century; recognition of Aboriginal inherent jurisdiction; a new machinery of government to replace the Department of Indian Affairs and Northern Development, with two federal departments, one dealing with services, the other with relations; a treaty commissioner to handle comprehensive claims and a tribunal for specific claims; effective financial mechanisms; redistribution of land and resources; and a network of healing centres and lodges.

In 2006, the Assembly of First Nations (AFN) conducted a report card analysis of the federal government's progress on the RCAP recommendations. According to the AFN report card, the only A grade went to designating June 21 of each year as National Aboriginal Day. An F grade was assigned to 37 indicators of progress in complying with the recommendations. Canada's failure to act, the AFN concluded, earned it a failing grade overall.

To date, the government has been slow in responding to the spirit of RCAP. Nevertheless, the report's recommendations secured a blueprint for a new social contract. They also secured a minimum starting point for future negotiations based on standards to measure, compare, and criticize. For example, *Gathering Strength, Canada's Aboriginal*

Action Plan (1997) was designed to renew the government's partnership with Aboriginal peoples, strengthen Aboriginal governance, support strong and healthy communities, and develop a new fiscal relationship, in large part by building on the RCAP principles of mutual respect, mutual recognition, mutual responsibility, and sharing. By serving as a catalyst and an inspiration for setting a new course in government policies, a threshold in restructuring Aboriginal peoples–Canada relations has been crossed with no turning back.

To sum up: Historically, Canada's Aboriginal policy can be described as a contested and evolving site, involving conflicting agendas, competing priorities, and divided loyalties whose cumulative effect has had a negative impact on Aboriginal peoples (Frideres, 2011). Admittedly, overt policies of integration and assimilation have been shelved in favour of those that recognize Aboriginal rights for purposes of entitlement and engagement. Sections 25 and 35 of the 1982 *Constitution Act* have expanded areas of jurisdiction that once were denied or constrained under the colonialist era. Reforms are increasingly structural, collaborative, and cooperative, producing a shift in focus from welfare to self-governance; from dependence to self-determining autonomy; from government assistance to power-sharing; from paternalism to partnership; and from a perception of Aboriginal peoples as a minority with needs to a peoples with rights.

Yet the process remains uneven because a commitment to commit is neither a sign of conviction nor a signal for action (Bird et al., 2002). Moves forward in this game of political cha-cha-cha are matched by steps backward or sideways, as governments balk, duck, and elude. Rhetorics of change rarely match the realities of implementation. For some, everything has changed because governments have taken Aboriginal demands too seriously: Critics have pounced on the so-called Aboriginal orthodoxy that currently informs official government policy because of its misguided notion that Aboriginal peoples are—or once were—sovereign nations with justifiable claims as parallel societies (Flanagan, 1999, 2001). For others, however, nothing has changed in terms of goals: Attainment of Aboriginal self-sufficiency on government terms continues to underpin official Aboriginal policy—a situation that some find insulting and paternalistic. As a participant in an EKOS focus group study (2004) observed:

> The Government is telling us that we need to be self-sufficient! Who is it that introduced drugs and alcohol to us? Who is it that told us that our beliefs and language were something to be ashamed of? Who is it that abused us in residential schools? Now we have to be self-sufficient? Maybe, but they have no right to tell us this . . .

In short, while most Canadians dismiss colonialism as an unfortunate relic of the past, Eurocentric attitudes and discriminatory practices continue to box in Aboriginal realities. And despite growing Aboriginal challenges to the rules that inform the conventions rather than simply the conventions that refer to the rules, only the means to government goals have changed, according to Aboriginal critics (Alfred, 2005; J. Green, 2003), with open assimilation strategies giving way to more covert strategies of control that consolidate a neo-colonialist framework of containment.

RENEWING THE RELATIONSHIP

Aboriginal peoples do not like to see themselves as a social problem. Without denying the many challenges that confront Aboriginal communities, they contend that material poverty is not necessarily responsible for their marginalization. Powerlessness associated with (neo-)colonization and denial of Aboriginal rights is just as problematic (Adams, 1999). Equally demoralizing are stereotypes that portray Aboriginal peoples as hopeless welfare dependants or helpless slaves of customs, whose cultures preclude a secure and satisfying coexistence in Canadian society. Contrary to popular perception, Aboriginal peoples have struggled to halt the vicious cycle of exclusion and demeaning clientelism that has historically entrapped them (see R.O. Porter, 2005, for an overview). Collectively and individually, they have explored ways to survive by asserting control over their lives. In rejecting those political and social arrangements that once colonized and controlled, arrangements are proposed that not only advance Aboriginal interests but also challenge and transform those foundational principles that govern Canada's constitutional order (Maaka & Fleras, 2005). In other words, it is not a case of solving the "Indian problem," but one of fixing a broken relationship. Three key planks secure a platform for renewing the relation along postcolonial lines: (1) taking aboriginality seriously, (2) promoting self-determining autonomy through Aboriginal models of self-governance, and (3) acknowledging Aboriginal title and treaty rights by way of specific and comprehensive claims.

Taking Aboriginal Difference Seriously

Aboriginal peoples define themselves as different and deserving of differential status and treatment (Macklem, 2001). They categorically reject the view of themselves as Canadian citizens who happen to live on reserves. Nor do they approve of being labelled as just another ethnic or immigrant minority. In contrast to immigrants, who voluntarily chose to be part of Canada, Aboriginal peoples were forcibly incorporated into the Canada-building project and now want to "get out" by reconfiguring their relational status. Aboriginal peoples claim to be a de facto sovereign political community (peoples) whose inherent and collective rights to self-government (nationhood) are guaranteed not because of need, disadvantage, or compensation, but by virtue of aboriginality as principle. As the original occupants, whose inalienable rights have never been extinguished by treaty or conquest, Aboriginal peoples do not seek sovereignty per se. Rather, they *are* sovereign because of ancestral occupation and *have* sovereignty because of Aboriginal and treaty rights. All that is required are appropriate arrangements to put this principle into practice for purposes of recognition, reward, and relationships.

The centrality of **Aboriginal (peoples) rights** underpins the notion of Aboriginal difference (Alfred, 2005; Belanger, 2008; D. Turner, 2006). Aboriginal rights encompass those entitlements that ensure their survival as peoples, including the right to ownership of land and resources; the right to protect and promote language, culture, and identity; the right to political voice and self-governance; and the right to Aboriginal models of self-determination (McKee, 1996). The rights of Aboriginal peoples are regarded as *sui generis*, that is, they differ from ordinary citizenship rights by virtue of Aboriginal peoples' status as the original occupants (Borrows & Rotman, 1997). These *sui generis* rights are collective and inherent: *collective* in that Aboriginal communities can exercise jurisdiction over the individual rights of members of these communities; *inherent* in that they are not delegated by government decree but are intrinsic to Aboriginal peoples because of first principles, reflecting either natural law or spiritual decree. Inherency suggests that the legitimacy of Aboriginal governance does not flow from sources such as the Crown, Parliament, or the Constitution. Legitimacy is derived instead from original occupancy, is bequeathed by the Creator, reflects the consent of the people, complies with treaties or international law, and may never be extinguished even with explicit consent (Bell, 1997). According to Elijah Harper,

> Self-government is not [something] that can be given away by any government, but rather . . . flows from Creator. Self-government . . . is taking control and managing our own affairs, being able to determine our own future and destiny . . . It has never been up to the governments to give self-government. It has never been theirs to give (as cited in the Royal Commission on Aboriginal Peoples, 1992, p. 19).

The concept of aboriginality underlies the notion of Aboriginal rights (Maaka & Fleras, 2005). Strictly speaking, the word "aboriginality" is the nominalization of the adjective "aboriginal" (refers to the state of being aboriginal or pertaining to Aboriginal peoples). The relationship of aboriginality to aboriginal parallels that of ethnicity to ethnic. Both aboriginality and ethnicity refer to the process of a "shared awareness of ancestral commonalities as a basis for entitlement or engagement." In the case of aboriginality, this difference is justified by the primacy of original occupancy, together with the corresponding rights and power that flow from this status. Aboriginality asserts a special relationship between Aboriginal peoples and the state with respect to the complementary set of unsurrendered rights and unextinguished powers that inform this relationship. Aboriginal peoples have long insisted on recognition of their difference, including: (1) Aboriginal peoples are different, constitutionally speaking; (2) their difference must be protected in constructing a new social contract; (3) Aboriginal difference must be taken seriously as grounds for living together separately; and (4) it must be taken into account as the basis for rewards, recognition, and relations-repair (Macklem, 2001). Not unexpectedly, programs and policies that apply to non-Aboriginal minority groups are dismissed as inapplicable and counterproductive in light of Aboriginal difference as peoples and as nations.

To summarize, Aboriginal peoples have claimed the right to be different as well as the right to be the same. Equality of treatment (formal equality) is critical; so too is the demand for group-differentiated rights (equality of outcomes) because of their unique constitutional status as original occupants. Equal treatment, to be sure, but also treatment as equals by taking Aboriginal difference seriously. Demands go beyond the symmetrical notion of diversity implied by multiculturalism (all differences are equally different). Such equality suppresses Aboriginal difference by glossing over their unique status, history, culture, and relationships (Kernerman, 2005; Turner, 2006). Without difference, Aboriginal peoples have no more moral authority than other Canadians to challenge the political agenda and transform the constitutional order. Aboriginal peoples do not see any contradiction in insisting on a "first among equals" status. As far as they are concerned, an asymmetrical status is compensation for the loss of land, lives, and livelihood. Canadian politicians and policy makers rarely dispute the validity of Aboriginal rights for self-determining autonomy. Only the nature and scope of these rights is debated.

Self-Determining Autonomy through Aboriginal Self-Governance

Aboriginal peoples are in the midst of a drive to regain control over their lives and life chances. The powerful expression of aboriginality rejects the legitimacy of existing political relations and mainstream institutions as a framework for living together. Also rejected is the relevance and moral authority of those structures that once colonized Aboriginal peoples. Proposed instead is the restoration of an inherent and collective right to Aboriginal models of self-determining autonomy over land, identity, and political voice. Since the Penner Report of 1983, the policy lens for framing Aboriginal peoples–Canada relations has been "self-government"—and more recently "self-determination" (Christie, 2002). Key elements of this self-determination project include control over the process and power of local governance, sharp curtailment of state jurisdiction while enhancing Aboriginal control, the attainment of cultural sovereignty, and a realignment of political relations around a nation-to-nation format in key jurisdictional areas related to power, privilege, and resources (Maaka & Fleras, 2008). (See online Insight 7.5.)

Aboriginal leaders have endorsed the principle of self-determining autonomy. Its value lies in breaking the cycle of deprivation and dependency, in moving beyond the colonialist mentality of the *Indian Act*, and in its embrace of an Aboriginal renaissance as a spearhead for renewal and reform. Aboriginal models of self-determining autonomy will vary and are expected to evolve in line with community needs (social, economic, cultural) and local circumstances (rural or urban). Some will reflect a government model, others an Aboriginal model, and still others will combine elements of both, with differences being contextual rather than categorical, that is, in accordance with community levels of local development rather than ideology. A few Aboriginal models are looking for complete independence; others want a fundamental restructuring of their relationship within a reconstituted Canada; many want some kind of accommodation within the existing federal system, because they lack any viable alternatives; and still others want a limited autonomy involving negotiated agreements that are mostly administrative in nature, that is, delegation of government power to manage local services (Kulchyski, 2005).

Four models of self-determining autonomy can be theorized: (1) statehood, a sovereign country with absolute independence, no external interference, and a final say over both internal and external affairs; (2) nationhood, a de facto sovereignty with province-like powers and jurisdiction over all internal matters; (3) municipality-hood, a community-based level of self-determining autonomy, retaining control over local affairs but limited by interaction with comparable mainstream bodies; and (4) institution-hood, having meaningful decision-making powers through institutional inclusion or parallel institutions (see also O'Regan, 1994). Table 7-1 summarizes these possibilities with respect to varying categories of self-determining autonomy and its expression through levels of sovereignty.

TABLE 7-1	Models of Self-Determining Autonomy
Statehood	**Nationhood**
absolute (*de jure*) sovereignty	relative (de facto) sovereignty
Community/municipality-level	**Institution-level**
nested (community-based) sovereignty	nominal (as if) sovereignty

Generally speaking, Aboriginal claims for self-determining autonomy are consistent with the "nationhood" model of "domestic dependent nations" in the United States. American First Peoples do not possess external sovereignty (e.g., they cannot raise an army or establish diplomatic relations with foreign countries). Nevertheless, these "domestic dependent nations" retain considerable control over internal affairs, at least in theory if not always in practice, subject to certain restrictions at the federal and state levels. To date, with the possible exception of the Nisga'a settlement, the Canadian government has endorsed a level of self-determining autonomy whose authority is beyond a municipality but less than a nation or province. Aboriginal leaders publicly endorse a model somewhere between nationhood/provincehood and statehood but appear willing to compromise, depending on particular circumstances.

Few should be surprised that the politics of aboriginality and self-determining autonomy entail debates over self-governance (Fleras, 2000). Canada itself is a territorial-based sovereignty involving a principled allocation of power between federal and provincial jurisdictions, and this division of jurisdictions is being played out at the level of Aboriginal self-government. Aboriginal self-government is already an emerging reality in Canada (Hylton, 1994/1999). In acknowledging Aboriginal peoples as historically self-governing, the Penner Report of 1983 proposed the concept of Aboriginal self-government as a constitutionally entrenched and distinct order of governance in Canada, with its own negotiated jurisdictions and fiscal arrangements (Christie, 2002). The government agreed, but only to self-government within the Canadian federation. Passage of the 1984 *Cree Naskapi (of Quebec) Act* put into practice the concept of Aboriginal self-government legislation in Canada (Price, 1991). Establishment of self-government in 1986 by the Sechelt of British Columbia's west coast also proved to be a pioneering move. Rather than being part of a broader land claims agreement, the Sechelt agreement involved specifically designed legislation to move beyond the federal *Indian Act*. But the Nisga'a Final Agreement confirms the arrival of a powerful new self-governance (the creation of Nunavut as a northern territory in 1993 does not qualify as self-government per se, but as public government, since non-Inuit residents can participate in the political process), one that is autonomous in its own right, yet shares in the sovereignty of Canada by way of overlapping and exclusive jurisdictions (Dufraiment, 2002). (See online Debate 7.3.)

Debates over self-governance often pivot around the politics of jurisdiction (Fleras, 1996, 2000). The politics of jurisdiction are open to negotiations in three dimensions: what is "mine," what is "yours," and what is "ours"—ranging from shared arrangements on the one hand to exclusive tribal control over land ownership and membership, up to and including autonomy, on the other. Core jurisdictions include those matters of vital political, economic, cultural, and social concern to Aboriginal peoples (Royal Commission on Aboriginal Peoples, 1996b). Peripheral jurisdictions include those realms with an impact on adjacent jurisdictions or that attract federal/provincial interest. Jurisdictional matters are expected to vary from band to band; nevertheless, they are likely to include control over (1) the delivery of social services such as policing, education, and health and welfare; (2) resources and use of land for economic regeneration; (3) the means to protect and promote distinct cultural values and language systems; (4) band membership and entitlements; and (5) local expenditures according to Aboriginal priorities rather than those of the government or bureaucracy. This is not to say that all Aboriginal communities possess the developmental capacity to fully engage in self-government, as related costs and responsibilities are daunting. But many do, and are casting about for ways to establish arrangements that will divest all vestiges of **internal colonialism** in exchange for self-rule.

Aboriginal Development: An Economic or a Political Solution?

Common sense would dictate that economic development on Canada's reserves depends on creating jobs, generating income, and encouraging business start-ups. The thinking is along these lines: There is a problem of not enough jobs and income, so let's get some businesses going on the reserve. But important research in the United States suggests that this jobs-and-income approach may provide some short-term successes in Aboriginal communities, but rarely does it generate meaningful and sustained development. Even those tribes with abundant natural resources or high rates of education or the largest amount of financial capital are unlikely to excel in the long run.

In a series of studies conducted by Cornell and Kalt (2003), a *political solution* must precede any sustainable economic growth. Put bluntly, by creating an environment in which businesses, investment, and humans can flourish, a nation-building approach is the solution. According to Cornell and Kalt, economic success stories belonged to those tribes who exercised a robust level of de facto sovereignty, namely, a degree of self-determining autonomy (de facto sovereignty in fact and practice) over the right to govern their affairs and make decisions, control resources, and determine their futures. Yet assertions of sovereignty in fact or practice will have little impact on

socioeconomic conditions in the absence of an effective governance capacity. The governing institutions through which sovereignty is exercised include those that provide (1) stable institutions and policies, (2) fair and effective dispute resolutions, (3) a separation of politics from business management, (4) a competent bureaucracy, and (5) a cultural match (the consistency of cultural values with decision making).

In short, sovereignty as self-determining autonomy is the starting point; without it and effective governing institutions, successful and sustained development is unlikely. Key questions need to be addressed to form the basis for a developmental strategy:

- What kind of society does the tribe want to build?
- What does it want to change, what is it hoping to preserve, and what is it willing to give up?
- What are its developmental priorities (e.g., health) and concerns (e.g., environmental impact)?
- What assets can it work with?
- What constraints does it confront?

Answers to these questions are crucial: Without a sense of strategic direction, the danger is that the tribe will find itself in a reactive mode, responding to the agenda of others instead of actively pursuing its goals in halting the impoverished conditions on the reserve.

The range and scope of self-governing jurisdictions has yet to be decided. Of particular concern is the question of magnitude. Should Aboriginal self-government be focused on a national organization or, alternatively, on local bodies that reflect variations in culture and levels of development (Bern & Dodds, 2000)? An intermediate position is gaining favour: namely, Aboriginal "nations," that is, a sizable body of Aboriginal peoples with a shared sense of common identity that constitutes a predominant population (rather than every community) in a certain territory (Royal Commission on Aboriginal Peoples, 1996b). Aboriginal communities across Canada can be collapsed into between 60 and 80 historically based Aboriginal nations, based on economies of scale and natural ties, thus reviving the nation-way in which Aboriginal peoples once were organized. The expanding population of Aboriginal peoples in the cities poses a fresh challenge that will necessitate a new social contract for sharing political and economic power (J. Green, 2003).

Not everyone is jumping aboard the self-governance bandwagon. A few Aboriginal leaders have sounded a note of caution; for Taiaiake Alfred (2005), self-government as a catalyst for political and economic change is not the answer without a corresponding decolonization of minds along traditional Aboriginal lines. Otherwise, Alfred argues, it's just another form of cooptation at the expense of Aboriginal difference, autonomy, and empowerment. Non-Aboriginal opinion is often confused and rarely enthused (Widdowson & Howard, 2002; see also Cairns, 2005). Concerns are raised over costs, feasibility, effectiveness, degree of legitimacy, and belief that self-government is not the cure to all problems. Some see Aboriginal self-government as a "recipe" for social disunity; others query the soundness of a system based on race and separate status; yet others believe Aboriginal "nations" lack the capacity to be self-determining and exercise sovereignty; and still others express concerns over the cost of implementation (Anderssen, 1998; Gibson, 1998; Widdowson, 2003). Government spending on Aboriginal peoples is already deemed to be out of control, including billions spent on provincial jurisdictions such as education and healthcare, but with no guidelines for what to expect or how to spend.

Appeals to Aboriginal self-governance are also criticized as a simplistic solution to a complex problem. Its espousal by those Aboriginal elites (and their lawyers and consultants) who are removed from urban realities and out of touch with local needs rarely inspires confidence. Equally discomfiting are the micro-politics. Reserves may be so rife with corruption and mismanagement, including basic transparency and accountability procedures, that even Aboriginal organizations express concern over the transfer of yet more power to already dysfunctional communities (Ayed, 1999). As well, there is growing concern that some Aboriginal peoples are manipulating claims to self-governing sovereignty as a smokescreen to justify illegal activities, including the slaughter of endangered species and creation of online gambling and casinos (Hamilton, 2005). No less worrying are the dangers of a new Aboriginal bureaucracy and increased dependency on federal transfers, resulting in a yet larger Aboriginal "grievance industry" that enriches a few at the expense of many (Fiss, 2005a, 2005b; Helin, 2006; Widdowson & Howard, 2008).

Of particular concern is the spectre of dissolving Canada. Will Aboriginal self-governance structures transform Canada into a Swiss-cheese confederacy, one that is full of holes, but with no unifying centre to hold it together? Contrary to popular belief, however, most Aboriginal proposals are not interested in making a total break with Canadian society (Royal Commission on Aboriginal Peoples, 1996b). With few exceptions, Aboriginal demands for self-governing autonomy rarely extend to calls for political independence or territorial autonomy. Proposed instead is a relationship of relative and relational autonomy within a non-dominating framework of power-sharing and partnership (Scott, 1996). This excerpt from the RCAP report (1996b) should allay alarmist fears about "death by dismemberment":

> To say that Aboriginal peoples are nations is not to say that they are nation-states seeking independence from Canada. They are collectivities with a long shared history, a right to govern themselves and, in general, a strong desire to do it in partnership with Canada. (p. xi)

In other words, neither inherent self-government nor claims to Aboriginal sovereignty are synonymous with secession or independence. Advocated instead is a de facto sovereignty—one in name and function rather than structure—whereby Aboriginal peoples are treated *as if* sovereign for purposes of entitlement and engagement. The intent of a de facto sovereignty is not to demolish Canada but to dismantle those components of Canada that have dislodged Aboriginal peoples from their rightful place as First Nations (Borrows & Rotman, 1997). Aboriginal peoples are not attempting to turn back the clock by removing the settler and immigration population. On the contrary, they want to repatriate that part of their spiritual and cultural homeland whose sovereignty was never relinquished but prevails as the basis for living separately together. Admittedly, attainment of Aboriginal status as peoples or nations will require a reversal of those colonialist assumptions that historically have denied and excluded. Still, mounting pressure for new governance arrangements may prove unstoppable as Canada embraces a postcolonial social contract for living together (Maaka & Fleras, 2008).

Aboriginal Title and Treaty Rights

Moves toward a new social contract are anchored in the recognition, definition, and implementation of Aboriginal title and treaty rights (Russell, 2005). Enforcement of federal treaty obligations is particularly important in advancing Aboriginal interests and aspirations. **Treaties** were seen as a fundamental component of Aboriginal diplomacy with European powers. The British, in particular, insisted on observing legalities. Treaties represented practical nation-to-nation relationships between European colonizers and tribes. They also demanded a principled approach to determining ownership of private property, as only land that had been properly acquired (without encumbrances) could be sold, mortgaged, used as collateral, or employed in a productive manner in a free enterprise economy (Walkom, 1998). Treaties continue to be regarded as ongoing and organic agreements that reaffirm the distinctive legal status of Aboriginal nations. With treaties, Aboriginal peoples possess a constitutional right to carry on traditional harvesting practices for moderate livelihood, with governments having to justify any restrictions they wish to impose on this right by way of consultation, consent, and compensation (Manfredi, 2004).

Perceptual differences and a conflict of interest informed the treaty-making process (McKee, 1996). European authorities tended to see treaties as legal surrenders of Aboriginal land and authority in exchange for reserves, goods, and services. Treaties would provide the Crown with legal title to underoccupied land, foster peaceful settlement, avoid costly wars, and deter foreign annexation or expansion (Price, 1991). In short, treaties extinguished Aboriginal peoples' sovereignty (to the extent it existed). But others see it differently: For Aboriginal peoples, treaties reaffirmed their autonomy as political communities.

According to international law, a treaty is a formally ratified agreement incorporating a nation-to-nation relationship between sovereign entities. Treaties were viewed as semi-sacred and mutually binding contracts involving a reciprocal exchange of rights and responsibilities. As far as Aboriginal leaders are concerned, governments remain bound to honour the contractual obligations of these treaties—if only to preserve the honour of the Crown. To date, Canada's courts have shown little inclination to see treaties as international agreements preferring, instead, to define them as unique contractual agreements involving mutually binding obligations and the exchange of rights (Brooks, 1998).

Specific Treaty Claims Two types of treaty rights exist. One is based on specific claims to existing treaty violations, and the other involves comprehensive modern-day land claims (or regional settlements). A series of treaties was signed between 1763 and 1867 involving representatives of the Crown and Aboriginal nations. The earliest treaties resembled peace and friendship compacts to facilitate trade, secure allies, and pre-empt European rivals (McKee, 1996). Later treaties involved exchanges of land for goods and services. Between 1867 and 1923, 11 numbered (1–11) treaties were signed, involving a surrender of Aboriginal interest in land to the Crown across much of the Prairies and parts of the Northwest Territories, British Columbia, and Ontario. These historical Indian treaties set out the obligations and benefits for both parties to the agreement. Aboriginal peoples surrendered title to land and resources. In return, they received reserve lands, agricultural equipment, ammunition, annual payment, access to services, and clothing. Their right to hunt and fish on Crown land remained in effect as long as these lands remained unoccupied. The Crown also promised schools on reserves or teachers when requested. As an example, consider the terms of agreement between the Crown and the First Nations of Manitoba and the Northwest Territories:

- Aboriginal tribes would relinquish all their rights and title to the great region from Lake Superior to the foot of the Rocky Mountains.
- Land would be set aside as reserves for homes and agriculture. This land could not be sold without Indian consent and then only for their benefit.
- Indians would be granted the right to hunt and fish over these Crown lands until sold into private hands.
- An annual payment of $5 would be made for each man, woman, and child ($25 for chief, $15 for councillor). Suitable clothing, medals, and flags to the chiefs would be provided.
- To assist in agricultural endeavours, each band would receive implements, herds, and grain.
- Schools would be established on reserves.
- Sale of alcohol on reserves would be prohibited (see Price, 1991).

Noble intentions were one thing; implementation proved another. The treaty process was often marred by such willful duplicity and callous expediency that it hardly seemed worth its weight in paper (Price, 1991). Most grievances reflected federal failures to abide by treaty promises. With the passage of time, benefits were pared back or simply ignored. Miserly payouts proved a sore point. Another source of grievance entailed the unauthorized and uncompensated whittling away of reserve lands because of fraud, expropriation, or government theft. Disputes over reserve boundaries proved a constant source of friction. No less devastating was the misappropriation of Aboriginal monies from government sale of resources or mineral rights held in trust by the Crown.

Specific treaty claims are aimed at righting historical wrongs associated with treaty deception and Crown double dealing. To restore Crown honour, the courts have instructed the federal government to display a "fair, large, and liberal interpretation" of treaty provisions by giving Aboriginal peoples the benefit of the doubt. In the words of Chief Justice Beverley McLachlin: "Put simply, Canada's Aboriginal peoples were here when Europeans came, and were never conquered" (as cited in Fenwick, 2005), thus putting the onus on the "honour of the Crown" to deal generously with Aboriginal claims. Settling a specific land claim entails a four-stage process: (1) review (a submitted claim is vetted by Indian and Northern Affairs Canada to determine its validity, then forwarded to the Justice Department to determines its chances of winning in court. The vast majority of claims filed since 1973 are mired at this preliminary stage); (2) negotiation; (3) ratification (once a deal is struck it must be ratified by the First Nations community, and sometimes requires provincial approval, and finally, federal ratification), and (4) implementation (funds and land are transferred to the community). Hundreds of outstanding specific claims exist, ranging in scope from expropriations for hydro lines to reserve boundaries and actual land parcels, including much of downtown Toronto (Maccharles, 2005). In May 2008, the House of Commons gave final approval to establish an independent Specific Claims Tribunal, including $2.5 billion over ten years for resolving specific claims of $150 million or less (Curry, 2008). Unlike the advisory Indian Claims Commission, the Specific Claims Tribunal is an independent body empowered to make binding decisions about claims and compensation (Delic & Abele, 2010). According to government statistics, there are fewer than 600 claims currently in progress (down from the more than 800 in 2007), with another 75 in litigation.

Comprehensive Claims Comprehensive claims consist of modern-day treaty arrangements for establishing certainty over disputed ownership of land. Since 1973, 21 modern treaties have been negotiated, beginning with the James Bay and Northern Quebec Agreement in 1976 for most of the territorial north, particularly the Yukon, most of northern Quebec, and parts of British Columbia (Abele, 2004). Rather than redressing the specific claims of existing treaties, comprehensive (land claims) treaties address the need to establish broadly based agreements over *who owns what* with those Aboriginal nations that have never signed a treaty in the past (Purvis, 1999). Securing certainty of control over "untreatied" land and resources is imperative. For the Crown, certainty of ownership is a prerequisite for investment and development purposes. For Aboriginal peoples, clarifying the rights of ownership secures a potential economic base for prosperity and survival. Negotiated settlements provide Aboriginal communities with constitutionally protected rights to wildlife harvests, resource management, some subsurface mineral rights, and regulated development (Land & Townshend, 2002). Economic benefits can be derived by renting out lands and resources at rates that are favourable to Aboriginal interests. Benefits can also be achieved through local development (in tandem with public or private interests) at a pace that reflects community priorities and developmental levels.

The resolution of land claims settlements in Canada is predicated on the principle of **Aboriginal title**. Broadly speaking, Aboriginal title specifies Aboriginal rights of use over land and resources whose ownership (title) has not yet been legally extinguished and transferred to the Crown (Knafla & Westra, 2010). The principle itself revolves around the question of who occupied the land prior to the unilateral assertion of Crown ownership. If Aboriginal peoples can prove that they had continuous and exclusive occupation of the land prior to European contact, they can claim Aboriginal title; otherwise, the land reverts to Crown ownership. Because it has no counterpart in English common property law, Aboriginal title is unlike other forms of property ownership, hence it is *sui generis*: Aboriginal title cannot be surrendered or transferred to any individual but only to the Crown, is sourced in original occupancy, and is collectively held in perpetuity for the benefit of future owners.

How does Aboriginal title apply to Canada? The Calder decision of 1973 may have acknowledged the possibility of Aboriginal title to unceded (unextinguished) land. A Supreme Court ruling (the Sparrow decision) in 1990 gave practical effect to constitutional guarantees of existing treaty and Aboriginal rights (Rotman, 2004). But it was the Delgamuukw ruling in 1997 that really advanced the cause of Aboriginal title, when the Supreme Court overturned an earlier British Columbia court decision that dismissed Aboriginal claims to land title as impossible to determine, even if they existed. Under Delgamuukw, the court ruled that Aboriginal peoples have a constitutional and exclusive right of use and ownership to land, if they can prove that they occupied it prior to European arrival. Delgamuukw also advanced the concept of Aboriginal title by expanding the support base for proving ownership. To assist in proving claims, oral traditions are now admissible as evidence in deciding Aboriginal title, in effect tipping the burden of proof over to the Crown.

Subsequent Supreme Court rulings have also strengthened the Aboriginal hand. Notwithstanding some judiciary back-pedalling, the government acknowledges a moral and legal duty to meaningfully negotiate (not just pay lip service to consult) before permitting developmental activities on disputed land. Nor can the government issue licences for mining or logging to private developers while the disputed land is under negotiation (Makin, 2005). Until Aboriginal title is settled, in other words, not a single tree can be felled by Crown authorities without *consultation, consent, and compensation*—even in cases where infringements on Aboriginal title lands are for public purposes or national interests (Matas, Anderssen, & Fine, 1997). Finally, rather than restricting land use to traditional hunting and foraging practices, Aboriginal claimants can use the land or resources in almost any way they wish, except in a destructive sense that may imperil future use (Gray, 1997).

REMAKING CANADA: CONTESTED INTERESTS

Historically, Canada and other settler societies sought to eliminate the "Indian problem" by way of assimilation, forced migration, bureaucratic indifference, or outright suppression (Churchill, 2004; McRoberts, 2003). The present may be no less single-minded, albeit more subtle. In reaction, Aboriginal peoples in Canada and throughout the world have taken the initiative in politicizing their demands for a radical restructuring of society along the lines of a new social contract (Fleras & Elliott, 1992; Niezen, 2003). The focus of a new social contract has shifted from one that seeks survival to one that challenges the distribution of power within a new constitutional order. The terrain is increasingly contested. Aboriginal leaders have relied on various tactics and strategies to get the message across. Political authorities, ever distrustful and fearful of losing power or control, have responded with a host of delaying or defusing tactics (Sissons, 2005).

Aboriginal Initiatives: Tactics and Strategies

The politics of "relations repair" are sharply contested. Principles and philosophies span the spectrum from "radical" to "moderate": At one end are those who believe in revolutionary changes for advancing Aboriginal peoples' claims to self-determining autonomy (Alfred, 2005; Mercredi & Turpel, 1993). At the other are the moderates who endorse a conciliatory, incremental approach that cuts deals, enhances local autonomy, improves job opportunities, and fosters dialogue with private sectors (Fontaine, 1998; see also Gray, 1997). In between are those who don't know, who don't care, or who are more concerned with "getting on" than with "taking a stand."

Aboriginal initiatives tend to focus on land and resources (Kulchyski, 2005). Without land, any hope of economic development is seriously compromised, as is Aboriginal peoples' capacity to protect language and culture, speak the language of nationhood, or assert self-determining autonomy in any meaningful fashion (of course, Aboriginal land continues to have spiritual and social significance above and beyond the practical [Little Bear, 2004]). Whether to protect land or promote issues, Aboriginal initiatives for change are generally pursued through conventional channels of dialogue, consultation, and persuasion, with central policy structures. Tactics include recourse to Parliament, the existing court system, public opinion polls, and special interest/lobby groups, such as the Assembly of First Nations. Courts are preferred venues for exerting pressure on the government to honour its constitutional obligations, while also providing a forum for articulating Aboriginal issues. Lacking the reach of wealth and government power, Aboriginal peoples must rely on the powers of persuasion and moral rectitude through the courts, litigation, and the law (Wilkins, 2004). And court decisions from Calder to Sparrow to Delgamuukw have secured redress for historical inequities as grounds for advancing collective interests. Aboriginal leaders have also relied on international fora and agencies for assistance. They have gone to the United Nations, to Britain, even to the Vatican in the hopes of righting historical wrongs. These tactics have attained a measure of success, partly because of Canada's vulnerability to international criticism and censure.

Alternative strategies have been adopted as well. This cannot come as a surprise: after all, the use of conventional channels involves working within a colonialistic framework that (1) historically oppressed Aboriginal peoples, (2) is constructed in a way that unreflectively advances mainstream interests, and (3) is prone to protecting the system against challenge and change (see J. Green, 2003). Failure of political and constitutional channels to adequately address local grievances and national concerns has culminated in activist protest, ranging from acts of civil disobedience to threats of violence in some cases. Flamboyant and theatrically staged protests involving the mass media are particularly important in tweaking the conscience of a publicity-conscious government. By startling a complacent public into awareness or action, the use of negative publicity to embarrass the government has proven especially effective because of Canada's much ballyhooed commitment to human and individual rights (see Marcus, 1995). Finally, there have been occasional threats to employ violence if necessary. Yet the threat of violence has rarely moved beyond rhetoric and, when employed as at Oka or Burnt Church or Caledonia, is often defensive in nature. How long this non-violence will persist is open to conjecture, given the urgency of Aboriginal grievances, the impatience of younger activists, and perceptions of federal foot dragging and stonewalling (see online Case Study 7.4).

Aboriginal demands are consistent with their articulated status as "nations within." Central to their aspirations is the middle way—to strike a balance between extremes. Aboriginal peoples don't want to separate from Canada in the territorial sense, yet they also reject any move toward assimilation with a corresponding diminution of their unique status as self-determining political communities. A separate country is not on the agenda. What is proposed instead is a consensual partnership involving a sharing of jurisdiction in some areas such as health, but exclusive jurisdiction in other areas such as culture—with just enough room to ensure Aboriginal self-determining autonomy (Erasmus & Sanders, 2002). A commitment to Aboriginal models of self-governance is endorsed as a compromise between the extremes of separatism and absorption.

In other words, balance and compromise are key. Aboriginal peoples want to be modern by capitalizing on political and economic power for rebuilding strong communities. But being modern is not the same as abandoning traditional values and the practices of the past as a framework for the present (Alfred, 1999, 2005; Dean & Levi, 2006). Aboriginal peoples are pragmatists who wish to achieve a working balance between the cultural and spiritual values of the past without rejecting the technological benefits of modern society. They are not against development per se (unless attained at the cost of sacrificing uniqueness, authenticity, and spirituality), but insist on controlling benefits from local developmental projects.

Government Responses

Many Canadians fret over the unconventional nature of Aboriginal proposals. But Aboriginal demands are not radical when compared to the alternatives: They rarely invoke the overthrow of political institutions since it's hardly in their best interests to destroy the fiduciary (special) relationship that informs their existence. Few actively espouse the dismemberment of Canadian society or the imposition of Aboriginal cultural values. Endorsed instead is a restructuring of relations to ensure that (1) Aboriginal rights are taken seriously, (2) Aboriginal models of self-determination by way of self-governance are implemented, and (3) Aboriginal title and treaty rights are recognized. If these demands appear threatening to Canadians or if they seem unrealistic in light of contemporary realities, consider the options: A continuation of ineffectual government interference and paternalistic handouts is not the answer. No more effective is throwing more money at the problem or expanding the legion of experts for yet more top-down solutions (see online Insight 7.5). In short, the costs of re-priming the relationship may be formidable; however, they're nowhere near as daunting as the costs of doing things the same way.

Central authorities for the most part have stumbled in repairing the relational status of Aboriginal peoples. Political sectors have come under attack for caving in to Aboriginal demands while sacrificing national interests through restitutional expenditures and power giveaways. Conversely, they have also been criticized for sacrificing Aboriginal interests in pursuit of national goals (Adams, 1999). The promises of lofty rhetoric notwithstanding, there remains a noticeable lack of political will for "walking the talk"

(Macklem, 2001; Weaver, 1993b). Instead of a principled approach to addressing the issues, what prevails is the equivalent of a political samba: Every step forward is matched by one step back and two steps sideways. Politics and initiatives continue to be driven by public opinion polls, despite known deficiencies in mass surveys (Ponting, 1997; Purvis, 1999). Canadians appear to be broadly supportive of Aboriginal concerns and sympathetic to Aboriginal problems (Environics Institute, 2010b). But public support may be superficial, tentative, and conditional, thus making any government fearful of moving too quickly. Inasmuch as the intent is to simply rearrange the furniture without altering the floor plan of a sinking relationship, the government's Aboriginal agenda appears more concerned with appearances than with substance.

Mixed messages prevail. Political awareness is growing that the Crown has acted irresponsibly in dealing with Aboriginal peoples, in effect reneging on the trust implicit in this relationship. Political authorities appear receptive to Aboriginal claims—if only to avert a crisis of legitimacy and restore some semblance of political tranquility—albeit without enthusiasm or commitment. Awareness and acceptance are growing in acknowledging that Aboriginal peoples (1) are a distinct society, (2) possess a threatened culture and society, (3) depend on government trust and responsibilities for survival, (4) desire more control in line with local priorities, and (5) prefer to achieve their goals in partnership with central authorities.

But enthusiasm wanes with the prospect of putting the principles of power-sharing and partnership into a meaningful reality and measurable practice. Policy officials are understandably wary of dissolving conventional patterns of domination for the uncharted waters of a new constitutional order. The Crown is often unwilling to negotiate Aboriginal issues except when compelled to do so by the threat of unfavourable litigation (Rotman, 2004). The principle of Aboriginal self-governance is endorsed not as an independently sourced inherent right, but as a political concession, both contingent (qualified) and delegated on a band-to-band basis, with accountability to Parliament and the Constitution. (By contrast, an inherent right is not conditional but derived from the lives, laws, and traditions of Aboriginal communities and their sovereign and prior occupation of Canada, which neither unilateral assertion of Crown sovereignty over Canada nor subsequent infringements by the Canadian state have extinguished [Harris-Short, 2007]). Claims to Aboriginal self-governance may be acceptable, but only when they do not affect most Canadians, do not involve exorbitant sums of money, do not endorse any fundamental shift in power, and cannot be used as leverage in neutralizing the Québécois threat of secession (Widdowson, 2003).

In brief, aboriginality as principle and practice poses an unprecedented challenge for the balancing act in any society constructed around compromises. Few politicians can afford to cavalierly dismiss aboriginality or deny the existence of Aboriginal peoples' rights. By the same token, they can't afford to be seen as capitulating to Aboriginal demands. A willingness to compensate Aboriginal peoples for historical wrongs does not extend to bankrupting Canada. What prevails instead are debates over how to re-calibrate the relationship without shearing Canada's social fabric in the process. Nonetheless, although the most egregious expressions of colonialism have been abolished, the debate over the place of Aboriginal peoples in Canada remains so steeped in the foundational principles of a colonial constitutional order that many despair of transformational change (Alfred, 2001; Denis, 1997). The legacy of "whiteness" continues to shape how the legal system identifies, interprets, and enforces Aboriginal rights—proof, yet again, that Canadian law is neither neutral nor impartial, but an instrument for advancing mainstream interests under the guise of neutrality and fairness (Asch, 1997). The words of Noel Lyons (1997) are especially timely in emphasizing the contradictions of working within the very system that created the problem in the first place:

> As long as the process continues to be defined by rules and standards set by the dominant society, no measure of real self-government is possible because the process itself is a denial of the inherent rights of self-government of Aboriginal peoples. In other words, we cannot de-colonize peoples by relying on the rules and standards that were used to colonize them in the first place . . .

How is this neo-colonial relationship expressed (Denis, 1996, 1997)? Neo-colonialism works on the assumption that people may appear to be free by virtue of living in a system that is ostensibly neutral and based on universalistic principles. But this neutrality is an illusion, as hidden agendas continue to control and contain, albeit in an indirect manner (Adams, 1999). For example, the Delgamuukw ruling may have acknowledged Aboriginal title as an exclusive and collective right to ownership of land and its use. But this entitlement does not come into play without Aboriginal proof of title to land—an often expensive and lengthy undertaking (Christie, 2005). An extraordinarily high level of proof is required. According to Chief Justice Beverley McLachlin (R. v Bernard, 2005; R. v Marshall, 2005), Aboriginal claimants must prove exclusive physical possession, establish a substantial connection to the land, demonstrate direct lineage with the original inhabitants of the land, and avoid claims that do not reflect a "logical evolution" of activities from traditional times. As a result, a right to fish or hunt for moderate livelihood may be acceptable because of its traditional nature. Constructing casinos or bingo halls is not.

Clearly, then, Aboriginal peoples–Canada relations remain rooted in the colonialist assumption that the Crown knows what is best, is the final authority with the last say, and owns all the land outright. Even the courts are complicit in upholding unilateral Crown assertion of sovereignty over Aboriginal peoples and their territories. This assertion raises an awkward and embarrassing question: On what moral grounds can Canada define Aboriginal title as a legal burden on the Crown? Could it not be the case that the Crown imposes a burden on unsurrendered Aboriginal land, thus shifting the onus of proof on the Crown to prove its case? As Sharon Venne (1998) points out, there is no legal proof for ascertaining the legality of the Crown's unilateral assertion over Aboriginal peoples and their lands. Such neo-colonial arrogance, Venne asserts, is nothing more than political mumbo-jumbo dressed up in "hocus pocus" rules and regulations designed by the colonizers to dispossess Aboriginal peoples of land and resources.

To be sure, the courts have conferred on Aboriginal peoples a "*sui generis* legal status" based on their occupation of Canada prior to the Crown's unilateral assertion of sovereignty over Canada (Murphy, 2001, p. 110). They have ruled for the need to reinforce Crown fiduciary obligations by restricting Crown infringement on Aboriginal rights. The courts also have insisted that judicial decisions are not a substitute for Aboriginal policy, but a framework for negotiating Aboriginal peoples–Crown relations (Harty & Murphy, 2005, p. 39). Nevertheless, the courts are not prepared to challenge the colonialist assumptions that privilege the undisputed primacy of the Crown's claims to absolute sovereignty (Harris-Short, 2007). How could it be otherwise? Both the Crown and the judicial system are systemically rooted in the foundational principles of a Eurocentric and colonial constitutional order. Court judges consist of persons who are by training, personal history, and inclination more in tune with mainstream rhythms, ordering principles, and institutions rather than with Aboriginal realities (Wilkins, 2004, p. 293).

In short, the foundational premises of a colonial social contract are doing a disservice in establishing an agenda for living together differently. This social contract is based on a brand of liberal universalism that leaves little room for taking differences seriously, distrusts the notion of self-determining autonomy for Aboriginal communities, and privileges individual rights to choose over collective rights to survive (Peach, 2005). The application of universal norms and individualistic values embodied in the Charter to self-governing Aboriginal communities are fundamentally at odds with their social and cultural values (Harris-Short, 2007). The pervasive Eurocentrism that informs a neo-colonial political architecture has had the effect of (1) dismissing Aboriginal rights, values, or traditions as irrelevant or inferior; (2) normalizing Eurocentric ways of seeing and doing as natural and inevitable; and (3) asserting the superiority and dominance of conventional patterns and institutional structures. The framing of issues from a Eurocentric perspective draws attention to some aspects of reality as normal and necessary, but others as not; defines some aspects of reality as acceptable and desirable, but not others; and imposes a preferred reading of reality by emphasizing commonalities and similarities at the expense of deep differences (Maaka & Fleras, 2005). But for Aboriginal peoples to be equal they must be different, and their differences must be taken seriously as a blueprint for relationships, rights, and recognition (see Denis, 1996). Otherwise, there is a risk of being muscled into agreements that say more about securing a neo-colonial status quo rather than advancing a postcolonial social contract (S. Venne, 1998).

TOWARD A POSTCOLONIAL CANADA: TWO STEPS FORWARD . . .

> Canada is a test case for a grand notion—the notion that dissimilar people can share lands, resources, power, and dreams while respecting and sustaining their differences ("A Word from the Commissioners", in *Highlights from the Report of the Royal Commission on Aboriginal Peoples* 1996b, p. ix).

Indigenous peoples around the world are in the midst of a powerful social movement to reclaim what rightfully belongs to them (Maaka & Fleras, 2005). (See online Insight 7.6.) In many cases, land and natural resources are of primary concern; in other cases, reclamation of culture, spirituality, and language are central; in all cases, repairing the relations is central in constructing a postcolonial social contract (Maaka & Anderson, 2007). Canada, too, is struggling to recast its relationship with Aboriginal peoples. Growing awareness of massive disparities has combined with mounting resentment and emergent political realities to intensify political and public awareness of Aboriginal issues. Government initiatives to engage with Aboriginal peoples in improving their collective lot reflect an unprincipled combination of principle and ideology with realpolitik ("pragmatism") and appeasement (in which political authorities appear to act from fear of aboriginal extremism in order to ensure peace at any costs [Widdowson & Howard, 2008]). Not surprisingly, projections vary in transforming the relational status of Aboriginal peoples from colonized subjects to self-determining nations, with some proposing to work within the system, others outside of it, and still others in transforming it along postcolonial lines.

A sense of perspective is useful. A generation ago, most Canadians would have cringed at the prospect of discovering some Aboriginal ancestry; at present, they are scouring their closets in hopes of unearthing an ancestor they can claim as their own (Kulchyski, 2005). Not long ago, Canada believed it had moral authority and developmental progress on its side; after all, Canada saw itself as a white-man's country, with a God-given duty to control, co-opt, and convert those less fortunate. How times have changed: In rejecting the notions that "white is right" and "white is might," Aboriginal peoples now claim the high moral ground once occupied by those who justified their superiority by reference to "white" or "might" (Cairns, 2003). The distance travelled has been impressive. In the space of just over four decades, Aboriginal peoples have recoiled from the brink of legal extinction to reclaim a pivotal role in the reconstruction of Canadian society. Such a reversal originated and gained legitimacy when the "costs" of excluding Aboriginal peoples from the national agenda proved unacceptably high in social, political, and economic terms (Fleras & Krahn, 1992).

But while the rhetoric of transformation may be compelling, it may also be premature. Aboriginal moves to redefine their relationship with the people of Canada are fraught with ambiguity and confusion because of competing paradigms, hidden agendas, and entrenched interests. The most egregious colonialist practices and structures may have been discarded; nevertheless, Canada's constitutional order continues to promulgate principles that suppress Aboriginal rights. Of particular relevance is the imposition of one legal and sovereign political authority in a given territory under a single nationality, and universal citizenship that reduces all differences to equal status before the law (Harty & Murphy, 2005; McRoberts, 2003). Political authorities continue to call the shots by endorsing the foundational principles of a neo-colonial settler society, while Aboriginal values and aspirations are overwhelmed by the priorities and constraints of the majority "whitestream" (Denis, 1996). Although Canada's colonialist approach to Aboriginal affairs is explicitly repudiated, the fundamental objective of government policy—to eliminate the "Indian problem" by fostering European-style governance models—has barely budged with the passage of time (Alfred, 2005; Ponting, 1986). Only the means have changed, with crude assimilationist strategies replaced by more sophisticated tactics that not only co-opt Aboriginal discourses for self-serving purposes but also have the neo-colonial effect of advancing a corporatist agenda.

Recent developments are pointing to yet another paradigm shift in Aboriginal peoples–Canada relations. This proposed paradigm shift is gathering momentum partly in response to escalating Aboriginal pressure, partly to deflect a growing crisis in state legitimacy. In that no consensus prevails as to what should replace the paternalism of a patronizing past, instead of a paradigm shift, what we have is a paradigm "muddle." On one side is the dead weight of the *Indian Act*; on the other side are the progressive themes enshrined in the RCAP report. On one side are the "old rules of the game," many of which appear to be drawing to a close, but not without a struggle; on the other side is a new postcolonial paradigm that lacks both the political will and the critical mass of support to take hold. (See Table 7-2.) To no one's surprise, proposals for change are imbued with an air of ambivalence as colonialist paradigms grind up against postcolonizing realities, as the old collides with the new without displacing the other—resulting in discordant amalgams of the progressive with the regressive. Such a neo-colonial state of conflict is likely to persist until such time as conventional thinking accepts a unifying "vision" of Canada as a multilayered partnership of two founding peoples—Aboriginal and non-Aboriginal (French and English colonizers)—each sovereign in its own right yet sharing in the sovereignty of postcolonial Canada (see online Insight 7.7).

TABLE 7-2	**Redefining the Social Contract: Evolving Paradigms in the Relational Status of Aboriginal Peoples**		
	COLONIAL PARADIGM (old social contract– from *Indian Act* to White Paper)	**NEO-COLONIAL PARADIGM** (current social contract based on the principle of indirect rule)	**POSTCOLONIAL PARADIGM** (proposed social contract based on RCAP principles + constructive engagement)*
Status	Children	Citizens plus	Peoples/nations/ political communities
Rights	Wards of the state	Delegated rights and responsibilities	Inherent and collective indigenous rights
Entitlements	Social problems with needs	A minority problem with rights	Indigenous peoples with rights
Nature of relationship	Parent-child guardian-ship	Participation in gov-ernment initiatives	Nation to nation; government to government; peoples to peoples
Rules of engagement	Paternalistic (govern-ment "doing for" Aboriginal peoples)	Partnership (senior-junior partners)	Partnership (Abo-riginal peoples work with government)
Power distribution	Power deficit	Delegate power	Power sharing
Policy approach	Canada knows what is best (obey/conform)	Canada knows what is best but has duty to consult	Indigenous peoples know what is best— challenge + change
Policy goal	Assimilation (protec-tion until absorption and normalization)	Integration (conditional autonomy + state determination)	Relational self-determining autonomy without domination
Underlying policy assumptions	Absorption	Modernize	Indigenize— indigenous differ-ence as basis for rewards, recogni-tion, and relations
Animating logic	Eliminate "Indian problem"	Control problem by coexistence	Seek co-sovereign coexistence
Anticipated outcomes	Individual self-sufficiency	Community self-sufficiency	Self-determining autonomy as basis for living separately together

* See online Insight 7.7.

Solving the So-called Indian Problem: Assimilation? Autonomy? Accommodation?

As noted at the outset of this chapter, Aboriginal peoples often live in a world of problems. These problems range from the socioeconomic and the cultural to those dealing with health issues related to well-being and violence. To be sure, variations in socioeconomic status, gender, age, proximity to major centres, and location (off-reserve or on reserve) ensure that some individuals and communities experience problems more intensely than others, who lead healthy and prosperous lives. The range of problems confronting Aboriginal communities raises a number of questions: What are the causes? Who is responsible? Why? How can solutions consistent with the problem definition be achieved? To date, three ideal-typical models can be discerned for addressing the "Indian problem": *assimilation* ("be more like us"), *autonomy* (from "strategic separation" to "away from you"), or *accommodation* ("integration" or "in-between").

Assimilation Model: Living Together Equally

At one end of the debate continuum are those who endorse an assimilation model as a realistic solution to the "Indian problem" (Fiss, 2005a, 2005b; Flanagan, 1999; Gibson, 2009a, 2009b). The assimilation model is predicated on the assumption that Aboriginal peoples are themselves

the architects of their misfortune because of their continuing distance—geographically, legally, socially, and culturally—from Canadian society. They must take responsibility for solutions by becoming more thoroughly modern through exposure and involvement in the mainstream, while discarding those social patterns and cultural values at odds with contemporary Canadian realities.

No less problem inducing is the special status enjoyed by Aboriginal peoples (see Widdowson & Howard, 2008). Assimilationists argue that for true equality, the racist and counterproductive edifice of laws and programs for Aboriginal peoples (from reserves to Indian and Northern Affairs Canada) must be abolished in favour of normal citizenship. Insofar as all Canadians are fundamentally alike and equal before the law (Gibson, 2005), preferential treatment on the basis of race is morally wrong, bad policy, and socially divisive (Fiss, 2004). Particularly noxious is the *Indian Act*, with its imposition of outdated property rights that hobble reserve residents from using their land and houses in economically productive ways (Flanagan et al., 2010. Moreover, critics argue, the Canadian government spends up to $9 billion per year shoring up Aboriginal difference, with little to show for the expenditure except third-world living standards, a glaring lack of accountability and

(Continued)

transparency in spending, and Aboriginal demands for more and more (Fiss, 2005b). Worse still, a culture of dependency prevails. According to Calvin Helin (2006), the federal government has created a situation whereby all wealth in Aboriginal communities reflects transfer payments or welfare, thus reinforcing a dependency mindset at the expense of self-reliance as a community value.

For assimilationists, then, the solution to the "Indian problem" points to absorption into Canadian society: The strategies are three-fold: First, to eliminate the collectivist mindset that underpins these special provisions and preferential status, while exposing Aboriginal peoples to the balm of modernist values pertaining to individualism, competition, and private property rights (Fiss, 2004; Flanagan, 2001). Second, to wean Aboriginal peoples away from those "artificially preserved" cultural values and social patterns that no longer resonate with meaning in a twenty-first century society but preclude their ability to participate in a modern economy (Widdowson & Howard, 2008). Third, to explore Aboriginal peoples to the discipline of the market—most notably, a conversion into municipal level of elected government that generates income from taxing individualized property rights rather than relying on federal transfers for wealth creation (Fiss 2005b).

Autonomy Model: Living Separately Together

At the other end of the debate is the autonomy model (see Alfred, 2005). In that Aboriginal peoples continue to suffer the consequences of being forcibly incorporated into someone else's political project, the "Indian problem" is really the Indians' "Canada problem," and any solution must begin by challenging those (neo-) colonialist arrangements that created the problem in the first place, including those constitutional barriers that continue to box in Aboriginal communities along neo-colonial lines, while conditioning Aboriginal mindsets to think like the colonizers (Alfred, 2005). Autonomists endorse Aboriginal peoples' claims as sovereign political nations with inherent and collective rights to Aboriginal models of self-determining autonomy over land, identity, and political voice. Government policy must play its part in securing the inherent and treaty rights of Aboriginal peoples, according to the autonomists. That is, the federal government is pressured to honour its fiduciary responsibilities; protect the legitimacy of Aboriginal difference as a basis for recognition, reward, and relationship; and uphold Aboriginal sovereignty and models of self-determining autonomy to ensure the goal of living separately together.

The logic behind the autonomist claim is consistent with the principles of dependency theories: That is, sustained contact with the West, with its corresponding pressures to assimilate and modernize, creates more problems than solutions through dependency and underdevelopment (see also Helin, 2006). Poverty and powerlessness will not disappear with better opportunities or increased expenditures. A "throwing of money at a problem" approach may be effective in the short run, yet it downplays the structural (and more costly) roots of Aboriginal problems, namely, the lack of power and resource control. Significant improvements will materialize only when Aboriginal peoples secure a degree of autonomy, including access to power-sharing, an equitable share of revenue from reserve resources, and Aboriginal title to land—as aptly captured by Matthew Coon Come, former Grand Chief of the Grand Council of the Crees in Quebec:

> But without adequate access to lands, resources, and without the jurisdictions required to benefit meaningfully and sustainably from them . . . no number sustainably from them . . . no number of apologies, policies, token programs, or symbolic healing funds are going to remedy this fundamental socio-economic fact. (as cited in Barnsley, 1999, p. 1)

Different models of autonomy can be discerned. A "soft" autonomy model proposed by Cornell and Kalt (2003) and Graham and Levesque (2010) is based on a nation-building approach to development. It proposes a degree of de facto sovereignty, in which Aboriginal communities take charge of what happens on reserves to create sustainable growth that addresses the causes of problems, not just the symptoms. Others reject this materialist model of autonomy. For Alfred (2005), the route to autonomy lies in rejecting co-optation into mainstream society by political concessions or economic development. In asking the question of how to decolonize a Canada constructed on colonialism, Alfred emphasizes

instead the need to delegitimize colonization by decolonizing Aboriginal minds through the rejuvenation of tradition ("heeding the voices of the ancestors") and spirituality.

Accommodation Model: Living Together with Differences

In between these positions are those who endorse the principle of Aboriginal autonomy within the wider framework of Canadian society (see Cairns, 2005; Parkin, 2001). An accommodation model represents a compromise that balances the strengths of autonomy and assimilation models while rejecting the weaknesses of each. Aboriginal problems reflect an interactional frame: Although Aboriginal communities are the site of social problems, it's neither an "Indian problem" nor a Canada problem, but rather an "Indian"–Canada problem. According to accommodationists, Aboriginal peoples must assume responsibility for the choices they make and the predicament in which they find themselves. However, as sociologists are prone to say, peoples' options and choices do not originate in a political, historical, or economic vacuum, but within the broader context, with resulting restrictions and impositions. A degree of autonomy is critical in breaking the bonds of dependency and constructing self-reliance—not in the individual sense but through interdependence with other Aboriginal communities and society at large (Helin, 2006). In other words, for accommodationists, it's the relationship that is broken and in need of repair to bring about mutual adjustment.

(Continued)

Consider the accommodation solution proposed by Alan Cairns (2000) in his book *Citizens Plus: Aboriginal Peoples and the Canadian State*. The term "citizen plus" was first articulated in the *Hawthorne Report* of 1966 (Cairns participated in the commission that produced the report). The report emphasized that Aboriginal peoples have not only the same rights as all Canadians but also additional rights because of their historical and treaty status (Hawkes, 2000). According to Cairns (2000, p. 86), a commitment to "citizen plus" provides the framework for solving complex Aboriginal problems without destroying Canada in the process. In rejecting a nation-to-nation paradigm, it provides a middle ground that recognizes both Aboriginal difference and rights (thus rejecting assimilation) without forsaking a commitment to belonging and citizenship in Canada and the legitimacy of the Canadian state to survive (thus rejecting autonomy). In doing so, a citizen plus model provides a vehicle for Aboriginal peoples to ameliorate the conditions imposed by colonialism without relinquishing the benefits of citizenship in a modern state. In other words, Aboriginal self-determining autonomy as a third order of governance cannot be about separation but about incorporation—about "getting in" rather than "getting out" in hopes of completing the "circle of confederation" (as cited in Hawkes, 2000, p. 142).

To sum up: Three ideal-typical explanatory frameworks provide competing models for defining and solving the so-called Indian problem. The assimilationist model argues that normalizing the status of Aboriginal peoples as citizens and taxpayers, together with their absorption into mainstream society, provides the most workable solution. According to the autonomy model, Aboriginal peoples' problems arise from too much absorption into a system that doesn't work for them. As a result, the solution rests in advancing an Aboriginal right to self-determining autonomy by establishing as much distance as possible from mainstream society. The accommodation model seeks a compromise to these two options. Aboriginal peoples require a degree of autonomy to ensure self-determination and the protection of their rights, but not at the expense of disengaging from mainstream society in terms of belonging and commitment.

All three models concur that problems exist in Aboriginal communities, but disagree in framing the issue. Are Aboriginal peoples a *minority* with needs? A *peoples* with rights? Or *citizens* with rights and responsibilities? For assimilationists, the problems are seen as *needs* that require modern solutions; for autonomists, the existence of problems reflects a violation of their rights that must be restored for any sustainable renewal; and for accommodationists, solving the problems is all about repairing the *relationship* in ways workable, necessary, and fair. Table 7-3 compares these models by way of select criteria pertaining to problem, solution, and outcomes. It should be noted that other models exist that do not necessarily fit into one of these three models.

TABLE 7-3	Framing the "Indian Problem": Competing Models		
	Assimilation	**Autonomy**	**Accommodation**
Responsibility for problem	Blame the victims	Blame the system	Blame the relationship
Problem source	"Indian problem" = exceptionalism (= differential treatment) + Tribalism + collective rights + parallel society status (difference and isolation) + pre-modern Aboriginal culture, traditions, society, location	White problem = forcible incorporation into whiteness/capitalism resulting in dependency + underdevelopment + loss of authenticity	The relationship is broken. White–'Indian' problem
Solution	Modernize by becoming *more like us*: • Discipline of market • Municipalization (tax-based governance) • Property rights • Relocation • Removal of special status (i.e., *Indian Act*, Indian and Northern Affairs Canada) • Capacity building • Individual rights	Indigenize by becoming *less like you* + Aboriginal renewal (retribalize)	Repair the relationship
Means	Address *needs* by eliminating special status and preferential treatment	Recognize Aboriginal *rights* to self-determining autonomy at cultural, social, political, economic levels	Interdependence: citizens but with distinct rights
Results	Equal citizenship	Coexistence as equals	Citizen plus
Outcomes	Living together similarly (colonialism—we know what is best mentality)	Living separately together (postcolonialism)	Living together with differences (neo-colonialism—indirect rule)

Chapter Highlights

• Canadians often perceive Aboriginal peoples as "troublesome constituents" who create problems or have problems in need of solutions through government intervention. Yet the depressed social and economic conditions that confront many Aboriginal communities may be a "Canada problem," insofar as Aboriginal peoples were forcibly incorporated into a system that continues to deny, exclude, or exploit.

- Aboriginal policy has evolved through several stages: accommodation, assimilation, integration, devolution, and conditional autonomy. Perceptions of Aboriginal peoples as allies, children, citizens, minorities, and peoples appear to coincide with this evolution.
- Aboriginal resistance has shifted from a focus on cultural survival and formal equality to a highly politicized demand for radical renewal through relations-repair, based on recognition of Aboriginal title and treaty rights, Aboriginal models of self-determining autonomy at self-government levels, and taking Aboriginal difference seriously.
- Efforts to decolonize the Aboriginal agenda are widely anticipated as necessary and overdue; nevertheless, proposals for re-constitutionalizing the foundational principles of Aboriginal peoples–state relations must contend with political and bureaucratic interests, both of which resist fundamental change for fear of destabilizing the status quo.
- The concept of constructive engagement provides an ideal model for establishing a new set of foundational principles to govern Aboriginal peoples–Canada relations. Still, it remains to be seen if the creation of a more positive relationship for remaking Canada along post-colonial lines can overcome the foundational rules of a (neo-)colonial constitutional order.

For further study, you can access the Case Studies referenced in this chapter at **www.pearsoncanada.ca/fleras**.

Review Questions

1. Outline the current demands of the Aboriginal peoples with respect to improving their relational status in Canadian society. How do Aboriginal demands compare with the solutions proposed by the federal government?

2. Demonstrate how and why the assimilationists differ from the autonomists in defining and solving the so-called Indian problem. Indicate the underlying assumptions, problem definition, proposed solution, and anticipated outcome. Does a commitment to accommodation provide a compromise position?

3. Briefly discuss the shifts in Canada's Aboriginal policy in terms of goals, means, and ends, and explain how these shifts have contributed to the muddles in Aboriginal peoples–government relations.

4. To borrow a phrase from Charles Dickens, for Aboriginal peoples in Canada, this is both "the best of times" and "the worst of times." Indicate how this applies to the current status of Aboriginal peoples–Canada relations.

5. Compare the *Indian Act* of 1876 with the 1996 Report of the Royal Commission on Aboriginal Peoples in terms of underlying assumptions, problem definition, proposed solutions, and anticipated outcomes. Discuss your findings.

6. While most Canadians dismiss colonialism as an unfortunate relic of the past, Eurocentric attitudes and discriminatory practices continue to reinforce Aboriginal realities at present. Only the means have changed, according to Aboriginal critics (Alfred, 2005; J. Green, 2003), with open assimilation strategies giving way to more covert strategies of control that consolidate a neo-colonialist framework of containment. Explain, with examples.

7. If de facto sovereignty is a precondition for development, it stands to reason that Canadian government policy must focus on advancing Aboriginal nation-building rather than take a jobs-and-income approach. To what extent has the government been successful in advancing Aboriginal nation-building?

Endnotes

1. The expression "foundational principles" (like the concept of root causes) refers to those ideologies, structures, and systems that inform the institutions of family, the community, the market, and the state.

Links and Recommendations

FILMS

Finding Dawn (2006)

A moving NFB documentary that exposes the anguish of those affected by missing and murdered Aboriginal women. It also emphasizes what family and friends are doing to commemorate the deaths of these women.

Reel Injun's (2009)

A biting yet humorous look at media portrayals of Aboriginal peoples over the years.

Dances with Wolves (1990)

The film that really disrupted conventional stereotypes of Native Americans and the American Cavalry during the taming of the Wild West.

Once Were Warriors (1994)

A gritty and disturbing look at inner-city life among the indigenous peoples of New Zealand.

Whale Rider (2002)

A gentle and moving film that addresses some of the challenges confronting rural Maori as they move into the twenty-first century.

Two Worlds Colliding (2004)

An interesting National Film Board study of the crisis in Saskatoon after the discovery of the frozen bodies of two Aboriginal men on the outskirts of the city raised the possibility of dishonourable police conduct.

Additional films that take a more indigenous perspective include *Dance Me Outside* (1994), *Smoke Signals* (1998), and *Powwow Highway* (1989).

BOOKS

Visions of the Heart (3rd ed.), by David Long and Olive Patricia Dickason (2011). This book is a splendid collection of articles by both Aboriginal and non-Aboriginal scholars, who collectively address the challenges confronting Aboriginal peoples as well as make proposals for transformative change.

Racism, Colonialism, and Indigeneity in Canada, by Martin J. Cannon and Lina Sunseri (2011). This book is a fine collection of previously published materials on the politics of indigeneity, many by indigenous scholars and activists, who explore the intersection of race with colonialism in shaping Aboriginal peoples' lives.

Aboriginal Peoples in Canada (8th ed.), by James Frideres and Rene Gadacz (2008). This book is pretty much the classic in this field for those who want an overview.

Aboriginal Self-Government in Canada (3rd ed.), edited by Yale Belanger (2008). This book is an excellent collection of articles that address the politics of Aboriginal self-government in Canada.

A Poison Stronger Than Love, by Anastasia Shkilnyk (1985). This book is an unflinching indictment of the destruction inflicted by well-meaning government initiatives on an Aboriginal community in Northern Ontario—in the process giving credence to the expression "the banality of evil."

The Politics of Indigeneity: Challenging the State in Canada and Aotearoa New Zealand, by Roger Maaka and Augie Fleras (2005). An overview of indigenous peoples politics is provided by comparing the politics of aboriginality in Canada with those of Maori tribes in New Zealand.

This Is Not a Peace Pipe, by Dale Turner (2006). This book acknowledges the need for indigenous knowledge to complement Eurocentric intellectual traditions as a basis for cooperative coexistence.

Wasase: Indigenous Pathways to Action and Freedom, by Taiaiake Alfred (2005). Alfred continues his argument that the decolonization of Aboriginal peoples should avoid playing the government's self-government game, but focus on "respecting the wisdom of the Elders" as grounds for living separately together.

MAGAZINE

Windspeaker. This monthly newspaper is highly recommended as a source of information about Aboriginal peoples from an Aboriginal perspective.

WEBSITES

Indian and Northern Affairs Canada—A useful site providing a government-based overview of its relationships and responsibilities with the First Nations:
   www.ainc-inac.gc.ca

Assembly of First Nations—A perspective from a status-Indian viewpoint:
   www.afn.ca

Congress of Aboriginal Peoples—Represents the views of off-reserve and Métis peoples:
   www.abo-peoples.org

Native Women's Association of Canada—Aboriginal women's perspectives are emphasized:
   www.nwac.ca

CHAPTER 8

The Quebec Question:
The Canadian Quandary

Official Bilingualism: Has It Helped?

Canada can be described as officially bilingual, with national language policies that are simultaneously a source of unity and disunity, of pride and dismay. Problems of communication and cohesion can be expected in a country with two major languages, where over three-quarters of the population speak one language and less than one-quarter the other. The problem is compounded by a geographic divide. Nearly 4 million Quebec francophones are largely monolingual. If Montreal is excluded, the vast majority of Quebecers do not speak English. Twenty million English-speaking Canadians are no less monolingual, including about 90 percent of those outside the National Capital Region, New Brunswick, and the Nickel Belt in Ontario (Office of the Commissioner of Official Languages, 2006/7). Such a communication divide is costly: It not only intensifies the inwardness of the "solitudes within" but also amplifies the challenges of living together differently.

Canada is not the world's only officially bilingual country. Many European countries are committed to the principles of official bilingualism/ multilingualism, including the Netherlands (Dutch and Frisian) and Malta (English and Maltese), while Belgium and Luxembourg embrace three official languages. Nor should we assume that other official bilingualisms are modelled after Canada's federal model of linguistic duality. Official bilingualism (or multilingualism) itself comes in different shapes and sizes, and is expressed most frequently at individual, territorial, and institutional levels. Under **individual bilingualism**, each person is expected to become proficient in two or more languages of the country. Minorities in many countries have little choice except to learn the dominant language alongside their own if they hope to prosper. **Territorial bilingualism** is another option; it reflects a division of language use along geographical lines. For example, Belgium and Switzerland are divided into linguistic regions, each with its own predominant official language (Linden, 1994). Finally, there is **institutional bilingualism** with its focus on incorporating official languages at organizational levels, including dual language workplaces and delivery of bilingual services.

(Continued)

All three models of bilingualism flourish in Canada. There exists a territorial bilingualism, namely, the division of Canada into two language heartlands—Quebec and the rest of Canada—with a limited number of bilingual districts adjacent to Quebec, such as the National Capital Region (Ottawa) and New Brunswick. Individual bilingualism also exists in Canada. About 17 percent of Canada's total population defined themselves as having some degree of fluency in both languages, up from 13 percent in 1971, including 38 percent of the residents in Quebec and 33 percent in New Brunswick. Examples of both individual and territorial bilingualism extend to minority language minorities, including francophones across Canada and anglophones in Quebec. Officially, however, Canada endorses an institutional bilingualism, which obligates language duality in federal and federally regulated workplaces and service delivery. Passage of the ***Official Languages Act*** (1969/ 1988) acknowledged the equal and official status of French and English as languages of communication in federal institutions across the country or in regions designated as bilingual (Annual Report, 2005/6).

Canada's experiment with institutional bilingualism began in the 1960s. Efforts to strengthen French language rights in exchange for social peace culminated in a quintessential Canadian compromise: recognition of the right of federal public servants in 1966 to work in either French or English. In confirming the conclusions of the Royal Commission on Biculturalism and Bilingualism, passage of the *Official Languages Act* in

1969 formalized linguistic duality as a fundamental principle of Canadian society. Provisions of the Act acknowledged the presence and legitimacy of both French and English as Canada's official languages, with the courts and Parliament designated as bilingual, in addition to all federal government institutions. Bilingualism was expressed in federal documents, signs in national parks, and federally chartered passenger vehicles, from Air Canada planes to shuttle buses at Point Pelee National Park. A commercial dimension prevailed as well. To be sure, the Act did not require everyone to learn two languages; on the contrary, while protecting the rights of minority language communities across Canada, it guaranteed the rights of unilingual Canadians to remain monolingual (Office of the Commissioner of Official Languages, 2009/10). In keeping with the theme of respect, fairness, and inclusiveness, the *Official Languages Act* of 1988 addressed the following rights:

1. The right of Canadians to use French or English as the language of work in federal organizations and designated bilingual regions (including the National Capital Region, Montreal, New Brunswick, and parts of Quebec [Gaspé] and Ontario);

2. The right of all Canadians to receive federal services in either language at designated federal institutions where numbers warranted or demand was significant;

3. The protection of minority language rights (English in Quebec, French outside of Quebec). Under the Act, parents who speak one of the official

languages have the right to educate their children in either language, provided of course that both numbers and demand warrant establishing minority language education facilities. In taking positive actions to promote the minority language community, the Act consolidated both anglophone and francophone control over education and school boards in contexts where they constitute a viable minority population.

4. Equal opportunities of employment and advancement for French and English speakers in the public service. For example, the federal public services classifies positions along four lines (with positional breakdowns in brackets for 2007): bilingual French *and* English essential (40.2 percent), English essential (51.2 percent), French essential (4 percent) and French or English essential (4.4 percent) (Office of the Commissioner of Official Languages, 2006/7). French speakers (francophones) accounted for just over 30 percent of the core federal public service, while English speakers (anglophones) occupied the remaining positions. A similar ratio also reflected the distribution of French- and English-speaking management levels.

How should we assess **official bilingualism**—as a success or a failure? As a benefit or a cost? Should success be defined by tangible markers and verifiable outcomes? Or is success better measured through intangibles that advance Canada's national identity and

intercommunity dialogue (Office of the Commissioner of Official Languages, 2006/7)? Responses vary: On one side, there is much to like about official bilingualism. A 2004 United Nations Development Programme Report cited the global potential of Canada's unique federalism as a model for protecting minority language rights. On the other side, debates over linguistic duality continue to infuriate and divide the country. Quebecers dismiss official bilingualism as a plot of appeasement, bereft of any legitimacy or relevance; in turn, English-speaking Canadians appear equally unhappy over Canada's language duality, because of inconvenience and costs. This opinion piece from the *National Post* is evocative (Editorial, 2007):

> . . . Canadian bilingualism policy appears to be consuming a great deal of money and providing little visible progress. The francophone communities outside Quebec remain on life support; their members use French with each other but generally feel uncomfortable conducting trade or socializing in English. Anglos in Quebec retain their embattled but entrenched status. Overwhelmingly, Canada remains a land whose linguistic map is simple and sharply divided. As a social engineering project, the effort to turns us all into patriotic polyglots has failed.

The Debate Revisited box at the end of this chapter provides a broader assessment of official bilingualism from the vantage point of *consequences* (what the *Official Languages Act* of 1969 has accomplished) in light of its *intent* (what the Act really intended to do).

INTRODUCTION: FRENCH–ENGLISH RELATIONS: "WHAT IS CANADA FOR?"

Canada is widely regarded as one of the world's best places to live. According to a United Nations quality-of-life ranking, Canada's lofty position is secured by a combination of tangible measures such as educational and income attainment, in addition to less quantifiable markers including a commitment to tolerance, equal opportunity, safety, and freedom. Yet for all its resources and resourcefulness, Canada stands in danger of splintering along ethnic fault lines. Canada is not alone in this predicament. Around the world, the forces of ethnicity (as well as language, region, and religion) pose a greater threat to territorial integrity than does the danger of external invasion (Taras & Ganguly, 2009). Ethnic upheavals from within have displaced traditional cross-border wars involving the forcible capture of coveted territory. Nor is there any evidence that ethnic conflicts diminish when countries modernize or become globally connected. No matter how much effort is expended in securing a common citizenship, traditional loyalties and reassuring identities rarely vanish, while multicultural add-ons or inclusive inserts do little to placate ethnic nationalists. The potential for conflict is further sharpened in those contexts where nation-based minorities have been forcibly incorporated into a society at the expense of collective concerns. Tensions are stretched by a conflict of interests: Central authorities claim they represent society at large; by contrast, leaders of "internal nations" proclaim that only they can (a) speak for the "nation within," (b) galvanize public support to prove it, and (c) promote autonomy up to and including independence if necessary (McRoberts, 2003). The end result of these competing claims is nothing short of a bottleneck of mutual incomprehension.

The proliferation of ethnonational conflicts may well pose a definitive challenge for the twenty-first century (Maclure, 2004; see also Gagnon, Guibernau, & Rocher, 2003). Perhaps nowhere is this more the case than in Canada, where French–English relations (or, more accurately, French- and English-speaking relations) have coexisted uneasily since 1841, when Upper and Lower Canada combined into an incipient nation-state, a tinderbox aptly described by Lord Durham as the equivalent of "two nations warring in the bosom of a single state." Interactions since then pivot around a series of metaphors—from stretches of sullen isolation ("two solitudes") to periods of convulsive social transformation (the Quiet Revolution), with occasional bursts of violence to punctuate the indifference ("two scorpions in a bottle"). In between are positions of incredulity or incomprehension (Gordon, 2006), a stance stunningly captured by Alice Simard, mother of former Quebec Premier Lucien Bouchard, when she admitted despite annual holidays in Florida: "I've never met an English-speaking Canadian, but I'm sure they're as nice as any other foreigner" (as cited in *Report on Business*, January 1996). She is hardly alone in her solitude. Many Canadians cannot even communicate across the French–English divide outside of a bilingual belt that runs from Longlac and the National Capital Region to the Eastern Townships and New Brunswick. This communication gap is costly: Acrimonious debates have contributed to an impasse so profound and defiantly deep that bridging the Quebec–Canada divide may yet prove an exercise in futility (Gagnon et al., 2003; Gibbins & Laforest, 1998).

Points of conflict are varied and numerous. They range in scope from debates over collective versus individual rights to issues of jurisdiction ("who owns/controls what"), with convoluted provincial–federal squabbling in-between to complicate matters. Of particular note are clashes over the politics of language. Whereas an official bilingualism reinforces the right of individuals to choose their language—a right many English-speaking Canadians can readily identify with—Quebec's French-only policies advance the collective language rights of a francophone community that comprises a robust majority in Quebec, but a beleaguered minority in North America. The courts have acknowledged the inherent conflict between these competing rights. Yes, Quebec has the right to protect French, even with unorthodox methods if necessary, according to the Supreme Court, but not at the expense of individual rights for English-speaking Quebecers, as entrenched in the *Charter of Rights and Freedoms* (Annual Report 2005/6).

But the sharpest clashes tend to coalesce around the politics of **sovereignty**. Quebec's aspirations to sovereign ("autonomous") status often elicits conflicting reactions (Gagnon & Iacovino, 2007): English-speaking Canadians cannot understand why Quebec "wants out"; hard-line Quebecers can't comprehend why anyone would force them to "stay in." English-speaking Canadians are perplexed by Quebec's insistence on special status when clearly it's just another province; conversely, Quebecers are no less infuriated by English Canada's refusal to recognize Quebec for what it is: a **distinct society** or nation (Potter, 2006). As far as they're concerned, the Québécois constitute a powerful political community that claims sovereignty (nationhood) by virtue of a common history, a collective vision, shared grievances, and a distinctiveness because of traditional ancestry. A commitment to Canada may be acceptable, even desirable, but not if it infringes on Quebec's sovereign interests (Kymlicka, 1998b). Sovereignty per se may not be the preferred option under these conflicting circumstances, except as a benchmark by which other options are measured. Nevertheless, it remains a theoretical (and menacing) possibility. Failure to foster a *rapprochement* between these conflicting perspectives has propelled Canada perilously close to the brink. Time will tell if Prime Minister Stephen Harper's announcement in November 2006, recognizing Quebec as a "nation within a united Canada" will quell nationalist ambitions or create more quandaries (see Richer, 2007).

The antagonism between the French and English is thought to reflect a mutual dislike (Griffiths, 2008). Language has long been a source of conflict because the Canadian state cannot be neutral when it comes to public communication (Choudhry, 2007). In that a decision must be made as to which language(s) will prevail in conducting state business, users of the preferred language will invariably enjoy benefits and advantages, with the result that language conflict is inevitable when the stakes are so high. For a certain segment of the Quebec population, English is the enemy and the language of the conqueror, according to the *La Presse* editorial-page editor, rather than a tool for advancement or communication (as cited in Hamilton, 2008a). Attitudes in some cases have barely budged from the days when anglophones were seen as pampered yet ruthless tyrants anxious to squash the French. Even today, the English are perceived as callously insensitive and incapable of empathizing with a threatened language and culture. Not surprisingly, Quebecers perceive English-speaking Canada as a remote, even unfriendly place, with its own set of priorities and preoccupations, few of which apply to Quebec (Conlogue, 1997; Gagnon, 1996).

English-speaking Canadians are no less dismissive of Quebec's claims and criticisms. Despite Quebec's contribution to contemporary Canada (Courchene, 2009), Quebecers are caricaturized as narrow-minded ideologues whose rabid jingoism represses as it excludes. The sometimes absurd zeal of Quebec's language police confirms a suspicion that French is wielded as a weapon to humiliate the *anglais* rather than a resource to protect the *français*. Often outdated and stereotypical views of Quebecers as a closed society persist, a perception that glosses over Quebec's decade-long efforts to reinforce its status as one of the most minority rights–oriented province in Canada (Brooks, 2004; but see Quebec Human Rights Commission, 2011). These misplaced accusations of closed-mindedness are not without logic. Quebecers act defensively because they are boxed into a corner, thereby reinforcing a siege (or fortress) mentality around Quebec's claims to nationhood (Seguin, 2001). As a francophone island in the anglophone ocean of North America—both outnumbered and clinging to a small patch of homeland which they can call home—Quebecers are doubly conflicted: They must not only parry anglophone assimilation threats but also absorb those immigrants whose religious commitments pose a threat to Quebec's hard-won secular liberalism (Fraser, 2006). The prospect of balancing these competing challenges is fraught with peril, as noted in the 2008 report of the Bouchard-Taylor Commission on Reasonable Accommodation (see also Chapter 11). Put bluntly, Quebec must strike a balance between securing its future identity as a francophone and secular-liberal society with remaining a welcoming community for ethno-religious minorities.

Conflicting models of French–English relations together with the politics of pluralism in a fiercely French society have proven disruptive, and this chapter wades into the tricky waters of the Quebec question against the backdrop of a Canada quandary. This chapter examines the constitutional crisis that imperils Canada's national unity by exploring the politics of French–English relations in Canada. The dynamics of this relationship are shown to be informed by (1) Quebec's simultaneous status as a majority and a minority; (2) competing nationalisms, including ethnic, civic, and Aboriginal; (3) a vision of Quebec's place in Canada that differs from that of English Canada and varies within Quebec itself; and (4) a federal governance structure no longer as relevant in the twenty-first century as it was in the past. Debates over bilingualism and binationalism are framed within the broader context of Canadian federalism, the emergence and growing politicization of ethno-religious minorities in seeking a reasonable accommodation, and Quebec's determination to protect and promote its French character. Prospects for arriving at a mutually satisfactory solution remain elusive because of radically different visions for defining Quebec's place within the constitutional framework. That is, Quebec may want to stay in Canada, but on its own constitutional terms; by contrast, English Canada wants to dictate the terms of Quebec's staying, in effect exposing deficiencies in Canada's governance architecture as grounds for *rapprochement* (see Gagnon et al., 2003). A reinvented federalism along the lines of an asymmetrical multinationalism may prove Canada's best hope for survival (Ignatieff, 2005).

A note on terminology: This chapter addresses the relationship of French-speaking Canadians in Quebec (the Québécois or Quebecers) with the English-speaking Canadians who live in the rest of Canada but are symbolically centred in Canada's National Capital Region. (It is both interesting and curious that references to French and English are themselves a European transplant that persist into the twenty-first century). Within

Quebec itself there are additional solitudes, such as Québécois of "old stock" on one side, English-speaking anglophones on another, and allophones (with neither French nor English as a first language) on still another. Nearly 1 million racialized minorities in Montreal may find themselves outside the Québécois mainstream despite efforts by the government toward inclusiveness. The 1 million French-speaking persons outside of Quebec are no less isolated, including the 500 000 Franco-Ontarians and 300 000 Acadians in New Brunswick, who occupy a unique legal status as **official language minorities**. A reluctance by Quebec to endorse the struggles of other francophone communities attests to divergences of outlook and aspirations.

The term "English-speaking" also requires some clarification. Rather than a conventional ethnic group with a shared history and attributes, this category provides a label of convenience to describe those Canadians who reside primarily outside Quebec, rely on English as the primary language of communication, and generally subscribe to the Charter principles and principles of an official Multiculturalism as a governance model. English language minorities who live in Quebec are often called anglophones. Allophone is the term used for those immigrants and refugees in Quebec whose first language is neither French nor English. According to the Quebec government website, 6 percent of the population speaks a language other than French (which is spoken by 83 percent of the population) or English at 10 percent of the population. As well, 40 percent of Quebec's population can speak English and French (a figure that rises to 53 percent in Montreal), while 13 percent can speak a third language. Finally, references to English–French relations (or Ottawa–Quebec relations or Quebec–Canada relations) are employed as a proxy in referencing the relationship between French-speaking Quebec and English-speaking Canada.

QUEBEC IN A FEDERAL CANADA: PROVINCE OR PEOPLES/NATION?

Federalism is the most visible and distinctive element in Canadian political life. More than in most other advanced industrial countries, our politics have been conducted in terms of the conflicts between regional and language groups, and the struggles between federal and provincial governments . . . The very structure of Canadian federalism, with its ebb and flow of power between federal and provincial governments, has been at the head of our political debates. Indeed, for many observers, what makes Canada distinct is the highly decentralized character of its federal system (Simeon & Robinson, 2004, p. 101)

Quebec is historically a part of Canada's federalist system. But many of Canada's constitutional conundra reflect competing views of federalism as governance (Kymlicka, 1998b). The *Constitution Act* (formerly known as the *BNA Act*) of 1867 established **federalism** as a framework for balancing conflicting interests. On one side were those who wanted a centralized system as a bulwark against American might; on the other side were proponents of a decentralized arrangement that acknowledged the fundamental duality of two peoples (LaSelva, 2004). The political compromise established a federal system that constitutionally entrenched Quebec's linguistic, legal, and social distinctions, in effect confirming Quebec's distinct status in Confederation without undue interference from Ottawa over internal matters (Burgess, 1996). This arrangement also set the stage for one of Canada's longest-running debates: How to live together differently within the seemingly opposed forces of Canada-building versus Quebec-building.

In light of this constitutional tension, both the French and English sectors are locked into seemingly unflattering images of the other as racist, rigid, and unreasonable. Each regards its counterpart as the "problem," because of divergent models of Canada and Quebec's place within the constitutional order (Kernerman, 2005; McRoberts, 1997). English-speaking Canadians tend to support a Trudeau-inspired model of Canada as a contract, with its focus on a strong central government, equality of provinces with no special status for Quebec, a commitment to multiculturalism and official bilingualism, and primacy of individual rights and liberal universalism principles. Such a model has less currency in Quebec, where a compact commitment prevails that includes a strengthened cultural homeland, protection for the French language, assimilation of immigrants, and special arrangements for Quebec within a more flexible federalism. The emergence and growing popularity of a coalition model of Canadian federal society creates a dynamic that may prove to be the salvation of Canada.

Much of the tension reflects different interpretations of federalism and Quebec's place in a federated context (Harrison & Friesen, 2004). Is the federal system properly envisaged as a "contract" between central authorities and the provinces? Or is Canada better seen as a "compact" between the French and English? Or should the relationship be reframed as a "coalition" involving a tri-national alliance that incorporates Aboriginal peoples alongside both the French and English? The interplay of these competing perspectives—contract, compact, and coalition—animates the dynamics that propel the politics of French–English relations.

Canada as Contract

The **Canada as a contract** model envisions Canada as a federalist system of ten equal provinces under a central authority in Ottawa. A contract exists between the provinces (of which Quebec is one) and the federal government. The provinces (including Quebec) as well as the central authority in Ottawa are sovereign within their own jurisdictions as set out in the *Constitution Act* of 1867; neither can usurp the authority or powers of the other. Not surprisingly, the defining narrative behind Canadian history can be interpreted as a struggle between the provinces and Ottawa over control of jurisdictions, with the balance of power in recent years tilting toward the provinces.

Two variations of the contract thesis exist. First, provinces are equal to each other (including Quebec), but subordinate in status and power vis-à-vis the federal government. The privileging of Ottawa as "first among equals" is justified because of its responsibility for advancing Canada's national interests both at home (through comprehensive social programs) and abroad (through diplomatic or military initiatives). Second, federalism is defined as an arrangement of relatively autonomous provinces that have freely entered into accord with the federal government. Under the terms of the agreement, Ottawa has assumed those duties and responsibilities that go beyond the interests and capacities of the provinces. As a result of this freely agreed-upon division of power, both the provincial and federal jurisdictions are equal in status, with an attendant alignment of power and authority as outlined by constitutional decree (also known as *symmetrical federalism*—see Simeon & Robinson, 2004). Quebec is perceived as equivalent to the other provinces in legal status even if some minor concessions may be invoked to promote Quebec's distinctiveness in Canada (Kernerman, 2005, p. 46).

Canada as Compact

A second vision interprets **Canada as a compact** between English-speaking and French-speaking Canadians. The "two founding nations" model sees federalism as a pact between the French and English, a pact that was generally endorsed by English political elites under the prime ministership of Lester B. Pearson (Harty & Murphy, 2005). This vision of Canada from a Quebec viewpoint is strongly endorsed by the Québécois, who reject definitions of themselves as ethnic minorities or as mainstream Canadians who happen to speak French and live in Quebec (Gagnon & Iacovino, 2007). Even the notion of Quebec as a province in the conventional sense is dismissed. Proposed instead is a vision of Quebec as a peoples or a "distinct society" with inherent rights to nationhood by virtue of popular sovereignty. Charles Taylor captures this ethos:

> . . . Quebec is not a province like the others. As a jurisdiction at the heart of the French zone in convergence, it has responsibilities and challenges unlike those of other provinces . . . This is not to say that each and every province is not also different from others in its own way. But only Quebec is different in this way: that it sustains a society converging on French within a continent in which English massively predominates (as cited in Chambers, 1996).

According to the compact thesis, Canada is not a union of one central authority with ten equal provinces, including Quebec. Yes, there should be equality among provinces, but Quebec is fundamentally different from the others because its status as a nation/province, in effect putting pressure toward a flexible (or asymmetrical) federalism (Harty & Murphy, 2005; Simeon & Robinson, 2004). Accordingly, Canada represents a compact, or "covenant," between the French and English, one that is rooted in constitutional law and long-standing political agreement. Insofar as Confederation constituted a response to these internal rifts (LaSelva, 2004), Quebec entered into the agreement with assurances that it would retain its status as a nation and entitlements as a **charter member** of the Confederation. Quebecers continue to see themselves as a "people" with a shared language, culture, and homeland rather than another province with equal rights or an ethnic group whose differences are charming but irrelevant. They claim to constitute an internal nation as well, not only deserving of recognition of their differences, but also entitled to those self-governing powers equivalent to that of English Canada (Harty & Murphy, 2005; McRoberts, 2003). Predictably, then, the language of nationhood remains critical in advancing Quebec's interests because (1) it provides a standing and legitimacy within the international community, (2) it distinguishes Quebec's claims from those of ethnic minorities, (3) it imparts a sense of history and authenticity to Quebec's demands, and (4) it equalizes the bargaining power between Quebec and Ottawa (Kymlicka, 1998b). (See online Insight 8.3.) In November 2006, the House of Commons voted in favour of a motion introduced by Prime Minister Stephen Harper to recognize the Québécois as a "nation within a united Canada" (Thompson, 2006).

Canada as Coalition

A new and more inclusive vision of Canada is slowly gaining traction. According to this line of rethinking, Canada is neither a contract between a centre and the provinces nor an exclusive compact between the English and the French. Instead, it proposes **Canada as a coalition** comprising a tri-national partnership of the French, the English, and Aboriginal peoples, each of whom is sovereign in its own right yet sharing in the sovereignty of Canada as a whole (Kymlicka, 2001; Royal Commission on Aboriginal Peoples, 1996). As a result, Canada is envisaged as a community of communities incorporating territorially grounded "nations" and culturally specific "peoples" with claims to nationhood and self-determining autonomy.

To be sure, a radical restructuring of Canada along the lines of a three-nation state has yet to be formulated (McRoberts, 2001). At minimum, this coalition will require a highly decentralized framework for three national communities to exist in a loose but mutually productive alliance that acknowledges relative autonomy yet mutual interdependence (Gibbins & Laforest, 1998; Laforest, 1998). Under such a confederal arrangement, most of the functions performed by Ottawa would be transferred to Quebec and to Aboriginal nations, except for those pertaining to foreign affairs, currency, and defence. And while their jurisdiction would transcend that of a province, neither Quebec nor Aboriginal nations would be sovereign in the conventional sense of territorial autonomy. The key to making this model work is predicated on the principle of severing the link between nation and state as a framework for national self-determination (Kymlicka, 1998b). Peoples within a **multinational federation** do not need sovereign-state status to flourish; rather, they require a meaningful self-determining autonomy over jurisdictions under their control (Maaka & Fleras, 2005). But cobbling together such a coalition may prove infuriating when different political communities (or nations), each of which claims to be sovereign in its own right, compete for the same territorial homeland (see online Case Study 8.1).

THE POLITICS OF FRENCH–ENGLISH RELATIONS: BRINKMANSHIP OR BLUFF?

French–English relations remain as brittle as ever. On one side the old guard persists. A politically charged environment is filled with suspicions and threats but remarkably little dialogue, and what little there is may be more accurately described as a *dialogue des sourds* (dialogue of the deaf), with both sides continuing to talk past each other in a spiral of mutual incomprehension (Conlogue, 1997; McRoberts, 1997). On the other side, there are signs that debates from the past are just that. Young Québécois and new Quebecers seem less obsessed with issues such as a distinct society, the language wars, and more flexible federalism. According to Gilles Gagné, professor of sociology at Laval University, "Young people today have no use for the old arguments. They don't hate the English; they don't care about the latest fight with Ottawa," preferring instead to talk about the environment, the distribution of wealth, and issues of social justice in a global market economy (as cited in Gordon, 2005). To be sure, a lot of Quebecers, both young and old, may support independence in the abstract, but few have the appetite for yet another round of the turmoil that convulsed Quebec during the referendum crises (*Economist*, 2005).

Three scenarios can be projected from this disarray of reactions. First, Canada is presiding over a turbulent period of profound social change from which it will emerge a strengthened and restructured union. Second, we are witnessing the transformation of Canada into an unbalanced federalism of relatively autonomous political entities without much centre or rationale. Third, it will be back to business as usual once all the bluff and bluster subside. Of course, no one can predict which scenario will prevail, but questions remain: What, then, do the Québécois want? Conversely, what is English-speaking Canada willing to concede in addressing these demands? Admittedly, we could just as easily reverse the question by asking what English-speaking Canadians want, and how the Québécois would accommodate these demands. We should also remember that the intent behind the question "What does Quebec want?" should not be misinterpreted. While there may be a bullying inference that Quebec has no reason to complain since it occupies an enviable position in Canadian society with a freedom to express what in other countries might be ruthlessly suppressed as insolence or treason, no such slight is intended here.

Quebecers' Aspirations: From Status Quo to Independence

It is unfair to imply that the Québécois have a uniform set of expectations and aspirations—at least no more so than English Canada can speak with a singular voice and vision (Gagnon & Iacovino, 2007). Like English-speaking Canada, Quebec too has been buffeted about because of changes and challenges to its identity and unity (Harrison & Friesen, 2004; M. Venne, 2001). Quebecers have lost the certainties and securities of a world defined by rigid Catholic-dominated social orders of religion and class. The shock waves created by the Quiet Revolution continue to reverberate, prompting many Québécois to cast about for a fixed reference point.

Quebec's sense of nationhood also continues to evolve. In shifting from a defensive, inward-looking community to an increasingly open and cosmopolitan society (Salee & Coleman, 1997), Quebec's emergent nationalism is more liberal and tolerant than ever. It is couched in secular and universalistic terms, but it does not abandon a commitment to French language, culture, and interests both in Canada and abroad (Harty & Murphy, 2005). Unlike conventional ethnic nationalisms, Quebec's more civic-oriented nationalism reflects a willingness to integrate immigrants into society with full democratic citizenship rights. Such a transition is not without glitches. Debates in Quebec vacillate between democratic impulses for inclusiveness and universal citizenship on one side, and anxieties over losing its distinctiveness, identity, and political relevance on the other side. That is, how to integrate newcomers without eroding Quebec's French character in the process?

According to Gerald Bouchard of the Bouchard-Taylor Commission, Quebec's insecurities reflect its dual status as a politically mature majority in its homeland (72 percent of Quebec is francophone), but a fragile minority within the broader North American context (Ha, 2007). This "split persona" is not only fuelling a backlash against minorities, but may also account for Quebecers' ambivalence in seeking a new political contract with Canada—of moving forward yet demanding retention of the past, of refusing to be incorporated yet fearful of exclusion, and of committing to Quebec without relinquishing attachment to Canadianness (M. Venne, 2001). Rather than a sign of confusion or indecision, such ambiguity underpins Quebecers' perceptions of themselves as a minority-ized majority. Those who misread these conflicting signals—who fail to appreciate Quebec's insecurities as a minority and its preoccupation with survival by not playing the victim and invoking a frozen-in-time heritage—run the risk of looking soft when it comes to the nuanced politics of Quebec identity (Hamilton, 2008b). (See online Insight 8.2.)

Responses to what Quebec wants vary widely, ranging from endorsement of the status quo or moderate renewal within the existing framework to advocacy of a radical restructuring of Quebec's relationship with Canada, up to and including the point of outright secession (Gray, 2001). Quebecers are attached to Canada, but this attachment comes with strings attached. Opinions and responses depend on how survey questions are asked: When asked to choose between complete independence and the status quo, a majority of Quebec respondents prefer the status quo. When offered more choice than these two extremes, the majority opt for some kind of renewed federalism or sovereignty association (Greenspon, 1998). Ambiguities often reflect situational circumstances, such as the decline in support for sovereignty following the 11 September 2001 terrorist attack (Mackie, 2001). Consider the shift in Quebecer identity as measured in a Léger poll involving a representative sample of 1016 Quebec residents conducted between 18 October and 22 October 2001. Responses to the question "Do you consider yourself to be . . ." proved instructive in 2005 as well. See Table 8-1.

Clearly, many Quebecers embrace a multidimensional commitment to Quebec and Canada. Other studies acknowledge how the advantages of belonging to Canada are recognized by Quebecers. According to a study by the Centre for Research and Information on Canada (2005), nearly 67 percent of Quebecers agree that being part of Canada allows Quebec to bask in Canada's international stature; 65 percent believe that protection of Charter rights represents an advantage for Quebec; 64 percent acknowledge the benefits of transfer payments; 62 percent acknowledge the benefits of the protection from terrorism; and 46 percent even feel that being part of Canada is beneficial for the protection of Quebec's language and culture.

Young Quebecers (between the ages of 18 and 34) are no less supportive of key Canadian values and Canada's achievements. In a study conducted by the Centre for Research and Information on Canada (2006) involving 1212 Quebec young adults of anglophone, francophone, and allophone background, almost all agreed that Canada has a positive international reputation, nearly two-thirds endorse Canada's public policies for sharing wealth as improving the quality of life, and just over half support federalism as a useful framework for living together with differences. Yet identity and attachment to Canada and Quebec remain multifaceted, as Table 8-2 shows.

TABLE 8-1	Quebecers' Identity, 2001 and 2005		
	Feb. 2001 (%)	Oct. 2001 (%)	Aug. 2005 (%)
Solely a Quebecer	24	15	19
A Quebecer first, then a Canadian	25	32	43
Both a Quebecer and a Canadian	26	32	21
A Canadian first, then a Quebecer	15	13	11
Solely a Canadian	8	7	5
Sources: Léger Marketing (2001); Centre for Research and Information on Canada (2005).			

TABLE 8-2	**Quebecers' Identity, Based on Language Background**		
	Francophones (%)	Anglophones (%)	Allophones (%)
Solely a Quebecer	26	2	5
A Quebecer first, then a Canadian	39	9	9
Both a Quebecer and a Canadian	20	32	30
A Canadian first, then a Quebecer	10	31	25
Solely a Canadian	3	22	22
Source: Centre for Research and Information on Canada (2006).			

In short, Quebecers appear to embrace (at least) two political loyalties, and this dual allegiance may not be captured by reference to either Canadian federalism or Québécois nationalism (Webber, 1994). Québécois attachment to Canada may be real and powerful, but is conditional on Canada's acceptance of Quebec as a homeland of last resort. Quebecers may not want to leave Canada, but neither do they want to appear weak or vacillating by caving in to federalist bullying or anglo-arrogance. Responses also reflect a fundamental ambivalence toward Canada: Canada may be my country, it is said, but Quebec is my homeland. Or as quipped by Yvon Descamps, a French-Canadian comedian, in pinpointing the contradiction: "They want an independent Quebec inside a united Canada" (as cited in The Globe and Mail, 18 June 1994). In that ambiguity is at the core of Québécois aspirations and opinions, those leaders who intuitively grasp the politics of ambivalence will reap the spoils, and those who don't, won't (Gibbins & Laforest, 1998).

Broadly speaking, all Quebecers appear anxious to maintain the French character of their society. They want English-speaking Canada to recognize them as equals, preferably through formal recognition of Quebec's distinctiveness (Potter, 2006). Endorsed is a set of arrangements for preserving Quebec's distinctiveness as the homeland of last resort in North America. But agreement about goals does not always translate into consensus over means (Fournier, 1994). On the one side are the moderates who generally prefer accommodation within the framework of Canada. Proposed is a strengthening of Quebec's position within a modified federalist system, in large part by reinforcing its presence in Ottawa while expanding Quebec's access to power and resources. A new constitutional division of jurisdiction is proposed to ensure that each level of government controls what it does best. Moderates may even define themselves as "soft" sovereigntists, but disagree with the principle of separation, preferring instead a kind of flexible federalism that ensures power, autonomy, and identity.

On the other side are those nationalist perspectives that espouse a sovereign status for Quebec. Even here, there is little consensus over the concept of sovereignty. Meanings are bandied about without much regard for precision, with the result that references to sovereignty continue to generate more heat than light. Is it a desire to be left alone, or for Quebec to leave Canada, or vice versa, or a new social contract for rejoining Canada (Walkom, 2001)? For some, sovereignty is defined as a final authority that tolerates no external interference over internal matters; for others, sovereignty refers to arrangements between fundamentally independent political communities involving patterns of relative autonomy within a context of relational interdependence (Maaka & Fleras, 2005; see also Scott, 1996). The distinction between separation and sovereignty is subtle but real. Many believe that Quebecers already possess sovereignty because of constitutional guarantees that uphold Quebec's status as a founding nation. Secession, by contrast, is advocated by a small but vociferous segment of the population. Secessionist moves come in different packages, ranging from outright separation to sovereignty association, with most proposals entailing some degree of political autonomy without loss of close economic ties, such as free trade and common currency. In brief, reference to sovereignty is not merely a softer version of separation. Nor is it a sign of confusion in the minds of the Québécois. Rather, it is a nuanced reading of Quebec's constitutional home in the Canadian federal system. Or as Quebec Premier Jean Charest put it in response to a question about an independent Quebec: "The Liberal Party has always endorsed the legitimacy of the sovereign project including Quebec's means to achieve this goal, yet insist that Quebec is better off in a united Canada" (see Leblanc, 2006).

To be sure, some may believe that the spectre of separation is a spent force (Koven, 2007; Patriquin, 2007). The separatist-based Parti Québécois (PQ) not only finished third in the last provincial election, but several surveys also indicate dwindling public support for a sovereigntist agenda (down to 32 percent); nearly half of the PQ voters want to delete sovereignty from the party's options; and nearly 86 percent say they are proud to be Canadian (compared with 93 percent who say they are proud to be Quebecers) (Gagnon, 2007). Still, hardcore separatists haven't given up the struggle for Québécois sovereignty. After all, they argue, Quebec possesses a broad industrial base for wealth creation (Quebec's economy is the thirtieth largest in the world), a healthy government structure, a shared sense of culture and community, and autonomous sources of revenue. By contrast, federalism does not pay, since staying in Canada creates needless duplication and jurisdictional gridlock. Besides, many *indépendantistes* are tired of being stigmatized as a costly or inconvenient minority. They prefer a space to call their own, where they are the majority and call the shots. Quebecers want to be in the big league—a nation within a state—not just an outmaneuvred administrative subunit of Canada (Latouche, 1995). Or, as put by Louise Beaudoin of the PQ, "I want to be a majority in my own country" (Editorial, 1995). Admittedly, attainment of sovereignty is not without economic and social sacrifices, yet ethnicities everywhere have shown a willingness to absorb costs in exchange for heroic ideals. Nor will sovereignty solve all of Quebec's problems—a point that even the hawkish former Quebec premier Jacques Parizeau conceded—but it will normalize an awkward situation by creating a new political framework for living together separately.

An Official Response to Quebec's Aspirations

In August 1998, Canada's longest-running political drama took a controversial twist in the aftermath of the 1995 referendum (Rocher & Verrilli, 2003). To avert the possibility of yet another separatist scare, the federal government put three issues to the Supreme Court test: (1) Can Quebec legally and unilaterally secede from Canada? (2) Does international law regarding the right of self-determination condone the right to unilateral secession? (3) Which body of law would take precedence in case of conflict between domestic and international interpretation? The verdict was differently interpreted: To the delight of federalists, Canada's Supreme Court ruled unanimously in rejecting Quebec's claims to unilaterally secede from Canada. Any decision to declare Quebec's independence must be balanced by the realities of a federal system, consistent with constitutional principles and rule of law, and must protect the rights of Aboriginal peoples and minorities (Watson, 2008). But the ruling was hardly a victory for federal forces. To the Québécois' delight, the nine judges also made it clear that if a majority of Quebec voters embraced secession, the federal and provincial governments would have to negotiate the complex process of divorce. This ruling has also confirmed the PQ credo that Quebec people have the inalienable right to freely decide the political and legal status of Quebec in or out of Canada.

Not all Quebecers shared this enthusiasm (Rocher & Verrilli, 2003). The *Clarity Act*'s focus on legal procedures and the workings of the referendum tended to gloss over the key problem: that is, a redefining of Quebec's relational status with the rest of Canada. The Act also glossed over the crux of the conflict between the French and English: Why do claims to sovereignty continue to appeal to some Quebecers, and what can be done to address these concerns and aspirations? Criticism aside, however, the *Clarity Act* provides an example of the compromises that constitute the balancing act called Canada. The government's *Clarity Act* suggests the possibility of a negotiated divorce. That is, the federal government will enter into negotiations for separation if a clear majority of Quebecers decides to leave in response to a clear question. In amending the country's basic governing charter for engineering its own partition, Canada would represent one of the few countries in the world to orchestrate its own demise. Given this concession that Canada is divisible, albeit on shifting ground rules established by the federal government (what will determine what constitutes a clear question or clear majority, and on what grounds?), a major constitutional crisis is looming. To the extent that Canada is exploring the possibility of balancing unity with difference against a backdrop of **differentiated citizenship**, Canadians are once again rewriting the rules for living together differently across a deeply politicized society.

RETHINKING FRENCH–ENGLISH GOVERNANCE: TOWARD A MULTINATIONAL CANADA

What is wanted is a larger bed (more space for each partner), maybe even twin beds. But there is definitely a desire to continue sharing the bedroom. This is a marriage not of passion but of reason and convenience—a fine arrangement based on common history, shared interests, and mutual respect (Lysiane Gagnon, 1996).

Tension between Canada's French- and English-speaking communities is as old as the country itself (Kernerman, 2005). Québécois Canadians have complained of second-class status ever since the British defeat of French forces on the Plains of Abraham outside Quebec City in 1759. English Canada interprets Quebec's demands for more power and autonomy as little more than political blackmail and economic extortion (see Donolo & Gregg, 2005; Koven, 2007; Wong, 1998). Not surprisingly, Canada is widely perceived as forever hovering on the brink of self-implosion despite an abundance of riches that is the envy of many. None other than Pierre Elliott Trudeau once pounced on this skepticism and negativity when he said, "We peer so suspiciously at each other that we cannot see that we Canadians are standing on the mountaintop of human wealth, freedom, and privilege" (as cited in H. Porter, 2005).

Is Canada on the verge of realigning its relationship with Quebec (Courchene, 2007)? Admittedly, the picture at present is transitional, yet there is room for guarded optimism.

Canada's federal system is remarkably flexible and adaptive in endlessly tweaking the balance of power between self-rule and shared rule (Cairns, 2000; Chrétien, 1999). De facto arrangements have been in place since 1995 that recognize the uniqueness of Quebec as a distinct society with wide-ranging powers of self-determining autonomy (Dion, 2005). Quebec has its own pension plan and its own system of private law and civil code, levies its own income tax, and exercises a degree of control over immigration that is unprecedented for any federal system (Auboin, 2006; McRoberts, 1996). According to Stéphane Dion (2005), a former constitutional advisor for the federal Liberal government and leader of the Liberal Party, in many ways Quebec resembles a quasi-state, with controlling powers for setting provincial priorities and negotiating jurisdictions. In other words, with or without constitutional guarantees, Quebec is acting as if it were a distinct society by exercising a range of sovereignty-like powers.

National reaction to the quasi-autonomous status of Quebec is ambivalent. Canadians are not necessarily against ad hoc arrangements that cater to Quebec's demands for distinctiveness. The stumbling block resides in moves to explicitly legalize Quebec as a people with a distinct society status (Kymlicka, 2004). According to Charles Taylor (1993), English-speaking Canadians may be willing to accept negotiated and pragmatic arrangements that recognize Quebec's special place in Confederation (Editorial, 1997), but many balk at the idea of formalizing any arrangements that (1) oppose conventional views of Canada (as a social contract); (2) violate certain values related to formal equality (the principle of equal provinces); (3) involve a massive transfer of power to Quebec; (4) create imbalances within Canada's federal system because of preferential treatment; and (5) contravene core constitutional values related to individual versus collective rights. Too much formal recognition may compel Canadians to confront the French–English elephant in the constitutional room that no one wants to talk about. And doing nothing, as David Cameron of the University of Toronto explains, means that the ongoing drama in French–English relations can be seen as a tension to be played out for its endless possibilities rather than a problem to be solved once and for all.

What now? For some, one way of "solving" a complex problem is by ignoring it—despite the propensity of Canada's news media to twist everything into a unity crisis, thus overdramatizing the normal disagreements of any functioning democracy (Dion, 2005). For others, the national unity dilemma is the consequence of secessionist forces that have influenced the public agenda by propagating misconceptions about Quebec's place in Canada (e.g., English Canada as unsympathetic to Quebec's aspirations) (Cardozo & Musto, 1997). Effective communication may solve the problem without the need for constitutional change. For yet others, however, a workable accommodation between Ottawa and Quebec is unlikely without a major reappraisal of Canada's governance structures and processes. Jurisdiction repair is the key. On the one hand, Quebec is demanding more autonomy as a distinct society; on the other hand, Canadian provinces (especially those from the west) want more power-sharing at the federal level—in effect reinforcing a need for a more flexible, asymmetrical federalism (Kernerman, 2005; Taylor, 1993). In the case of Quebec, an asymmetrical federalism acknowledges that Quebec's jurisdictional powers and relationships in a federal governance differ in certain respects from those in the other provinces (Young, 2005).

Flag-waving or finger-pointing will not solve what many perceive as a governance problem rather than a simple case of mutual pigheadedness. The challenge is clearly laid out: Can two relatively autonomous political communities, each claiming sovereignty, learn to share a common political space over a shared homeland without self-destructing in the process (see Shipler, 2001)? Perhaps Canada's current governance structures cannot cope with the deeply divided demands of a tri-national society. Just as the concept of provinces may be increasingly antiquated and irrelevant (Diamond, 1997), so too are there problems with national governance structures designed for a fundamentally different Canada (Gillies, 1997). This should come as no surprise: The prospect of uncritically relying on a nineteenth-century political framework for solving the twenty-first–century problems of a multination state is hardly a realistic option, especially in the face of free-wheeling global forces and inward-looking identity politics. Engin Isin (1996) of York University writes of the need to reconsider the Quebec question within the shifting parameters of the new world order:

> [P]olitical boundaries no longer represent the social and economic realities facing Canadian provinces today. Loyalties of Canadian citizens and their sense of belonging are divided along other lines than the nineteenth-century territorial boundaries represented by the provinces. There are many other territorial identities and regions that are articulated into the different spheres of the global economy, rendering provincial loyalties and identities increasingly not only banal but counter-productive. (p. 6)

In other words, the Quebec question is really a Canadian quandary—in part because Canada's governance structures are saddled with ideological baggage from the Victorian era. As a system of governance for creating decentralized political units to foster democracy and respond locally, a province-based federalism may have worked in the past (McRoberts, 2003). But the emergence of Quebec nationalism and the vibrancy of Aboriginal nationalisms have exposed flaws in the arrangement (Gibbins & Laforest, 1998; Kymlicka, 2001). As long as Canada is defined as a provincially (or territorially) based federalism rather than a multinational federation, a constitutional impasse will persist (Gagnon & Iacovino, 2007). An antiquated model of society-building that equated good governance with a common culture, language, and citizenship cannot possibly address the demands of a Canada that is multilayered and deeply divided (Rimmer, 1998). Proposed instead is a multinational political covenant, one in which the constituent units include peoples or nations in addition to provinces or regional entities (McRoberts, 2001, 2003; Resnick, 2000). The need to configure a new constitutional order around national communities instead of provinces only—to acknowledge that the Québécois and Aboriginal peoples are Canadian but through membership in their groups (Kernerman, 2005)—is captured by Will Kymlicka (1998b), who writes

> So we must accept as given both that there will be minority nationalisms in Canada, and that these national loyalties will be territorially defined. We need to accept, in other words, that Canada is and will remain a *multination* state—a federation of peoples, if you will—in which people's national identity differs from, and may conflict with, their identity as Canadian citizens. (p. 20)

It remains to be seen if Canada can construct a "nested" federation of diverse nations and different citizenships that is responsive to the demands and realities of the nations within (Fleras & Elliott, 1992; Gagnon & Iacovino, 2007; Wilson, 2008). In time, perhaps, and with the appropriate architecture, the "multi-solitudes within" will come to realize that this regrettable necessity called Canada is not such a bad deal after all.

Official Bilingualism: Spanning the Solitudes or Sinking the Ship? A Canadian Covenant or Political Expediency?

Over 40 years of official bilingualism have proven inconclusive as a tool for national unity. Has official bilingualism contributed to Canadian unity by consolidating Quebec's place in Canada? Or is linguistic duality little more than an open sore, with biculturalism as the scab that many pick at? Are the costs justified in light of seeming paltry returns in advancing linguistic duality (about 17 percent of Canadians claim to be bilingual [self-reported] with most in Quebec. Or should its worth be measured in less tangible terms, such as in improving the tenor of French–English relations? Paradoxes prevail: How is it that Canadians are generally supportive of an official languages policy, and yet, as Graham Fraser (2006) points out, universities continue to treat French as a foreign language like German?

Canada is officially bilingual in name and commitment. Polls routinely indicate that Canadians are supportive of bilingualism, since ". . . living in a country with two official languages is one of the things that really defines what it means to be a Canadian" (as cited in Office of the Commissioner of Official Languages, 2004, p. 16). But reality does not always match the rhetoric, despite the fact that Canada's language policies are often the only connection between two largely unilingual societies (Fraser, 2006). Notwithstanding a sea-to-sea commitment to linguistic duality, the reality of bilingualism is restricted instead to (1) federal and federally

regulated institutions, (2) communities designated as bilingual reflecting a high proportion of French-speaking residents, such as Eastern and Northern Ontario, (3) the delivery of some essential provincial services, and (4) select schoolchildren in larger urban centres. Paradoxically, a commitment to bilingualism appears to be declining among young Canadians, despite a heavily financed federal Action Plan in 2003 to "bilingualize" 50 percent of all high school graduates by 2113 (Jaimet, 2007). Rates of bilingual competence vary across Canada: According to Statistics Canada and the Office of the Commissioner of Official Languages (OCOL), bilingualism in major cities varies from high rates in Montreal (53 percent), Moncton (47 percent), and Ottawa-Gatineau (44.2 percent) to low rates in Vancouver (7.5 percent), Edmonton (7.7 percent), and Toronto (8.5 percent) (Office of the Commissioner of Official Languages, 2006/7).

Federal services continue to fumble their language responsibilities. Despite the creation of a bilingual federal service, offices and facilities providing official language services vary by province, with 68.4 percent of New Brunswick offices offering bilingual services while the comparable figure in Saskatchewan is only 15.4 percent (Office of the Commissioner of Official Languages, 2006/7). Consider specific institutions: With a network of 7000 offices across Canada, Canada Post is ideally situated to put the principles of institutional bilingualism into practice. Nevertheless, a sample of designated bilingual offices exposed glaring deficiencies in staffing, questionable services delivered in person or by telephone, and the entrenchment of an inward-looking organizational culture that compels citizens to adapt to the bureaucracy rather than vice versa (Annual Report, 2009/10). In short, official bilingualism has not moved much beyond the domain of government and administration (Gunter, 2010). Yes, it may be a prerequisite for those planning careers in the military, public service, or federal politics, but little incentive is found elsewhere, thus squandering an opportunity for bridge-building across the linguistic divide (G. Fraser, 2006).

The government's Action Plan for Official Languages, unveiled in 2003, sought to address these shortcomings. The Action Plan reaffirmed Canada as a bilingual country, the promotion of bilingualism across Canada, and the guarantee of equality between French and English languages (Government of Canada, 2003). The Action Plan also expanded official languages funding and promotion in education and community programs by way of $750 million over five years. To date, according to the Commissioner of Official Languages, the Action Plan has shown some concrete results in some areas (like justice) but little in other areas (such as the language of work and services) because of budget cuts that compromised programs and the capacity of institutions to fulfill their obligations (Office of the Commissioner of Official Languages, 2006/7). Nor has there been

much success to date in implementing certain programs promised in the successor to the Action Plan, the Roadmap for Canada's Linguistic Duality 2008–2013) (Office of the Commissioner of Official Languages, 2009/10).

At the provincial level, only New Brunswick is officially bilingual, thanks in part to its large Acadian population. Even there, hostilities have erupted between French-speaking Acadians, who want to expand French-language services, and the English-speaking majority, who prefer the status quo (Carlson, 2010). Language policies in the federally administered territories also capture the spirit of the *Official Languages Act*. The Northwest Territories has acknowledged both French and English as official languages in addition to nine Aboriginal languages, while Nunavut is home to three official languages—English, French, and Inuktitut. Outside of New Brunswick and Quebec, English remains the semi-official language of communication in the delivery of service, commerce, administration, and provincial court activities.

The English-speaking provinces have wavered in their commitment to implementing minimal concessions to official language minorities, despite constitutional guarantees to that effect (Office of the Commissioner of Official Languages, 2005/6). For example, passage of the *French Language Services Act* (Bill 8) in 1986 enshrined the delivery of limited French language services when warranted by demand (that is, where the French-speaking population stands at 5000 or more, or represents 10 percent of the population). Yet Ontario refuses to formally guarantee

(Continued)

bilingual rights across the province, citing economic (too costly), political (too undemocratic), cultural (too confusing), and social (too divisive) factors.

Quebec is an official *unilingual* province. With the passage of the **French Language Charter (Bill 101)** in 1977, French became the official language of commerce, education, political, and public communication in Quebec. The Charter proclaimed that all Quebecers had the right to work, shop, study, and be administered to in French all the time; that French was the only language needed on commercial signs in the province (with a few exceptions); and that children of new immigrants who attended public schools had to study in French until the postsecondary level (Government of Canada, 2003). The rationale behind Bill 101 was largely about power: The combination of labour unions, professionals, and intellectuals enlisted language legislation to displace the powerful English-speaking elite by severing the dynamics of power and social relations that had thwarted the upward mobility aspirations of the Québécois (Salee, 2003). Despite the shift in ground rules and balance of power, Quebec's anglophones continue to be guaranteed a strong institutional network of English-language services in health, universities, and education—an equivalent that is rarely extended to francophones in other provinces (Seguin, 2001). To the delight of some and the dismay of others, who accused the *French Language Charter* of being racist or a prelude for launching Quebec independence, the opposite effect was

achieved. This exercise in language engineering not only put Quebecers at ease by nurturing a collective confidence (although worries persist that immigrants, especially those in the Montreal region, prefer English), but also deprived the separatists of a rationale for bifurcating Canada into two (Auboin, 2007; Fraser, 2006).

Central to any assessment is the need to critically deconstruct the *Official Languages Act*. What did the Act say it would do? What did it really intend to do? And what has it done as a result of forces and consequences beyond control? References to success or failure will also reflect and vary with (1) the criteria employed for evaluation, (2) the definition of key terms and concepts, and (3) the phrasing of questions on (and timing of) national surveys. Both political and public responses involve a mixture of support, rejection, expediency, and indifference. Critics tend to exaggerate the costs of official bilingualism; supporters prefer to inflate its benefits. A broad spectrum of opinion is evident. On one side, Max Yalden, a former Commissioner of Official Languages, has praised the *Official Languages Act* as one of the most innovative social reforms in a democratic society. An official bilingualism may not be the perfect answer; nevertheless, it may yet prove its worth in managing those tensions that provoke Canadians. On the other side, bilingualism is chided for failing to unite Canadians or to avert a constitutional crisis (Reid, 1993). In between are the critics who pounce on official bilingualism for not making Canadians more bilingual—in contrast with Quebec's success in advancing French (by way of admittedly controversial legislation). Others applaud the expansion of bilingualism across Canada, but worry that the costs may not justify the results, especially since the number of bilingual speakers in Canada outside Quebec has remained relatively constant.

Does official bilingualism contribute to or detract from Canada-building? Much depends on how Canada is defined: as a multicultural contract or a binational compact. Those who embrace a view of Canada as a multicultural contract tend toward a more positive spin. Official bilingualism originated in large part to counter the surge of nationalism in Quebec by offering Quebec the promise of participation and opportunity throughout all of Canada. But those who endorse a binational view of Canada as a compact dismiss bilingualism as little more than a "conflict management" strategy for defusing Quebec's constitutional demands (Fraser, 2006). According to the binationalists, the *Official Languages Act* borders on a dangerous irrelevancy: irrelevant, because it doesn't address the real issues; dangerous, because it distracts from the issues at hand. The national unity question is addressed, in other words, not by making Quebec more distinctive or by power-sharing, but by making the rest of Canada more like Quebec, thus putting Quebecers more at ease.

A paradox is in play. Instead of creating a more bilingual Canada, Trudeau's commitment to official bilingualism may have inadvertently reinforced a kind of serial monolingualism.

Federal institutions were transformed into vehicles for serving unilingual Canadians in their own language rather than putting the burden on individuals to change (McRoberts, 1997). But, while this transformational dynamic appealed to many English-speaking Canadians and their view of Canada, a commitment to "multiculturalism within a bilingual framework" fizzled in Quebec. Trudeau's efforts at depoliticizing Quebec's nationalism badly miscalculated the depth of Quebec's national aspirations (LaSelva, 2004). Bilingualism as a national unity strategy failed to dampen Quebec's nationalism; if anything, Kenneth McRoberts (1997) notes, it consolidated Quebec's resolve to see itself as a peoples by relying on the language of nationhood to gain legitimacy.

The conclusion seems inescapable: Moves to integrate Quebec into the national political community by way of language policies may be useful but ultimately insufficient in advancing a national unity strategy unless supplemented by power-sharing arrangements that ensure Quebec's status as *maîtres chez nous*. The irrelevance of official bilingualism is conveyed by political philosopher Charles Taylor (1993), who acknowledges that the key issue is not about the number of bilingual speakers. Rather, it is about whether there will be enough francophones in the next generation to perpetuate a dual language heritage. To ensure the survival of Quebec's French face, a meaningful and self-determining autonomy is required that secures for Quebec those powers of decision making over matters that mean the most.

Chapter Highlights

- Canada officially represents a society that subscribes to "multiculturalism within a bilingual framework." Its French–English duality constitutes a defining yet contested characteristic that secures a national identity yet fosters resentment and conflict.
- Official bilingualism does not appear to have been a resounding success in improving Quebec–English Canada relations. Official bilingualism is widely viewed within Quebec as appeasement without power. Still, under official bilingualism all Canadians have the right to work or receive services at the federal level in the official language of their choice.
- A central question in this chapter is "What is really going on in terms of Quebec–Ottawa relations?" Answers to this question suggest the usefulness of seeing Canada from a variety of diverse perspectives, including Canada as a contract, a compact, and a coalition.
- The politics of Quebec's diversity agenda is informed by (1) Quebec's simultaneous status as a majority and a minority; (2) competing nationalisms, including ethnic, civic, and Aboriginal; (3) a vision of Quebec's place in Canada that differs from that of English Canada and varies within Quebec itself; and (4) a federal governance structure that stifles its collective aspirations.
- What do the Québécois want? While answers are varied and reflect a certain degree of ambiguity, emphasis points to a new social contract that will enhance the distinct and sovereign character of Quebec's identity, language, and culture.
- The Quebec question is really a Canadian quandary. That is, existing federal arrangements cannot handle the nationalist aspirations of Quebec, suggesting instead an overhaul of federalism along a redesigned multinational governance structure and process.

For further study, you can access the Case Studies referenced in this chapter at **www.pearsoncanada.ca/fleras**.

Review Questions

1. Compare and contrast the differing visions of Canada with respect to English–French relations. Which do you think is the most correct reading of Canadian society?

2. The Quebec question may be a Canadian quandary. For some, Canada is the problem that Quebec is trying to solve. For others, Quebec is the problem that Canada is trying to solve. How would you respond to each of these assertions?

3. If someone were to ask you what you thought Quebec wants, how would you respond?

4. Has an official bilingualism contributed to or detracted from national unity? Discuss.

Links and Recommendations
FILM

There are many films that provide insight into Quebec. One of the most recent and best is *The Barbarian Invasions* (2003), a film that simultaneously celebrates the Quebec character while satirizing government and societal shortcomings.

BOOKS

Beyond Obligations. Annual Report 2009–2010 Volume 11, Office of the Commissioner of Official Languages (2010). An overview and assessment of how bilingualism is playing out in Canada by evaluating the performance of institutions, reporting to Parliament, and responding to complaints.

Vive Quebec! New Thinking and New Approaches to the Quebec Nation, edited by Michel Venne (2001). A robust defence of Quebec nationalism.

Beyond the Impasse: Toward Reconciliation, edited by Roger Gibbins and Guy Laforest (1998). A look at the perils and promises associated with reconciling French–English relations.

The Conditions of Diversity in Multinational Democracies, edited by Alain-G. Gagnon, Montserrat Guibernau, and Francois Rocher (2003). An examination of how the politics of difference are played out against the backdrop of multinational societies.

Federalism, Citizenship, and Quebec: Debating Multinationalism, by Alain-G. Gagnon and Rafaelle Iacovino (2007). An exploration of multinationalism governance with respect to Quebec's place in Canada.

WEBSITES

Office of the Commissioner of Official Languages—Visit this site for information on Canada's official languages and official bilingualism:
   www.ocol-clo.gc.ca

Expansionist Party of the United States—A series of arguments in favour of Quebec independence are presented on one of the party's webpages:
   www.expansionistparty.org/ForQCsep.html

CBC Indepth: Parti Québécois Timeline—This site presents key events in the history of the Parti Québécois, the political wing of Quebec's separatist movement, from its inception in 1967 to 2005:
   www.cbc.ca/news/background/parti_quebecois

CHAPTER 9

Immigrants and Immigration

DEBATE

The Refugee Determination Process: Is It Working?

Debates over refugees perplex and provoke as few other issues can or have. The numbers say it all: In 2008, there were a total of 34 million forcibly displaced persons of concern. This total included 10.5 million **refugees/asylum seekers**, 14.5 million internally displaced persons, and 6.5 million stateless persons (United Nations High Commissioner for Refugees, 2008). (The United Nations High Commissioner for Refugees [UNHCR] was established in 1950 with a three-year mandate to process European refugees.) By the end of 2009, the number of forcibly displaced persons had risen to 43 million.

According to UNHCR figures, Afghanistan remains the leading country of origin for refugees at 2.79 million, followed by Iraq at 1.9 million, and Palestine at 536 000 (excluding the 2.1 million Palestinians displaced by wars since 1948). Pakistan continues to be the asylum country with the largest overall number of refugees (1.8 million), followed by the Syrian Arab Republic (1.1 million) and Islamic Republic of Iran (980 000). Countries with the largest number of internally displaced persons include Colombia (3 million), Iraq (2.6 million), and Democratic Republic of Congo (1.5 million). Thailand is the country with the largest number of stateless persons (3 million). Finally, the displacement of 30–50 million persons because of environmental crises and natural disasters has prompted fears that ecological refugees may outnumber political refugees and persons in need of protection, with estimates of nearly 1 billion eco-refugees by 2050 because of the consequences of global warming.

No less significant are changing patterns of displacement. Nearly 80 percent of the world's refugees have fled to developing world countries, imposing an overwhelming burden on those jurisdictions least capable of addressing this humanitarian crisis (UNHCR Antonio Guterres in News Stories 16 June 2009). At 377 000 persons in 2009, the number of asylum seekers in industrialized nations has remained relatively stable in recent years (UNHCR, Briefing Notes, 23 March 2010). About 45 percent of asylum seekers to industrialized countries fled to Asia and the Middle East, while 29 percent went to Africa. Nevertheless, the United States remained first as the preferred destination country, with 49 000 asylum applicants; France was second, with 42 000 applicants. Canada ranked third among receiving countries, with 33 000 applicants (a 10 percent decrease from 2008). It should be noted that in 2010, the number of refugee claimants to Canada dropped to 22 000, or 23 percent of the industrial world's total, putting it in fifth place.

These numbers make the conclusion seem inescapable: The refugee crisis is real, its impact on countries and the global order is inestimable, and its omnipresence is unlikely to dissipate in the future. Dealing with the refugee crisis involves debates over constructing a system that not only deters "unwanted" claimants but also establishes a transparent protocol for deciding who is a refugee.

Canada is no less exempt from this crisis. But while other countries are struggling to staunch the flow of refugees, Canada has a framework in place that ostensibly provides a principled way of determining who is or is not a refugee. On the surface, establishing a system that is fair, fast, and final would seem simple enough (Showler, 2005, 2009). And in many ways, Canada's system is globally admired as a model to praise or emulate. In reality, the system is subject to relentless scrutiny and withering criticism (Bissett, 2009; Gallagher, 2008b; Moens & Collacott, 2008; Stoffman, 2002, 2009), as the following questions imply:

- Can the refugee determination system distinguish genuine cases from bogus applicants? Is the refugee determination system subject to abuse and breakdown, resulting in a safe haven for terrorists and a quick-fix channel for queue jumpers? (See online Insight 9.3.)
- How do we distinguish refugees fleeing persecution from immigrants

seeking opportunity from those grey zones where persecution is rife and the economy is dire, thereby making it nearly impossible to establish motives (Refugees, 2007)?

- Has the system proven effective in balancing national interests with the rights of refugees (Adelman, 2004)?
- How can an overburdened system— one that was established to process a trickle of Cold War dissidents— address a burgeoning caseload involving new and bewildering complexities (Spencer, 2003)?
- Can the system overcome media-driven images of **refugee claimants** as little more than self-serving queue-jumpers, and gate-crashers (see Dench, 2007)?

Canadians appear to be of mixed minds when it comes to the refugee question. Widespread acceptance of Vietnamese refugees in the 1970s is offset by the blistering attacks on the 600 Chinese "boat people" who landed on the British Columbia coast in 1999 (Hier & Greenberg, 2002) and, to a lesser extent, political and public reaction to 76 Tamil asylum seekers who arrived ten years later in the same port space (Fleras, 2010c). (See online Case Study 11.6.) Support is overwhelming for refugees who are seen as legitimate victims of state oppression. For example, for its work with international refugees, Canada received the UN Nansen medal in 1986—the first and so far the only country to earn such an accolade. But the welcome mat is fraying for refugees who are smuggled in, arrive unannounced without

(Continued)

documentation, who appear to be shopping around for the best deal, come across as economic opportunists circumventing conventional channels of entry, and who abuse the system through endless appeals and delays. Perceptions of control appear to be critical. As long as they are in charge of "who gets in," Canadians admire themselves as generous patrons to genuine victims. But any departure from the norm—that is, asylum seekers who self-select themselves for admission based on *their* needs (Simmons, 2010)—and Canadians bristle at the prospect of being taken advantage of.

Clearly, then, Canadians are conflicted over the current refugee determination system, with growing calls for "a major rethink" of how to manage the crisis. Much of the conflict over the politics of refugee determination pivots around two philosophical axis points (Plaut, 1989). On one side is *a restrictive* perspective that endorses a skeptical mentality toward refugee claims. According to this "guilty until proven innocent" approach, measures are required to thwart the entry of "bogus" refugees who imperil Canada's national interests, and to expedite their expulsion for unfounded claims (Collacott, 2006; Gallagher, 2004). But compared with other developed countries, Canada is perceived as soft on "irregular" migrants in search of permanent-resident status. Loopholes in the determination process are exploited by desperate refugees, while the system itself is subject to abuse by opportunistic lawyers, ruthless smugglers, gullible refugees, political interests, and bungling **Immigration and Refugee Board of Canada (IRB)** members (Bauer, 1994;

Gallagher, 2008b). Three options are proposed for tightening the admission process: (1) Detain undocumented asylum seekers until proof of person is established; (2) establish a firewall that excludes as many refugees as possible, then deal with genuine cases as they arise; or (3) redesign Canada's refugee program by selecting (sponsoring) only those from refugee camps around the world (Stoffman, 2002).

An *expansionist* mindset disagrees, proposing instead a generous acceptance of refugees that is in line with Canada's humanitarian and human rights commitments. The objective is to cast as wide a net as possible for refugees, then dispose of those who don't fit. According to this line of logic, all refugees should be assumed innocent and given the benefit of the doubt until they are proven guilty. After all, there is no such thing as an illegal migrant, since all asylum seekers are within their rights by international law to seek political asylum. Admittedly, proof of authenticity may be awkward without identity papers; yet playing by the rules by patiently standing in a queue is rarely an option. Such is the nature of any flight from persecution and chaos that few can afford the luxury of asking for papers or permission. The necessity to produce "satisfactory identity documents" negatively affects those refugee groups who come from countries without such official documents, where no government authority exists to issue such documents, where certain groups such as women or rural residents cannot access such documentation, and where simply asking for such documentation is likely to arouse suspicion or incur reprisals. (Keep in mind that it was the refugees' identity that put them at risk in the first place [Canadian Council for Refugees, 2000]). Additional deterrents to flight are no less daunting, including pre-boarding detection barriers, passport and visa control systems, carrier sanctions and fines, internment in some cases, and often flawed systems for processing claimants (Adelman, 2004; Kumin, 2004). In short, refugee claimants as protected persons deserve the benefit of the doubt, on the assumption that it is better to err on the side of generosity (i.e., to accept 99 bogus refugees) than to incorrectly reject a genuine case.

In keeping with this expansionist ethos, Canada is casting its refugee net ever more broadly. A 1986 Supreme Court decision ruled that everyone who landed in Canada was entitled to due process when claiming refugee status. There is growing acceptance of certain groups who do not strictly comply with the definition of persecution, but need *protection* because they experience refugee-like conditions, such as political oppression or environmental disaster. In May 1997, Canada expanded its definition of refugee status to include those internally displaced because of war or terrorism and in need of temporary protection from a dangerous situation (Stoffman, 1997; Waldie, 1998). Refugee status may be granted to minorities, such as the Roma ("gypsies"), who fail to receive state protection from public discrimination. Gender is also proving to be grounds for refugee status, reflecting patterns of persecution that affect women only, including cases of abusive domestic situations, exposure to mutilation, or forced marriage

and sterilization (Kumin, 2001). Finally, even rejected claimants or those who commit a serious crime may escape deportation if they risk injury upon return, fear becoming victims of crime in their homeland, or if their Canadian-born children would suffer from removal.

Such inclusiveness is not without costs or questions. How far can the refugee determination net be stretched before it unravels? Two projections prevail: Those who criticize government policy as either too restrictive or too generous tend to see hidden agendas behind every move to expand or constrict. Critics are so contemptuous of the refugee determination system that they would slough it off as a bad joke were it not dealing with life-threatening outcomes and society-destroying issues. The entire process is inundated with excess capacity; refugee workers are overworked; claimants encounter lengthy delays; and the system itself not only is prone to gaffes and subject to abuse because of political patronage in staffing the IRB, but also exposes Canadians to security risks (Collacott, 2006; Francis, 2002). By contrast, those who endorse government policy are reluctant to tamper with success. Flaws and glitches notwithstanding, Canada's refugee processing program is globally admired for its openness and generosity in providing the benefit of the doubt to those in need. Yet even supporters would acknowledge that Canada cannot possibly accept all refugees without self-imploding in the process, unless it secures its borders against the random flow of desperate people (Crepeau & Nakache, 2006).

(Continued)

To be sure, Canada is hardly alone in confronting this challenge. Comparable fears and concerns prevail throughout the Western world—too many refugees, too few resources, too slow a system, too inefficient a process, and too few deported (Showler, 2005). These "irregular" movements convince governments to erect new barriers to deter the unwanted. But these obstructionist measures have the perverse effect of ramping up a massive industry in the smuggling and trafficking of humans across international borders (Guterres, 2007). Not surprisingly, key questions need to be addressed: To what extent are global dynamics challenging Canada's capacity for coping with the worldwide movements of peoples (Castles & Miller, 2009)? How workable and fair is Canada's approach to the entry and acceptance of refugees? Does Canada as an affluent society have an obligation to be more generous when dealing with refugees? Or should priority be assigned to protecting Canada's security and sovereignty? Is the system too strict or not restrictive enough? On what grounds can any assessment be made? Who says so, and why? The Debate Revisited box at the end of this chapter will provide some additional insights.

INTRODUCTION: THE PARADOXES OF IMMIGRATION

The conclusion cannot be avoided: In this globalized era of human uprootedness and migration, the movement of people is not an anomaly but a normal process that may prove impossible to curb or control. (Pecoud & de Guchteneire, 2005)

The twenty-first century may well become defined by the movement of peoples from one country to another, from one continent to another (Guterres, 2007). With up to 200 million people on the move outside of their homeland—a population equivalent to that of Brazil, the world's fifth most populous country—it is safe to say that few countries have been untouched by international migration (Kapur, 2005; Papademetriou, 2003; Simmons, 2010). Humans from around the world are in a constant quest to improve their lives, to flee from confining environments, and to escape from natural and social disasters. People are being "pushed" from their homelands because of political oppression, ethnic conflicts, demographic pressure, and economic stagnation (Castles & Miller, 2009). They also are "pulled" to other countries to take advantage of opportunity and freedom— or to seek out adventure and excitement. In some cases, people are seeking asylum by fleeing persecution, human rights abuses, and armed conflicts; in other cases, they are escaping hardship and the uncertainties of life in developing countries with weak economies and unstable political systems (Refugees, 2007). The foreseeable future looks even less promising: Climate change and natural disasters will make existence increasingly unsustainable, while the growing awareness of gaps between the rich and poor will induce many to pull up roots and seek fortunes elsewhere, despite exposure to risks when crossing borders (Guterres, 2007).

In short, the world is increasingly inundated with new and more complex patterns of displacement and migration (Massey, 2009; Pecoud & de Guchteneire, 2005). As the nature of these border crossings varies, so too does the proliferation of terms to account for the variety, as Table 9-1 shows.

TABLE 9-1	Types of Migrants

Immigrants

- Born elsewhere
- Arrive voluntarily
- Entitled to permanent status
- Associated with economic benefits or family reunification

Refugees

- Forced to flee their home country
- Cannot return because of a well-founded fear of persecution based on race, ethnicity, etc. (convention refugees)
- May be in need of protection and cannot be returned because of safety concerns (protected persons)

Asylum seekers

- Seek sanctuary (safe keeping) in another country by declaring refugee status

Internally displaced persons

- Forced to flee their home, but remain located in their home country

Stateless persons

- Not considered a national by any state

Evacuees

- Temporarily evacuated from a crisis zone, but must return once hostilities subside

Guest workers/temporary workers

- Enter another country on a temporary basis and are expected to leave upon completion of their job or expiry of their work visa

Professional transients

- Legally relocate from one country to another to take advantage of job opportunities; they are highly skilled but may be contractual temporary workers

Nowhere are the politics of immigration more striking than in Canada (Li, 2003). As Stephen Gallagher (2008b) observes, Canada may be the only country in the world where mass immigration constitutes an article of faith, embodies a policy norm, and is integral to its national identity. Canada's immigration program has garnered widespread popularity and public support, in addition to praise as a success by international standards (Reitz, 2010). On the whole, Canada has become a more vibrant and dynamic society because of immigrants (Ibbitson, 2005b). In their role as builders of Canada, immigrants have not only contributed but continue to contribute to national identity. They have also bolstered the Canadian economy, both abroad and domestically (Halli & Driedger, 1999; Hiebert & Ley, 2006). In light of increased global competition for the brightest and the best, immigrants may provide a solution to the problems of an aging population, shrinking birth rate, diminishing tax base, and skills shortage in a global and information-based economy. No less critical is their contribution to re-energizing Canada's economy by virtue of their consumer spending, optimistic outlook, and entrepreneurial spirit (Walton-Roberts,

2011). However counterintuitive it may seem, a fundamental mindset shift is overdue: Canada needs immigrants more than immigrants need Canada.

Canadians for the most part have embraced immigration with the kind of civility and open-mindedness that is becoming a national trademark (Adams, 2007). While many European countries are rethinking their commitment to immigration in light of post-9/11 security concerns, Canada continues to maintain historically high levels. Canada's intake of just over 252 000 migrants in 2009 (and nearly 281, 000 in 2010—the highest single year total in 50 years) constitutes 0.8 percent of the total population—making Canada one of the largest per capita immigrant-receiving countries in the world relative to the size of its population. By contrast, the United States issued about 1.1 million permanent residence visas (green cards) representing about 0.4 percent of the population in 2009, while Australia admitted 224 000 immigrants in 2008/9 which is just over 1 percent of the total population (Reitz, 2010). Canadians also appear favourably disposed to immigration. A recent Nanos Research poll for Policy Options conducted by telephone with 1008 randomly selected Canadians in late May/early June 2010 indicated that Canadians overwhelmingly support immigration as a positive feature. The poll found that 81.4 percent agreed (65.3 percent) or somewhat agreed (16.1 percent) that immigration reflects a positive feature about Canada, while only 16 percent disagreed or somewhat disagreed with this statement. The poll also demonstrated that (1) immigration is thought to strengthen the economy; (2) the government should do more through language and labour market support to assist immigration settlement into Canada; and (3) immigrants do a good job of fitting into Canada (Nanos, 2010).

As well, Canada remains a destination of choice for international immigrants. According to an international survey commissioned by the Historica-Dominion Institute (2010) in partnership with the Munk School of Global Affairs and Aurea Foundation, more than half the people (53 percent) from the world's 24 leading economies say they would abandon their homelands and move to Canada if they could. This tilt toward Canada is most noticeable in the emerging economies of the G20: A whopping 77 percent of Chinese would immigrate to Canada if they had a choice, followed by 71 percent of Mexicans, 68 percent of Indians, 64 percent of Turks, and 62 percent of both the Polish and South Africans. Respondents to the survey expressed overwhelmingly positive attitudes about Canada's welcoming and tolerant treatment of newcomers. A full 86 percent of respondents said that Canada is a country where rights and freedoms are respected; 79 percent said Canadians are tolerant of those from different racial and cultural backgrounds; 79 percent said that Canada has one of the best qualities of life in the world (in 2009, the UN Human Development Index ranked Canada fourth, behind Norway, Australia, and Iceland); and 72 percent said Canada is welcoming to immigrants.[1] Unlike many European countries, moreover, Canada possesses neither an anti-immigrant political party nor an active racist skinhead movement. The results of this survey bode well for Canada's efforts to attract highly educated immigrants in the looming global talent wars.

The conclusion seems inescapable: Canada remains a country of choice for those looking to improve fortunes, to reunite with family and relatives, and to escape political repression. But there is a darker side to this bucolic picture: Canada may be a land of immigrants, yet it remains sharply conflicted over the pros and cons of immigration. Put bluntly, Canada's immigration policy is thought to be out of control with respect to "how many," "what kind," "where from," and "what for," with a corresponding negative impact on both new Canadians and Canadian society (Bissett, 2008; Grubel & Grady, 2011). Those on the right complain of too many of the "wrong kind"; those on the left complain of not enough of the "right kind"; and those in the middle may be confused over "what kind" is right. Still others criticize Canada's immigration program as unfair and inefficient and in need of a major overhaul, despite a glowing international reputation as a principled framework that is being copied elsewhere, including the United Kingdom (Canadian Press, 2007a) and more recently in Germany. Of particular concern is the trend toward temporary foreign workers to address short-term labour needs at the expense of Canada's long-term interests (Hennebry, 2010).

Criticism over immigration paradoxes cannot be brushed off. Immigration may be inseparable from the quality of life in Canada; after all, Canada's standard of living will depend on immigration to offset the diminishing returns of an aging population and declining birth rate (Ibbitson, 2005a). The labour by irregular migrants is critical in shoring up the middle-class lifestyle that Canadians crave (Hiebert, 2006). Yet the promise and productivity of immigration are lost in a welter of debates over fiscal uncertainty, corporate downsizing, job losses, economic restructuring, and political expediency (Li, 2003). Yes, up to 40 percent of new immigrants may possess university degrees, but a similar percentage also have fewer than 13 years of education, speak neither French nor English, and lack the credentials for full employment (Hawthorne, 2007). Immigration may have facilitated a robust consumer economy in Canada's gateway cities of Vancouver and Toronto, but associated costs cannot be discounted, including congestion, shortage of affordable housing, and strains on social service delivery (Ley & Hiebert, 2001). Double standards are no less unmistakable: Immigrants are rebuked for stealing jobs from "real" Canadians, yet rejected as "freeloading parasites" if unemployed. Put bluntly, Canadians remain "reluctant hosts" who appear welcoming at times, truculent at other times, but whose ambivalence—even hostility—toward certain foreign-born individuals is palpable beneath a folksy veneer of tolerance.

Just as Canadians are perplexed by the politics of immigration, so too are newcomers experiencing glitches in the process. "Getting in" is one thing. "Settling down," "fitting in," and "moving up" have proven more challenging than most would have imagined. Immigrants come to Canada with the best of intentions for making a positive contribution to Canada and for themselves (Isajiw, 1999). Yet Canada has not always proven itself the haven that many had expected. True, both immigrants and refugees possess the rights of citizenship and the multicultural right to inclusiveness. Nevertheless, many continue to encounter obstacles that intensify levels of immigration frustration, up to and including violence turned inward (suicide) or outwards (domestic abuse) (DiManno, 2007; see also Biles & Burstein, 2003). Formidable barriers exist in a society whose welcome mat is yanked out from underneath at the slightest provocation. And Canada's much vaunted tolerance has been put to the test in the aftermath of 9/11 amidst fears that loose entry regulations and lax enforcement may foster a haven for terrorist groups (Thompson, 2001). As a result, antipathy toward new Canadians sometimes borders on the xenophobic or apoplectic, with calls for rigorous screening procedures, including DNA testing, immigrant and citizenship tests, and vigorous deportation procedures.

Admittedly, the introduction of various government programs has facilitated the process of immigrant integration and settlement (Halli & Driedger, 1999; Wayland, 2006). But in a country whose national agenda is dominated by Aboriginal politics and

Québécois nationalism, dangers lurk in excluding immigrants from meaningful national dialogue over the following key questions:

- Why should Canada accept immigrants?
- Who should be encouraged to come to Canada?
- How many immigrants (if any) should be accepted?
- Which category of immigrant is preferred: family, economic, or refugee?
- What kind of diversity can immigrants bring with them?
- How do we balance long-term goals for Canada-building with short-term responses to specific needs?
- In what way do immigrants contribute to or detract from Canada-building?
- What is the best way of integrating immigrants—by dwelling on differences or emphasizing commonalities?

These questions cannot be left unanswered in the pursuit of an immigration policy of mutual benefit. Responses often elicit intense emotions—even spasms of hysteria—that often defy rational discussion. The sensitivity of the topic can generate hostility because immigration politics upset cherished notions of national unity and identity; require difficult political decisions and tradeoffs at individual or institutional levels; and may expose hypocrisies of governance or political commitment (Papademetriou, 2003). Nevertheless, answers to these questions require a level of deliberation that must transcend political slogans or public posturing (see also Swain, 2007).

Problem or solution? Cost or benefit? Good or bad or in between (see Chomsky, 2007; Swain, 2007)? It is within the context of concern and criticism, of progress and stalemate, of conviction and confusion that this chapter explores the politics of immigration. By looking at immigration's impacts and implications for Canada-building and for new Canadians, it examines the political and social dimensions of immigration with respect to principles and politics, patterns and programs, both in the past and at present. The chapter begins by theorizing the concept of Canada as an **immigration society**, followed by a look at Canada's immigrant diversity in terms of shifting patterns. It continues with a closer examination of the laws and policies that governed the entry of immigrants into Canada. Particular attention is aimed at the politics of "entry," as this category has evolved over time, thus raising the question of whether the current model and program of immigration is the best one for Canada in light of emergent realities. Many of the controversies associated with immigration are discussed as well, including who gets in, on what grounds, from where, what for, and at what level of acceptance. Criticism of Canada's refugee determination process poses awkward but important questions: Who is a refugee? How do we find out? Is the system fair? Is it working? How can it be improved? The difficulties endured by immigrants in adjusting to Canadian society—that is, settling down, fitting in, and moving up—confirm what many suspect: From afar, Canada's status as an immigration society sparkles; up close, it loses some of its sheen and lustre.

A word of caution: A chapter on immigration, immigrants, and refugees could not possibly address all topics without stretching its resources to the point of superficiality and gloss. Emphasis is focused primarily on the needs and concerns of immigrants and their descendants from so-called non-conventional countries of origin, in terms of their adjustment to Canadian society under a bewildering array of policy circumstances, institutional barriers, and social pressures. Specific groups are not dealt with per se. The intent is to provide a comprehensive overview of immigrants and refugees *as if* they constituted a relatively uniform category for analytical purposes. Admittedly, this ideal-typical stance runs the risk of oversimplification, reductionism, excessive analysis, or essentializing (treating everyone in a category in a fixed, homogeneous, and deterministic fashion). Still, there are many benefits in embracing the big picture while holding constant the range of internal diversity because of race, ethnicity, age, gender, sexual preference, and social class.

CANADA: AN IMMIGRATION SOCIETY

Canada embraces a diverse tapestry of immigrants and refugees from different parts of the world. Because of a robust immigration program, Canada constitutes a staunchly heterogeneous society whose reputation as a multicultural mosaic needs little propping up. Canada's ethnic composition has undergone a radical transformation since the passage of the *British North America (Constitution) Act* of 1867 when only 8 percent of Canada's population was of neither British nor French ancestry (Palmer, 1975). Between 1896 and 1914, the balance began to shift when up to 3 million immigrants—many of them from Central and Eastern Europe—arrived to domesticate the West. Immigration increased substantially prior to and just after World War I, reaching a peak of just over 400 000 in 1913, followed by an all-time low of just 7600 immigrants in 1942. The post–World War II period resulted in yet another "exodus" from the war-devastated countries of Europe, but sources of immigration since the 1980s have shifted as well—in the process rekindling controversy over the politics of "who gets in, why, and how." Data from Statistics Canada provide an overview of immigration patterns and immigrant diversity for the period 2001 to 2006.

Immigration Facts and Figures

- According to 2006 Census data (Statistics Canada, 2006a), approximately 6.2 million immigrants (foreign born) live in Canada, drawn from more than 200 countries of origin. The foreign born now account for 19.8 percent of the total Canadian population—a figure that has grown steadily in recent years. Only Australia, with 22.2 percent of its population as foreign born, outpaces Canada.

- Birthplace of Canadian immigrants: Asia and the Middle East (2.5 million); Europe (2.3 million); Africa (375 000); Caribbean and Bermuda (318 000); United States and South America (both 250 000); Central America (130 000); and other (59 000).

- Canada's population stood at about 31.2 million, with an annual intake of around 250 000 immigrants between 2001 and 2006 (or more accurately 1.1 million between January 1, 2001, and May 16, 2006, during which the population of Canada grew by 1.6 million). Compare this total to an average of 126 000 per year in the 1980s, 144 000 in the 1970s, and 137 000 in the 1960s.

- Between 2001 and 2006, Canada's foreign-born population increased by 13.6 percent, while the growth rate for the Canadian-born population was only 3.3 percent. By 2025, immigrants will account for all of Canada's population increase (birth rates will be offset by death rates as Canadian women continue to reproduce at levels below the replacement rate).

- Recent immigrants (between 2001 and 2006) from Asia and the Middle East comprise the largest portion of newcomers (58.3 percent) to Canada. European immigrants comprise the second-largest group of recent newcomers at 16.1 percent, followed by South and Central America at 10.8 percent, Africa at 10.6 percent, and the Caribbean at 8.9 percent. In 1971, those from Europe accounted for 61.6 percent of newcomers, while only 12.1 percent were born in Asia.

- Canadians reported speaking more than 200 different languages, with the most common, in descending order, being English, French, Chinese, Italian, and German.

- Of the 1.1 million immigrants between 2001 and 2006, 581 000 (in rounded-off figures) settled in Ontario, 194 000 in Quebec, and 178 000 in British Columbia. These three provinces received 85.8 percent of recent immigrants, with Ontario leading the way with 54.9 percent, followed by Quebec at 17.5 percent and British Columbia at 16 percent. Only 855 recent immigrants settled in Prince Edward Island and 1440 in Newfoundland and Labrador, between 2001 and 2006.

- Immigration has contributed greatly to the cosmopolitan mix of Canada's urban space (McIsaac, 2003). In 2006, 97.2 percent of recent immigrants who had landed in the previous five years lived in an urban community or Census Metropolitan Area. In total, 95 percent of all foreign-born residents are urban.

- Nearly 70 percent of all recent immigrants live in the "MTV" cities of Montreal, Toronto, and Vancouver. Fully 16.6 percent of newcomers live in smaller Census Metropolitan Areas like the Waterloo Region or Calgary.

- Both absolute numbers and relative percentages make Toronto, Montreal, and Vancouver more diverse than provincial or national averages. In 2006, 3.9 million foreign-born residents lived in these three cities, comprising 62.9 percent of all Canada's immigrants. Toronto was home to 2.3 million foreign-born residents, or 45.7 percent of its population; Vancouver had 831 000, or 39.6 percent of its total; and Montreal had 740 000, or 20.6 percent of its total.

- Most immigrants reported positive impressions of their move to Canada. Asked why they came to Canada, the largest number of responses cited their children's futures, reuniting with family and close friends, and the quality of life.

- The majority of foreign-born persons (85 percent) who were eligible for citizenship in 2006 had become naturalized ("citizens").

Clearly, then, Canada can be described as a society of immigration and immigrants. Canada is also one of the few countries in the world that qualifies as *an immigration society* in the normative sense of the expression. With nearly 200 million migrants on the move, such a statement may strike one as odd. But the centrality of immigrants to contemporary existence notwithstanding, few societies have acknowledged the reality and importance of immigration, in part out of fear of disrupting national identities, exposing weaknesses in national governance and security, and undermining state capacity for enforcing unpopular laws. Not surprisingly, migrants in search of jobs or a new life tend to be seen as problems to be solved through programs or services rather than as victims of "failed societies" related to the larger issue of transnational global capital and its impact on those that are most impoverished (Simmons, 2010).

In short, many societies may qualify as a society of immigrants along descriptive lines; few, however, can claim to be a prescriptively immigration society in terms of normative standards. The United States and Australia are two other notable immigration societies, as are Brazil and Argentina, several Latin American countries, and most recently, New Zealand (Hiebert, Collins, & Spoonley, 2003). An immigration society can be defined as one that takes a principled and proactive approach to immigration based on four distinguishing criteria (see also Ucarer, 1997):

- Policies and principles regulate the entry of immigrants into the country.
- Programs are in place to facilitate the integration and settlement of immigrants.
- Immigrants are entitled to all rights, including permanent residence and citizenship.
- Immigration and immigrants are viewed as an asset for society-building.

Canada clearly subscribes to each of these attributes, at least in principle if not always in practice. By contrast, countries such as Germany tended to deny the need for or existence of immigrants, while rejecting their status as immigration societies. If anything, such countries defined themselves as "complete societies" (Castles & Miller, 2009)—as ethnically rooted with a shared sense of history, culture, and destiny, and an exclusive concept of citizenship that excluded outsiders, and as countries that exported surplus populations (Sykes, 2008, p. 11; Zick, Pettigrew, & Wagner, 2008). Immigration was reduced to an anomaly that did not contribute to national identity or society-building. Policies were devised to stabilize inflows, limit long-term stays, discourage permanent residence, restrict participation and involvement, label newcomers as guest workers, and withhold citizenship and attendant rights (Pecoud & de Guchteneire, 2005). For example, foreigners and their children were generally excluded from citizenship even if born and raised in Germany; paradoxically, those of German parentage (ancestry) were automatically granted citizenship regardless of how long they had lived outside of Germany (Modood, 2003).

To be sure, this mindset is changing across Europe. Formerly anti-immigrant countries have little option now except to embrace immigration as a means to offset the effects of an aging population, a plummeting birth rate, costly welfare programs, a shortage of skilled professional workers, and obligations under EU membership (Munz & Ohliger, 2003). Since 2000, the restrictions for citizenship have been lifted for children born of lawfully resident foreign parents in Germany (Macklin & Crepeau, 2010). Passage of the *Immigration Act* of 2005 also established provisions for a single statutory framework for managing immigration into Germany, including the *Residence Act*, which regulates the residence status and integration of foreigners (Germany.info, 2007). Nevertheless, any transitioning from a society of emigrants to an immigrant society will prove challenging, as both mindsets and institutions must rethink the paradox of needing immigrants but not wanting them (*Economist*, 22 October, 2010).

Getting In: Early Practices, Evolving Trends

Canada is frequently praised—or occasionally pilloried—as a society of immigrants (Foster, 1998). With the exception of Aboriginal peoples, all Canadians are immigrants or descendants of immigrants. Immigration has played a pivotal role in Canada's national development and will continue to do so in the foreseeable future (Ibbitson,

2005b). The increasingly unfettered movements of people, ideas, labour, and investment because of globalization will see to that. But Canadians seem curiously ambivalent about immigration and immigrants, despite a long-standing reliance on immigrant labour as a catalyst for development and capitalist expansion (Bolaria & Li, 1988).

The content and direction of Canadian immigration practices have evolved over time (Boyd & Vickers, 2000; Foster, 1998; Knowles, 2007). Initial moves for governing the admission of foreign individuals reflected a combination of ideological considerations, political expediency, international obligations, and the colonialist requirements of a hinterland economy. Outcomes were decided by an interplay of factors, including racism and ethnocentrism, the agricultural bias of Canada's early immigration policies, the pivotal role of private and business interests, Canada's Commonwealth commitments as part of the British Empire, and high levels of out-migration to the United States. Historically, the Canadian state grappled with conflicting interests, that is, how to preserve its whiteness while securing an adequate supply of migrant labour without embracing an overtly racist immigration program (Thobani, 2000b, 2007). This conflict of interest transformed immigration policy and practice into a contested site, with competing interests jockeying to impose their agenda.

Until the late nineteenth century, immigration into Canada was largely informal and highly discretionary (Meyers, 2002). Initial practices regarding whom to let in and whom to keep out could be described as essentially racist in orientation, assimilationist in objective, nativist in content, and exclusionary in outcome (Abu-Laban, 1999; Wallis & Fleras, 2008). To the extent that rules existed, immigration regulations reflected a distinction between preferred versus non-preferred "races" (Elabor-Idemudia, 1999; Thobani, 2000b). A preference for more assimilable whites, namely, those from Britain and Northern Europe, contrasted with the dismissal of inferior "races" as contrary to Canada's climate or cultural values (Simmons, 2010). As much energy was expended in keeping out certain "types" as was in encouraging others to settle. The 1869 *Immigration Act* and subsequent amendments, including the 1910 *Immigration Act*, excluded undesirables, such as criminals, the mentally unfit, the diseased, nationalities unlikely to assimilate, and city dwellers. Strict limitations were imposed on the Japanese, Chinese, and East Asians, in part through head taxes or regulations such as the Continuous Journey Rule that required all immigrants to travel directly from their country of origin or citizenship with a through ticket purchased in the home country. The fact that steamships required refuelling at some point before arriving at Vancouver or Halifax ensured a de facto exclusion behind a facade of *de jure* neutrality.

A "racial pecking order" of preference prevailed (Lupul, 1988; Walker, 1997). In keeping with a dominant perception of Canada as "a white man's country," preferred categories of immigrants were drawn from the so-called superior stock of Western Europe. This category was virtually exempt from entry restrictions except for certain formalities to ensure restriction of those defined as diseased, deranged, and dangerous. At the bottom of this pecking order were blacks and Asians, both of whom were seen as inherently inferior and ultimately unassimilable. The Irish, too, were deemed to be culturally and economically dangerous people—a poor, ignorant, and knavish people with "papist" religious convictions and prone to crime and joblessness. In between these two poles were the non-preferred classes, consisting of immigrants from Eastern and Middle Europe and Russia. While admiring them for their brawn and industry, Canadians also harboured a degree of suspicion toward these "dangerous foreigners," particularly those Bolsheviks who dared to challenge the principles of free enterprise (Avery, 1995). A special "restricted" permit class controlled the entry of Jews and Mediterranean peoples.

Once preferred sources dwindled, other Europeans began to look better. Canada's first immigration minister, Clifford Sifton, made virtue of necessity in 1896 when he encouraged immigrants from Eastern Europe to settle the west, despite a chorus of criticism over compromising national interests. Sifton resolutely opposed the import of urban factory workers, many of whom were seen as degenerate, susceptible to economic unrest, or fodder for radical agitators. Most immigrants were expected to settle, to farm, and to secure a rural economic base for Canada (Knowles, 2007). The agricultural bias of early immigration was eloquently expressed when Sifton mused about "stalwart peasants in a sheepskin coat, born on the soil, whose forefathers had been farmers for 10 generations, with a stout wife and a half-dozen children."

But not all immigrants saw themselves as tillers of soil. Over time, migrants shifted from agriculture to wage employment in labour-intensive industries such as railroad construction, mining, and construction work (Avery, 1995). Nor did all immigrants look to Canada as the promised land. It took a lot of convincing to get people to come; even more inducements were required to make them stay, thanks to the vagaries of Canada's physical terrain and climatic rigors. Many new Canadians promptly emigrated to the United States—between 1851 and 1948, almost as many left for the United States as immigrated to Canada (Beaujot, 1999; Isajiw, 1999) while during the 1971 to 1981 decade, there were almost half as many long-term departures (636 000) as permanent arrivals (1 429 000)—in effect reinforcing a perception of Canada as little more than a transfer point between America and Europe (Whitaker, 1991). This trend persists into the present, according to a Statistics Canada study, including the departure of one-third of all mature male immigrants within 20 years of arrival (Thompson, 2006).

A commitment to immigration for Canada-building exposed two thorny problems: the need for cheap labour and the necessity of a means for rapid removal of immigrants when no longer required (Walker, 2001b). Political parties engaged in endless polemics over who was desirable or assimilable, preferred or non-preferred (Thobani, 2000a, 2000b). But all agreed that Canada's survival depended on excluding those workers who were perceived as unsuitable to Canadian conditions, who were thought to be incapable of assimilating into prevailing norms of decency and democracy, and who posed a threat to Canadian values and institutions. Non-preferred immigrants were tolerated as long as they quietly toiled away in remote regions and at tasks deemed too demeaning and demanding for white Canadians (e.g., railways, mines, lumber camps, domestic work). Nowhere was this more evident than in the treatment of Asian "guest workers" or "sojourners," such as the Chinese and Indians, many of whom were tolerated merely as "fodder" for Canadian capitalist expansion—a tap to be turned on when needed, turned off when not.

Three insights can be gleaned from this overview of early migration. First, diverse interests tended to sway public reaction and political response to immigrants and immigration. For example, business and powerful transportation companies supported immigration on the grounds that a prosperous local economy required a steady supply of migrant labour. By contrast, organized labour and public sentiment generally favoured a restriction of those immigrants who depressed wages, increased job insecurity, and threatened to "lower [the] Canadian standard of living" (Avery, 1995; see also Stoffman, 2003). The government found itself sandwiched in between, sometimes aligning with one side, then the other; at other times capitulating to private or to public interests as the circumstances dictated.

Second, early immigration practices reflected practical considerations that coincided with Canada's economic needs. Immigrants were selected on the basis of their ability to fill slots in the expanding economy. When Chinese migrants were required for railroad building, the taps were turned on; when they were no longer required, the taps were turned off. The expediency of a taps-on and taps-off approach assured an uneven immigration intake based on advancing national interests. Settlement of the Prairies required large numbers, with immigration peaking at 400 870 in 1913; by contrast, wars and Depression conditions resulted in declining figures, bottoming out in 1942 at 7576 immigrants. This stop-and-go mentality exposed Canada to criticism that it was merely operating a guest worker system; that is, foreigners were welcome when the economy boomed, but unwelcome otherwise.

Third, the acceptance of immigrants was driven by a hard-boiled pragmatism. Canada "needed" workers and settlers for the backbreaking toil of taming the wilderness. To an extent that few would care to admit, the practical aspects of Canada's immigration policy remain in effect. Canada wants immigrants for largely self-serving reasons, including to (1) offset the effects of an aging population and declining birth rate, (2) ensure a sufficient tax base to underwrite increasingly costly services, (3) expand the size of the domestic market, (4) establish profitable international linkages, and (5) stimulate sustained economic activity through production and consumption. Actively courted are those business immigrants who are willing to invest in Canada or to create employable industries. No less critical a factor is the need for cheap and disposable labour. The importation of temporary agricultural workers and domestic live-in caregivers are but two instances of how Canada creates a "guest worker" program to establish a pool of disposable workers (Fleras, 2010a). Canada, of course, is not the only country whose immigration practices reflect political calculation and economic expediency. European countries have demonstrated all too readily their eagerness to accept immigrants as guest workers to feed a labour-starved economic boom, but an equal disdain for them during the downturn.

Overhauling the Program: Contemporary Policies

Immigration into Canada remained expansionist beyond World War I. Entry criteria in 1931 embraced British subjects, American citizens, dependants of permanent residents in Canada, and agriculturalists, while discouraging migrants from Southern and Eastern Europe and prohibiting entry of Asians between 1923 and 1947 (Castles & Miller, 2003). But dampened rates of immigration with the onset of the Great Depression lasted until the end of World War II. To take advantage of the postwar economic boom, a 1947 immigration policy specified who could get in, namely: (1) British subjects and American citizens, if they met standards of health and character; (2) those who were qualified to work in labour-starved primary industries; (3) sponsored relatives from those European countries like Greece or Italy with strong family connections; and (4) refugees and displaced persons under international supervision. And while guilt over Canada's heartless denial of sanctuary for Holocaust victims during the war helped to fuel the immigration boom (Thompson, Herd, & Weinfeld, 1995), immigration was locked into a cycle of exclusion that privileged whiteness (Gwyn, 2000), as the distinction between preferred and non-preferred races continued to be made. Orders to maintain an eye on Canada's absorptive capacity were strictly enforced, with quotas still applying for most non-Europeans, despite a growing demand for skilled and unskilled labour from those quarters of the world that historically fell outside the usual sources (Foster, 1998).

By 1962, Canadian immigration laws experienced a shift of paradigmatic proportions. Canada became one of the first countries in the world to announce that ". . . any suitable qualified person from anywhere in the world" would qualify for entry, based primarily on personal merit and societal contribution. In embracing an ostensibly colour-blind commitment, Canada's immigration selection process was deracialized by shifting the selection criteria from national origin and ethnicity to those of skills, education, and experience (Gwyn, 2000; Hawkins, 1974; Mackey, 1998). Class rather than race emerged as the pivotal criterion for entry, once economic necessity overwhelmed restrictions based on racist ideology and national origins (Ralston, 1999). Regulations were introduced emphasizing labour market needs and family relations, while independent-class immigrants were admitted on the strength of their technical/professional qualifications. With further reforms in 1967, criteria for entry were justified on four major immigrant classes: family, assisted relatives, independents, and refugees. A points system of evaluation was introduced: Both independent and assisted-relative applicants were numerically assessed against the demands of occupation, education, and language expertise. A formally colour-blind immigration policy reduced the relevance of race as a criterion for entry. Still, the system was not entirely free of systemic bias. A points system continued to favour class-advantaged male applicants with access to educational credentials in those countries with Canadian embassies for processing applications (Abu-Laban, 1999; Thompson, 2006).

For the most part, Canada's immigration program was largely reactive in responding to domestic realities and international pressures. But passage of the *Immigration Act* in 1978 formalized a shift in rationale. The Act not only codified the grounds for admission into Canada but also articulated a principled framework for balancing the goals of (1) reunifying families, (2) protecting legitimate refugees, and (3) enhancing Canada's prosperity and global competitiveness. Immigration policy and programs focused on protecting national interests, ensuring sufficient immigrants for Canada's economic growth, reuniting families, and providing a safe haven for those in need of protection (Citizenship and Immigration Canada, 2001). The federal government retained primary responsibility for the selection of immigrants and setting of policy, while maintaining consultation/negotiations with the provinces over policy agenda, immigration levels, and settlement measures (Taylor, 2005).

In short, immigration policy proposed to balance the principled with the practical to ensure fairness without loss of control. Compromises focused on balancing the humanitarian goals of family reunification and refugee protection with labour market needs and the economic contribution of immigrants (Grant & Oertel, 1999). On one side, a commitment to humanitarian values resulted in high numbers from the refugee and family reunification classes, even in the face of mounting criticism. On the other side, a reliance on high immigration totals reflected a commitment to moderate and controlled intake as a catalyst for sustained economic growth. Prior to the late 1980s, immigration policies tended to respond to shortages or surpluses in the labour market. This "taps-on, taps-off" approach was challenged by focusing on immigration as an economic driver. Immigrants did not just serve the needs of labour, according to this line of thinking, they also represented consumer and investors with the "critical mass," the "buying power" and "connections" to improve Canada's economic performance. The relatively high and constant rates of immigration during the 1990s, recessionary pressures and public disgruntlement nothwithstanding, were justified on these grounds.

A further realignment was reflected by the passage of the ***Immigration and Refugee Protection Act*** in 2002. As the first major change to Canada's immigration program since 1978, the Act sought to tighten up the immigration program by (1) imposing more restrictions on entry; (2) focusing on the recruitment of immigrants who can integrate quickly into the workplace and society; (3) shifting from a strict points system to an emphasis on flexible and transferable skills and income-generating potential; (4) insisting on knowledge of an official language; and (5) firming up sponsorship rules to ensure a more evenly shared burden of the costs in resettlement. Changes to the processing of refugees were introduced as well, including a one-step process involving single-member panels with limited avenues of appeal (Dauvergne, 2004). Dennis Coderre (2003), then Minister of Citizenship and Immigration, defended the rationale behind the new immigration law:

> Our strategy is designed to strike a balance between attracting workers with flexible skills, reuniting families and being tough on those who pose a threat to Canadian security, all the while maintaining Canada's humanitarian tradition of providing a safe haven to people in need of protection. (p. 5)

Passage of the Act was not without criticism (*Canadian Issues*, 2005). Not everyone endorsed the focus on human capital attributes rather than occupational demand as the basis for admission into Canada. Critics charged that the system was elitist and counterproductive, resulting in a shortage of skilled tradespeople and blue-collar workers such as truck drivers, but a surplus of foreign-trained professionals who could not crack a highly regulated job market. Critics were also unhappy with refugee restrictions (Bissett, 2008; Dench, 2007). (See online Case Study 9.4.) The subsequent introduction of a safe third-country agreement with the United States was criticized for compromising the safety of refugee claimants—an argument supported by a Supreme Court ruling in late 2007—in part because the United States offers less protection than Canada, frequently detains asylum seekers without identity papers, does not recognize refugee criteria such as gender persecution, and withholds social assistance or work permits to claimants for the first six months (Maccharles, 2004). Finally, critics questioned the Act's emphasis on security as compromising the basic civil rights of immigrants and refugees (Crepeau & Nakache, 2006). Passage of Bill C-36 and the issuing of security certificates enable the government to detain, arrest, and deport immigrants or refugees based on suspicion of terrorism or secret evidence that suspects cannot access (Beare, 2003). In addition, the criteria are vaguely worded, are not accompanied by any burden of empirical proof, and do not set explicit time limits for detentions or decisions (Wayland, 2006).

Overview: Historical Trends into Contemporary Patterns

An overview of immigration history should make it abundantly clear: The content, dynamics of, and rationale behind immigration into Canada have evolved over time (Knowles, 2007). The logic governing immigration today differs in terms of focus, rationale, underlying assumptions, and anticipated outcomes from the dynamic that drove immigration in the past. The nature of immigrants with respect to origins, requisite skills, and expectations has shifted as well. Changes in immigration patterns are no less evident—both more transient and complex than in the past—with periods of sojourning increasingly more common in a world of circular migration, dual citizenship, and trans-national communities (Willis & Yeoh, 2000). Comparing the past with the present yields the following historical trends (see also Boyd & Vickers, 2000):

- From a highly subjective emphasis on racial and national origins as criteria for selection to an immigration program that is principled, transparent, and espouses the principle of colour-blindness in attracting the best and brightest.

- From a reliance on European sources of immigrants to those from Asia and other so-called non-conventional origins.

- From emphasizing the importance of rural-based agricultural/primary industry immigrants to focusing on immigrants who are globally connected, highly educated, and professionally skilled and who do not require costly resettlement services.

- From a focus on immigration in term of an absorptive capacity model ("taps-on, taps-off") to immigration as a model for "sustained economic growth."

- From a labour market model of immigration to that of a "human capital model," thus shifting the emphasis from matching immigrants with worker shortages to that of attracting newcomers with education, flexible and transferable skills, and language competence who can quickly integrate into a knowledge-based economy or quickly adapt to changing economic environments (Beach, Green, & Reitz, 2003; Weber, 2005).

- From a loosely monitored administrative system with relatively open borders to a tightly regulated and politically charged system involving different levels of government, both federal and provincial.

- From a focus on whom to keep out to an emphasis on whom to let in, including a greater emphasis on skilled professionals and entrepreneurial talent who do not require costly resettlement services.

- From a settlement immigration model based on immigrants as potential citizens and Canada-builders to a more customized immigration model, including a growing reliance on temporary foreign workers for short-term economic results (Fleras, 2010a).

Despite these shifts in trends, three themes appear to be constant. First, immigration remains a response to Canada's demands for labour (see Li, 2003). The prime objective has never wavered: to supply a labour pool, first for agriculture and settlement, then for industrialization, and currently for professionally skilled jobs. The fact that the preferred requirements have varied from one historical context to the next does not invalidate this underlying logic. A bimodal dynamic prevails. While the immigration program is focused on recruiting the best and the brightest from the global south, businesses in Canada are no less eager to secure cheap labour in their efforts to pare costs and remain globally competitive (Hiebert & Ley, 2006). Second, the nature and characteristics of immigration and immigrants reflect both internal and external pressures often beyond federal control. Whereas in the past, Canada's membership in the Commonwealth dictated whom to keep out, current immigration programs and patterns are influenced by global labour shortages in key economic sectors, competition on the global markets, the demands of an aging population, a shrinking labour force, shifts in source countries, and improvements in communication and transportation networks (Simmons, 2010). Third, much of the political and public discourses behind immigration reflect an unspoken assumption: immigrants are a burden on Canadian society whose costs must be minimized for ongoing acceptance. To be sure, there are "good" immigrants who are economically productive, readily self-sufficient, and can easily integrate without draining public resources (Abu-Laban, 1999). But "bad" immigrants are increasingly demonized as problems who do a disservice to Canada Bissett, 2008). Such a polarization is reflected in the politics of who gets into Canada.

WHO GETS IN?: CANADA'S IMMIGRATION PROGRAM

Canada's immigration policy is guided by three broad objectives: to reunite families, fulfill Canada's international obligations and humanitarian traditions with respect to refugees, and promote a vibrant economy. These objectives are reflected in the three main admission categories for entry into Canada on a permanent basis, namely, family-class immigrants, refugee class immigrants, and economic (or independent) immigrants (Schellenberg & Maheux, 2007). Table 9-2 provides an overview of Canada's immigration program in 2009 by way of admission class and totals.

TABLE 9-2	Immigrants by Admission Class and Totals, 2009	
		% of all immigrants
Family class (total	**65 187**	**25.9%**
Spouses and partners	43 887	
Sons and daughters	3025	
Parents/grandparents	17 175	
Others (including children)	1100	
Economic (independent) class (total)	**153 458**	**60.9%**
Federal skilled workers	40 729	
Business immigrants (investors, self-employed, entrepreneurs)	3423	
Provincial/territorial nominees	11 799	
Live-in caregivers	6272	
Canadian Experience Class	1774	
Total of principal applicants under the economic category	(63 997)	
Total of spouses and dependants under the economic category	(89 461)	
Refugees and protected persons class (total	**22 844**	**9.1%**
Government assisted	7425	
Privately sponsored	5036	
Landed in Canada	7202	
Refugee dependants	3181	

Other	10 635	4.1%
Humanitarian/compassionate cases	10 223	
Total	**252 124**	**100%**
Temporary foreign workers and foreign students		
Temporary foreign workers	178 640 (boosting overall total of temps in Canada to 282 771)	
International students	85 131 (boosting overall total of international students in Canada to 196 227)	
Total	**263 771**	

Source: Citizenship and Immigration (2009), permanent residents and temporary residents by category.

Categories of Admission

Family Class The family class recognizes the need for families to stay together to improve their integration into Canada. Families can employ two basic entry strategies (Thomas, 2001). They can migrate as a unit by relying on the skills and resources of the principal applicant to qualify for admission under the skilled worker point system (see Table 9-3). Or, one member of a family (or domestic unit) might migrate first, then send for the remaining members once citizenship or permanent residency is established. Under this chain migration strategy, immediate members of the family—a spouse (or fiancé), parents, grandparents, dependent and unmarried children under 19 years of age, and orphaned brothers, sisters, nieces, nephews, and grandchildren—are allowed automatic entry into Canada provided, of course, they are of good health, pass security checks, and are without a criminal record. Processing times for family-class sponsorship can vary: Based on a combination of all world regions, 50 percent of cases involving spouses/partners and dependent children are finalized within six months. By contrast, according to Citizenship and Immigration Canada, it takes 30 months to finalize 50 percent of admissions related to parents or grandparents (Wayland, 2006). To ensure family relationships are authentic, especially for those from Africa, the Caribbean, India, and Pakistan, individuals may be asked to prove identity through DNA testing (Jimenez, 2004). Sponsors must agree to support their sponsored family after they become permanent residents. Non-immediate members of a family as defined by Canada, such as aunts or uncles, must partially rely on points for entry.

Economic (Independent) Class The economic class (including federal skilled workers and business people such as entrepreneurs, self-employed individuals, and investors) has emerged as a major source of landing for immigrants. In contrast to the period between 1980 and 1995, when most immigrants entered Canada on the strength of family relations, nearly 60 percent of immigrants currently fall into the economic category. As Canada increasingly looks for those immigrants with higher skill levels whose costs of training and

TABLE 9-3	The Skilled Worker Point System
Maximum points allowed	**Criteria for points**
Education—25 points	25 points for education (maximum for Ph.D. or M.A., 5 points for high school diploma)
Language skills—24 points	24 points for language proficiency (up to 16 points for first official language—reading, writing, speaking, understanding; up to 8 points for the second official language)
Work experience—21 points	21 points for work experience (top points for 4 years of experience in a highly skilled occupation, 15 points for one year)
Employment status—10 points	10 points for arranged employment in Canada
Age—10 points	10 points for age (maximum points for those between 21 and 49; 2 points less each year over 49 or under 21 years of age)
Adaptability—10 points	10 points for adaptability (5 points for full-time job experience in Canada; 5 points for full-time study in Canada; 5 points for having a close relative in Canada, 5 points for a spouse with a university degree)

education are borne outside this country, this trend is likely to continue (Weinfeld & Wilkinson, 1999). Keep in mind that, strictly speaking, the totals for the economic class include spouses and dependants who are not preselected on a skills basis, with the result that in 2009 about 40 percent of immigrants who entered under the economic class (or just under 25 percent of the total immigrant intake) were processed as principal applicants.

A point system is applied that assesses the principal applicant on the grounds of job-related experience, age, official-language knowledge, and education. The candidate may also undergo an assessment for adaptability. The number of points required for entry is currently pegged at 67 points for skilled workers and the self-employed. Applicants from the business class (both investor and entrepreneur) can earn up to 35 points for their commercial experiences and connections. Assisted relatives also receive credit as nominated immigrants (5 points), but require additional points elsewhere to qualify. Everyone in this category must pass the usual health and security clearances. Each adult applicant must also pay a $500 application fee ($100 for children), in addition to a $490 right-of-landing fee (until recently, $975) to a maximum of four members per family. The landing fee was waived for refugees in 2000. The point system is outlined in Table 9-3.

In response to criticism that a human capital model of immigration isn't working, Canada's immigration program has adopted a more strategic approach for defining who gets in (Lowe, 2008). In 2008, Citizenship and Immigration Canada established rules that restricted the entry of federal skilled workers to those (a) with an offer of arranged employment, (b) applicants legally residing in Canada for at least one year, or (c) with demonstrated skills in one of 38 (now 29) priority jobs in hopes of unblocking an unmanageable backlog and processing delays (Alboim, 2009; Nakache & Kinoshita, 2010). Passage of Bill C-50 enables the immigration minister to prioritize applicants from the Federal Skilled Workers Program in response to labour shortages in select occupations. Applicants who fall outside of these three categories are not processed, while those already in the queue but lacking one of the 29 occupational designations must further bide their time. Immigration Minister Jason Kenney justified this move when he claimed,

Before we changed the system, we had to process every application received. Since many more people applied every year than could be accepted, a backlog was created. Now that we are processing *only those applications that meet specified criteria*, our Government is making significant progress in reducing the backlog (as cited in Marketwire, 2009, emphasis mine).

Predictably, the fast tracking of those deemed to be skilled in designated occupations has dramatically reduced waiting times for entry approval, according to Vancouver-based immigration lawyer Richard Kurland (Greenaway, 2010).

The economic class includes the *business subcategory*—namely, investor, entrepreneur, and self-employed. The "entrepreneurial" program selects immigrants with an ability to establish a new business or buy equity (at least 33 percent) into a qualifying business that they must manage and that will create at least one full-time job for a non-family member. To qualify under the self-employed category, an applicant must possess (1) an appropriate business acumen, (2) artistic qualifications, or (3) a net worth to be able to either establish or buy a business that will make a contribution to the Canadian economy or to Canada's artistic and cultural (sports) life. Under the "investor" program, applicants must meet the usual immigration criteria in addition to demonstrating a net worth of $1.6 million legally acquired. In exchange for investing $800 000 in a Canadian fund for five years (the principal amount is then returned) a business applicant receives permanent resident status. Thousands of applicants have taken advantage of this program since its inception in 1986, including just over 3400 in 2009. But the program has also been plagued by charges of fraudulent abuse, cumbersome delays (up to five years to process applicant files), and gross mismanagement that undermines potential benefits (Ley & Hiebert, 2001).

Another subcategory of the economic class is *provincial nominees*. Early provincial nominee programs originated as niche initiatives responding to specific regional labour market needs (Alboim, 2009). But the numbers of provincial nominees has grown exponentially in recent years from fewer than 500 in 2000 to just over 22 000 in 2008—in part because the program is designed to overcome long delays and a backlog of immigrants via the federal pipeline (Taylor, 2009). All provinces have an agreement with the federal government that permits each of them to nominate and recruit immigrants who are willing to settle in that province through requirements established by each province. The Provincial Nominee Program (PNP) allows provinces to priority process Canadian immigrant applicants for the province in which they plan to work and live. The program also allows employers to recruit foreign workers based on their ability to contribute to the economic development of that particular province. To apply under the PNP, applicants must be nominated by a Canadian province or territory; possess the necessary skills, experience, and education to make an immediate economic contribution; and be prepared to assume permanent residency in Canada. The federal government continues to maintain control over PNP admissions by stipulating that all applicants must pass a medical examination, and security and criminal checks (Nakache & Kinoshita, 2010).

The introduction of the *Canadian Experience Class (CEC)* in 2008 reflects yet another move toward "designer" immigrants (Simmons, 2010; Sweetman & Warman, 2010). Under the CEC, international students who have graduated from a Canadian university and temporary workers with the qualifying work experience and competence in English or French can apply for permanent residency without having to leave Canada. To qualify for permanent residency, a highly skilled temporary worker must have two years of full-time (or equivalent) Canadian work experience in a managerial, professional, or technical/skilled occupation (e.g., carpenter, welder, pipefitter). But the program has come under criticism because the transition to permanent residency is only at the high end, thus excluding those with "lower skill levels" (e.g., meat packers, food plant workers, kitchen staff). For a foreign graduate from a Canadian post-secondary institution (with at least two years of full-time study), the program requires one year of full-time (or equivalent) skilled work experience in Canada. International students are a main target for CEC; after all, they are highly skilled, possess Canadian credentials, and reduce settlement costs due to their familiarity with Canadian society (Simmons, 2010). While only 1774 principal applicants under CEC were processed in 2009, totals could eventually expand to about 25 000 per year, or about 10 percent of Canada's overall immigration intake (see online Case Study 9.5).

Refugees and Protected Persons Class The refugee category is the third category of landing. Refugees are accepted as part of Canada's humanitarian and legal obligations to the world community. Since 1951 (or more accurately 1969, when it signed the 1951 UN Convention on Refugees), Canada has performed admirably in protecting refugees, especially in comparison with countries that perfunctorily deny entry or routinely deport those seeking asylum. Canada has officially admitted over half a million refugees during this period of time, with recent annual intakes ranging from 20 000 to 35 000—an impressive total in its own right, but a modest dent in global volumes.

Three categories of refugees exist, none of which requires points for entry. One category consists of sponsored refugees who are selected abroad. These "assisted" refugees are preselected either by government officials on their ability to establish themselves in Canada (Government Assisted Refugees) or by private agencies, individuals, clubs, or church groups (Privately Sponsored Refugees), with private sponsors obligated to provide support for up to ten years. Both government and privately sponsored refugees automatically receive landed immigrant (or permanent residence) status upon arriving in Canada. They also receive assistance through government programs once they arrive.

The second category consists of refugee claimants (Landed in Canada Refugees or inland protected persons) who arrive unannounced by foot, boat, or plane, often without documentation such as passports, and claim refugee status from within Canada (Dempsey & Yu, 2004). According to the Canadian Council of Refugees (2007), most (62 percent in 2006) claims in Canada are made from within Canada at an immigration office (about one-third at the Etobicoke office, which covers Toronto). Only about 20 percent of claims are made at a land border. Once a refugee is in Canada, a set of refugee determination protocols is activated (see Wayland, 2006). The current three-step system—(1) eligibility determination, (2) refugee status determination, and (3) permanent residency—consists of a so-called simplified procedure that purports to balance fairness with efficiency (see online Insight 9.3). In contrast to sponsored refugees, refugee claimants are not entitled to all the benefits and social services that Canadians enjoy until the establishment of permanent residency status. In 2007, the top ten sources of refugees by country, number of claimants, and acceptance rates (in brackets) were as follows:

1. Mexico, 7047 (10 percent accepted)
2. Haiti, 3713 (50 percent accepted)
3. Colombia, 2636 (78 percent accepted)
4. China, 1462 (65 percent accepted)
5. United States, 968 (5 percent accepted)
6. Sri Lanka, 811 (88 percent accepted)
7. Nigeria, 762 (44 percent accepted)
8. India, 557 (12 percent accepted)
9. Israel, 395 (17 percent accepted)
10. Pakistan, 359 (50 percent accepted

The third category involves those rejected refugee claimants who are granted protection under a Pre-Removal Risk Assessment (i.e., protected persons will not be deported to their home country if the removal exposes them to danger) (Wayland, 2006).

Canada and the United States: Doing Immigration Differently

Canada and the United States may be described and prescribed as immigration societies. And yet the immigration patterns with respect to number and types in Canada and the United States continue to reflect striking differences despite the two countries sharing commonalities (see Table 9-4).

TABLE 9-4	Annual Immigration to the United States, 2002–2006
All new lawful permanent residents	1 000 000
Employer sponsored	163 000
Family sponsored	649 000
Other	210 000
Temporary workers and dependants	321 000
Unauthorized/undocumented	500 000 (Pew Institute Hispanic Centre estimate)
TOTAL	1 800 000 (approx. per year)

- The average annual intake of immigrants (legal and permanent) into the United States between 2002 and 2006 was about 1 million. Canada's intake is smaller at about 250 000 per year, but Canada's population is one-tenth the size of the US population.

- Immigrants are defined as foreign-born persons with lawful permanent resident status. About 60 percent of immigrants (permanent residents) to the United States are not new entrants but those adjusting from temporary to permanent status. With few exceptions, those on temporary permits in Canada must apply from outside.

- Unlike in the United States, with its focus on family sponsorship, most immigrants to Canada arrive via economic class.

- The United States attracts a disproportionately higher number of undocumented persons than Canada.

Sources: As cited in Migration Policy Institute (2007), and based on 2005 and 2006 Yearbook of Immigration Statistics published by Office of Immigration Statistics. Available online.

TABLE 9-5	Attitudes toward Immigrants/Immigration	
	Canada	**United States**
Assessing government management of immigration	Good/fair (59%)	Good/fair (34%)
	Poor/very poor (35%)	Poor/very poor (63%)
Are there too many immigrants?	Yes (24%)	Yes (48%)
Is immigration more of a problem than an opportunity?	Yes (25%)	Yes (54%)
Do immigrants take away jobs?	Yes (32%)	Yes (44%)
Do legal immigrants increase crime?	Yes (29%)	Yes (23%)
Do illegal immigrants increase crime?	Yes (51%)	Yes (58%)
Source: Transatlantic Trends (2010).		

In addition to differences in flows, sources, and qualifications, Canadians and Americans appear to possess strongly divergent attitudes toward immigrants in terms of numbers, management, costs, and benefits, as demonstrated in Table 9.5.

THE BENEFITS AND COSTS OF IMMIGRATION

Immigration has long proven a defining characteristic of Canada (Ibbitson, 2005b). From Canada's earliest days as a nation through to its involvement in the global transformations of recent decades, immigration has advanced Canada's social, economic, and cultural development. Canadians have reacted to immigrants and immigration in different ways, ranging from enthusiasm and endorsement on the one hand to resentment and hostility on the other, with a combination of indifference, resignation, and indecision in between. As well, it is difficult to determine what it is about immigration or immigrants (including refugees) that Canadians dislike or approve—is it the diversity or the politics or the processing system?

The Benefits of Immigration

For some, Canada's immigration and refugee programs are positively endorsed as a model of decorum, reflecting both the epitome of Canada's values and its maturity as a nation. Immigrants and refugees built this country, according to this line of thinking, and Canada's prosperity and identity will continue to depend on their industry and enthusiasm. Studies in other parts of the world, such as Australia, New Zealand, and the United States, confirm that, on balance, immigrants are a net contributor to society—demographically, socially, culturally, and economically (Castles & Miller, 2009; Fleras & Spoonley, 1999; Hiebert et al., 2003). The same conclusions apply to Canada (Halli & Driedger, 1999): Immigrants create more jobs than they take; as consumers, they provide markets for Canadian goods; they are more likely to start businesses than other Canadians; they are better qualified in terms of education; they realign the demographics by offsetting the effects of an aging population and declining birth rates; and they pay more in taxes than they accept in social services. Immigrants not only do the drudge work that Canadians disdain but also ease labour shortages during phases of capitalist expansion (it is estimated that all new labour market growth by 2011 will come from immigrants; Taylor, 2005). Immigrants tend to possess drive and vitality, with boundless energy and optimism, and a willingness to take entrepreneurial risks by capitalizing on international links to improve Canada's competitive position in a global economy. Finally, despite financial and social costs related to initial settlement in Canada, immigrants are the same people who will keep the economy afloat so that Canadians can retire comfortably (Hiebert & Ley, 2006). In general, then, rather than crippling the economy, immigrants inject a much-needed kick-start because of their commitment, connections, and cash.

The Costs of Immigration

Others disagree with this positive picture, and point out how arguments cited in defence of immigration neither stand up to empirical scrutiny nor have a logical basis (Centre for Immigration Policy Reform, 2010; Francis, 2002; Stoffman, 2003). Criticisms of immigration include: (1) Immigration rules are unjust, prone to abuse, and difficult to enforce (e.g., they are open to the reckless issuing of ministerial permits in exchange for favours or to facilitate entry or stay [Francis, 2005]); (2) the immigration program is manipulated to accommodate crass political considerations rather than national interests (e.g., electoral politics may help explain why political parties maintain high levels of immigration in Canada while avoiding any reference to immigration issues or any criticism of immigrants.); (3) newcomers continue to be duped and exploited by unscrupulous immigration consultants (Rankin, 2007); and (4) immigration is feared as a portal for entry of extremists and terrorists (Moens & Collacott, 2008). As proof that the system is "broken" or "breaking" (or perhaps just groaning under the weight of its own success), the backlog of applicants for entry into Canada now stands at just under 1 million, so that it may take up to six years to get an applicant into the pipeline (compared to approximately six months' wait time for an Australian application) (Hawthorne, 2008).

Immigrants are criticized for the "problems" they *allegedly* bring into Canada. Some of the allegations put forward are that immigrants are using their ties abroad to establish illegal international distribution systems for contraband drugs, loan-sharking, extortion rackets, prostitution, and the smuggling of "human cargo" into Canada. (Studies indicate that immigrant youth are not only less likely to commit crime, because of bonds and commitments, but also may be responsible for reducing Canada's crime rates [Dinovitzer, Hagan, & Levi, 2009; Jimenez, 2009].) And in the security-conscious post-9/11 era, some immigrants are accused of using Canada as a launching pad for recruitment, fund raising, and staging grounds for terrorist attacks, both abroad and at home (Moens & Collacott, 2008). For critics, then, immigrants and immigration are essentially an investment option for Canada, to be measured in cost–benefit terms and evaluated accordingly (Bissett, 2008): If the costs are too high, pare back or bail out.

Currently, one of the more contentious aspects of immigration is its highly urbanized character. Nearly all immigrants settle in urban centres (primarily the MTV cities of Montreal, Toronto, and Vancouver), while avoiding wide swaths of Canada that are in need of what immigrants have to offer, prompting debate over how to spread the wealth more evenly across Canada. That immigrants and refugees are drawn to large urban regions is understandable (Hiebert, 2000). Cities provide the networks, supports, and resources that facilitate the adjustment and integration of immigrants and refugees. Thus, they prove to be irresistible as a magnet for incoming immigrants and refugees. For example, about one-half of all immigrants to Toronto cite family and community as the chief reason for selecting that city (only about a quarter cite economic or work reasons). By contrast, immigrants are reluctant to settle in the Atlantic provinces because the cities lack a critical mass of their "own kind" (Ibbitson, 2004). To date, debates over creating a more geographically balanced distribution of migrants and minorities across Canada have proven futile, despite proposed government incentives to do so, with some arguing that such a move would be contrary to Canada's constitutional mobility rights even if new Canadians proved receptive to the idea (see also Biles & Burstein, 2003). Recent evidence indicates a modest increase in immigration to cities such as Charlottetown and Moncton, with a decline in immigration to cities such as Toronto (20 percent fewer immigrants in 2007 than in 2006) and Vancouver (1 percent less in 2007 than in 2006).

The Benefits and Costs: A Balanced View

In assessing immigration as either a benefit or cost, a sense of balance is critical. Immigration is about benefits *and* costs (see online Insight 9.2). For example, economic benefits are not distributed equally; some regions and sectors receive a disproportionate share of both costs and benefits. Some parts of the economy (e.g., real estate or immigration lawyers) benefit from immigration and others (e.g., manual workers) suffer (Stoffman, 2003), but the average person may be largely unaffected. Immigration may increase Canada's population and the size of its economy but not necessarily increase its standard of living (Centre for Immigration Policy Reform, 2010). Certain immigrants provide immediate benefit (especially economic-class immigrants), while some may not (refugee class) because of their circumstances, and others do so indirectly or over time (family-class immigrants) (Li, 2003). Long-term gains may be undeniable, but short-term costs may sting and are often offloaded by Ottawa to provinces, municipalities, and institutions (Grubel & Grady, 2011). Moreover, immigration policies and patterns cannot be a benefit to all: Migration may be good for the host country, which wants the brightest and the best, but less than ideal for the sending country, which is depleted of the very personnel it needs for societal improvement (Kapur, 2005; Pecoud & de Guchteneire, 2005). Such a complex assessment makes it doubly important to appreciate the pros *and* cons of immigration.

In short, the benefits of immigration are unmistakable, but so too are the costs. As a result, those who obsess about the negative (threats to national unity, identity, and security) are no less ideologically myopic than those supporters who rhapsodize about the positive (Castles & Miller, 2003). Nor should response or assessment be based entirely on utilitarian terms of liability or asset. The importance of immigration to Canada goes beyond the question of demography or economy; issues related to Canada-building are involved as well (Halli & Driedger, 1999; Ibbitson, 2005b). Evolving patterns of immigration have irrevocably transformed the very concept of Canada as a British colony. The watering down of the historical duality that once defined "Canadianness" because of immigration has re-sculpted the political contours of Canada's social landscape into a cosmopolitan kaleidoscope of cultures, colours, and connections, with striking implications for national unity and identity. Or as former minister of Citizenship and Immigration Sergio Marchi once commented in connecting immigration with national identity:

> Immigration is fundamentally about nation-building—about deciding who we are as Canadians and who we want to become . . . We need a clear and practical vision of the kind of nation we want to build (Marchi, 1994, p. iii; *Immigration*, 2003).

Attitudes toward Immigrants and Immigration

Attitudes and reactions toward immigrants and immigration vary. Many people are supportive of immigrants and refugees as hard-working and positive contributors to society (Nanos, 2008). But Canadians are openly critical of immigrants who do not add "value" to Canada or, worse still, prove a drain on its resources (Blackwell, 2004). Canadians may resent the presence of refugees who jump the queue to get in, but approve of their availability as cheap and disposable labour in factories, restaurants, fields, and homes (Canadian Council for Refugees, 2000). Others dislike what they see as threats to Canada's economy; for example, immigrants may depress wages by creating more supply than demand in the labour market (Stoffman, 2003, 2007). Context is critical in making these assessments: Canadians may not be unduly upset over immigration when the economy is booming; however, concerns escalate when the economy cools and (1) competition intensifies for good jobs and scarce resources; (2) immigrant labour becomes a permanent underclass; and (3) imbalances appear in education, welfare, and service demands, and income distribution (Goldsborough, 2000). The changing ethnic mix is endorsed as enriching the Canadian landscape; yet fears mount over possible social friction when immigrants reject core Canadian values (see Adams, 2007).

To date, surveys indicate that Canadians are generally supportive of immigration and the benefits that immigrants bring, although they don't want current levels increased (Nanos, 2010; Transatlantic Trends, 2010). A survey by the Strategic Counsel for *The Globe and Mail* and CTV in April 2008 involving 1000 Canadians aged 18 years and over also reinforced what other polls have confirmed: Canadian attitudes toward immigrants and visible minorities are generally positive but remain conditional and contradictory, with attitudes varying along socioeconomic and locational lines, as demonstrated in Table 9-6.

In the face of such complexity and inconsistencies, Canadians tend to hold conflicting perceptions of immigrants. On one side are images of immigrants as the rich and pampered who buy their way into Canada. On the other side are images of immigrants as desperate people who have fled their homes and are now struggling to survive as best they can (Kazemipur & Halli, 2003; see also Montreuil & Bourhis, 2004). In between are images of immigrants as opportunists who are taking advantage of Canadian generosity to advance their interests. Canadians tend to be comfortable with immigrants who are poor, appear to be grateful for the opportunity, and are willing to start at the bottom as cooks, labourers, and farmhands. Immigrants are "acceptable" if (1) their cultural practices are compatible with Canada's; (2) they know their place by acknowledging their status as "guests" in Canada and fit in accordingly; and (3) they appreciate that immigration policy must advance national interests rather than cater to minority demands. Canadians are less sure of how to "cope" with those immigrants who are affluent, confident, assertive, and highly

TABLE 9-6	The Complexities of Attitudes toward Immigration and Immigrants

Question 1. Latest Census: 5 million Canadian citizens are members of visible minority groups. Do Canadians view this as positive or negative?

Positive	48%
Negative	9%
Not sure	42%

Those with household incomes over $100 000 were more positive (61 percent) than those with household incomes under $50 000 (40 percent). Those who lived in communities of a million or more were more positive (54 percent) than those in communities of under 30 000 (33 percent).

Question 2. Do Canadians agree or disagree . . . We make too many accommodations to visible minorities?

Totally agree (too many concessions)	61%
Totally disagree	36%

Those who were aged 50 years and older were in greater agreement (68 percent) than those between 18 and 34 (53 percent). Those with high school or less education were in greater agreement (72 percent) than those who graduated from college or university (55 percent). Gender differences were relatively small.

Question 3. Is accepting new immigrants of diverse ethnic and religious backgrounds a defining and enriching part of our Canadian identity?

No (weakens Canadian identity)	30%
Yes (strengthens Canadian identity)	61%
Don't know	9%

Those with household incomes under $50 000 were more likely to say no (33 percent) than those with incomes over $100 000 (25 percent). Those who lived in communities under 30 000 were more likely to say no (34 percent) than those in communities of over a million (28 percent).

Question 4. Do Canadians feel that new immigrants hold on to their customs and traditions for too long?

Yes (too long)	45%
No (immigrants integrate)	47%

Those with household incomes under $50 000 were more likely to say yes (52 percent) than those with household incomes over $100 000 (34 percent). Those who lived in communities under 30 000 were more likely to say yes (54 percent) than those in communities over a million (42 percent).

Source: Strategic Council (2008).

qualified; unwilling to put up with slights or slurs as the price of admission or staying; and, as professional transnationals, are willing to shop their talents wherever the global economy will take them. This immigrant-by-convenience mentality has elicited a sharp rebuke from *National Post* columnist, George Jonas (2006):

> It was only in the last thirty years that a new type of immigrant emerged: the immigrant of dubious loyalty . . . The new immigrant seemed ready to share the West's wealth but not its values. In many ways he resembled an invader more than a settler or refugee. Instead of making efforts to assimilate, he demanded changes in the host culture. He called on society to accommodate his linguistic and religious requirements.

Let's be realistic: No person, no matter how opposed to immigration in principle or practice, is without some sympathy for the plight of the world's poorest. Similarly, no person, regardless of pro-immigrant sympathies, can dismiss its negative impact on some sectors of society (Millman, 1997). Somewhere between the "yeas" and the "nays" are those who see the interplay of costs and benefits. The in-between sector takes a practical outlook on immigration. With an intake of approximately 250 000 new Canadians each year, some with clearly different cultures, experiences, and expectations, a degree of friction and annoyance is inevitable. So too is the likelihood of crowding, pressure on existing services, inflated markets, sporadic crime surges, and congested roads. Costs cannot be ignored: A country cannot expect to have a policy of immigration-driven sustained economic growth without some negative repercussions. Cultural clashes are inescapable as well. A sense of proportion is badly needed. If Canadians value the cultural and economic benefits associated with immigration, they must be prepared to shoulder the costs. A step back from the fray provides a reminder that immigration *is* a benefit that invariably accompanies a cost for someone, somewhere, sometimes.

For the in-betweens, then, immigration is neither a sacred cow immune to criticism nor a convenient scapegoat to blame for Canada's problems (see online Debate 9.1). People who occupy an informed middle ground acknowledge the partial validity of arguments both for and against. They acknowledge that costs accompany benefits; for example, there is much of value in Canada's principled (rule-based, transparent, and accountable) approach toward immigration; nevertheless, a proliferation of rules can create bureaucracy, red tape, and inflexibility because of high volumes, in the process eliminating room for discretionary decisions except at political levels where such interference can prove costly (Thompson, 2005). In other words, assessments about the costs and benefits of immigration are rarely right or wrong, but both right and wrong, depending on the context, criteria, and consequences, with the result that inflated claims on both sides of the debate often conceal whatever truths they contain.

IMMIGRANT EXPERIENCES IN CANADA

> Every act of immigration is like suffering a brain stroke: One has to learn to walk again, to talk again, to move around the world again, and, probably most difficult of all, one has to learn how to re-establish a sense of community. (Vivian Rakoff, as cited in Fulford, 2003)

The model of immigration settlement based on the European experience may no longer apply (Frideres, 2005; Suarez-Orozco & Suarez-Orozco, 2001). The European model saw immigration settlement as a one-way upwardly mobile journey resulting in permanent residence in the adopted country. But in a world of globalization and transnational localities, immigrants are increasingly expressing multiple attachments and multiple homelands—one place oriented, the other people oriented (Cheng, 2005; Satzewich & Wong, 2006)—creating new wrinkles in the adjustment process as some groups rapidly integrate while others don't. The new global context demands a fresh outlook on immigration—from new explanatory frameworks to innovative policy responses—one that acknowledges both its multidimensional and dynamic nature, including its cross-border movements and transmigrant networks (Fleras, 2011b; Massey, 2009; Simmons, 2010; Spoonley, 2010).

Put succinctly, it's no longer acceptable to see immigration as a fixed pattern of relocation between A and B. Instead, current immigration patterns reflect complex and fluid fields of flow involving different actors, across different domains, and at different levels (Simmons, 2010). Rather than a simple one-way movement of people in search of permanent residency, immigration must be framed as a complex and drawn-out transformational process involving a host of political and social factors, with economic and cultural consequences for both the sending and receiving country (Castles & Miller, 2009). The process itself can be envisaged as falling along a continuum from pre-migration preparation at one end to post-migration integration at the other end, with transitional phases in-between, as demonstrated in Table 9-7.

Canada's immigration policy continues to emphasize the settlement of new Canadians in terms of settling down, moving up, and fitting in. Settlement itself involves a three-stage process: (1) immediate needs for assistance and reception; (2) intermediate needs for accessing the labour market, housing, health services, and so on; and (3) long-term needs in which immigrants strive for integration into Canadian society and the economy (see Table 9-7) (Wayland, 2006). In hopes of equipping migrants with the tools to settle down, both the governmental and non-profit sectors offer language training, employment

TABLE 9-7	Life Course Transition of an Adult Immigrant with Children		
Pre-migration >	**Settlement >**	**Adaptation >**	**Integration**
Conditions in homeland (political, economic, etc.)	Basic language	Language skills	Citizenship
Status and experiences in home country (social class, education level, resources, resourcefulness)	Housing	Career	Participation in politics and civic life
Skill sets (labourer, entrepreneur, professional)	Employment	Networks	Adjustment to host country (from acceptance to marginalization)
Reasons for leaving the country (push and pull)	Education	Community	
Necessary attributes: (a) motivation to move (b) resources to do so), and (c) be admissible	Social services	Sense of identity	
Transition experiences (good, easy, etc.)	Readiness of receiving country (policies, programs, opportunities)	Knowledge of Canada	
Entry formalities, including application	Immigrant resources for settling in (supports, language competence)	Implications for the human services sector	

Sources: Kunz (2005); Segal et al. (2010); Simmons (2010).

counselling, and translation services. Settlement services are predominantly delivered by immigrant-serving groups such as the Kitchener-Waterloo Multicultural Centre, who rely heavily on government funding to defray the costs of service delivery (see also the *Our Diverse Cities* series, volumes 1–4, published by Metropolis, available online at **www.metropolis.net**). Admittedly there are glitches: In most provinces, settlement services are available only to permanent residents or **convention refugees**; as a result, years of residence may be required for a refugee claimant before eligibility for these services (Wayland, 2006; Zaman, 2006. As well, the federal government has waffled over increased funding for settlement and language services since 1995, preferring instead to devolve responsibility for settlement to the private sector or the provinces.

That immigrants are a dynamic mix of tradition and **modernity** (Halli-Vedanand, 2007) ensures the emergence of new immigrant experience (Pendakur & Pendakur, 2004). Some immigrants are primed for success; others are being squeezed out of the picture because of discrimination, racism, and prejudice; and still others are just muddling through. For some immigrants, the immigration process is filled with hope and opportunity; for others, it is fraught with danger and disappointment; for still others, it is a combination of hope and despair (Suarez-Orozco & Suarez-Orozco, 2001). The immigrant experience may prove less gratifying than originally anticipated—particularly as elders drift apart from the junior generation, as younger women chafe over traditional roles and pervasive paternalism, and as educated elites become estranged from the community at large (Handa, 2003). No less immobilizing are the pangs of homesickness. Andrei Codrescu (1995) writes of the bittersweet, near-death experiences of his Romanian mother:

> Most people come here because they are sick of being poor. They want to eat and they want something to show for their industry. But soon enough it becomes evident to them that these things are not enough. They have eaten and they are full, but they have eaten alone . . . This time they are lacking something more elusive than salami and furniture. They are bereft of a social and cultural milieu . . . Leaving behind your kin, your friends, your language, your smells, your childhood, is traumatic. It is a kind of death. (p. 47)

For others, the immigrant experience provides a payoff but is not without penalties:

> Many of us were greeted with a myriad of challenges when we arrived, but we decided to take things one day at a time. We missed our home countries but then we find opportunities here that we may not have had back home. There are some values here that we appreciate and would like to add to the values back home that we still hold on to. On the other hand, many of us still cannot help missing home because there are certain values over there that we just cannot find here. Sometimes acceptance and closeness become very limited to us. We have friends here but even when you get close, it does not feel like the closeness back home. (Peprah, 2005).

Often there is a flipside to immigration that exposes its challenges and obstacles. Naheed Mustafa (2007) writes in response to the death of a young Muslim woman from Brampton, Ontario:

> To say immigration is transformative is a gross understatement. Families leave everything and everyone they know and move to a foreign place where they become blank slates. The support of the extended family is gone, the cocoon of well understood social norms is cast off and parents and their children stand out in the open waiting for a new life to start . . . But while parents want economic opportunities and a solid education for their children, they are wary of the siren call of the "West." They want change but not too much change.

Many new Canadians appear to be relatively satisfied with the quality of life in Canada (Adams, 2007). The General Social Survey indicated that 84 percent of immigrants who arrived between 1990 and 2003 expressed strong or somewhat strong feelings of belonging to Canada, compared with 85 percent of all Canadians (Omidvar, 2010). Many immigrants appreciate the opportunities and services available to them and their children, the promise of human freedom, and sufficient market transparency to succeed. According to the 2005 Longitudinal Survey of Immigrants to Canada (see Schellenberg & Maheux, 2007), what immigrants like best about Canada are the climate and physical environment (19.1 percent), cultural aspects (freedom, rights, etc.) (14.4 percent), safety (11 percent), peace and political stability (10.4 percent), and educational opportunities (9.9 percent). Paradoxically, however, what they most dislike (aside from the 19 percent who do not dislike anything) are the climate and physical environment (26.7 percent), lack of employment opportunities (17.4 percent), and high taxes (11.1 percent). Yes, material well-being and quality of life are perceived to have improved compared with their homelands, but many immigrants will confront a series of problems that have accompanied them into Canada or encounter problems upon entry and settlement (Jimenez, 2006). Few could possibly anticipate the obstacles that need to be surmounted:

> Let's face it, a lot of "us" never considered, when we decided to emigrate, what it would really be like once the dust of moving had settled—especially the psychological adaptations that would be required of us, our children, and future generations. (Singh, 2000, p. 2)

Problems may arise because of personal shortcomings related to culture shock, lack of political power, loss of economic well-being, personal isolation, lack of support from the homeland, and discriminatory barriers that preclude entry or acceptance. Surveys repeatedly indicate that securing employment (preferably jobs in one's field of experience or expertise) is the largest settlement-related problem for new Canadians (Wayland, 2006). Other common obstacles include learning a new language, getting used to the weather, adapting to new cultural values, and accessing language training, housing, and healthcare services (Schellenberg & Maheux, 2007). Immigrants confront numerous challenges and criticisms; after all, living in a new country can be daunting, especially in the context of major cultural differences.

Patterns of settlement may expose immigrants to double standards. Immigrants might be inclined to maintain some semblance of their traditions and culture because of the culture shock or fears of racism, and the need for continuity, assistance, and meaning at a time of rapid change. However, doing so may subject immigrants to criticism for sticking with their own kind at the expense of integrating into Canada. Yet if they integrate and immerse themselves in the host community at large, at the expense of their authenticity, they may be accused of "selling out" to the system. The persistence of immigrant enclaves has also raised questions about Canada's "welcome mat." To what extent are these enclaves the result of racist and exclusionary practices such as housing discrimination? Or do they reflect an immigrant preference for familiar community (Novac, 1999; Yelaja & Keung, 2005)? In either case, as more new arrivals speak neither French nor English and settle in suburban enclaves behind language barriers or low-paid work, officials must work harder to integrate them by expanding spaces and places for interaction (Reinhart, 2007; Siemiatycki, 2007).

Settling Down

Generally speaking, the primary concerns of new Canadians are practical and survival related. In contrast with the more political demands of Canada's founding peoples for self-determining autonomy, immigrants and refugees are more concerned with the pragmatic issues related to "getting in" by way of equality, participation, and acceptance. They don't want a separate existence that rejects their adopted homeland but want inclusion in Canada, whether that means opting for residence in their own immigrant communities because of convenience or comfort, or pressuring institutions to accommodate their cultural and religious identities (*Canadian Issues*, 2005). Foremost is the desire to "put down roots" by "settling down," "fitting in," and "moving up" in Canadian society, without necessarily severing ties with their cultural tradition. More specifically, immigrant needs can be itemized as follows:

1. A labour market with opportunity and a workplace without discrimination.
2. The expansion of opportunities in the labour and education markets as well as improved access to housing, government institutions, social services, and mass media.
3. Conferral of full citizenship rights, including the right to move, participate, and criticize.
4. Access to the best of Canada without diminishing their children's sense of cultural identity.
5. The capability to express themselves in terms of their identity without paying a penalty in the process.
6. Respect for their differences as a legitimate and valued part of society.

In short, immigrants and their descendants want the best that both worlds have to offer. They want to be treated as individuals by being accepted for what they do rather than being lumped together into an amorphous mass on the basis of who they are. Conversely, they also want appreciation for who they are culturally, without sacrificing meaningful involvement in society. Full citizenship rights are important, but no less so is respect for their cultural worth as a people with a meaningful past—yet no less Canadian.

But what new Canadians want is not necessarily what they get. Immigrant qualifications continue to be dismissed, education degrees devalued, and overseas experience discounted as next to worthless (Drummond & Fong, 2010; Finnie & Meng, 2002). Foreign education counts for about half of the value of Canadian schooling in terms of earning power, while foreign experience has little market value in Canada (one year overseas = one-third of a year in Canada). Refusal to recognize the credentials of new Canadians costs Canada billions in lost revenue (Conference Board of Canada, 2004), in effect reinforcing the idea that non-recognition is really a Canada problem rather than an immigrant problem (Wayland, 2006). In other words, immigrants may be selected for their skills, credentials, and work experiences; yet Canadian employers don't want to use these or don't know how to. Not surprisingly, as labour sociologist Jeffrey Reitz (2005) puts it, the success of Canada's immigration policy will be measured by institutions that link workers to jobs by providing for an international transferability of skills, credentials, and experience.

Despite the much-hyped reference to Canada as a land of opportunity, thousands of immigrants can't find meaningful work in Canada (Basok & Bastable, 2009; Schellenberg & Hou, 2005). As noted earlier, the most common barriers to working include: (1) lack of Canadian work experience, (2) lack of recognition of foreign credentials and work experience, (3) lack of knowledge about the Canadian economy and the unwritten labour market codes that take time to learn, and (4) increased competition with a growing educated Canadian labour force (Alboim & McIsaac, 2007). Not surprisingly, highly skilled immigrants find themselves segregated in menial and unskilled occupations with little in the way of security or prospects for promotion. A Longitudinal Survey of 12 000 immigrants who arrived in Canada in 2000/1 found that only 40 percent of skilled principal applicants worked in the occupations for which they were trained, which means that 60 percent can be deemed as downwardly mobile (Alboim & McIsaac, 2007). Understandably, frustration levels mount:

> Many individuals feel that they were duped into coming to Canada, but do not want to face the shame of returning to their homelands. They settle for underemployment and hope that their children's luck will be better. Other migrants move to the United States where accreditation processes are perceived to be swifter. (Wayland, 2006, p. 77)

No less harrowing for skilled and professional immigrants is the closed-shop mentality of licensed occupations that continue to impose restrictions and deny accreditation. This bottleneck that prevents professionals from gainful employment may reflect a fundamental disconnect: The federal government controls immigration, but the provinces control the licensing, while the professional bodies control who gets in (see online Case Study 5.1).

Moving Up

Equally demanding are the challenges in moving up (Ruddick, 2003). Immigrants once spent several years earning less than the average Canadian, but over time would achieve or surpass the average (Ley & Hiebert, 2001). Now it may take up to ten years for immigrants to match Canadian-born incomes. For example, immigrants who came to Canada before 1981 earned more upon arrival and took less time to catch up; by contrast, those who arrived after 1981, especially racialized (visible) minorities, tend to have higher unemployment rates and lower employment incomes, despite higher education levels (Galabuzi, 2007; Harvey, Siu, & Reil, 1999; Ley & Hiebert, 2001; Pendakur & Pendakur, 2004; 2010).

To be sure, the picture is more complex than many critics say. According to a Statistics Canada study of Canada's immigrant labour markets in 2006, new immigrants (less than five years in Canada) have unemployment rates three times higher than Canadian-born residents, despite much higher educational levels for those between 25 and 54. However, within ten years of their arrival, immigrants have the same job prospects as Canadian-born workers, thanks to increased experience and improved language skills. In other words, foreign credentials matter, but employers are more interested in those competencies (speaking without a foreign accent) for which qualifications often serve as a proxy. Not surprisingly, the strongest predictor of economic success are neither credentials nor degrees but abilities in one of Canada's two official languages. And not just basic French or English competencies in reading and writing, it is argued, but a nuanced level of sophistication for solving problems and getting along (Banting, Courchene, & Seidle, 2007).

How do we account for these disparities? According to Jeffrey Reitz (1998) of the University of Toronto, lower entry-level earnings are determined as much by institutional structures, local labour market conditions, and protectionism on the part of employers and professional bodies as they are by prejudicial attitudes and lack of human capital.

Foremost among structural factors are the changing racial and ethnic composition of the immigrant population, the attendant racism that comes with diversity, the inability of employers to evaluate foreign credentials and educational degrees (resulting in a corresponding discounting of these skills), communication problems for non-English and non-French–speaking immigrants, and changes in the labour market because of economic globalization and knowledge-based economies (Biles & Burstein, 2003). Increased employment and earnings are often linked with language proficiency in one of Canada's two official languages. Yet many immigrants have neither French nor English as a first language, even as the federal government is scaling back its English as a second language (ESL) program and restricting access to it to permanent residents and convention refugees (Wayland, 2006). As well, the managers of unionized workplaces may find their hands tied when it comes to hiring skilled workers with overseas experience, because collective agreements with entrenched seniority rights stipulate that they recruit from within the bargaining unit when filling positions (James, 2005). Clearly, then, settlement structures and reception models are key to reducing poverty and improving productivity: The better the reception models in terms of integration into social and economic networks, the greater the success of immigrant adaptation (Abu-Laban, Derwing, & Mulder, 2004).

Fitting In

The challenges of fitting in are no less complex. Customary family relations and status are challenged and transformed in the new country, resulting in intergenerational conflicts (Tyyska, 2008). For immigrant youth, the pressures may be punishing (Handa, 2003): They must adjust to a new country, cope with the pressures of prejudice and racism during their formative years of identity construction, become involved with routines and friendships, and learn a new language quickly enough to finish high school and compete with their Canadian-born peers for places in post-secondary education (it generally takes five to seven years to develop English language equivalency for success at school). Immigrant and refugee schoolchildren are subject to a host of conflicting demands and pressures. Some may perform poorly because of racial stereotyping, low teacher expectations, curricula and textbooks at odds with minority experiences, and lack of positive role models among school staff (L. Brown, 2005). And most need to negotiate the demands of a mainstream peer culture whose values of independence and competition may conflict with the cultural norms (from interdependence and cooperation to obedience) of family and community (Anisef & Kilbride, 2003; Handa, 2003; Tyyska, 2008). Young women, as the moral guardians of the culture and nation, are particularly vulnerable, as Mythili Rajiva (2005) says:

> Girls are expected to maintain cultural practices that are sometimes no longer relevant in their homeland countries, and are certainly not widely accepted in Canadian society. This includes concerns with dress and behaviour; peer socializing (at night, at parties, and school dancing); growing independence at adolescence (which is often not part of immigrant community understandings of adolescence); and perhaps most importantly, interacting with members of the opposite sex and having romantic relationships with boys who are not part of the community. (p. 27)

There is value in understanding immigrants as gendered subjects who are differently located with respect to identity construction, experiences, and opportunity and outcomes (Tastsoglou, Ray, & Preston, 2005; Zaman, 2006).

Intergenerational family tensions are inevitable as parents and offspring struggle to find a workable balance between the permissiveness of Canada and the more conservative traditions of new immigrant groups (Handa, 2003). In many cases, the immigrant story contains two broad narratives: adult immigrants who falter in making the transition, and their offspring who tend to successfully adjust (Sykes, 2008). Immigrant parents may feel alienated from a language and culture that confuses them, especially when parental authority is questioned, whereas their immigrant children assimilate rapidly, which enables them to assume an assertiveness and independence that inverts conventional roles (Lupa, 1999). (See online Case Study 4.1.) Parents are forced to strike a Faustian bargain: All parents desire a better future for their children, but attainment of this success tends to undermine parental authority and family cohesion (Suarez-Orozco & Suarez-Orozco, 2001). And immigrant women may be the real victims (Rajiva, 2005). Thousands of new Canadians are living in quiet desperation and depression, suffering in silence behind walls of social alienation, financial pressure, family turmoil, and cultural mores that isolate and foreclose avenues of help (Reinhart & Rusk, 2006).

For refugees, the situation is decidedly grimmer. Traumatized by emotional and psychological abuses en route to Canada, refugees are still expected to adapt to Canada's unique social, cultural, and geographic climate with only minimal outside assistance. Refugees may have complex needs, with widely varying educational and literacy levels, and much to learn in a relatively short period of time—about everything from awareness of community support agencies to issues of abortion, contraception, same-sex relations, domestic violence, child supervision, divorce, and child custody (Etherington, 2005). The impact of the cultural shock may be unsettling because of exposure to radically different lifestyles, mixed messages and conflicting expectations, rapid social change, and an inhospitable climate. Worse still, refugee families may remain separated for lengthy periods of time because of delays in acquiring permanent residence for the sponsoring family member or inability to pay processing fees that must accompany each application (Wayland, 2006). The transitional stresses that accompany refugee claimants are compounded by their language difficulties, shame at their inability to work, and low self-esteem because of loss of control over their destiny. As expressed by one refugee from Central America who fell into an abusive relationship: "I was from a country where I was the daughter of a middle-class professional. Here, I was no one. Refugee is such a negative word. People saw me as garbage" (as cited in White, 1999).

PROSPECTS: NEEDING IMMIGRATION, EMBRACING IMMIGRANTS?

How should we assess Canada's record as an immigration country? Few countries have demonstrated the same degree of generosity, inclusiveness, and tolerance that Canada has, especially with the introduction of the *Canadian Charter of Rights and Freedoms* and official Multiculturalism. Canada's commitment is reflected in the positioning of immigration within the context of Canada-building. Canada's record may not be perfect in this regard, but surely it is less imperfect than other countries in living up to an ideal, as articulated by this 1862 pamphlet to entice prospective German settlers:

Canada is the land of peace, order, and abundance . . . The immigrant when he arrives is protected and guided by government officials . . . Canada is about the only country in which the . . . immigrant practically as well as before [the] law is seen as immediately equal to the native born. (as cited in Avery, 1995, p. 239)

The immigration process activates a "social contract" between immigrants that involves a two-way process of mutual accommodation (Frith, 2003; Parekh, 1997; Spencer, 2003). Canada expects immigrants to identify with core cultural values, make a positive contribution, participate through involvement, and abide by the laws of society. Immigrants, in turn, expect fair treatment through the removal of discriminatory barriers, the conferral of citizenship rights, the creation of welcoming communities, and the right to identify with the cultural tradition of their choice (Volpe, 2005). In short, coming to Canada activates a social contract in which immigrants trade talents for responsibilities, while Canada exchanges safety and security for rights.

Yet another dimension to assessing immigration requires attention: Canadians for the most part have not yet fully confronted the reality and challenges of immigrant integration as a two-way process of mutual adjustment (see Modood, 2003). Reluctance to endorse measures that encourage inclusiveness and accommodation is but one sign of this denial. Another sign is a belief that some immigrant groups are making demands that are culturally, socially, and politically unacceptable, although Tariq Modood (2005) argues that these groups are only seeking social space and respectful endorsement of their cultural heritage—a right that is implied in an official Multiculturalism. Growing anti-immigrant sentiment is yet another possibility, although any backlash will be constrained by (1) human rights codes that prohibit the public articulation of racist views, (2) a pervasive liberalism within the political culture, and (3) a lack of institutional power base to fortify racist exclusion. In other words, there is not much likelihood of reverting to an openly racial basis for either the selection of immigrants or their treatment once they are in Canada. Still, immigrants continue to experience barriers that deny or exclude. Although immigrants may not be second-class citizens under the law, nevertheless, they remain so in public perception and national discourses. Such mixed messages of denial and exclusion reflect badly on Canada's much-vaunted reputation as an immigrant society that abides by the principles of multiculturalism.

DEBATE REVISITED

The Refugee Determination Process: A Functioning Dysfunction?

How should the refugee determination process be assessed—is it in disarray or as good as it gets? Reaction is mixed: Many, including the United Nations High Commissioner on Refugees, believe Canada's refugee determination process to be one of the world's most generous. For some, this generosity is to be celebrated as a source of pride (Mawani, 1997); for others, it proves that Canadians are being taken for a ride (Collacott, 2006). Those who think

(Continued)

the system is excessively generous point out that Canada accepts refugee claimants at six times the international norm. Of the 95 500 refugees who made claims to the Immigration and Refugee Board of Canada between 1993 and 1997, 42 percent were accepted (down from the 84 percent in 1989), 33 percent were rejected, and 25 percent were neither finalized nor ineligible. In 2003, the figure for acceptance remained at 42 percent, with 42 percent rejected and 18 percent abandoned, but reinforcing critics' view that claimants are using the refugee system for backdoor entry into Canada (Jimenez, 2004). In 2010, the acceptance rate dipped to 38 percent.

Canada is the only country to recognize conventional refugees from Brazil, Costa Rica, Israel, Jamaica (and several other Caribbean countries), Republic of Korea, and the Philippines (Gallagher, 2008b). How can this anomaly be explained? Why does Canada recognize more conventional refugees from Cuba, Lebanon, Mexico, Pakistan, Peru, and Romania than all other countries combined? Does it make sense to focus on claims of persecution based on membership in certain groups, including a German family who wanted to home-school their children, homosexuals in Mexico who recently received approval for gay marriages, and white South Africans fearing black violence? That claims from citizens of democratic societies such as Israel, the United Kingdom, and the United States are accorded due process is proof of a broken system. And with the number of claimants continuing to grow, there are fears that the system may self-implode from taking on too much with too few resources.

The best spin on the 42 percent acceptance rate believes these numbers are a reflection of Canada's commitment to assist the world's most unfortunate. The worst spin suggests that Canada's refugee determination system is absurdly dysfunctional—especially since Canada does not share a border with a refugee-producing country, thus negating any justification for such numbers. According to critics, unlike most countries that vigorously weed out "fake" asylum seekers, everyone who lands in Canada is entitled to due process by a tribunal (Gallagher, 2004). Numerous loopholes and vulnerabilities are exploited that can prove costly once legal, welfare, and administrative costs are factored in (Stoffman, 1997). Operating an asylum-processing system and processing refugees does not come cheaply. That being the case, critics argue, why not accept all refugee claimants and dispense with the costs involved in deporting the few who fail to comply? The savings, time, and energy could then be used to improve settlement of "legitimate" refugees plucked from overseas camps.

Others, including refugee lawyers and advocacy groups, see the 42 percent acceptance rate as exceptionably low. Canada's refugee determination system is accused of being racist and discriminatory, both deliberately and systemically (Canadian Council for Refugees, 2000). Practices with an inadvertent yet negative impact on refugees may include an insistence on documentation, a narrow definition of family, racial profiling in selection processes, and the skewed distribution of visa posts. And despite moves toward improving training, eliminating political patronage, and strengthening the criteria for appointment, arbitrariness remains a problem, including a publicized case wherein one of two nearly identical Palestinian brothers was accepted by one board member, while the other was rejected by another board member. Or consider this stunning revelation: Refugee approval rates not only vary from city to city but also from board member to board member, with some having approval rates of 81 percent, while five members have a zero percent approval rate (Jimenez, 2004). Not surprisingly, the practice of refugee determination appears to be dictated more by political objectives and personal politics than by humanitarian concerns, and a tendency to treat refugees as a social problem rather than as humans in distress (Dench, 2004).

An intermediate position is echoed by those who contend that the current system is ensnared in a paradox. However well intentioned, the Supreme Court Singh decision of 1985 resulted in the clogging up of the refugee determination process. (The Singh ruling stated that anyone who so much as steps on Canadian soil is entitled to due process of law.) Instead of being efficient and fair, the system has become legal limbo, with numerous avenues of appeals and lengthy administrative backlogs that invariably raise public ire (Simpson, 2000). Contradictions are at play: Canada's refugee determination processes may not respond quickly enough to those in genuine need of protection (the victims of war and oppression in refugee camps)—in the process encouraging a vast and profitable underground migrant smuggling system (Bell & Jimenez, 2000).

Conversely, it may respond too generously to those who lie and cheat to get in, with the result that a beleaguered refugee determination system is gored by the paradox of processing those who neither require nor deserve Canada's protection. However generous and compassionate, such a perverse dynamic will invariably generate bottlenecks in a system designed to rule over matters of life and death, without compromising Canada's national interests (see online Debate 9.1).

Yes, there is much to commend in Canada's refugee determination system; nevertheless, improvement is necessary if Canada is to maintain its status as the true north strong and free. The challenge is no longer how to design the perfect refugee determination system that balances the real with the ideal, but how to create one that is politically, socially, and ethically acceptable (Kumin, 2004). Moral quandaries abound: while Canadians do not want Canada to become a haven for terrorists because of misplaced generosity or inadequate screening procedures, they squirm at the prospect of sending people back to torture or death. Canadians may resent refugees who prove to be a social or medical burden, particularly those refugees who arrive in Canada without proper identification (SES Canada Research, 2003), yet balk at the prospect of deporting them to a cruel fate (Duffy, 1999). As Janet Dench (2007) points out, refugees are people who have no choice except to flee. Canadians by contrast do have a choice: to welcome refugees as human beings in need of protection or to abandon them by pulling up the drawbridge.

Chapter Highlights

- Canada is sociologically regarded as an immigrant society. That is, it has an immigration program in place, sees immigrants as a national asset, confers rights, and encourages settlement and citizenship.
- Canada routinely ranks high among countries with respect to immigration on a per capita basis, with the result that the foreign born account for nearly 20 percent of the population.
- Immigration currently averages about 250 000 people per year, with the majority arriving from Asia, Africa, and South and Central America. Most immigrants prefer Ontario and British Columbia; Toronto, Montreal, and Vancouver are all major immigrant targets.
- In the past, immigration practices were highly racist in terms of who got in. At present, Canada's immigration policy can be described as relatively colour-blind, with a focus on sustaining economic growth.
- Immigrants can be admitted on three grounds: family-reunification class, economic class (which includes the business class and is based on a point system), and refugee class.
- The spectacular expansion of the temporary foreign workers program elicits praise from Canadian businesses but concerns from those who worry that Canada's long-term interests are sacrificed for short-term gains.
- Canadians appear divided in their reaction to immigration, with some seeing it as a problem, others as a solution, and still others as both a problem and a solution, depending on the context, consequences, and criteria.
- Immigration comes with benefits and costs. Benefits are numerous but impact differently on different sectors of society and the economy. The costs are no less real for some Canadians.
- Immigrant needs and aspirations have been misportrayed. Most want to put down roots in their adopted country, contribute to its growth, receive benefits that all Canadians are entitled to, and get the best for their children without losing their distinctiveness.
- Refugees continue to be seen as a problem, especially those who are unsponsored. Canada may have a relatively high rate of acceptance of refugee claimants, but most agree that the refugee determination system is broken (i.e., overworked and under-resourced).

For further study, you can access the Case Studies referenced in this chapter at **www.pearsoncanada.ca/fleras**.

Review Questions

1. Briefly compare the concept of immigration in the past with the post-1978 immigration policy in terms of underlying assumptions, goals, methods, and outcomes.
2. Discuss the benefits and drawbacks of increased immigration to Canada.

3. Discuss the aspirations of immigrants in terms of needs and goals. What kinds of barriers exist that preclude attainment of these goals?

4. Critics of immigration point out that Canada has too many immigrants who are derived from the wrong classes and come from the wrong countries. Respond to these criticisms.

5. Point out the issues that contribute to a "refugee crisis" in Canada.

6. Is the current model and program of immigration the best one for Canada, in light of emergent realities? If you were the Immigration Minister, what changes would you make, based on doing what is workable, necessary, and fair?

7. In his book *Immigrants: Your Country Needs Them*, Philippe Legrain (2007) asks some interesting questions that should elicit personal reflection and classroom debate:

   (a) How far should immigrants adapt to society, and vice versa?

   (b) How much immigrant diversity can a society embrace? How much unity does it need?

   (c) Does an immigrant society require shared values and culture for survival? If yes, what are they?

   (d) Should immigrants be left to their devices in settling down or should government intervention be promoted?

   (e) Should immigrants be allowed to live separate lives in ethnic enclaves or should they be encouraged to interact?

   (f) Should immigrants be allowed to live where they want, or does the government have the right to distribute immigrants more evenly across the country?

Endnotes

1. The findings are based on an Ipsos poll conducted on behalf of the Historica-Dominion Institute between 12 and 22 May 2010. An international sample of 18 624 adults aged 18+ were interviewed in a total of 24 countries. Approximately 1000+ individuals participated on a country-by-country basis, with a margin of error of +/− 3.1 percentage points 19 times out of 20 per country. In 11 countries, a sample of 500 respondents participated, with a margin of error of +/− 4.4 percentage points 19 times out of 20 for each of these countries.

Links and Recommendations

FILMS

Who Gets In (1991)

   A National Film Board documentary about immigration into Canada—somewhat dated, but still packs a wallop.

Dirty Pretty Things (2002)

   A searing look at what undocumented refugees in London, England, must sometimes do to survive. See also *Spare Parts* (2006).

The Refugees of the Blue Planet (2006)

A powerful look at how environmental disasters are impacting on human populations and displacing them from their homelands.

BOOKS

Destination Canada: Immigration Debates and Issues, by Peter S. Li (2003). A popular book that offers a balanced view of immigration as a cost and/or benefit to Canada.

Strangers at Our Gates: Canadian Immigration and Immigration Policy, 1540–2006, by Valerie Knowles (2007). A detailed and historical account of the history of immigration in Canada.

"They Take our Jobs!" and Twenty Other Myths about Immigration, by Aviva Chomsky (2007). The author looks at and debunks 21 popular myths and misconceptions about immigration and immigrants in the United States.

Managing Two Worlds: The Experiences and Concerns of Immigrant Youth in Ontario, edited by Paul Anisef and Kenise Murphy Kilbride (2003). An original work based on a collaborative research effort, this book provides valuable insights into the settlement experiences of immigrant and refugee youth.

Transnational Identities and Practices in Canada, edited by Vic Satzewich and Lloyd Wong (2006). This collection of articles explores how and why members of immigrant groups maintain connections with the homeland, and what this transnationalism means for the immigrants themselves and for Canadian society.

Immigration and Canada: Global and Transnational Perspectives, by Alan B. Simmons (2010). An excellent book that explores Canadian immigration within the broader context of world issues and transnational migrations.

WEBSITES

Citizenship and Immigration Canada—Canada's official site for immigration:
www.cic.gc.ca

Immigration Law in Canada (Federal Publications Inc.)—Books on immigration laws in Canada:
http://fedpubs.com/subject/immig_law.htm

About.com Immigration Issues—For various issues relating to immigration in Canada, the United States, and abroad:
http://immigration.about.com

PART 3

Living Together with Differences in a Multiculturally Inclusive Canada

The upsurge of racial pride and ethnic affiliation in Canada and abroad is well documented (Isajiw, 1997). Religious and ethnocultural minorities are demanding respectful recognition of their identities, seeking the right to full and equal participation in society, and insisting that institutions make reasonable accommodations to ensure inclusiveness. In the face of these spiralling and sometimes contradictory demands, pluralistic societies confront a dilemma when grappling with the challenge of cooperative coexistence. A principled framework must be established for constructing a functioning society out of culturally diverse populations without compromising a commitment to either common values or individual rights (Sellers, 2005). But the interplay of competing agendas may disrupt the dynamics of any balancing act: On one side is a liberal commitment to the individuality of autonomy and equality; on the other side is a society-building imperative to impose a uniformity of language, culture, and identity over a heterogeneous population (Baubock, 2005; May, 2004; Pearson, 2001); on yet another side is a multicultural adherence to the principle of respecting differences without undermining a commitment to inclusiveness and equality (Siddiqui, 2008).

Countries such as Australia (May, 2004) and New Zealand (Pearson, 2001; Spoonley, 2005) must cope with the politics of diversities and difference related to (1) the influx of immigrants, (2) the proliferation of identity politics, (3) the politicization of ethnicity as a social force, (4) the appearance of anti-racism movements, and (5) the ascendancy of ethnic and indigenous nationalisms. Central authorities have responded to this unprecedented surge of diversities and difference in a variety of ways, ranging from indifference or rejection to tolerance or acceptance (Fleras, 2009a; Kobayashi, 1999; Willett, 1998). Historically, however, the presence of cultural diversity was widely perceived as a threat to effective governance. Recognition of these differences, it was thought, could culminate in social fragmentation, block the creation of a cohesive and stable society, and jeopardize the attainment of national identity and unity. Not surprisingly, state authorities tended to either ignore, isolate, or suppress differences in the hopes of enhancing a ruling class hegemony (Jakubowicz, 2005). Strategies to bolster national unity and identity were varied, but invariably included (1) centralization of political power to ensure mainstream control; (2) imposition of a dominant legal tradition and judicial system; (3) official language laws; (4) a nationalized system of compulsory education; (5) adoption of state symbols for celebrating the dominant group's history; (6) seizure of so-called empty lands in the name of progress or national interests; and (7) restriction of immigrants to clones of the majority sector.

But what was a self-evident truth in the past is fiercely contested at present. In contrast to the past, when the concept of good governance and cultural diversity were deemed to be mutually exclusive, new ground rules are emerging that challenge this perception. Alternatives for redefining majority–minority relations have evolved, in part because traditional formats such as assimilation no longer offer a moral compass for living together with differences equitably and in dignity, in part to defuse minority challenges to the prevailing status quo. Instead of assimilation as a framework for managing diversity, a commitment to the principles and practices of **multiculturalism** has increasingly moved to the fore as grounds for cooperative coexistence (Fleras, 2009a. In acknowledging that national unity and identity do not require a singular identity or denunciation of diversity—after all, people are known to have multiple identities and conflicting affiliations without sinking into personal incoherence or social chaos—a commitment to multicultural principles has resulted in government programs to assist in the settlement of migrants, to acknowledge their contribution to society, and to educate the general public about the benefits of a pluralistic society (May, 2004).

Of those societies at the vanguard in advancing a multicultural governance, few can match Canada's blistering pace (Fleras, 2002). With the emergence of Toronto and Vancouver as dynamically cosmopolitan cities, Canada has transformed itself into one of the world's most ethnically diverse societies without collapsing into a welter of interethnic conflicts. The entrenchment of multiculturalism at constitutional and statutory levels has further reinforced its legacy as Canada's key contribution in advancing global peace (Foster, 2005; James, 2005). In short, just as Canada is defined as an immigration society, so too does it qualify as a normatively multicultural society: (1) it has put in place multicultural policies and programs for managing diversities; (2) it considers the multicultural management of diversities as Canada-building; (3) it acknowledges the rights and legitimacy of all Canadians regardless of their race, ethnicity, national origins, or immigrant status; (4) it recognizes that multiculturalism provides both a social climate and the aspirational framework for enhancing minority integration; and (5) it has established programs to facilitate the integration of new Canadians (Fleras, 2011a).

Forty years of **official Multiculturalism** have confirmed what many now routinely endorse: the right of people to identify with the cultural tradition of their choice without sacrificing full and equal participation in society because of ethnic differences. Canada's official Multiculturalism has served admirably as a catalyst for defusing intergroup tensions by promulgating the once unthinkable—that diversities and difference are compatible with good governance, provided that ground rules are in place. A commitment to Multiculturalism embraces the notion that people have multiple identities, that equitable outcomes can be achieved without denying cultural differences, that culturally diverse people can coexist without conflict if an overarching vision prevails, and that respect for differences cannot transpire without a commitment to social justice, political equality, and full and equal participation (see also Rodriguez-Garcia, 2010). Under the banner of an official Multiculturalism, Canadians are accepted as racially or ethnically different yet no less Canadian, with a corresponding package of citizenship rights and entitlements regardless of origin, creed, or colour. To be sure, Canadians are not nearly as multicultural as their collective pride would imply; in some ways they are less diversity driven than their melting pot neighbours to the south (Abu-Laban & Gabriel, 2002; Jedwab, 2002; Reitz & Breton, 1994). Still, the promotion of multiculturalism has accelerated a reshaping of Canada in ways that have evoked international acclaim, in effect reinforcing Canada's lofty ranking as a leading light in advancing a living together with differences equitably and in dignity.

It is one thing to promote a multiculturalism policy that *endorses yet neutralizes* diversity and difference as a legitimate component in Canada-building. It may be something altogether different to transform this principle into workable practices that make an appreciable difference. The challenge is threefold: first, how to create an inclusive society in which minority women and men can maintain their identities without foreclosing hard-fought equality rights within the framework of a functioning governance; second, how to create an inclusive Canada that is both safe for difference and safe from difference without trampling on individual rights and cultural differences or imperilling the long-term prospects of a cohesive Canada; third, how to incorporate Multiculturalism into the broader scheme of things? That is, if race and ethnic relations are ultimately unequal relations, what is the role of multiculturalism in creating and maintaining inequality as well as in challenging and transforming it?

This final section responds to these challenges by exploring the politics and practices of multiculturalism within the context of an inclusive Canada-building. Chapter 10 examines official Multiculturalism as a formal strategy for proactively managing diversities and differences as "different" yet "equal." The chapter begins by theorizing multiculturalism as governance, examines multiculturalism from different frames of reference, with particular emphasis on Multiculturalism as policy and practice for improving the integration of minorities and migrants. It concludes by demonstrating how Multiculturalism can be interpreted as a progressive yet flawed social experiment for democratic governance in ways both constructive and integrative, yet fractious and controversial. Chapter 11 emphasizes the practice of multiculturalism in terms of putting inclusivity to work at institutional levels. Initiatives are in place to (1) improve minority access, representation, and equitable treatment at institutional levels, (2) create institutions that are reflective of, respectful of, and responsive to differences, and (3) formulate institutional services that are available, accessible, and appropriate. But barriers created by organizational structures and individual mindsets have compromised moves toward institutional inclusivity at the level of media and education. The final chapter, Chapter 12, looks at the politics of diversity and difference with respect to Canada-building. A commitment to Canada's Difference Model is transforming Canada into what many see as the world's foremost postnational society—one whose design and dynamics differ from those of conventional nation-states. The prospect of constructing an inclusive citizenship that acknowledges diverse experiences and realities yet acknowledges people's commonalities as Canadians provides a fitting reminder. Canada is by no means a perfect society when it comes to managing diversity and difference; nevertheless, it may well qualify as one of the least imperfect in perfecting the art of living together with differences.

CHAPTER 10

Multiculturalism as Canada-Building Governance

The Politics of Multiculturalism:
European Rejection, Canadian Embrace

References to Multiculturalism as policy and philosophy have come under intense scrutiny. From the Antipodes to Europe, multiculturalism is experiencing a crisis of legitimacy. Policies and ideologies that once embraced multiculturalism as a framework for cooperative coexistence are now dismissed as irrelevant or inferior, a failure or a threat (Gregg, 2006). In the aftermath of 9/11, the Madrid and London bombings, and politicized assassinations of high-profile Dutch personalities including Pym Fortune and Theo van Gogh, multiculturalism in Europe is criticized for everything from the spate of terrorist attacks to the fostering of cultural separatism, political fragmentation, and social ghettoization. A resonant note of dismay is captured by Trevor Phillips, chair of Britain's Commission for Racial Equality, when he accused the British of "sleepwalking into segregation": "We focused far too much on the 'multi' and not enough on the common culture—thereby allowing **tolerance** to solidify into isolation rather than insisting on sharing common values without losing a sense of uniqueness." More recently, in an address to the country's conservative Christian Democratic Union in October 2010, German Chancellor Angela Merkel dismissed "multikulti" as a failure for its role in aborting the integration of immigrants—sentiments similarly echoed in early 2011 by French President Sarkozy and British Prime Minister Cameron.

In brief, multiculturalism may have reigned supreme in Europe for 20 years, but not anymore, and a commitment to multicultural governance is increasingly ridiculed as a deadly liability instead of an empowering solution. Having outworn its welcome and ostensibly outlived its usefulness, multiculturalism is increasingly maligned as either a good idea gone bad or, alternatively, a bad idea that has unfolded precisely as predicted. But while Europe's love affair with multiculturalism has tanked, the situation in Canada differs sharply. Canada's multiculturalism appears to be relatively untouched by criticism or backlash, while support for immigrants and immigration remains at an all-time high (Jedwab, 2006; Nanos, 2010). For example, according to a survey by the Centre for Research and Information on Canada involving a representative sample of 2032 randomly selected individuals in August 2005, Canadians clearly embrace multiculturalism as a defining characteristic of Canada, while linking immigration with a host of positive social, economic, and cultural advantages (see Dasko, 2005; Seidle, 2007b; Siddiqui, 2010). An Angus Reid poll in 2010 reinforced high levels of support for multiculturalism (54 percent), albeit along the lines of a melting pot version rather than a mosaic model. Not surprisingly, with multiculturalism ranking as the second-greatest source of pride about Canada after democracy/freedom (Adams, 2007, p. 96), Canadians are genuinely puzzled by the intensity of European vitriol, especially since core Canadian policies related to multiculturalism and immigration enjoy substantial public consensus, while sporadic criticisms rarely yield much political traction (Soroka, Johnston, & Banting, 2006).

How do we account for this multicultural divide? Why is Canada seemingly immune to calls for retrenchment of multiculturalism, whereas European jurisdictions are circling the proverbial wagons against what many perceive as excessive (Muslim) immigration and politically correct multiculturalism (Hage, 2006; Joppke, 2007)? How reasonable is the backlash in Europe? Is the backlash little more than a code for Islamophobia, which is prompted by a combination of fear of Muslim terrorism, concerns over Muslim rejection of gender and gay rights, and worries about being "swamped" by Muslims should Turkey enter the European Union (Hage, 2006)? Should Canada be worried as well, and begin to reassess its much-ballyhooed commitment to an official Multiculturalism? Is there something about Canada—its people or its policies or its priorities or placement—that transforms multiculturalism into a dynamic that benefits as it solves? Or is Canada riding a lucky streak because of a fortuitous combination of history and geography (Kymlicka, 2004)? The Debate Revisited box at the end of this chapter provides some possible answers.

INTRODUCTION: LIVING TOGETHER WITH DIFFERENCES: PUZZLES, PARADOXES, AND PROSPECTS

People overseas marvel at two dimensions of Canadian society. First, how can Canada maintain its independence and integrity despite proximity to the world's most powerful economic and military machine? That Canadians have retained their distinctiveness and autonomy under the shadow of this colossus is remarkable. That they have managed to secure an enviable standard of living is yet more astonishing. Second, how does Canada remain united and prosperous when confronted by the politics of a multilayered diversity? Consider the pushes and pulls: English-speaking Canadians seem to be perpetually embroiled with the Québécois over language issues; Aboriginal assertiveness has profoundly challenged the very notion of "what Canada is for"; and Canada annually accepts thousands of immigrants and refugees from around the world without spiraling out of control. And yet, despite the tripwires of balancing diversity with unity, Canada has managed to cobble together a society that now ranks as one of the most prosperous and progressive.

There are no simple explanations to either of these observations; nevertheless, a commitment to multiculturalism may prove the common denominator. Canada represents one of several democratic societies that have capitalized on multicultural principles as a principled paradigm for living together with differences (Adams, 2007; Tierney, 2007). Originating in part to harmonize competing ethnicities without losing control of the overall agenda, official Multiculturalism has been perpetuated for a variety of political and economic considerations involving state functions, private interests, and electoral survival (Wood & Gilbert, 2005). Multiculturalism continues to provide an aspirational blueprint: it serves as a normative framework for "managing" diversity by seeking to reconcile (balance) cultural diversity with social inclusion, economic equality and political cohesion (also Rodriguez-Garcia, 2010). A combination of demographic and political upheavals in recent years has further reconfigured Canada's multicultural agenda in ways inconceivable even a generation ago (Hiebert, Collins, & Spoonley, 2003; Kymlicka, 2007; Moosa, 2007; Ujimoto, 2000).

Reaction is mixed to what many perceive as one of the world's most powerful social forces at present (Savard & Vignezzi, 1999). As Tyler Cowen (1999) concludes:

> Based on the dual ideals of peace and *multiculturalism*, Canada is one of mankind's greatest achievements. It is comparable to the notable civilizations of the past, and indeed exceeds most of them in terms of stability, living standards, and civil liberties. (emphasis mine)

For some, multiculturalism represents a late–twentieth century experiment for rewriting the rules of social and political engagement in an age of migration (Gagnon & Iacovino, 2007). Others prefer to dismiss it as a modernist anachronism in a postmodern world of fluidity, multiplicity, and unpredictability (Duncan, 2005). Still others recognize both its potency and impotence in addressing the challenges of "getting along." In light of these disparities in reactions, who can be surprised when Multiculturalism is pilloried as Canada's "biggest mistake" (Hitchens, 2010; Kay, 2008), yet triumphalized as a "quiet revolution" equivalent in status and stature to three other societal transformations—the French, American, and Russian revolutions (Sandercock, 2006).

However much revered or vilified, an official Multiculturalism is prone to paradoxes (Banting, Courchene, & Seidle, 2007; Khan, 2005). At the core of this paradox is a proposed balancing of the act between unity (commonality) and difference. Put bluntly, too much multiculturalism (differences) and not enough monoculturalism (unity) may destabilize a society to the point of dismemberment. Conversely, too much unity but too little in the way of differences can create a one-size-fits-all leviathan that stifles as it standardizes (Fish, 1997). Yet there are challenges in the absence of measurable values for operationalizing "unity" with "difference." That is, what is the appropriate balance, who says so, on what grounds, and how can we find out? For some, official Multiculturalism may advance the society-building goals of cultural identity, social justice, citizenship, national unity, societal integration, and equality. For others, Multiculturalism may have the sincerest intentions of creating a just and inclusive Canada, but its logic can be manipulated to foster inequality, separate ethnic silos, and intergroup friction (Kostash, 2000; Valpy, 2007). The solution appears straightforward enough: Establish a rules-based framework and normative standards that can engage difference as different yet equal, without eroding the goals of national unity, identity, and prosperity in the process. But in seeking to make Canada safe for difference, yet safe from difference (see Schlesinger Jr., 1992), what sounds simple in principle may collapse in practice.

In acknowledging a domain rife with confusion, contestation, and contradiction, this chapter explores the politics of multiculturalism in Canada by (1) theorizing it, (2) examining it at different levels of meaning, (3) analyzing the diverse perceptions and critical reactions, and (4) evaluating its role in Canada-building. Emphasis is on unpacking the different levels of meaning, including multiculturalism as (1) fact (what empirically is); (2) ideology (what ought to be); (3) policy (what is about to be); (4) practices (what really happens); and (5) critical discourse (what must be) (Fleras, 2002). A theorizing of multiculturalism as governance yields three basic models—conservative, liberal, and plural—each of which differs in advancing a framework for an inclusive and cooperative coexistence. Insofar as migrant and minority relations are fundamentally unequal relations, the chapter reinforces a main theme of this book: the role of Canada's official Multiculturalism in creating and/or changing patterns of inequality. Particular attention focuses on historically analyzing Multiculturalism by way of evolving stages, namely, ethnicity, equity, civic, and integration. A discussion of both public attitudes and scholarly criticism makes the conclusion abundantly clear: The prospect of living together with differences equitably and in dignity may be gravely compromised without an official Multiculturalism.

THEORIZING MULTICULTURALISM

The Multiculturalism Paradox: Not Meaning What It Says; Not Saying What It Means

To say we live in a multicultural world is surely a statement of understated proportions. Our world is characterized by immigrant-driven demographic diversity, a growing commitment to multiculturalism as a basis for living together differently, and the codification of multicultural principles for managing difference. To be sure, the post-9/11 epoch has played havoc with the principles and practices of multiculturalism. With reactions ranging from outright hostility to studied indifference, questions abound: Can an official Multiculturalism provide a bulwark against the sense of alienation and exclusion that many believe motivates disaffected second-generation youth into anti-social activities? Can Multiculturalism be held accountable for so-called integration failures related to home-grown terrorism (Jakubowicz, 2007; see also Biles & Spoonley, 2007)? Is Multiculturalism meant to address racialized and immigrant inequality, or is it a cynical ploy to disguise inequities behind a facade of orchestrated platitudes (Thobani, 2007)? How potent is Multiculturalism as an instrument of change: Does it promise more than it can deliver (a kind of "sheep in wolf's clothing") or, alternatively, does it accomplish more than it is willing to admit ("a wolf in sheep's clothing") (Fleras, 2007c)? The dearth of consensus in responding to these questions makes it abundantly clear: Theorizing multiculturalism has proven an enigmatic and elusive exercise. Too often, debates over Multiculturalism are a matter of semantics rather than of substance because of its uncanny knack for meaning everything, yet nothing, depending on the context. Political and philosophical debates over multiculturalism are so fractured—ranging from questions of how to balance collective and individual rights to debates over establishing a framework for equality between groups without sacrificing individual freedoms within groups—that agreement is virtually impossible. Confusion is further sowed by people's seeming inability to distinguish between the ideal and the real, that is, between what an official Multiculturalism says it's doing and (1) what it really is doing, (2) what people think it's doing, (3) what people think it should be doing, and (4) what a state-endorsed multiculturalism can realistically do. Any theorizing of multiculturalism is compromised by failure to distinguish between and among each of these operative levels.

The conclusion seems inescapable: Despite continued popularity and support (at least in Canada), repeated reference to multiculturalism has not congealed into any agreement over definition, attributes, or applications (Biles, 2002). Instead, references have revealed an uncanny knack of meaning different things to different people, depending on whatever the context allows (Fleras, 2002). This should come as no surprise; after all, if the concept of culture is widely regarded as one of the most complex concepts in the English language, it stands to reason that *multi*culture should prove equally elusive. The term itself has absorbed such a mélange of meanings that many despair of any clarity or consensus (Caws, 1994). Championed yet maligned, idealized as well as demonized, multiculturalism simultaneously evokes a two-edged preference for consensus as well as criticism and change; of conformity yet diversity; of control yet emancipation; of exclusion yet participation; of compliance yet creativity (see Vasta & Castles, 1996). For some, multiculturalism is synonymous with Canada's official version, so that alternative readings are simply unthinkable. For others, multiculturalism is a transformative discourse that poses a critical challenge to the cultural status quo (Goldberg, 1994b; May, 2002). For others still, multiculturalism goes beyond a political or cultural project to embrace crossings and connections, as individuals routinely traverse cultural borders by way of multiple affiliations and hybridic identities (Handa, 2003; Qadeer, 2007). For others yet, multiculturalism refers to the coexistence of diverse cultures in society, either in territorially separate locales or sharing the same space, with corresponding implications for unity and interactivity (Gwyn, 2001a, 2001b).

Of particular importance are references to multiculturalism as governance. Multiculturalism as governance entails establishing relationships between the rulers (the governing) and the ruled (the governed) for living together with differences, in dignity and equitably, in ways workable, necessary, and fair. The range of models that fall under a multicultural governance umbrella are three-fold (Fish, 1997; Fleras, 2009b; Sandercock, 2003):

- At one end are *conservative* models of multiculturalism as governance. This largely assimilationist and weaker version of multiculturalism is anchored in the need (whether by submission or absorption) to respect common values and shared monocultural principles as the basis for a cohesive society, although cultural diversities are tolerated in the private sphere (Rodriguez-Garcia, 2010). According to a culture-blind equality that defines everyone as equal regardless of race or ethnicity, a conservative model of multiculturalism believes that a society of many cultures is possible as long as cultural differences are rejected as grounds for recognition and reward. After all, if everyone is equal before the law, then everyone is entitled to the same treatment—no more, no less (Neill & Schwedler, 2007). Three premises inform this multiculturalism-as-melting-pot model of governance: (1) our similarities as individuals outweigh our differences as group members; (2) nobody should be denied or excluded because of racial and ethnic differences; and (3) within reasonable limits and the rule of law, a commitment to commonalities can craft a progressive and prosperous society.

- Stronger models point to a *liberal* multiculturalism. With its lukewarm endorsement of diversity and difference along the lines of liberal universalism, a liberal model of multiculturalism believes that a society of many cultures is possible as long as people are treated the same as a matter of course, but differently when situations dictate otherwise. This multiculturalism-as-a-kaleidoscope model of governance acknowledges the need to recognize and respect cultural differences (within limits) without sacrificing minority rights to equality and opportunity. To the extent that cultural differences are recognized to ensure reasonable accommodation and institutional inclusion, the recognition of diversities must (1) conform with mainstream values and constitutional principles, (2) neither break the law nor violate people's rights, and (3) comply with the principle of agreeing to disagree because an intolerance of tolerance is unacceptable in a multicultural society.

- Finally, *plural* models of multiculturalism endorse a no-holds-barred allegiance to embracing difference as a basis for multicultural governance. A plural multicultural model takes cultural differences seriously even if they challenge existing patterns of power and privilege while fostering different group rights, differential citizenship, illiberal outlooks, separate institutional development, and hermetically sealed communities (May, 2002). This "strong" multiculturalism recognizes the legitimacy of cultural differences and ethnoreligious communities in the public sphere (in institutions, for instance) (Grillo, 2007). In that all cultures are seen as equally worthwhile under a multiculturalism-as-mosaic model of governance, a coexistence of culturally different communities is endorsed, with or without bridging devices to unify. (It could be argued that a plural multiculturalism can also include segregrationist or exclusionary versions characterized by separation between communities, essentialist readings of difference that foster inequality and restrictive access to citizenship (Rodriguez-Garcia, 2010). It remains to be seen if any society can be constructed around the radical relativism of a strong multiculturalism: Survival would be at best provocative; at worst, precarious. Table 10-1 provides a quick comparison of the three models of multiculturalism as governance.

In short, models of multiculturalism as governance span a spectrum of meanings, implications, and scenarios. Multiculturalism itself is loosely defined as a normative framework and political program to improve the incorporation/integration of migrants and minorities along conservative, liberal, or plural lines. Admittedly, the distinctions among these models of multicultural governance are more categorical (analytical) rather than contextual (lived), with the result that most jurisdictions embody an inconsistent package of multicultural do's and don'ts. Nevertheless, distinctions exist. Both liberal and (to a lesser extent) conservative models tend to create conditions for securing the status quo by facilitating the more gentle integration of newcomers and minorities into the existing social and cultural framework. By contrast, plural models tend to promote the long-term maintenance of multiple and separate cultures by allowing a degree of control over internal religious, political, and cultural affairs. Clearly, then, competing models make it difficult to theorize multiculturalism, given the plethora of conflicting discourses and hidden agendas. Still, there is no paucity of questions pertaining to multiculturalism as governance:

1. Is multiculturalism primarily about culture-conscious equity or culture-blind equality? Is it about treating people equally regardless of their differences, or about treating people as equals precisely because of those differences that are disadvantaging?

TABLE 10-1	Models of Multiculturalism as Governance		
Conservative multiculturalism	**Liberal multiculturalism**	**Plural multiculturalism**
"Melting pot model = culture/difference-blind"	**"Kaleidoscope model = culture/difference-tolerant"**	**"Mosaic model = culture/difference-conscious"**
A belief that a society of many cultures is possible, but only if ethnocultural differences are rejected as irrelevant for attainment of full equality and participation. (They are permissible but only in the private or personal spheres.) True equality arises from treating everyone the same (equal treatment), regardless of their racial or ethnocultural differences. In that everyone is fundamentally the same and the same before the law, no one should be excluded because of their differences; nor should anyone be accorded special treatment on that basis.	A belief that a society of many cultures is possible when cultural differences are tolerated or respected; but normally such differences are rejected as a basis for advancing equality or special treatment unless circumstances dictate otherwise. Members of culturally diverse minorities are treated equally (the same) as a matter of course, but treated *as equals* (differently or equivalently) when necessary by taking their differences into account. In short, a liberal model endorses a commitment to culture/difference-blind as a rule; culture/difference-conscious as an exception.	A belief that a society of many cultures is possible, but only if people's cultural differences are taken seriously as well as taken into account up to and including (1) special treatment, (2) autonomous institutions, (3) separate communities, and (4) collective group rights. In other words, differences matter and society must be reconfigured accordingly to ensure that minorities are treated *as equals* (equivalently).

2. Is multiculturalism about society-in-difference or difference-in-society? Does multiculturalism as governance endorse a particular vision of the good society and then ask how much difference can be incorporated within the limits of this vision? Or does it accept the priority of cultural differences, then redesign the good society accordingly (Sandercock, 2003)?

3. Is multiculturalism about difference or disadvantage? About recognition or redistribution (Banting et al., 2007)? Does multiculturalism as governance celebrate differences as ends in themselves? Or does it emphasize the removal of discriminatory barriers to ensure inclusive equity for those whose cultural differences have proven disadvantageous?

4. Is multiculturalism a radical policy departure (a new normative framework for integrating minorities into society along more equitable lines) or more of the same, albeit with fancier labels (and little more than assimilation in slow motion)?

5. Can a commitment to multiculturalism tolerate intolerance? That is, can a multicultural governance thrive in a context in which people agree to disagree? Can it flourish when certain groups disagree with the principle of agreeing to disagree? (See online Debate 10.1.)

6. Is multiculturalism about promoting cultural identity or social equality or national interests? Is the issue one of fostering a social climate conducive to the retention of

cultural identity? Should the focus be on social equality by ensuring that everyone is equal before the law, regardless of race or ethnicity? Or should multiculturalism be concerned primarily with advancing national interests by combining respect for diversity within a framework of shared values (Granatstein, 2007; Runnymede Trust, 2000)?

7. How gender neutral is multiculturalism as governance? Do some versions of multiculturalism embrace an androcentric tendency to condone cultural and religious practices that are at odds with women's **gender equity** rights (Reitman, 2005; Stein, 2007)? (See online Debate 10.2.)

8. Is multiculturalism about universality or particularity? Does a multicultural governance endorse the universality principle, that what we have in common as rights-bearing individuals is more important—at least for purposes of entitlement and recognition—than what divides us into culturally distinct groups? Or does it reject the universality of liberalism by privileging the particularism of ethnicity and group rights as a basis for belonging and governance (Hall, 2000)?

9. Is multiculturalism about "us" or "them"? Should a multicultural governance focus on addressing the concerns of minority women and men? Or should it aim at sensitizing the mainstream mindset by focusing on removing those prejudicial and discriminatory barriers that preclude minority integration?

10. Is a commitment to multiculturalism relevant or irrelevant? Has multiculturalism outlived its usefulness as a twentieth-century modernist project? In a globalizing world of transmigration and diaspora, does it still make sense to endorse a multicultural governance when immigrant realities are no longer tied to place (Fleras, 2011b)?

11. Is it possible to create a more "religion-friendly" model of multiculturalism? Or must a commitment to religion as a publicly legitimate player be rejected because of Canada's commitment to secularism and separation of church and state (Bramadat & Seljak, 2005, 2008; Kymlicka, 2003; Modood, 2003; Seljak, 2009)?

12. Should the multiculturalism in a multicultural governance be concerned with making society safe *from* diversities, yet safe *for* diversities? Or should it focus on making diversities safe *from* society as well as safe *for* society?

To the extent that no consensus prevails, disagreement flourishes. Multiculturalism may be seen as a blueprint for facilitating the integration of minorities into an inclusive-leaning society. Yet there is no agreement over the role of multiculturalism in promoting integration, whether multiculturalism fosters or obstructs the integration process, and how much each side needs to concede as part of the mutual accommodation process (Jedwab, 2005). In other words, if minority-majority relations are fundamentally unequal relations, does multiculturalism create or reinforce this inequity, or does it challenge and change it? There is even less agreement regarding what multiculturalism is doing, what it's really doing, and what it should be doing or is capable of doing in a liberal-capitalist society (Duncan, 2005). Responses will vary with the frame of reference (official Multiculturalism versus popular multiculturalism), the level of analysis (micro versus macro), a proposed vision of society (a **mosaic** or kaleidoscope or melting pot), and the role of multiculturalism in achieving an inclusive society (positive or negative).

The conclusion is inescapable: multiculturalism is experiencing an identity crisis (what is it in the context of the twenty-first century?) and a crisis of confidence (what should it be doing in light of post-9/11 realities?). Multiculturalism can mean whatever people want it to mean—a kind of "floating signifier" in which many meanings and references can be absorbed or dispersed without much fear of contradiction (Gunew, 2004)—and it is precisely this ambiguity that is proving both a strength and a weakness in theorizing multiculturalism (Modood, 2005; Willett, 1998). Any theorizing must begin by a distinguishing of the general (multiculturalism as the informal, the interpersonal, the contextual) from the specific (multiculturalism as the formal, the official, the principled). At the general level, multiculturalism can be defined as a belief that people can live together with their differences at personal, institutional, and national levels, provided that an overarching vision is in place, as are a set of rules for constructively *engaging differences as different yet equal.* More specifically, official Multiculturalism can be defined as a package of policies and programs for society-building around the institutional integration of minorities through the removal of discriminatory barriers. That's the theory. What about the reality in Canada?

MULTICULTURALISM IN CANADA

How would you respond to the question, "Is Canada a multicultural society?" To qualify, a multicultural society is one that minimally subscribes to the following attributes: (1) differences are defined as an asset and opportunity; (2) minorities are seen as contributing to society-building; (3) policies and programs supporting the inclusion of differences are in place at institutional levels; (4) governments not only endorse differences as part of the national identity but also take an active role in facilitating the integration of migrants and minorities; and (5) sufficient resources are available for transitioning diversity ideals into daily practice. Yet framing Canada as a multicultural society will also vary with how multiculturalism is defined, including these different levels of meaning:

1. An *empirical fact* (what is)
2. An *ideology* (what ought to be) with a corresponding array of ideas and ideals
3. An explicit government *policy* and programs (what is proposed)
4. A set of *practices* for promoting political and minority interests (what really is)
5. A *critical discourse* with a commitment to challenge and change (what must be)

Failure to separate these analytically different levels of meaning can create confusion because of the tendency people have to talk past each other—using the same words but speaking a different language.

Multiculturalism as Fact

As fact, multiculturalism makes an empirical statement about "what is." It may be stating the obvious, but the obvious is sometimes overlooked for precisely that reason; that is, most countries are ethnically diverse, composed of people from a variety of different backgrounds who speak, think, worship, and act differently. Nearly all countries comprise different racialized and ethnic groups whose identities are stoutly defended and demanding of recognition or resources. Members of these minority groups often wish to retain aspects of their culture, yet are equally anxious to reap the benefits of full societal involvement.

Employed in the descriptive sense of the term, few would dispute the "fact" of Canada as a multicultural society. The existence of Aboriginal peoples, French and English charter group members, and multicultural minorities attests to this empirical fact of reality (Elliott, 1983). Adding to this multilayered variety is the realization that Canadians have been drawn from 170 different countries and speak over 200 different languages (Kalbach & Kalbach, 1999). Recent immigration patterns suggest a continuation of this diversity trend (see Chapters 1, 4, and 9 for breakdowns of ethnic diversity in Canada).

Multiculturalism as Ideology

Unlike its descriptive counterpart, multiculturalism as an **ideology** refers to a prescriptive statement of "what ought to be." It prescribes a set of beliefs about creating a society of many cultures in which people cooperatively coexist without capitulating to chaos. Canadians have long prided themselves on being a tolerant society, with numerous national polls demonstrating consistent public support for Canada's multicultural mosaic. To be sure, this endorsement varies with time and place, often lacks enthusiasm, is conditional, and is easily revoked when costs outstrip benefits. Nevertheless, multiculturalism remains pivotal as a defining characteristic, an embodiment of "Canadianness," and proof that living in a pluralistic society provides a richer experience than in a monocultural society (Kymlicka, 2005). In general, references to a multicultural ideology acknowledge that a society of many cultures is better than monocultural society; a commitment to multicultural principles is preferred over assimilation as a policy alternative; and culturally diverse communities can coexist as long as certain ground rules prevail.

Several assumptions underlie a multicultural ideology. First, a belief that people are social beings whose well-being depends on a shared cultural identity. Minority cultures constitute living and lived-in realities that are valued in their own right, while imparting a sheen of security during times of stress or social change (Kymlicka, 1995). Affiliation with one's cultural kind does not imply an element of mental inferiority, stubbornness, or lack of patriotism. Rather, these differences are important and of benefit to both individuals and society at large if properly "managed." Second, multiculturalism does not dismiss difference as contrary to the goals of national unity or societal progress. Instead, cultural differences are endorsed as integral components of a national mosaic, a reflection of the Canadian ideal, and a source of unity and strength. Third, a multicultural ideal builds upon the principles of **cultural relativism**. This doctrine holds that all cultural practices are relative to a particular time and place, take their meaning from this context, and must be understood accordingly. That is not to say that everything *is* equally good; nor is anyone espousing the philosophy that "anything goes." On the contrary, a critically informed relativism approaches diversity *as if* it were an equally valid expression of the human experience. Fourth, a commitment to multiculturalism is predicated on the premise that those confident in their cultural background will concede a similar tolerance to others (Berry, Kalin, & Taylor, 1977). Or as Trudeau explained back in 1971, if national unity is to mean anything in the deeply personal sense, it must be anchored in confidence in one's own identity, for it is out of this respect for others that a sharing of ideas and assumptions is fostered (see Forbes, 2007).

There is yet another ideological slant to multiculturalism. Rather than a "happy face" ideology around the virtues of tolerance and celebrating diversity, an official Multiculturalism can be interpreted as a hegemonic discourse in advancing dominant ideology ("ruling elites controlling unruly ethnics"). Much of what passes for multiculturalism is little more than an exercise in conflict resolution and impression management whose primary goal is to "cool out" those troublesome constituents who are problems or create problems (Bannerji, 2000; Thobani, 2007). On one side, the ideas and ideals associated with multiculturalism are critical in securing an unequal status quo behind the folksy facade of national interests. On the other side, it embraces an ideology that promotes the interests of vested groups at the expense of the population at large. In short, the ideological aspect of multiculturalism reflects its status as false consciousness. Multiculturalism not only dulls the public senses to the continuing marginalization of migrants and minorities—a kind of opiate of the masses—but also lulls people into a false sense of security by conveying the impression of improvement. Emphasis on the "culture" in multiculturalism also has the effect of papering over the structural sources of division and disadvantage in society. To the extent that nothing of substance happens under a multicultural watch, although many are convinced that something does, no one should underestimate the power of a hegemonic ideology to divide and distract (see Ley, 2005).

Multiculturalism as Policy

Policy considerations are central to any official Multiculturalism (Magsino, 2000). Governments throughout the world have embarked on official strategies for controlling immigration, managing ethnic relations, accommodating differences, "cooling out" troublesome constituents, and integrating ethnocultural minorities into the mainstream (Hudson, 1987). Policy frameworks such as assimilation or segregation, which may have worked in the past, are increasingly inadequate for addressing contemporary minority demands. By contrast, multiculturalism represents an aspirational blueprint for living together with differences. It provides a principled framework for specific government initiatives to transform multicultural ideals into official programs and practice. In that Multiculturalism promotes the right to be different yet the same, as well as the right to be the same yet different, a new symbolic order is projected, one that addresses the integration of migrants and minorities by respecting differences while removing discriminatory barriers (Banting et al., 2007). Multiculturalism can also be interpreted within a broader normative framework that justifies the promotion of diversity programs without fear of inciting public concern over yet more government intrusion. This normative framework may not be openly articulated; nevertheless, it supplies the "underlying agenda" that legitimizes policy initiatives for enhancing a multicultural society–building project.

To say that Canada is officially Multicultural is extolling the obvious. Yet the irony is improbable. From its inception in 1971, when it barely garnered a paragraph in Canada's national newspaper, official Multiculturalism has evolved to the point where it constitutes a formidable component of Canada's national identity. It has profoundly altered how Canadians think about themselves and their relationship to the world (Forbes, 2007; Temelini, 2007; see also Henshaw, 2007, for the 1930s origins of multicultural thinking). Forty years of official Multiculturalism have proven pivotal in orchestrating a national consensus around majority acceptance of minority participation. Multiculturalism as a policy originated in the quest for integrative society-building functions. It continues to persist for precisely the same reasons, namely, the integration of migrants and minorities by modifying the rules of inclusion and settlement (Kymlicka, 2001). The goal of Multiculturalism has never wavered from its underlying commitment, which is the possibility of living together with differences, without the differences getting in the way of equal involvement or social order. Only the means for achieving the "cultural," the "social," and "national interests" have changed, evolving in response to demographic upheavals and political developments, with ethnicity-based solutions giving way to equity-grounded reforms and, more recently, the promotion of citizenship, belonging, and cohesion. For the sake of simplicity, these shifts can be partitioned into four overlapping policy stages: *ethnicity*, *equity*, *civic*, and *integrative*.

Ethnicity Multiculturalism Canada's official Multiculturalism arose following the publication of the Report of the Royal Commission on Bilingualism and Biculturalism in 1969. The findings of the Royal Commission had concluded that Canada comprised a multicultural commonwealth of "other ethnics," albeit within the bicultural (or binational) framework of two founding peoples. Various ethnic minority groups, especially the Ukrainians and Germans, had lobbied vigorously, arguing that their languages and cultures were as vital as Quebec's to Canada-building (Jaworsky, 1979; see also Lupul, 2005; Temelini, 2007). They rejected the notion of Canada as the union of two founding nations, with its implication that some Canadians were more deserving than others. Proposed instead was a descriptive ideal that captured the contribution of the "other ethnics" to the cultural enrichment of a bicultural Canada. Pressure to create a symbolic multicultural order was further heightened by the need to depoliticize the autonomist forces of Québécois nationalism in the aftermath of the Quiet Revolution (Breton, 1989). Finally, with "Britishness" losing its saliency in Canada and elsewhere (see Jakubowicz, 2005), Multiculturalism emerged as an ideological glue for bonding Canadians, based on a vision of Canada as a multicultural mosaic of equality-seeking individuals rather than a colonial outpost.

A commitment to multiculturalism within a bilingual framework was subsequently articulated by the Liberal government when Prime Minister Pierre Elliott Trudeau rose in Parliament on 8 October 1971 and declared his government's intentions to embrace "multiculturalism within a bilingual framework." As many have noted, multiculturalism originated in response to Trudeau's disdain for both British and French nationalism, whose ethnonational tyrannies compromised individual rights and the right of choice. Trudeau sought to abolish culture and rootedness as justification for superior entitlement. By putting all Canadians on an equal footing regardless of their culture or immigrant status, Trudeau's goal was a Canada in which members of different nationalities intermingled as neighbours on a common territory, without discarding their distinct cultural identities *if they chose to do so* (Cameron, 2004; Forbes, 2007). For Trudeau, the linking of individual rights with equal status under multiculturalism would "strengthen the solidarity of the Canadian people by enabling all Canadians to participate fully and without discrimination in defining and building the nation's future." Four major principles secured this aspirational aim to realign Canada along multicultural lines:

• *Equality of status*: Canada does not have an official culture; all cultures are equal.

• *Canadian identity*: Diversity lies at the heart of Canadian identity.

- *Personal choice*: Individuals have the right to identify with the cultural tradition of their choice.
- *Protection of individual rights*: Individuals have the right to be free from discrimination.

To put these principles into practice, the government proposed initiatives to (1) assist those cultural groups that demonstrated a commitment to share and contribute to Canada; (2) assist the members of all cultural groups to overcome cultural barriers to full participation in Canadian society; (3) promote creative encounters and exchanges among all Canadian cultural groups in advancing national unity; and (4) assist immigrants to acquire at least one of Canada's official languages to ensure full and equal participation.

In short, an ethnicity multiculturalism was not about celebrating ethnocultural differences; if anything, it hoped to eliminate those cultural prejudices that denied or excluded. A commitment to ethnocultural preservation was not high on the multicultural agenda— at least not beyond an initial commitment when powerful ethnic lobbyists prevailed. Ethnicity multiculturalism went beyond a simple "be nice to different people" focus, with emphasis instead on improving minority and migrant integration into an inclusive society (Donaldson, 2004). It sought not only to promote national unity, in the belief that those secure in their culture would reciprocate accordingly, but also to simultaneously make ethnicity irrelevant as an indicator of privilege or a marker of identity for ranking Canadians or allocating power (Kruhlak, 2003). To the extent that cultural diversity was respected and protected, ethnicity multiculturalism focused on integrating new Canadians through their ethnic identity rather than offering unqualified preservation of their differences. Conditions applied to this social contract, including: (1) all new Canadians should have a primary commitment to Canada; (2) all new Canadians must accept Canada's fundamental structures, principles, and values; (3) all new Canadians had the right to identify with the culture of their choice, provided these choices did not violate people's rights, break the law, or contravene core constitutional values; and (4) all new Canadians had the right to share their cultural differences with other Canadians (Cardozo & Musto, 1997).

Equity Multiculturalism The focus of official Multiculturalism shifted noticeably by the early 1980s. Instead of emphasizing the centrality of identity and ethnicity, Multiculturalism discourses embraced the more equity-driven concerns of racialized immigrants. The often different requirements of visible minority immigrants, compared to those of European "ethnics," proved more perplexing. For new immigrants, their visibility complicated the process and prospect of integration; as a result, the need for dismantling racial barriers to opportunity had to prevail over the celebration of their cultural differences (McRoberts, 1997). The earlier emphasis on ethnicity and identity as keys to integration was subsequently replaced by a commitment to equity, social justice, and institutional inclusiveness (Agocs & Boyd, 1993; Donaldson, 2004). Funding allocations were adjusted accordingly. Rather than simply doling out vast sums to ethnocultural organizations or events, as had hitherto been the case, authorities shifted toward equity goals related to anti-racism, race relations, and removal of discriminatory barriers at institutional levels.

Subsequent developments further advanced the political profile of official Multiculturalism. The *Canadian Charter of Rights and Freedoms*, which came into effect in 1985, constitutionally entrenched Multiculturalism as a distinguishing feature of Canadian life. The emergence of Multiculturalism as a tool of interpretation at the highest levels of constitutional decision making reinforced its status as a fundamental characteristic of Canada. Its prominence was further advanced when Canada became the world's first and only officially Multicultural country with the passage of the *Canadian Multiculturalism Act* in 1988. Passage of the Act aspired to promote cultures, reduce discrimination, and accelerate institutional inclusiveness through the "preservation and enhancement of Canadian multiculturalism." In that the *Canadian Multiculturalism Act* completed the Canada-building project associated with the passage of the *Official Languages Act* of 1969, the Statement on Multiculturalism in 1971, and its enshrinement in the *Constitution Act* of 1982, its significance cannot be understated. Each of these initiatives converged to create a distinctly Canadian society based on the integrative principle that individuals are self-defining and morally autonomous agents who should participate equally regardless of differences (Breton, 2001).

Civic Multiculturalism With the election of the Liberals in 1993, the fortunes of official Multiculturalism began to decline. The stand-alone but short-lived Department of Multiculturalism and Citizenship was subsequently deprived of its lofty status and folded into the super-ministry of Canadian Heritage under a Secretary of State (Multiculturalism and Canadian Identity). In an era of government cutbacks, Multiculturalism proved a soft target, attracting criticism from both the right and the left (Bibby, 1990; Bissoondath, 1994), despite its ongoing commitment to social equality and cultural respect. Concerns that Multiculturalism was losing its popularity because it lacked relevance for both mainstream and racialized Canadians prompted calls for rethinking the multicultural agenda. A more inclusive multiculturalism—civic multiculturalism—began to emerge, directed at a shared national unity by "break[ing] down the ghettoization of multiculturalism," as aptly phrased by Hedy Fry (1997), former minister for Multiculturalism.

A repackaged Multiculturalism program was formalized in 1996 around three strategic goals: (1) civic participation (full and equal involvement), (2) social justice (equitable treatment), and (3) identity (fostering a Canada in which all Canadians feel a sense of attachment and belonging regardless of their background). In 2002, four priority objectives were articulated: (1) fostering cross-cultural understanding and awareness of racism, (2) combating racism and discrimination, (3) promoting shared citizenship, and (4) developing more responsive and representative institutions (Department of Canadian Heritage, 2005). To achieve these objectives, the Multiculturalism programs focused on the following: (1) institutional change (inclusiveness through removal of discriminatory barriers); (2) federal institutional change (integrating diversity into policies, programs, and services); (3) combating racism (including removing discriminatory barriers, and promoting anti-racism programs and cross-cultural understanding); and (4) civic engagement (promoting active and shared citizenship as well as building capacity for minorities to participation in public decision making) (Canadian Heritage, 2005/6). In short, a **civic multiculturalism** was oriented toward Canada-building by way of shared citizenship, with an emphasis on fostering a sense of belonging, a civic engagement, an active involvement in community life, and a shared awareness of Canadian identity and Canada's national interests.

Integrative Multiculturalism Multiculturalism has evolved into a new phase whose operative focus is integration. In reacting to perceived fears of social fragmentation and ethnic isolation because of differences in immigrant values and social patterns, the minister for Citizenship, Immigration, and Multiculturalism, Jason Kenney, has proposed a fundamental shift toward immigrant integration and community cohesion in hopes of depoliticizing diversities and difference while de-radicalizing the threat of homegrown extremism (Freeze, 2008; Kunz & Sykes, 2007). In a speech entitled, "Good Citizenship: the Duty to Integrate," Kenney argued that any embrace of diversity must be balanced by a prior commitment to value consensus, that is, ". . . on the political values that are grounded in our history, the values of liberal democracy rooted in British Parliamentary democracy that precisely have given us the space to accommodate such diversity" (as cited in Marwah & Triadafilopoulos, 2009). Not surprisingly, according to the *Annual Report on the Operation of the* Canadian Multiculturalism Act *2008–2009*, the government has implemented a unity and diversity approach to multiculturalism around three main policy objectives: (1) to build an integrated and socially cohesive society by promoting civic literacy and engagement among all Canadians; (2) to make federal institutions more responsive to Canada's diverse populations through removing discriminatory barriers and fostering intercultural understanding; and (3) to promote Canadian values abroad by engaging in international discussions on multiculturalism and diversity (Citizenship and Immigration Canada, 2010).

To sum up, Canada's official Multiculturalism represents a complex and contested policy that has evolved over time in response to social and political changes (Seiler, 2002). Despite shifts in emphasis—from ethnicity to equity to civic to integrative—an official Multiculturalism has never wavered from its central mission: an inclusive Canada-building through immigrant integration (Kymlicka, 1998a, 2001). An official Multiculturalism as governance represents a politically driven commitment for building an inclusive society through removal of prejudice and discriminatory barriers, so that no one is excluded from full and equal participation because of race or ethnicity. Only the means have changed over time. Table 10-2 compares and contrasts the different stages in the evolution of Canada's official Multiculturalism, keeping in mind the inevitability of simplification when comparing ideal-typical categories in a world that is contextual rather than categorical.

A policy overview also exposes another dimension of Canada's official Multiculturalism: A state-backed Multiculturalism is *not* about (1) celebrating differences, (2) promoting ethnic minorities or group rights, (3) fostering parallel communities, (4) transforming structures or challenging liberal democratic principles, (5) addressing politicized or deep differences, or (6) advocating an "anything goes" mentality. Rather, Canada's official Multiculturalism promotes a principled governance framework that establishes the rules for living together with differences (1) without the differences getting in the way of living together; (2) by making society safe for differences and safe from differences; and (3) by creating an accommodating social climate and responsive institutional framework that (a) rejects racism and racial discrimination, (b) endorses the principles of equity regardless of ethnic background, and (c) fosters an environment in which newcomers feel a sense of interconnectedness to Canada and other Canadians. And most important, in advancing the principle of inclusion through the removal of discriminatory barriers and a respect for cultural differences, an inclusive multiculturalism emphasizes the centrality of political equality, social justice, and full participation as the governance model for living together with diversities and differences (Rodriguez-Garcia, 2010).

TABLE 10-2	Policy Shifts in Canada's Official Multiculturalism: A Work In Progress			
	Ethnicity multiculturalism (1970s)	Equity multicul- turalism (1980s– early 1990s)	Civic multicul- turalism (1995–2005)	Integrative multicultural- ism (2006– present)
Dimension	Cultural	Structural	Social	Societal
Focus	Respecting differences	Fostering equality	Living together	Integration
Mandate	Ethnicity	Race relations	Civic culture	Citizenship
Magnitude	Individual adjustment	Institutional accommodation	Full engage- ment	National safety/security
Problem	Prejudice	Racism/ discrimination	Exclusion	Segregation/ extremism
Solution	Cultural sensitivity	Removal of barriers	Inclusion	Shared Cana- dian values
Outcomes	Cultural capital	Human capital	Social capital	National com- munity
Key metaphor	"Mosaic"	"Level playing field"	"Strengthening the bonds"	"Strangers becoming neighbours"

Multiculturalism as Practice

Glowing accolades about celebrating and sharing cannot disguise what many have long suspected: The implementation of multiculturalism as ideology does not always translate into practices consistent with policy principles. Multiculturalism as practice refers to its application for advancing a broad range of goals, agendas, and priorities. Politicians and bureaucrats look upon multiculturalism as a resource with economic or political potential to be exploited at national or international levels for practical gain. To the dismay of many, Canada's official Multiculturalism originated as a political program to achieve political goals in a politically astute manner (Peter, 1978). The governing apparatus of the Canadian state relied on Multiculturalism to fulfill a variety of legitimating functions involving national unity, economic prosperity, and electoral survival (see also Bharucha, 2000). At its inception, official Multiculturalism hoped to formulate a new founding myth of Canada as a land of opportunity and equality, thus uniting all Canadians at a time of political turmoil, but without any fundamental redistribution of power (Helly, 1993). It also sought to shore up electoral strength in urban Ontario, to counterbalance Western resentment over perceived favouritism toward the Québécois, to preempt the encroachment of American cultural values, and to thwart intergroup strife because of competing priorities. In short, official Multiculturalism parlayed a potential weakness into strength without sacrificing a commitment to social cohesion, national identity, domestic peace, economic advantage, and global status (Kurthen, 1997).

The politics of multiculturalism are closely linked with party politics. From nomination struggles to ethnic coalitions, multicultural politics at the crassest level reflect a belief in ethnic support as relevant for (re-)election. The vast majority of Canada's multicultural minorities are concentrated in the MTV centres of Montreal, Toronto, and Vancouver—a trend likely to be amplified by future immigration patterns. (For example, the percentage of immigrants in Ontario ridings based on 2004 electoral boundaries included Scarborough Rouge River at 66.8 percent and Scarborough Agincourt at 64.5 percent (Jedwab, 2005). Or consider that 37 of the 44 ridings in the Toronto region voted Liberal in the 2003 federal election (repeated again in 2006), thanks in part to the immigrant vote. But new Canadians are increasingly voting Conservative. In the 2008 federal election, the Conservatives scored wins in six ridings with visible minority/immigrant populations of 20 percent or more. Moreover, 33 percent of immigrants voted for the Conservatives in the 2008 election, compared with 38 percent for the Liberals (a drop from 55 percent in 2000). This trend continued into the 2011 federal election in which the Conservatives capitalized on the ethnic vote to a resounding win, including 30 of the 44 seats in the greater Toronto region (Swan, 2011). Interestingly, new legislation proposed by the Conservatives would add 30 seats to the House of Commons, with all new urban ridings consisting predominantly of large immigrant/visible minority populations (Ibbitson & Friesen, 2010). The continuing heterogeneity of Canada's population will further prompt political parties to pursue the multicultural vote through promises of increased representation, funding, and employment equity initiatives.

Also widely touted is the commercial potential of multiculturalism. Former prime minister Brian Mulroney promoted a business model of multiculturalism rooted in economic rationality and self-interest in his "Multiculturalism Means Business" speech at a Toronto conference in 1986. The commercial value of multiculturalism remains stronger than ever because of the demands of a global economy. Diversity and the market are closely intertwined because capitalizing on differences is seen as good for the economy, especially when 40 percent of Canada's GDP is export based:

> The ethnocultural diversity of Canada's population is a major advantage when access to global markets is more important than ever to our economic prosperity. Protecting this advantage means that steps to eradicate racism are essential. Canada cannot afford to have any of its citizens marginalized. As a knowledge-based economy in an increasingly global marketplace, every mind matters. All Canadians must have the opportunity to develop and contribute to their full potential. (Canadian Heritage, 2001)

Multiculturalism continues to be promoted as a valuable export, just as staple products were in the past (Abu-Laban & Gabriel, 2002). By enhancing Canada's sales image and competitive edge in a global economy—particularly by cultivating and tapping into the lucrative Asian market—references to multiculturalism are touted as having the potential to harness lucrative trade contracts, establish international linkages and mutually profitable points of contact, attract members of the transnational elite, and penetrate export markets. By playing the "ethnic harmony card," the promotion of multiculturalism as an ideology of cooperative coexistence and worldly cosmopolitanism provides reassurance for nervous investors and fidgety capital (Mitchell, 1993). Finally, as the globalization of capitalist market economies continues to expand, multiculturalism may well provide the networking for confronting the challenges of a shifting and increasingly borderless reality that may be the twenty-first century norm. The conclusion seems inescapable: In that multicultural priorities will continue to be driven by an economic agenda more interested in improving Canada's competitive advantage than in securing institutional inclusiveness, the business side of Multiculturalism should never be discounted.

Multicultural minorities are no less inclined to adopt multiculturalism as a resource for attaining practical goals (Burnet, 1981; Qadeer, 2007). Minorities have basic needs: As a group, they want to become established, expand economic opportunities for themselves and their children, eliminate discrimination and exploitation, and retain access to their cultural heritage without loss of citizenship rights. Multiculturalism is employed as a tool for meeting these needs through elimination of discriminatory barriers in employment, education, housing, and criminal justice. After all, racialized minorities and immigrants may have the same rights as all Canadians, including the right to be free of discrimination. But they must live (from survive to prosper) in a racialized Canada that is *neither designed for their use or advancement nor reflective of their experiences, realities, or aspirations.* With official Multiculturalism, minority women and men are empowered with a platform and a tool for staking out their claims while articulating their demands alongside those of Aboriginal peoples and the Québécois. Multiculturalism also empowers an otherwise powerless sector with the leverage to prod or provoke central policy structures. By holding central authorities accountable for failure to connect multicultural ideals with everyday results, appeals to official Multiculturalism are thus calculated to extract public sympathy and global scrutiny—in the same way as Canada's Aboriginal peoples have relied on international fora (such as the United Nations) to leverage concessions from the federal government. For minorities, then, the driving force behind multiculturalism is equality, not diversity; integration, not isolation; and inclusion, not separation. (See Chapter 11 for additional material on the practice of multiculturalism at institutional levels.)

Multiculturalism as Critical/Transformative Discourse

An inclusive multiculturalism is not the only multicultural game in town (Fleras, 2009a). Different multicultural discourses can be discerned that challenge, resist, and transform rather than advocate consensus, conformity, and control. As a transformative discourse of resistance, **critical multiculturalism** challenges the authority and legitimacy of the status quo by contesting the prevailing distribution of power and privilege. A critical multiculturalism transcends the simple construction of identities, celebration of differences, or commitment to tolerance. It goes beyond a United Colors of Benetton pluralism with its corporate-orchestrated tastes, appearances, sensations, and colours—a consumer-driven approach to ethnic diversity that does little to transform institutional inequalities (May, 2004).

The politicization of culture is proposed as grounds for living together differently. As a philosophy of criticism and protest, critical multiculturalism views cultural institutions (like education or media) as fundamentally racist in that they privilege Western values at the expense of minority struggles, identities, and aspirations (Early, 1993). Criticism is directed at the legacy of European ethnocentrism, with its cramming of difference into a single paradigm, its positing of Europe as the apex of evolutionary progress, its self-appointed right to do what it pleases, and its sanitizing of Western exploitation and human rights abuses (Stam & Shohat, 1994). Differences do not merely exist under critical multiculturalism; they are a critical part of the struggle to create a new public culture (Kurien, 2006). Inasmuch as minority interests are openly contesting the shaping of institutional knowledge from education to media, the politics of critical multiculturalism are transformative in content and style (Frederickson, 1999).

To be sure, critical multicultural discourses exist in Canada (Thobani, 2000a, 2000b). But transformative multiculturalisms receive much more publicity in the United States, where challenging the "dominant silencing of diversity" (Eisenstein, 1996, 2004) fosters a framework by which new identities are (re)formulated, new communities are constructed, knowledge and power are contested, and Eurocentric universalisms are exposed for what they are: self-serving discourses in defence of dominant ideology. In contrast with Canada's consensus-oriented inclusive multiculturalism, the postmodernist discourses that animate America's critical multiculturalism subvert as they resist. A critical multiculturalism transcends the constraints of official policy initiatives, primarily because it's unhampered by the demands and accountabilities of the political process or electoral pandering. In challenging the prevailing distribution of social power, the counter-hegemonic discourses of critical multiculturalism oppose Eurocentricity by relativizing the white capitalist patriarchy with its exclusionary designs on the "other" (Eisenstein, 1996; Giroux, 1994).

By contrast, Canada's Multiculturalism model is essentially an inclusive society-building exercise that seeks to depoliticize (rather than celebrate) differences through institutional accommodation and removal of discriminatory barriers. It is proposed that better conditions for living together with differences can be achieved by ensuring that everyone is treated equally and that no one is excluded because of their differences, yet acknowledging that differences may be taken into account when necessary to ensure treatment as equals. An inclusive multiculturalism is grounded in the liberal universalist credo that our commonalities as rights-bearing, equality-seeking individuals are more important than that which divides us through group membership. The logic of a consensus (or inclusive) multiculturalism is concerned with drawing people into the framework of an existing Canada ("fitting in") rather than in bringing about transformative social change. Its focus on changing attitudes instead of structure makes it abundantly clear: Canada's official Multiculturalism may be interpreted as a discourse of domination whose primary goal is to cool out potentially troublesome constituents. Clearly, then, a "playful" inversion underscores these dueling discourses. Rather than making difference safe from society as well as safe for society, as is the case with critical multiculturalism, official Multiculturalism purports to depoliticize difference by making society safe from difference yet safe for difference. Table 10-3 provides a brief comparison.

TABLE 10-3 Duelling Multiculturalisms	
Canada's official (consensus) multiculturalism	**Critical multiculturalism in the United States**
Modernist project (unity; universalism)	Postmodernist (diversity; particularism)
Society-building	Society dismantling
Depoliticizing differences	Politicizing differences
Consensus	Challenge
Controlling	Empowering
Fitting in	Getting out
Hegemonic (making Canada safe from difference)	Counter-hegemonic (making difference safe from the United States)

PUBLIC PERCEPTIONS/CRITICAL REACTIONS

Of the conceptual tripwires and cultural landmines strewn across the Western landscape in recent years, few have triggered as much vitriol or controversy as multiculturalism (Gilroy, 2004; Possner, 1997). Timing in particular has played politics with a modernist project that many regard as passé for the post-9/11 (and 7/7 in London) realities of the twenty-first century. The introduction of multiculturalism as a popular and political discourse may have originated in an era of optimism and reform, but it is badly listing at present because of concerns over security (Rex & Singh, 2004; see also Gregg, 2006). What started out as a society-building idea with noble intentions (to assist newcomers into Canada) has evolved into a flashpoint for tension. On one side are those advocates who continue to worship at the altar of multiculturalism; on another side are those who recoil at the very prospect of foisting yet more mystification on an unsuspecting public; on yet another side are those critics who sneer at something so irrelevant or counterproductive (see Ley, 2005).

Public Perceptions

Public perception of multiculturalism in Canada is varied. Some Canadians are vigorously supportive; others are in total rejection or denial; still others are indifferent; and yet others are plainly uninformed (see Cardozo & Musto, 1997; Cameron, 2004). For some, multiculturalism is at the root of many of Canada's problems; for others, multiculturalism is too often scapegoated for everything that goes wrong when minorities are involved (Kymlicka, 2007; Siddiqui, 2007). The majority appears to be caught somewhere in between, depending on their reading of multiculturalism and its contribution (or lack thereof) to Canadian society. Variables such as age, income, level of education, and place of residence are critical in gauging support, with higher levels of approval among the younger, more affluent, better educated, and urban (Anderssen & Valpy, 2003). While many may be critical of Canada's official Multiculturalism—after all, it's a proven scapegoat for the sins of a society undergoing rapid changes and increased diversity (Ley, 2007)—few Canadians actually know what federal and provincial governments are doing to promote the idea, prompting this reaction from Jack Jedwab, the executive director of the Association for Canadian Studies: "People don't know that much about the policy. There's a giant leap—probably one of the biggest public policy gaps that I've seen—between the extent to which people know about the policy and the regular criticism of it." (as cited in Boswell, 2010). To the extent that many Canadians are unsure of what Canada's official Multiculturalism is trying to do, how, and why, the prospect of living differently together equitably and in dignity is compromised.

Public support for official Multiculturalism is open to debate. Opinion polls are known to provide different answers, depending on the kind of questions asked. Nevertheless, national surveys on multiculturalism suggest a solid base of support often in the 60 to 70 percent range (ACS/Environics, 2002; Angus Reid Group, 1991; Berry, 2006; Cardozo & Musto, 1997; Dasko, 2005; Jedwab, 2005; Nanos, 2010). Yet support for official Multiculturalism is not as transparent as the data suggest. First, Canadians may be supportive of multiculturalism, but only on principle or as a demographic fact: At the same time, they may reject Multiculturalism as official policy or mistakenly conflate

Multiculturalism with unpopular government programs like employment equity. Second, support is not the same as enthusiasm: Canadians appear to embrace multiculturalism as a reality to be tolerated rather than an ideal to be emulated or a passion to be pursued. Third, support or rejection tends to be selective and inconsistent: Most Canadians support some aspect of multiculturalism, but are conflicted over issues of accommodation (Collacott, 2006; Jedwab, 2004) or unintended consequences; they may harbour worries over Multiculturalism as the thin edge of the wedge for justifying practices at odds with mainstream values or for fostering conditions that breed terrorism, discourage integration, or encourage ghettoization (Baubock, 2005; Friesen, 2005). Fourth, support is conditional: Canadians are prepared to accept Multiculturalism if costs are low and demands are reasonable for assisting new Canadians to settle in, removing discriminatory barriers, learning about others, and promoting tolerance (Gwyn, 1996). Support is withdrawn when endorsement is seen as eroding Canada's sense of national unity and identity, challenging authority or core values, curbing the integration of cultural communities, criticizing the mainstream, breaking the law, or acquiescing to the demands of particular groups (Simpson, 2005).

Critical Reactions

Official Multiculturalism is unevenly supported across Canada (Duncan, 2005). Residents of Ontario and western Canada appear receptive to Multiculturalism, but the Québécois and Aboriginal peoples have spurned it (Bouchard & Taylor, 2008; Breton, 2001; Ignace & Ignace, 1998; Kymlicka, 2001). The concerns of "nations within" go beyond those of disadvantage or difference but focus, instead, on the injustices and disempowerment resulting from Canada's society-building project (Baubock, 2005). Instead of self-defining themselves as immigrants who want to "get in" (using the language of multiculturalism), both Aboriginal peoples and the Québécois prefer the language of nationalism, that is, "getting out" (Maaka & Fleras, 2005; Murphy, 2005). An official Multiculturalism cannot possibly address the demands of fundamentally autonomous political communities; nor is it equipped to handle the highly politicized discourses of challenge and transformation (McRoberts, 2001). Still, Quebec possesses its own program of official multiculturalism entitled *interculturalism*, with its connotation of an interactive process of participation, engagement, and social exchange (Rodriguez-Garcia, 2010). (See online Insight 8.3.)

Many political observers and social critics have criticized Canada's multicultural agenda (see Fleras, 2002, for a review). Multiculturalism is seen as divisive because of its tendency to tolerate practices incompatible with Canada's central core. It is also accused of hypocrisy in offering the illusion of tolerance while punishing behaviour at odds with core values (Stoffman, 2002, 2007). Some dismiss official Multiculturalism as a bad idea that's performing as poorly as many had predicted. It originated to pander to ethnic interests, persists as little more than an opiate for the masses, and remains a divisive force in Canadian society. Others are no less dismissive of Multiculturalism, calling it a good idea gone bad. Still others dismiss Multiculturalism as a largely aspirational document: It not only fails to clearly articulate objectives and expectations but also lacks the force of implementation and enforcement. Noble intentions aside, critics contend, Multiculturalism continues to undermine the common good, in large part because both politicians and minority leaders have hijacked it for ulterior purposes. Even the much-touted mosaic metaphor comes in for criticism. Canada's multicultural discourses remain rooted in an understanding of ethnicity as primordial and essentialized rather than flexible, dynamic, and relational. Membership and participation in this mosaic locks individuals into hermetically sealed groups that are isolated from the rest of society—to the detriment of Canadian unity.

Still others pounce on official Multiculturalism regardless of what it does or doesn't do. Multiculturalism has been accused of being too radical or too reactionary, of promoting too much or not enough change, of promising more than it can deliver (a sheep in wolf's clothing) or delivering more than bargained for (a wolf in sheep's clothing). And while Multiculturalism may be embraced by many as a strength to be admired, it may be demonized and dismissed by others as a weakness to be condemned or exploited, as noted by Irshad Manji (2005):

> As Westerners bow before multiculturalism, we anesthetize ourselves into believing that anything goes. We see our readiness to accommodate as a strength—even a form of cultural superiority . . . Radical Muslims, on the other hand, see our inclusive instincts as a form of corruption that makes us soft and rudderless. They believe the weak deserve to be vanquished. Paradoxically, then, the more we accommodate to placate, the more their contempt for our "weakness" grows. And the ultimate paradox may be that in order to defend our diversity, we'll need to be less tolerant. (p. A19)

Academic opinion is mixed (see May, 2002). Critics on the left have pounced on Multiculturalism as ineffective except as a mantra for politicians to trot out for publicity purposes. Multiculturalism is criticized as a colossal hoax perpetuated by vested interests to ensure minority co-optation through ideological indoctrination (false consciousness) (Thobani, 1995). Excessive emphasis on diversity and culture and insufficient focus on racism and racialized structures pose a serious challenge to inclusion and justice. As a capitalist plot to divide and distract the working classes, Multiculturalism is condemned for ghettoizing minorities into occupational structures and residential arrangements, thereby lubricating the prevailing distribution of power and wealth behind a smokescreen of well-oiled platitudes (Bannerji, 2000; Dei, 2000). Not surprisingly, Multiculturalism is rejected as little more than an interim measure for absorbing minorities rather than an authentic policy alternative—an "assimilation in slow motion" behind a facade of diversity intentions. Or to put a none too fine spin on it, Multiculturalism represents a clever device by ruling elites to control unruly ethnics (Hage, 1998).

Those on the right repudiate Multiculturalism as a costly drain on resources that runs the risk of eroding national unity. Worse still, Stewart Bell writes in *Cold Terror: How Canada Nurtures and Exports Terrorism around the World* (2004), the openness of Multiculturalism makes Canada vulnerable to infiltration by terrorists (Collacott, 2006). Moderates may be unsure of where to stand. Official Multiculturalism may sound good in theory, but implementation may falter because of difficulties in balancing unity with diversity. For example, while its intent may be to facilitate the integration of immigrants and secure their loyalty, Multiculturalism may have the perverse effect of strengthening immigrants' attachment to their homeland by way of diasporic nationalisms (Kurien, 2006). Conversely, while Multiculturalism may provide minorities with a platform for promoting distinctiveness, the very act of participation may have the reverse effect of absorbing minorities into the dominant culture (Pearson, 2001). Or alternatively,

Multiculturalism is long on principle and promise, but has proven short on delivery except to convey an air of mutual indifference in which Canadians share geographic and political space but little else (Ignatieff, 2001).

The conclusion seems inescapable: In its role as the self-appointed catalyst for social engineering, multiculturalism has attracted its share of criticism—even in the country where it was first articulated and is most fully institutionalized (Ley, 2005). National shortcomings for some reason tend to polarize around the multicultural management of minority relations (Siddiqui, 2007). This is hardly surprising, since criticism and contro- versy are generated by the disconnect between what an official Multiculturalism says it does versus (1) what it really means to do, (2) what it really does, (3) what it can realis- tically do, and (4) what the public and critics think it should be doing compared to what they think it is doing or is meant to do. For example, Multiculturalism is so ill defined that immigrants are understandably confused about what is permissible and what is not, thus encouraging a belief that Canada is committed to accepting and adapting to what- ever customs they bring with them into the country Not surprisingly, when asked how he saw Multiculturalism 20 years after its inception, Trudeau responded that it had been twisted to celebrate differences rather than to improve newcomer integration into Canada—the original intent was not for newcomers to retreat into their ethnic corners, but to enjoy full participation through creative encounters (as cited in Cobb, 1995).

But while much of this criticism may be valid, it is not entirely accurate (see also Ryan, 2010). Criticism of Multiculturalism may not reflect a looming backlash any more than silence is proof of its acceptance. To the extent that criticism is vocal, the disgrun- tlement may arise from growing discontent among the already disenchanted rather than a new legion of malcontents. And it is difficult to determine what exactly people dislike about Multiculturalism—the principle, the policy, the practice? A sense of perspective is helpful: In that both critics and supporters gloss over the underlying logic of Multicul- turalism, those who stoutly defend Multiculturalism at all costs are as ideological as those who disparage it for lacking any redeeming value. In that there are many publics, all with different expectations and needs, the impact of official Multiculturalism is nei- ther all good nor all bad; rather, it may be both good and bad, depending on the context, criteria, and consequences. In other words, as demonstrated below, Multiculturalism may be both good *and* bad simultaneously, liberating yet marginalizing, unifying yet divisive, inclusive yet exclusive, beneficial yet costly. Consider the following paradoxes:

- On one side, an official Multiculturalism is dismissed as divisive in that it undermines the basis of Canadian unity and identity (see also Ryan, 2010). Too literal an interpre- tation of multiculturalism can generate reified and essentialist group distinctions that foster group stereotyping and negative out-group sentiments at odds with the attain- ment of social cohesion and national unity (see Verkuyten, 2007). On the other side, Canada's official Multiculturalism is unifying in that it creates a blueprint for an inclu- sive Canada. A 2011 study by the European Commission concluded that Canada ranked third among 29 countries for the strength of integration policies and commit- ments (Jedwab, 2011). The virtues of sharing, interaction, and participation points to Multiculturalism as Canada-building by improving the process of integration for minorities rather than condoning the creation of segregated ethnic communities with separate power bases (Kostash, 2000; McRoberts, 2004).

- On one side, Multiculturalism may be seen as regressive in its ghettoizing or stigmatizing of minorities. Neil Bissoondath (1994) has castigated a Multiculturalism that aids in the containment and control of migrants and minorities while essentializing their identities in some frozen past. On the other side, Multiculturalism has proven integrative in reversing discrimination by creating a commitment to institutional inclusiveness. In building bridges rather than erecting walls, Canada's Multiculturalism encourages minority women and men to become involved, construct productive lives, and contribute to society (McGauran, 2005). Compared with immigrants in other countries, new Canadians are more likely to become citizens, engage in the political process, perform better in the economy (especially in the second generation), and experience social acceptance (Kymlicka, 2011). By incorporating efforts to remove discrimination, nurture civic engagement, foster cross-cultural understanding, and promote responsive institutions, Multiculturalism connotes a process for making the mainstream more inclusive rather than making minorities more multicultural (see Chan, 2003/4).

- On one side, Multiculturalism is criticized for not taking differences seriously because of preference for an empty pluralism. On the other side, Multiculturalism is criticized for taking differences too seriously, thus imperilling Canadian unity and identity. In reality, Multiculturalism is not about promoting diversity, but about unity through removal of differences-based discrimination. Multiculturalism provides a social climate that not only encourages an individual to affiliate with the cultural tradition of his or her choice but also ensures that cultural differences do not interfere with getting along, settling down, and fitting in.

- On one side, Multiculturalism may be accused of being a symbol without substance—a frivolous diversion with no power to challenge or transform. On the other side, Multiculturalism has presided over a radical remaking of Canada—from a transplanted mono-colonial enclave to a cosmopolitan society of many cultures and colours—in part by incorporating the symbols of diversity into the narratives of Canadian "nationhood" (Will Kymlicka in Gregg, 2006).

Table 10-4 captures the dialectics of an official Multiculturalism as simultaneously positive/beneficial and negative/costly. The left-hand column reflects the perceptions of those who believe that the consequences of Multiculturalism (both intended and inadvertent) are largely negative; as a result, Multiculturalism deserves criticism because of the costs it imposes and the problems it creates. On the other side are those who believe that the intent of Multiculturalism is positive; accordingly, Multiculturalism deserves support because of the benefits it inspires and the solutions it provides for living together with differences equitably and in dignity. The end result? Depending on the context and criteria, the impact of Multiculturalism can be both a problem and a solution that entails both costs and benefits.

In short, the impact and implications of official Multiculturalism are double-edged. In the same way that ethnicity can empower or divide, depending on the particular frame of reference, so too can a commitment to Multiculturalism both enhance and detract. Positive and negative effects coexist uneasily. That the benefits of Multiculturalism cannot be discounted reflects the ability of the powerless to convert the very tools for controlling them into levers of resistance and change (Pearson, 1994). Yet recourse to official Multiculturalism can depoliticize the potency of difference by channelling it into the private or personal. Far from being a threat to the social order, Canada's official

TABLE 10-4	Appraising Official Multiculturalism: Costs and Benefits	
Costs	**Benefits**
Divisive	**Inclusive**
• Destabilizes/conflicts	• Creates an inclusive Canada
• Undermines liberal values	• Emphasizes immigrant integration
• Erodes national unity/identity	• Fosters unity amid diversity
• Fosters "us" vs. "them" mentality	• Depoliticizes differences to reduce potential conflict
	• Removes difference-based barriers to full participation
Ghettoizing	**Integrating**
• Is inward looking	• Focuses on social, cultural, and economic integration
• Delays integration	• Provides anyone with opportunity
• Leads to ethnic enclaves	• Allows anyone to be Canadian regardless of race or ethnicity
• Fosters extremism	• Emphasizes a commitment to liberal universalism (we are basically alike as individuals)
• Essentializes by locking in	• Focuses on intergroup sharing, interaction, creative encounters, participation
Un-Canadian	**Pro-Canadian–building**
• Tolerates illiberal values	• Rejects differences that break the law, violate others' rights, and contravene core constitutional values
• Provides smokescreen for questionable values	
Exercise in political correctness	**Correcting for bias**
• Creates a reluctance to criticize	• Respects differences to ensure people feel good about themselves and reciprocate to others
• Creates a reluctance to say anything negative about government's diversity policies	
• More diversity = more uniformity	• Minimizes the language of hatred in public
Hoax as hegemony	**Catalyst for change**
• Acts as opiate of the masses	• Is a two-way process of mutual adjustment
• Creates false consciousness	• Is not transformational change but does modify existing arrangements
• Creates the illusion of inclusion	
• Creates the expectation of equality	• Focuses on changing attitudes and institutional reform
• Whitewashes racist past/present	
• Reduces racism to individual pathology	• Promotes the principle of reasonable accommodation
• Cools out troublesome constituents	
• Is impression management	• Makes racism unacceptable in Canada
• Is a political act to achieve political goals in a politically acceptable manner	

Multiculturalism constitutes a discourse in advancing the 1867 *Constitution Act* principle of "Peace, Order, and Good Government." Depending on where one stands on the political spectrum, this is a cause for concern or contentment.

A sense of perspective is useful. Multiculturalism is not the cause of Canada's problems, any more than it can be the cure-all (Belkhodja et al., 2006). There is no risk of Canada unravelling because of Multiculturalism: The politics of a "distinct society" and the "nations within" will see to that first. Nor should we get worked up over the absence of a common culture—as if Multiculturalism destroyed what never existed except, perhaps, within the context of a transplanted British Empire. Perhaps Canada's core value is the absence of any common culture except those shared values pertaining to basic decency, a respect for rule of law, a commitment to individual equality, and a constant quest for identity (see Sajoo, 1994). Difference, not uniformity, is Canada's strength, and to expect otherwise is unrealistic in a multilayered and deeply divided society organized around overlapping citizenships of the First Nations, the Québécois, and multicultural minorities. Disagreement and conflict are inevitable in such a deeply divided context. Just as shared ethnicity does not entail a unanimity of vision (Bissoondath, 1994), so too can a multicultural society survive on a multiplicity of voices and visions—provided that we agree on the principle of agreeing to disagree.

MULTICULTURALISM: DOING IT THE CANADIAN WAY

A commitment to multiculturalism has contributed to Canada's image as a progressive society. Some measure of proof is gleaned from accolades by high-flying personalities, including Bono of U2, who claims the world "needs more Canadas," and the Aga Khan, who extols Canada as the most "successful pluralist society" in the world (see Biles, Tolley, & Ibrahim, 2005, p. 25). Canada's lofty status as an enlightened multicultural society with an enviable standard of living is further confirmed by several UN panels. Finally, when compared with others, Canadians themselves seem to express markedly more positive attitudes toward immigration, multiculturalism, and difference, while taking pride in Canada's reputation as an open and inclusive society (Jedwab, 2005; Nanos, 2010).

Canada's worldwide reputation as a beacon of tolerance in an intolerant world is largely deserved. The fact that Canada has escaped much of the inter-ethnic strife that currently convulses many countries speaks well of its stature in proactively working through differences. The majority of Canadians, especially the younger and the well educated, are relatively open to diversity, with pride in Canada's multicultural heritage as a long-term investment in constructing a more vibrant society (see SBS, 2008; Anderssen & Valpy, 2003). Canada's success in integrating immigrants scores high by international standards, while official Multiculturalism may well prove pivotal in facilitating successful outcomes (Kymlicka, 2008). This tolerance is paying dividends abroad: According to an international survey commissioned by the Historica-Dominion Institute (2010) in partnership with the Munk School of Global Affairs and Aurea Foundation, more than half the people (53 percent) from the world's 24 leading economies say they would abandon their homelands and move to Canada if they could. Both potential and landed immigrants display high levels of pride in Canada (Adams, 2007) because of its freedom and democracy, quality of life, and tolerance for diversities—with the vast majority of newcomers taking out Canadian citizenship as soon as they can qualify (Bloemraad, 2006).

Other markers of success include the following:

- Compared with immigrants in other countries, Canadian immigrants are much more likely to be involved in the political process as voters, party members, and candidates who are actively recruited by political parties.
- The children of immigrants in Canada have better educational outcomes than the children of immigrants in any other Western democracy; as well, these second-generation Canadians outperform children of Canadian parents in terms of educational outcomes.
- The absence of immigrant ghettos in Canada would suggest high levels of social/ geographical integration. To be sure, immigrant/ethnic enclaves are common, but they embody a fundamentally different logic and different dynamics.
- Increasing levels of inter-racial marriage attest to growing immigration integration along multiculturalism lines (Kymlicka, 2008).

However, even whole-hearted support for multiculturalism is no excuse for glossing over its imperfections. In contrast with the grisliness of reality elsewhere, a commitment to multiculturalism stands as a paragon of virtue. But compared with the ideals enshrined in multiculturalism, Canadians could be doing better in the art of living together with differences. Furthermore, everyone agrees that there are enough loopholes in official Multiculturalism to dishearten even the most optimistic. Few would deny its vulnerability to manipulation by politicians and minority leaders. And when carelessly bandied about, its potential to deter, divide, diminish, or digress cannot be dismissed.

But carping criticism is no more helpful than unstinting praise. Evaluating multiculturalism is not simply a case of either/or, but both/and with respect to costs and benefits. Multiculturalism cannot be reduced to either a cost or a benefit, but as a benefit that accompanies a cost, depending on the context, consequences, or criteria. Moreover, criticism is one thing; proposals for alternatives to multiculturalism are quite another. Critics may relentlessly attack multiculturalism as regressive or irrelevant. But critiques rarely offer constructive criticism in proposing positive alternatives that are workable, necessary, and fair (Ford & Delaney, 2008). If a commitment to multiculturalism is incompatible with living together with differences, what other options are there? Let's be candid: Multiculturalism is hardly an option in a modern Canada because of its politicized diversities, robust immigration programs, and competing citizenships. Neither assimilation nor isolation stands much chance of survival in our politicized era. A much-touted return to traditional values for cementing Canadians into a unified and coherent whole sounds good in theory (Bibby, 1990; Bissoondath, 1993, 1994). In reality, such wishful thinking may camouflage a wistfulness for a golden age that never existed.

Forty years ago, Canada blazed a trail in establishing a framework for living together with differences. Has it been worth it? On balance, yes. Multiculturalism established a national agenda for engaging difference that strikes many as consistent with Canada's liberal–democratic framework. A governance framework has evolved that to date has managed to balance difference with unity—even if that balancing act is a bit wobbly at times. Such an endorsement may not sound like a lot to those with unrealistically high expectations; nevertheless, the contributions of multiculturalism should not be diminished by unfair comparison with utopian standards. A sense of proportion is required. Just as multiculturalism cannot be blamed for everything that is wrong in Canada, so too should Canadians stay clear of excessive praise in a country where equality and inclusiveness are unevenly applied. The nature of its impact and implications falls somewhere in between the poles of unblemished good and absolute evil. Multiculturalism is neither the root of all Canada's problems nor the all-encompassing solution to problems that rightfully belong elsewhere. It is but one component—however imperfect—for improving the integration of migrants and minorities by balancing the competing demands of diversity with unity.

Multiculturalism, in short, remains an option of necessity for a changing and diverse Canada (Ley, 2005). As a skilful blend of balances in a country built around compromises, multiculturalism symbolizes an innovative if imperfect social experiment for living together with differences. Multiculturalism has excelled in extricating Canada from its colonialist past and elevating it to its much-ballyhooed status as a trailblazer for constructive engagement. Under the circumstances, it is not a question of whether Canada can afford multiculturalism. More to the point, Canada cannot afford *not to* embrace multiculturalism in advancing political unity, social coherence, economic prosperity, and cultural enrichment. That is not to say that the coast is clear or that Canadians can rest on their laurels. Still, the entrenchment of multiculturalism has elevated Canada to the front ranks of society—not a perfect society by any stretch of the imagination—but possibly one of the world's least imperfect societies.

DEBATE REVISITED

Accounting for the Transatlantic Divide: Has Multiculturalism Failed in Europe or Has Europe Failed Multiculturalism?

With the hardening of European arteries toward immigration and the Islamic "other," the politics of multiculturalism have catapulted to the forefront of twenty-first century challenges (Fleras, 2009b; Goodspeed, 2006; Hansen, 2007; Morphet, 2007; Saunders & Haljan, 2003). How do we account for the continued popularity of multiculturalism in Canada in contrast to its declining fortunes in European societies? Is it because of good luck, good foresight, sound policies, historical trends? A bit of context might help:

The side-by-side/live-and-let-live multiculturalism in European societies tended to disengage immigrants from full and equal citizenship rights. Immigrants were rarely seen as potential permanent residents, but rather as guest workers who would eventually leave upon completion of their work. Thus, Europe's embrace of multiculturalism was predicated on a removal logic: Guest workers and their families required retention of their cultural and language skills for readjustment upon return to their home countries. For

(Continued)

example, children in Dutch schools learned Turkish or Moroccan in primary schools, while many lived in ethnic enclaves that encouraged an inward-looking isolation—not out of any inclusivity commitment but to facilitate their exit to a homeland. Furthermore, the benign neglect of immigrant communities was justified on the grounds that European countries did not see themselves as immigrant societies and thus felt minimal responsibility to actively integrate immigrants (guest workers) into the social fabric.

The end result? The segregation of differences into semi-autonomous ethnic silos culminated in a visionless coexistence of separate groups with little or no inter-ethnic interaction (much less creative encounters) among them. Nor was there much incentive for migrants to identify with a Europe that denied them citizenship or exposed them to marginality. Without an overarching vision for living together differently, what eventually emerged was a living arrangement that amounted to a serial monoculturalism (Sen, 2006). Under a serial monoculturalism, which acknowledged rather than accepted differences, the social and economic integration of migrants and minorities stalled, resulting in the marginalization of too many immigrants—further reinforcing public fears that multiculturalism was co-opted by radical politics for the dismantling of liberal–democratic values (Hurst, 2006; Kymlicka, 2011).

The situation in Canada differs (Fleras, 2007c; Kymlicka, 2004, 2005). First, in contrast to European countries that tend to see themselves as complete societies with established identities (Verkuyten, 2007), Canada defines

itself as an unfinished project in progress. Canada also defines itself as an immigration society: immigrants to Canada are seen as assets rather than burdens, crucial to Canada-building rather than a national liability, and as potential citizens rather than a permanent underclass. Multiculturalism, in turn, provides a tool to facilitate the integration of new Canadians by improving their chances of settling down, fitting in, and moving up. Not surprisingly, as a low cost risk, Multiculturalism is more likely to enjoy public support when immigrants are seen as bona fide permanent residents with access to full and equal citizenship rights. Support is also bolstered when there are principled rules regarding the acceptability of immigrant cultural practices. To the extent that cultural differences are respected under Canada's official Multiculturalism, this commitment is conditional: That is, cultural differences are tolerable but cannot break the law, violate individual rights, or contravene core constitutional values. In that a commitment to Multiculturalism reflects and reinforces Canada's status as an immigration society, while securing the creation of a national identity based on tolerance, its legitimacy is all but assured (Fleras, 2009a).

Second, the link between immigration and multiculturalism is mutually enhancing. A robust immigration program not only creates a need for multiculturalism governance, it also depends on multiculturalism for success. Conversely, Canada's Multiculturalism program could hardly flourish outside the context of a proactive and comprehensive immigration program. Not surprisingly, the multicultural response to immigration represents a low-risk option for living together with differences (Kymlicka, 2005). The political and social architecture is in place to manage the risk by ensuring that immigrants are legal, liberal, and equipped. Immigrants to Canada arrive through conventional channels, most share liberal values with the rest of Canada, and many are well educated and primed to work in Canada's post-industrial economy. The fact that Canada does better than other countries when measured on the grounds of immigrant participation, citizenship, pride of country, and levels of trust attests to its popularity and success (Bloemraad, 2006). Compare this situation with those European countries that are in close proximity to poor, unstable countries from North Africa or the Middle East, whose young inhabitants want opportunities, whether as legal migrants, illegal workers, guest workers, or asylum seekers. Predictably, then, this disconnect undermines public support for multiculturalism when immigrants are associated with illiberal practices at odds with mainstream norms and values, when immigrants are viewed as illegal by entry or unwelcome for the long haul, and when they are perceived as ill-equipped for coping with the demands of contemporary society (see Calder & Ceva, 2011).

Third, Canada's continued embrace of multiculturalism may not reflect commitment or insight. Rather, the accidents of geography and history may prove the critical factor (Kymlicka, 2004). Canada is so geographically isolated from the mass migration centres of the world (for example, North Africa, the Middle East, and Central America) that it rarely must worry about porous borders (but see Hier & Greenberg, 2002). Canada can afford to cherry pick whom it wants as new residents, while disbarring those whose differences are too different. As well, the serendipity of timing is pivotal. The emergence and entrenchment of multiculturalism reflected an era when most immigrants were from Europe, with a willingness to comply with Canada's liberal values and rights-based framework (Granatstein, 2007). As a result, once immigration shifted toward more culturally contentious non-European sources, Canadians had already internalized a familiarity with and fondness for multiculturalism and its role in enhancing a culture of minority rights (Kymlicka, 2004, 2007).

Fourth, support for multiculturalism is further bolstered by implicit rules for "drawing the multicultural line." Unlike the perceived anything-goes excesses of some multicultural regimes, Multiculturalism in Canada is about limits and boundaries. Difference may be tolerated under an inclusive multiculturalism, but this tolerance is conditional and principled: That is, cultural differences must be freely chosen, cannot break the law, violate individual rights, preclude individuals from full and equal involvement, or contravene core constitutional values. Furthermore, differences should not be expressed through inward looking ethnic enclaves or politicized for public power grabs, but de-politicized as a basis or dialogue, interaction, and understanding. Even passage of the 1988 *Canadian Multiculturalism Act*

(Continued)

sought to integrate new Canadians into the mainstream through their ethnic identity rather than offer unqualified preservation of their differences. Clearly, then, the multiculturalism in Canada's official Multicultural governance is not what it appears to be. More accurately, multiculturalism transforms differences into discourses about social equality and human rights rather than celebrations of diversity. In doing so, multiculturalism is rendered an indispensable component in advancing Canada's inclusiveness agenda for living together with differences, in dignity and equitably.

Chapter Highlights

- This chapter emphasizes the politics of official Multiculturalism as a politically motivated framework for living together with differences within the context of Canada-building.
- Societies differ in their responses to the growing presence of immigrant minorities. Options include (1) exclusion and expulsion, (2) tolerant indifference toward the culturally distinct, (3) non-recognition of guest workers as *persona non grata*, and (4) the institutional inclusion of minorities under the banner of multiculturalism.
- Is Canada a multicultural society? Responses to this question vary with different levels of meaning implicit within multiculturalism, that is, as a sociological fact, an ideological system of beliefs and values, a set of policies involving government–minority relations, a renewable resource in serving political and minority interests, or a critical discourse that challenges as it resists.
- Canada's inclusive Multiculturalism is based on the principle of mutual adjustment: that is, you adapt, we adjust/we adapt, you adjust. According to this inclusive multicultural model, a society of many cultures can exist as long as people's cultural differences do not get in the way of equality, participation, and citizenship. To the extent that cultural differences are tolerated, individuals are permitted to identify with the cultural tradition of their choice, provided this affiliation does not violate human rights, laws of the land, or core constitutional values.
- Canadian Multiculturalism has historically been concerned with improving minority equality and participation in society, initially through elimination of ethnocentric biases (ethnicity), then through the removal of discriminatory barriers and institutional accommodation (equity), followed by enhancing moves to bolster a sense of belonging and citizenship (civic), and currently a focus on integrating newcomers into a cohesive Canada.
- At once an asset as well as a hindrance, Multiculturalism has been regarded as both a source of social tension and an innovative means for minority conflict management. Neither a problem nor a solution, its influence exists somewhere in between—that is one component for engaging diversity in a complex yet unequal context.

- Multiculturalism is usually criticized as being divisive, regressive, or incompetent. Multiculturalism can also be shown to be unifying, progressive, and effective. The degree of criticism or praise of multiculturalism varies, depending on one's vision of Canadian society and the perceived role of multiculturalism in fostering that vision.
- The multicultural paradox is self-evident: Too many differences can create anarchic conditions that inhibit the effective functioning of a social system, while too many restrictions make a mockery of multicultural principles. Nevertheless, the question arises: Where do we draw the line? Who says so, and why?

For further study, you can access the Case Studies referenced in this chapter at **www.pearsoncanada.ca/fleras**.

Review Questions

1. Indicate how multiculturalism differs from other blueprints for managing race and ethnic relations (consult Chapter 1).
2. Compare and contrast the different phases in the development of Canada's multiculturalism policy in terms of objectives, assumptions, means, and outcomes.
3. Is Canada a multicultural society? "Yes," "no," "maybe," or "it depends"? Be sure to focus on the different levels of meaning associated with multiculturalism (consult Chapter 1).
4. Demonstrate some of the benefits and costs associated with Canada's official Multiculturalism. Defend whether you believe multiculturalism is a solution to the problem of unequal relations or more of a problem rather than a solution.
5. Multiculturalism is about knowing limits and drawing lines as a basis for living together with our differences. Explain, and provide an example to illustrate how much diversity a multicultural society can tolerate before self-destructing.
6. Racialized minorities and immigrants may have the same rights as all Canadians, including the right to be free of discrimination, but they find that they must live (from surviving to thriving) in a Canada that is *neither designed for their use nor reflects their experiences, realities, or aspirations*. Explain.
7. It's been said that multiculturalism rarely means what it says or says what it means, so that it can mean whatever people want it to mean depending on the context. As a result, multiculturalism can by used to mean everything, yet nothing. Explain these two sentences and use examples to illustrate your explanation.

Links and Recommendations

BOOKS

Politics in the Vernacular: Nationalism, Multiculturalism, and Citizenship, by Will Kymlicka (2001). Will Kymlicka provides an excellent overview of multiculturalism in Canada.

Multiculturalism and the History of Canadian Diversity, by Richard Day (2000). As the title implies, the book explores multiculturalism from a historical perspective, in effect reminding us that multiculturalism did not magically appear in 1971.

Where Race Does Not Matter: The New Spirit of Modernity, by Cecil Foster (2005). Another interesting take on race relations by arguing that Canada is increasingly approaching the status of a colour-blind society because of multiculturalism.

The Politics of Multiculturalism: Cross-National Perspectives in Multicultural Governance, by Augie Fleras (2009). Pardon the bias, but this book is highly recommended in addressing the politics of multiculturalism as they apply to Canada, the United States, New Zealand, Australia, the United Kingdom, and the Netherlands.

JOURNAL

Journal of International Migration and Integration, volume 3, no. 3/4 (2002). Check out this journal for more about the multicultural backlash in Europe.

WEBSITES

Canadian Heritage—The official website for Canada's official Multiculturalism provides a lot of information, albeit from a government slant:
   www.canadianheritage.gc.ca

Citizenship and Immigration Canada: Multiculturalism Annual Report—This website publishes the latest *Annual Report on the Operation of the* Canadian Multiculturalism Act:
   www.cic.gc.ca/english/resources/publications/multi-report2010/index.asp

Wikipedia provides useful insights into multiculturalism, including comparisons and criticisms of multiculturalism in the United States and Australia:
   http://en.wikipedia.org/wiki/Multiculturalism

CHAPTER 11

Multiculturalism at Work: Institutional Inclusivity as Reasonable Accommodation

DEBATE

Putting Reasonable Accommodation to the Test

The politics of **reasonable accommodation** add yet another wrinkle to Canada's multicultural debates (Adams, 2007). As explained by the deputy minister of Canadian Heritage in a briefing to the federal Secretary of State for Multiculturalism, "There is now a sense of urgency to more clearly define and explain the principle of reasonable accommodation, as alarming shifts regarding the split between 'them' and 'us' may occur" (as cited in Wente, 2007b). Not surprisingly, an increasingly secular and diverse Canada joins a list of other countries in confronting an existential paradox (Gray, 2007). As Canada becomes less formally religious, religious minorities are becoming more demanding in asserting religious rights, including the right to express this religiosity. In that this politicization increases the potential for intergroup strife, Canadians of all sacred and secular stripes are under pressure to rethink the notion of reasonable accommodation (Cahill, Bouma, Dellal, & Leahy, 2006). That is, just as the Canadian state expects religious and ethnocultural minorities to reasonably accommodate into society, so too do minorities expect the state to make reasonable accommodation of their interests and concerns as well.

In the debate about how far Canada should go in accommodating diversity, responses vary. How much accommodation should be reciprocated: that is, what can "they" expect of "us" versus how much should "we" expect of "them"? What do people mean when they say that immigrants should fully accommodate (or adapt): Should immigrants discard all outward signs of religiosity, from hijabs to kirpans, or does accommodation entail adopting core Canadian values, including acceptance of religion as a private matter and respect for religious dissidents? Or is such a stance another example of imposing Eurocentric values in seeming opposition to the principles of Canada's official Multiculturalism? To what extent are Canadians too accommodating of diversity—or not accommodative enough—thus compromising the integration of newcomers into Canada?

(Continued)

Surveys indicate that Canadians in general, although Quebecers to a lesser extent, are supportive of ethnocultural and religious minorities (Jedwab, 2007). Nevertheless a hardening of Canada's tolerance threshold is apparent. A poll of 1083 Canadians in the summer of 2007 by SES Research for Policy Options exposed the depth of division. Over half (53.1 percent) of respondents indicated that immigrants should adapt fully to culture in Canada, 18 percent believed it is reasonable to accommodate religious and ethnic minorities, and 21.3 percent fell in between (MacDonald, 2007). In Quebec the figures for accommodation proved even more intransigent, including 76.9 percent (no), 5.4 percent (yes), and 12.9 percent (maybe). The 16 October 2007 issue of *La Presse* reinforced these findings when results of its own poll virtually opposed any religious and cultural concession to immigrants and racialized minorities. Such resistance does not bode well, especially since the Quebec government plans to increase the number of immigrants in the province by 50 000 annually from 2012 to 2015, primarily to offset a skilled labour shortage and declining birth rates ("Québec Souhaite," 2011).

Tensions came to a boil when the staunchly francophone town of Herouxville passed a municipal ordinance that proposed a ban on those cultural practices at odds with the townfolk's culture (Abu-Laban & Abu-Laban, 2007). (See also online Insight 8.2.) But Ontario is no less exempt from the politics of reasonable accommodation. Consider the pre-election frenzy over the pros and cons of public funding of religious or ethnic schools in 2007 (Fulford, 2007; Jonas, 2007). For some, the funding of faith- and ethnic-based schools reflects the principles of an inclusive multiculturalism; for others, such a proposal is so divisive that it will foster segregation, weaken the public school system by siphoning off badly needed funds to religious schools, and undermine social cohesion by promulgating beliefs contrary to Canada's core constitutional values (see Bhabha, 2007). Still others agree in principle with extending the funding, but worry about imposing undue hardships on the public system in terms of costs, implementation, and consequences. And while faith/ethnic-based schools are not necessarily divisive per se, it is argued, the logic behind publicly funding these schools may well exert a divisive impact.

Who's right? Who's wrong? The fact that each position is consistent with specific readings of multiculturalism reinforces the importance of deconstructing the politics behind reasonable accommodation. Put bluntly, does true inclusion entail treating everyone *equally*; that is, treating everyone the same, regardless of their differences? Or does it reside in treating peoples as *equals* by taking their differences into account precisely because they are disadvantaging? And while both the Canadian state and religious/ethnic minorities concur with the principle to reasonably accommodate to each other, what exactly constitutes an "accommodation" that is "reasonable"? The Debate Revisited box at the end of this chapter will continue this discussion and deconstruct the concept of reasonable accommodation.

INTRODUCTION: PUTTING MULTICULTURALISM INTO PRACTICE

Canada's historical track record on race relations is spotty at best. Prejudice and discrimination meant that a belief in diversity and difference was perceived as inimical to Canada-building. Cultural differences were deemed incompatible with the good governance principles of "Peace, Order, and Good Government" as set out in the preamble to the 1867 *Constitution Act*. Immigrants and racialized minorities were expected to blend into the existing societal framework as the price of admission into Canada. With the inception of official Multiculturalism, however, institutional response to difference has improved. Diversity and difference are currently touted as an integral and legitimate component of Canada's social fabric, with untapped potential for improving national identity, wealth creation, and international standing. Multicultural differences are no longer dismissed as a bothersome anomaly with no redeeming value outside a personal or private context. On the contrary, the ongoing reconstruction of Canadian society is now primed for putting multiculturalism to work at institutional levels (Zachariah, Sheppard, & Barrett, 2004).

There is much to commend in institutions becoming more multiculturally responsive. At a time when both the workforce and the community at large are increasingly diverse and demanding, only the pace of change or the scope of adjustments should remain open to debate (Diller, 2004). Public and private institutions are increasingly anxious to enhance overall effectiveness by including all Canadians who have something to contribute. No more so than in Canada's cities, where the vast majority of immigrant and racialized Canadians live (Andrew, 2004; Frideres, 2006). Municipalities are under pressure to create welcoming communities through governance programs that not only remove discriminatory barriers but also enhance access, participation, and inclusivity (*Our Diverse Cities*, 2004, 2006, 2007). For urban service organizations, a commitment to multiculturalism can reap institutional dividends by easing workplace tensions, generating creative synergies, and facilitating community access by improving the quality of service delivery. For private companies, the inclusion of diversity is tantamount to money in the bank. Corporations increasingly rely on the language skills, cultural knowledge, life experience, and international connections that people of diversity bring to the workplace. Diversity connections can also provide the catalyst for internationalizing domestic businesses, thus improving competitive advantage in global markets.

However valued and overdue, preliminary efforts at putting multiculturalism to work at institutional levels have proven uneven. The commitment may be there, but with neither the political will for implementation nor the resources for enforcement, a reality gap looms (see online Insight 11.1). Of particular note are service-oriented institutions such as media, education, and policing, each of which is under pressure to move over and make institutional space. Their mandate as agencies of socialization and social control not only strikes at the hub of social existence but also influences the degree to which people are in harmony with their communities or alienated from them (see online Insight 11.2). Media and education furnish the "blueprint" for acceptable behaviour; the police, in turn, control the limits of unacceptable behaviour by enforcing the rules (see online Insight 11.3). Failure of each of these institutions to balance multicultural imperatives with organizational realities runs the risk of marginalizing untapped talent, shortchanging the delivery of services, and compromising both institutional effectiveness and efficiency.

This chapter discusses the politics of putting multiculturalism into practice by way of **institutional inclusivity**. It examines how major institutions are responding to the demands of difference through inclusive policies and programs for reasonable accommodation, both internally (organizational cultures, rules, and workforce composition) and externally (service delivery and community relations). Attention is focused on the institutions of the media and education, with respect to how they have addressed the challenges of implementing multicultural principles, in the process revealing both the pitfalls and promises of institutional inclusivity as well as the complexities and contradictions. Both institutions are analyzed on the basis of those barriers that complicate the attainment of inclusivity (for improving minority access, equity, and representation); what has been accomplished to date in accommodating difference (in creating a respectful, reflective, and responsive workplace/classroom); and what still needs to be done for improving patterns of inclusivity (in terms of services that are available, accessible, and appropriate). The conclusion should come as no surprise: Institutions have responded differently to the demands of diversity. Progress intermingles with inertia to create a confusing picture that speaks volumes about the politics of putting principles into practice. In other words, institutions may have come a long way from an exclusionary past; nonetheless, they still have a long way to go before inclusion is a reality.

INSTITUTIONAL INCLUSIVITY: POLITICS, PRINCIPLES, AND PRACTICE

The emergence of "inclusivity" as a popular buzzword poses a key question: What exactly does the term (as well as "inclusiveness" and "inclusion") mean? Is it about assimilation or integration? about diversity or disadvantage? about culture-blind or culture-conscious initiatives? about reform or radical change (Mittler, 2000; Ratcliffe, 2004; Winter, 2001)? Is inclusivity primarily about managing minorities (i.e., utilizing cultural differences to bolster the bottom line), or is it about engaging differences to promote social justice (Wrench, 2007)? Is it about being nice to minorities; replacing white personnel with minority hires; accelerating the promotion of minorities along the corporate ladder; or celebrating differences to enliven a dull corporate culture? For some, inclusivity involves a process by which institutions adjust institutional design, operation, and outcomes to make them more respectful of, responsive to, and reflective of difference (Keung, 2004). For others, it's about establishing a new framework that improves minority access, representation, and equity within the workplace, while enhancing the availability, access, and appropriateness of service delivery for minority communities (Fleras, 2006). For still others, inclusivity is about rethinking the value of diversity—not as a problem to solve or a challenge to surmount but as an asset for improving the workplace climate and the delivery of social services—one in which both workers and clients feel recognized and respected (culturally safe) rather than excluded or at risk (Fleras & Spoonley, 1999).

The politics of inclusivity can be tricky. Underemphasizing the relevance of diversity when required may be as discriminatory as overemphasizing it when not. Excluding minorities from full and equal involvement can generate conflict, yet incorporating differences can be equally disruptive to intergroup relations—at least in the short run (see Putnam, 2007). Fostering an inclusive workplace climate requires a careful reassessment of rules, procedures, and outlooks; nevertheless, changes of this magnitude may imperil the bottom line. The adjustment process must not only occur at the level of institutional structure and individual mindsets but also concentrate on the relationships within (the workplace environment) and connections without (clients). Finally, institutions must balance legitimate employment and equity concerns with an equally legitimate Charter-right requirement for institutions to reasonably accommodate worker needs. Such varied demands confirm the complexities of inclusivity in a world where accommodating reasonably does not come naturally.

Having good intentions is one thing, putting inclusive principles into institutional practice another. Institutions are complex, often baffling landscapes of domination, power, and control, often pervaded by prejudice, nepotism, patronage, and the "old boys" network. Mainstream institutions are neither neutral in design nor value-free in process, but structurally Eurocentric and constructed for advancing majority interests and priorities, either deliberately or systemically (Harris, 1995). Moves to inclusivize are rarely simple or straightforward; rather, they are fraught with ambiguity and tension because of individual resistance, structural barriers, and institutional inertia. Conservatives confront progressives in a struggle for control of the agenda. Despite both internal and external pressures to change, conventional views remain firmly entrenched as vested interests balk at discarding the tried and true. Newer visions are compelling but lack the critical mass to scuttle traditional ways of "doing business." The interplay of these juxtapositions can be disruptive as institutions evolve into a "contested site" involving competing world views and opposing agendas.

Defining "Institutional Inclusivity"

"Institutional inclusivity" can be defined as a process for modifying institutional design, organization, and outcomes with an eye toward (1) creating a workplace climate that is respectful, reflective, and responsive to diversity and difference; (2) ensuring a workforce that is representative and equitably treated and rewarded; and (3) by providing a service that is accessible, available, and appropriate (i.e., respectful and responsive).

What constitutes an inclusive institution? Responses entail the possibility of four analytically distinct models of inclusivity (Humpage & Fleras, 2001). (See Table 11-1.) An *equality* model attempts to ensure equal treatment for all by modifying existing institutional arrangements through removal of discriminatory barriers. By ensuring that no one is penalized or rewarded because of their race and ethnicity, this colour-blind model proposes a level playing field where all can participate equally, regardless of race or ethnicity. By contrast, an *equity* model acknowledges the possibility of incorporating diversity into institutional rules, agendas, and priorities on the grounds that minorities need to be treated equally (the same) regardless of their race or ethnicity, but also as

TABLE 11-1	Models of Institutional Inclusivity	
Equality	**Equity**
Treating everyone the same (equally) by creating a level playing field where no one is rewarded or penalized for who they are	Treating individuals as equals by taking differences into account when necessary through reasonable accommodation
(difference/colour/culture-blind)	(culture/colour/difference-tolerant)
Parallel	**Autonomy**
Constructing institutions by, for, and about minorities, but modelled after mainstream institutions	Constructing separate (or stand-alone) institutions that reflect, reinforce, and advance minority realities, experiences, and priorities
(culture/colour/difference-conscious)	(culture/colour/difference-mandatory)

equals (differently) when required, precisely because of their diversity-induced disadvantages. Initiatives for "minority-izing" institutions range from including more minorities at all institutional levels to the incorporation of minority symbols and priorities in redefining "how we do things around here."

Two additional models can be discerned. Both are predicated on the premise that no amount of organizational tweaking will create a truly inclusive institution, given the racialized nature of mainstream institutions. In arguing that only a degree of autonomy will do, the creation of *parallel* institutions reflects a need for minorities to work apart by constructing structures that are modelled after mainstream institutions, but operated entirely by, for, and about minority women and men. Examples include the establishment of Aboriginal policing services that incorporate aboriginality ("being Aboriginal") into the peacekeeping process (Public Safety, 2007). The proliferation of ethnic and multicultural media as a viable alternative to the negativity of mainstream media is yet another application (see online Insight 11.5). Proposals for *autonomous* institutions entail the creation of "separate" institutions based on the principle that certain minorities have the right to construct self-determining structures that reflect their realities, reinforce their priorities, and advance their interests—even if these do not necessarily conform with mainstream expectations (Chung, 2005). The emergence of Islamic-focus schools is one example explored in online Case Study 11.7. Another example is explored in Debate 7.3, which looks at the emergence of Aboriginal models of self-determining autonomy.

In defining an inclusive institution, much will depend on the model of inclusivity that is applied. With respect to *equality* and *equity* models of inclusivity, five criteria prevail, namely: *workforce representation, organizational rules and operations, workplace climate, service delivery,* and *community relations.*

- First, an institution's workforce should be representative, that is, relatively proportional to the composition of the regional labour force, acknowledging, of course, both extenuating social and cultural factors to account for discrepancies. Such a numerical accommodation applies not only to entry-level jobs but also across the board to include all managerial levels.

- Second, institutional rules and operations cannot hinder minority recruitment, selection, training, promotion, and retention. This commitment to rooting out both open and **systemic discrimination** demands a careful scrutiny of company policy and procedures.

- Third, the institution must foster a workplace climate conducive to minority well-being and success. At minimum, such a climate cannot tolerate harassment of any form; at best, diversity is actively promoted as normal, necessary, and beneficial to productive functioning (Wrench, 2007).

- Fourth, an inclusive institution ensures a delivery of its services that is community-based, culturally sensitive, and multiculturally responsive (Fleras, 2006). This multi-cultural commitment to culturally sensitive services entails an institutional willingness to engage as partners in genuine dialogue with the community at large. Outcomes must be based on bilateral decision-making rather than be unilaterally imposed.

- Fifth and finally, institutions do not operate in a social or political vacuum. Some degree of community input, power sharing, and public accountability is critical if productive lines of communication are to be secured (Fleras, 2006b).

Just as inclusivity at institutional levels can be defined by select criteria, so too can the factors and forces that impede the inclusion process be delineated (Conference Board of Canada, 2004). To some extent, these barriers represent the flip side of those dimensions that constitute an inclusive institution, including: *people*, *hierarchy*, *bureaucracy*, *corporate culture*, and *occupational subcultures*.

- People as institutional actors are a prime obstruction, especially when their self-interest is threatened because of preferential treatment to others (Thomas, Mills, & Mills, 2004). That revelation should come as no surprise. Unless convinced or compelled, few individuals are inclined to relinquish power or share privilege without a struggle.

- Inclusivity may be derailed by institutional structures such as hierarchy. Those in higher echelons may "talk the walk" of inclusivity, but fail to "walk the talk" when it comes to practice or implementation. Middle and lower management may be less enthused about proposed changes, preferring instead to cling to traditional authority patterns. Those at the bottom of the corporate pecking order may be least receptive to institutional change, and act accordingly to subvert or ignore it (see Kanter, 1977).

- Bureaucracy is a major inhibitor. Larger systems operate on bureaucratic principles of rational control to ensure standardization and regulation. Such a controlling imperative is not conducive to inclusivity, especially if diversity is perceived as disruptive, imposed, and irrelevant.

- Barriers implicit within corporate cultures prevail as well. Corporate cultures may recoil from adjustment when faced with a perceived threat to the bottom line or the "way we do things around here." Institutions instead reveal an uncanny knack of becoming ends in themselves over time by satisfying only their own criteria for excellence at the expense of clients or workers.

- Occupational subcultures may derail the best of intentions to accommodate. Those informal groupings that characterize all organizations not only exercise control over members' behaviour, because of common values and shared experiences, but also resist moves to accommodate, for fear of losing status or power.

The rest of the chapter will examine how mainstream institutions have risen to the challenge of inclusivity. With successes marred by failures, the verdict is mixed. This assessment is especially true of Canada's mainstream media and education system where a commitment to institutional inclusivity has shown promise and progress, but also resistance to change (see also online Insights 11.2 and 11.3 on inclusivity and policing).

MEDIA PORTRAYING MINORITIES: THE (MIS)REPRESENTATIONAL BASIS OF MEDIA–MINORITY RELATIONS

With the possible exception of schools and the criminal justice system, few institutions have attracted as much criticism and concern as the mainstream media (see also Cottle, 2005; Henry & Tator, 2006; Mahtani, 2008; Murray, 2009). Passage of the *Canadian Multiculturalism Act* in 1988 obligated all government agencies, and Crown corporations such as the CBC, to improve minority access, equity, and representation. As well, private media have come under both internal and external pressure to reflect the culture and colour of Canada. Despite improvements, however, the mainstream media have been singled out as visibly negligent in responding positively to Canada's evolving diversity (Fleras & Kunz, 2001; Mahtani, 2002). Media (mis)treatment of minorities in Canada remains mixed at best, deplorable at worst (Fleras, 2007; Jiwani, 2006; Kelley, 2006). Criticism applies across the board, from a dearth of minority employment opportunities to negative media portrayals of minorities. The media have been reproached for biased and inaccurate coverage of Aboriginal peoples and racialized minorities, many of whom continue to be insulted, stereotyped, caricaturized, and "miniaturized" as inferior or irrelevant (see also Suro, 2009). The cumulative impact of this dismissive treatment is unmistakably unmulticultural; after all, what most people know about diversity and difference is gleaned from media messages rather than first-hand experiences.

Why should mainstream media be under such scrutiny? To say the media are powerful and pervasive is merely stating the obvious. This potency reflects an agenda-setting ability to articulate *who is important, what is acceptable in society, and whose voices shall be heard* (Fleras, 2004a). The media not only construct those images that define acceptability, importance, or desirability; they also confer legitimacy on this "media-ted" reality through selective exposure and positive reinforcement. The ideological basis of reality construction is doubly articulated. As discourses in defence of dominant ideology, the media are ideological in reflecting and advancing the ideas and ideals of the dominant sector, while dismissing alternative perspectives as inferior or irrelevant (Abel, 1997). The media are ideological in a second way: They organize ("frame") information in ways that draw attention to some aspects of reality as normal and necessary, yet siphon attention away from other aspects of reality (Fleras, 2010c; see also Entman, 1993). The end result? Public discourses are generated in which certain persons or objects are "normalized" as acceptable and desirable, whereas others are demonized or marginalized. To be sure, the media do not necessarily set out to control by ideological indoctrination; nevertheless, the cumulative impact of negative images and deflating messages exerts a controlling effect on those victimized by unflattering portrayals.

Should Canadians care that the world is pervaded and transformed by media images that deny or exclude? The control of knowledge and its dissemination through media messages is fundamental to the exercise of societal power (Jiwani, 2006). Media messages not only assist in the identification and construction of what it means to be a Canadian but also in defining who is entitled to claim Canadianness (Bullock & Jaffri, 2000). The consequences of media distortion cannot be underestimated. In a world where meaningful encounters with Aboriginal peoples and racialized minorities may be uncommon or superficial, mainstream media may constitute the public's primary source of information about minorities or diversities. Not surprisingly, the images that constitute the representational basis of media–minority relations have come under scrutiny (Fleras 2011a). How do the media portray Aboriginal peoples and racialized minority women and men? In what ways do media images of minorities say more about the mainstream and its fears or fantasies? Are prevailing images the result of conscious or unconscious decisions? Do the media have a responsibility and role in facilitating the integration of migrants and minorities (Fleras, 2004). What, if anything, has been or can be done to improve this level of representation (see also Spoonley & Butcher, 2009)? Answers to these questions inform the content of this section.

Normalizing Invisibility, Problematizing Visibility

Historically, the mainstream media tended to misrepresent minorities by over-representing them in domains that don't count (from crime to athletics) while under-representing them in areas that do count (from business to decision making). More specifically, this mistreatment of minority women and men was classified into four categories, namely, *invisibility*, *stereotypes*, *problem people*, and *whitewashing* (Fleras & Kunz, 2001). This assessment was true for all mainstream media processes, including newscasting, advertising, filmmaking, and TV programming. The extent to which these classificatory frames persist into the present is worrying, particularly with certain media such as newscasting that continue to problematize visibility while normalizing invisibility.

Frame No. 1: Invisibility Numerous studies have confirmed what many regard as obvious: Canada's multicultural diversity is poorly reflected in media processes and outcomes. Visible minorities are reduced to an invisible status through under-representation in programming, staffing, and decision making. Even substantial representation in the media may be misleading if minority women and men are pigeonholed into a relatively small number of programs or into a limited number of roles, such as entertainers or athletes. Consider the plight of African Americans on television. Shows whose casts include blacks are common enough, especially those involving workplace dynamics such as *ER*. Yet dramas are rarely constructed around black stories in the belief that there is no sizable demographic audience for this kind of material. As a result, TV sitcoms tend to be segregated into all-white casts and all-black casts, while minorities such as Latinos/Latinas, Asians, and Aboriginal peoples are under-represented proportional to their numbers in real life (Kamalipour & Carilli, 1998).

It would be inaccurate to say that the news media ignore minorities. A "shallows and rapids" treatment is a more accurate appraisal; that is, under normal circumstances, minorities are ignored or rendered irrelevant by the mainstream press (shallows). Otherwise, coverage is guided by the context of crisis or calamity, involving natural catastrophes, civil wars, and colourful insurgents. When the crisis subsides or persists too long, media interest wanes. Admittedly, conflicts and problems occur in minority communities; nevertheless, the absence of balanced coverage may distort public perceptions of minority experiences and aspirations. This distortion may not be deliberately engineered. Rather, the flamboyant and sensational are accorded disproportionate coverage to satisfy audience needs and sell copy, without much regard for the effects on the lives of those sensationalized. The media may shun responsibility for their discriminatory impact, arguing that they are reporting only what is newsworthy. Deliberate or not, however, such a one-dimensional focus on negativity has had the systemic effect of negatively portraying minorities as "troublesome constituents" (see online Insight 11.4).

Minorities are also made invisible by being reduced to the level of adornments to amuse, distract, or embellish. This decorative aspect is achieved by casting minorities in stereotypical roles, that is, associated with the exotic and sensual, portrayed as congenial hosts for faraway destinations, enlisted as superstar boosters for athletics and sporting goods, or ghettoized in certain marketing segments related to rap or hip hop. Most minority roles on television consist of bit parts, either as background scenery or as foils to sharpen white characters and characteristics. Blacks on television are locked into roles as entertainers or athletes, with little emphasis on intellectual or professional prowess, much less any recourse to positive role models to which minority youth can aspire outside athletics or entertainment (Edwards, 2000). Such restrictions may prove inherently satisfying to mainstream audiences who historically have enjoyed laughing at or admiring minorities cast as breezy entertainment. And yet the laugh-tracking of minorities is not without consequences. This depoliticizing of minorities by "playing 'em for laughs" reassures mainstream audiences that everybody still knows their place.

Frame No. 2: Stereotypes Minorities have long complained of stereotyping by the mainstream media (Azam, 2000; Stam & Miller, 2000). People of colour were historically portrayed in a manner that played into prevailing prejudices. Liberties with minority depictions in consumer advertising were especially flagrant. In an industry geared toward image and appeal, the rule of homogeneity and conservatism prevailed. People of colour were rarely depicted in the advertising of beauty care and personal hygiene products. So entrenched was the image of "whiteness" as the preferred standard of beauty that advertisers wanted their products sanitized and bleached of colour for fear of lost revenue (Bledsloe, 1989). Elsewhere, images of racial minorities were steeped in unfounded generalizations that accentuated the comical or grotesque. This stereotyping fell into a pattern. People from the Middle East continue to be portrayed as tyrannical patriarchs or ruthless fanatics with a bent for linking terrorism with religion (Elmasry, 1999; Karim, 2002). Asians have been typecast either as sly and cunning or as mathematical whizzes, Latinos/Latinas as hot blooded. Blacks in prime-time shows remain stuck as superheroes/athletes or sex-obsessed buffoons surrounded by a host of secondary characters such as hipsters, outlaws, and "gangstas."

Consider how the media have portrayed Canada's Aboriginal peoples. Images of Aboriginal peoples as the "other"—a people removed in time and remote in space—are filtered through Eurocentric lenses (Lambertus, 2004). Representations range from their valorization as "noble savages" and "primitive romantics," including spiritual mystics and environmental custodians, to their debasement as "villains" or "victims" with the stigma of "problem people" or "menacing subversives" sandwiched in between (see Alia & Bull, 2005; Goodall, Jakubowicz, & Martin, 1994; see also Blythe, 1994). Film portrayals embraced a mythical image of an imaginary warrior who traversed the Great Plains between 1825 and 1880 (Francis, 1992), while the standard for the generic North American Indian was packaged from a so-called Indian Identity Kit (Berton, 1975), which consisted of the following items, few of which were even indigenous to Aboriginal peoples prior to European settlement: wig with hair parted in the middle into hanging plaits; feathered war bonnet; headband (a white invention to keep the actor's wig from slipping off); buckskin leggings; moccasins; painted-skin teepee; and a tomahawk and bows and arrows. This one-size-fits-all image applied to all First Peoples, regardless of whether they were Cree or Salish or Ojibwa or Blackfoot, in effect reinforcing a "seen one Indian, seen them all" mentality.

Collectively, these images reinforce the notion of Aboriginal peoples as an alien species whose histories began with the arrival of whites, and whose reality makes sense only within the context of settler interaction (see Razack, 2002). Collective resistance to their colonization is rarely depicted, in effect depoliticizing Aboriginal concerns and contributions to Canada, although individual acts of protest may be acknowledged. News stories involving Aboriginal assertion are framed as a narrative involving a conflict of interest between the opposing forces of mayhem and stability (Abel, 1997). Aboriginal activism is portrayed as a departure from established norms, while protesters are reduced to dangerous militants or irrational ideologues (Miller, 2005). The subsequent demonizing of Aboriginal activism marginalizes the legitimacy of dissent, trivializes Aboriginal issues, and distracts from the issues at hand. To be sure, the media have begun to invert conventional stereotypes, with much greater emphasis on First Peoples' courage or compassion compared with the rapacious greed of white settler colonization (think *Dances with Wolves*). Nevertheless, there is a long way to go, as Maurice Switzer (1997), a member of the Elders' Council of the Mississaugas of Rice Lake First Nations at Alderville, Ontario, writes in *Aboriginal Voices*:

> The country's large newspapers, TV and radio news shows often contain misinformation, sweeping generalizations and galling stereotypes about natives and native affairs. Their stories are usually presented by journalists with little background knowledge or understanding of aboriginals and their communities . . . As well very few so-called mainstream media consider aboriginal affairs to be a subject worthy of regular attention. (pp. 21–22)

Why such stereotyping? Stereotyping simplifies the process of representation. A pool of Aboriginal stereotypes provides a convenient shorthand for audiences to relate to because they share common cultural codes. Reliance on these simplistic and reductionist images creates readily identifiable frames (or tropes) that advance story lines, plot twists, or character development. Over time, these stereotypes solidify into definitive statements about "reality" and, while not "real" in the conventional sense, stereotypes are real in their social consequences. In other words, rather than an error in perception, stereotyping constitutes a pattern of thought control through the internalizing of negative images (Churchill, 1999). By projecting whiteness onto the Aboriginal "other," such stereotyping may also contribute to the construction of white identities. To the extent that whites have long resorted to fantasies or anxieties about the "other" as a basis for collectively defining who they are in relation to the world around them, media images really do say more about the "us" than the "them."

Frame No. 3: Problem People Minority women and men are frequently depicted as troublesome constituents who "are problems," "have problems," or "create problems" (Fleras, 2004a). As "problem people" they are taken to task by the media for making demands at odds with national unity, identity, or prosperity. Portrayal of Canada's Aboriginal peoples is instructive, especially when they are depicted as (1) a threat to Canada's territorial integrity or national interests (Nisga'a Final Settlement); (2) a risk to Canada's social fabric (from Oka to Caledonia); (3) an economic liability (the costs associated with land claims settlement or compensation for victims of residential schools); and (4) a problem for the criminal justice system (a disproportionate number of Aboriginal prison inmates) or an unfair player (cigarette smuggling or illegal online gambling operations). Compounding this negativity are repeated references to Aboriginal reliance on welfare, alcohol dependency and substance abuse, a perceived laziness and lack of ambition, and an inclination to mismanage what little they have. The combined impact of this negativity borders on "propaganda": Canada's First Peoples are villainized as "troublesome constituents" whose demands for self-determining autonomy pose a threat to society. Success stories are rarely reported and the few exceptions that make it into the news simply confirm the rule.

Non-Aboriginal minorities are also problematized by the media. People of colour, both foreign and Canadian born, are targets of negative reporting that dwells on costs, threats, and inconveniences. Media reporting of refugees usually refers to illegal entries and the associated costs of processing and integrating them into Canada (Fleras, 2010b). (See online Insight 11.6.) Canada's refugee determination system is repeatedly criticized for allowing entry of refugees who pose a security threat. Immigrants are routinely cast as potential troublemakers who steal jobs from Canadians, cheat on the welfare system, take advantage of educational opportunities, lack commitment to Canada, engage in illegal activities such as drug trafficking or smuggling, imperil Canada's unity and identity by refusing to discard their culture, and undermine its security by spawning homegrown terrorists (Karim, 2006). This negativity is reinforced when stories are framed around minority challenges to the prevailing distribution of power and privilege in Canada (Jiwani, 2006).

Nowhere is this negativity more evident than in media coverage of Muslims or those of Arabian appearance (Canadian Islamic Congress, 2005; see also Suro, 2009). Positive and normalizing images of ordinary Muslims or Arabs are almost non-existent in the mainstream media (Alliance of Civilizations, 2006; Starck, 2007). Coverage of Muslims as violent and irrational is heavily skewed toward international conflicts, without providing a historical context (Manning, 2006). For the news media, the debate over the so-called clash of civilizations—Islamic versus Western—tends to frame their coverage accordingly, that is, protagonists ensnared in global geopolitics (in the same way the Cold War once served as a framing function for geopolitical developments) (Seib, 2004/5). News frames routinely portray Muslim/Arab males as tyrants or terrorists, while Muslim/Arab women are pitied as burqa-bearing submissives at odds with modern realities. For example, the following patterns frame news media coverage of Islam, according to the Runnymede Trust (2000), an independent British think tank:

1.   Islam is seen as a monolithic bloc and impervious to change.

2.   As the "other," Islam lacks values in common with other cultures.

3.   Islam is irrational, barbaric, and sexist, hence inferior to the West.

4.   Islam is violent and aggressive, and its support of terrorism poses a threat.

5.   Islam can be manipulated for political and military advantage.

6.   Because of its inferiority, Islamic criticism of the West is rejected.

7.   Hostility toward Islam justifies the discrimination and exclusion of Muslims.

8.   Hostility toward Islam and Muslims is justified.

9.   Islam is incompatible with tolerance and pluralism.

Predictably, then, the mainstream media stand accused of racism for using loaded terminology (Islam as extremist, fundamentalist, terrorist, or primitive) to advance simplistic and negative stereotypes (deSouza & Williamson, 2006). The combination of insult and injury, together with diminished self-esteem, fosters resentment and rage over what many see as race-baiting propaganda. Such racialized one-sidedness also intensifies the risk of racial tensions and increased discrimination. In light of Islamophobic (Islam-fearing) coverage, visual images involving Muslims immediately trigger a subliminal negativity:

> A bearded Middle Eastern looking man wearing a black cloak and turban can trigger an entire series of images of a fanatical religious movement, of airplane hijackings, of western hostages held helpless in dungeons, of truck bombs killing hundreds of innocent people, of cruel punishment sanctioned by Islamic law, and of suppression of human rights—in sum of intellectual and moral regression. (Karim, 2006, p. 118)

Not surprisingly, perhaps, when a Gallup poll asked 10 000 respondents in predominantly Muslim countries what the West could do to improve relations with the Muslim world, 47 percent (the single largest response) said the Western media must stop disrespecting Islam by portraying Muslims as inferior or threatening (Alliance of Civilizations, 2006).

Frame No. 4: Whitewashing In contrast to the past, when racialized minorities remained outside the preferred advertising "demographic," mainstream media are under pressure to "move over and make space" because of government regulation, minority assertiveness, and commercial imperatives. Nowhere is this more so than in advertising or programming, where the escalation in the quality and quantity of minority appearances is unmistakable. And yet media acceptance comes with strings attached. Minority women and men are air-brushed by being restricted to ornamental levels that cannot be taken seriously. Minorities are rendered acceptable by the media if their appearance or actions are whitewashed to coincide with mainstream expectations (norms) or values. To achieve this goal of acceptability, those minorities whose differences are perceived as problematic are sanitized for mainstream palettes. This depolitizicing by whitewashing may prove inherently satisfying to mainstream audiences. But minority concerns are compromised by a Eurocentric whitewashing that not only essentializes cultural differences into a single perspective but also negatively portrays the "other" as inferior or irrelevant (Shohat & Stam, 1994). The ethnocentrism of a white superiority complex may not be openly articulated by media "whitewashing." Rather it is assumed and nor-malized as the unquestioned norm that depoliticizes as it whitewashes. The fact that an ethnocentric media bias exists is not the problem; after all, bias is inevitable because all social constructions reflect the values and agendas of those who create them. Rather, the problem lies in media coverage that is so blind to its bias that it cannot admit to this eth-nocentrism, preferring instead to hide behind claims of objectivity and neutrality (Fleras 2011a; Maracle, 1996). (See online Insight 11.5.)

Accounting for the Problem: The Media as "Soft" Propaganda

Many reasons account for media mistreatment of minorities (Alia & Bull, 2005). These span the spectrum, from hard-boiled business decisions that reflect the realities of mar-ket forces, to a lack of cultural awareness, to deep-seated prejudice among media per-sonnel. Questions invariably arise: Does media mistreatment of minorities imply the presence of prejudiced personnel or structural discrimination? Is it a case of unwittingly cramming minority realities into Eurocentric categories as a basis for description or evaluation? Or does it reflect a preference to act out of self-interest by kowtowing to the dictates of the marketplace, especially during periods of economic uncertainty or corpo-rate restructuring? Confusion and uncertainty are the rule rather than the exception. Key personnel may be unsure of how to integrate Canadians of colour into the media without being accused of paternalism or tokenism. Even sensitive presentations must grapple with dilemmas as varied as the following: (1) how to portray other cultures whose prac-tices conflict with Canada's democratic principles without reinforcing stereotypes or ethnocentrism; (2) whether to emphasize only positive minority stories or to include both positive and negative, thereby reinforcing their status as "troublesome constitu-ents"; and (3) whether cultural differences can be presented without polarizing the world into us versus them (see McAndrew, 1992). Unsure of what to do or how to do it, media decision-makers may avoid diversity topics for fear of career-curbing mistakes.

Media executives concede the importance of improving the quantity and quality of minority representations. The combination of a growing ethnic market and an increased competition for consumer loyalty and dollars has sounded the death knell for monocul-tural media. But moves to convey a positive minority image generally misfire. Media efforts to improve minority representation may be greeted with disdain or coolness. Positive portrayals and inclusive programming may be dismissed as window-dressing, condescending, tokenistic, or "politically correct." A no-win situation may prevail. Portrayals of minorities in high status and stable relationships (as in the *Cosby Show*) are rebuked for creating unrealistic and unattainable expectations that can only foster resentment. These mixed messages put the media in a double bind, that is, in a lose-lose situation where they are damned if they do, damned if they don't. Bewildered and taken aback by criticism regardless of what they do, the media recoil for fear of detonating yet another cultural landmine through negative publicity or inciting consumer revolt that could impede corporate profits or implode on personal careers.

The representational basis of media–minority relations is tainted by prejudice and racism—at times deliberate, at other times inadvertent. Systemic biases are especially powerful in shaping what we see or hear. At the core of systemic bias is a tacitly assumed

Eurocentrism—a set of beliefs about the superiority of Westocentric values and practices that is so pervasive as to escape detection. With Eurocentrism, reality is automatically interpreted from a mainstream point of view as natural and normal, while minority perspectives are dismissed or demeaned accordingly (Shohat & Stam, 1994). Take the news media (Herman & Chomsky, 1988): They are profoundly ideological in that they privilege (or normalize) the corporate perspective as normal and acceptable, and discredit minority viewpoints as inferior or irrelevant (Fleras, 2007a). News media are also ideological in that they themselves are loaded with ideological assumptions that influence how news stories are "framed." The framing of news provides a handy reference point for quickly defining issues around a preferred reading (Entman, 1993). But this "framing" experience is neither neutral nor natural; rather, it reflects the interests of those who own or control the media. The controlling of thought without peoples' awareness of what is happening reinforces the status of news as a hegemonic discourse in defence of dominant ideology.

Put bluntly, hegemonic news media constitute an exercise in "soft" or "systemic" propaganda (Fleras & Kunz, 2001). (See online Insight 11.4.) Media are not propaganda in the conventional sense of flagrant and deliberate brainwashing, that is, the news media don't go out of their way to deny or exclude. Nevertheless, applying mainstream news norms to coverage of minorities as troublesome constituents may have a discriminatory effect, however inadvertently or impersonally (keep in mind that some minorities are more vulnerable than others to negative media coverage). For example, are negative depictions of Muslims and Islam reflective of racist decision-makers who deliberately amplify Islamophobia through exaggerated and sensationalized coverage? Or do we have a case of institutionalized ("soft") propaganda, insofar as this negativity is conveyed not through biased coverage but through coverage that is systemically biasing by virtue of its one-sidedness and consequences. That is, rather than something deliberate and malevolent, this typecasting of Muslims as problem people reflects the nature of mainstream news media to Eurocentrically frame (or problematize) all Muslims as troublesome constituents.

In short, the media do not deliberately set out to disseminate propaganda or willfully control people's thoughts. But media coverage can be deemed propaganda by virtue of how information is processed ("framed"): Some aspects of reality are presented as normal, acceptable, and desirable, while other aspects are dismissed as inferior, irrelevant, or dangerous. In effect, this framing encourages a preferred reading of reality consistent with how the media want audiences to see reality without their awareness and as if it were from no perspective at all ("seeing like the media or media gaze" [Fleras, 2011a]). Coverage can also be deemed propaganda because it reflects the inevitable consequences of creating one-sided messages that consistently support one point of view to the exclusion of others. Consider the following:

- In that news media tend to focus on conflict as newsworthy or to frame issues around a conflict narrative, thus advancing institutional interests rather than the public good, news media can be interpreted as institutionalized or systemic propaganda.

- In that Eurocentric whiteness is routinely privileged as the tacitly assumed norm by which others are judged or interpreted, the news media engage in systemic propaganda.

- In that the news media invariably frame minority women and men as "troublesome constituents" in opposition to the Canadian norm, a soft propaganda is at play.
- To the extent that the media routinely portray minorities as having problems or creating problems, this one-sided depiction constitutes systemic propaganda.
- In that the shallow pluralism endorsed by a pro-white Eurocentric media neither takes differences seriously (except as a problem to be solved) nor takes difference into account (except as a source of conflict and confrontation), the liberal universalism implicit in mainstream news media reflect soft propaganda.

To be sure, no one is saying that the news media are propaganda per se. Perhaps it's best to say that mainstream news media may be interpreted *as if* they were soft (systemic) propaganda when judged by what they *really* do and the consequences they create rather than what they *say* they do and the outcomes they propose.

Inclusivizing the Media

The mainstream media in Canada are under pressure to make appropriate adjustments (Fleras, 2006). Multicultural minorities and Aboriginal peoples have asked some tough questions of the media over their commitment to inclusivity. Demands for change include the following proposals: the incorporation of minority perspectives into the media process, more multicultural programming, balanced and impartial newscasting, and sensitivity training for journalists and decision makers (Abel, 1997). To some extent, many changes are already in progress (Hier, 2008; but see Mahtani, 2008). The government Task Force on Broadcasting Policy, co-chaired by Gerald Caplan and Florian Sauvageau in 1986, singled out the need to include Aboriginal peoples and racial minorities (Raboy, 1988). The 1988 *Broadcasting Act* has come out in favour of "cultural expression" by expanding air time for ethnic and racialized minorities. Reforms include sensitivity training for program and production staff, language guidelines to reduce race–role stereotypes, and monitoring of on-air representation of historically disadvantaged people. Rules are in place to deter abusive representations of individuals on the basis of race or ethnicity as well as age, gender, religion, or disability. In advertising too, racial minorities are appearing more frequently across a broader range of products and services. Companies that utilize diversity are now perceived as sophisticated and cosmopolitan unlike their all-white counterparts, who come across as staid and outdated. Demographics may be pushing the changes: When immigrants and racialized minorities compose nearly 50 percent of the populations in Vancouver and Toronto, the media are under pressure to acknowledge difference.

Institutional inclusivity does not come easily to the media. A conflict of interest is proving a stumbling block. The commercial media do not see themselves as reform agencies to promote progressive change or to accommodate diversities, even if they may have a social responsibility to do so. They are a business whose *raison d'être* is simple: to make money by connecting audiences to advertisers through ratings. Institutional practices that once worked to generate revenues (e.g., stereotyping) will be retained; those that don't will be discarded. Such a bottom-line mentality—with its preference for morselization over context, conflict over cooperation, and personalities over issues—will invariably be at odds with minority demands for balanced and contextual coverage (see Atkinson, 1994). For example, all media storytelling, from news and weather to TV programming, reflects a conflict format (We Interrupt the News/Youth Force, 2001). The one-sidedness of conflict tropes exert a negative impact on those minorities without the positive images to counterbalance their media status as problem people. The irony seems inescapable. The very changes that minorities want of the media—responsible coverage of minority interests, less sensationalism, more context, toned-down language, and less stereotyping—are precisely the tools that keep the media financially afloat.

Modest improvements in the quality and quantity of minority coverage notwithstanding (see Spoonley & Butcher, 2009), the mainstream news media have fumbled the inclusivity challenge in two ways: first in a systemically biasing way that frames minorities as troublesome constituents; second, in their failure to frame "deep" diversities except as a conflict or problem (Fleras, 2004a, 2006). This assessment should come as no surprise. The news media are fundamentally racialized because as institutions they are neither neutral nor universalistic. Rather, they are deeply and fundamentally ideological by way of racialized rules, practices, discourses, and rewards that (both deliberately or inadvertently) reinforce white interests and Eurocentric agendas. The end result? By framing diversity and difference around conflict or problem frames to the exclusion of alternative frameworks—that is, by normalizing invisibility while problematizing visibility—news media coverage of minorities has proven systemically biasing rather than systematically biased (Everitt, 2005). Framing initiates a process for organizing information that privileges some aspects of reality and disprivileges other aspects, in the hopes of encouraging a preferred reading.

Clearly, media advances are interposed with media stagnation. In theory, both the quality and quantity of media representations have improved. In reality, however, the picture remains as blurry as ever, with modest improvements in quantity undermined by continuing misrepresentations in quality. This suggests that media representations of minority women and men are couched in compromise—that is, advances in some areas are offset by stalemate in others. It also suggests that the media will continue as a contested site for control of the agenda, with advocates for the establishment in competition with activist forces. At the core of this contestation process is power. Until the issue of power is resolved—in terms of who owns it, who has access to it, and whose values will dominate—the representational basis of media–minority relations will remain riddled with ambiguity and frustration (see online Insight 11.6).

MULTICULTURAL AND ANTI-RACIST EDUCATION

Some of the most interesting advances in inclusivity involve the educational system (Ghosh & Abdi, 2004). This commitment to **multicultural education** represents a significant shift from the past. Education has, for the most part, reflected a fundamental commitment to monoculturalism, with schooling of children largely inseparable from their absorption into the mainstream (Alladin, 1996). Canada (like Australia and New Zealand) originated as a local outpost for British cultural expansion, with its goal to assimilate both the indigenes and immigrants into the colonial hierarchy of cultural power (Jakubowicz, 2005). But times are changing. Schooling and education are widely committed to the inclusivity principles of multiculturalism by way of different models to achieve this goal. On one side are diversity models of multicultural education (enrichment, enlightenment, embracive, and empowerment), with their emphasis on changing individual attitudes through exposure to cultural differences. On the other side are anti-racist models that focus on transforming structures by challenging those systems that uphold power and difference. In both cases, the concept of monocultural education comes under attack.

Monocultural Education

Historically, a monocultural education system prevailed in Canada. All aspects of schooling, from teachers and textbooks to policy and curriculum, were aligned with the principles of anglo-conformity. From daily routines to decision making at the top, education was organized to facilitate cultural indoctrination and societal assimilation of minority students. These reproductive functions were accomplished in a direct manner by way of Eurocentric course content, pedagogical styles, and methods of evaluation. Indirect and largely unobtrusive measures were also employed. The school system screened out certain information by projecting certain types of knowledge as necessary and normal, others as inappropriate. Issues were framed in a way that gave prominence and conferred cultural legitimacy to some, but ignored others. Through schooling, in other words, the reproduction of the ideological and social order was realized without much public awareness or open debate. In linking power with culture, schooling and education evolved into a site for the reproduction of social inequality by denying equal opportunity and fostering outcomes at odds with certain minority students (Dei, 1996a). Anything that veered outside this anglocentric framework was ignored as irrelevant or dangerous and punished accordingly

But the demographics are changing. About 20 percent of students in public, elementary, and secondary schools are of visible minority or immigrant status—with projections of a numerical majority by 2017 (Areepattamannil, 2005). The figures for Toronto are even more impressive, with racial and ethnic minorities constituting nearly 50 percent of secondary students. But fears persist that schools are failing to provide a positive learning environment that values cultural diversity while enhancing educational credentials. In addition, children of economically deprived immigrant and racialized minority groups are not doing as well in school as their Canadian-born peers, with lower achievement in test scores, grades, graduation rates, and college applications. This is particularly true for those children who have settled in Canada with non-existent or interrupted education, with the result that the education system is staggering under the weight of schooling the unschooled (Mahoney, 2007). Such underachievement comes with a hefty price tag: When children of colour leave school without the basic tools for job success or learning skills, the underachievement affects everything, from their quality of life to social inclusion to self-esteem. In other words, the educational system must become more representative of, reflective of, and responsive to the differences that inform and advance a changing Canada (Areepattamannil, 2005).

Few openly endorse the explicit assimilationist model that once informed educational circles. But the fact that, foundationally, it continues to persist says a lot about the power and pervasiveness of Eurocentric institutions. A commitment to assimilation remains an unspoken but powerful ethos at all schooling levels—not in the openly monocultural sense of deliberate indoctrination, but through the logical (or systemic) consequences of a racialized schooling system (Banks & Banks, 1997; May, 1999). As a result, the site encompassed by schooling and education is increasingly transformed into a contested space, involving the struggles between those who endorse the monocultural status quo versus the historically excluded who seek inclusivity (Giroux, 1994). Not surprisingly, a dual dynamic is apparent: Education plays both a conservative and a progressive role in society, with the concept of multicultural education somehow straddling this oppositional dynamic. A more radical extension of multicultural education known as anti-racist education provides a challenge to the limitations of multicultural education as well as the inequities that persist both within and outside the education system.

Models of Multicultural Education

The impetus for multicultural education constitutes a departure from conventional ways of doing things. Its introduction has not only challenged how schools should relate to difference but has also raised questions about the dynamics of formal education in a changing and diverse society. In striving to be inclusive of difference, multicultural education encompasses a variety of policies, programs, and practices for engaging difference within the school setting to ensure that differences do not disadvantage students. It also seeks to incorporate all students by modifying existing content and protocols to ensure better involvement and success. But what sounds good in theory may falter in practice because of entrenched interests and structural barriers that blunt, deflect, absorb, or crush any significant move toward meaningful inclusivity.

Different models of multicultural education can be observed, ranging in scope and comprehensiveness from "moderate" to more "radical" approaches: *enrichment, enlightenment, embracive,* and *empowerment.* As we shall see later in the chapter, an anti-racism approach is pushing the envelope of accommodation even further.

Enrichment Model An enrichment multicultural education is aimed at all students. Students are exposed to a variety of different cultures to enhance knowledge of and appreciation for cultural diversity. For example, the Ontario government has introduced a First Nations perspective into grades one to twelve as part of a revamped social studies curriculum, including social studies, history, geography, and Canadian and world studies courses (L. Brown, 2005). The curriculum is enriched with various multicultural add-ons. Special days are set aside for multicultural awareness; projects are assigned that reflect multicultural themes; and specific cultures are singled out for intensive classroom study. Additional perspectives include a focus on healthy identity formation, cultural preservation, intercultural sensitivity, stereotyping awareness, and cross-cultural communication. A desirable side effect of the enrichment process is greater tolerance, enhanced sensitivity, and more harmonious intercultural relations. A less beneficial consequence is a failure to initiate sweeping institutional changes, much less challenge the racism within and outside the school.

The enrichment model is widely accepted because of its non-threatening nature. Yet, this very innocuousness has brought it into disrepute with critics. Enrichment styles have been criticized as too static and restrictive in scope because of their emphasis on *diversity* (rather than *difference*) that is, on the exotic components of a culture that everyone can relate to, rather than to more substantive issues such as values and power relations. Diverse cultures are studied at the level of material culture, stripped of their historical context, and discussed from an outsider's point of view (Mukherjee, 1992). However well intentioned, a "samosas, saris, and steel bands" style may inadvertently trivialize or stereotype by over-romanticizing minorities or a timeless past. That these concerns have yet to be allayed to everyone's satisfaction points to the elusiveness of a proposed balancing act.

Enlightenment Model A second approach that is compatible with the first is an enlightenment model of multicultural education. This approach is similar to the enrichment model insofar as both seek to modify people's attitudes by changing how they think about diversity. Enlightenment models are less concerned with celebrating differences as a basis for attitudinal change. The focus is on enlightening students about race relations in society. Enlightenment models go beyond the description of specific cultures; endorsed, instead, is a broader, analytical approach toward diversity not as a "thing" but as a relationship, both hierarchical and unequal. Attention is directed to how minority–majority relations are created and maintained as well as what would be required to challenge and transform these predominantly unequal relationships. Stronger versions may expose students to Anglo-European complicity in crimes of racism, dispossession, and imperialism and the corresponding concentrations of power in white hands. Specific group victimization may be included, for example, genocide against First Peoples, while the achievements of indigenous and immigrant peoples are emphasized, as a corrective to their being whitewashed as failures or threats.

Embracive Model Both enrichment and enlightenment models focus on directly changing students' mindsets toward diversity and difference. An embracive model is directed at transforming the culture of the classroom. In rejecting the Eurocentricity that still infuses the classroom—from pedagogy and curriculum to patterns of student–teacher interaction—an embracive model acknowledges the obvious in inclusivity: that excluding diverse cultural values from the classroom can prove alienating for foreign students and racialized minority students. Proposed instead is a commitment to take cultural differences seriously and to take them into account in crafting a more inclusive classroom environment. Of particular note in advancing classroom inclusivity is the introduction of different ways of knowing and bodies of knowledge that do not necessarily fit into a conventional framework. A multicentric approach is promoted that acknowledges multiple ways of knowing and making sense of the world rather than privileging Eurocentricity as the sole source of valid and legitimate knowledge, traditions, and experiences (Dei et al., 2000). In short, a classroom that is embracive of cultural differences is more likely to create a more inclusive learning and interactive environment that respects and engages all students.

Empowerment Model Both the enrichment and enlightenment styles of multicultural education concentrate on the needs of non-minority pupils. In contrast to them, the empowerment model is directed essentially at the needs of minority students. The minority-focus empowerment model is predicated on the belief that monocultural school systems are failing minority pupils. Minority students do not see themselves represented in a Westocentric curriculum that rarely acknowledges minority achievements and contributions to society. What minority students require is an inclusive curriculum that incorporates the values they bring to school for improving successful learning outcomes (Dei, 1996b); a school context that capitalizes on minority strengths and learning styles as a basis for achievement; and a platform for minority stories to be told in their own voices, while repudiating the white-centredness of school knowledge as the only legitimate form of culture (McCaskill, 1995; Mukherjee, 1992).

Empowerment models come in different shapes. On one side of the empowerment model is the creation of culturally safe places within the existing school system. On the other side is the creation of separate schools for minority pupils, such as Aboriginal youth or youth at risk (L. Brown, 2005). A minority-centred school provides an alternative learning environment by catering to students for whom mainstream schools are inappropriate, even with thoughtful reforms (Dei, 1996b, 2005; Duffy, 2004). For example, an Africentric or African-focused school arrangement seeks to improve academic and social achievement for students at risk by emphasizing the centrality of black experiences in social history, by utilizing black role models as teachers and black teachers as role models, and by customizing content to appeal to those minority students who are alienated and disengaged from a Eurocentric educational system (see online Case Study 2.4). Examples also include an Ojibwa-focused school, housed in a wing of a school run by the Toronto District School Board, which has been in operation as Toronto's only official school of its type for 30 years without controversy (Brown, 2007). More empowering still are Islamic-focused schools (see online Case Study 11.7).

Another example of empowerment education is reflected in Aboriginal peoples' struggles to gain control of Aboriginal education. Since the early 1970s, Aboriginal peoples have sought to implement a variety of reforms involving the need to (1) decentralize the educational structure, (2) transfer funding control to local authorities, (3) devolve power from the centre to the community, and (4) empower parents to assume increased responsibility for their children's education. Aboriginal grievances and concerns over education are understandable. Federally directed native education sought to disrupt the cultural patterns of Aboriginal children, then expose them to the values and priorities of the West, often in schools off-reserve and away from community, friends, and relatives. The rigid assimilationism and abusive consequences of residential schools have been amply documented (Miller, 1999).

Other consequences are less direct but no less real in denying Aboriginal experiences, as the Métis scholar Paul Chartrand (1992, pp. 8–9) says: "It is easy to assert power over others if they are made to feel they have no identity, they have no past, or at least no past that matters." As a corrective to these historically imposed disadvantages, the aims of Aboriginal-controlled education are bicultural. First, it seeks to impart those skills that Aboriginal children will need to succeed in the outside world. Second, it hopes to immerse children in an environment that is unmistakably Aboriginal in content and style. The key is to produce children who possess a strong sense of who they are and where they come from, without forsaking the skills to compete in the dominant sector (Rushowy, 2001).

In summary, the introduction of multicultural education has transformed schools into much more inclusive places than in the past. Admittedly, multicultural education has been criticized from all sides. Some denounce it because the celebrating of diversity is perceived as a soft option contrary to the goals of a "real" education that prepares children for citizenship and the marketplace. Others attack multicultural education as hegemonic distraction that does nothing to challenge structural inequalities. The focus on diversity rather than difference conceals relationships of inequality within contexts of power. Worse still, although it conveys the impression (or illusion) that something is being done, the status quo remains undisturbed. And while the partial validity of these criticisms

TABLE 11-2	**Models of Multicultural Education**			
	Enrichment	**Enlightenment**	**Embracive**	**Empowerment**
Solution	Tolerance	Insight	Differences	Achievement orientation
Focus	Experience	Analysis	Exposure	Personal capacity–building
Goal	Undo prejudice	Remove ignorance	Cultural accommodation	Bicultural competence
Outcome	Culture awareness	Diversity literacy	Multi-perspectives	Improvement of life chances
Means	Celebrating differences	Race relations	Curriculum/pedagogy	Building of self-confidence
Target	Students	Students	Classroom culture	Minority students

cannot be denied, they ignore how multicultural education has the potential to shift the very foundations of both education and society by transferring diversity from the margins to the centre of the agenda (Gay, 1997; Ghosh & Abdi, 2004).

Table 11-2 provides an ideal-typical comparison of enrichment, enlightenment, embracive, and empowerment models of multicultural education along diverse criteria. Each of these ideal-typical models of multicultural education differ in terms of how they define the major problem, underlying assumptions regarding how and why the problem persists, and what needs to be done as solutions to create anticipated outcomes consistent with the problem definition.

Anti-racist Education

Multicultural education revolves around a philosophy of personal transformation. It consists of activities and curricula that promote an awareness of diversity in terms of its intrinsic value to minorities or to members of society at large. To the extent that diversity is celebrated, however, it is largely seen as a colourful add-on to an otherwise Euro-centric agenda (Zine, 2002). The aim of multicultural education is largely attitudinal, that is, to enhance individual sensitivity by improving knowledge about cultural differences (enrichment) and race relations (enlightenment). But there is no proof that enriched or enlightened attitudes will lead to behavioural changes, much less challenge issues of power, difference, and social inequality. Nor is there any evidence to suggest that a "food court and festival" multicultural education will address the major challenges in education at present—creating schools where all children are valued and respected, feel a sense of belonging, and have access to education that responds to diverse needs of different students (Ghosh, 2002; McGregor, 2002).

By contrast, **anti-racist education** takes its cue from anti-racism in general: that is, a commitment to actively challenge, resist, and transform the system by actioning the removal of racially discriminatory barriers at interpersonal and institutional levels both within education and outside. Anti-racist education begins with the assumption that minority underachievement is not necessarily caused by cultural differences. Nor will cross-cultural understanding contribute to any fundamental change in uprooting the structural roots of inequality unless issues of power and subordination are addressed (Kivel, 1996; Zine, 2002). Improving minority status is contingent on removing the behavioural and structural components of racial inequality both within and outside the education system, along with the power and privileges that sustain racism through institutional policies and procedures. Sweeping changes are needed—not tinkering with multicultural add-ons.

Anti-racist education can be defined as a proactive and process-oriented approach that balances the value of difference with a sharing of power and corresponding structural changes (Dei, 2000, 2007). Five processes prevail in advancing an anti-racist education that is both inclusive and equitable: (1) critical insight into those intersecting disadvantages that students bring into the classroom; (2) an informed discourse that focuses on race and racism as issues of power and inequality rather than matters of cultural difference; (3) a deconstruction of existing school practices to uncover the structural roots of monoculturalism and inequality; (4) a de-centring of Eurocentric knowledge by incorporating minority perspectives into all aspects of teaching and learning; and (5) a challenge to the status quo by fostering engagement and empowerment through political and social activism (Dei, 1996a).

In short, anti-racist education differs from multicultural education—at least for purposes of analysis. An anti-racist education questions the foundational principles of education. It calls into question the constitutional framework of schooling by politicizing the very basis of what passes for knowledge. The pedagogy becomes political (Giroux, 1999) when it addresses how the production of knowledge, social identities, and social relations has historically privileged some and disprivileged others. Under an anti-racist education, both students and teachers are offered the opportunity to see how culture is organized, who is authorized to speak about different forms of culture, which cultures are acceptable, and which are unworthy of public esteem. They also come to understand how power operates in the interests of dominant social relations; what needs to be done to challenge a Eurocentric constitutional order; and how these unequal relations can be transformed to create an inclusive Canada. Taken together, the goal of anti-racist education is to delegitimize those white privileges at the heart of contemporary society by "interrogating" the system of power relations that continue to deny or exclude. Table 11-3 provides a quick summary and comparison of multicultural and anti-racist education along ideal-typical lines.

TABLE 11-3	**Multicultural and Anti-Racist Education: A Comparison**	
	Multicultural education	**Anti-racist education**
Focus	Culture	Structure
Objective	Cultural sensitivity	Discriminatory barriers
Concerns	Ethnocentrism	Racism
Goals	Change individuals	Transform the system
Means	Attitudes	Behaviour
Scope	Student	Institutions
Style	Accommodation/reform	Challenge/resistance/transformation
Outcome	Celebrating differences	Promoting equity

Deconstructing Reasonable Accommodation: Doing What Is Necessary, Workable, and Fair?

Controversies over multicultural inclusivity reflect the politics of reasonable accommodation (Abu-Laban & Abu-Laban, 2007). Such a discursive shift should come as no surprise: Although Canada's official Multiculturalism is predicated on promoting inclusivity, namely, a two-way process of integration ("you adapt, we adjust/we adapt, you adjust") through reasonable accommodation (within limits and without undue hardship), Canadians tend to be confused over references to "reasonable" and "accommodation," "within limits," and "undue hardship." Questions abound: Is there a principled basis for defining reasonable accommodation with respect to institutional services that are responsive, reflective, and respectful? In creating *reasonable accommodation within limits and without undue hardship*, who decides, why, and on what grounds? According to a UN report (2006), while employees have a duty to accommodate diversity or disability, it is the claimant's responsibility to justify the "reasonable," whereas institutions must assume responsibility for justifying "undue hardship" and "within limits."

Debates in the United States are helpful in untangling these conundra. The concept of reasonable accommodation sprang into prominence over religious-based discrimination in the employment sector (United Nations, 2006). It was subsequently applied to the disability context, culminating in the 1990 *American Disability Act*, which

called on employers to reasonably accommodate qualified applicants or employees with disabilities. Under this Act, reasonable accommodation consists of any institutional adjustment—from building design to job duties—that does not inflict undue hardship on the accommodating agent (Goren, 2007). In determining whether an accommodation poses an undue hardship on the employer or service provider, the following factors are pivotal: (1) the nature and cost of the accommodation vis-à-vis institutional size, budget limitations, employee numbers, and types of facilities; and (2) the degree to which the accommodation could substantially alter the job requirement or the nature of the operation (Epilepsy Foundation, 2007). To ensure reasonableness, an underlying proportionality test is implied, one that balances burdens with benefits for all persons affected by the proposed adjustment (United Nations, 2006). In short, the "reasonable" in reasonable accommodation is not an empty qualifier, but central in securing the legitimacy of the adjustment process (Grey, 2007).

Similarly in Canada, the obligation to provide reasonable accommodation is enshrined within federal and provincial human rights legislation, in addition to judicial interpretation of the non-discrimination clause of the Charter (United Nations, 2006). According to the Ontario Human Rights Code, institutions have a duty to abolish those practices and programs that may exert a discriminatory impact on minorities. Toward that end, the Supreme Court has ruled that refusal by institutions such as school boards to reasonable accommodation violates the constitutional rights of Canadians, namely the religious freedom guaranteed by the Charter (Abu-Laban & Abu-Laban, 2007). Finally, the *Employment Equity Act* of 1996 obligates employers to reasonably and proportionately accommodate persons from designated groups. In deciding whether an accommodation would impose undue hardship, the factors of *health*, *safety*, and *cost* must be considered, ranging from disproportionate costs to impeding an enterprise's operation (Bouchard & Taylor, 2008). As well, there are limits to inclusivity under a reasonable accommodation. Accommodations for consideration must reject concessions that violate the rights of individuals (especially accommodations that victimize the most vulnerable members of a group), break the law, or contravene core constitutional values.

Let's put all this into perspective: Reasonable accommodation entails a process of making institutions more inclusive by making them more reflective of, responsive to, and respectful of diversity. It consists of any modification to service delivery or employment context that secures equal opportunities for qualified minority women and men, in part by treating minorities equally ("the same"), in part by treating them as equals ("differently") when necessary. Modifications include those pertaining to the application process to expand the applicant pool; accommodations on the job to take distinctive needs into account; and ongoing adjustments to ensure that all workers enjoy equal benefits and privileges (Epilepsy Foundation, 2007).

Two dimensions prevail in fostering reasonable accommodation—the reactive and the proactive: (1) reactive: the removal of discriminatory barriers, and (2) proactive: the implementation of positive measures (affirmative action or employment equity) to improve institutional access, representation, and equity in training, participation, rewards, and advancement (United Nations, 2006). Failure to provide reasonable accommodation at reactive and proactive levels can be construed as discriminatory and un-Canadian (European Union, 2005).

Chapter Highlights

- The concept of putting multiculturalism to work is concerned primarily with engaging diversity at the level of institutional inclusion. The media and education are but two of the institutions that must respond to a changing and diverse society.
- Institutional inclusivity is concerned with modifying institutional structures and values to ensure the full and equal participation of all Canadians. It is also concerned with improving an organization's representation, workplace climate, operational procedures and rules, and service delivery in a multicultural society. The most common barriers to institutional accommodation are people, hierarchy, bureaucracy, corporate culture, and occupational subculture.

- Models of inclusiveness can range from those that work within the existing system (reform and minority-ization) to those that posit alternative institutional solutions (parallel and separate).
- Canada's media industry has been remiss in responding to the challenges of diversity and institutional inclusiveness. Such an omission creates problems, as the media possess the capacity for defining public discourses regarding what is acceptable, normal, and necessary.
- Recent initiatives to create an inclusive and multicultural media are to be applauded. But accommodation is slow and gradual because of numerous points of resistance at individual and institutional levels.
- Four models of multicultural education can be observed. The enrichment model is concerned primarily with enhancing knowledge of and appreciation for cultural diversity. The enlightenment model is focused on informed understanding of Canadian race, ethnic, and Aboriginal relations. The embracive model focuses on attitude modification through a classroom environment in which cultural differences are celebrated and respected. An empowerment model is geared toward empowering racial minorities and Aboriginal peoples by modifying the curriculum and pedagogy to reflect a minority focus.
- Anti-racist education differs from multicultural education. It is concerned with isolating and challenging expressions of racism and racial discrimination at personal and institutional levels through direct action.
- The politics of reasonable accommodation are central to any debate over institutional inclusivity. This is particularly true with the prospect of reasonably accommodating ethno-religious minorities in a Canada that in principle is predominantly secular.

For further study, you can access the Case Studies referenced in this chapter at **www.pearsoncanada.ca/fleras**.

Review Questions

1. Compare and contrast the different models of multicultural education in terms of assumptions, objectives, and intended effects.

2. It's been argued that multicultural education is concerned with changing the person, while anti-racist education is more focused on transforming the system. Discuss this argument, by comparing anti-racist education with multicultural education with respect to focus, objectives, concerns, scope, and outcomes.

3. How are multicultural minorities and Aboriginal peoples portrayed by the media? Why? How does this portrayal present a problem in Canada's multicultural society?

4. Indicate what, if anything, can be done to improve media images of multicultural minorities and Aboriginal peoples. Keep in mind both the commercial and organizational context in which changes must occur.

5. What does the concept of institutional inclusivity mean? What are the components of an inclusive institution? What barriers exist that may preclude the institutional inclusion of diversity?

6. What does the concept of reasonable accommodation mean? How are the politics over reasonable accommodation played out in Ontario with respect to the proposed public funding of faith- and ethnicity-based schools?

Links and Recommendations

BOOKS

Religion and Ethnicity in Canada, edited by Paul Bramadat and David Seljak (2005). This book is one of the few in the field, and an excellent one at that.

Race, Ethnicity, and Difference: Imagining an Inclusive Society, by Peter Ratcliffe (2004). This book explores the exclusion of minorities in contemporary society, the barriers that put and keep them there, and what needs to be done to achieve institutional inclusion.

Our Diverse Cities, volumes 1–4, by Metropolis (2004, 2006, 2007). This examination of what both large- and medium-sized cities in Canada are doing to facilitate the integration of newcomers is available online at **www.metropolis.net**.

Education and the Politics of Difference: Canadian Perspectives, by Ratna Ghosh and Ali A. Abdi (2004). This book is an excellent introduction to the politics of multicultural education, especially because it reminds us that bigotry rather than difference is the enemy of a multicultural society, and that a multicultural education must go beyond tolerance and focus on justice, rights, and resources as an ethical response to racialized minorities if Canadians want to deepen the meaning of democracy and equality.

Islamic Peril: Media and Global Violence, by Karim Karim (2002). This book is a searing indictment of how Islam and Muslims are demonized by the news media—either directly or by association.

FILMS

Reel Injuns (2009)

Cree filmmaker Neil Diamond provides a biting yet sometimes hilarious look at the often racist film depictions of Aboriginal peoples in Canada and the United States. Read Pierre Berton's book *Hollywood's Canada* to expand your understanding of what and why.

WEBSITES

The websites listed in Chapter 10 are applicable here. Here are other recommendations.

For media, two sites are outstanding in providing insights into how mainstream media (mis)represent minorities:

Diversity Watch:

www.diversitywatch.ryerson.ca

Media Awareness Network:

www.media-awareness.ca

For multicultural and anti-racist education, a useful overview of current activities in this area is provided by the following website Canadian Education Trend Report: Anti-Racism and Multicultural Education.

www.safehealthyschools.org/whatsnew/racism.htm

Aboriginal Canada Portal—Issues of community and restorative justice for Canada's Aboriginal peoples are found at this website:

www.aboriginalcanada.gc.ca

CHAPTER 12

This Adventure Called Canada-Building

DEBATE

Rethinking Citizenship in a Postnational Canada

Canadians take quiet pride in themselves as citizens of a widely admired society. About 85 percent of all immigrants who permanently settle in Canada take the oath of **citizenship**, putting Canada at the forefront of the global citizenship sweepstakes (Kymlicka, 2003; Seidle, 2007a; Tran, Kustec, & Chui, 2005). This is hardly surprising: A Canadian citizenship entitles its bearer not only to rights and privileges, but also to membership in what many regard as one of the world's best places to live. Admittedly, until the *Citizenship Act*, which came into effect in January 1947 (Bloemraad, 2007), there was no such thing as a Canadian citizen, apart from a Commonwealth context. To the extent that such a category existed, "Canadians" were defined as British subjects who happened to be living in Canada, with a corresponding obligation to conduct themselves accordingly. In other words, citizenship, such as it was, prevailed primarily as a subset of British subjecthood (Macklin & Crepeau, 2010)

But passage of the *Citizenship Act* announced that Canadians were no longer simply transplanted British "expats." With the *Citizenship Act*, Canadian citizenship acquired autonomous legal existence, although Canadians remained linked to Britain (Bloemraad, 2007; Macklin & Crepeau, 2010). A new kind of belonging was proposed, one that embraced the realities of Canada rather than those of the United Kingdom. The goal of citizenship sought to integrate all Canadians into a single body politic, in large part by ignoring any distinction between Canada-born and foreign-born as a basis for citizenship. The boldness of this universalistic embrace cannot be underestimated. In an era when differences invariably denoted inferiority or exclusion, passage of the *Citizenship Act* embraced all citizens regardless of who they were or where they were from. The Act also redefined what it meant to be a Canadian, secured the right to full participation for citizens, and specified a citizen's commitments and obligations to Canada. But the challenges of globalization and cultural diversity have increasingly disrupted conventional assumptions pertaining to the primacy of the nation-state, how individuals negotiate their place and sense of belongings within a local and transnational context, and the relative cohesion and universalism of citizenship (Ang, 2011). This transformation makes it doubly important to rethink not only what it means to be a citizen at a national and global level, but also

(Continued)

what entitlements and patterns of belonging are possible in light of ongoing social changes and cultural diversities.

The Dimensions of Citizenship: Legal and Social

The concept of citizenship consists of two dimensions: the legal and the social. In legal parlance, citizenship entails formal membership in a politically constituted community (Delanty, 2000). A legal–political contract is established involving a transaction of mutual benefit to all parties, including a reciprocal exchange of rights and duties that connects individuals with membership in the state (Hebert & Wilkinson, 2002; Squires, 2007a). Individual citizens rely on the state to protect their rights and freedoms; in turn, the state expects that individual citizens fulfill certain duties, obligations, and responsibilities. For citizens of Canada, these rights and freedoms include equality rights, democratic rights, legal rights, mobility rights, language rights, a right of return to Canada from overseas travel, freedom of religion, freedom of expression, and freedom of assembly and association. (According to the *Canadian Charter of Rights and Freedoms*, only three rights are reserved exclusively for citizens: the right to vote and stand for election; the right to an education in a minority (English or French) language; and the right to enter and remain in Canada [Macklin & Crepeau, 2010].) In return, Canadian citizens are obliged to obey Canadian laws, participate in the democratic process, respect the rights and freedoms of others, and recognize Canada's linguistic duality and multicultural heritage.

People can acquire citizenship in two ways: at *birth* and by *naturalization* (Macklin & Crepeau, 2010). Citizenship by *birthright* is transmitted by descent from a citizen, with the result that citizenship is restricted to those who share a common bloodline or who can trace their genealogy to a citizen. All states allow their citizen parents to automatically pass their citizenship on to their children, according to Macklin and Crepeau (2010), but will vary in the number of generations across which a person living abroad can transmit citizenship by descent.[1] Citizenship by birthright can also be acquired from birth on the territory of the conferring citizenship state. Relatively few states (e.g., Canada and the United States) tolerate automatic and unconditional citizenship by birth on their territory. Countries like the United Kingdom and Australia allow citizenship by birth, but only if one of the parents holds lawful resident status. Citizenship by birth on territory may also be open to members of former colonies (Bell, 2004). By contrast, citizenship by *naturalization* involves the process of formal acquisition by someone who is not a citizen by birth. It is offered to those newcomers who are legal residents, fulfill certain residency requirements, make an effort to acquire citizenship, and acknowledge a commitment to the rule of law and shared values of the country in question.

But citizenship is not just about the legalities of membership and relationship to the state. Citizenship also incorporates a social dimension with respect to belonging and entitlements. The debate over belonging is based on who can belong as citizens, how and why, and what kind of entitlements ("rights") flow from this relationship. Common to each of these citizenship regimes is the primacy of universality as a basis for belonging and entitlement. A **universal citizenship** can be defined as one that treats all citizens the same, since everyone is thought to belong in the same way. Each citizen is entitled to the same benefits and rights—and stands in the same relation to the state—regardless of race or ethnicity. Entitlements because of difference are ignored under a universal citizenship: Just as people's differences cannot be used to exclude, so too should their differences not entitle them to special privileges or preferential treatment. A universal citizenship also rejects any type of entitlement rooted in collective or group rights as contrary to the principle of individual equality before the law. Promotion of group differences on racial or ethnic grounds—even in the spirit of inclusiveness and progress—can only undermine bonds of loyalty, unity, and identity.

Challenges to the Concept of Universal Citizenship

However enlightened for its times, the concept of universal citizenship has come under attack (Bosniak, 2000; Harty & Murphy, 2005; Kernerman, 2005; Yuval-Davis, 2007). Frameworks that may have worked in the past have proven cumbersome in addressing the highly politicized and collective claims of national minorities and indigenous peoples. In a world

of migration and multiple identities, the idea of a universal citizenship comes across as increasingly antiquated and counterproductive, although some would argue that increased diversification intensifies its relevance and importance (Kymlicka, 2003). Instead of a passive citizenship with its concept of membership in a homogeneous cultural group and corresponding sense of loyalty and duty, argue Yvonne Hebert and Alan Sears in their 2004 report *Citizenship Education*, contemporary citizenship involves a more dynamic dimension in a democratic state than widely envisaged. As Hebert and Wilkinson (2002) write:

> Citizenship is in transformation, its meaning is expanding, and interest in the subject is exploding. Citizenship has moved from being closed to being opened, from exclusion to inclusion. Once having had a unitary meaning, citizenship is now diffuse, multiple, and ever-shifting. Originally defined clearly by geographical borders and a common history, citizenship is increasingly in question . . . the transformation of citizenship is important, for it concerns who we are, how we live together, and what kind of people our children are to become. (p. 1)

The politics of citizenship in Canada are attracting attention—no more so than in the quest to balance particularistic entitlements and customized belonging with the unifying framework of universal citizen rights. The Debate Revisited box at the end of this chapter will further examine this issue.

INTRODUCTION: NEW GAME, NEW RULES, NEW OUTCOMES

Adventure, n. a daring enterprise (*Concise Oxford Dictionary*)

That we live in a period of convulsive social change is surely beyond dispute. Canada is currently in the midst of a social and demographic revolution so profound in its impact and implications that it threatens to sever the very moorings that formerly anchored it into place. Everything is changing so quickly that nothing is certain or predictable except a pervasive sense of confusion or uncertainty. What once were endorsed as universal truths are no longer accepted as morally valid or socially relevant. What once were defined as vices are increasingly embraced as virtues; perceived strengths, in turn, collapse into weaknesses as the politics of difference scuttles traditional assumptions about right and wrong. For example, in rejecting a belief that differences are incompatible with good governance, Canada now abides by the principles of an inclusive multiculturalism as a principled framework for living together differently (Fleras, 2009b). Admittedly, the transformational process has proven more bumpy than many imagined. Rules of the established order rarely apply in an age of difference and change, while vested interests tend to resist the establishment of new rules. The old order may be eroding but retains a critical mass of inertia; by contrast, the new order is compelling yet lacks the critical mass to dislodge the old.

Transformative changes of such magnitude require a mastery of context and perspective. Compared with societies that are plagued by human and natural misery, Canada's relentless inspection of itself reflects the indulgence of a country that by any measure is a "solution in search of a problem." The challenge of **Canada-building** may pale in comparison to that of India. With its 1 billion people, 16 official languages, and 5 major religions, India's survival as a modern democracy is a twenty-first century success story. Or consider Indonesia, with its 200 million people spread across 17 000 islands, representing 300 ethnic groups and 500 languages/dialects (Gee, 1998). Still, no one should casually dismiss the challenges that confront a deeply divided and multilayered Canada. Canada-building is complicated by factors as disparate as an expansive geography, a debilitating colonial history, an unwieldy and fractious regionalism, an unhealthy proximity to the United States, the potentially divisive politics of nationalism, and astonishing levels of immigrant diversities (Hiller, 2000). A cooperative coexistence is complicated by the interplay of Aboriginal peoples politics, the continuing divide between Quebec and the rest of Canada, and the growing presence and politicization of immigrant Canadians. Canada's commitment to inclusiveness as grounds for living together with differences further reinforces the country's status as a "contested site" involving a competitive struggle over power, privilege, and resources.

In short, Canada appears to be cresting the wave of a brave new adventure. This "adventure called Canada" (as a former Governor General of Canada once deftly put it) involves a series of interrelated but incomplete and competing society-building projects. The challenge lies in transforming this sprawling but narrowly populated land mass into a moral community of citizens with a shared sense of core values, a common vision, a sense of belonging, and a singularity of collective purpose. Foremost is the ongoing business of constructing a sense of cohesion, commitment, and identity from the threads of history, change, and diversities. Of equal importance to the national project is the sorting out of jurisdictions and entitlements around a three-nations model of Canada. The politics of Canada-building are sharply contested by the interplay of Canada's three major Ethnicities all with competing agendas, unique histories, distinct legal statuses, and different entitlements (see Jenson, 2002). Sorting through each of these different demand levels—and doing so simultaneously by accommodating diverse ways of accommodating difference—may reflect Canada's definitive challenge and crowning glory.

Reactions over the politics of Canada-building vary. That much can be expected in a society in which the politicization of difference has profoundly challenged the very notion of "what Canada is for"—a nation of nations? a community of communities? a category of convenience for self interested individuals? For some, the prospect of a multicultural society within the framework of a tri-national state equips Canada with the flexibility to withstand the stresses of uncertainty and change. Others disagree, and continue to embrace attitudes and projections seemingly inconsistent with twenty-first century realities. In trying to turn back the clock, they want to fortify Canada against the intrusions of a changing and diverse world. Still others fall somewhere in between. They may be mentally predisposed for change, yet are baffled by the prospect of applying yesterday's solutions to today's problems. There is mounting dismay that the promising diversity initiatives of the 1970s and 1980s—from multiculturalism to employment equity—have capitulated to a pessimism that nothing works and nobody cares (see also Friesen, 2005; Kitaro, 1997). With everything up for grabs and nothing taken for granted, only one thing appears certain: Canada's **society-building** skills will be sorely tested in the attempt to reconcile the often competing demands of unity with those of difference in a freewheeling yet interconnected global world

The politicization of difference has made it abundantly clear: If improperly managed or left entirely to market forces, the politics of difference can provoke and partition. But with the appropriate architecture in place, dissimilar peoples can learn to share land, power, and resources while respecting their differences as grounds for a sustainable coexistence. There is much of value with such an assessment, and this concluding chapter explores the possibilities of a Canada at a critical juncture in its (r)evolutionary development. The chapter will examine how this adventure called Canada-building is fraught with perils and pitfalls, yet full of promise and potential. Reference to the **"Canadian Way"** implicit within **Canada's Difference Model** offers a blueprint for addressing the challenges of a deeply divided and multilayered society. A reassessment of Canada's so-called weaknesses as a postmodern strength is shown to have transformed Canada into a postnational society. This transformational paradox is captured by debates over the politics of citizenship, with proponents of a universal citizenship clashing with advocates of an inclusive citizenship in defining belonging and entitlements. The chapter concludes accordingly. Canada is hardly perfect in managing race, ethnic, and Aboriginal relations. Nevertheless, it may be less imperfect than the rest, partly because Canada possesses the right kind of "imperfections" for living together with differences in the twenty-first century.

CANADA-BUILDING: AN UNFINISHED WORK IN PROGRESS

Can a modern (European-based) constitution recognize and accommodate cultural diversity? This is one of the most difficult and pressing questions of the political era we are entering at the dawn of the twenty-first century. (James Tully, 1995, p. 1)

Canada sits among a handful of settler-based countries in the vanguard that is constructing coherent yet pluralistic societies. Canada's status as a global trailblazer for constructively engaging differences stems from the unorthodox way it has gone about solving its largely atypical problems (see Saul, 1998). The contours of Canadian society are realigning along pluralistic lines, signalling a departure from earlier eras when government agendas routinely privileged the authority of mainstream rules, monocultural values, and dominant institutions (Kymlicka, 2003). But a profound cultural and demographic shift is uprooting Canada's Eurocentric moorings. As a result of challenges to its constitutional order, Canadians are experiencing what Michael Adams (1997) calls a "sea change" in Canada's social values—from an authoritarian, top-down pyramid to a more horizontal "pancake" model anchored in flexibility and openness.

The challenges of a diversifying and changing Canada are proving a governance conundrum. A proliferation of divided loyalties has complicated the search for national unity—especially when Canada's major Ethnicities envision their commitment to Canada as conditional and contingent on claims that must be differently accommodated (Kymlicka, 2001). Aboriginal peoples are no longer willing to remain on the peripheries of Canada. They instead are actively and openly competing for recognition and resources as part of an ongoing reformulation of Canada's Aboriginal peoples–state relations. The proposed restructuring of Quebec–Ottawa relations within a renewed federalism has proven frustratingly elusive, with little in the way of a permanent resolution. But the two interdependent solitudes have such a vested interest in staying together that this mutual dependency may well yield the flexibility and compromise to shore up an awkwardly coherent coexistence. The politics of Canada's multicultural agenda are no less potent. A commitment to the ideals of cultural identity, social equality, and civic citizenship has catapulted official Multiculturalism to the forefront of strategies for addressing immigrant concerns, albeit not without criticism (Fleras, 2009b; Zachariah, Sheppard, & Barrett, 2004).

The politics of working through differences has profoundly transformed Canada (Magnet, 2004; Parkin, 2003). In ways unimaginable and yet inescapable, the Canada of today differs from the country of a generation ago, not to mention that of a century ago. Many of these changes are reflected, reinforced, and advanced at (1) policy levels for constructing engaging difference, (2) institutional levels with respect to reasonable accommodation, (3) the level of a more tolerant cultural climate, and (4) the symbolic level in terms of identity. Even the discourses around race, ethnic, and Aboriginal relations are changing. References to race, ethnicity, and aboriginality are no longer framed as a "thing" (noun) but as a "process" (verb) undergoing continuous changes, challenges, and contestation. Consider the following discursive shifts in redefining Canada's evolving response to the dynamics of race, ethnic, and Aboriginal relations:

- *National Vision: From British Colony to Cosmopolitan Kaleidoscope.* From a vision of Canada as a tightly scripted "white-man's country," where everyone knew their place, to its emergence as a tri-national and multicultural work in progress where nothing is certain because everything is contested and negotiable.

- *Models of Governance: From Uniformity to Multiculturality.* From monoculturalism as a framework for living together to the principles of multiculturalism in advancing a multicultural governance of difference and diversity. From a one-size-fits-all formula for

Canada-building, including a universal citizenship with similar rights and obligations, to the idea of customizing arrangements in response to Canada's multilayered differences.

- *Status of Minorities: From Margins to Mainstream.* From the marginalization and inferiorization of those outside an Anglo-Canadian profile—including Aboriginal peoples, racialized minorities, and immigrant Canadians—to their centrality as key players in reshaping the political, social, and cultural contours of Canadian society.

- *Institutions: From Exclusion to Inclusivity.* From institutions that ordinarily and routinely excluded minorities because of their differences to an emphasis on institutional inclusivity ("incorporation") through reasonable accommodation that is respectful of, reflective of, and responsive to differences by way of services that are available, accessible, and appropriate.

- *Status of Diversity: From Indifference to Difference.* From a rejection of difference as irrelevant, inferior, and contrary to good governance, to an endorsement of differences, albeit at a superficial level ("pretend pluralism"), in defining who gets what (Bannerji, 2000).

- *Tolerance Levels: From Open Dislike to Openness.* From an intolerance of others as a badge of pride as might be expected of a white Canada, to an embrace of tolerance as profoundly central to Canada's identity as a multiculturally cosmopolitan society (Foster, 2005).

- *Patterns of Entitlement: From Inequality to Equity.* From an endorsement of inequality as inevitable, normal, and necessary to a commitment to the principle of equity, including recognition of collective rights and group-specific measures as well as the need to take people's differences into account for true equality and inclusiveness.

- *From Race-Conscious to Race-Blind to Race-Sensitive.* From a Canada that explicitly excluded others because of race to one that believes race no longer matters because of Canada's commitment to the principles of a colour-blind society. From an era when race mattered (stigma) to one where it shouldn't matter but it does (perception) to one with a growing awareness that it will matter because a colour-blind Canada neither exists nor should exist if differences are taken seriously (race-sensitive).

- *Levels of Intervention: From Laissez-Faire to Macro-Management.* From a government reluctance to get involved in managing the dynamics of race, ethnic, and Aboriginal relations, to the centrality of government intervention in micro-managing limits and macro-managing priorities, reflecting an awareness that market forces alone cannot bring about justice and equality.

- *Expanding Rights: From Whites to Humanity.* From a Canada that routinely denied and excluded others because of national origins (as well as gender) to a Canada that many see as a pacesetter in protecting and promoting the principle of **human rights**, both individual and collective—at least in theory if not always in practice (see online Insight 12.1).

- *Rethinking Canada-Building: From Modernity to "Postnationality."* From a commitment to Canada as a modernist ("centralized and uniform") project to its endorsement as a postnational ("decentralized and differenced") society, culminating in a distinctively Canadian Way for constructively engaging difference. Of particular note is recognition of Canada's Difference Model, with its commitment to differential accommodation in advancing a postnational future (see the next section).

The Canadian Way and Canada's Difference Model: Differential Accommodation

Canada is widely regarded both nationally and internationally as a world leader when it comes to constructively engaging diversity. Canada's experiment in accommodating differences—including Aboriginal peoples, Québécois, and increasingly politicized multicultural minorities—has produced over 140 years of relatively peaceful coexistence (Kymlicka, 2004; LaSelva, 2004; see also Bickerton & Gagnon, 2004). As well, Canada is perceived as a model for managing intergroup differences in those countries that, too, are grappling with the politics of differences. The challenge is relatively straightforward: to balance these fundamental yet opposed differences in a way that most Canadians find acceptable, that provide a blueprint for living together despite deep differences, and that consolidate a commitment to Canada without undermining the integrity of parts (McRoberts, 2003). Responses to this challenge entail the concept of the Canadian Way and Canada's Difference Model for managing diversities. The former is implicit in the latter, and together they provide a solution to the key challenge of the new millennium: How can different ways of accommodating difference coexist in deeply divided and multilayered societies without a capitulation to chaos?

The Canadian Way: Principle and Process The Canadian Way may mean a lot of things, depending on the speaker, context, or intended audience, but most references involve *content* and a *process*. As content, the Canadian Way articulates a commitment to the principles of *differences* and *inclusiveness* as a basis for democratic governance. In contrast to the past, when a monocultural governance sought to uphold a white Canada while working to assimilate or exclude minorities and differences, the Canadian Way embraces the possibility of creating a prosperous and cohesive Canada by injecting a diversity dividend into the national agenda (Kymlicka, 2003). A principled commitment to diversity and difference does not necessarily compromise an equally strong attachment to national unity and respect for core Canadian values, as pointed out by Canadian Heritage (2001):

> Canada's approach to diversity is based on the belief that the common good is best served when everyone is accepted and respected for who they are, and that this ultimately makes for a resilient, more harmonious, and more creative society. This faith in the value of diversity recognizes that respect for cultural distinctiveness is intrinsic to an individual's sense of self-worth and identity, and a society that encourages achievement, participation, attachment to country and a sense of belonging.

The Canadian Way also endorses a principled process for meeting the evolving challenges of diversities (Kymlicka, 2001). Mechanisms and arrangements have been introduced to facilitate engagement and community without violating individual rights and national interests. An extensive legal framework exists to promote the principles of diversity and individual rights—from official Multiculturalism to the *Canadian Charter of Rights and Freedoms* to the *Employment Equity Act*. Structures are in place so that disagreements can be resolved through negotiation and compromise instead of through resorting to a rigid dogmatism. Individuals who believe their rights have been violated can appeal to federal and provincial human rights commissions for redress.

Two preconditions inform this process. First, there must be a society-wide commitment to the principle of agreeing to disagree, so that differences of opinion can be articulated, discussed, and adjusted accordingly. Second, the process of negotiated compromise requires an institutional framework that creates relatively open lines of communication. Or as Will Kymlicka (2001) writes in defending process as the heart of the Canadian Way:

> Canada has a legal framework for discussing issues of diversity. Policies of multiculturalism, federalism and Aboriginal rights give the relevant groups a seat at the table and constitutional legitimacy to their identities and interests. Many countries have no framework for the majority and minority to sit down and discuss how to live together. (p. A15)

Thus, reference to the Canadian Way connotes the pragmatic ways in which Canadians address the challenge of difference in a multilayered and deeply divided society. Canada incorporates what might be called a pluralistic model for managing diversities, and its strength lies in differently working through problems rather than applying a one-size-fits-all solution, of seeking compromises rather than unilaterally imposing fixtures, and of balancing diverse interests in a state of creative tension rather than seeking definitive answers.

Canada's Difference Model: Differential Accommodation Canada may be one of the only countries in the world that must simultaneously address the interests, agendas, and demands of three major ethnicities—namely, Aboriginal peoples, charter groups, and multicultural minorities. The genius of Canada's Difference Model is its willingness to recognize the legitimacy of three mutually exclusive yet principled policy platforms. Canada's Difference Model for managing diversities is not just about accommodating difference. More to the point, *it's about accommodating different ways of accommodating difference*. In creating a society based on compromise, a Difference Model acknowledges that (1) Canada's major ethnicities possess fundamental divergent agendas and priorities because of different sociological status, patterns of belonging, and corresponding entitlements; (2) any policy solutions must be customized to accommodate the difference between voluntary minorities who want to "get in" versus forcibly incorporated peoples who want to "get out"; and (3) proposed outcomes must coincide with the constitutional status of each major ethnicity without breaching the principle of unity within diversity. In addition, Canada's Difference Model must also balance oppositional tensions and choices resulting from competing values, including uniformity versus diversity; individual rights versus group rights; formal equality (symmetry or equal treatment) versus substantive equality (asymmetry or special treatment); and personal freedom versus national security (Jenson & Papillon, 2001).

Three ethnicity levels of differential accommodation are addressed in Canada's Difference Model:

1. One ethnicity level is represented by Aboriginal peoples, who claim to be sovereign peoples with the right of self-determining autonomy over land, identity, and political voice (Maaka & Fleras, 2008). A package of priorities is proposed whose foundational principles promote power-sharing and a partnership based on a government-to-government relationship. To the extent that Canada is grappling with decolonizing its relationship with the descendents of the original inhabitants, in part by promising a more positive alternative, the contours of a new postcolonial social contract are taking shape.

2. Another ethnicity level is represented by the Québécois, who, like Aboriginal peoples, claim to be sovereign in principle. Québécois demands pivot around putting this principle into practice in a way that acknowledges a compact view of Canada, Quebec's status as a distinct society, and Québécois demands of mastery over their own house (Gagnon, Guibernau, & Rocher, 2003). English-speaking Canada appears to be moving in the direction of a more flexible federalism, one that recognizes Quebec as more than a province but less than a separate nation-state, although there is reluctance to constitutionally entrench this shift for fear of blowing out of proportion the fictions that paper over Canada's contradictions.

3. At yet another ethnicity level are immigrant and multicultural minorities, who want equality and inclusion yet respect for their cultural differences, without paying a penalty in the process (James, 2005; see also Abu-Laban & Gabriel, 2002). The combination of initiatives, from anti-racism to employment equity, reinforce the notion of Canada as a society of many cultures, in which people's cultural differences cannot preclude full participation and equal citizenship rights as a matter of course, while still acknowledging that differences can be taken into account when necessary.

To be sure, references to Canada's Difference Model tend to overstate this country's outcomes in the diversity sweepstakes. The most egregious expressions of colonialism in Canada may have been eradicated; nevertheless, Canada's Difference Model is largely silent about challenging the foundational principles that govern the country's constitutional order. For example, Ontario's *Mining Act* of 1873 still allows mining companies (or any adult with a prospector's licence) to prospect anywhere for subsurface minerals—even when trampling on Aboriginal lands or yet-to-be-resolved land claims. In keeping with this colonial infrastructure, there remains a refusal or incapacity, because of costs and consequences, to take Aboriginal difference seriously. Yes, Aboriginal self-government is in place, but not necessarily Aboriginal *models* of self-determining autonomy. True, Quebec is now recognized as a nation and a distinct society, but neither concession is constitutionally entrenched. Nor is there much enthusiasm for seriously re-engaging Aboriginal peoples or the Québécois as fundamentally autonomous political communities, both sovereign and sharing sovereignty by way of separate and interlocking jurisdictions. It is similar with immigrant and multicultural minorities: A commitment to institutional inclusivity may reflect the principles of multiculturalism, but too often, only in the very narrow sense of replacing white incumbents with minority hires within the existing framework of rules, structures, and priorities. Inasmuch as the status quo remains largely intact, with changes only to the practices referring to the rules instead of foundational rules that inform practices and conventions, the challenge of living together with differences remains as complex as ever.

TOWARD A POSTNATIONAL CANADA: NATION OR NOTION?

Increasingly, we are cultural Canadians: Canadian by willpower rather than by policy. We feel attached to Canada because we like the smell of it. It is an affair of the heart. The process is ephemeral, not mechanical, but no less real. Get used to it. We live in an age of intangibles, and our love of country is as intangible as it is profound. (Edward Greenspon, editor of *The Globe and Mail*, 2001)

The world is engulfed by two mutually exclusive yet inextricably linked forces. On the one hand are the universalizing (and homogenizing) forces of a freewheeling global market economy. Transnational movements of goods and services are conducted with seemingly minimal regard for societal boundaries (Castles & Miller, 2009). Advances in information technology tend to render national borders increasingly porous and difficult to monitor and control. On the other hand, the fragmenting forces of insurgent ethnic identities are poised to dismember and destroy. Radical ethnicities and ethnic national-isms appear to be largely indifferent or hostile to the legitimacy of the nation-state, preferring instead a commitment to challenge, resist, and transform regardless of conse-quences (Ignatieff, 2005). This interplay of centrifugal ("push out") and centripetal ("pull in") forces promises to reshape the political contours of societies large and small, in the process contesting the concept of "what society is for."

On balance, Canada appears to have been relatively successful in balancing these global forces with those of national interests and minority rights, even if the juggling act tends to be wobbly at times. Such an achievement in Canada-building is not to be sneered at, given the enormity of the challenges. Unlike the more **complete (or civilizational) societies** of Europe (Castles & Miller, 2009), Canada *represents* an idea and a set of ide-als rather than a people with a history, language, and culture, and it is this fundamental ambiguity that underscores the contradictions in Canada-building. "Canada is not a real country," as former Quebec premier Lucien Bouchard once taunted English-speaking Canadians, but a collection of shreds and patches with no real historical or cultural reason to claim nationality or peoplehood. Outside of Quebec, Canadians have little in common—no shared ancestors or genetic pool, no origin myths, and few common rituals—except perhaps a commitment to public institutions such as universal healthcare. Or rephrased, Canada is not so much a mosaic of culturally distinct tiles, but a complex matrix of wiggly lines and contested angles in response to the demands of multiple identities and competing sovereignties under a single polity. That is, it's a notion, not a nation.

This assessment of Canada as all "lines" and "angles" may not flatter. Yet these very vulnerabilities may yield a host of possibilities for crafting a new kind of Canada. That is, Canada may be poised on the brink of becoming the world's first postnational soci-ety. Consider the contrasts: A "national" society embraces the principles of modernity and modernism as the basis for modern governance. As an Enlightenment project, mod-ernity rejected religion as a legitimate form of social authority, embraced reason and scientific inquiry as the organizing principle of social life, sought to develop universal categories of explanation and rationalization, strove for the attainment of absolute truth (universally valid foundations for human knowledge based on reason and science), and embraced a belief in history as having direction or purpose (Dustin, 2007). Applied to society, an embrace of modernity and modernism reflected the ideals and attainment of a unitary, centralized, and homogenized nation-state under control of a dominant national group, which used its privileged status and power to impose nationhood through its language, culture, history, symbols, and so on (Kymlicka, 2004, 2007). A national (or modern) society also embraced as a basis for society-building a commitment to a master narrative (uniformity), a coherent state identity (homogeneity), universalism (rules apply to all), centrality (to ensure conformity and control), clarity (rather than ambiguities), a low threshold for uncertainties, and a belief in merging nation (peoples) with state (a people) (Dustin, 2007). Or, put alternatively, society-building adhered to the principle of rational

370 Part Three: Living Together with Differences in a Multiculturally Inclusive Canada

instrumentality, with its McDonaldized commitment to reducing costs by improving efficiency, predictability, and standardization (Ritzer, 2008). (See online Debate 12.2.)

By contrast, the world we inhabit at present is an untidy one. Established rules, values, and institutions are struggling to construct more flexible modes of governance to cope with new and fluid realities that have yet to gain mainstream traction (Ang, 2011). The double binds are numerous: In a globalizing world of capital flows and people movement, the nation-state is losing its salience as governance space for fostering human security and community, yet it's also proving impossible to ignore as an instrument of intervention and regulation. In a world of transmigration (transnationalism), hybridity, and diaspora, it no longer makes sense to talk of multiculturalism or citizenship as forms of governance when people's notions of identity and affiliation are increasingly untied from place. A static and categorical multiculturalism as governance and discursive construct is increasingly incapable of capturing the immensely more complex and dynamic world of diversities within diversities (multiversal or super-diversity) within shifting contexts of power and inequality (Fleras, 2011b). The interplay and dynamics of unsettled boundaries, uncertain loyalties, and fragile identities is consequential in deconstructing the monocultural ideal of the nation-state as a unity-in-diversity. As Ien Ang (2011) argues, it is now time to recast the nation-state as a socially constructed and imaginary ideal, both unstable and evolving with no foreseeable closure in sight.

Just as we are in a profoundly postmulticultural era, so too does postnational society invoke the postmodernist principle of "doing things differently." In a multiversal era of politicized differences within differences that challenges the foundational principles of a conventional societal order, it is futile or repressive to endorse modernist goals of clarity, coherence, centralized authority, commonality, and consensus. The lofty position of a monocultural nation-state as the privileged unit of sovereign identity and agency—a bounded entity with territorial integrity and historical continuity—is sharply being eroded by rampant internal fragmentation and thoroughly porous borders (Ang, 2011). Traditional criteria for defining a nation-state are contested, including the goal of matching territory ("state") with that of culture, identity, a people, and history ("nation"). In contrast to a monocultural nation-state, a postnational society espouses a multiculturality that repudiates (1) the idea that the state is possessed by a single national group (but rather espouses the idea that it belongs equally to all citizens); (2) assimilationist policies that force minorities to hide their identities (but rather accords equal recognition and respect for difference and diversity) and (3) institutional practices that exclude or deny (in favour of those that improve equal involvement and full citizenship rights) (Kymlicka, 2007). In place of centralized and fixed mono-uniformity is a sense of impermanence, fragmentation, and mutability, reflecting a radically skeptical world where everything is relative and contested, because nothing is absolute and definitive (Bauerlein, 2001; Dustin, 2007; Gwyn, 1996). With postnationality, in other words, weaknesses morph into society-building strengths; conversely, strengths drift into weaknesses within contexts of transformative changes.

In short, by challenging the rules upon which convention is based rather than simply the practices that refer to the rules (Angus, 2002), a postnational society proposes a new game with a different set of rules for belonging, identity, and unity. This line of reasoning applies to Canada in how it manages the politics of difference without destroying

TABLE 12-1	The Nation-State versus the Notion-State	
Modern nation-state	**Postnational society (notion-state)**
Society = striving completion	Society as ongoing social construction/unfinished project in progress
All-encompassing narrative: "We are all one people"	Multiple voices, multiple identities, multiple loyalties
Making society safe from difference	Making difference safe from society
One-way adjustment: "Our way, the right way"	Inclusive two-way adjustment/reasonable accommodation: You adjust, we adapt; we adjust, you adapt"
Coherent and singular national identity	Splintered and contested national identity
Conformity and standardization: "Treat everyone the same"	Inclusive diversity: "Treat others equally and as equals" + accommodate different ways of accommodating differences
Centralized command and pyramidal control	Decentralized and devolved (flattened) control
Conflate nation with state, including universal citizenship model of belonging, identity, and entitlement	Society as a nation of nations, community of communities, diversities within diversities, including customized citizenship models of belonging, entitlement, and identity
A monocultural society that at best acknowledges a pretend (superficial) pluralism	A difference-driven society that takes difference seriously
Society-building = problem to be solved	Society-building = tension to be managed/negotiated
A commitment to a nation (common history, cultures, peoples, territory)	A commitment to a notion (a set of ideas and ideals)

itself in the process. Instead of a definitive centre that categorically defines and controls, Canada is constructed around a society-building process that accommodates different ways of accommodating difference with respect to belonging, entitlements, and identity. Rather than something natural or normal with a shared history, geography, or ethnicity ("nation"), Canada is defined as an ongoing social construction ("notion")—a project or convention created by individuals and groups, evolving and relative to a particular time and place, and subject to reformative change—as this quote aptly conveys: "Canada is a kind of model for the 21st century, in which a nation defines itself not as a piece of geography or a race of people but as a political and cultural and existential concept" (John Gray, as cited in Whittington, 1998).

A brief comparison (see Table 12-1) demonstrates the ideal–typical contrasts between the modernist nation-state project and the postnational (notion-state) model— keeping in mind that Canada is only beginning to disengage from modernity toward postmodernity as a society-building blueprint.

Building Canada: Perfecting Imperfections

A rewriting of the rules for differently living together allows Canada to claim status as one of the world's first postnational societies (see Gwyn, 1994, 1996). The lightness of being that is associated with Canada's postnationality may provide a prototype for the ideal twenty-first century society by the simple expedient of transforming weaknesses into strengths because of shifting circumstances. The fact that Canada represents a political union born out of economic necessity rather than a national spirit or violent struggle may work in its favour. The endless debates over power and jurisdictions may have morphed into a kind of glue for binding Canadians together. Of course, debates over Canada's unity and identity often perplex and provoke, even infuriate those with a keen sense of what Canada is for. But the paradox of a rolling Canadian identity provides a resiliency and flexibility that avoids being locked into the rigidities of the past (see Castles & Miller, 2009). This notion of Canada as "tension to be negotiated rather than a problem to be solved" mentality may have also bolstered its reputation as an open and tolerant society, with a commitment to constructively engaging difference as a virtue to be nurtured rather than a vice to be spurned.

Put bluntly, in a world of diversity, uncertainty, and change, Canada's atypicalness may be its strength. Canada's seeming vulnerability—its decentralized unity and diversity-based identity—may prove a tower of strength in a world where rigidity and authority are incompatible with the freewheeling demands of a global market economy characterized by the international movement of people and ideas (Simmons, 2010). Perhaps this penchant for snatching virtue from vice defines and distinguishes Canadians in promoting postnationalist ways of living together differently in a deeply divided and multilayered Canada. Canadians may well possess the kind of temperament best suited for the postmodern realities of the twenty-first century, namely, a dedication to pragmatism, a commitment to civility and tolerance, and a willingness to compromise for the sake of the whole. In a world where rules and conventions are being turned inside out, Canada's threshold for uncertainty and tolerance of ambiguity may provide just the right amount of resilience to bend, not break. In an era where a passionate attachment to homeland or culture may maim or destroy, its redemption may reflect a willingness to "cut some slack" when necessary. In renegotiating the meaning of Canadianness by way of rights, principles, obligations, and rules of engagement (MacQueen, 1994), a commitment to compromise may prove our lasting contribution to world peace, as eloquently expressed by Adrienne Clarkson, former Governor General of Canada:

> It's a strength and not a weakness that we are a permanently incomplete experiment built on a triangular foundation—aboriginal, francophone, and anglophone. What we continue to create, today, began 450 years ago as a political project . . . It is an old experiment, complex, and, in worldly terms, largely successful. Stumbling through darkness and racing through light, we have persisted in the creation of a Canadian civilization (as cited in Canadian Heritage, 2001).

The conclusion is inescapable: This adventure called Canada-building remains a work in progress. Canada may not be a real country in the complete sense of the term, but rather an ongoing and unfinished project that must be continually willed into action. As a social construction of ideas and ideals—a space of travelling cultures—Canada cannot rest on its laurels. On the contrary, as a work in progress, it must always define, modify, and change in line with changing circumstances (see also Sandercock, 2003). That it has managed to transform this indeterminacy into contemporary strengths— even if out of necessity rather than principle—must surely say something about Canada's commitment for constructively engaging difference. In other words, Canada appears to have just the right kind of imperfections for harnessing the resources and resourceful-ness needed to meet the challenges of an increasingly postnational global era. The words of Professor Xavier Arbos, a Catalan and president of the International Council for Canadian Studies, strike as reassuring and rewarding: "Canadians have reasons to be proud of a country that is balanced, democratic, a country that cares, where there is less violence . . ." Canada may not be perfect, he adds, but it looks a lot better than most.

From Universal to Inclusive Citizenship: Putting Canada's Difference Model to the Test

For some, a universal citizenship must prevail in Canada. Only a universal citizenship can perform the twin tasks of protecting Canada's national inter-ests while ensuring protection of the fundamental rights of all loyal Canadi-ans. Equality and progress reflect the renunciation of differences to ensure that everyone is equal before the law with the same rights, entitlements, and obligations regardless of their differ-ences. A citizenship splintered into "this" and "that" cannot possibly fulfill its basic function of creating shared loyalty, common identity, patriotic commitment, and those unifying sym-bols for bonding citizens into a single framework. Without the shared values of a universal (common) citizenship for bonding and bridging, the danger of society splintering into a series of fractured communities is all too real. Moreover, reference to a differentiated citizenship is deemed as un-Canadian since (1) some individuals are treated more equally than others, (2) special group rights are elevated over individ-ual rights, and (3) the legitimacy of the political community at large is com-promised. To be sure, a universal citi-zenship may acknowledge the need

to invoke special treatment for the his-torically disadvantaged, but only if the measures are temporary, specific to the problem, and reflect need rather than racial factors.

For others, a more differentiated citizenship is required in Canada. A one-size-fits-all unitary citizenship no longer resonates with relevance within the context of Canada's multilayered and deeply divided society (Hebert & Wilkinson, 2002; Redhead, 2003). Entitlements under a "universal" citi-zenship often fail certain marginalized minorities because they privilege for-mal equality rights (equal treatment) over substantive equity rights (treatment as equals), thus ranking all individuals as similar for political or economic purposes, regardless of circumstances or commitments (Schouls, 1997). As Iris Marion Young (1990) has argued, a universal conception of citizenship is unfair when applied to unequal con-texts, that is, treating all citizens—regardless of race, class, or gender—as disembodied individuals in the abstract rather than as disadvantaged minorities in a real world. Moreover, Canada can no longer be defined in terms of singularity—one nation, one identity,

(Continued)

one culture, or one belonging (Hebert & Wilkinson, 2002). In a world of globalization and transmigratory connections, many individuals retain meaningful relations to more than one state, and acknowledge this reality through the acceptance of dual or multiple citizenships (Fleras, 2011b; Macklin & Crepeau, 2010; Simmons, 2010). Identities today are openly and politically plural, with people belonging to many different groups and defining themselves in terms of these multiple affiliations without necessarily experiencing contradiction or rejecting commonalities (Karim, 2006; Mawani, 2008).

Proposed instead of a universal citizenship is an **inclusive citizenship**. An inclusive citizenship combines the rights of universal citizenship with the differentiated claims of Aboriginal peoples, national communities, and multicultural minorities (Harty & Murphy, 2005). With an inclusive citizenship, different patterns of entitlement and belonging are endorsed based on the principle of accommodating diverse ways of accommodating difference.

Four types of citizenship entitlements and belonging can be differentiated under an inclusive citizenship: *equity, multicultural, self-determining,* and *transmigratory* (or *transnational*)—each of which reflects a reading of Canada as a multilayered and deeply divided society.

- *Equity Entitlements*: Those immigrants and descendants of immigrants who have been historically disadvantaged because of their differences may require a different set of entitlements to ensure full citizenship rights. Equity citizenship entitlements are aimed at improving institutional access and societal integration through the removal of discriminatory barriers and the introduction of proactive programs such as employment equity.

- *Multicultural Entitlements*: Both racial and cultural minorities may require some degree of official protection of their ethnocultural heritage. Multicultural citizenship goes beyond a demand for cultural rights or acceptance of cultural differences as a value. Rather, it entails new forms of inclusion involving recognition and the promotion of previously marginalized cultures on the assumption that membership in a living and lived-in cultural reality provides individuals with meaningful choices to maximize freedom (Allegritti, 2010; Kymlicka, 1992). In contrast to liberalism and universal citizenship, an inclusive multicultural citizenship insists on the need to recognize the cultural embeddedness of citizenship while taking steps to take cultural differences seriously through the political integration of all citizens—a process that involves a dialogue between central authorities and previously excluded groups (Allegritti, 2010).

- *Self-Determining Entitlements*: Another type of citizenship entitlement involves Aboriginal peoples and the Québécois. Both Aboriginal peoples and minority nations like the Québécois have different group-specific needs, aspirations, status, and experience; as a result, citizenship entitlements must be customized accordingly. As peoples or nations, their demands as citizens go beyond universal citizenship. They include claims upon the state for control over land, culture, language, and identity; the right to self-government and jurisdiction over matters of direct relevance; and a transfer of power from central authorities (devolution) rather than mere political representation or institutional accommodation (Kymlicka, 1992). Belonging to Canada is indirect, that is, through membership in First Nations communities rather than through individual citizenship.

• *Transmigratory (Transnational) Entitlements*: Transmigratory citizenship refers to the possibility of dual or even multiple citizenships, both concurrently and without contradiction (Dijkstra, Geutjen, & Ruijter, 2001). The theory of a postnational (or transnational) citizenship in a global era is predicated on three realities: (1) the eroding sovereignty of states; (2) less constraining geography because of technology; and (3) the capacity of people to maintain multiple links between their homeland and the host country (Simmons, 2010). In an age of migration where up to 200 million people may be on the move at any time and connections are a mouse click away, new patterns of belonging may reflect loyalty to the home country and the adopted country (Kymlicka, 2003). Immigrants in the past may have traditionally discarded the old by severing ties with the homeland and embracing the new. But the combination of modern communications technologies with relatively cheap air travel reinforces both the possibility of return migration and the greater likelihood of multiple loyalties and belongings (Castles & Miller, 2009; Squires, 2007a; Yuval-Davis, 2007).

The concept of an "inclusive" citizenship emphasizes the validity of both universal rights and customized citizenship entitlements. To be sure, an inclusive citizenship is not about a different set of citizenship rights for different groups of citizens. More accurately, it is about accepting that, in addition to universal citizenship rights, different groups of Canadians can claim patterns of entitlements and belonging consistent with their diverse status, aspirations, and experiences. In visualizing citizenship as a rope of interwoven strands, one of these strands emphasizes universal citizenship rights with respect to individual equality and equality before the law. Another strand focuses on those citizenship entitlements that take differences seriously, together with the need to take differences into account for meaningful equality. Admittedly, the balancing act implicit in fostering a "differentiated universalism" (Squires, 2007a) will prove difficult and awkward, as Ruth Lister (1997) concludes, since neither is sufficient in its own right but requires the other to complete it:

> [R]ejecting the "false universalism" of traditional citizenship theory does not mean abandoning citizenship as a universalist goal. Instead, we can aspire to a universalism that stands in creative tension to diversity and difference and that challenges the divisions and exclusionary inequalities which can stem from diversity. (p. 66)

(Continued)

Is Canada ready for a formally articulated inclusive citizenship? Not every Canadian will be comfortable with the notion of citizenship as (1) differentiated by way of different entitlements and belongings, (2) inclusive of differences yet united in purpose, (3) responsive to both individual and collective group rights, and (4) allowing a primary affiliation with the whole while retaining membership in the parts without fear of contradiction or chaos. Questions will prevail: Is it possible to create a national citizenship in a global world of transnational communities and diasporic migrants (see also Harty & Murphy, 2005; Kernerman, 2005)? Is it possible for Canadians to take advantage of such crossings and connections to embrace specific affiliations without compromising a commitment to commonalities? Or is Canada destined to become a space of travelling cultures and people with varying degrees of attachment and commitment (Sandercock, 2003)—a hotel of convenience in which people come and go as they please, without obligations or duty (Kent, 2008)?

Like it or not, approve or disapprove, the future of a postnational Canada entails customizing different models of belonging and entitlements. In an era of transnationalism and diasporic dispersion where people no longer identify exclusively with one country, preferring instead multiple identities and intersecting allegiances that transcend national boundaries (Dijkstra et al., 2001; Satzewich & Wong, 2006), Canada must acknowledge the reality of comings and goings if it wants to attract the brightest and the best. This is no time to impose the modernist notion of a unitary Canadian citizenship, with a dash of multicultural colour thrown in for good measure. A one-size-fits-all citizenship is unlikely to appeal in a deeply divided and multilayered Canada where some are banging on the door to "get in" while others are breaking down the door to "get out." Yes, it will take time to convince Canadians that people are alike in different ways yet different in similar ways. Nevertheless, the postnational goal of belonging differently together without drifting apart will depend on accepting this seeming paradox—that true equality arises from treating both individuals and groups equally (the same) as a matter of course but treating them as equals (differently) when the situation calls for it.

Chapter Highlights

- Canada can be envisaged as a work in progress with respect to managing race, ethnic, and Aboriginal relations. While the project remains unfinished (as one might expect of a journey with no goal), Canada has evolved from an intolerant and exclusive British colony to a postnational society based on a commitment to doing it differently.
- Conventional ways of thinking about citizenship (universal citizenship) are being challenged by the concept of customized citizenship rights based on different notions of belonging and entitlements. An inclusive citizenship seeks to combine the unitary with the customized as a basis for living together across a deeply divided Canada.

- Canada's Difference Model and the Canadian Way are widely touted as Canada's main contributions to cooperative coexistence, in large part by acknowledging the challenges of accommodating different ways of accommodating diversity rather than relying on a single one-size-fits-all standard.
- Canadians possess a relatively high threshold for ambiguity and change because of historical precedents. Such flexibility not only allows weaknesses to be transformed into strengths but also may secure Canada's status as the world's first postnational society.

For further study, you can access the Case Studies referenced in this chapter at **www.pearsoncanada.ca/fleras**.

Review Questions

1. One of the key themes in this chapter is the notion that Canada has been able to transform weaknesses into strengths. Describe what is meant by this claim, and provide several examples of snatching virtue (strengths) from vice (weaknesses) that have contributed to Canada-building.

2. Compare and contrast the different types of citizenship that are brought to bear in living together with our differences. Utilize the categories of underlying assumptions and anticipated outcomes as criteria for comparison.

3. What is meant by the expression "Canada's Difference Model"? How does the notion of "Canada's Difference Model" relate to the concept of the Canadian Way?

4. Evidence suggests that Canada may be advantageously positioned to redefine itself as the world's first postnational society. Comment on what constitutes a postnational society, how a postnational society differs from a modern society, and how Canada appears to fit this new model of societyhood.

Endnotes

1. Until 2009, the *Citizenship Act* of 1977 conferred conditional citizenship to a child born abroad to a person also born abroad to a Canadian citizen, provided that this child took active steps before 28 years of age to manifest their connection to Canada. Amendments in 2009 stipulated that a child born abroad to a Canadian citizen will acquire Canadian citizenship but cannot transmit Canadian citizenship to their children (Macklin & Crepeau, 2010).

Links and Recommendations

BOOKS

Immigration and Canada, by Alan Simmons (2010). This excellent book compels the reader to rethink Canadian immigration by contextualizing it within a global framework.

The Age of Migration, by Stephen Castles and Mark Miller (2009). Now in its fourth edition, this book remains the standard for analyzing patterns of immigration around the world.

In Defence of Multicultural Citizenship, by S. Harty and M. Murphy (2005). As the title implies, the authors provide a robust defence of a differentiated yet inclusive citizenship.

WEBSITES

Citizenship and Immigration Canada—The official website:
www.cic.gc.ca

Justice Laws Website—For a review of the *Citizenship Act* in Canada and for Canada's human rights legislation:
http://laws.justice.gc.ca

Canadian Policy Research Networks—For a general overview of citizenship and diversity and for more on Canada's Difference Model, see Jane Jenson and Martin Papillon's article, *The Changing Boundaries of Citizenship: A Review and a Research Agenda*:
www.cprn.org/doc.cfm?doc=182&l=en

Canadian Citizenship Test—All prospective citizens of Canada must answer 20 multiple-choice questions. Do you think you could pass the test? Check it out.
www.v-soul.com

Canadian Human Rights Commission—This site includes the activities and rulings of the Commission:
www.chrc-ccdp.ca

International Council for Canadian Studies—If your interest lies in the notion of Canada as a postnational society, the *International Journal for Canadian Studies*, Volume 25, 2002, might be useful:
www.iccs-ciec.ca

Glossary

Aboriginal peoples Aboriginal peoples represent the descendents of the original (indigenous) occupants of Canada who have been colonized and forcibly incorporated into Canadian society, but now want to "get out" of this arrangement by redefining their relational status in society. *See also* Aboriginality; Aboriginal (peoples') rights.

Aboriginal (peoples') rights The entitlements that Aboriginal peoples possess by virtue of their original occupancy of the land. These rights are unique to Aboriginal peoples; secure the basis for rewards, recognition, and relationships; and include the right to Aboriginal models of self-determining autonomy over jurisdictions related to land, identity, and political voice. *See also* Aboriginal peoples, Aboriginality.

Aboriginal self-governance Aboriginal peoples claim that, as fundamentally autonomous political communities ("nations"), they have a right to govern themselves in ways that reflect their realities, reinforce their experiences, and advance their interests. *See also* Governance, Self-government.

Aboriginal title A constitutional recognition that Aboriginal peoples continue to own those lands and resources that they have occupied continuously for centuries. The Crown cannot encroach upon lands that have not been lawfully surrendered without meaningful consultation, negotiation, consent, and compensation.

Aboriginality Used in a descriptive sense, aboriginality ("being Aboriginal") describes the principle by which a politicized awareness of original occupancy provides a moral basis for entitlement and recognition. The politicization of "being Aboriginal" involves the politics of transformative change—not only in challenging the legitimacy of the sovereign

state as the paramount authority but also in advancing innovative patterns of belonging that embody the post-sovereign notion of the "nations within." *See also* Aboriginal peoples, Aboriginal (peoples') rights, Aboriginal self-governance.

Androcentrism A tendency for men to see the world from their point of view as normal and necessary; to assume that others are seeing the world in the same way; and to dismiss other perspectives as inferior or irrelevant.

Anglo-conformity An expectation that minorities under British colonial rule must outwardly conform to mainstream (British) culture and society. *See also* Assimilation.

Anti-racism A commitment to identify, isolate, and challenge racisms through direct action at individual and institutional levels.

Anti-racist education An educational discourse and practice that seeks to challenge and transform those institutional structures and patterns of behaviour that continue to uphold power imbalances within and outside the school system.

Assimilation A complex and dynamic process in which minorities begin to lose their distinctiveness through absorption into dominant society. As policy or political framework, assimilation can refer to those formal government initiatives for absorbing minority populations into the mainstream. *See also* Anglo-conformity.

Asylum seeker A person who flees one country and seeks refuge and protection in another country by claiming refugee status.

Bilingualism Entails the coexistence of two languages at *territorial*, *institutional*, or *individual* levels. Canada is officially bilingual at federal institutional levels, but of the ten provinces only New Brunswick is provincially bilingual. Under an official bilingualism, minority language rights (French outside Quebec, English in Quebec) are protected.

Bill 101   Also known as the 1977 *French Language Charter*, which made French the official language of public communication in Quebec.

Canada as a coalition   An interpretation of Canada as a partnership involving at least three nations: the French-speaking, the English-speaking, and Aboriginal peoples.

Canada as a compact   An interpretation of Canada as a covenant (special relation) between Quebec and the rest of Canada. According to the compact vision, the Québécois are neither an ethnic minority nor a province, but a distinct people with claims to nationhood because of a common homeland, culture, language, and identity, with a status equivalent to that of the English as a founding (charter) group. *See also* Charter members/groups, Canada as a contract, Canada as a coalition.

Canada as a contract   An interpretation of Canada and its federalist system as a contract between the federal authorities and 10 equal provinces. A contract model tends uphold the federal sector as dominant because of its national responsibilities. However, other versions claim equal status for provinces and the federal sector.

Canada-building   *See* Society-building.

Canada's Difference Model   Widely regarded as a progressive model for simultaneously accommodating different ways of accommodating racial, ethnic, and aboriginal difference, Canada's Difference Model acknowledges the need to customize policy and programs to meet the distinctive aspirations of Canada's three major "Ethnicities": Aboriginal peoples, the Québécois, and multicultural minorities. *See also* Canadian Way.

Canadian Charter of Rights and Freedoms   When it came into effect in 1985, the Charter constitutionally entrenched the right of individuals to be free of unnecessary state intrusion. The concept of collective rights is also endorsed as a reasonable limitation on individual rights if demonstrably justified in a free and democratic Canada.

Canadian Multiculturalism Act   *See* Official Multiculturalism.

Canadian Way   A discourse that espouses Canada's commitment to difference (content) and dialogue (process) as a model for living together with differences in a deeply divided and multi-layered society. *See also* Canada's Difference Model.

Capitalism   An economic (and social) system organized around the rational pursuit of profit.

Charter members/groups   The 1867 *British North America Act* (now *Constitution Act*) enshrined the rights of the French settlers and English colonizers as the founding members of Canadian society, with a corresponding right to establish agendas and set priorities.

Citizenship   A legal contract establishing a reciprocal exchange of rights and duties between a person and the state in which he or she lives. A social dimension of citizenship pertains to issues of belonging, identity, rights, and entitlements. *See also* Inclusive citizenship.

Citizenship Act   Passage of this Act in 1947 established citizenship as something distinctively Canadian in terms of identity and rights, thereby replacing the earlier notion that Canadians were simply transplanted British subjects.

Civic multiculturalism   An emphasis on Canada's Multiculturalism policy and program that focuses on the language of inclusion by way of citizenship, belonging, and participation.

Civic nationalism   A contested term usually employed to demonstrate state initiatives in building a cohesive society, civic nationalism is concerned with creating a community of individuals who belong together by virtue of (1) possessing equal rights, (2) a common loyalty to shared values, rule of law, and institutions, and (3) a willingness to coexist in a spirit of "live and let live." Compare with "ethnic nationalism," with its emphasis on membership by blood.

Class   An aggregate of persons who occupy a similar status or stratum in society because of similarities in power, wealth, or status. Marxists see class in terms of people's relationship to the means of productive private property (namely, owners versus workers). Those of a Weberian bent see class as a complex interplay of factors such as wealth, power, and prestige, in effect leading to different class systems, including the always popular categories of upper, middle, and lower class.

Collective definition   A distinct if somewhat underutilized approach to the study of race and ethnicity, collective definition endorses a view of race, ethnic, and Aboriginal relations as dynamic and contested. Sectors ("dualisms") within both the dominant and subdominant groups compete with each other to define the situation differently and act accordingly, thereby creating complex intergroup dynamics that pull in seemingly opposite directions *See also* Dualism.

Colonialism   A violent and traumatic process reflecting a specific era of European expansion and settlement over so-called underutilized lands. European powers forcibly exploited indigenous peoples by appropriating land and resources, extracting wealth, and capitalizing on cheap labour, while invoking racial doctrines to justify and explain their removal, exploitation, or extermination.

Complete (or civilizational) society   A term that describes the settled countries of Europe. European societies tend to see themselves as culturally and demographically finished projects, with a corresponding rejection of society-building through immigration or diversity.

Comprehensive claims   A modern-day equivalent of nineteenth-century treaty agreements in which the Crown acquired certainty of ownership over large blocks of Aboriginal land, while Aboriginal communities received rights to smaller sections of land (reserves),

allocation of services, money, and goods, and access to Crown land resources. In contrast to nineteenth-century agreements, however, comprehensive treaties tend to include protocols for establishing Aboriginal self-governing arrangements as well as rights to co-manage natural resources and revenue-sharing from resource extraction.

Conditional autonomy   The current phase in the evolving government policy toward Aboriginal peoples. Unlike previous phases that emphasized the elimination of all things Aboriginal, a commitment to conditional autonomy acknowledges the rights of Aboriginal peoples as nations within, with a collective right to self-determining autonomy (albeit, within limits and with strings attached) over land, identity, and political voice.

Conflict theory   Based on the idea that societies are sites of inequality, with the result that confrontation, competition, and change are inevitable, in part because diverse groups compete for scarce resources in contexts that privilege some groups but not others. *See also* Internal colonialism.

Constitutional order   A tacitly assumed framework for the principled distribution of power and authority in society. Those foundational principles that govern the social, political, and economic order of society operate at relatively high levels of generality, with the result that they often are beyond examination or criticism. *See also* Governance, Aboriginal self-governance.

Constructive engagement   A new (postcolonial) social contract for redefining the relationship of Aboriginal peoples to society at large. Constructive engagement is premised on the notion that competitive or confrontational models are not conducive to living together differently. Proposed instead is a model of cooperative coexistence that not only endorses Aboriginal peoples as fundamentally autonomous political communities—sovereign in their own right while sharing sovereignty over society—but also embraces the postcolonial principles of power-sharing and partnership. *See also* Postcolonial social contract, Aboriginality.

Constructivist explanation   A framework for explaining ethnicity by reference to its socially constructed character. Rather than something real, natural, or inevitable, ethnicity constitutes a social convention created by individuals who make meaningful choices within broader contexts. *See also* Primordial explanation.

Convention refugees   Refugees who are selected and sponsored for entry into Canada because they fulfill the UN criteria for refugee status.

Critical multiculturalism   A commitment to difference politics that promotes an agenda to challenge, resist, and transform those prevailing patterns of power and privilege that marginalize minority women and men.

Cultural relativism   A belief that the merit and worth of cultures and cultural practices are relative to the society in which they exist. As a result, all cultural practices should be analyzed and assessed on their own terms rather than by some arbitrarily selected external criteria. It is widely (but incorrectly) thought that, in the absence of absolute standards, cultural relativism embraces the idea that all cultural practices are good and valid—even those in violation of human rights. A critical cultural relativism argues that, for purposes of assessment and change, all cultural practices should be seen *as if* good and valid.

Depoliticizing ethnicity   A process by which the potency of ethnicity or difference is "neutered" by eroding its potential for intergroup strife. Ethnicity is relegated to the private or personal domain, and is thus dislodged from the competition for power and privilege in the public sphere.

Devolution   The practice of transferring responsibilities and structures to the local level on the assumption that those closest to the community have a better grasp of local concerns than do remote bureaucrats. Devolution rarely involves the transfer of power but often entails the offloading of administrative duties to the periphery.

Difference   In contrast to the empirical descriptor "diversity," difference is employed in the more politicized sense to convey the placement of different groups along a hierarchy of dominance and subdominance that is undergoing constant evaluation and adjustment within unequal contexts.

Differentiated citizenship   The idea that the social contract implicit in belonging to society must be customized to reflect the different realities, experiences, and needs of Canada's major Ethnic groups. *See also* Citizenship, Inclusive citizenship.

Discourse   Ways of thinking and talking about the world based on how reality is identified, named, classified, and interpreted.

Discrimination   Often viewed as the behavioural counterpart of prejudice (attitudes), discrimination consists of actions that have an adverse effect (whether deliberate or not) of denying or excluding someone because of who they are. Discrimination can be expressed at different levels, ranging from the personal, intentional, and direct to the impersonal, inadvertent, and systemic. *See also* Racism.

Discursive   *See* Discourse.

Distinct society   The concept of distinct society is usually applied to describe the political aspirations of the Québécois. The Québécois assert that they constitute a "distinct society," that is, a historical people with a unique language, culture, and identity, whose homeland of last resort is Quebec.

Diversity   A descriptive and depoliticized statement of demographic fact about differences, namely, a reference to separate states of being in which people are slotted into a pre-existing category. Compare with "difference" and its connotation of politicized diversity or the contextualizing of diversity within contexts of power and inequality.

Dominant group   The collectivity of persons in society with the institutionalized authority not only to preserve the prevailing distribution of power, privilege, and property, but also to impose its standard and culture as the norm by which to judge and evaluate others.

Dualism   A term at the core of collective definition perspective, the concept of dualism suggests a series of binary divisions (factions) within both the dominant and subdominant sectors of society. *See also* Collective definition.

Employment equity   This concept can be interpreted as a principle (or philosophy) or a policy (or program) with a corresponding set of programs and practices. As a *principle*, employment equity embraces the notion of institutional inclusion by improving the hiring and treatment of minorities through removal of discriminatory barriers and implementation of proactive programs. As a *policy*, it refers to official government policy of Canada's *Employment Equity Act* of 1986/96, with its commitment to institutional inclusiveness for the historically disadvantaged.

Entitlement   The conferral of certain rights and privileges (who gets what) to members of a group.

Equity   The belief that true equality rests on recognizing the relevance of context, the importance of taking differences into account, and a balancing of individual with collective rights. A commitment to equity acknowledges the primacy of equal results (not just equal opportunity) to ensure that members of a group have a fair share of scarce resources.

Essentializing   A belief in unchanging human characteristics that are (1) uniform and stable within a certain category of persons, (2) immutable and impervious to social context or historical modification, and (3) determinative of peoples thoughts and actions. The fluid and relational aspects of identity formation are ignored while the homogeneity of the group is emphasized.

Ethnic cleansing   As a variant of genocide, it involves a deliberate process to eliminate an ethnic group from a particular locale through either outright killing or forced expulsion.

Ethnic groups   Communities of "like-minded" individuals with a shared awareness of a common identity, language, history, and culture, together with a sense of group belonging based on perceived ancestral links.

Ethnic nationalism   People who share an ancestrally based identity can be mobilized into an action group (social movement) for defence of homeland, language, culture, and autonomy. Those related by blood can claim a right to speak the language of nationhood, express a fierce loyalty to their sense of peoplehood, and insist on their status as peoples with an inherent right to self-determining autonomy, including secession. *See also* Civic nationalism, Nationalism.

Ethnicity   A principle by which socially distinct groups of individuals are defined, differentiated, and organized around a shared awareness of their common ancestry because of culture, physical attributes, language, historical experiences, homeland, and birthright. Ethnicity not only secures a basis for community and identity, but also provides a rationale for mobilizing "like-minded" people into action for advancing social, political, and cultural interests.

Ethnocentrism   A universal tendency to see and interpret reality from a particular cultural perspective as normal, necessary, and natural, with a corresponding inclination to dismiss or denigrate others as inferior or irrelevant and to judge other practices or beliefs by one's own cultural standards. Ethnocentrism can also include a belief in the superiority of one's culture, values, assumptions, and world view. *See also* Eurocentric.

Eugenics   A science and a social movement that attained considerable popularity during the first decades of the twentieth century, eugenics advocated improving the quality of the human species through selective reproduction. Eugenics encouraged the creation of large families among the socially superior, while discouraging breeding within so-called inferior stock (i.e., the poor or minorities).

Eurocentrism   A belief in the moral superiority of European thoughts and practices as the norm or standard by which others are judged and interpreted. Also a tendency to see and interpret the world through European eyes as natural and normal, assume others are doing so as well, and dismiss those that don't as mistaken or a threat. *See also* Ethnocentrism.

Everyday racism   Consists of large unconscious speech patterns and daily actions that deny and exclude.

Federalism   A political arrangement with a relatively well-defined division of jurisdiction and authority between the centre and the subunits. As noted by others, federalism involves two levels of governance with a corresponding division of constitutional powers to govern. One level is concerned with the country as a whole; the other with the localized concerns of provinces or states.

Feminism   A widely varied ideology and social movement that espouses the equality and worth of women. Feminisms range from those that reject the existing system as patriarchal, racist, or classist to those that are willing to work within the system by removing discriminatory barriers to equality. Feminisms also vary, depending on whether the differences between men and women are perceived as absolute or relative.

Formal equality   An equality that is based on strict mathematical equivalence; that is, because everyone is equal before the law everyone should be treated the same, regardless of their differences. Often associated with the principle of equal opportunity. *See also* Equity.

French Language Charter   Also known as Bill 101, the 1977 Charter that made French the official language of public communication in Quebec.

Functionalism   A sociological perspective (or theory) that sees society as a complex and integrated totality composed of interrelated parts that individually and collectively contribute to the stability and survival of society.

Gender equity   Acknowledges that achievement of de facto equality must entail special measures—from the elimination of discriminatory barriers to ensuring inclusion principles within the design and delivery of services and programs—to correct historical imbalances and social disadvantages that preclude women from competing on a level playing field.

Gendered inequality   A belief that inequality between women and men is not just about individual attitudes but structural and structured, that is, is embedded within the design, organization and functioning of society. *See also* Patriarchy.

Gendered society   An acknowledgment that all human societies are fundamentally informed by and divided along lines that marginalize or exploit women while bolstering the interests, privilege, and power of men as natural and normal.

Genocide   An orchestrated effort by the state or those acting on its behalf or approval to eradicate members from a devalued group occupying the same territory. Although current debates revolve around the centrality of "intent" as crucial to any definition, genocide in a broader sense can also be indirect, unintended or unconscious, and not openly violent in process. *See also* Ethnic cleansing.

Governance   A political framework that defines the relationship between the ruled and the rulers in terms of how authority is divided, power is distributed, and valued resources are allocated within a particular jurisdiction. The term "government" refers to specific forms of this relationship. *See also* Aboriginal self-governance.

Harassment   A type of discrimination in which persistent and unwelcome actions are directed at individuals by those who ought to know better.

Hate racism   An open dislike of others because of who they are or what they do.

Hegemonic   *See* Hegemony.

Hegemony   The changing of people's attitudes—without their being aware of it—whereby those in positions of power are able to secure control and cooperation through consent rather than coercion.

Human rights   Inalienable (inherent) entitlements that all persons have by virtue of their status as human beings.

Hybridic ethnic identity   *See* Postmodern ethnic identity.

Identity politics   Also known as politics of recognition, identity politics incorporates a broad range of attachments and activities based on the shared experiences of an identifiable group. Members of that constituency assert or reclaim their distinctiveness not only to ensure that they are recognized and accorded respect *on their own terms*, but also to challenge dominant group characterizations of them.

Identity thesis   An attempt to explain the surge in and popularity of ethnicity by pointing out how ethnic group membership provides a buffer for coping with the demands of an urban context.

Ideological racism   A racism that reflects, reinforces, and advances society-wide ideas and ideals (including beliefs and values about what is normal, desirable, and acceptable) that have a negative or controlling effect on a devalued group. *See* Ideology.

Ideology   Defined in its broadest sense, ideology refers to a complex set of ideas and ideals that attempts to explain, justify, and perpetuate a specific set of circumstances. Employed in a critical sense, ideology consists of those beliefs that rationalize the prevailing distribution of power, privilege, and resources in society by bolstering the cultural patterns of the dominant sector as natural or normal, while dismissing or demeaning subdominant patterns.

Immigrant   Persons born overseas but voluntarily residing in a new country, with a right to permanent residency on the grounds of labour market contribution or family reunification. With the possible exception of Aboriginal peoples, all Canadians are immigrants or descendants of immigrants.

***Immigration Act,* 1978**   Although superseded by the *Immigration and Refugee Protection Act* of 2002, this Act continues to provide the ideological underpinnings of Canada's immigration policies, programs, and practices. The focus is on finding a working balance between humanitarian and pragmatic concerns while protecting Canada's national interests and international commitments.

Immigration and Refugee Board of Canada (IRB)   An agency of approximately 180 political appointees who sit in single-person tribunals to determine whether individual asylum seekers qualify for entry into Canada as legitimate refugees.

Immigration and Refugee Protection Act   This 2002 Act replaces the 1978 *Immigration Act.* Emphasis is increasingly aimed at addressing Canada's security concerns without sacrificing conventional humanitarian commitments and a commitment to Canada-building through immigrant-driven economic growth.

Immigration society   A society that takes a principled and proactive approach to immigration and immigrants. Policies and programs exist to regulate the entry of immigrants, programs are in place to assist the integration and settlement of immigrants, immigrants are entitled to all rights and privileges, and immigration is viewed as an asset or resource for society-building.

Inclusive citizenship   A belief that citizenship in Canada must be customized to reflect the distinctive needs and aspirations of Aboriginal peoples, national communities such as the Québécois, and historically disadvantaged multicultural minorities. In many ways consistent with the core principle of Canada's Difference Model, namely, a commitment to accommodate different ways of accommodating differences.

Inclusive multiculturalism   *See* Integrative multiculturalism.

Indigenous peoples   *See* Aboriginal peoples.

Indigenous rights   *See* Aboriginal (peoples') rights.

Individual bilingualism   A type of bilingualism whereby each person is expected to become proficient in two or more languages of a country.

Institutional bilingualism   A type of bilingualism that focuses on incorporating official languages at organizational levels, including the use of dual language workplaces and delivery of services.

Institutional inclusivity   The idea that mainstream institutions must move over and make space for the historically disadvantaged through reasonable accommodation. At one level, inclusivity is about increased minority presence through removal of discriminatory barriers and the introduction of proactive measures to create services that are available, accessible, and appropriate. At another level, inclusivity is about redesigning institutional structures, values, and practices in ways reflective of, respectful of, and responsive to minority differences.

Institutional power   The ability to influence others because the influence is deeply embedded within the foundational principles of the constitutional order and backed up by the coercive authority of the state.

Institutional racism   Those organizational policies, programs, and practices that openly deny or inadvertently exclude minorities from full and equal participation.

Instrumentalist explanation   In explaining the surge and popularity of ethnicity, the instrumentalist approach argues that people collectively mobilize under the banner of an ethnicity as a show of collective strength in a competitive world.

Insurgent ethnic identity   A politicized ethnic identity involving a strong identification with one's own group, often accompanied by an intense dislike of others, who are seen as inferior, irrelevant, or a threat.

Integration   A model of race and ethnic relations as well as a policy framework for managing diversity that involves a set of policy ideals and practices opposing the principles of segregation or separation. As governance, integration involves a commitment to incorporate minorities into the mainstream as equals without sacrificing their distinctive identities. Integration can also refer to a process in which different cultures fuse as "paints in a bucket" to create a distinct cultural amalgam.

Integrative multiculturalism   Canada's official Multiculturalism is not about celebrating differences but about ensuring institutional inclusivity through removal of discriminatory barriers.

Interactionism   A sociological perspective that envisions society as an ongoing human accomplishment, involving a dynamic process whereby social reality is created and recreated by individuals who engage in meaningful interaction. Also called "symbolic interactionism."

Internal colonialism   A fundamentally exploitative relationship in which indigenous peoples are forcibly incorporated into a system not of their own making with a corresponding loss of land, identity, and political voice.

Intersectional analysis   A theoretical approach to the study of inequality that incorporates the interplay of gender with race, ethnicity, and class in defining outcomes. Gender is superimposed on and intersects with race, ethnicity, and class to create interlocking patterns of domination that intensify the exclusion or exploitation.

Islamophobia Fear of Islam, whereby Muslim religion is racialized as a threat to security and Islamic-based cultures are demonized as barriers to integration.

Lived ethnic identity   A kind of ethnic identity that is lived out on a full-time basis. Compare with "symbolic ethnic identity."

Marxism   A philosophy or ideology based on interpreting the work of Karl Marx. According to Marxism, both the dynamics of history and the organization of society can be understood as an ongoing and evolving clash between the ruling (capitalist) class and the working class in the competition for scarce resources.

Melting pot   A metaphor used to describe the preferred ideal in American race and ethnic relations. The concept of a melting pot suggests the fusion of minority differences to create a new and improved national culture. The ideal, however, does not match the reality for many racial minorities who, by choice or by circumstances, remain unmeltable. *See also* Mosaic, Integration.

Merit/Meritocracy   The act of rewarding a person on the basis of credentials or achievement. Three features make a judgment meritocratic: the measurement of achievement against a commonly accepted scale applied to all candidates; assurances that every candidate is measured impersonally on the basis of performance rather than personality; and the selection of examiners on the basis of their excellence and impartiality. *See also* Modernity.

Minority group   Any socially defined category of individuals who are perceived as different and inferior and treated accordingly by the majority. References to minorities are about power relations, not about numbers. *See also* Subdominant group, Visible minorities.

Misogyny   Hatred of women.

Modernity   A world view based on the legitimacy of scientific inquiry and rationality as the organizing principle for thought, action, and social life. Modernity is viewed as the triumph of the universal over the particular, citizenship over identity, individual rights over tribal rights, and reason over emotion. Additional features include a belief in (1) the attainment of absolute knowledge in the social sciences, (2) an unfolding of history in the direction of progress, (3) universal categories of experience, (4) explanation through grand theory, and (5) the centrality of reason and science for solving problems and improving society.

Mosaic   A metaphor to describe the ideal arrangement of unity within diversity involving various racial and ethnic groups in Canada. The proposed image is that of a patterned entity comprising disparate and distinct elements arranged into a cohesive and recognizable whole. Proponents admire the positive images associated with the mosaic; detractors denounce it as a gross distortion that neither fits reality nor escapes the conceptual trap of framing cultural diversity as frozen in time and fixed in place.

Multicultural education   A philosophy of education based on the belief that schooling should not only reflect, reinforce, and advance cultural diversity within the classroom, but also improve student's receptivity to cultural differences. Four key models exist—enrichment, enlightenment, embracive, and empowerment—each of which can be contrasted to the other in terms of underlying assumptions, styles, and proposed outcomes.

Multicultural minorities   Those non-French and non-English immigrants and descendants of immigrants whose priorities and interests differ from the more politicized concerns of Aboriginal peoples. *See also* People of colour, Visible minorities.

Multiculturalism   A belief that a society of many cultures is possible as a basis for "living together with differences" under four ideal-typical scenarios: (1) differences are rejected or (2) differences are tolerated or (3) differences are taken into account or (4) differences are taken seriously. Different levels of meaning of multiculturalism can be discerned, including multiculturalism as a statement of empirical fact; a set of ideals; an official policy; a set of practices; and a critique. *See also* Official Multiculturalism.

Multinational federation   A proposed political arrangement that rejects the current system of provincial-based federalism. Proposed instead is a federalism that acknowledges Canada as a multi-layered coalition of different nations. *See also* Canada as a coalition.

Nation   A politicized community of "like-minded" people who share a common homeland, language, identity, set of grievances, and cultural and historical symbols. Unlike a *state*, which is essentially a political and administrative system, a *nation* consists of people who believe they are fundamentally different, express a political consciousness as a distinct people, insist on self-determination at social and cultural levels, propose political autonomy on those grounds, and claim to speak the language of nationhood (Snyder, 2000). Both Québécois and Aboriginal peoples prefer to see themselves as "nations" within the framework of Canadian society.

Nationalism   A political/ideological expression of a community of people who, by virtue of shared destiny, common history, common ancestry, and homeland, have the right to call themselves a nation with an attendant right to claim self-determining autonomy ("self-rule") up to and including independence. *See also* Ethnic nationalism, Civic nationalism.

Nations within   A term normally employed to describe Aboriginal ambitions for self-determination in Canada. The "nations within" concept acknowledges the relative autonomy of Aboriginal peoples but does not advocate outright secession or independence. *See also* Self-government.

Normative racism   Reflects a largely unconscious bias toward others because of prevailing cultural values, beliefs, and norms. *See* Ideological Racism

Official bilingualism   *See* Bilingualism, *Official Languages Act.*

Official language minorities   French-speaking Canadians who live outside Quebec and English-speaking Canadians who reside in Quebec have certain rights that provide them with access to services in their language (where numbers warrant), in addition to rights to exercise control over institutions such as education.

Official Languages Act   Passage of this Act in 1969/1986 established Canada as an officially bilingual society. The Act ensures bilingual services and workplaces within federal institutions across the country, while protecting the language rights of official-language minorities (French outside Quebec, English in Quebec).

Official Multiculturalism   The transformation of multicultural principles into official policy began with an all-political party agreement in 1971, followed by the entrenchment of multiculturalism in the *Canadian Charter of Rights and Freedoms* in 1982, and enshrinement with the passage of the *Multiculturalism Act* in 1988. As an aspirational blueprint, an official Multiculturalism embraces the principle of an inclusive Canada by making society safe *for* differences, yet safe *from* differences.

Patriarchy   The notion of society as designed by, for, and about men so that the constitutional order (in terms of core values, key institutions, and distribution of power) reflects, reinforces, and advances male privilege and power.

People of colour   *See* Visible minorities, Multicultural minorities, Racialized minorities.

Pluralism   The belief that culturally different groups can coexist in society and that such a condition is both attainable and socially beneficial. The principles of multiculturalism represents one variant of a pluralist society.

Polite racism   A dislike of others that is indirect because it is coded in euphemistic language.

Politicization   The process by which issues are taken out of the personal or private domain and drawn into the public domain in the competition for valued resources.

Postcolonial social contract   A proposed restructuring of Aboriginal peoples–state relations that rejects the colonial assumptions of the past in favour of a new constitutional arrangement involving the foundational principles of partnership, power sharing, radical participation, and a commitment to respect, recognition, and restoration.

Postcolonialism   The "post" in postcolonialism is not intended in the sense of "over" or "after." More accurately, it reflects a commitment to challenge the persistent neo-colonialism that governs the foundational principles of a society's constitutional order.

Postmodern ethnic identity   A kind of ethnic identity based on a dynamic integration of past with the present and the situational. A hybridic notion of "who am I" is constructed that is fluid, contextual, and multiple, without reflecting a sense of contradiction or confusion in the process. Also called "hybridic ethnic identity."

Postmodern(ism)   A discourse that rejects the modernist claim for a unified and organized way of thinking about the world from a fixed and objective point of view. By challenging the (im)possibility of absolute knowledge in the field of social sciences, postmodernism argues that there is no such thing as objective reality with a rational core of meaning in the centre, but only discourses about reality, whose truthfulness reflects social location and power relations. Postmodernism also espouses a mind-dependent world where there is no centre of authority, only different viewpoints where everything is relative and true because nothing is absolutely knowable, and where nothing is neutral or impartial because every-thing/everyone is located in time and space.

Power   In everyday language, the ability to make others do what they normally wouldn't want to do. Power should not be thought of as a thing, but as a process inherent to relation-ships. The relational nature of power shifts from context to context, suggesting that minorities can wield power in certain situa-tions, although access to institutionalized power (power backed by the coercive author-ity of the state) remains elusive.

Prejudice   A set of biased and generalized prejudgments of others based on faulty, unfounded, and inflexible generalizations. Rather than being viewed as a purely psycho-logical phenomenon involving an irrational mindset of the ignorant, prejudice should be interpreted in sociological terms, insofar as it originates when the dominant sector invokes negative ideas to justify and entrench its power and privilege.

Primordial explanation   A perspective that explains the staying power of ethnicity by reference to some deep biological yearning (or hard-wiring) that compels people to seek out their "own kind" as a basis for belonging, entitlement, and identity. *See also* Constructiv-ist explanation.

Profiling   *See* Racial profiling.

Protected Persons   *See* Refugee.

Race   Currently defined as a biologically based social construct involving the classifica-tion of persons (typology) into hierarchical categories (taxonomy) on the basis of real or imagined characteristics. Race has neither empirical validity nor scientific value; never-theless, people continue to believe it does and

act accordingly with terrifying real effects, thus reinforcing the sociological axiom that phe-nomena do not have to be real to be real in their consequences.

Racial profiling   Discriminatory actions by those in positions of authority that rely on stereotypes of race to negatively target group members, ostensibly for reasons of security or law and order.

Racial typologies   Classifications whereby racial groups are evaluated and hierarchically arranged in ascending and descending orders of superiority or inferiority to justify patterns of privilege and power.

Racialization   A socially constructed process whereby certain groups are negatively defined (or raced) as different or inferior and subject to differential and unequal treatment.

Racialized inequality   The lack of equality that reflects the embedding of race-based (dis)advantages within the institutional struc-tures of society. Rather than being neutral and value-free, society is designed and organ-ized in a way that reflects, reinforces, and advances as normal and necessary the interests of those with the power to define or control it.

Racialized minorities   This term is increas-ingly preferred over "visible minorities" or "people of colour" because it acknowledges how attaching a race label to minorities reflects a socially constructed process rather than a description of reality out there based on alleged biological traits. Racialization also acknowledges that there is no such thing as race but only individuals who are defined along racial grounds by those with the power to make such labels stick.

Racialized stratification   A hierarchical ranking of racial and ethnic minorities in ascending/descending order based on the crite-ria of income, education, or social class. Think of Canada as "layered" into "strata" in terms of how different minorities fare in the compe-tition for valued resources, with "whites" on top and groups such as First Nations and racialized minorities near the bottom.

Racism   Racism refers to a relatively organized set of ideas and ideals (ideology) that asserts or implies natural superiority of one group over another in terms of entitlements and privileges, together with the institutionalized power to put these beliefs into practice in a way that denies or excludes those who belong to a devalued category.

Reasonable accommodation   Institutional adjustments (within limits and without undue hardship) to improve the full and equal participation of those historically excluded.

Refugee   Defined by the United Nations as a person who flees his or her country because of a well-grounded fear of persecution based on race, national origins, religious background. By focusing on factors largely beyond a person's control, the grounds for admission have expanded in recent years; for example, Canada now extends the concept of refugee status to include gender-based persecution.

Refugee claimants   Unlike convention refugees who are privately sponsored or government selected, these asylum seekers arrive unannounced and invoke their right to claim refugee status. Also called "in-Canada refugees" or "protected persons."

Reifying   Exercising the belief in unchanging human characteristics that are uniform and stable within a certain category and impervious to social context or historical modification.

Resource mobilization theory   Accounting for ethnicity by acknowledging how like-minded people will mobilize into action groups to improve their competitive edge in the competition for scarce resources.

Reversing discrimination   In contrast to reverse discrimination, which argues that special rights for minorities are a kind of discrimination in reverse, reversing discrimination contends that special measures for minority women and men are intended to reverse (remove) the discrimination that historically has denied or excluded them.

Scientific racism   The belief that racial capacities between populations (or races) could be measured and evaluated by intelligence tests, especially the IQ (Stanford-Binet) test.

Segregation   The process and practice of separating groups on the basis of race or culture. This *separation* can occur voluntarily or involuntarily, can involve formal or informal measures, and may be interpreted as empowering or disempowering.

Self-determination   *See* Self-determining autonomy.

Self-determining autonomy   As fundamentally autonomous political communities that are sovereign and share sovereignty over the land, Aboriginal peoples claim to have inherent and collective rights to Aboriginal models for controlling jurisdictions (or domains) of immediate concern related to land, identity, and political voice. Recourse to self-determining autonomy is not the same as independence; rather it involves a commitment to restructure the foundational principles of a colonial constitutional order along the lines of a new (postcolonial) social contract.

Self-government   A term that is usually employed within the context of Aboriginal demands for Aboriginal models of self-determining autonomy. Aboriginal peoples claim that self-government provides the political expression of their demand for control over internal affairs. *See also* Aboriginal self-governance.

Separation   *See* Segregation.

Sexism   A belief in the superiority of men over women. *See also* Androcentrism, Patriarchy.

Situational ethnic identity   *See* Symbolic ethnic identity.

Social Contract   *See* Postcolonial social contract.

Social Darwinism   A doctrine of racial superiority that reworked some of Darwin's ideas on evolution and applied them to group relations. With its notion of a struggle for survival and survival of the fittest, the world under social Darwinism was portrayed as an arena where populations are locked in mortal combat over competition for scarce resources. Those with the adaptive skills survive and prosper, according to social Darwinists; those without are doomed.

Society-building   The ongoing process by which contemporary societies use policies and programs to create political and moral communities of individuals in the face of internal demands and external pressures. The term "nation-building" may also be used because most states (or societies) are seeking to become more nation-like.

Sovereignty   The exercise of exclusive and final authority over land, peoples, rules, and all legal and political matters within a strictly bounded territory. For some, sovereignty is about borders; for others, especially Aboriginal peoples, it is about establishing productive and meaningful relations with society at large.

Specific treaty claims   Refers to the need for reparations involving Crown breaches of existing treaty provisions. *See also* Treaties, Comprehensive claims.

State   A political, legal, and administrative unit that claims to exercise final authority over a specific territory, monopolizes the legitimate use of force to enforce decisions and keep the peace, and is governed by authorities who purport to represent the inhabitants.

Stereotype   A shorthand way of classifying social reality into convenient categories on the basis of common properties. As a generalization, it provides an oversimplification or exaggerated version of the world, reflecting preconceived and unwarranted notions that apply to all members of the devalued group.

Subdominant group   Also called subordinate, subdominant groups stand in an unequal relationship to dominant groups because of differences in power, privilege, and wealth.

Subliminal racism   A subconscious racism involving deeply entrenched prejudices that individuals are unaware of but that influence beliefs and behaviour. This unconscious racism is often masked by principled arguments that endorse the principle of equality but reject the means to achieve that goal by appealing to a higher or alternative value to justify the (in)action.

Substantive equality (equity)   Based on the idea that differences sometimes have to be taken into account in achieving an equality that goes beyond theory. This colour-conscious approach to equality appears to be at variance with colour-blind notions whereby everyone is thought to be equally the same and treated accordingly. *See also* Equity.

Symbolic ethnic identity   (Also called "situational ethnic identity") A process in which an individual retains a cognitive or emotional affiliation with a cultural past while continuing to fully participate in the wider society.

Symbolic interactionism   *See* Interactionism.

Systematic racism   A direct attempt by institutions, employing explicit rules and deliberate practices, to prevent the full and equal participation of minorities.

Systemic discrimination   Based on the principle that bias and barriers may be inherent within the normal functioning of an institutional system. Systemic discrimination reflects a biasing process in which the rules or practices of an institution when evenly and equally applied may exert an inadvertent negative effect or consequences on certain minorities who are excluded or penalized through no fault of their own.

Systemic racism   *See* Systemic discrimination.

Territorial bilingualism   A type of bilingualism that reflects a division of language use along geographical lines. For example, Belgium and Switzerland are divided into linguistic regions, each with its own predominant official language.

Tolerance   A dislike of other practices, but a willingness to put up with these dislikes in the name of public peace or social justice. Tolerance is about indifference rather than acceptance.

Transnational ethnic identity   An ethnic identity reflecting the way globalization has changed the conventional notions of belonging that linked a person's identity with a particular place. Rather than treating homeland country as an either–or dichotomy, a transnational ethnic identity captures new notions of multiple homelands and multiple attachments.

Treaties   Transactions between the Crown and Aboriginal peoples involving an exchange of rights, duties, and obligations. Treaties of alliance and friendship exist, nevertheless, most treaties involve a transaction in which Aboriginal peoples surrender large tracts of land in exchange for goods and services in perpetuity, and rights of use of unoccupied or underutilized Crown land.

Universal citizenship   The idea that everyone in Canada belongs in the same way, as individuals with identical rights, duties, and obligations.

Visible minorities   The term is used to designate those who are non-white, non-Aboriginal, non-Caucasian in origin or identity (regardless of place of birth), and those who are defined as such by the government or have agreed to this label for purposes of employment equity or census taking. This term is used interchangeably with "people of colour" or, increasingly, "racialized minorities."

White Paper   A bill tabled by the Liberal government in 1969 to abolish Aboriginal peoples as a distinct status group in Canada. The bill proposed to repeal the *Indian Act*, dismantle the Department of Indian Affairs, and mothball the reserves by allocating land to Aboriginal peoples on an individual basis to do as they want. Aboriginal leaders strongly resisted the White Paper, a move that many see as the catalyst that mobilized Aboriginal peoples into action for redefining their relational status in Canada.

References

Abel, Allen. 2001. "P Is for Prejudice." *Saturday Night*, June 23/30.

Abel, Sue. 1997. *Shaping the News: Waitangi Day on Television*. Auckland, NZ: Auckland University Press.

Abele, Frances. 2004. *Urgent Need, Serious Opportunity: Towards a New Social Model for Canada's Aboriginal Peoples*. CPRN Social Architecture Papers. Research Paper F/39. April.

Abele, Frances, Russell LaPointe, and Michael Prince. 2005. "Symbolism, Surfacing, Succession, and Substance: Martin's Aboriginal Policy Style," in *How Ottawa Spends*. B. Doern (ed.). Pp. 99–121. Montreal/Kingston: McGill-Queen's University Press.

Abella, R.S. 1984. *Report of the Royal Commission on Equality in Employment*. Ottawa: Minister of Supply and Services.

Aboriginal Institutes' Consortium. 2005. *Aboriginal Institutions of Higher Education: A Struggle for the Education of Aboriginal Students, Control of Indigenous Knowledge and Recognition of Aboriginal Institutions: An Examination of Government Policy*. Toronto: Canadian Race Relations Foundation.

Abraham, M.E.S. Chow, L Maratou-Alipranti, and E Tastsoglou. 2010. *Contours of Citizenship: Women, Diversity, and the Practices of Citizenship*. Burlington, VT: Ashgate Publishing.

Abu-Laban, Yasmeen. 1999. "The Politics of Race, Ethnicity, and Immigration," in *Canadian Politics*. J. Bickerton and A.-G. Gagnon (eds.). Peterborough, ON: Broadview Press.

Abu-Laban Y., and B. Abu-Laban. 2007. "Reasonable Accommodation in a Global Village." *Policy Options* (September), 28–33.

Abu-Laban, Y., T. Derwing, and M. Mulder. 2004. "Why Canada Should Accept Refugees." *Canadian Issues* (March), 33–36.

Abu-Laban, Yasmeen, and Christina Gabriel. 2002. *Selling Diversity: Immigration, Multiculturalism, Employment Equity, and Globalization*. Peterborough, ON: Broadview Press.

Achenbach, Joel. 2004. "Brain Trust Can't Pin Down Race." *Toronto Star*, 16 October.

ACS/Environics. 2002. "Public Opinion Poll." *Canadian Issues* (February), 4–5.

Adams, Howard. 1999. *Tortured People: The Politics of Colonization*. Penticton, BC: Theytus Books.

Adams, Michael. 1997. *Sex in the Snow: Canadian Social Values at the End of the Millennium*. Toronto: Penguin.

Adams, Michael. 2007. *Unlikely Utopia*. Toronto: Penguin.

Adelman, Howard. 2004. "Introduction." *Canadian Issues* (March), 3–4.

Adorno, T.S. et al. 1950. *The Authoritarian Personality*. New York: Harper and Row.

African Canadian Legal Clinic. 2006. *Bill C-27 and the Issue of Female Genital Mutilation*. Available online at **http://www.aclc.net**

Agnew, Vijay (ed.). 2007. *Interrogating Race and Racism*. Toronto: University of Toronto Press.

Agocs, Carol, and Monica Boyd. 1993. "Ethnicity and Ethnic Inequality," in *Social Inequality in Canada* (2nd ed.). J. Curtis et al. (eds.). Pp. 330–352. Toronto: Prentice-Hall.

Agrell, Siri. 2010. "Number of Mixed-Union Couples on the Rise." *The Globe and Mail*, 21 April.

Aguirre, Adalberto Jr., and Jonathan Turner. 1995. *American Ethnicity: The Dynamics and Consequences of Discrimination*. New York: McGraw Hill.

Akdenizli, Banu. 2008. *Democracy in the Age of New Media: A Report on the Media and the Immigration Debate*. Los Angeles: The Brookings Institute. University of Southern California, Norman Lear Centre.

Alboim, Naomi. 2009. *Adjusting the Balance: Fixing Canada's Economic Immigration Policies*. Toronto: Maytree Foundation.

Alboim, Naomi, and Elizabeth McIsaac. 2007. "Making the Connections: Ottawa's Role in Immigrant Employment." *IRPP Choices, 13*(3). Available online at **http://www.irpp.org/choices/archive/vol13no3.pdf**

Alcoba, Natalie. 2007. "Culture Not Behind Girl's Death, Brother." *National Post*, 13 December.

Alfred, Taiaiake. 1999. *Peace, Power, and Righteousness: An Indigenous Manifesto*. Toronto: Oxford University Press.

Alfred, Taiaiake. 2001. "Mexico Laps Canada in Fight for Rights Recognition." *Windspeaker*, April.

Alfred, Taiaiake. 2005. *Wasase: Indigenous Pathways to Action and Freedom*. Peterborough, ON: Broadview Press.

Alfred, Taiaiake, 2008. *Anishnabek Outlaw Term "Aboriginal."* 27 June. Available online at **http://www.taiaiake.com/28**

Alia, Valeria, and Simone Bull. 2005. *Media and Ethnic Minorities*. Edinburgh: Edinburgh University Press.

Al-Krenawi, Alean, and John R Graham (eds.). 2003. *Multicultural Social Work in Canada*. Toronto: Oxford University Press.

Alladin, Ibrahim. 1996. "Racism in Schools: Race, Ethnicity, and Schooling in Canada," in *Racism in Canadian Schools*. I. Alladin (ed.). Pp. 4–21. Toronto: Harcourt Brace.

Allegritti, Inta. 2010. "Multiculturalism and Cultural Citizenship," in *Cultural Citizenhip and the Challenges of Globalization*. W. Ommundsen et al. (eds). Cresskill, NJ: Hampton Press.

Allemang, John. 2005. "The Limits of Tolerance." *The Globe and Mail*, 24 September.

Allen, Robert. 1993. *His Majesty's Indian Allies: British Indian Policy in the Defence of Canada, 1774–1815*. Toronto: Dundurn Press.

Alliance of Civilizations. 2006. *Research Base for the High-Level Group Report: Analysis on Media*. New York: United Nations.

Allport, Gordon. 1954. *The Nature of Prejudice*. New York: Doubleday and Company.

Alumkal, Antony W. 2008. "Analyzing Race in Asian American Congregations." *Sociology of Religion*, 69(2), 151–168.

Amarasingam, Amarnath. 2008. "Religion and Ethnicity among Sri Lankan Tamil Youth in Ontario." *Canadian Ethnic Studies*, 40(2), 149–169.

Amnesty International. 2004. *Stolen Sisters: Discrimination and Violence Against Indigenous Women in Canada*. London, UK: Author.

Andersen, Margaret L., and Patricia Hill Collins (eds.). 1998. *Race, Class, and Gender: An Anthology* (3rd ed.). Belmont, CA: Wadsworth.

Andersen, Margaret L., and Patricia Hill Collins (eds.). 2007. *Race, Class, and Gender: An Anthology* (6th ed.). Belmont, CA: Wadsworth.

Anderson, Kay. 2007. *Race and the Crisis of Humanism*. New York: Routledge.

Anderson, Kim. 2000. *A Recognition of Being: Reconstructing Native Womanhood*. Toronto: Sumac Press.

Anderson, Kim. 2009. "Leading by Action: Female Chiefs and the Political Landscape," in *Restoring the Balance*. G Valaskakis et al. (eds.). Pp. 99–124. Winnipeg: University of Manitoba Press.

Anderssen, Erin. 1998. "Canada's Squalid Secret: Life on Native Reserves." *The Globe and Mail*, 12 October.

Anderssen, Erin, and Michael Valpy. 2003. "Face the Nation: Canada Remade." *The Globe and Mail*, 6 June.

Andrew, Caroline. 2004. "Introduction." *Our Diverse Cities, 1*(1), 8–11.

Ang, Ien. 2011. "Ethnicities and Our Precarious Future." *Ethnicities, 11*(1), 37–41.

Angus, Ian. 2002. "Cultural Plurality and Democracy." *International Journal of Canadian Studies* 25.

Angus Reid Group Inc. 1991. *Multiculturalism and Canadians: Attitude Study, 1991*. National survey report submitted to the Department of Multiculturalism and Citizenship.

Angus Reid. 2010. "More Canadians Questioning the Benefits of Immigration. Survey Poll." 14 September.

Anisef, Paul, and Kenise Murphy Kilbride (eds.). 2003. *Managing Two Worlds: The Experiences and Concerns of Immigrant Youth in Ontario*. Toronto: Canadian Scholars Press.

Annual Report. 2005/6. "Annual Report on Official Languages." Ottawa: Public Service Human Resources Management Agency of Canada.

Annual Report. 2009/10. *Beyond Obligations: Volume 11: An Overview and Assessment of How Bilingualism Is Playing Out in Canada by Evaluating the Performance of Institutions, Reporting to Parliament, and Responding to Complaints*. Ottawa: Office of the Commissioner of Official Languages.

Ansley, Bruce. 2004. "Stealing a March." *Listener NZ*, 15 May.

Applebaum, Barbara. 2010. *Being White, Being Good*. Toronto: Lexington Books.

Areepattamannil, Shaljan. 2005. "Wanted: More Multicultural Teachers for Our Rainbow Classrooms." *The Globe and Mail*, 7 September.

Asch, Michael. 1997. *Aboriginal and Treaty Rights in Canada: Essays on Law, Equality, and Respect for Differences*. Vancouver: UBC Press.

Ashini, Napes. 2002. "Niassinam: Cariboo and F16s," in *Nation to Nation*. J. Bird et al. (eds.). Pp. 74–81. Toronto: Irwin.

Assante, Molefi Kete. 2003. *Erasing Racism: The Survival of the American Nation*. Amherst, NY: Prometheus Books.

Atkinson, Joe. 1994. "The State, the Media, and Thin Democracy," in *Leap into the Dark: The Changing Role of the State in New Zealand Since 1984*. A. Sharp (ed.). Auckland, NZ: Auckland University Press.

Auboin, Benoit. 2006. "Identity Fatigue." *Maclean's*, 11 December.

Auboin, Benoit. 2007. "Bill 101: A Gift We Never Expected." *Maclean's*, 13 August.

Augoustinos, M., and K.J. Reynolds (eds.). 2001. *Understanding Prejudice, Racism and Social Conflict*. Thousand Oaks CA: Sage.

Avery, Donald H. 1995. *Reluctant Hosts: Canada's Response to Immigrant Workers, 1896–1994*. Toronto: McClelland & Stewart.

Aydemir, A., and M. Skuterud. 2004. "Explaining the Deteriorating Entry Earnings of Canada's Immigrant Cohorts: 1996–2000." Family and Labour Studies Division, Statistics Canada. 11F0019MIE. No. 225.

Ayed, Nahlah. 1999. "Self-Government a Mess, Native Coalition Testifies." *Toronto Star*, 3 March.

Azam, Sharlene. 2000. *Rebel, Rouge, Mischievous Babe: A Book about Real Girls and the Myths We Ask Teens to Believe*. Toronto: HarperCollins.

Back, Les. 2002. "The New Technologies of Racism," in *A Companion to Race and Ethnic Studies*. D.T. Goldberg and J. Solomos (eds.). Pp. 365–378. Malden, MA: Blackwell.

Backhouse, Constance. 1999. *Colour-Coded: A Legal History of Racism in Canada: 1900–1950*. Toronto: University of Toronto Press.

Bakanic, Von. 2009. *Prejudice: Attitudes about Race, Class, and Gender*. Upper Saddle River, NJ: Pearson Prentice Hall.

Banaji, Mahazir. 2003. "Colour Blind?" *This Magazine*, January/February.

Banks, J.A., and C.A. McGee Banks (eds.). 1997. *Multicultural Education: Issues and Perspectives*. Toronto: Allyn and Bacon.

Bannerji, Himani. 2000. *The Dark Side of the Nation*. Toronto: Canadian Scholars' Press.

Banting, Keith, Thomas J. Courchene, and Leslie Seidle (eds.). 2007. *Belonging? Diversity, Recognition, and Shared Citizenship in Canada*. Montreal: Institute for Research on Public Policy (IRPP).

Banton, Michael. 1987. *Racial Theories*. Cambridge: Cambridge University Press.

Banton, Michael. 2000. "Racism Today." *Ethnic and Racial Studies*, *22*(3), 606–615.

Banton, Michael. 2005. "Historical and Contemporary Modes of Racialization," in *Racialization*. K. Murji and J. Solomos (eds.). Oxford, UK: Oxford University Press.

Barker, M. 1981. New Racism. London: Junction Books.

Barkun, Michael. 1994. *Religion and the Racist Right: The Origins of the Christian Identity Movement*. Chapel Hill, NC: University of North Carolina Press.

Barnsley, Paul. 1999. "Cree Chief Slams Gathering Strength." *Windspeaker*.

Barrett, Stanley R. 1987. *Is God a Racist? The Right Wing in Canada*. Toronto: University of Toronto Press.

Barrett, Stanley R. 2007. "The Role of Violence in the Far Right in Canada," in *Racial, Ethnic, and Homophobic Violence*. M. Prum et al. (eds.). Pp. 73–82. New York: Routledge-Cavendish.

Barth, Frederick. 1969. *Ethnic Groups and Boundaries*. Boston: Little, Brown.

Basok, Tanya, and Marshal Bastable. 2009. "Knock, Knock, Knockin' on Heaven's Door": Immigrants and the Guardians of Privilege in Canada. *Labour/Le Travail*, *63*, 207–219.

Bass, Gary J. 2006. "What Really Causes Civil War?" *New York Times Magazine*, 13 August.

Baubock, Rainer. 2005. "If You Say Multiculturalism Is the Wrong Answer, Then What Was the Question You Asked?" *Canadian Diversity*, *4*(1), 90–94.

Bauder, Harald. 2003. "Equality, Justice, and the Problem of International Borders: The Case of Canadian Immigration Regulation." *ACME*, *2*(2), 167–182.

Bauder, Harald. 2008. "Dialectics of Humanitarian Immigration and National Identity in Canadian Public Discourse." *Refuge*, *25*(1), 84–94.

Bauer, William. 1994. "How the System Works." *The Globe and Mail*, 12 November.

Bauerlein, Mark. 2001. "Social Constructionism: Philosophy for the Academic Workplace." *Partisan Review, 68*(2), 228–241.

Beach, Charles, M. Alan, G. Green, and Jeffrey G. Reitz (eds.). 2003. *Canadian Immigration Policy for the 21st Century.* Kingston, ON: John Deutsch Institute for the Study of Economic Policy, Queen's University.

Beare, Margaret. 2003. "Policing with a National Security Agenda." Commissioned by the Department of Canadian Heritage for the National Forum on Policing in a Multicultural Society.

Beaujot, Roderic P. 1999. "Immigration and Demographic Structures," in *Immigrant Canada*. S. Halli and L. Driedger (eds.). Toronto: University of Toronto Press.

Behrens, G. 1994. "Love, Hate, and Nationalism." *Time*, 21 March.

Belanger, Yale. 2008. *Aboriginal Self-Government in Canada* (3rd ed.). Saskatoon: Purich Publishing.

Belkhodja, Chedly et al. 2006. "Introduction: Multicultural Futures: Challenges and Solutions?" *Canadian Ethnic Studies, 38*(3), ii–v.

Bell, Catherine. 1997. "Métis Constitutional Rights in Section 35(1)." *Alberta Law Review, 36*(1), 180–204.

Bell, Derrick A. 2006. "Foreward: The Perils of Racial Prophecy," in *Images of Color, Images of Crime: Readings* (3rd ed.). Coramae R. Mann, Marjorie S. Zatz, and Nancy Rodriguez (eds.). Cary, NC: Roxbury Publishing Company.

Bell, Michael. 2004. "Tripping Up on the Dual Citizenship." *The Globe and Mail*, 29 July.

Bell, Stewart, and Marina Jimenez. 2000. "Canada Should Go Overseas to Select Refugees, System's Critics Say." *National Post*, 31 March.

Bell-Fialkoff, Andrew. 1993. "Ethnic Conflict." *The World and I* (July), 465–477.

Bem, Sandra Lipsitz. 1994. "In a Male-Centered World, Female Differences Are Transformed into Female Disadvantages." *The Chronicle of Higher Education* (17 August), B1–2.

Benson, Rodney. 2010. *What Is News Diversity and How do We Get It? Lessons from Comparing French and American Immigration Coverage.* News and Inclusion Symposium. Stanford University. March.

Berkeley, Rob. 2010. "It Ends Here: Generation 3.0." *Bulletin* (361, Spring). Available online at **http://www.runnymedetrust.org**

Bern, John, and Susan Dodds. 2000. "On the Plurality of Interests: Aboriginal Self-Government and Land Rights," in *Political Theory and the Rights of Indigenous Peoples.* D. Ivison et al. (eds.). Pp. 163–182. Oakleigh, Australia: Cambridge University Press.

Berry, Brian, and Eduardo Bonilla-Silva. 2007. "'They Should Hire the One with the Best Score': White Sensitivity to Qualification Differences in Affirmative Action Hiring Decisions." *Ethnic and Racial Studies, 31*(2), 215–242.

Berry, John. 2006. "Mutual Attitudes among Immigrants and Ethnocultural Groups in Canada." *International Journal of Intercultural Relations, 30*, 719–734.

Berry, John W., Rudolph Kalin, and Donald M. Taylor. 1977. *Multiculturalism and Ethnic Attitudes in Canada.* Ottawa: Ministry of Supply and Services in Canada.

Berton, Pierre. 1975. *Hollywood's Canada: The Americanization of Our National Image.* Toronto: McClelland & Stewart.

Bhabha, Faisal. 2007. "Don't Fear Religious Schools." *National Post*, 24 August.

Bharucha, R. 2000. *The Politics of Cultural Practice: Thinking through Theatre in an Age of Globalization.* Hanover, NH: University Press of New England.

Bhavnani, R., H.S. Mirza, and V. Meetoo. 2005. Tackling the Roots of Racism. Lessons for Success. Bristol, UK: Joseph Rountree Foundation and Polity Press.

Bibby, Reginald W. 1990. *Mosaic Madness: The Potential and Poverty of Canadian Life.* Toronto: Stoddart.

Bickerton, J., and A.-G. Gagnon (eds.). 2004. *Canadian Politics.* Peterborough, ON: Broadview Press.

Biddiss, Michael D. (ed.). 1979. *Images of Race.* New York: Holmes and Meier.

Biles, John. 2002. "Everyone's a Critic." *Canadian Issues* (February), 35–38.

Biles, John, and Meyer Burstein. 2003. "Immigration: Economics and More." *Canadian Issues* (April), 13–15.

Biles, John, and Paul Spoonley. 2007. "Introduction: National Identity: What Can It Tell Us about

Inclusion and Exclusion?" *National Identities, 9*(3), 191–195.

Biles, John, Erin Tolley, and Humera Ibrahim. 2005. "Does Canada Have a Multicultural Future?" *Canadian Diversity, 4*(1), 23–28.

Binder, Leonard (ed.). 1999. *Ethnic Conflict and International Politics in the Middle East.* Florida: University Press of Florida.

Bird, John, Lorraine Land, and Murray Macadam. 2002. *Nation to Nation: Aboriginal Sovereignty and the Future of Canada* (2nd ed.). Toronto: Irwin.

Bishop, Anne. 2005. *Beyond Token Change: Breaking the Cycle of Oppression in Institutions.* Halifax: Fernwood.

Bissett, James. 2008. "Demography Is Destiny: Toward a Canada-First Immigration Policy." Canadian Centre for Policy Studies. Available online at **ww.policystudies.ca/documents/ Demography_is_Destiny.pdf**.

Bissett, James. 2009. "The Current State of Canadian Immigration Policy," in *The Effects of Mass Immigration on Canadian Living Standards and Society.* Herbert Grubel (ed). Pp. 3–38. Calgary: Fraser Institute.

Bissett, James. 2010. *Abusing Canada's Generosity and Ignoring Genuine Refugees.* Frontier Centre for Public Policy. Policy Series No 96. October.

Bissoondath, Neil. 1993. "A Question of Belonging: Multiculturalism and Citizenship," in *Belonging: The Meaning and Future of Canadian Citizenship.* William Kaplan (ed.). Kingston/Montreal: McGill-Queen's University Press.

Bissoondath, Neil. 1994. *Selling Illusions: The Cult of Multiculturalism.* Toronto: Stoddart.

Blackduck, Alison. 2001. "Indigenous Landscape is Looking Very Bleak." *Toronto Star*, 12 July.

Blackwell, Tom. 2000. "Judge Rules Métis Don't Need License to Hunt in Ontario." *National Post*, 21 January.

Blackwell, Tom. 2004. "Ontario Cracks Down on Migrant Sponsors." *National Post*, 26 November.

Blank, Rebecca M., Marilyn Dabady, and Constance Citro (eds.). 2004. *Measuring Racial Discrimination.* Washington, DC: The National Academies Press.

Blauner, Rob. 1972. *Racial Oppression in America.* New York: HarperCollins.

Blauner, Rob. 1994. "Talking Past Each Other: Black and White Languages," in *Race and Ethnic Conflicts.* Fred L. Pincus and Howard J. Ehrlich (eds.). Pp. 18–28. Boulder, CO: Westview Press.

Blaut, James M. 1992. "The Theory of Cultural Racism." *Antipode, 23*, 289–299.

Bledsloe, Geraldine. 1989. "The Media: Minorities Still Fighting for Their Fair Share." *Rhythm and Business Magazine* (March/April), 14–18.

Bleich, Erik. 2006. "On Democratic Integration and Free Speech: Response to Tariq Modood and Randall Hansen." *International Migration*, 17–32.

Block, Sheila. 2010. "How Do Race and Gender Factor into Income Inequality?" *Canadian Centre for Policy Alternatives*, 2 June.

Block, Sheila, and Grace-Edward Galabuzi. 2011. "Canada's Color-Coded Labour Market: The Gap for Racialized Workers." *Canadian Centre for Policy Alternatives*, March.

Bloemraad, Irene. 2006. *Becoming a Citizen: Incorporating Refugees and Immigrants in the United States and Canada.* Berkeley, CA: University of California Press.

Bloemraad, Irene. 2007. "Citizenship and Pluralism: Multiculturalism in a World of Global Migration," in Citizenship and Immigrant Incorporation. G. Yurdakul and M. Bodemann (eds). Pp. 57–74. New York: Palgrave Macmillan.

Blumer, Herbert, and Troy Duster. 1980. "Theories of Race and Social Action," in *Sociological Theories: Race and Colonialism.* UNESCO ed. Paris. 211–238.

Blythe, Martin. 1994. *Naming the Other: Images of the Maori in New Zealand Film and Television.* Metuchen, NJ: Scarecrow Press.

Bolaria, B. Singh, and Peter S. Li. 1988. *Racial Oppression in Canada* (2nd ed.). Toronto: Garamond Press.

Boldt, Edward. 1993. *Surviving as Indians: The Challenges of Self-Government.* Toronto: University of Toronto Press.

Bonilla-Silva, Eduardo. 1996. "Rethinking Racism: Toward a Structural Interpretation." *American Sociological Review.*

Bonnett, Alastair. 2000. *Anti-racism.* London: Routledge.

Borrows, John, and Leonard Rotman. 1997. "The Sui Generis Nature of Aboriginal Rights: Does It Make a Difference?" *Alberta Law Review, 36*, 9–45.

Bosniak, Linda. 2000. "Citizenship Denationalized." *Indiana Journal of Global Legal Studies, 7*(2), 447–509.

Boston, Jonathon. 2005. *The Policy Implications of Diversity*. Paper presented to the NZ Diversity Forum, at Te Papa Museum, Wellington, August 23rd.

Boswell, Randy. 2010. "Canadians Split on 'Common Culture.'" *The Vancouver Sun*, 21 April.

Bouchard, Gerard, and Charles Taylor. 2008. "Building the Future: A Time for Reconciliation." Abridged Report of the Commission for Reasonable Accommodation of Religious and Cultural Minorities.

Boyd, Monica. 2006. "Social Mobility or Social Inheritance. Unpacking Immigrant Offspring Success." Paper presented to the Annual Meetings of the Canadian Association of Sociology and Anthropology, York University. June 1–3.

Boyd, Monica, and Deanna Pikkov. 2008. "Finding a Place in Stratified Structures: Migrant Women in North America," in *New Perspectives on Gender and Migration*. N. Piper (ed.). Pp. 19–58. New York: Routledge.

Boyd, Monica, and Michael Vickers. 2000. "100 Years of Immigration in Canada." *Canadian Social Trends* (Autumn), 2–12.

Brace, C. Loring. 2005. *"Race" Is a Four-Letter Word: The Genesis of the Concept*. New York: Oxford University Press.

Brady, Margaret. 2001. "A Separate Health Crisis." *National Post*, 19 July.

Bramadat, Paul, and David Selijak (eds.). 2005. *Religion and Ethnicity in Canada*. Toronto: Pearson Longman.

Bramadat, Paul, and David Seljak (eds). 2008. *Christianity and Ethnicity in Canada*. University of Toronto Press.

Brattain, Michelle. 2007. "Race, Racism, and Antiracism: UNESCO and the Politics of Presenting Science to the Postwar Public." *The American Historical Review, 112*(5).

Braziel, Jana Evans, and Anita Mannur. 2003. "Nation, Migration, Globalization: Points of Contention in Diasporic Studies," in *Theorizing Diaspora: A Reader*. J.E. Braziel and A. Mannur (eds.). Pp. 1–22. Oxford: Blackwell.

Breton, Eric. 2001. "Canadian Federalism, Multiculturalism, and the Twenty-First Century." *International Journal of Canadian Studies, 21*(Spring), 160–175.

Breton, Raymond. 1989. "Canadian Ethnicity in the Year 2000," in *Multiculturalism and Intergroup Relations*. James Frideres (ed.). Pp. 149–152. New York: Greenwood Press.

Breton, Raymond, Wsevolod W. Isajiw, Warren E. Kalbach, and Jeffrey G. Reitz. 1990. *Ethnic Identity and Equality: Varieties of Experience in a Canadian City*. Toronto: University of Toronto Press.

Bristow, Peggy (coordinator), Dionne Brand, Linda Carty, Afua A. Cooper, Sylvia Hamilton, and Adrienne Shadd. 1993. *We're Rooted Here and They Can't Pull Us Up: Essays in African Canadian Women's History*. Toronto: University of Toronto Press.

Broadbent, Alan. 2009. "Now Is the Time." *Maytree Opinion, 10* (July).

Brock, Kathy L. 1991. "The Politics of Aboriginal Self-Government: A Paradox." *Canadian Public Administration, 34*(2), 272–285.

Brooks, Stephen. 1998. *Public Policy in Canada: An Introduction*. Toronto: Oxford University Press.

Brooks, Stephen. 2004. "Political Culture in Canada: Issues and Directions," in *Canadian Politics* (4th ed.). J. Bickerton and A.-G. Gagnon (eds.). Pp. 55–78. Peterborough, ON: Broadview Press.

Brown, David. 1989. "Ethnic Revival: Perspectives on State and Society." *TWQ, 11*(4), 1–17.

Brown, Louise. 2005. "Amid Debate, Race-based School Thrives." *Toronto Star*, 15 September.

Brown, Louise. 2007. "Cultural Oasis Nurtures Students." *Toronto Star*, 29 November.

Brown, Maureen J. 2004. *In Their Own Voices: African-Canadians in the Greater Toronto Area Share Experiences of Police Profiling*. Commissioned by the African-Canadian Community Coalition on Racial Profiling.

Brown, Michael. 2005. *Whitewashing Race. Myth of a Color-Blind Society*. Berkeley, CA: University of California Press.

Brown, Murphy. 2005. "Ways to Go to Equality." *Share*, 17 March.

Brown, Rupert. 2010. *Prejudice: Its Social Psychology* (2nd ed.). Wiley-Blackwell.

Buckley, Helen. 1992. *From Wooden Ploughs to Welfare: Why Indian Policy Failed in the Prairie Provinces*. Toronto: McMillian Collier.

Bullock, K.H., and G.J. Jaffri. 2000. "Media (Mis)representations: Muslim Women in the Canadian Nation." *Canadian Woman Studies, 20*(2), 35–40.

Bunzl, Matti. 2005. "Between Anti-Semitism and Islamophobia: Some Thoughts on the New Europe." *American Ethnologist, 32*(4), 499–508.

Bureau of Public Affairs, US Department of State. 2010. Trafficking in Persons: Ten Years of Partnering to Combat Modern Slavery (Fact Sheet). Washington: US State Department. Available online at **http://www.state.gov/r/pa/scp/fs/ 2010/143115.htm**

Burgess, Michael. 1996. "Ethnicity, Nationalism, and Identity in Canada–Quebec Relations: The Case of Quebec's Distinct Society." *Journal of Commonwealth and Comparative Politics, 34*(2), 46–64.

Burnet, Jean. 1981. "The Social and Historical Context of Ethnic Relations," in *A Canadian Social Psychology of Ethnic Relations*. Robert C. Gardiner and Rudolph Kalin (eds.). Pp. 17–36. Toronto: Methuen.

Butler, Don. 2008. "'Over Racism' Rife at Justice, Senators Told." *Ottawa Citizen*, 6 February. Available online at **http://www.canada.com/ ottawacitizen/news/story.html?id=63063ebb-edf8-4b0c-845a-475547c81188**

Byrne, Bridget. 2010. *White Lives: The Interplay of "Race," Class, and Gender in Everyday Life*. New York: Routledge.

Cahill, D., G. Bouma, H. Dellal, and M. Leahy. 2006. *Religion, Cultural Diversity, and Safeguarding Australia*. Published by the Department of Immigration and Multicultural and Indigenous Affairs and Australian Multicultural Foundation.

Caines, Lisa. 2004. "The Deep Roots of Prejudice." *Research*, Spring: 38.

Cairns, Alan. 2000. *Citizens Plus: Aboriginal Peoples and the Canadian State*. Vancouver: UBC Press.

Cairns, Alan. 2003. "Aboriginal Peoples in the Twenty-First Century: A Plea for Realism," in *A Canadian Social Psychology of Ethnic Relations*. Robert C. Gardiner and Rudolph Kalin (eds.). Pp. 17–36. Toronto: Methuen.

Cairns, Alan C. 2005. *First Nations and the Canadian State: In Search of Coexistence*. Kingston: Queen's University Institute of Intergovernmental Relations.

Calder, Gideon, and Emaneula Ceva (eds). 2011. *Diversity in Europe: Dilemmas of Differential Treatment in Theory and Practice*. New York: Routledge.

Cameron, Elspeth. (ed.). 2004. *Multiculturalism and Immigration in Canada: An Introductory Reader*. Toronto: Canadian Scholars' Press.

Canadian Council for Refugees. 2000. *Report on Systemic Racism and Discrimination in Canadian Refugee and Immigration Policies*. In preparation for the UN World Conference Against Racism, Racial Discrimination, Xenophobia and Related Intolerance. Montreal.

Canadian Council for Refugees. 2001. "Refugee Women Fleeing Gender-Based Persecution." Available online at **http://www.ccrweb.ca/ genderpers.html**

Canadian Feminist Alliance for International Action [CFAFIA]. 2008. *Women's Inequality in Canada*. Submission of CAFAFIA to the UN Committee on the Elimination of Discrimination Against Women on the occasion of the Committee's Review of Canada's 6th and 7th Reports.

Canadian Heritage. 2001. *Canadian Diversity: Respecting Our Differences*. Ottawa.

Canadian Heritage. 2005/6. "Annual Report on the Operation of the Canadian *Multiculturalism Act*." Available online at **http://www.pch.gc.ca/progs/multi/reports/ ann2005-2006/index_e.cfm**

Canadian Islamic Congress. 2005. "Anti-Islam in the Media." Summary of the Sixth Annual Report for the Year 2003. 31 January. Available online at **http://www.canadianislamiccongress.com/ rr/rr_2003.php**

Canadian Issues. 2005. "Immigration and the Intersections of Diversity." Spring.

Canadian Labour Congress. 2008. "Equality, Once and For All." Available online at **http://canadianlabour.ca/en/womens_ economic_equa**

Canadian Press. 2005. "Canada Least Racist Nation But Problems Exist, Chan." *Hamilton Spectator*, 16 March.

Canadian Press. 2007a. "Immigration Policies Need Changing, Flaherty Advised." *KW Record*, 1 September.

Canadian Press. 2007b. "More New Canadians Forced to Use Food Banks." Reprinted in *The Record*, 8 November.

Canadian Press. 2010. Affirmative Action at Issue by Steve Rennie. In the *Waterloo Region Record*, 23 July.

Canadian Race Relations Foundation. 2003. *Facts about Racism and Policing*. Available online at **http://www.crr.ca**

Canadian Race Relations Foundation. 2008. *What Is Canadian Racism? A National Symposium.* Calgary, AB. 30 April to 2 May.

Cannon, Martin J., and Lina Sunseri (eds.). 2011. *Race, Colonialism and Indigeneity in Canada.* Toronto: Oxford University Press.

Caplan, Gerald. 2005. "The Genocide Problem: Never Again or All Over Again." *The Walrus,* 68–76.

Caplan, Gerald. 2007. "Talk but No Action on Genocide." Cited in Carol Goar. *Toronto Star*, 25 April.

Caplan, Gerald. 2010. "Honour Killings in Canada: Even Worse Than We Believe." *The Globe and Mail,* 23 July.

Cardinal, Harold. 1969. *The Unjust Society.* Edmonton: Hurtig.

Cardozo, Andrew. 2005. "Multiculturalism vs. Rights." *Toronto Star*, 15 September.

Cardozo, Andrew, and Luis Musto (eds.). 1997. *Battle over Multiculturalism: Does It Help or Hinder Canadian Unity?* Ottawa: Pearson-Shoyama Institute.

Carlson, Kathryn Blaze. 2010. "New Brunswick New Centre of French-English Tensions." *National Post*, 31 July.

Carment, David. 2007. "Exploiting Ethnicity: Political Elites and Domestic Conflict." *Harvard International Review, 28*(4).

Caselli, Francesco, and Wilbur John Coleman II. 2006/2010. *On the Theory of Ethnic Conflict.* Working Paper No. 12125 for National Bureau of Economic Research Cambridge MA.

Cassin, A.M., T. Krawchenko, and M. VanderPlaat. 2007. *Racism and Discrimination in Canada. Laws, Policies, and Practices.* Atlantic Metropolis Centre. Multiculturalism and Human Rights Research Reports. No 3. Ottawa: Department of Canadian Heritage.

Castells, Manuel. 1997. *The Power of Identity.* Oxford: Blackwell.

Castellano, Marlene Brant. 2009. "Heart of the Nations: Woman's Contribution to Community Healing," in *Restoring the Balance.* G. Valaskakis et al. (eds.). Pp. 203–236. Winnipeg: University of Manitoba Press.

Castles, Stephen, and Mark J. Miller. 2003. *The Age of Migration* (3rd ed.). New York: Guildford Press.

Castles, Stephen, and Mark J. Miller. 2009. *The Age of Migration. International Population Movements in the Modern World* (4th ed.). New York: The Guilford Press.

Caulfield, Timothy, and Gerald Robertson. 1996. "Eugenics Policies in Alberta: From the Systematic to the Systemic." *Alberta Law Review, 35*(1), 59–81.

Caws, Peter. 1994. "Identities: Cultural, Transcultural, and Multicultural," in *Multiculturalism: A Critical Reader.* D.T. Goldberg (ed.). Pp 371–378. Oxford: Blackwell.

CBC News. 2010. "Rights Icon Desmond Gets N.S. Apology." 16 April. Available online at **http://www.cbc.ca/news/canada/nova-scotia/story/2010/04/15/ns-desmond-apology-dexter.html**

CBC News. 2010. "Montreal Teen Arrest Rate Double for Blacks." 26 May.

CBC News. 2010. "Canada Falls Short on Aboriginal Rights: Report." 27 May.

Centre for Immigration Policy Reform. 2010. *Policy Statement.* Available online at http://www.immigrationreform.ca

Centre for Research and Information on Canada. 2005. "Portraits of Canada: Backgrounder, Quebecers See Advantages in Key National Public Policies." Ottawa.

Centre for Research and Information on Canada. 2006. "Quebec Youth Support Key Canadian Values: Backgrounder." Montreal.

Centre for Social Justice. 2010. *Aboriginal Issues.* Available online at **http://www.socialjustice.org**

Chambers, Gretta. 1996. "Distinct Clause Needs Study, Not Merely Semantic Jigging." *The Globe and Mail*, 22 April.

Chan, Raymond. 2003/2004. "A Message from the Minister of State (Multiculturalism)." *Annual Report on the Operation of the Canadian Multiculturalism Act.* Ottawa.

Chan, Wendy, and Kiran Mirchandani. 2002. "From Race and Crime to Racialization and Criminalization," in *Crimes of Colour: Racialization and the Criminal Justice System in Canada.* W. Chan and K. Mirchandani (eds.). Pp. 9–23. Peterborough, ON: Broadview Press.

Chandler, J.J., and C Lalonde. 1998. Cultural Continuity as a Hedge Against Suicide in Canada's First Nations. *Transcultural Psychiatry, 35*(2), 191–219.

Chartrand, Paul. 1992. "Aboriginal Self-Government: The Two Sides of Legitimacy," in *How Ottawa Spends: A More Democratic Canada . . . ?* Susan D. Phillips (ed.). Pp. 231–256. Ottawa: Carleton University Press.

Chartrand, Paul L., and Albert Peeling. 2004. "Sovereignty, Liberty, and the Legal Order of the 'Freemen' (Otipahemsu'uk): Towards a Constitutional Theory of Métis Self-Government." *Saskatchewan Law Review, 67*(1), 339.

Cheng, Hau Ling. 2005. "Constructing a Transnational, Multilocal Sense of Belonging: An Analysis of Ming Pao (West Canadian Edition)." *Journal of Communication Inquiry, 29*(2), 141–159.

Chomsky, Aviva. 2007. *"They Take Our Jobs!" And 20 Other Myths about Immigration.* Boston: Beacon Press.

Choudhry, Sujit. 2007. "Does the World Need More Canada? The Politics of the Canadian Model in Constitutional Politics and Political Theory." *I-CON, 5*(4), 606–638.

Chrétien, Jean. 1999. "Federalism Reigns for Most Who Live in Democracies." *Canadian Speeches: Issues of the Day, 13*(4), 62–64.

Christiansen, Thomas, and Christine Reh. 2009. *Constitutionalizing the European Union.* Basingstoke, UK: Palgrave Macmillan.

Christchurch Press. 2010. "Black Farmers Win $1.8b [NZ] Discrimination Case." 20 February.

Christie, Gordon. 2002. *Challenges to Urban Aboriginal Governance.* Presented to the Institute for Intergovernmental Relations. Queens University. 1 November.

Christie, Gordon. 2005. "Aboriginal Resource and Subsistence Rights after Delgamuukw and Marshall," in *Advancing Aboriginal Claims: Visions, Strategies, Directions.* Kerry Wilkins (ed.). Saskatoon: Purich Publishing.

Chung, Andrew. 2005. "A Call for 'Separateness.'" *Toronto Star*, 8 October.

Chung, Andrew. 2010. "Police Profiling 'Alarming' in Montreal." *Toronto Star*, 9 August.

Churchill, Ward. 1999. *Fantasies of the Master Race: Literature, Cinema, and the Colonization of North American Indians.* Winnipeg: Arbeiter Ring.

Churchill, Ward. 2002. *Perversions of Justice Indigenous Peoples and Angloamerican Law.* San Francisco: City Lights Publishers.

Churchill, Ward. 2004. *Kill the Indian, Save the Man: The Genocidal Impact of American Indian Residential Schools.* San Francisco: City Lights Publishers.

Citizenship and Immigration Canada. 2001. "Pursuing Canada's Commitment to Immigration." *The Immigration Plan for 2002.* Ottawa.

Citizenship and Immigration Canada. 2009. "Facts and Figures 2009—Immigration Overview: Permanent and Temporary Residents." Ottawa.

Citizenship and Immigration Canada. 2010. *The Current State of Multiculturalism in Canada and Research Themes on Canadian Multiculturalism.* Available online at **http://www.cic.gc.ca**

Clarfield, Geoffrey. 2007. "Where Tribe Is Everything." *National Post*, 15 December.

Clark, Bruce, 1990. *Native Liberty, Crown Sovereignty: The Existing Aboriginal Right of Self-Government in Canada.* Kingston, ON: McGill-Queen's University Press.

Clark-Avery, Kristen. 2007. "Introduction." *Souls: A Critical Journal of Black Politics, Culture, and Society, 9*(1), 1–3.

Closs, William J. 2003. "Racial Profiling Guidelines Ensure Fairness for All." *Kingston Whig-Standard*, 16 May.

Closs, William J., and Paul F. McKenna. 2006. "Profiling a Problem in Canadian Police Leadership: The Kingston Police Data Collection Problem." *Canadian Public Administration, 49*(2), 143–160.

Coates, Rodney D. 2008. "Covert Racism in the USA and Globally." *Sociology Compass, 2*(1), 208–231.

Cobb, Chris. 1995. "Multiculturalism Policy May be Outdated, Says MPs." *Ottawa Citizen*, 4 July.

Coderre, Dennis. 2003. "Interview with the Minister of Immigration and Citizenship." *Canadian Issues* (April), 4–7.

Codrescu, Andrei. 1995. "Faux Chicken & Phony Furniture." *Utne Reader* (May/June), 47–48. Originally published in the *The Nation*, 12 December 1984.

Cohen, Randy. 1999. "Cut Rate Rationale." *NY Times Magazine*, 18 July.

Collacott, Martin. 2006. "A Refugee System in Need of Overhaul." *National Post*, 9 March.

Collett, Elizabeth. 2010. "Europe: A New Continent of Immigration," in *Rethinking Immigration and Integration: A New Centre-Left Agenda.* Olaf Cramme and Constance Motte (eds.). Pp. 10–18. London, UK: Policy Network.

Collier, Paul. 2007. "Ethnic Civil Wars: Questioning the Received Wisdom." *Harvard International Review, 28*(4).

Colour of Poverty Campaign. 2007. "Understanding the Racialization of Poverty in Ontario: Fact Sheets." Available online at **http://www.colourofpoverty.ca**

Conference Board of Canada. 2004. *The Voices of Visible Minorities: Speaking Out on Breaking Down Barriers.* September.

Conference Board of Canada. 2008. *Renewing Immigration: Toward a Convergence and Consolidation of Canada's Immigration Policies and Systems.* Ottawa: Author.

Conlogue, Ray. 1997. "Arrêt! You Are Entering a French-Speaking Area." *The Globe and Mail*, 22 March.

Connor, Walker. 2000. "National Self-Determination and Tomorrow's Political Map," in *Citizenship, Diversity, and Pluralism*. A. Cairns, J.C. Courtney, Peter MacKinnon, Hans J. Michelmann, and David E. Smith (eds.). Pp. 163–176. Montreal/Kingston: McGill-Queen's University Press.

Cooke, Martin et al. 2007. "Indigenous Well-Being in Four Countries: An Application of the UNDP's Human Development Index to Indigenous Peoples in Australia, Canada, New Zealand and the United States." *BMC International Health and Human Rights*, 7(9). Available online at **http://www.biomedcentral.com/1472-698X/7/9**

Cooke, Martin, and Jennifer McWhirter. 2010. "Public Policy and Aboriginal Peoples in Canada: Taking a Life Course Perspective." *Canadian Public Policy*.

Cooper, Afua. 2006. *The Hanging of Angelique.* Toronto: HarperCollins.

Cornell, Stephan, and Douglas Hartmann. 1998. *Ethnicity and Race: Making Identities in a Changing World.* Thousand Oaks, CA: Pine Forge Press.

Cornell, Stephen, and Douglas Hartmann. 2007. *Ethnicity and Race. Making Identities in a Changing World.* Thousand Oaks, CA: Sage.

Cornell, Stephan, and Joseph P Kalt. 2003. *Sovereignty and Nation-building: The Development Challenge in Indian Country Today.* Joint Occasional Papers on Native Affairs NO 2003-03. Originally published in the American Indian Culture and Research Journal 1998.

Cose, Ellis. 1997. *Color-Blind: Seeing Beyond Race in a Race-Obsessed World.* New York: HarperCollins.

Cotler, Irwin. 2004. Presentation to the Ontario Bar Association, June 17. Available online at **http://www.oba.org/en/gen/sep04/speaking.aspx**

Cotler, Irwin. 2007. "The New Antisemitism: An Assault on Human Rights," in *Antisemitism:*

The Generic Hatred. M. Fineberg et al. (eds.). Pp. 15–33. Portland, OR: Vallentine Mitchell Publishers.

Cottle, Simon. 2005. *Ethnic Minorities and the Media.* Maidenhead, UK: Open University Publication.

Council of the European Union. 2004. *Draft Conclusions of the Council and the Representatives of the Governments of the Member States on the establishment of Common Basic Principles for immigrant integration policy in the European Union.* **http://ec.europa.eu/justice/funding/2004_2007/doc/council_conclusions_common_basic_principles.pdf**

Courchene, Thomas. 2007. "Introduction and Overview," in *Canada: The State of the Federation: Annual Review.* Pp. 1–23. Queen's University, Kingston: Institute of Intergovernmental Relations.

Courchene, Thomas. 2009. "Where Would Canada Be without Quebec?" *The Globe and Mail,* 29 October.

Covering Immigration: An International Media Dialogue [Draft Agenda Notes]. 2009. New York: French–American Foundation.

Cowen, T. 1999. "Cashing in on Cultural Free Trade: Don't Give Us Shelter: A U.S. Economist Sings the Praises of Canadian Artists." *National Post,* 24 April.

Crawford, Beverly. 2006. "The Causes of Cultural Conflict: An Institutional Approach." Available online at **http://repositories.cdlib.org/cgi/viewcontent.cgi?article=1058&context=uciaspubs/research**.

Crawford, Beverly, and Ronnie D. Lipschutz (eds.). 1998. *The Myth of "Ethnic Conflict": Politics, Economics, and "Cultural" Violence.* University of California International and Area Studies Digital Collection. Research Series #98.

Crepeau, Francois, and Delphine Nakache. 2006. "Controlling Irregular Migration in Canada: Reconciling Security Concerns with Human Rights Protection." *IRPP Choices, 12*(1).

Cross, Pamela. 2007. "Violent Partners Create War Zone for Women." *Toronto Star,* 6 July.

Cudmore, James. 2001. "Inuk Accuses Ottawa of Discrimination." *National Post,* 22 March.

Cummings, Joan Grant. 2007. "Foreword," in *Theorizing Empowerment.* N. Massaquoi and N.N. Wane (eds.). Pp. xiii–xiv. Toronto: Inanna Publications.

Curran, Peggy. 2010. "Young Blacks More Apt to be Pulled Over by Police, Report." *Montreal Gazette*, 10 August.

Curry, Bill. 2008. "Native Band Sues for $550 Billion, Saying Mine Sites Belong to Them." *The Globe and Mail*, 14 May.

Curry, Bill. 2010. "Natives Fear Renewed Push for Privatized Land Ownership." *The Globe and Mail*, 1 September.

Curtis, Michael. 1997. "Review Essay. Antisemitism: Different Perspectives." *Sociological Forum, 12*(2), 321–327.

Da Costa, Kimberly McClain. 2007. *Making Multiracials: State, Family, and Market in the Redrawing of the Color Line*. California: Stanford University Press.

Dalmage, Heather M. (ed.). 2004. *The Politics of Multiculturalism: Challenging Racial Thinking*. Albany: State University of New York.

Das Gupta, Tania. 2009. *"Real" Nurses and Others. Racism in Nursing*. Halifax: Fernwood.

Das Gupta, Tania, Carl E. James, Roger Maaka, Grace Edward Galabuzi, and Chris Anderson (eds.). 2007. *Race and Racialization: Essential Readings*. Toronto: Canadian Scholars' Press.

Dasko, Donna. 2005. "Public Attitudes toward Multiculturalism and Bilingualism." Canadian and French Perspectives on Diversity Conference, 16 October 2003. Ottawa: Canadian Heritage for the Minister of Supply and Public Works.

Dauvergne, C. 2004. "Why Judy Sgro Is Just Plain Wrong—No One Is Illegal." *The Globe and Mail*, 2 August.

Davis, Angela. 1998. "Masked Racism: Reflections on the Prison Industrial Complex." *Colorlines*, Fall, 1–4. Available online at **http://www.colorlines.com**

Davis, Kingsley, and Wilbert E. Moore. 1945. "Some Principles of Stratification." *American Sociological Review* 5: 242–249.

Day, Richard. 2000. *Multiculturalism and the History of Canadian Diversity*. Toronto: University of Toronto Press.

Deak, Istvan. 2002. "The Crime of the Century." *New York Review*, 26 September: 48–50.

Dean, Bartholomew, and Jerome M. Levi (eds.). 2006. *At the Risk of Being Heard: Identity, Indigenous Rights, and Postcolonial States*. University of Michigan Press.

Deckha, Maneesha. 2010. Gender, Culture, and Violence: Toward a Paradigm Shift? *Equity Matters*. Fedcan Blog. Available online at **http://blog.fedcan.ca/2010/02/18/**

Dei, George Sefa. 1996a. "Black/African-Canadian Students' Perspectives on School Racism," in *Racism in Canadian Schools*, I. Alladin (ed.). Pp. 2–61. Toronto: Harcourt Brace.

Dei, George Sefa. 1996b. *Anti-racism Education: Theory and Practice*. Halifax: Fernwood.

Dei, George Sefa. 2000. "Contesting the Future: Anti-racism and Canadian Diversity," in *21st Century Canadian Diversity*. S. Nancoo (ed.). Pp. 295–319. Toronto: Canadian Scholars' Press.

Dei, George Sefa. 2004. "Why I Back School Board Plan." *Toronto Star*, 26 November.

Dei, George Sefa. 2005. "Anti-racist Education— Moving Yet Standing Still. Editorial Commentary." *Directions, 3*(1), 6–9.

Dei, George Sefa. 2006. "On Race, Anti-racism, and Education." *Directions, 3*(1), 27–34.

Dei, George J. Sefa. 2007. "Speaking Race: Silence, Salience, and the Politics of Anti-racist Scholarship," in *Race and Racism in 21st Century Canada*. S.P. Hier and B.S. Bolaria (eds.). Pp. 53–66. Peterborough, ON: Broadview Press.

Dei, George Sefa et al. 2000. *Removing the Margins: The Challenges and Possibilities of Inclusive Schooling*. Toronto: Canadian Scholars' Press.

Delaney, Joan. 2008. "Fear of Extinction Leads to Francophone Multicultural Malaise." *Epoch Times*, 27 March–2 April.

Delanty, Gerard. 2000. *Citizenship in a Global Age: Society, Culture, Politics*. Philadelphia: Open University Press.

Delic, Senada, and Francis Abele. 2010. "The Recession and Aboriginal Workers," in *How Ottawa Spends 2010/2011*. G.B. Doern and C. Stoney (eds). Pp. 187–216. Montreal and Kingston: McGill-Queen's University Press.

Dempsey, Colleen, and Soojin Yu. 2004. "Refugees to Canada: Who Are They and How Are They Faring?" *Canadian Issues* (March), 5–10.

Dench, Janet. 2004. "Why Take Refugees?" *Canadian Issues* (March), 11–13.

Dench, Janet. 2007. "The Safe Country Dilemma: Why Offering Asylum Is an Obligation." *The Globe and Mail*, 6 December.

Denis, Ann. 2008. "Intersectional Analysis: A Contribution of Feminism to Sociology." *International Sociology, 23*(5), 677–694.

Denis, Claude. 1996. "Aboriginal Rights in/and Canadian Society: A Syewen Case Study." *International Journal of Canadian Studies, 14*(Fall), 13–34.

Denis, Claude. 1997. *We Are Not You: First Nations and Canadian Modernity.* Peterborough, ON: Broadview Press.

Denton, Nancy A., and Stewart E. Tolnay (eds.). 2002. *American Diversity: A Demographic Challenge for the Twenty-First Century.* Albany: State University of New York.

Department of Canadian Heritage. 2005. *Canada's Diversity: Respecting Our Differences.* Annual Report on the Operation of the Canadian *Multiculturalism Act 2000–2004.* Ottawa: Minister of Public Works and Government Services.

Department of Indian Affairs and Northern Development. 1997. *Socioeconomic Indicators in Indian Reserves and Comparable Communities.* Ottawa: Author.

Department of Justice. 2009. *Family Violence. Overview Paper.* Available online at **http://www.justice.gc.ca/eng/pi/fv-vf/facts-info/fv-vf/index.html**

DeSouza, Ruth, and Andy Williamson. 2006. "Representing Ethnic Communities in the Media." *AEN Journal, 1*(1). Available online at **http://www.aen.org.nz/journal/1/1/williamson_desouza.html**

Deutsche, Welle. 2010. *Berlin Announces Plans to Promote Integration and Attract Skilled Workers.* Available online at http://www.dw-world.de

Deveaux, Monique. 2006. *Gender and Justice in Multicultural Liberal States.* New York: Oxford University Press.

Devine, Fiona, Miles Savage, John Scott, and Rosemary Crompton. 2005. *Rethinking Class: Culture, Identities, and Lifestyle.* New York: Palgrave Macmillan.

Diamond, Jack. 1997. "Provinces Are Archaic: More Power to Cities." *The Globe and Mail,* 26 May.

Dickason, Olive. 1992. *Canada's First Nations: A History of Founding Peoples from Earliest Times.* Toronto: McClelland & Stewart.

Dijkstra, S., K. Geutjen, and A. De Ruijter. 2001. "Multiculturalism and Social Integration in Europe." *International Political Science Review, 22*(1), 55–84.

Diller, Jerry V. 2004. *Cultural Diversity: A Primer for the Human Services* (2nd ed.). Belmont, CA: Thompson–Brooks/Cole.

DiManno, Rosie. 2007. "Kept the Faith for the Sake of Aqsa Parvezes." *Toronto Star,* 15 December.

Dinovitzer, Ronit, John Hagan, and Ron Levi. 2009. "Immigration and Youthful Illegalities in a Global Edge City." *Social Forces, 88*(1), 337–372.

Dinsdale, Peter. 2009. "Urban Aboriginals: The Policy Void at the Centre of Canadian Politics." *Inroads: A Canadian Journal of Public Opinion,* 22 June.

Diocson, Cecilia. 2005. "Filipino Women in Canada's Live-in Caregiver Program." *Philippine Reporter* (March), 16–31.

Dion, Stephane. 2005. "Nothing Can Justify Secession in Canada." *Toronto Star,* 30 October.

DiversiPro. 2007. *Research on Settlement Programming through the Media.* Available online at **http://atwork.settlement.org**

DiversityInc. 2008. "Hate Groups in America Surging: New Southern Poverty Law Center Report." Available online at **http://www.diversityinc.com/public/3190.cfm**

Doane, Ashley. 2006. "What Is Racism?" *Racial Discourse and Racial Politics, 32*(2–3), 255–275.

Doane, Ashley. 2007. "The Changing Politics of Color-Blind Racism." *The New Black: Alternative Paradigms and Strategies for the 21ˢᵗ Century Research in Race and Ethnic Relations, 14,* 159–174.

Donaldson, Ian. 2004. "Identity, Intersections of Diversity, and the Multicultural Program." *Canadian Diversity, 3*(1), 14–16.

Donolo, Peter, and Allan Gregg. 2005. "What Regional Tensions?" *The Globe and Mail,* 22 September.

Dosman, Edgar. 1972. *Indians: The Urban Dilemma.* Toronto: McClelland & Stewart.

Douglas, Debbie. 2005. Cited in "Award Winner Battles for Immigration Workers," by Debra Black. *Toronto Star,* 9 March.

Dovidio, John et al. 2010a. "Prejudice, Stereotyping, and Discrimination: Theoretical and Empirical Overview," in *The Sage Handbook of Prejudice, Stereotyping, and Discrimination.* J.F. Dovidio et al. (eds.). Pp 3–28. Thousand Oaks, CA: Sage.

Dovidio, John et al. 2010b. "Understanding Bias toward Latinos: Discrimination, Dimensions of Difference, and Experiences of Exclusion." *Journal of Social Issues, 66*(1), 59–78.

Dow, Steve. 2003. "Racism in the Net." Available online at **http://www.smh.com.au**

Driedger, Leo. 1989. *The Ethnic Factor: Identity in Diversity.* Toronto: McGraw-Hill Ryerson.

Drost, Herman, Brian Lee Crowley, and Richard Schwindt. 1995. *Marketing Solutions for Native Poverty.* Toronto: CD Howe Institute.

Drummond, Don, and Francis Fong. 2010. "An Economics Perspective on Canadian Immigration." *Policy Options* (July/August).

Du Bois, W.E.B. 1940. *Dusk of Dawn.* New York: Harcourt, Brace.

Duffy, Andrew. 1999. "Ex-Prostitute with AIDS Wins Deportation Delay." *Windsor Star*, 20 November.

Duffy, Andrew. 2004. "Struggle for Success." *Toronto Star*, 25 September.

Dufraiment, Lisa. 2002. "Continuity and Modification of Aboriginal Rights in the Nisga'a Treaty." *UBC Law Review, 35*(2), 455–477.

Duncan, Howard. 2005. "Multiculturalism: Still a Viable Concept for Integration?" *Canadian Diversity, 4*(1), 12–14.

Duncan, Howard. 2006. "Diasporas and Transnationalism." *Metropolis World Bulletin, 6*, 2.

Duncanson, John, Dale Ann Freed, and Chris Sorensen. 2003. "There's Racism All Over the Place." *Toronto Star*, 26 February.

Dunn, K.M., N. Klockerm, and T. Salabay. 2007. "Contemporary Racism and Islamophobia in Australia." *Ethnicities, 7*(4), 564–589.

Dunphy, Bill. 2003. "Immigrant Poverty Rate Soaring." *Hamilton Spectator*, 20 June.

Durie, Mason. 2005. "Race and Ethnicity in Public Policy: Does It Work?" *Social Policy Journal of New Zealand, 24*, April.

Dustin, Donna. 2007. *The McDonaldization of Social Work.* Aldershot, UK: Ashgate.

Early, G. 1993. "American Education and the Postmodernist Impulse." *American Quarterly, 45*(2), 220–221.

Easteal, Patricia. 1996. *Shattered Dreams: Marital Violence Against Overseas-Born Women in Australia.* Canberra: Australia National University Press.

Economist. 2005. "Peace, Order, and Rocky Government." 3 December.

Economist. 2009. "The Price of Prejudice." 17 January.

Economist. 2010. "*Multikulturell Wir*?" 13 November.

Editorial. 1995. *The Globe and Mail*, 1 March.

Editorial. 1997. *The Globe and Mail*, 16 September.

Editorial. 2003. *Canadian Issues*, Special Issue, April.

Editorial. 2005a. "Equal Opportunity, Equal Justice for All." *Toronto Star*, 12 May.

Editorial. 2005b. "Fighting Racism." *Share*, 17 March.

Editorial. 2007. "You Can't Engineer Language." *National Post*, 28 December.

Editorial. 2008. "Disturbing Trends in Poverty Rates." *Toronto Star*, 24 February.

Editorial. 2010a. "Racial Profiling Study Demands Action." *Montreal Gazette*, 10 August.

Editorial. 2010b. "Viola Desmond's Stand." *Toronto Star*, 19 April.

Edwards, Harry. 2000. "Crisis of Black Athletes on the Eve of the 21st Century," in Sport and the Color-Line. *Black Athletes and Race Relations in 20th Century America.* P.B. Miller and D.K. Wiggins (eds.). p 345–350. New York: Routledge

Eisenstein, Zillah. 1996. *Hatreds: Racialized and Sexualized Conflicts in the Twenty-first Century.* New York: Routledge.

Eisenstein, Zillah. 2004. *Against Empire: Feminism, Racism, and the West.* New York: Zed Books.

EKOS. 2004. *Fall 2003 Survey of First Nations People Living On-Reserve.* Integrated Final Report by EKOS Research Associates. March.

Elabor-Idemudia, Patience. 1999. "The Racialisation of Gender in the Social Construction of Immigrant Women in Canada: A Case Study of African Women in a Prairie Province." *Canadian Woman Studies, 19*(3), 38–44.

Elliott, Jean Leonard. 1983. *Two Nations, Many Cultures: Ethnic Groups in Canada.* Toronto, ON: Prentice-Hall.

Elmasry, M. 1999. "Framing Islam." *Kitchener-Waterloo Record*, 16 December.

El-Tablawy, Tarek. 2005. "Female-led Muslim Service Sparks Anger." *Toronto Star*, March.

Endelman, Todd M. 2005. "Anti-Semitism in Western Europe Today," in *Contemporary Anti-Semitism.* D. Penslar et al. (eds.). Pp. 64–79. Toronto: University of Toronto Press.

Entman, Robert. 1993. "Framing: Toward a Clarification of a Fractured Paradigm." *Journal of Communication, 43.*

Entman, Robert, and Andrew Rojecki. 2001. *The Black Image in the White Mind. Media and Race in America.* Chicago: University of Chicago Press.

Environics Institute. 2010a. Urban Aboriginal Peoples Increasingly Significant Presence in Canadian Cities Today [Press release]. 6 April.

Environics Institute. 2010b. *Urban Aboriginal Peoples Study*.

Epilepsy Foundation. 2007. "Reasonable Accommodation (ADA Title 1)." Available online at **http://www.epilepsyfoundation.org/living/wellness/employment/accommodation.cfm**

ERASE Racism. 2005. "What Is Institutional Racism?" Available online at **http://www.eraseracismny.org**

Erasmus, G., and J. Sanders. 2002. "Canadian History: An Aboriginal Perspective," in *Nation to Nation: Aboriginal Sovereignty and the Future of Canada*. John Bird, Lorraine Land, and Murray MacAdam (eds.). Toronto: Irwin Publishing.

Essed, Philomena. 1991. *Understanding Everyday Racism: An Interdisciplinary Study*. Newbury Park, CA: Sage.

Essed, Philomena. 2002. "Everyday Racism," in *A Companion to Race and Ethnic Studies*. D.T. Goldberg and J. Solomos (eds.). Pp. 202–216. Malden, MA: Blackwell.

Este, David. 2008. Cited in "Immigrant Men Learn How to Broaden Paternal Role," by Andrea Gordon. *Toronto Star*, 17 May.

Etherington, Frank. 2001. "Immigrant Women Face Double Burden if Abused." *KW Record*, 4 September.

Etherington, Frank. 2005. "Newcomers Have Complex Needs." *KW Record*, 19 March.

European Union. 2005. "European Union Disability Discrimination Project." Available online at **http://www.euroddlaw.org**

Everitt, Joanna. 2005. "Uncovering the Coverage: Gender Biases in Canadian Political Reporting." Breakfast on the Hill Seminar Series sponsored by SSHRC. 17 November.

Ewan, E., and S. Ewan. 2006. *Typecasting: On the Arts and Sciences of Human Inequality*. New York: Seven Stories Press.

Farley, John E. 2005. "Race, Not Class: Explaining Racial Housing Segregation in the St. Louis Metropolitan Area, 2000." *Sociological Focus*, 38(2), 133–150.

Feagin, Joe. 2006. *Systemic Racism: A Theory of Oppression*. New York: Routledge.

Feagin, Joe, and José Cobas. 2008. "Latinos/as and White Racial Frame: The Procrustean Bed of Assimilation." *Sociological Inquiry* 78(1):39–53.

Fekete, Liz. 2009. A Suitable Enemy. Racism, Migration, and Islamophobia in Europe. London, UK: Pluto Press.

Fekete, Liz (ed.). 2010. *Alternative Voices on Integration*. Institute of Race Relations.

Fenwick, Fred. 2005. *Supreme Court Confirms Duty to Consult with Aboriginal Peoples: Haida Nation v. British Columbia*. Available online at **http://findarticles.com/p/articles/mi_m0OJX/is_5_29/ai_n25106350/**

Ferber, Abby L. 1998. *White Man Falling: Race, Gender, and White Supremacy*. Boston: Rowman & Littlefield Publishers.

Fernando, Shanti. 2006. *Race and the City: Chinese-Canadian and Chinese-American Political Mobilization*. Vancouver: UBC Press.

Finnie, Ross, and Ronald Meng. 2002. "Are Immigrants' Human Capital Skills Discounted in Canada?" Ottawa: Statistics Canada, Business and Labour Market Analysis Division.

Fish, Stanley. 1997. "Boutique Multiculturalism, or Why Liberals Are Incapable of Thinking about Hate Speech." *Critical Inquiry* (Winter), 378–395.

Fishman, Mark. 1980. Manufacturing News. Austin, TX: University of Austin Press.

Fiss, Tanis. 2004. *Apartheid: Canada's Ugly Secret*. Calgary: Centre for Aboriginal Policy Change.

Fiss, Tanis. 2005a. *Dividing Canada: The Pitfalls of Native Sovereignty*. Calgary: Centre for Aboriginal Policy Change.

Fiss, Tanis. 2005b. *Road to Prosperity: Five Steps to Change Aboriginal Policy*. Calgary: Centre for Aboriginal Policy Change.

Flanagan, Tom. 1999. *First Nations? Second Thoughts*. Montreal/Kingston: McGill-Queen's University Press.

Flanagan, Tom. 2001. "Property Rights on the Rez." *National Post*, 11 December.

Flanagan, Tom, Chistopher Alcantara, and Andre Le Dressay. 2010. *Beyond the Indian Act: Restoring Aboriginal Property Rights*. Montreal and Kingston: McGill-Queen's University Press.

Fleras, Augie. 1987. "Redefining the Politics over Aboriginal Language Renewal: Maori Language Schools as Agents of Social Change." *Canadian Journal of Native Studies*, 7(1), 1–40.

Fleras, Augie. 1993. "From Culture to Equality: Multiculturalism as Ideology and Policy," in *Social Inequality in Canada* (2nd ed.). James

Curtis, Edward Grab, and Neil Guppy (eds.). Pp. 330–352. Toronto: Prentice-Hall.

Fleras, Augie. 1996. "The Politics of Jurisdiction," in *Visions of the Heart: Canadian Aboriginal Issues*. David Long and Olive Dickason (eds.). Pp. 111–143. Toronto: Harcourt Brace.

Fleras, Augie. 2000. "The Politics of Jurisdiction," in *Visions of the Heart: Canadian Aboriginal Issues* (2nd ed.). David Long and Olive Dickason (eds.). Toronto: Harcourt.

Fleras, Augie. 2001. *Social Problems in Canada: Constructions, Conditions, and Challenges* (3rd ed.). Don Mills, ON: Pearson Education.

Fleras, Augie. 2002. *Engaging Diversity: Multiculturalism in Canada: Politics, Policies, and Practices*. Scarborough, ON: Nelson.

Fleras, Augie. 2003. *Mass Media Communication in Canada*. Scarborough ON: Nelson.

Fleras, Augie. 2004a. *The Conventional News Paradigm as Systemic Bias: Rethinking the Misrepresentational Basis of Newsmedia–Minority Relations*. Paper presented to the Media, Minorities, and Integration Conference at Siegen University, Germany. Proceedings published under Rainer Geissler and Horst Pottker.

Fleras, Augie. 2004b. "Racializing Culture/Culturalizing Race: Multicultural Racism in a Multicultural Canada," in *Racism, Eh? A Critical Interdisciplinary Anthology of Race and Racism in Canada*. C.A. Nelson and C.A. Nelson (eds.). Pp. 429–443. Concord, ON: Captus Press.

Fleras, Augie. 2005. "Institutionalizing Racism/Racializing Institutions." *Directions: Research and Policy on Eliminating Racism. Canadian Race Relations Foundations*, 2(2), 18–24.

Fleras, Augie. 2006. "Media and Minorities," in *Media and Migration: A Comparative Perspective*. R. Geissler and H Pottker (eds.). Pp. 179–222. Berlin: Transcript Publishers.

Fleras, Augie. 2006b. *Towards a Cultural Empowerment Model for Mental Health Services*. Paper presented to the Mental Health Conference by Centre for Research on Health and Education Services, Wilfrid Laurier University, Waterloo, Ontario, December.

Fleras Augie. 2007a. *Aboriginal and Ethnic Media*. Paper presented at the Media and Migration Conference at the University of Dortmund, Germany, June.

Fleras, Augie. 2007b. *Multiculturalisms in Collision: Transatlantic Divides, Intercontinental Discourse*. Paper presented at the Universities of Augsburg and Nuremberg (Erlangen) Germany, June.

Fleras, Augie. 2007c. *Newsmedia as Systemic Propaganda*. Paper presented to the "20 Years of Propaganda Model Conference." University of Windsor, 16 May.

Fleras, Augie. 2008. *The Politics of Re/Naming*. Paper Commissioned by the Department of Justice and Delivered at the Ninth National Metropolis Conference in Halifax, 6 April.

Fleras, Augie. 2009a. *The Politics of Multiculturalism: Cross National Perspectives in Multicultural Governance*. New York: Palgrave Macmillan.

Fleras, Augie. 2009b. "Towards an Indigenous Grounded Analysis Policymaking Framework." (with Roger Maaka) *International Indigenous Policy Journal* (online). Volume 1.

Fleras, Augie. 2010a. *Customizing Immigration, Commodifying Migrant Labour*. Paper presented at the Conference on the 25 Years of Canadian Studies at the University of Augsburg, Germany, December 9.

Fleras, Augie. 2010b. *Framing the Other Within. Newsmedia Coverage of Immigrants and Immigration in Canada*. Paper presented at the New Zealand/Canada Conference at Victoria University in Wellington, New Zealand, 18 February.

Fleras Augie. 2010c. *Indigenizing Policymaking by Mainstreaming Indigeneity*. Paper presented at the New Zealand/Canada Conference at Victoria University, Wellington, New Zealand. February 17. Subsequently published in the *Australasian Canadian Studies*, 27(1–2), 55–84.

Fleras, Augie. 2011a. *The Media Gaze: Representations of Diversity in Canada*. Vancouver: UBC Press.

Fleras, Augie. 2011b. *The Politics of Multicultural Governance in a Globalizing World: A Case for Multiversalism and Multiculturalism in Canada*. Paper presented at the Conference commemorating 15 Years of Canadian Studies at the University of Matanzas, Cuba, 24 February.

Fleras, Augie, and Jean Leonard Elliott. 1992. *The Nations within: Aboriginal-State Relations in Canada, the United States, and New Zealand*. Toronto: Oxford University.

Fleras, Augie, and Vic Krahn. 1992. *From Community Development to Inherent Self-Government:*

Restructuring Aboriginal–State Relations in Canada. Paper presented at the Annual Meetings of Learned Societies. Charlottetown. June.

Fleras, Augie, and Jean Lock Kunz. 2001. *Media and Minorities: Misrepresenting Minorities in a Multicultural Canada.* Toronto: TEP.

Fleras, Augie, and Paul Spoonley. 1999. *Recalling Aotearoa: Indigenous Politics and Ethnic Dynamics in New Zealand.* Auckland: Oxford University Press.

Flynn, J.R. 1984. "The mean IQ of Americans: Massive Gains 1932 to 1978." *Psychological Bulletin, 95*(1), 29–51.

Folson, Rose Baaba. 2005. *Calculated Kindness: Global Restructuring, Immigration, and Settlement in Canada.* Halifax: Fernwood.

Fontaine, Phil. 2003. "Native Status Not an Obstacle." Letter to the *National Post*, 3 November.

Forbes, Hugh Donald. 2007. "Trudeau as the First Theorist of Canadian Multiculturalism," in *Multiculturalism and the Canadian Constitution.* S. Tierney (ed.). Vancouver: UBC Press.

Ford, Caylan, and Joan Delaney. 2008. "Is Official Multiculturalism Failing in Its Own Heartland?" *Epoch Times*, 17 February.

Forsythe, David P. 2006. *Human Rights in International Relations.* New York: Cambridge University Press.

Foster, Cecil. 2005. *Where Race Does Not Matter: The New Spirit of Modernity.* Toronto: Penguin.

Foster, Lorne. 1998. *Turnstile Immigration: Multiculturalism, Social Order, and Social Justice in Canada.* Toronto: Thompson Education.

Fournier, Pierre. 1994. *A Meech Lake Post-mortem: Is Quebec Sovereignty Inevitable?* Montreal: McGill-Queen's University Press.

Fox, Nick J., and Katie J. Ward. 2008. "What Governs Governance, and How Does It Evolve? The Sociology of Governance-in-Action." *British Journal of Sociology, 59*(3), 519–538.

Francis, D. 1992. *The Imaginary Indian: The Image of the Indian in Canadian Culture.* Vancouver: Arsenal Pulp Press.

Francis, Diane. 2002. *Immigration: The Economic Case.* Toronto: Key Porter.

Francis, Diane. 2005. "Immigration Issues Should Be Probed." *National Post*, 28 April.

Frankenberg, Ruth (ed.). 1993. *White Women, Race Matters: The Social Construction of Whiteness.* Minneapolis: University of Minnesota Press.

Fraser, Graham. 2004. "Premiers Reminded of Suicide Epidemic." *Toronto Star*, 26 September.

Fraser, Graham. 2006. *Sorry, I Don't Speak French: Confronting the Canadian Crisis That Won't Go Away.* Toronto: McClelland & Stewart.

Fraser, John. 2006. "The Toxic Tower." *The Globe and Mail*, 24 June.

Frederickson, G.M. 1999. "Mosaics and Melting Pots." *Dissent* (Summer), 36–43.

Frederickson, G.M. 2002. *Racism: A Short History.* Princeton, NJ: Princeton University Press.

Frederico, Christopher, and Samantha Luks. 2005. "The Political Psychology of Race." *International Journal of Political Psychology, 26*(6), 661–674.

Freeland, Benjamin. 2010. "Gains in Native Entrepreneurship Impeded by Lack of Education." *The Globe and Mail*, 1 September.

Freeze, Colin. 2005. "Criminals with Refugee Claims Are Well-Versed on Their Rights." *The Globe and Mail*, 18 April.

Freeze, Colin. 2008. "Heritage Department Takes Aim at Religious Radicals." *The Globe and Mail*, 1 September.

Frideres, James S. 1998. *Native Peoples in Canada: Contemporary Conflicts* (5th ed.). Toronto: Prentice-Hall.

Frideres, James S. 2005. "Ethnogenesis: Immigrants to Ethnics and the Development of a Rainbow Class Structure." *Canadian Issues* (Spring), 58–60.

Frideres, James. 2006. "Cities and Immigrant Integration: The Future of Second and Third-Tier Cities." *Our Diverse Cities, 2*, 3–8.

Frideres, James. 2011. *First Nations in the Twenty-first Century.* Toronto: Oxford University Press.

Frideres, James S., and René R. Gadacz. 2008. *Aboriginal Peoples in Canada* (7th ed.). Scarborough: Pearson Education Canada.

Friends of the Simon Wiesenthal Center for Holocaust Studies. 2008. "Letter to the president of the University of Toronto." *National Post*, 5 February.

Friesen, Joe. 2005. "Blame Canada (for Multiculturalism)." *The Globe and Mail*, 20 August.

Friesen, Joe. 2010a. "For Aboriginal Women Especially, It Pays to Have a University Degree." *The Globe and Mail*, 8 April.

Friesen, Joe. 2010b. "Tories Take Aim at Employment Equity." *The Globe and Mail*, 22 July.

Frith, Rosaline. 2003. "Integration." *Canadian Issues* (April), 35–36.

Fry, Hedy. 1997. "Liberal Party: A Continued Commitment to the Ideals of Multiculturalism," in *Battle over Multiculturalism: Does It Help or Hinder Canadian Unity?* Andrew Cardozo and Luis Musto (eds.). Ottawa: Pearson-Shoyama Institute.

Fukuyama, Frances. 1994. "The War of All against All." *New York Times Book Review*, 10 April.

Fulford, Robert. 2003. "From Russia, with Stories: David Bezmozgis Captures the Essence of Immigrant Life in His New Fiction." *National Post*, 27 May.

Fulford, Robert. 2007. "It Isn't Written in Stone." *National Post*, 27 August.

Gagnon, Alain-G., M. Guibernau, and F. Rocher. 2003. *The Conditions of Diversity in Multinational Democracies*. Montreal: Institute for Research on Public Policy.

Gagnon, Alain-G., and Raffaelle Iacovino. 2007. *Federalism, Citizenship, and Quebec: Debating Multinationalism*. Toronto: University of Toronto Press.

Gagnon, Lysiane. 1996. "Sorry to Be Boring, but Quebec Loves Its Constitutional Contradictions." *The Globe and Mail*, 6 July.

Gagnon, Lysiane. 2007. "Autonomy: Saving Face in Quebec." *The Globe and Mail*, 20 August.

Galabuzi, Grace-Edward. 2006. *Canada's Economic Apartheid: The Social Exclusion of Racialized Groups in the New Century*. Toronto: Canadian Scholars' Press.

Gallagher, Charles A. 2007. *Rethinking the Color Line: Readings in Race and Ethnicity* (3rd ed.). New York: McGraw-Hill.

Gallagher, Margaret. 2005. "Who Makes the News." *Global Media Monitoring Project*.

Gallagher, Stephen. 2003. "Canada's Dysfunctional Refugee Determination System." Occasional Paper, No. 78 of the Fraser Institute.

Gallagher, Stephen. 2004. "Canada and the Challenge of Asylum Migration." *Canadian Issues* (March), 43–44.

Gallagher, Stephen. 2008a. *Canada and Mass Immigration: The Creation of a Global Suburb and Its Impact on National Unity*. Available online at http://www.immigrationwatchcanada.org

Gallagher, Stephen. 2008b. *Mass Migration in Canada*. Paper presented to the Canadian Immigration Policy Conference. Sponsored by the Fraser Institute. Montreal, 4 June.

Garner, Steve. 2007. *Whiteness: An Introduction.* New York: Routledge.

Garvey, John, and Noel Ignatieff. 1996. *Race Traitor*. New York: Routledge.

Gay, G. 1997. "Educational Equality for Students of Color," in *Multicultural Education*. J. Banks and C. Banks (eds.). Pp. 195–228. Toronto: Allyn and Bacon.

Gee, Marcus. 1998. "Is This the End for Suharto?" *The Globe and Mail*, 14 January.

Gee, Marcus. 2001. "Debunking the Race Myth." *The Globe and Mail*, 15 February.

Geissler, Rainer, and Horst Pöttker (eds.). 2006. *Mass Media Integration. Media and Migration: A Comparative Perspective*. Berlin: Transcript.

George, Usha. 2006. "Immigration Integration: Simple Questions, Complex Answers." *Canadian Diversity, 5*(1), 3–6.

Ghosh, Ratna. 2002. *Redefining Multicultural Education* (2nd ed.). Toronto: Nelson.

Ghosh, Ratna, and Ali A. Abdi. 2004. *Education and the Politics of Difference: Canadian Perspectives*. Toronto: Canadian Scholars' Press.

Gibb, Heather. 2010. "Missing from Temporary Foreign Worker Programs: Gender Sensitive Approaches." *Canadian Issues* (Spring), 94–98.

Gibb, J.T., and L. Huang. 2003. *Children of Color: Psychological Intervention with Culturally Diverse Youth* (2nd ed.). San Francisco: Jossey-Bass.

Gibbins, Roger, and Guy Laforest (eds.). 1998. *Beyond the Impasse: Toward Reconciliation.* Montreal: Institute of Research for Public Policy.

Gibson, Gordon. 1998. "Nisga'a Treaty: The Good, the Bad, and the Alternative." *The Globe and Mail*, 13 October.

Gibson, Gordon. 2005. "Canada's Apartheid World." *The Globe and Mail*, 15 July.

Gibson, Gordon. 2009a. *A New Look At Canadian Indian Policy: Respect the Collective—Promote the Individual*. Calgary: Fraser Institute.

Gibson, Gordon. 2009b. "The Politics of Canadian Immigration Policy," in *The Effects of Mass Immigration on Canadian Living Standards and Society*. H Grubel (ed). Calgary: Fraser Institute.

Gillborn, David. 2006. "Rethinking White Supremacy: Who Counts in 'White World.'" *Ethnicities, 6*(3), 318–340.

Gillespie, Marie. 1996. *Television, Ethnicity, and Cultural Change.* London: Routledge.

Gillette, Aaron. 2007. *Eugenics and the Nature–Nurture Debate in the Twentieth Century.* New York: Palgrave Macmillan.

Gillies, James. 1997. "Thinking the Unthinkable and the Republic of Canada." *The Globe and Mail,* 28 June.

Gilroy, Paul. 2004. *After Empire: Melancholia or Convivial Culture?* London: Routledge.

Giroux, H.E. 1994. "Insurgent Multiculturalism as the Promise of Pedagogy," in *Multiculturalism: A Critical Reader.* D.T. Goldberg (ed.). Pp. 325–343. Oxford: Blackwell.

Giroux, H. 1999. "Rewriting the Discourse of Racial Identity: Towards a Pedagogy and Politics of Whiteness." *Harvard Educational Review, 67*(2), 285–320.

Giroux, Henri. 2008. *The Terror of Neoliberalism: Authoritarianism and the Eclipse of Democracy.* Boulder CO: Paradigm Press.

Glasser, Theodore L., Isabel Awad, and John W. Kim. 2009. "The Claims of Multiculturalism and the Journalists' Promise of Diversity." *Journal of Communication, 59,* 57–78.

Glazer, Nathan. 1997. *We Are All Multiculturalists Now.* Cambridge, MA: Harvard University Press.

Glazer, Nathan. 2010. "Democracy and Deep Divides." *Journal of Democracy, 21*(2).

Goar, Carol. 2005. "Nation Ignores U.N. Criticism." *Toronto Star,* 11 November.

Goldberg, David Theo. 1993. *Philosophy and the Politics of Meaning.* Oxford: Basil Blackwell.

Goldberg, David Theo. 1994a. "Introduction: Multicultural Conditions," in *Multiculturalism: A Critical Reader,* D.T. Goldberg (ed.). Pp 1–44. Cambridge, MA: Basil Blackwell.

Goldberg, David Theo. (ed.). 1994b. *Multiculturalism: A Critical Reader.* Malden, MA: Blackwell.

Goldberg, David Theo. 2002. "Racial States," in *A Companion to Racial and Ethnic Studies.* D.T. Goldberg and J. Solomos (eds.). Pp. 233–258. Malden, MA: Blackwell.

Goldberg, David Theo. 2005. "Racial Americanization," in *Racialization.* K. Murji and J. Solomos (eds.). Pp. 87–102. Oxford: Oxford University Press.

Goldberg, David Theo, and John Solomos (eds.). 2002. *A Companion to Racial and Ethnic Studies.* Malden, MA: Blackwell.

Goldberg, Jonah. 2006. "Racism by Any Other Name," *National Review Online.* 15 November.

Goldsborough, James. 2000. "Out of Control Immigration." *Foreign Affairs* (September/October), 89–101.

Goodall, Healther, Andrew Jakubowicz, and Jeannie Martin. 1994. *Racism, Ethnicity, and the Media.* Australia: Allen & Unwin.

Goodspeed, Peter. 2006. "Death of Multiculturalism." *National Post.* 25 November.

Gordon, Andrea. 2008. "Immigrant Men Learn to Broaden Paternal Role." *Toronto Star,* 17 May.

Gordon, Sean. 2005. "A New Kind of Sovereigntist." *Toronto Star,* 30 October.

Gordon, Sean. 2006. "The Two Solitudes as Far Apart as Ever." *Toronto Star,* 30 September.

Gordon, Sean. 2010. "Claims of Racial Bias Dog Police in Montreal." *The Globe and Mail,* 10 August.

Goren, William D. 2007. "Concept of Undue Hardship and Reasonable Accommodation in the Employment Context." Available on line at **http://www.mediate.com/articles/gorenW2.cfm**

Gorski, Paul. 2004. *Language of Closet Racism: An Introduction. Race, Racism, and the Law. Speaking Truth to Power.* Available online at **http://academic.udayton.edu**

Gosine, Andil. 2003. "Myths of Diversity." *Alternatives Journal, 29*(1), 1–4.

Gottschalk, Peter, and Gabriel Greenberg. 2008. *Islamophobia: Making Muslims the Enemy.* Toronto: Rowman and Littlefield Publishers.

Government of Canada. 2003. "The Next Act: New Momentum for Canada's Linguistic Duality, The Action Plan for Official Languages." Ottawa.

Government of Canada. 2005. "A Canada for All: Canada's Action Plan Against Racism." Available online at **http://www.pch.gc.ca/multi/plan_action_plan/tous_all/index_e.cfm**

Government of Canada. 2010. "Aboriginal People as Victims of Crime." Available online at **http://www.victimsweek.gc.ca**

Grabb, Ed, and Neil Guppy (eds.). 2010. *Social Inequality in Canada. Patterns, Problems & Policies* (5th ed.). Toronto: Pearson.

Graham, John, and Francois Levesque. 2010. *First Nations Communities in Distress: Dealing with Causes, Not Symptoms.* Ottawa: Institute on Governance.

Graham, Katherine A.H. 2007. "Introduction." *Our Diverse Cities: Ontario, 4*(Fall), 3–6.

Granatstein, J.L. 2007. *Whose War Is It? How Canada Can Survive in the Post 9/11 World.* Toronto: HarperCollins Publishers.

Grant, Hugh M., and Ronald R. Oertel. 1999. "Diminishing Returns to Immigration? Interpreting the Economic Experience of Canadian Immigrants." *Canadian Ethnic Studies, 31*(3), 56–66.

Graham, John, and Francois Levesque. 2010. *First Nations Communities in Distress: Dealing with Causes, Not Symptoms.* Ottawa: Institute on Governance.

Gray, Jeff. 2007. "Countries around the World Are Wrestling with Religious Rights." *The Globe and Mail*, 10 September.

Gray, John. 1997. "AFN Rivals Embody Competing Visions." *The Globe and Mail*, 28 July.

Gray, John. 1998. "Mining Companies Reluctant to Invest after Ruling." *The Globe and Mail*, 9 June.

Gray, John. 2001. "Separatists Have Never Agreed on the Route." *National Post*, 13 January.

Green, Joyce. 2003. "Decolonizing in the Age of Globalization." *Canadian Dimension* (March/April), 3–5.

Green, Joyce (ed). 2007. *Making Space for Indigenous Feminism.* London: Zed Books.

Green, Joyce. 2008. "Aboriginal Rights in a Neo-Liberal World." *Canadian Dimension* (March/April), 22–25.

Greenaway, Norma. 2010. "Wait Times Drop for Prospective Immigrants, Especially Skilled Workers: Analysis." *National Post*, 21 June.

Greenberg, Joshua. 2000. "Opinion Discourses and Canadian Newspapers: The Case of the Chinese 'Boat People.'" *Canadian Journal of Communication, 25*(4).

Greenspon, Edward. 1998. "Sovereignty Outlook Weakening." *The Globe and Mail*, 2 April.

Greenspon, Edward. 2001. "Building the New Canadian Identity." *The Globe and Mail*, 10 November.

Gregg, Allan. 2006. "Identity Crisis: Multiculturalism: A Twentieth-Century Dream Becomes a Twenty-first-Century Conundrum." *The Walrus* (March), 28–38.

Grey, Julius. 2007. "The Paradoxes of Reasonable Accommodation." *Policy Options* (September), 34–40.

Griffiths, Rudyard. 2008. "The Country's Two Solitudes Are More Solitary by the Day." *The Globe and Mail*, 18 February.

Grillo, R. 2007. "An Excess of Alterity? Debating Difference in a Multicultural Society." *Ethnic and Racial Studies, 30*(6), 979–998.

Gross, Michael L. 1996. "Restructuring Ethnic Paradigms: From Premodern to Postmodern Perspectives." *Canadian Review of Studies in Nationalism, 23*(1–2), 51–65.

Grubel, Herbert. 2005. "Immigration and the Welfare State in Canada: Growing Conflicts, Constructive Solutions." *Public Policy Sources, 84.* Available online at **http://www.fraserinstitute.org/ Commerce.Web/publication_details.aspx? pubID=3096**

Grubel, Herbert. 2009. *The Effects of Mass Immigration on Canadian Living Standards and Society.* Calgary: Fraser Institute.

Grubel, Herbert, and Patrick Grady. 2011. *Immigration and the Canadian Welfare State.* Calgary: Fraser Institute.

Guess, Teresa J. 2006. "The Social Construction of Whiteness: Racism by Intent, Racism by Consequence." *Critical Sociology, 32*(1). Available online at **http://crs.sagepub.com/cgi/content/ abstract/32/4/649**

Guibernau, Montserrat. 2007. *The Identity of Nations.* Malden, MA: Polity Press.

Guimond, Eric, Don Kerr, and Roderic Beaujot. 2004. "Charting the Growth of Canada's Aboriginal Populations: Problems, Options, and Implications." *Canadian Studies in Population, 31*(3), 55–82.

Gunew, Sneja. 2004. *Haunted Nations: The Colonial Dimension of Multiculturalism.* New York: Routledge.

Gunter, Lorne. 2009. "A Man's Home Is His Castle." *National Post.* 29 July.

Gurr, Ted Robert. 2001. *Peoples vs States: Minorities at Risk in the New Century.* Washington, DC: United States Institute for Peace.

Guterres, Antonio. 2007. "People on the Move— Ideally, Out of Choice." *The Globe and Mail*, 3 December.

Gwyn, Richard. 1994. "The First Borderless State." *Toronto Star*, 26 November.

Gwyn, Richard. 1996. *Nationalism without Walls: The Unbearable Lightness of Being Canadian.* Toronto: McClelland & Stewart.

Gwyn, Richard. 2000. "A Visionary Challenges Our Policy on Immigration." *Toronto Star*, 12 March.

Gwyn, Richard. 2001a. "Old Canada Disappears." *Toronto Star*, 21 March.

Gwyn, Richard. 2001b. "Racism Must Be Addressed." *KW Record*, 5 September.

Ha, Tu Thanh. 2007. "Quebecker's Insecurities Said to Fuel Backlash Against Minorities." *The Globe and Mail*, 15 August.

Habyarimana, James et al. 2008. "Is Ethnic Conflict Inevitable?" *Foreign Affairs*, July/August.

Hage, G. 1998. *White Nation: Fantasies of White Supremacy in a Multicultural Society.* Sydney, Australia: Pluto Press.

Hage, Ghassan. 2006. "The Doubts Down Under." *Catalyst Magazine*, 17 May.

Hagey, Rebecca. 2004. "Implementing Accountability for Equity." *Directions, 2*(1), 59–77.

Hall, Anthony J. 2000. "Racial Discrimination in Legislation, Litigation, Legend, and Lore." *Canadian Ethnic Studies, 32*(2), 119–137.

Hall, Stuart. 1996. "New Ethnicities," in *Stuart Hall in Critical Studies*, D. Marley and K.H. Chen (eds.). London: Routledge.

Halli, Shiva S., and Leo Driedger (eds.). 1999. *Immigrant Canada: Demographic, Economic, and Social Challenges.* Toronto: University of Toronto Press.

Halli-Vedanand, Shiva S. 2007. "The Problem of Second-Generation Decline: Perspectives on Integration in Canada." *International Migration and Integration* 8: 277–287.

Halstead, Mark 1988. *Education, Justice, and Cultural Diversity: An Examination of the Honeyford Affair, 1984–85.* London: Falmer Press.

Hamilton, Graeme. 2005. "'Sovereign' Reserve Hits the Jackpot." *National Post*, 18 July.

Hamilton, Graeme. 2008a. "Lost in Translation." *National Post*, 16 February.

Hamilton, Graeme. 2008b. "Quebec Still Faces Cultural Challenges." *National Post*, 24 May.

Hanamoto, Darrell. 1995. *Monitored Peril. Asian Americans and the Politics of Representation.* St. Paul, MN: University of Minnesota Press.

Handa, Amita. 2003. *Of Silk Saris and Mini-Skirts: South Asian Girls Walk the Tightrope of Culture.* Toronto: Women's Press.

Hannis, Grant. 2009. "Reporting Diversity in New Zealand: The 'Asian Angst' Controversy." *Pacific Journalism Review, 15(1)*, 114–128.

Hansen, Randall. 2007. "Diversity, Integration, and the Turn from Multiculturalism in the United Kingdom," in *Belonging?* K. Banting et al. (eds.). Pp. 351–386. Montreal: IRPP.

Harding, Sandra. 2002. "Science, Race, Culture, Empire," in *Companion to Racial and Ethnic Studies.* D.T. Goldberg and J. Solomos (eds.). Pp. 217–228. Malden, MA: Blackwell.

Harell, Allison, and Dietlind Stolle. 2010. "Diversity and Democratic Politics: An Introduction." *Canadian Journal of Political Science, 43*(2), 235–256.

Harris, Fred. 1995. *Multiculturalism from the Margins.* Westport, CT: Bergin and Garvey.

Harris, Paul. 1997. *Black Rage Confronts the Law.* New York: New York University Press.

Harris-Short, Sonia. 2007. "Self-Government in Canada: A Successful Model for the Decolonisation of Aboriginal Child Welfare," in *Accommodating Cultural Diversity.* S. Tierney (ed.). Hampshire, UK: Ashgate Publishing.

Harrison, Trevor W., and John W. Friesen. 2004. *Canadian Society in the Twenty-First Century: A Historical Sociological Approach.* Toronto: Pearson.

Harty, Siobhan, and Michael Murphy. 2005. *In Defence of Multinational Citizenship.* Vancouver: UBC Press.

Harvey, Edward B., Bobby Siu, and Kathleen D.V. Reil. 1999. "Ethnocultural Groups, Period of Immigration and Socioeconomic Situation." *Canadian Ethnic Studies, 31*(3), 95–108.

Hassan, Farzana. 2008. "Muslim Feminist Perspectives on International Women's Day." *Montreal Gazette*, 8 March.

Hawkes, David. 2000. "Review of Citizens-Plus." *Isuma* (Autumn), 141–142.

Hawkins, Freda. 1974. *Canada and Immigration.* Kingston: McGill/Queen's University Press.

Hawthorne, Lesleyanne. 2007. *Foreign Credential Recognition and Assessment: An Introduction.* Available online at **http://canada.metropolis.net/pdfs/Hawthorne_intro_en.pdf**.

Hawthorne, Lesleyanne. 2008. "The Impact of Economic Selection Policy on Labour Market Outcomes for Degree Qualified Migrants in Canada and Australia." *IRPP Choices, 14*(5). May. Available online at **http://www.cerium.ca**

Health Canada. 2006. *First Nations, Inuit, and Aboriginal Health: Suicide Prevention.* Available online at **http://www.hc-sc.ca**

Heath, A.F., and J.R. Tilley. 2005. "National Identity and Xenophobia in an Ethnically Divided

Society." *International Journal on Multicultural Societies, 7*(2), 119–132.

Heath, Anthony, and Sin Yi Cheung. 2007. "The Comparative Study of Ethnic Minority Disadvantage," in *Unequal Chances: Ethnic Minorities in Western Labour Markets.* A. Heath and S.Y. Cheung (eds.). Pp. 1–44. New York: Oxford University Press.

Hebert, Yvonne M., and Alan Sears. 2004. *Citizenship Education.* Toronto: Canadian Education Association.

Hebert, Yvonne M., and Lori Wilkinson. 2002. "The Citizenship Debates: Conceptual, Policy, Experiential, and Educational Issues," in *Citizenship in Transformation in Canada.* Y. Hebert (ed.). Pp 3–36. Toronto: University of Toronto Press.

Hechter, Michael. 1975. *Internal Colonialism: The Celtic Fringe in British National Development.* Berkeley, CA: University of California Press.

Heider, Karl. 1988. "The Rashomon Effect. When Ethnographers Disagree." *American Anthropologist.*

Helin, Calvin. 2006. *Dances with Dependency.* Vancouver: Orca Spirit Publishing.

Helly, Denise. 1993. "The Political Regulation of Cultural Plurality: Foundations and Principles." *Canadian Ethnic Studies, 25*(2), 15–31.

Helmes-Hayes, Rick, and James Curtis (eds.). 1998. *The Vertical Mosaic Revisited.* Toronto: University of Toronto Press.

Hennebry, Jenna. 2010. "Who Has Their Eye on the Ball? Jurisdictional Futbol and Canada's Temporary Foreign Worker Program." *Policy Options* (July/August).

Henry, Frances, and Carol Tator. 1993. "The Show Boat Controversy." *Toronto Star*, 28 May.

Henry, Frances, and Carol Tator. 2002. *Discourses of Domination: Racial Bias in the Canadian English-Language Press.* Toronto: University of Toronto Press.

Henry, Frances, and Carol Tator. 2003. *Racial Profiling in Toronto: Discourses of Domination, Mediation, and Opposition.* Final Draft Submitted to the Canadian Race Relations Foundation.

Henry, Frances, and Carol Tator. 2006. *The Colour of Democracy: Racism in Canadian Society* (3rd ed.). Toronto: Harcourt Brace/Nelson.

Henry, Frances, and Carol Tator (eds.). 2009. *Racism in the Canadian University: Demanding Social Justice, Inclusion, and Equity.* Toronto: University of Toronto Press.

Henry, Frances, and Carol Tator. 2010. *The Colour of Democracy. Racism in Canadian Society* (4th ed.). Toronto: Thomson Nelson.

Henshaw, Peter. 2007. "John Buchan and the British Imperial Origins of Canadian Multiculturalism," in *Canadas of the Mind.* N. Hillmer and A. Chapnick (eds.). Montreal/Kingston: McGill-Queen's University Press.

Herman, Ed, and Noam Chomsky. 1988. *Manufacturing Consent: The Political Economy of Mass Media.* New York: Pantheon Books.

Hesse, Barnor. 2004. "Discourses on Institutional Racism, The Geneology of a Concept," in *Institutional Racism in Higher Education.* I. Law et al. (eds.). Pp. 131–148. Sterling, VA: Trentham Books.

Hiebert, Dan. 2000. "Immigration and the Changing Canadian City." *Canadian Geographer, 44*(1), 25–43.

Hiebert, Dan. 2006. "Winning, Losing, and Still Playing the Game: The Political Economy of Immigration in Canada." *Journal of Economic and Social Geography, 97*(1), 38–48.

Hiebert, Dan, Jock Collins, and Paul Spoonley. 2003. *Uneven Globalization: Neoliberal Regimes, Immigration, and Multiculturalism in Australia, Canada, and New Zealand.* Working Paper Series No. 03-05. Research on Immigration and Integration in the Metropolis.

Hiebert, Dan, and David Ley. 2006. "Introduction: The Political Economy of Immigration." *Journal of Economic and Social Geography, 97*(1), 3–6.

Hier, Sean. 2008. "Racism, Media, and Analytical Balance," in *Communications in Question: Competing Perspectives on Controversial Issues in Communication Studies.* J Greenberg and C.D. Elliott (eds.). pp. 131–138. Toronto: Thomson Nelson

Hier, Sean, and B. Singh Bolaria. 2007. *Identity and Belonging: Rethinking Race and Ethnicity in Canadian Society.* Toronto: Canadian Scholars' Press.

Hier, Sean, and Joshua Greenberg. 2002. "News Discourses and the Problematization of Chinese Migration to Canada," in *Discourses of Domination.* F. Henry and C. Tator (eds.). Pp. 138–162. Toronto: University of Toronto Press.

Hier, Sean, and Kevin Walby. 2006. "Competing Analytical Paradigms in the Sociological Study of Racism in Canada." *Canadian Ethnic Studies, 38*(1).

Hiller, Harry. 2000. *Canadian Society: A Macro Analysis* (4th ed.). Toronto: Prentice-Hall.

Hinton, M., E. Johnston, and D. Rigney. 1997. *Indigenous Australians and the Law.* Sydney: Cavendish Publishing.

Historica-Dominion Institute. 2010. *What the World Thinks of Canada: Canada and the World in 2010, Immigration & Diversity.* Available online at **http://cms.juntos.ca/docs/Db-Historica Dominion/June_22_Canada_and_the_World_EN.pdf**

Hitchens, Christopher. 2010. "The Good Intentions Paving Company." *National Post,* 25 June.

Hochschild, Jennifer. 2002. "Affirmative Action as Culture War," in *A Companion to Racial and Ethnic Studies.* D.T. Goldberg and J. Solomos (eds.). Pp. 282–303. Malden, MA: Blackwell.

Hodgetts, Darrin, et al. 2005. "Maori Media Production, Civic Journalism and the Foreshore and Seabed Controversy in Aotearoa." *Pacific Journalism Review, 11*(2), 191–208.

Holdaway, Simon. 1996. *The Racialisation of British Policing.* New York: St. Martin's Press.

Holdaway, Simon. 2000. *Police Race Relations: Consultative Paper Written for the Commission on the Future of Multi-Ethnic Britain.* London, UK: Runnymede Trust.

Holdaway, Simon. 2003. "Police Relations in England and Wales: Theory, Policy, and Practices." *Policy and Society* 7:49–75.

Hommel, Maurice. 2001. "Escaping Poisonous Embrace of Racism." *Toronto Star,* 24 August.

hooks, bell. 1994. *Outlaw Culture: Resisting Representations.* New York: Routledge.

hooks, bell. 1995. *Killing Rage.* Boston: South End Press.

Hope or Heartbreak: Aboriginal Youth and Canada's Future [entire issue]. 2008. *Horizons, 10*(1).

Horton, James O., and Lois E. Horton. 2004. *Slavery and the Making of America.* New York: Oxford University Press.

Hudson, Michael. 1987. "Multiculturalism, Government Policy, and Constitutional Entrenchment—A Comparative Study," in *Multiculturalism and the Charter: A Legal Perspective.* Canadian Human Rights Foundation (ed.). Pp. 59–122. Toronto: Carswell.

Hum, Derek, and Wayne Simpson. 2000. "Not All Visible Minorities Face Labour Market Discrimination." *Policy Options* (December), 45–51.

Hum, Derek, and Wayne Simpson. 2005. *Economic Assimilation of Canadian Immigrants: Cross Sectional and Panel Data Estimates.* Final Report Presented to the Prairie Centre for Excellence in Research on Immigration and Integration.

Human Resources and Skills Development Canada. 2006. *Ten Years of Experience.* Ottawa: Author. Available online at **http://www.hrsdc.gc.ca/eng/lp/lo/lswe/we/review/2006/issues.shtml**

Humpage, Louise, and Augie Fleras. 2001. "Intersecting Discourses: Closing the Gaps, Social Justice, and the Treaty of Waitangi." *Social Policy Journal of New Zealand, 16,* 37–54.

Huntington, Samuel. 1993. *The Clash of Civilizations and the Remaking of World Order.* New York: Simon and Schuster.

Hurley, Mary C. 2009. *The Indian Act.* Parliamentary Information and Research Service. 23 November.

Hurst, Lynda. 2003. "A Critical Meaning of Bias." *Toronto Star,* 12 April.

Hurst, Lynda. 2006. "Discontent in Eurabia." *Toronto Star,* 11 February.

Hurtado, Aida. 1996. *The Color of Privilege: Three Blasphemies on Race and Feminism.* Michigan: University of Michigan Press.

Hurwitz, Jon, and Mark Peffley. 2010. "Race, Crime, and Punishment in the US Criminal Justice System." *Canadian Journal of Political Science, 43*(2).

Huston, Patricia. 1995. "Intellectual Racism?" *Canadian Medical Association Journal, 153,* 1219.

Hutchinson, John, and Anthony D. Smith (eds.). 1996. *Ethnicity.* Oxford: Oxford University Press.

Hylton, John H. (ed.) 1994/1999. *Aboriginal Self-Government in Canada: Current Trends and Issues.* Saskatoon: Purich Publishing.

Hyman, Ilene. 2009. *Racism as a Determinant of Immigrant Health.* Policy brief commissioned by the Public Health Agency of Canada and supported by Metropolis. Submitted 30 March.

Hyndman, Jennifer. 1999. "Gender and Canadian Immigration Policy: A Current Snapshot." *Canadian Woman Studies, 19*(3), 6–10.

Ibbitson, John. 2004. "Why Atlantic Canada Remains White and Poor." *The Globe and Mail,* 20 August.

Ibbitson, John. 2005a. "Canada's Immigration Challenge." *The Globe and Mail,* 11 March.

Ibbitson, John. 2005b. *The Polite Revolution: Perfecting the Canadian Dream.* Toronto: McClelland & Stewart.

Ibbitson, John, and Joe Friesen. 2010. "Conservative Immigrants Boost Tory Fortunes." *The Globe and Mail,* 4 October.

Ignace, M.B., and R.E. Ignace. 1998. "The Old Wolf in Sheep's Clothing: Canadian Aboriginal Peoples," in *Multiculturalism in a World of Leaking Boundaries.* D. Haselbach (ed.). Pp. 101–132. New Brunswick, NJ: Transaction Publishers.

Ignatieff, Michael. 1994. *Blood and Belonging: Journeys into the New Nationalism.* Toronto: Viking.

Ignatieff, Michael. 1995. "Nationalism and the Narcissism of Minor Differences." *Queens Quarterly, 102*(1), 1–25.

Ignatieff, Michael. 2001. "Human Rights and the Rights of the State: Are They on a Collision Course?" Hagey Lecture. University of Waterloo, 24 January.

Ignatieff, Michael. 2005. "The Coming Constitutional Crisis." *The Globe and Mail,* 16 April.

Imai, Shin. 2007. *The Structure of the Indian Act: Accountability in Governance.* Research Paper for the National Centre for First Nations Governance. July.

Immigration: Opportunities and Challenges. 2003. Editorial. Special issue of Canadian Issues (April).

Immigration and Refugee Board of Canada. 2007. *Immigration: Opportunities and Challenges.* Ottawa: Author.

INAC. 2003. Budget 2003. Backgrounder: Demographics.

INAC. 2004. *Sustainable Development Strategy 2004–2006: On the Right Path Together: A Sustainable Future for First Nations, Inuit, and Northern Communities.* Available at **www.ainc-inac.gc.ca/sd/sdd0406_e.html**

INCITE: Women of Color Against Violence. 2006. *Color of Violence: The INCITE Anthology.* Cambridge, MA: South End Press.

Indian and Northern Affairs Canada. 1995. *Inherent Right of Self-Government Policy.* Ottawa: Author.

Institute of Race Relations (IRR). 2010. *Racial Violence: The Buried Issue.* Available online at **http://www.irr.org.uk**

Isajiw, Wsevolod (ed.). 1997. *Multiculturalism in North America and Europe: Comparative Perspectives on Interethnic Relations and Social Incorporation.* Toronto: Canadian Scholars' Press.

Isajiw, Wsevolod W. 1999. *Understanding Diversity: Ethnicity and Race in the Canadian Context.* Toronto: Thompson Education.

Isin, Engin. 1996. "Global City-Regions and Citizenship," in *Local Places in the Age of the Global City.* D. Bell, R. Keil, and G. Wekerle (eds.). Montreal: Black Rose Books.

Jaimet, Kate. 2007. "Francophone Immigration Policy 'Stupid': Professor." *National Post,* 19 December.

Jain, Harish C. 1988. "Affirmative Action/ Employment Equity Programs and Visible Minorities in Canada." *Currents, 5*(1), 3–7.

Jain, Harish C., and Rick D. Hackett 1989. "Measuring Effectiveness of Employment Equity Programs in Canada: Public Policy and a Survey." *Canadian Public Policy, 15*(2), 189–204.

Jakubowicz, Andrew. 2005. "Multiculturalism in Australia: Apogee or Nadir?" *Canadian Diversity, 4*(1), 15–18.

Jakubowicz, Andrew. 2007. "Political Islam and the Future of Australian Multiculturalism." *National Identities, 9*(3), 265–280.

James, Carl. 1998. *Seeing Ourselves: Exploring Race, Ethnicity, and Culture* (2nd ed.). Toronto: Thompson Education.

James, Carl E. 2002. "Introduction: Encounters in Race, Ethnicity, and Language," in *Talking about Identity.* Carl James and Adrienne Shadd (eds.). Pp. 1–8. Toronto: Between the Lines.

James, Carl (ed.). 2005. *Possibilities and Limitations: Multicultural Policies and Programs in Canada.* Halifax: Fernwood.

James, Carl. 2008 "'It Will Happen without Putting in Place Special Measures': Racially Diversifying Universities," in *Racism in the Canadian University.* F. Henry and C. Tator (eds). Pp. 128–159. Toronto: University of Toronto Press.

James, Carl, and Adrienne Shadd (eds.). 1994. *Talking about Differences: Encounters in Culture, Language, and Identity.* Toronto: Between the Lines.

James, Carl, and Adrienne Shadd (eds.). 2001. *Talking about Identity: Encounters in Race, Ethnicity, and Language.* Toronto: Between the Lines.

Jaret, Charles. 1995. *Contemporary Racial and Ethnic Relations.* Scarborough, ON: Harper Collins.

Jaworsky, John. 1979. *A Case Study of Canadian Federal Government's Multicultural Policies.*

Unpublished MA Thesis. Political Science. Ottawa: Carleton.

Jean, Michaëlle. 2005. "The Government's Policy of Multiculturalism Encourages People to Stay in Ethnic Ghettos." *NovoPress.Info*, 27 September. Available online at **http://am.novopress.info/?p=987.**

Jedwab, Jack. 2002. "Melting Mosaic: Changing Realities in Cultural Diversity in Canada and the United States." *Canadian Issues* (February), 19–23.

Jedwab, Jack. 2004. "Notional Nations: The Myth of Canada as a Multinational Nation." *Canadian Diversity, 3*(2), 19–22.

Jedwab, Jack. 2005. "Neither Finding Nor Losing Our Way: The Debate over Canadian Multiculturalism." *Canadian Diversity, 4*(1), 95–102.

Jedwab, Jack. 2006. "Canadian Integration: The Elusive Quest for Models and Measures." *Canadian Diversity, 9*(1), 97–103.

Jedwab, Jack. 2007. "Canadian 'Separatists' Value Accommodation of Religious Minorities: Exploring the Relationship between Church–State Separation and Reasonable Accommodation." Montreal: Association for Canadian Studies.

Jedwab, Jack. 2011. "Multicultural vs Intercultural: A Superficial Exercise in Branding." *Montreal Gazette*, 7 March.

Jensen, Robert. 2009. *Racism Watch: In South Africa, Apartheid Is Dead, But White Supremacy Lingers On.* Available online at **http://www.trinicenter.com**

Jenson, Jane. 2002. *Citizenship: Its Relationship to the Canadian Diversity Model.* Paper for the Program and Policy Officers of the Department of Canadian Heritage. Ottawa.

Jenson, Jane, and Martin Papillon. 2001. "The Changing Boundaries of Citizenship: A Review and a Research Agenda." Available online at **http://www.cprn.org/doc.cfm?doc=182&l=en**

Jhappan, Radha. 1995. "The Federal–Provincial Power Grid and Aboriginal Self-Government," in *New Trends in Canadian Federalism.* F. Rocher and M. Smith (eds.). Pp.15–186. Peterborough, ON: Broadview Press.

Jimenez, Marina. 1999. "Immigration Rules Costing Canada Billions." *National Post*, 18 February.

Jimenez, Marina. 2004. "Tough Refugee Rules Create Agony for Parents." *The Globe and Mail*, 16 October.

Jimenez, Marina. 2006. "When Multi Morphs into Plural." *The Globe and Mail*, 8 December.

Jimenez, Marina. 2009. "Right Resume, Wrong Name." *The Globe and Mail*, 21 May.

Jiwani, Yasmin. 2001. "Intersecting Inequalities: Immigrant Women of Colour, Violence, and Health Care." Available online at **http://www.harbour.sfu.ca/freda/articles/hlth04.htm**

Jiwani, Yasmin. 2006. *Discourses of Denial: Mediations on Race, Gender, and Violence.* Vancouver: UBC Press.

Jiwani, Yasmin. 2010. "Erasing Race. The Story of Reena Virk," in *Reena Virk*, M. Rajiva and S. Batacharya (eds.). Pp. 82–121. Toronto: Canadian Scholars' Press.

Johnson, Genevieve Fuji, and R. Enomoto. 2007. "Preface," in *Race, Racialization, and Anti-racism in Canada and Beyond.* G.F. Johnson and R. Enomoto (eds.). Toronto: University of Toronto Press.

Jonas, George. 2006. "Anti-Semitism's Presentable Cousin." *National Post*, 20 January.

Jonas, George. 2007. "McGuinty Is a Child of the Times." *National Post*, 27 August.

Joppke, Christian. 2007. "Beyond National Models: Civic Integration Policies for Immigrants in Western Europe." *West European Politics, 30*(1), 1–22.

Kalbach, M.A., and W.E. Kalbach. 1999. "Demographic Overview of Ethnic Origins: Groups in Canada," in *Race and Ethnic Relations in Canada* (2nd ed.). Pp. 3–20. Toronto: Oxford University Press.

Kamalipour, Y.R., and T. Carilli (eds.). 1998. *Cultural Diversity and the U.S. Media.* New York: State University of New York Press.

Kanter, Rosabeth. 1977. *Men and Women of the Corporation.* New York: Vintage.

Kapur, Devesh. 2005. *Give Us Your Best and Brightest.* Washington, DC: Center for Global Development.

Karim, Karim. 2002. *Islamic Peril: Media and Global Violence.* Montreal: Black Rose Books.

Karim, Karim. 2006. "American Media's Coverage of Muslims: The Historical Roots of Contemporary Portrayals," in *Muslims and the News Media.* E. Poole and J.E. Richardson (eds.). Pp. 116–127. New York: I.B Taurus.

Karner, Christian. 2007. *Ethnicity and Everyday Life.* London: Routledge.

Kashima, Y., K. Fiedler, and P. Freytag (eds.). 2008. *Stereotype Dynamics: Language-Based Approaches to the Formation, Maintenance, and Transformation of Stereotypes.* New York: Lawrence Erlbaum Associates.

Kawakami, Kerry, Elizabeth Dunn, Francine Karmali, and John Dovidio. 2009. "Mispredicting Affective and Behavioral Response to Response." *Science, 323*(5911), 276–278.

Kay, Barbara. 2007. "The True Enemy: Human Tribalism." *National Post,* 18 December.

Kay, Jonathan. 2008. "Jonathan Kay Reads the Bouchard-Taylor Report on 'Reasonable Acommodation in Quebec.'" *National Post,* 24 May.

Kazemipur, A., and S.S. Halli. 2003. "Poverty Experiences of Immigrants: Some Reflections." *Canadian Issues* (April), 18–20.

Keevak, Michael. 2011. *Becoming Yellow: A Short History of Racial Thinking.* Princeton, NJ: Princeton University Press.

Kelley, Deidre M. 2006. "Frame Work: Helping Youth Counter Their Misrepresentations in Media." *Canadian Journal of Education, 29*(1), 27–48.

Kelly, Jennifer. 1998. *Under the Gaze: Learning to be Black in White Society.* Halifax: Fernwood.

Kent, Tom. 2008. "Canada Is Much More than a Hotel." *The Globe and Mail,* 15 April.

Kernerman, Gerald. 2005. *Multicultural Nationalism: Civilizing Difference, Constituting Community.* Vancouver: UBC Press.

Keung, Nicholas. 2004. "A Business Case for Diversity." *Toronto Star,* 6 May.

Keung, Nicholas. 2008. "Wait Time to Grow from 6 to 10 Years." *Toronto Star,* 26 May.

Kevles, Daniel J. 1995. *In the Name of Eugenics: Genetics and the Use of Human Heredity.* New York: Alfred A. Knopf.

Khan, Sheema. 2005. "The Sharia Debate Deserves Proper Hearing." *The Globe and Mail,* 15 September.

Khan, Sheema. 2010. "The Blame of Honour Crimes." *The Globe and Mail,* 22 June.

Khayatt, Didi. 1994. "The Boundaries of Identity at the Intersections of Race, Class, and Gender." *Canadian Woman Studies, 14*(2), 6–13.

Khoday, Amar. 2007. "'Honour Killings' Hide Racist Motives." *Toronto Star,* 8 March.

Khoo, S.-E, E. Ho, and C. Voigt-Graf. 2008. "Gendered Migration in Oceania: Trends, Policies, and Outcomes," in *New Perspectives in Gender and Migration.* N. Piper (ed.). Pp. 101–136. New York: Routlege.

Kil, Sang Hea. 2010. "Review of Whiteness: An Introduction. By Steve Garner." *Journal of Ethnic and Migration Studies, 36*(3), 538–538.

Kim, Won. 2006. "Racial Discrimination Is Bad for Your Health—Literally." *DiversityInc.,* 31 October.

Kinsella, Warren. 1994. *Web of Hate: The Far-Right Network in Canada.* Toronto: HarperCollins.

Kitaro, Harry. 1997. *Race Relations.* Englewood Cliffs, NJ: Prentice-Hall.

Kivel, Paul. 1996. *Uprooting Racism: How White People Can Work for Justice.* Philadelphia: New Society Publishers.

Kivisto, Peter, and Wendy Ng. 2005. *Americans All* (2nd ed.). Los Angeles: Roxbury.

Knafla, Louis A., and Haijo Westra. 2010. *Aboriginal Title and Indigenous Peoples. Canada, Australia, and New Zealand.* Vancouver: UBC Press.

Knowles, Valerie. 2007. *Strangers at Our Gates: Canadian Immigration and Immigration Policy: 1540–2006.* Toronto: Dundurn.

Kobayashi, Audrey. 1999. "Multiculturalism and Making Difference: Comments on the State of Multiculturalism Policy in Canada." *Australian-Canadian Studies, 17*(2), 33–39.

Kobayashi, Audrey. 2001. *"Race" and Racism in Canada.* Race Relations Training Module prepared for Human Resources Department Canada.

Kobayashi, Audrey. 2003. "Police Need Better Race Training, Expert: Accept Racism Exists Professor Urges." *Kingston Whig-Standard,* 13 June.

Kobayashi, Audrey. 2005. "Employment Equity in Canada: The Paradox of Tolerance and Denial," in *Possibilities and Limitations.* C. James (ed.). Pp. 154–162. Halifax: Fernwood.

Kobayashi, Audrey, and Genevieve Fuji Johnson. 2007. "Introduction," in *Race, Racialization, and Anti-racism in Canada and Beyond.* G.F. Johnson and R. Enomoto (eds.). Pp. 3–16. Toronto: University of Toronto Press.

Koenig, Matthias, and Paul de Guchteneire. 2007. *Democracy and Human Rights in Multicultural Societies.* Burlington, VT: Ashgate Publishing.

Koenigsberg, Richard. 2004. "Dying for One's Country: The Logic of War and Genocide." Available online at **http://home.earthlink.net/~libraryofsocialscience/dying_for.htm**.

Kogawa, Joy. 1994. *Itsuka.* New York: Doubleday.

Kostash, Myrna. 2000. *The Next Canada: In Search of Our Future Nation.* Toronto: McClelland & Stewart.

Koven, Peter. 2007. "Quebec Separatism Seen as Spent Force." *National Post,* 14 May.

Kruhlak, Orest. 2003. *Annual Shevchenko Lecture.* University of Alberta, Edmonton, 14 March.

Kulchyski, Peter (ed.). 1994. *Unjust Relations: Aboriginal Rights in Canadian Courts.* Toronto: Oxford University Press.

Kulchyski, Peter. 2005. "Bush Life." *Canadian Dimensions Magazine,* May/June.

Kumi, Phyllis. 2008. "Lessons from the 'Ghetto Dude' Affair." *Toronto Star,* 22 January.

Kumin, Judith. 2001. "Gender: Persecution in the Spotlight." *Refugee, 2*(123), 12–13.

Kumin, Judith. 2004. "Can This Marriage Be Saved? National Interest and Ethics in Asylum Policy." *Canadian Issues* (March), 14–17.

Kunz, Jean Lock. 2005. "Applying Life Course Lens to Immigration Integration." *Canadian Issues* (Spring), 41–43.

Kunz, Jean Lock, Anne Milan, and Sylvain Schetagne. 2001. *Unequal Access: A Canadian Profile of Racial Differences in Education, Employment, and Income.* Toronto: Canadian Race Relations Foundation.

Kunz, Jean, and Stuart Sykes. 2007. *From Mosaic to Harmony: Multiculturalism Canada in the 21st Century.* Ottawa: Policy Research Institute.

Kuokkanen, Rauna. 2007. *Reshaping the University: Responsibility, Indigenous Epistemes, and the Logic of the Gift.* Vancouver: UBC Press.

Kupu Taea. 2007. *Media & Te Tiriti o Waitangi. By the Media and Te Tiriti Project.* Available online at **http://www.trc.org.nz**

Kurien, Prema A. 2006. "Multiculturalism and American Religion: The Case of Hindu Indian Americans." *Social Forces, 85*(2), 723–741.

Kurthen, Hermann. 1997. "The Canadian Experiences with Multiculturalism and Employment Equity: Lessons for Europe." *New Community, 23*(2), 249–270.

Kymlicka, Will. 1992. "The Rights of Minority Cultures: Reply to Kukathas." *Political Theory, 20,* 140–145.

Kymlicka, Will. 1995. "Misunderstanding Nationalism." *Dissent* (Winter), 131–137.

Kymlicka, Will. 1998a. *Finding Our Way: Rethinking Ethnocultural Relations in Canada.* Toronto: Oxford University Press.

Kymlicka, Will. 1998b. "Multinational Federalism in Canada: Rethinking the Relationship," in *Beyond the Impasse.* R. Gibbins and G. Laforest (eds.). Pp. 15–50. Montreal: IRPP.

Kymlicka, Will. 2001. *Politics in the Vernacular: Nationalism, Multiculturalism, and Citizenship.* Toronto: Oxford University Press.

Kymlicka, Will. 2003. "Immigration, Citizenship, Multiculturalism: Exploring the Links." *The Political Quarterly,* 195–208.

Kymlicka Will. 2004. *The Canadian Model of Diversity in a Comparative Perspective.* Eighth Standard Life Visiting Lecture. University of Edinburgh. 29 April.

Kymlicka, Will. 2005. "The Uncertain Futures of Multiculturalism." *Canadian Diversity, 4*(1), 82–85.

Kymlicka, Will. 2007. *Multicultural Odysseys: Navigating the New International Politics of Diversity.* Oxford, UK: Oxford University Press.

Kymlicka, Will. 2008. *The Current State of Multiculturalism in Canada.* Ottawa: Multiculturalism and Human Rights Branch, Government of Canada.

Kymlicka, Will. 2010. "Testing the Liberal Multiculturalist Hypothesis: Normative Theories and Social Science Evidence." *Canadian Journal of Political Science, 43,* 257–271.

Kymlicka, Will. 2011. "Multiculturalism in Normative Theory and Social Science." *Ethnicities, 11*(1), 5–31.

Laforest, Guy. 1998. "Standing in the Shoes of the Other Partners in the Canadian Union," in *Beyond the Impasse: Toward Reconciliation.* R. Gibbins and G. Laforest (eds.). Pp. 51–82. Montreal: IRPP.

Lambertus, Sandra. 2004. *War Time Images, Peace Time Wounds: The Media and the Gustafsen Lake Standoff.* Toronto: University of Toronto Press.

Lamoin, Amy, and Cassandra Dawes. 2010. "Racism in Australia: Is Denial Still Possible?" *Race/Ethnicity: Multidisciplinary Global Perspectives, 3*(2).

Land, Lorraine, and Roger Townshend. 2002. "Land Claims: Stuck in Never-Never Land," in *Nation to Nation.* J. Bird, L. Land, and M. Macadam (eds.). Pp. 53–62. Toronto: Public Justice Resource Centre.

LaSelva, Samuel V. 2004. "Understanding Canada: Federalism, Multiculturalism and the Will to Live Together," in *Canadian Politics*. J. Bickerton and A.-G. Gagnon (eds.). Pp. 17–34. Peterborough, ON: Broadview Press.

Lasica, J. D. 1996. "Net Gain: Journalists in an Interactive Age." American Journalism Review (November), 20–33.

Latouche, Daniel. 1995. "Quebec, See under Canada: Quebec Nationalism in the New Global Age," in *Quebec: State and Society* (2nd ed.). A.-G. Gagnon (ed.). Pp. 40–63. Toronto: Nelson.

Leblanc, Daniel. 2006. "Sovereigntists Jump on Comments by Charest." *The Globe and Mail*, 11 July.

Leckie, Jacqui. 1995. "Silent Immigrants? Gender, Immigration and Ethnicity in New Zealand," in *Immigration and National Identity in New Zealand*. S.W. Greif (ed.). Pp. 50–76. Wellington, New Zealand: Dunmore Press.

Lee, Jo-anne, and John Lutz. 2005. "Introduction: Towards a Critical Literacy of Racisms, Anti-racisms, Racialization," in *Situating "Race" and Racisms in Time, Space, and Theory: Essays for Activists and Scholars*. J. Lee and J. Lutz (eds). Pp. 3–29. Montreal and Kingston: McGill-Queen's University Press.

Léger Marketing. 2001. Poll. October.

Legrain, Philippe. 2007. *Immigrants: Your Country Needs Them*. Princeton, NJ: Princeton University Press.

Le Guin, Ursula. 1975. "The Ones Who Walk Away from Omelas," in *The Wind's Twelve Quarters*. London: Orion Books.

Leigh, Darcy. 2009. Colonialism, Gender, and the Family in North America: For a Gendered Analysis of Indigenous Struggles. *Studies in Nationalism and Ethnicity, 9*(1), 70–88.

Lentin, Alana. 2004. "Racial States, Anti-racist Responses: Picking Holes in 'Culture' and 'Human Rights.'" *European Journal of Social Theory, 7*(4), 427–443.

Leonardo, Zeus. 2004. "The Color of Supremacy: Beyond the Discourse of 'White Privilege.'" *Educational Philosophy and Theory, 36*(2).

Leong, Melissa, and Glynnis Mapp. 2006. "Murders of Women Have South Asians Worried about Abuse." *National Post*, 7 November.

Lerner, Gerda. 1997. *Why History Matters: Life and Thought*. New York: Oxford University Press.

Levitt, Cyril. 1997. "The Morality of Race in Canada." *Society* (July/August), 32–37.

Lewis, Charles. 2008. "Race Disappears as Deciding Factor." *National Post*, 5 December.

Ley, David. 2005. *Post-Multiculturalism?* Working Paper No. 05-17. Research on Immigration and Integration in the Metropolis. Vancouver: Vancouver Centre of Excellence.

Ley, David. 2007. "Multiculturalism: A Canadian Defence." *Metropolis*.

Ley, David, and Daniel Hiebert. 2001. "Immigration Policy as Population Policy." *The Canadian Geographer, 45*(1), 120–125.

Li Peter. 1995. "Racial Supremacism under Social Democracy." *Canadian Ethnic Studies, 27*(1), 1–17.

Li, Peter S. 1998. *The Chinese in Canada* (2nd ed.). Toronto: Oxford University Press.

Li, Peter S. 1999. *Race and Ethnic Relations in Canada* (2nd ed.). Toronto: Oxford University Press.

Li, Peter S. 2003. *Destination Canada: Immigration Debates and Issues*. Toronto: Oxford University Press.

Li, Peter. 2007. "Contradictions of 'Racial' Discourse," in *Interrogating Race and Racism*. V. Agnew (ed.). Pp. 37–54. Toronto: University of Toronto Press.

Lian, Jason Z., and Ralph David Matthews. 1998. "Does the Vertical Mosaic Still Exist? Ethnicity and Income in Canada, 1991." *Canadian Review of Sociology and Anthropology, 35*(4), 461–477.

Lieberman, Robert. 2006. "Shaping Race Policies: the United States in Comparative Perspective. Princeton University Press. Reviewed by Erik Bleich." *Ethics & International Affairs, 20*(1), 133.

Linden, W. 1994. *Swiss Democracy*. New York: St. Martin's Press.

Lister, Ruth. 1997. *Citizenship: Feminist Perspectives*. London: Macmillan.

Little Bear, Leroy. 2004. "Aboriginal Paradigms: Implications for Relationships to Land and Treaty Making," in *Advancing Aboriginal Claims*. Kerry Wilkins (ed.). Pp. 26–38. Saskatoon: Purich Publishing.

Littleton, James (ed.). 1996. *Clash of Identities: Essays on Media, Manipulation, and Politics of the Self.* Toronto: Prentice Hall.

Liu, James H. et al. (eds.). 2006. *New Zealand Identities*. Wellington, NZ: Victoria University Press.

Loney, Martin. 1998. *The Pursuit of Division: Race, Gender, and Preferential Hiring in Canada.* Montreal/Kingston: McGill-Queen's University Press.

Long, David, and Olive Dickason. 2000. *Visions of the Heart: Canadian Aboriginal Issues* (2nd ed.). Toronto: Harcourt.

Long, David, and Olive Patricia Dickason. 2011. *Visions of the Heart* (3rd ed.). Toronto: Oxford University Press.

Lopes, Tina, and Barb Thomas. 2006. *Dancing on Live Embers: Challenging Racism in Organizations.* Toronto: Between the Lines.

Lowe, Sophia. 2008. *"Designer Immigrants": Eliminating Barriers.* Available online at **http://www.triec.ca**

Lowe, Sophia. 2010. "Rearranging the Deck Chairs? A Critical Examination of Canada's Shifting (Im)migration Policies." *Canadian Issues* (Spring), 25–28.

Lumb, Lionel. 2004. cited in *Ethnic and Visible Minorities in the Media—Media Awareness Network.* Available online at **http://media-awareness.ca**

Lupa, Alan. 1999. "When Generations and Cultures Clash." *Boston Sunday Globe*, 8 August.

Lupul, Manoly R. 1988. "Ukrainians: The Fifth Cultural Wheel in Canada," in *Ethnicity in a Technological Age.* Ian H. Angus (ed.). Pp. 177–192. Edmonton: Canadian Institute of Ukrainian Studies, University of Alberta.

Lupul, Manoly. 2005. *The Politics of Multiculturalism: A Ukrainian-Canadian Memoir.* Edmonton: Canadian Institute of Ukrainian Studies Press.

Lyons, Noel. 1997. "Feds Criticized." *Windspeaker.* 3 November.

Maaka, Roger, and Chris Anderson (eds.). 2007. *The Indigenous Experience.* Toronto: Canadian Scholars' Press.

Maaka, Roger, and Augie Fleras. 2005. *The Politics of Indigeneity: Challenging the State in Canada and Aotearoa New Zealand.* Dunedin, NZ: University of Otago Press.

Maaka, Roger, and Augie Fleras. 2008. "Contesting Indigenous Peoples Governance: The Politics of Self-Determination versus Self-Determining Autonomy," in *Aboriginal Self-Governmen in Canada: Current Issues and Trends* (3rd ed.). Y. Belanger (ed.), Saskatoon: Purich Publishing.

Mac an Ghaill, Mairtin. 1999. *Contemporary Racisms and Ethnicities: Social and Cultural Transformations.* Philadelphia: Open University Press.

Maccharles, Tonda. 2004. "Canada, U.S. in Refugee Deal." *Toronto Star*, 15 October.

Maccharles, Tonda. 2005. "High Court Supports Native Rights." *Toronto Star*, 19 November.

MacDonald, L. Ian. 2007. "SES—Policy Options Exclusive Poll: The Limits of Reasonable Accommodation." *Policy Options* (September), 1–5.

Macedo, Donaldo, and Panayota Gounari. 2006. "Globalization and the Unleashing of New Racism: An Introduction," in *The Globalization of Racism.* D. Macedo and P. Gounari (eds.). Pp. 3–24. Boulder, CO: Paradigm Publishers.

Mackey, Eva. 1998. *The House of Difference: Cultural Politics and National Identity in Canada.* London: Routledge.

Mackie, Richard. 2001. "Sovereignty Support Near Low, Poll Finds." *The Globe and Mail*, 26 October.

Macklem, Patrick. 2001. *Indigenous Difference and the Constitution in Canada.* Toronto: University of Toronto Press.

Macklin, Audrey. 1999. "Women as Migrants in National and Global Communities." *Canadian Woman Studies*, 19(3), 24–32.

Macklin, Audrey, and Frances Crepeau. 2010. "Multiple Citizenship, Identity, and Entitlement in Canada." *IRPP Study, 6*, June.

Maclure, Jocelyn. 2004. "Between Nation and Dissemination: Revisiting the Tension Between National Identity and Diversity," in *The Conditions of Diversity in Multinational Democracies.* A.-G. Gagnon et al. (eds.). Montreal: IRPP.

MacQueen, Ken. 1994. "I Am a Canadian. Don't Let Me Screw Up." *Kitchener-Waterloo Record*, 23 April.

Magnet, Joseph Eliot. 2004. *Modern Constitutionalism: Identity, Equality, and Democracy.* Toronto: Butterworths.

Magsino, R.F. 2000. "The Canadian Multiculturalism Policy: A Pluralist Ideal Revisited," in *21st Century Canadian Diversity.* S. Nancoo (ed.). Pp. 320–341. Toronto: Canadian Scholars' Press.

Mahoney, Jill. 2007. "Leaping Over Education Adversity." *The Globe and Mail*, 5 December.

Mahtani, Minelle. 2002. "Interrogating the Hyphen-Nation: Canadian Multicultural Policy and Mixed Race Identities." *Social Identities, 8*(1).

Mahtani, Minelle. 2008. "How Are Immigrants Seen—And What Do They Want to See. Contemporary Research on the Representation of Immigrants in the Canadian Language Media," in *Immigration and Integration in Canada*. John Biles et al. (eds.). Pp. 231–252. Montreal/Kingston: McGill-Queens University Press.

Maioni, Antonia. 2003. "Canadian Health Care," in *Profiles of Canada*. K. Pryke and W. Soderland (eds.). Pp. 307–326. Toronto: Canadian Scholars Press.

Manfredi, Christopher. 2004. "Fear, Hope and Misunderstanding: Unintended Consequences and the Marshall Decision," in *Advancing Aboriginal Claims*. Kerry Wilkins (ed.). Pp. 190–201. Saskatoon: Purich Publishing.

Manji, Irshad. 2005. "Not All Traditions Deserve Respect." *NY Times*. Reprinted in the *National Post*, 11 August.

Mann, Michelle M. 2005. *Aboriginal Women: An Issues Backgrounder*. Prepared for the Status of Women in Canada. Available online at **http://www.swc-cfc.gc.ca/pubs/ges_aboriginal/index_e.html**

Manning, Peter. 2006. "Australians Imagining Islam," in *Muslims and the News Media*. E. Poole and J.E. Richardson (eds.). Pp. 128–141. New York: I.B. Taurus.

Mansur, Salim. 2010. *The Muddle of Multiculturalism. A Liberal Critque*. Halifax: Atlantic Institute for Market Studies.

Maracle, Brian. 1996. "One More Whining Indian Tilting at Windmills," in *Clash of Identities*. J. Littleton (ed.). Pp 15–20. Toronto: Prentice-Hall.

Marchi, Sergio. 1994. "Sergio Marchi on Immigration." *OpenParliament*. Available online at **http://openparliament.ca/hansards/1023/96/only/**

Marcus, Alan Rudolph. 1995. *Relocating Eden: The Image and Politics of Inuit Exile in the Canadian Arctic*. Hanover, NH: The University Press of New England.

Marger, Martin. 1997. *Race and Ethnic Relations: American and Global Perspectives* (4th ed.). Toronto: Nelson/Thomson Learning,

Marger, Martin. 2001. *Race and Ethnic Relations: American and Global Perspectives* (5th ed.). Toronto: Nelson Thomson.

Marketwire. 2009. *Government of Canada Tables. 2010 Immigration Plan. Citizenship and Immigration, Canada*. Available online at **http://www.marketwire.com**

Martin, James G., and Clyde W. Franklin. 1973. *Minority Group Relations*. Columbus, OH: Charles E. Merrill Publishing Company.

Martin, Philip, Manolo Abella, and Christiane Kuptsch. 2005. *Managing Labour Migration in the Twenty-First Century*. Princeton, NJ: Yale University Press.

Marwah, Inder, and Triadafilos Triadafilopoulos. 2009. "Europeanizing Canada's Citizenship Regime? Canada Europe Transatlantic Dialogue: Seeking Transnational Solutions to 21st Century Problems." *Commentary* (May).

Mason, Gary. 2010. "Give First Nations the Power to Help Themselves." *The Globe and Mail*, 17 June.

Masood, Ehsan. 2008. "Muslims and Multiculturalism: Lesson from Canada." *Open Democracy*. Available online at **http://www.opendemocracy.net**

Massey, Douglas S. 2009. "The Political Economy of Migration in an Era of Globalization," in *International Migration and Human Rights: the Global Repercussions of U.S. Policy*. S. Martinez (ed.). Pp. 25–41. Berkeley, CA: University of California Press.

Matas, Robert, Erin Anderssen, and Sean Fine. 1997. "Natives Win on Land Rights." *The Globe and Mail*, 12 December.

Matsuoka, Atsuko, and John Sorenson. 1999. "Eritrean Women in Canada: Negotiating New Lives." *Canadian Woman Studies, 19*(3), 104–109.

Mawani, Aysha. 2008. *Transnationalism: A Modern Day Challenge to Canadian Multiculturalism*. Paper presented at the Annual Meeting of the International Communication Association, Montreal, May 22. Available online at **http://www.allacademic.com**

Mawani, Nurjehan. 1997. "Is Refugee Determination Fair?" *The Globe and Mail*, 13 December.

May, Harvey. 2004. *Broadcast in Colour: Cultural Diversity and Television Programming in Four Countries*. Australian Film Commission.

May, S. (ed.). 1999. *Critical Multiculturalism*. Madison, WI: University of Wisconsin Press.

May, Stephen. 2002. "Multiculturalism," in *A Companion to Racial and Ethnic Studies*. D.T. Goldberg and J. Solomos (eds.). Pp. 124–144. Malden, MA: Blackwell.

Mayer, Nonna, and Guy Michelat. 2001. "Subjective Racism, Objective Racism: The French Case." *Patterns of Prejudice, 35*(4).

McAndrew, Marie. 1992. "Combating Racism and Ethnocentrism in Educational Materials: Problems and Actions Taken in Quebec," in *Racism and Education: Different Perspectives and Experiences*. Ontario Teachers Federation (ed.). Pp. 49–60. Ottawa: Canadian Teachers' Federation.

McCaskill, Tim. 1995. "Anti-racist Education and Practice in the Public School System," in *Beyond Political Correctness*. S. Richer and L. Weir (eds.). Pp. 253–272. Toronto: University of Toronto Press.

McDougall, Gay. 2009. *Statement by the United Nations Independent Expert on Minority Issues on the Conclusion of Her Visit to Canada*. United Nations, Office of the High Commissioner on Human Rights, 23 October.

McGauran, the Honourable Peter. 2005. "The Australian Government Minister for Citizenship and Multicultural Affairs." *Canadian Diversity, 4*(1), 6–8.

McGill University. 1994. *Anti-racism and Race Relations*. Prepared by Monique Shebbeare. McGill's Equity Office, July.

McGregor, Gail. 2002. "Book Review of *Removing the Margins: The Challenges and Possibilities of Inclusive Schooling* (George Sefa Dei et al., 2000)." Available online at **http://www.aaanet.org/sections/cae/aeq/br/deietal.htm**

McHugh, Paul. 1998. "Aboriginal Identity and Relations: Models of State Practice and Law in North America and Australasia," in *Living Relationships*. K Coates and P. McHugh (eds.). Institute of Public Policy. Wellington, NZ: Victoria University of Wellington.

McIntosh, Peggy. 1988. *White Privilege and Male Privilege: A Personal Account of Coming to See Correspondences through Work in Women Studies*. Working Paper No. 189. MA: Wellesley College, Centre for Research on Women.

McIntyre, Sheila. 1993. "Backlash against Equality: The 'Tyranny' of the 'Politically Correct.'" *McGill Law Journal/Revue de Droit de McGill, 38*(1), 3–63.

McIsaac, Elizabeth. 2003. *Nation Building through Cities: A New Deal for Immigrant Settlement in Canada*. Ottawa: Caledon Institute.

McKee, Craig. 1996. *Treaty Talks in British Columbia*. Vancouver: UBC Press.

McKenna, Ian. 1994. "Canada's Hate Propaganda Laws—A Critique." *British Journal of Canadian Studies, 15*, 42.

McMullin, Julie. 2010. *Understanding Social Inequality in Canada. Intersections of Class, Age, Gender, Ethnicity and Race*. Toronto: Oxford University Press.

McRoberts, Kenneth. 1996. "Introduction (Citizenship and Rights)." *International Journal of Canadian Studies, 14*(Fall), 5–12.

McRoberts, Kenneth. 1997. *Misconceiving Canada: The Struggle for National Unity*. Toronto: Oxford University Press.

McRoberts, Kenneth. 2001. "Canada and the Multinational State." *Canadian Journal of Political Science, 24*(4), 683–713.

McRoberts, Kenneth. 2003. "Managing Cultural Differences in Multinational Democracies," in *The Conditions of Diversity in Multinational Democracies*. A.-G. Gagnon et al. (eds.). Pp. 1–14. Montreal: IRRP.

McRoberts, Kenneth. 2004. "The Future of the Nation State and Quebec–Canada Relations," in *The Fate of the Nation State*. M. Seymour (ed.). Montreal: McGill-Queen's University Press.

McVeigh, Robbie, and Ronit Lentin. 2006. "Situated Racisms: A Theoretical Introduction," in *Racism and Anti-racism in Ireland*. R. Lentin and R. McVeigh (eds.). Belfast, IE: Beyond the Pale Publications.

Mead, Walter Russell. 1993. "This Land Is My Land." *New York Times Book Review*, 7 November.

Meadows/Bridgeview, Marguerite. 2005. "The Model School, Islamic Style." *Time*, 11 June.

Medrano, J.D., and M. Koenig. 2005. "Nationalism, Citizenship, and Immigration in Social Science Research—Editorial Introduction." *International Journal on Multicultural Societies, 7*(2), 82–89.

Melchers, Ron. 2005. Cited in *Race Study Results under Fire*. Available online at **http://www.ottawamenscentre.com**

Melle, Tilden J. 2009. "Race in International Relations." *International Studies Perspectives, 10*, 77–83.

Mendelsohn, Matthew. 2003. "Birth of a New Ethnicity," in *The New Canadians*. E. Anderssen and M. Valpy (eds.). Pp. 59–66. Toronto: McClelland & Stewart.

Mendelson, Michael. 2006. *Aboriginal Peoples and Postsecondary Education in Canada*. Ottawa: Caledon Institute of Social Policy.

Mercredi, Ovide, and Mary Ellen Turpel. 1993. *In the Rapids: Navigating the Future of First Nations*. Toronto: Penguin Books.

Metropolis Presents. 2004. *Conference Notes on Media, Immigration and Diversity: Informing Public Discourse or Fanning the Flames of Intolerance?* March 30. Ottawa: National Library.

Meyers, Eytan. 2002. "The Causes of Convergence in Western Immigration Control." *Review of International Studies, 28*, 123–141.

Midlarsky, Manus. 2005. *The Killing Trap: Genocide in the Twentieth Century*. Cambridge, UK: Cambridge University Press.

Migration Policy Institute. 2007. "Annual Immigration to the United States." Fact Sheet No. 16, May.

Miles, Robert. 1982. *Racism and Migrant Labour*. London: Routledge and Kegan Paul.

Miller, J.R. 1989. *Skyscrapers Hide the Heavens: A History of Indian–White Relations in Canada*. Toronto: University of Toronto Press.

Miller, J.R. 1999. *The State, the Church, and Residential Schools in Canada*. Paper presented at a Conference on Religion and Public Life: Historical and Comparative Themes, Queen's University, 13–15 May. Available online at **http://www.anglican.ca/Residental-Schools/resources/miller.htm**

Miller, John. 2005. *Ipperwash and the Media: A Critical Analysis of How the Story Was Covered*. Paper prepared for the Aboriginal Legal Foundation in Toronto. Available online at **http://www.attorneygeneral.jus.gov.on.ca/inquiries/ipperwash/policy_part/projects/pdf/ALST_Ipperwash_and_media.pdf**

Millman, Jennifer. 2007a. "Affirmative Action News: Why Race Counts in School Segregation." *DiversityInc*, 12 November.

Millman, Jennifer. 2007b. "Why Color-Blind Isn't the Answer." *DiversityInc*, 24 July.

Millman, Joel. 1997. *The Other Americans: How Immigrants Renew Our Country, Our Economy, and Our Values*. New York: Penguin.

Milloy, Courtland. 2001. "Racism Still Lurks in US Corporate World." *KW Record*, 10 January.

Mills, Charles W. 1997. *Racial Contract*. Ithaca, NY: Cornell University Press.

Minister of Indian Affairs and Northern Development. 1997. *Gathering Strength, Canada's Aboriginal Action Plan*. Ottawa: Minister of Public Works and Government Services Canada.

Mitchell, Alana. 1998. "Sensitivity Required in Using Race Data." *The Globe and Mail*, 17 February.

Mitchell, Brenda. 1993. "Color Me Multicultural." *Multi-Cultural Review, 1*(4), 15–17.

Mittler, P. 2000. *Working toward Inclusive Education: Social Contexts*. London: Fulton.

Modan, Gabriella Gahlia. 2007. *Turf Wars. Discourse Diversity and the Politics of Place*. Malden MA: Blackwell Publishing.

Modood, Tariq. 2003. "Muslims and the Politics of Difference" *The Political Quarterly* (Special Issue), 100–115.

Modood, Tariq. 2005. *Multicultural Politics: Racism, Ethnicity, and Muslims in Britain*. Minneapolis, MN: University of Minnesota Press.

Modood, Tariq. 2007. "Multiculturalism and Nation-Building Go Hand in Hand." *Guardian Unlimited*, 23 May.

Moens, Alexander, and Martin Collacott (eds.). 2008. *Immigration Policy and the Terrorist Threat in Canada and the United States*. Calgary: Fraser Institute.

Montreuil, Annie, and Richard Y. Bourhis. 2004. "Acculturation Orientations of Competing Host Communities toward Valued and Devalued Immigrants." *International Journal of Intercultural Relations, 28*(6), 507–532.

Monture, Patricia. 2004. "The Rights of Inclusion: Aboriginal Rights and/or Aboriginal Women?" in *Advancing Aboriginal Claims*. Kerry Wilkins (ed.). Pp. 39–66. Saskatoon: Purich Publishing.

Monture-Angus, Patricia. 2002. *Journeying Forward: Dreaming First Nations' Independence*. Halifax, NS: Fernwood Publishing.

Moore, Robert. 1992. *Racism in the English Language*. New York: The Racism and Sexism Resource Center for Educators.

Moosa, Zohra. 2007. "Minding the Multicultural Gap." *Catalyst*, 16 March.

Morissette, Rene. 2008. Cited in "Highly Educated but Poorly Paid." Colin Perkel. *The Globe and Mail*, 1 May.

Morphet, Janet. 2007. "Embracing Multiculturalism: The Case of London," in *Migration and Cultural Inclusion in the European City*. William J.V.

Neill and Hanns-Uve Schwedler (eds.). Pp. 167–183. New York: Palgrave.

Morris, Barry, and Gillian Cowlishaw (eds.). 1997. *Race Matters: Indigenous Australians and "Our" Society*. Canberra, AU: Aboriginal Studies Press.

Morse, Bradford W. (ed.) 1985. *Aboriginal Peoples and the Law*. Ottawa: Carleton University Press.

Mothers United Against Racism. 2005. "The Police's Fight against Incivilities Encourages Racial Profiling and Harassment: Minority Mothers." Press release, 16 May.

Muharrar, Mikal. 2005. Cited in "Ethnic Profiling and Gang and Gun Violence," Patricia Hylton. *Pride* (October), 12–18.

Muir, Rick, and Margaret Wetherell. 2010. *Identity, Politics, and Public Policy*. London, UK: Institute for Public Policy Research.

Mukherjee. Alok. 1992. "Educational Equity for Racial Minorities and the School: The Role of Community Action," in *Racism and Education: Different Perspectives and Experiences*. Pp. 73–81. Ottawa: Ontario Federation of Students.

Munz, Rainer, and Rainer Ohliger (eds.). 2003. *Diasporas and Ethnic Migrants: Germany, Israel and Post-Soviet Successor States in Comparative Perspective*. Portland, OR: Frank Cass.

Murphy, Michael. 2001. "Culture and Courts: A New Direction in Canadian Jurisprudence on Aboriginal Rights?" *Canadian Journal of Political Science, 34*(1), 109–129.

Murphy, Michael (ed.). 2005. *Canada: The State of the Federation 2003: Reconfiguring Aboriginal–State Relations*. Published by the Institute of Intergovernmental Relations. School of Policy Studies. Kingston: Queen's University.

Murray, Catherine. 2009. "Designing Monitoring to Promote Cultural Divesification in TV." *Canadian Journal of Communication, 34*(4), 675–699.

Murray, Charles, and Richard J. Herrnstein. 1994. *The Bell Curve: Intelligence and Class Structure in American Life*. New York: The Free Press.

Mustafa, Naheed. 2007. "Aqsa Parvez's Death Lays Bare Flipside of Immigration." *Toronto Star*, 12 December.

Nagel, Joane, and Susan Olzak. 1982. "Ethnic Mobilization in the New and Old States: An Extension of the Competition Model." *Social Problems, 30*(2), 127–142.

Nakache, Delphine, and Paula J. Kinoshita. 2010. "The Canadian Temporary Foreign Worker Program," *IRPP Study* No. 5, May.

Nakhaie, Reza M. 2007. "Ethnoracial Origins, Social Capital, and Earnings." *International Migration and Integration, 8*, 307–325.

Nancoo, Stephen. 2004. *Contemporary Issues in Community Policing*. Mississauga, ON: Canadian Education Press.

Nanos, Nik. 2008. "Nation-Building through Immigration: Workforce Skills Come Out on Top." *Policy Options* (June), 30–32.

Nanos, Nik. 2010. "Canadians Strongly Support Immigration, But Don't Want Current Levels Increased." *Policy Options* (July/August).

National Film Board of Canada. 2006. *Race Is a Four-Letter Word* [Film].

Native Women's Association of Canada. 2004. *Background Document on Aboriginal Women's Health*. Ottawa: Author.

Neill, William J.V., and Hanns-Uve Schwedler (eds.). 2007. *Migration and Cultural Inclusion in the European City*. New York: Palgrave.

Nelson, Adie. 2009. *Gender in Canada* (4th ed.). Toronto: Pearson.

Neufeld-Rocheleau, Melody, and Judith Friesen. 1987. "Isolation: A Reality for Immigrant Women in Canada." *Saskatchewan Multicultural Magazine, 6*(2), 12–13L.

Newhouse, David, and Evelyn Peters. 2003. *Not Strangers in These Parts. Urban Aboriginal Peoples*. Ottawa: Policy Research Initiative.

Newhouse, David, Cora Voyageur, and Dan Beavon (eds.). 2007. *Hidden in Plain Sight. Contributions of Aboriginal Peoples to Canadian Identity and Culture*. Toronto: University of Toronto Press.

Niezen, Ronald. 2003. *The Origins of Indigenism: Human Rights and the Politics of Identity*. Berkeley: University of California Press.

Novac, Sylvia. 1999. "Immigrant Enclaves and Residential Segregation: Voices of Racialized Refugees." *Canadian Woman Studies, 19*(3), 97–103.

O'Doherty, Kieran, and Martha Augoustinos. 2008. "Protecting the Nation: Nationalist Rhetoric on Asylum Seekers and the Tampa." *Journal of Community & Applied Social Psychology, 18*, 576–592.

Office of the Commissioner of Official Languages. 2004. *Annual Report of the Office of the Commissioner of Official Languages*. Ottawa: Author.

Office of the Commissioner of Official Languages. 2006/7. *Annual Report of the Office of the Commissioner of Official Languages*. Ottawa: Author.

Office of the Commissioner of Official Languages. 2009/10. *Annual Report of the Office of the Commissioner of Official Languages*. Ottawa: Author.

O'Hara, Carolyn. 2005. "From Prussia with Hate." *New Statesmen*, 14 November, 38–39.

Okin, Susan (ed.). 1999. *Is Multiculturalism Bad for Women?* Princeton, NJ: Princeton University Press.

Olsson, Eva Karin. 2009. "Rule Regimes in News Organization Decision Making." *Journalism* 10(6), 758–776.

Omi, M., and H. Winant. 1994. *Racial Formation in the United States* (2nd ed.). New York: Routledge.

Omidvar, Ratna. 2010. "Canada's Immigration Score: Recommendations for a Win-Win." *Policy Options* (July/August).

Ominayak, Bernard, and Ed Bianchi. 2002. "Lubicon Cree: Still No Settlement after All These Years," in *Nation to Nation*. J. Bird et al. (eds.). Pp. 163–174. Toronto: Irwin.

Ommundsen, Wenche, Michael Leach, and Andrew Vandenberg (eds). 2010. "Multiculturalism and Cultural Citizenship," in *Cultural Citizenship and the Challenges of Globalization*. W. Ommundsen et al. (eds). Cresskill, NJ: Hampton Press.

O'Neill, Peter. 2008. "Canada Sets Example in Diversity: Jean." *Canwest News Service*, 6 May.

Ontario Human Rights Commission. 2003. *Paying the Price: The Human Cost of Racial Profiling*. Toronto: Author.

Ontario Human Rights Commission. 2005. *"Fishing without Fear." Report on the Inquiry into Assaults on Asian-Canadian Anglers*. Toronto: Author.

O'Regan, Tipene. 1994. *Indigenous Governance: Country Study—New Zealand*. Study prepared for the Royal Commission on Aboriginal Peoples. Ottawa.

Ornstein, Michael. 2006. *Ethno-Racial Groups in Toronto, 1971–2001: A Demographic and Socio-Economic Profile*. Toronto: Institute for Social Research.

Orwin, Clifford. 2010. "No Room at the Inn for Veiled Women? Get Real, Canada." *The Globe and Mail*, 30 March.

Our Diverse Cities. 2004. Volume 1, Number 1.

Our Diverse Cities. 2006. No 2. Summer.

Our Diverse Cities. 2007. No 4. Fall.

Paikin, Steve. 2010. "Racism, Then and Now." *The Agenda*. Aired on TVOntario, 10 April.

Palmer, Douglas L. 1996. "Determinants of Canadian Attitudes toward Immigration: More Than Just Racism?" *Canadian Journal of Behavioural Science, 28*(3), 180–192.

Palmer, Howard (ed.). 1975. *Immigration and the Rise of Multiculturalism*. Toronto: Copp Clark Publishing.

Paolucci, Paul. 2006. "Race and Racism in Marx's Camera Obscura." *Critical Sociology, 32*(4).

Papademetriou, Demetrios G. 2003. "Managing Rapid and Deep Change in the Newest Age of Migration." *The Political Quarterly* (Special Issue), 39–58.

Papillon, Martin. 2002. *Immigration, Diversity and Social Inclusion in Canada's Cities*. Discussion Paper F/27. Canadian Policy Research Network.

Papp, Aruna. 2010. *Culturally Driven Violence against Women: A Growing Problem in Canada's Immigration Communities*. Winnipeg: Frontier Centre for Public Policy.

Paradies, Yin C. 2006. "Beyond Black and White: Essentialism, Hybridity, and Indigeneity." *Journal of Sociology, 42*(4), 355–367.

Paradkar, Bageshree. 2000. "Suffering in Silence." *Toronto Star*, 24 June.

Parekh, Bhikhu. 1997. "Foreward," in *Ethnic Minorities in Britain*. T. Modood and R. Berthoud (eds.). London: Policy Studies Institute.

Parekh, Bhikhu. 2000. "Preface," in *The Future of Multi-Ethnic Britain—Report of the Commission on the Future of Multi-Ethnic Britain*. Bhikku Parekh (chair). London: Profile Books.

Parkin, Andrew. 2001. "Introduction," in *What Will Hold Us Together?* Centre for Policy Research in Canada.

Parkin, Andrew. 2003. *A Changing People: Being Canadian in a New Century*. CRIC Paper No. 9. Montreal: Centre for Research and Information on Canada.

Pascal, Julia. 2006. "What's in a Name?" *Catalyst*, 20 November.

Pascale, Celine-Marie. 2007. *Making Sense of Race, Class, and Gender: Common Sense, Power, and Privilege in the United States*. New York: Routledge.

Pateman, Carole. 1988. *Sexual Contract*. Cambridge, MA: Polity Press.

Patriquin, Martin. 2007. "The End of Separatism?" *Maclean's*, 13 August.

Pauktuutit. 2006. *National Strategy to Prevent Abuse in Inuit Communities and Sharing Knowledge, Sharing Wisdom*. Iqaluit, NU: Pauttutit Inuit Women of Canada.

Peach, Ian. 2005. "The Politics of Self-Government." *SIPP News* (Spring), 4–6.

Pearson, David 1994. *Canada Compared: Multiculturalism and Biculturalism in Settler Societies*. St. John's: Institute of Social and Economic Research, Memorial University.

Pearson, David. 2001. *The Politics of Ethnicity in Settler Societies*. London: Palgrave Macmillan.

Pecoud, Antoine, and Paul de Guchteneire. 2005. *Global Migration Perspectives*. No 27. Switzerland: Global Commission on International Migration.

Pecoud, Antoine, and Martin Geiger (eds.). 2010. *The New Politics of Migration Management. Actors, Discourses, and Practices*. New York: Springer.

Pendakur, Krishna. 2005. *Visible Minorities in Canada's Workplaces: A Perspective on the 2017 Projection*. Vancouver: Metropolis Project.

Pendakur, Krishna, and Ravi Pendakur. 2004. *Colour My World: Has the Majority–Minority Earnings Gap Changed over Time?* Working Paper No. 04-11. Research on immigration and integration in the metropolis. Vancouver: Vancouver Centre of Excellence.

Pendakur, Krishna, and Ravi Pendakur. 2011. *"Color by Numbers: Minority Earnings in Canada 1995–2005." Journal of International Migration and Integration* 12(3):305-329.

Pendakur, Ravi. 2000. *Immigrants and the Labour Force: Policy, Regulation, and Impact*. Montreal/Kingston: McGill-Queen's University Press.

Penslar, Derek J. 2005. "Introduction," in *Contemporary Antisemitism: Canada and the World*. D.J. Penslar (ed.). Toronto: University of Toronto Press.

Perigoe, Ross. 2006. *Muslims and Media*. Paper presented at the Congress, York University, Toronto, Ontario, May.

Perkel, Colin. 2008. "Highly Educated but Poorly Paid." *The Globe and Mail*, 1 May.

Perlmutter, David. 2000. *Policing the Media: Street Cops and Public Perception of Law Enforcement*. Thousand Oaks CA: Sage.

Perreaux, Les. 2010. "The Face of Quebec Revealed in Niqab Debate." *The Globe and Mail*, 20 March.

Perry, Alex, and Laura Blue. 2008. "The Demons That Still Haunt Africa." *Time Magazine*, January.

Peter, K. 1978. "Multi-cultural Politics, Money, and the Conduct of Canadian Ethnic Studies." *Canadian Ethnic Studies Association Bulletin, 5*, 2–3.

Peters, Evelyn. 2001. "Geographies of Aboriginal People in Canada." *Canadian Geographer, 45*(1), 138–144.

Peters, Evelyn, 2004. *Three Myths about Aboriginals in Cities. Breakfast on the Hill Seminar Series (25 March)*. Ottawa: Canadian Federation for the Humanities and Social Sciences.

Petrou, Michael and Luiza Ch. Savage. 2006. "Genocide in Slow Motion." *Maclean's*, 11 December.

Pew Forum on Religion and Public Life. 2007. *U.S. Religious Landscape Survey: Report 1: Religious Affiliation*. Available online at **http://religions.pewforum.org/reports**

Philip, M. Nourbese. 1996. "How White Is Your White?" *Borderlines, 37*, 19–24.

Phillips, Anne. 2007. *Multiculturalism without Culture*. Princeton, NJ: Princeton University Press.

Picard, Andre. 2005. "Health's a Black and White Issue: Colour-Blindness Is Killing Minorities." *The Globe and Mail*, 12 February.

Picca, Leslie Houts, and Joe Feagin. 2007. *Two-Faced Racism: Whites in the Backstage and the Frontstage*. New York: Routledge.

Piche Victor. 2010. *Global Migration Management or the Emergence of a New Restrictive and Repressive Migration World Order*. International Workshop—Institute for Migration and Intercultural Studies. University of Osnabruck, Germany, 13 November.

Pickering, Michael. 2001. *Stereotypes: The Politics of Representation*. New York: Palgrave.

Picot, G., F. Hou, and S. Coulombe. 2007. *Chronic Low Income and Low-Income Dynamics among Recent Immigrants*. Analytical Studies Branch

Research Paper Series 2007(294). Ottawa: Statistics Canada.

Pieterse, Jan Nederveen. 2007. *Ethnicities and Global Multiculture*. Lantham, MD: Rowman and Littlefield.

Pinker, Susan. 2008. *The Sexual Paradox: Extreme Men, Gifted Women and the Real Gender Gap*. Toronto: Random House.

Piper, Nicola. 2008. "International Migration and Gendered Axes of Stratification: Introduction," in *New Perspectives on Gender and Migration*. N. Piper (ed.). Pp. 1–18. New York: Routledge.

Piper, Nicola. 2010. "Temporary Economic Migration and Rights Activism: An Organizational Perspective." *Ethnic and Racial Studies, 33*, 108–125.

Plaut, Rabbi W. Gunther. 1989. "Unwanted Intruders or People in Flight." *Perception, 13*(2), 45–46.

Ponting, J. Rick. 1986. *Arduous Journey: Canadian Indians and Decolonization*. Toronto: McClelland & Stewart.

Ponting, J. Rick. 1997. *First Nations in Canada: Perspectives on Opportunities, Empowerment, and Self-Determination*. Toronto: McGraw-Hill Ryerson.

Ponting, J. Rick, and Roger Gibbins. 1980. *Out of Irrelevance: A Socio-Political Introduction to Indian Affairs in Canada*. Toronto: Butterworths.

Porter, Henry. 2005. "It's Great Up North." *Guardian Weekly*, 2–8 December.

Porter, John. 1965. *The Vertical Mosaic*. Toronto: University of Toronto Press.

Porter, Robert Odawi. 2005. *Sovereignty, Colonialism and the Indigenous Nations: A Reader*. Durham, NC: Carolina Academic Press.

Possner, Michael. 1997. "A Battlefield Primer on Multiculturalism." *A Review*, 12 July.

Potter, Andrew. 2006. "One of These Things Is a Lot Like the Others." *Maclean's*, 11 December.

Price, Richard. 1991. *Legacy: Indian Treaty Relationships*. Edmonton: School of Native Studies, University of Alberta.

Proudfoot, Shannon. 2010. "Diversity Can Be Good for Big Cities." *Vancouver Sun*, 13 April.

Public Safety Canada. 2007. *Aboriginal Policing Update, 1*(2).

Public Service Alliance of Canada. 2010. *A Critical Analysis of the Annual Report on Employment Equity in the Federal Public Sector Service 2008–09*. Available online at **http://www.psac-afpc.org**

Purich, Donald. 1986. *Our Land: Native Peoples in Canada*. Toronto: James Lorimer and Sons.

Purvis, Andrew. 1999. "Whose Home and Native Land?" *Time*, 15 February: 16–26.

Putnam, Robert. 2007. "*E Pluribus Unum*: Diversity and Community in the Twenty-First Century." *Scandinavian Political Studies, 30*(2).

Qadeer, Mohammad A. 2007. "The Charter and Multiculturalism." *Policy Options* (February), 89–97.

Qadeer, Mohammad A., and Sandeep Agrawal. 2009. "Ethnic Enclaves Bloom Amid City Landscape." *Toronto Star*, 5 July.

Qadeer, M.A., S. Agrawal, and A. Lovell. 2009. *Evolution of Ethnic Enclaves in the Toronto Metropolitan Area 2001–06*. [PowerPoint presentation].

Quebec Human Rights Commission. 2011. *Racial Profiling and Its Consequences*. Quebec City: Author.

"Québec Souhaite Ouvrir Ses Portes à 200 000 Immigrants D'Ici 2015." 2011. *RadioCanada.ca*. Available online at **http://www.radio-canada.ca/nouvelles/National/2011/04/14/003-immigration-quebec-orientations.shtml**

R. v Bernard. 2005. SCC (Supreme Court of Canada).

R. v Marshall. 2005. SCC (Supreme Court of Canada).

Raboy, M. 1988. *Missed Opportunities: The Story of Canada's Broadcasting Policy*. Montreal/Kingston: McGill-Queen's University Press.

Rajagopal, Indhu. 2006. *Hidden Academics: Contract Faculty in Canadian Universities*. Toronto: University of Toronto Press.

Rajiva, Mythili. 2005. *Bridging the Generation Gap*. Available online at **http://canada.metropolis.net/pdfs/Rajiva_e.pdf**

Rajiva, Mythili, and Sheila Batacharya (eds). 2010. *Reena Virk: Critical Perspectives on a Canadian Murder*. Toronto: Canadian Scholars Press.

Ralston, Helen. 1999. "Canadian Immigration Policy in the Twentieth Century: Its Impact on South Asian Women." *Canadian Woman Studies, 19*(3), 33–37.

Ramirez, Judith. 2001. "Canada at Forefront in Gender Guidelines for Refugee Status." *Toronto Star*, 4 May.

Rankin, Jim. 2007. "Series Exposed an Immigration Scam." *Toronto Star*, 30 December.

Rankin, Jim, and Betsy Powell. 2008. "Why the Difference for Non-Whites?" *Toronto Star*, 21 July.

Ratcliffe, Peter. 2004. *"Race," Ethnicity, and Difference: Imagining the Inclusive Society*. New York: Open University Press.

Razack, Sherene. 1994. "What Is to Be Gained by Looking White People in the Eye? Culture, Race, and Gender in Cases of Sexual Violence." *Sign* (Summer), 894–922.

Razack, Sherene (ed.). 2002. *Race, Space, and the Law: Unmapping a White Settler Society*. Toronto: Between the Lines.

Razack, Sherene. 2004. *Dark Threats and White Knights: The Somalia Affair, Peacekeeping, and the New Imperialism*. Toronto: University of Toronto Press.

Redhead, Mark. 2003. "Charles Taylor's Deeply Diverse Response to Canada's Fragmentation: A Project Often Commented on but Seldom Explored." *Canadian Journal of Political Science, 36*(1), 61–83.

Refugees. 2007. "Refugee or Migrant?" Published by UNHCR #148 (2).

Reid, Scott. 1993. *Lament for a Notion: The Life and Death of Canada's Bilingual Dream*. Vancouver: Arsenal Pulp Press.

Reinhart, Anthony. 2007. "A Nation of Newcomers." *The Globe and Mail*. 5 December.

Reinhart, Anthony, and James Rusk. 2006. "Immigrants Suffer in Silence within Walls of Suburbs." *The Globe and Mail*, 11 March.

Reitman, Oonagh. 2005. "Multiculturalism and Feminism: Incompatibility, Compatibility, and Synonymity?" *Ethnicities, 5*(2), 216–247.

Reitz, Jeffrey. 1998. *Warmth of the Welcome: The Social Causes of Economic Success for Immigrants in Different Nations and Cities*. Boulder, CO: Westview Press.

Reitz, Jeffrey. 2005. "Tapping Immigrant Skills: New Directions for Canadian Immigration Policy in the Knowledge Economy." *IRRP Choices, 11*(1). Available online at **http://www.irpp.org/choices/archive/vol11no1.pdf**

Reitz, Jeffrey. 2009. "Assessing Multiculturalism as a Behavioural Theory," in Multiculturalism and Social Cohesion. J. Reitz et al. (eds.). Pp. 1–43. New York: Springer Science+Business Media.

Reitz, Jeffrey. 2010. "Selecting Immigrants for the Short Term: Is it Smart in the Long Run?" *Policy Options* (July/August).

Reitz, Jeffrey, and Rupa Banerjee. 2007. "Racial Inequality, Social Cohesion, and Policy Issues," in *Belonging?* K. Banting et al. (eds.). Pp. 489–546. Montreal: IRPP.

Reitz, Jeffrey, and Raymond Breton. 1994. *The Illusion of Difference: Realities of Ethnicity in Canada and the United States*. Toronto: CD Howe Institute.

Rensberger, Boyce. 1994. "The Case for One Race." *Toronto Star*, 24 December.

Report of the Commission of Inquiry into Systemic Racism in Ontario's Criminal Justice System. 1995. Toronto: Queen's Printer of Ontario.

Resnick, Philip. 2000. "Civic and Ethnic Nationalism: A Canadian Perspective," in *Canadian Political Thought*. Ron Beiner and Wayne Norman (eds.). Toronto: Oxford University Press.

Resnick, Philip. 2001. *The Politics of Resentment: British Columbia Regionalism and Canadian Unity*. Vancouver: UBC Press.

Rex, John. 2004. "Multiculturalism and Political Integration in the Modern Nation State." Documentos CIDOB, *Dinamicas Interculturales*. Numero Uno.

Rex, John, and Gurharpal Singh. 2004. *Governance in Multicultural Societies*. London, UK: Ashgate.

Reyna, Christine, A. Tucker, W. Korfmacher, and P.J. Henry. 2005. "Searching for Common Ground Between Supporters and Opponents of Affirmative Action." *Political Psychology, 26*(5), 667–681.

Ricard, Danielle, and Rima Wilkes. 2008. *Newspaper Framing of Protest by Indigenous Peoples and the Construction of National Identity*. Available online at **http://www.allacademic.com**

Richards, John, and M. Scott. 2009. *Aboriginal Education: Strengthening the Foundations*. Ottawa: Canadian Policy Research Networks.

Richer, Jocelyne. 2007. "Quebec Wants to Define Nation Status." *The Globe and Mail*, 7 August.

Rimmer, Alan. 1998. "PQ Win Means Return to the Referendum Debate." *Echo* (December), 3–9.

Ritzer, George. 2008. *The McDonaldization of Society* (5th ed.). Los Angeles: Pine Forge Press.

Roberts, Julian V., and Ronald Melchers. 2003. "The Incarceration of Aboriginal Offenders: Trends from 1978 to 2001." *Canadian Journal of Criminology and Criminal Justice, 45*(2), 1–18.

Roberts, Lance W., and Rodney A. Clifton. 1990. "Multiculturalism in Canada: A Sociological Perspective," in *Race and Ethnic Relations in Canada*, Peter S. Li (ed.). Pp. 20–147. Toronto: Oxford University Press.

Rocher, Francois, and Nadia Verrilli. 2003. "Questioning Constitutional Democracy in Canada: From the Canadian Supreme Court Reference on Quebec Secession to the Clarity Act," in *The Conditions of Diversity in Multinational Democracies*. A.-G. Gagnon et al. (eds.). Pp. 207–240. Montreal: IRRP.

Rodriguez, Ilia. 2009. "'Diversity Writing' and the Liberal Discourse on Multiculturalism in Mainstream Papers." *The Howard Journal of Communication, 20*, 167–188.

Rodriguez-Garcia, Dan. 2010. "Beyond Assimilation and Multiculturalism: A Critical Review of the Debate on Managing Diversity." *International Migration and Integration, 11*, 251–272.

Rolfsen, Catherine. 2008. "After the Apology." *This Magazine*, September/October.

Rooney, Frances. 2008. "Viola Desmond, Unintentional Revolutionary." 29 January. Available online at **http://section15.ca/features/people/2008/01/29/viola_desmond/**

Roscigno, Vincent, J.L. Garcia, S. Mong, and R. Byron. 2007. "Racial Discrimination at Work: Its Occurrence, Dimensions, and Consequences. The New Black, Alternative Paradigms and Strategies for the 21st Century." *Research in Race and Ethnic Relations, 14*, 111–135.

Roth, Lorna. 1998. "Television Broadcasting North of 60," in *Images of Canadianess*. L. d'Haenens (ed.). Pp. 147–166. Ottawa: University of Ottawa Press.

Rothenberg, Paula S. (ed.). 2001. *Race, Class, and Gender in the United States* (5th ed.). New York: Worth Publishers.

Rotman, Leonard Ian. 1996. *Parallel Paths: Fiduciary Doctrine and the Crown–Native Relationship in Canada*. Toronto: University of Toronto Press.

Rotman, Leonard. 2004. "Let Us Face It, We Are All Here to Stay. But Do We Negotiate or Litigate?" in *Advancing Aboriginal Claims*. Kerry Wilkins (ed.). Pp. 202–240. Saskatoon: Purich Publishing.

Royal Commission on Aboriginal Peoples. 1992. *Framing the Issues: Discussion Paper No 1*. Ottawa: Royal Commission on Aboriginal Peoples.

Royal Commission on Aboriginal Peoples. 1996a. *Final Report*. Volume One, Chapter 13, "Conclusions" section 1. Primary source: DCS 1920 HC Special Committee.

Royal Commission on Aboriginal Peoples. 1996b. *People to People, Nation to Nation: Highlights from the Report on the Royal Commission on Aboriginal Peoples*. Ottawa: Minister of Supply and Services Canada.

Ruddick, E. 2003. "Immigrant Economic Performance." *Canadian Issues, 5*, 16–17.

Rummel, R.J. 2005. *Genocide: Meaning and Definition*. Available online at **http://www.hawaii.edu/powerkills/GENOCIDE.ENCY.HTM**

Runnymede Trust. 2000. *The Future of Multi-Ethnic Britain: Report of the Commission on the Future of Multi-Ethnic Britain*. London, UK: Profile Books.

Rushowy, Kristin. 2001. "Native Students Return to Roots at School in the Heart of the City." *Toronto Star*, 15 October.

Rushton, J.P., and A.R. Jensen. 2005. "Thirty Years of Research on Race Differences in Cognitive Ability." *Psychology, Public Policy, and Law, 11*, 235–294.

Rushton, Philippe. 1994. *Race, Evolution, and Behavior: A Life History Perspective*. New York: Transaction.

Rushton, Philippe. 1995. *Race, Evolution, and Behavior: A Life History Perspective*. New Brunswick, NJ: Transaction.

Rusk, James. 2005. "Conditions on Reserve 'Atrocious' Doctor Says." *The Globe and Mail*, 24 October.

Russell, Peter. 2005. *Recognizing Aboriginal Title: The Mabo Case and Indigenous Resistance to English-Settler Colonialism*. Toronto: University of Toronto Press.

RVH (Racism, Violence, and Health) Project. 2002/3. *Racism Makes You Sick—It's a Deadly Disease*. Halifax: Dalhousie University.

Ryan, Phil. 2010. *Multicultiphobia*. Toronto: University of Toronto Press.

Sajoo, Amyn B. 1994. "New Dances with Diversity." *Policy Options* (December), 14–19.

Salee, Daniel. 2003. "Transformative Politics: The State and the Politics of Social Change in

Quebec," in *Changing Canada: Political Economy as Transformation*. Wallace Clement and Leah Vosko (eds.). Pp. 25–50. Montreal: McGill/Queen's University Press.

Salee, Daniel, and William Coleman. 1997. "The Challenges of the Quebec Question: Paradigm, Counter-Paradigm, and the Nation-State," in *Understanding Canada*. W. Clement (ed.). Montreal/Kingston: McGill-Queen's University Press.

Saloojee, Anver. 2005. *Social Inclusion, Anti-racism, and Democratic Citizenship*. CERIS/Metropolis. *Policy Matters* (January).

Sammel, Ali. 2009. "Turning the Focus from 'Other' to Science Education. Exploring the Invisibility of Whiteness." *Springerlink*. Available online at **http://blogs.springer.com**

Samson, Colin. 2003. *A Way of Life That Does Not Exist: Canada and the Extinguishment of the Innu*. St. John's: ISER Books.

Samuel, Edith. 2006. *Integrative Antiracism: South Asians in Canadian Academe*. Toronto: University of Toronto Press.

Samuel, Edith, and Shehla Burney. 2003. "Racism, Eh? Interactions of South Asian Students with Mainstream Faculty in a Predominantly White Canadian University." *The Canadian Journal of Higher Education, 33*(2), 81–103.

Sandercock, Leonie. 2003. *Rethinking Multiculturalism for the 21st Century*. Working Paper No. 03-14. Research on Immigration and Integration in the Metropolis. Vancouver: Vancouver Centre of Excellence.

Sandercock, Leonie. 2006. *Mongrel Cities of the 21st Century: In Defense of Multiculturalism*. UBC Laurier Lecture.

Sarich, Vincent, and Frank Miele. 2004. *Race: The Reality of Human Differences*. Boulder, CO: Westview Press.

Sarick, Lila. 1999. "Serbian Community Feeling Betrayed." *The Globe and Mail*, 8 May.

Satzewich, Vic (ed.). 1998. *Racism and Social Inequality in Canada*. Toronto: Thompson Education.

Satzewich, Vic. 2000. "Whiteness Limited: Racialization and the Social Construction of 'Peripheral Europeans.'" *Histoire sociale/Social History, 23*, 271–290.

Satzewich, Vic. 2004. "Racism in Canada: Change and Continuity." *Canadian Dimensions* (January/February), 20.

Satzewich, Vic. 2007. "Whiteness Studies: Race, Diversity, and the New Essentialism," in *Race and Racism in 21st Century Canada*. S.P. Hier and B.S. Bolaria (eds.). Pp. 67–84. Peterborough, ON: Broadview Press.

Satzewich, Vic. 2011. *Racism in Canada*. Toronto: Oxford University Press.

Satzewich, Vic, and Nikolaos Liodakis. 2010. *"Race" and Ethnicity in Canada: A Critical Introduction* (2nd ed.). Toronto: Oxford University Press.

Satzewich, Vic, and William Shaffir. 2007/9. *Racism versus Professionalism: Claims and Counter-claims about Racial Profiling*. Paper presented to the Immigration, Minorities, and Multiculturalism in Democracies Conference, Montreal, October 24–27. Subsequently published in *Canadian Journal of Criminology and Criminal Justice* in April 2009.

Satzewich, Vic, and Lloyd Wong (eds.). 2006. *Transnational Identities and Practices in Canada*. Vancouver: University of British Columbia Press.

Saul, John Ralston. 1998. *Reflections of a Siamese Twin: Canada at the End of the Twentieth Century*. Toronto: Penguin.

Saunders, Barbara, and David Haljan (eds.). 2003. *Wither Multiculturalism? A Politics of Dissensus*. Leuven, BE: Leuven University Press.

Saunders, Doug. 2004. "Sacrificing Freedom for Equality." *The Globe and Mail*, 4 September.

Sauvageau, Florian, David Schneiderman, and David Taras. 2006. *The Last Word. Media Coverage of the Supreme Court of Canada*. Vancouver: UBC Press.

Savard, P., and B. Vignezzi. 1999. *Multiculturalism and the History of International Relations from the 18th Century Up to the Present*. Ottawa: Carleton University Press.

Sawchuk, Joe. 1998. *The Dynamics of Native Politics: The Alberta Métis Perspective*. Saskatoon: SK Publishing.

SBS (Special Broadcasting Service). 2008. "Multicultural Australia: A Nation of Paradoxes—Study Finds." [Press release].

Schachar, Ayelet. 2005. "Religion, State, and the Problem of Gender: Re-Imagining Citizenship and Governance in Diverse Societies." *McGill Law Journal, 50*, 49–88.

Schaller, Mark. 2004. "Terrorism in Youth." *Westcoast News*, 22 July.

Schellenberg, Grant, and Feng Hou. 2005. "The Economic Well-Being of Recent Immigrants to Canada." *Canadian Issues* (Spring), 49–52.

Schellenberg, Grant, and Helene Maheux. 2007. "Immigrants Perspectives on Their First Four Years in Canada." *Canadian Social Trends*, Catalogue no. 11-008. Ottawa: Statistics Canada.

Scheurich, J.J., and M.D. Young. 2002. "White Racism among White Faculty," in *The Racial Crisis in American Higher Education*. W.A. Smith, P.G. Altbach, and K. Lomotey (eds.). Pp. 221–239. Albany, NY: State University of New York.

Schick, Carol. 2008. "Keeping the Ivory Tower White: Discourses of Racial Domination," in *Rethinking Society in the 21st Century: Critical Readings in Sociology*. Michelle Webber (ed.). Markham, ON: IPP.

Schick, Carol, and Verna St. Denis. 2005. "Troubling National Discourses in Anti-racist Curriculum Planning." *Canadian Journal of Education*, *28*(3), 295–317.

Schlein, Lisa. 2005. "Disparity between Native and Non-Native Canadians Highlighted in UN Report." *Toronto Star*, 11 April.

Schlesinger, Arthur M., Jr. 1992. *The Disuniting of America: Reflections on a Multicultural Society*. New York: W.W. Norton.

Schoenfeld, Gabriel. 2004. *The Return of Anti-Semitism*. San Francisco: Encounter Books.

Schouls, Tim. 1997. "Aboriginal Peoples and Electoral Reform in Canada: Differentiated Representation versus Voter Equality." *Canadian Journal of Political Science, 24*(4), 729–749.

Scott, Craig. 1996. "Indigenous Self-Determination and the Decolonization of the International Imagination." *Human Rights Quarterly* 18: 815–820.

Scott, James C. 1998. *Seeing Like a State*. Princeton, NJ: Yale University Agrarian Press.

Scott, Marion. 2009. "Refugees to Canada in Catch-22 Situation." *Montreal Gazette*, 26 November.

See, Katherine, and William J. Wilson. 1988. "Race and Ethnicity," in *Handbook of Sociology*, Neil J. Smelzer (ed.). Pp. 223–242. Newbury Park: Sage.

Seguin, Rheal. 2001. "View of Language Laws Seen as Racist." *The Globe and Mail*, 26 March.

Seib, Philip. 2004/2005. "The Newsmedia and the Clash of Civilizations." *Parameters* (Winter).

Seidle, F. Leslie. 2007a. *Citizenship Rule and Naturalization Rates*. Paper prepared for the Bouchard-Taylor Commission on Reasonable Accommodation. 15 June.

Seidle, Leslie. 2007b. *Diversity, Recognition, and Shared Citizenship in Canada*. Paper presented to the Roundtable: The Future of Multiculturalism—A German-Canadian Debate. Berlin. 29 March.

Seiler, Tamara Palmer. 2002. "Thirty Years Later: Reflections on the Evolution and Future Prospects of Multiculturalism." *Canadian Issues* (February), 6–8.

Seljak, David. 2009. *Dialogue among the Religions in Canada*. Ottawa: Policy Research Initiative, Government of Canada.

Sellers, Frances Stead. 2005. "Multiculturalism." *Kitchener-Waterloo Record*, 25 August.

Semyonov, M., R. Raijman, and A. Gorodzeisky. 2008. "Foreigners' Impact on European Societies: Public Views and Perceptions in a Cross-National Comparative Perspective." *International Journal of Comparative Sociology, 49*(1), 5–29.

Sen, Amartya. 2006. *Identity and Violence: The Illusion of Destiny*. New York: W.W. Norton.

Senate Standing Committee on Human Rights. 2010. *Reflecting the Changing Face of Canada. Employment Equity in the Federal Public Service*.

SES Canada Research. 2003. "No Welcome Mat for Refugees without ID: Ontarians Want Refugees with False ID Sent Home." [Press release]. Available online at **http://www.sesresearch.com/news/press_releases/PR%20March%207%202003.pdf**

Shakir, Uzma. 2010. *Canada's Immigration Fall from Grace*. Toronto: Atkinson Charitable Foundation.

Shapiro, Thomas M. 2004. *Racial Inequality: The Hidden Cost of Being African-American*. New York: Oxford University Press.

Sheehy, Elizabeth. 2010. "Misogyny Is Deadly: Inequality Makes Women More Vulnerable to Being Killed." *Canadian Centre for Policy Alternatives Newsletter* (July/August).

Shipler, David K. 2001. "A Conflict's Bedrock Is Laid Bare." *New York Times*, 27 May.

Shkilnyk, Anastasia M. 1985. *A Poison Stronger Than Love*. New Haven, CT: Yale University Press.

Shoemaker, Pamela J., and Akiba A. Cohen. 2006. *News around the World*. New York: Routledge.

Shohat, Ella, and Robert Stam. 1994. *Unthinking Eurocentrism: Multiculturalism and the Media.* New York: Routledge.

Showler, Peter. 2005. "Refugee Laws Are Not the Problem." *The Globe and Mail*, 29 April.

Showler, Peter. 2009. "Fast, Fair, and Final: Reforming Canada's Refugee Sysytem." Toronto: Maytree Foundation.

Siddiqui, Haroon. 2007. "Don't Scapegoat Multiculturalism." *Toronto Star*, 10 June.

Siddiqui, Haroon. 2008. "In Quebec, Equality for Minorities Just Talk." *Toronto Star*, 25 May.

Siddiqui, Haroon. 2010. "Ranting from the right Deafens Canadians to Success of Pluralism." *Toronto Star*, 24 October.

Siemiatycki, Myer. 2005. "Introduction." *Canadian Issues* (Spring), 3–4.

Siemiatycki, Myer. 2010. "Marginalizing Migrants: Canada's Rising Reliance on Temporary Foreign Workers." *Canadian Issues* (Spring), 60–63.

Silk, Mark. 2008. "Islam and the American News Media Post-September 11." in Mediating Religion. J. Mitchell and S. Marriage (eds.). Pp. 73–88. New York: T and T Clark.

Silverberg, Christine. 2004. "After Stonechild: Rebuilding Trust." *The Globe and Mail*, 20 October.

Simeon, Richard, and Ian Robinson. 2004. "The Dynamics of Canadian Federalism," in *Canadian Politics.* J. Bickerton and A.-G. Gagnon (eds.). Peterborough, ON: Broadview Press.

Simmons, Alan. 2010. *Immigration and Canada. Global and Transnational Perspectives.* Toronto: Canadian Scholars' Press.

Simpson, Jeffrey. 2000. "Waiting for the Right Immigration Bill." *The Globe and Mail*, 2 April.

Simpson, Jeffrey. 2005. "There's a Lesson for All of Us from the Sharia Issue." *The Globe and Mail*, 14 September.

Sinha, Shalini. 2006. "Generating Awareness for the Experiences of Women of Colour in Ireland," in *Racism and Anti-racism in Ireland.* R. Lentin and R. McVeigh (eds.). Belfast, IE: Beyond the Pale Publications.

Sirna, Tony. 1996. "Creating a 'Society of Communities.'" *Communities Journal for Cooperative Living*, 50–53.

Sissons, Jeffrey. 2005. *First Peoples: Indigenous Cultures and Their Futures.* London: Reaktion Books.

Sivanandan, A. 2007. "Foreword," in *The End of Tolerance.* A. Kundnani (ed.). London, UK: Pluto Press.

Sivanandan, A. 2009. "Foreword," in *A Suitable Enemy.* L. Fekete (ed.). London, UK: Pluto Press.

Skidelsky, Robert. 2004. "The Killing Fields." *New Statesman*, 26 January.

Slattery, Brian. 1997. "Recollection of Historical Practice," in *Justice for Natives: Search for a Common Ground.* Andrea P. Morrison (ed.). Pp 76–82. Montreal/Kingston: McGill-Queen's University Press.

Small, Stephen. 2002. "Racisms and Racialized Hostility at the Start of the New Millenium," in *A Companion to Racial and Ethnic Studies.* D.T. Goldberg and J. Solomos (eds.). Pp. 259–281. Malden, MA: Blackwell.

Smith, Anthony D. 1993. "The Problem of Nationalist Identity: Ancient, Medieval, or Modern." *Ethnic and Race Relations.*

Smith, Anthony D. 1996. "LSE Centennial Lecture: The Resurgence of Nationalism? Myth and Memory in the Renewal of Nations." *British Journal of Sociology, 47*(4), 1–16.

Smith, D.E. 1999. *Writing the Social: Critique, Theory, and Investigations.* Toronto: University of Toronto Press.

Smith, Ekuwa. 2004. *Nowhere to Turn? Responding to Partner Violence against Immigrant and Visible Minority Women.* Ottawa: Canadian Council of Social Development.

Smolash, Wendy Naava. 2009. "Mark of Cain(ada). Racialized Security Discourse in Canada's National Papers." *University of Toronto Quarterly, 78*(2), 1–15.

Snyder, Jack L. 2000. *From Voting to Violence: Democratization and Nationalist Conflict.* New York: W.W. Norton.

Solomos, John, and Les Back. 1996. *Racism and Society.* London: Macmillan.

Solomos, John, and Martin Bulmer. 2005. *Researching Race and Racism.* New York: Routledge.

Soroka, Stuart, Richard Johnston, and Keith Banting. 2006. *Ties that Bind? Social Cohesion and Diversity in Canada.* Montreal: Institute for Research on Public Policy.

Sowell, Thomas. 2004. *Affirmative Action around the World: An Empirical Study.* New Haven, CT: Yale University Press.

Spencer, Sarah. 2003. "Introduction." *The Political Quarterly* (Special Issue), 1–24.

Spoonley, Paul. 1993. *Racism and Ethnicity in New Zealand*. Auckland, NZ: Oxford University Press.

Spoonley, Paul. 2005. "Multicultural Challenges in a Bicultural New Zealand." *Canadian Diversity* 4(1): 19–22

Spoonley, Paul. 2010. "Rethinking Immigration." Wellington: Asia New Zealand Foundation.

Spoonley, Paul, and Andrew Butcher. 2009. "Reporting Superdiversity: The Mass Media and Immigration in New Zealand." *Journal of Intercultural Studies, 30*(4), 355–372.

Squires, Judith. 2007a. "Negotiating Equality and Diversity in Britain: Towards a Differentiated Citizenship." *Critical Review of International Social and Political Philosophy, 10*(4), 531–559.

Squires, Judith. 2007b. *The New Politics of Gender Equality*. New York: Palgrave Macmillan.

Stam, R., and T. Miller. 2000. "Black America Cinema," in *Film and Theory: An Anthology*. R. Stam and T. Miller (eds.). Pp. 236–256. Oxford: Blackwell.

Stam, R., and E. Shohat. 1994. "Contested Histories: Eurocentrism, Multiculturalism, and the Media," in *Multiculturalism: A Critical Reader*. D.T. Goldberg (ed.). Pp. 296–324. Cambridge, MA: Blackwell.

Starck, Kenneth. 2007. *Perpetuating Prejudice or Merely Telling a Story? Media Portrayal of Arabs in the United States*. Paper presented to the Media-Migration-Integration Conference at the University of Dortmund, Germany, 22 June.

Stasiulis, Daiva K. 1990. "Theorizing Connections: Gender, Race, Ethnicity, and Class," in *Race and Ethnic Relations in Canada*. Peter S. Li (ed.). Pp. 69–305. Toronto: Oxford University Press.

Stasiulis, Daiva K. 1999. "Feminist Intersectional Theorizing" in *Race and Ethnic Relations in Canada* (2nd ed.). Peter Li (ed.). Pp. 347–397. Toronto: Oxford University Press.

Stasiulis, Daiva K., and Abigail B. Bakan. 1997. "Negotiating Citizenship: The Case of Foreign Domestic Workers in Canada." *Feminist Review, 57*, 112–139.

Statistical Analyis Unit. 2010. *Impact of the Employment Equity Act and the CHRC Employment Equity Program over the Years*. March.

Statistics Canada. 2002. *Ethnic Diversity Study*. Available online at **http://www.statcan.gc.ca/cgi-bin/imdb/p2SV.pl?Function=getSurvey&SDDS=4508&lang=en&db=imdb&adm=8&dis=2**

Statistics Canada. 2003. "Low-Income Rates among Immigrants." *The Daily*, 19 June. Available online at **http://www.statcan.gc.ca/daily-quotidien/030619/dq030619a-eng.htm**

Statistics Canada. 2005a. "Women in Canada: A Gender-Based Statistical Report." Catalogue No. 89–503 XIE.

Statistics Canada. 2005b. "Readmission to Saskatchewan Correctional Services among Aboriginal and Non-Aboriginal Adults, 1999/2000 to 2003/2004." *The Daily*, June 3. Catalogue No. 85-002-XIE20050028411.

Statistics Canada. 2006a. "Immigration in Canada: A Portrait of the Foreign-born Population, 2006 Census: Findings." Available online at **http://www12.statcan.ca/english/census06/analysis/immcit/ index.cfm**

Statistics Canada. 2006b. "Measuring Violence against Women: Statistical Trends." Catalogue No. 85-570.

Statistics Canada. 2007. "Study: Low-Income Rates among Immigrants Entering Canada." *The Daily*, 30 January.

Statistics Canada. 2008. "Aboriginal Peoples in Canada in 2006: Inuit, Métis, and First Nations, 2006 Census." Available online at **http://www12.statcan.ca/english/census06/analysis/aboriginal/index.cfm**

Status of Women Canada. 2007. *Gendering Canada's Refugee Process*. Available online at **http://www.swc-cfc.gc.ca/pubs/pubspr/0662435621/ index_e.html**

Steele, Shelby. 2006. *White Guilt*. New York: HarperCollins.

Stein, Janice Gross. 2007. "Religion versus the Charter." *University of Toronto Magazine* (Winter). Available online at **http://www.magazine.utoronto.ca/07winter/stein.asp**

Stein, Janice, David Robertson Cameron, John Ibbitson, Will Kymlicka, John Meisel, Haroon Siddiqui, and Michael Valpy. 2007. *Uneasy Partners, Multiculturalism and Rights in Canada*. Waterloo, ON: Wilfrid Laurier Press.

Steinberg, Stephan. 1989. *The Ethnic Myth: Race, Ethnicity, and Class in America* (2nd ed.). New York: Athenium.

Stepan, Nancy. 1982. *The Idea of Race in Science: Great Britain, 1800–1960*. London: Macmillan Press.

Sternberg, Robert J., and Elena Grigorenko. 1997. *Intelligence, Heredity, and Environment*. New York: Columbia University Press.

Steyn, Mark. 2006. "Keepin' It Real is Real Stupid." *Maclean's*, 2 October: 58–59.

Stocking, George. 1968. *History of Anthropological Theory*. New York: Free Press.

Stoffman, Daniel. 1997. "Making Room for Real Refugees." *International Journal* (Autumn), 575–581.

Stoffman, Daniel. 2002. *Who Gets In: What's Wrong with Canada's Immigration Program —and How to Fix It*. Toronto: McClelland & Stewart.

Stoffman, Daniel. 2003. "The Mystery of Canada's High Immigration Levels." *Canadian Issues* (April), 23–24.

Stoffman Daniel. 2008. "Truths and Myths about Immigration," in *Immigration Policy and the Terrorist Threat in Canada and the United States*. A. Moens and M. Collacott (eds). Pp. 3–21. Calgary: Fraser Institute.

Stoffman, Daniel. 2009. Are We Safe Yet? *The Walrus*. May.

Stokes, J., I. Peach, and R. Blake. 2004. *Rethinking the Jurisdictional Divide: The Marginalization of Urban Aboriginal Communities and Federal Policy Responses*. Public Policy Paper 28. Regina: Saskatchewan Institute of Public Policy.

Strategic Council. 2008. "A Report to *The Globe and Mail* and CTV: Attitudes Towards Canada's Growing Visible Minority Population." Toronto: Strategic Council.

Strauss, Julian. 2005. "Can They Build a Future?" *The Globe and Mail*, 28 October.

Strauss, Julian. 2006. "Is the Canadian Model for Relations with Aboriginals Beyond Repair?" *The Globe and Mail*, 16 January.

Suarez-Orozco, Carola, and Marcelo M. Suarez-Orozco. 2001. *Children of Immigration*. Cambridge, MA: Harvard University Press.

Sue, Derald Wing. 2003. *Overcoming Racism: The Journey to Liberation*. San Francisco: John Wiley and Sons.

Sun Media. 2007. "Racial Tolerance Report." Leger Marketing. January.

Surette, Ray. 2007. *Media Crimes and Criminal Justice: Images and Realities* (2nd ed.). Toronto: Wadsworth.

Suro, Roberto. 2008. *The Triumph of No: How the Media Influence the Immigration Debate*. A report by Governance Studies at the Brookings Institution and the Norman Lear Center at USC-Annenberg, 2008, Washington, DC.

Suro, Roberto. 2009. *Promoting Misconceptions. News Media Coverage of Immigration*. Los Angeles, CA: Centre for the Study of Immigrant Integration, University of Southern California.

Swain, Carole. 2002. *The New White Nationalism in America*. Cambridge: Cambridge University Press.

Swain, Carole. (ed.). 2007. *Debating Immigration*. New York: Cambridge University Press.

Swan, Michael. 2011. "Ethnic Vote Takes Harper to the Promised Land." *Catholic Register*, 3 May.

Switzer, Maurice. 1997. "The Canadian Media Have Declared Open Season on Indians." *Aboriginal Voices* (December): 8.

Sykes, Stuart. 2008. *A Story of Reefs and Oceans: A Framework for the Analysis of the "New" Second Generation in Canada*. Discussion Paper. Ottawa: Policy Research Initiative.

Tanovich, David M. 2006. *The Colour of Justice: Policing Race in Canada*. Toronto: Irwin Law.

Taras, Raymond C., and Rajat Ganguly. 2002. *Understanding Ethnic Conflict: The International Dimension* (3rd ed.). Montreal: Longman.

Taras, Raymond C., and Rajat Ganguly. 2009. *Understanding Ethnic Conflict: The International Dimension* (4th ed.). Montreal: Longman.

Tastsoglou, E., and V. Preston. 2006. "Gender, Immigration, and the Labour Market: Where We Are and What We Still Need to Know." *Ceris Policy Matters, 18*.

Tastsoglou, E., B. Ray, and V. Preston. 2005. "Gender and Migration Intersections in a Canadian Context." *Canadian Issues* (Spring), 91–93.

Tator, Carol, and Francis Henry. 2006. *Racial Profiling in Canada: Challenging the Myth of a Few Bad Apples*. Toronto: University of Toronto Press.

Tatum, Dale C. 2010. *Genocide at the Dawn of the 21st Century*. New York: Palgrave Macmillan.

Taylor, Charles. 1993. "The Deep Challenge of Dualism," in *Quebec: State and Society* (2nd ed.). A.-G. Gagnon (ed.). Pp. 82–95. Toronto: Nelson.

Taylor, Leanne, Carl James, and Roger Saul. 2007. "Who Belongs? Exploring Race and Racialization in Canada," in *Race, Racialization, and Anti-racism in Canada and Beyond*. G.F. Johnson and R. Enomoto (eds.). Pp. 151–178. Toronto: University of Toronto Press.

Taylor, Lesley Ciarula. 2009. "Best Immigrants Not a Priority." *Toronto Star*, 22 July.

Taylor, Peter Shawn. 2005. "Help Wanted." *Canadian Business* (March 14–27), 29–34.

Teelucksingh, Cheryl (ed.). 2006. *Claiming Space: Racialization in Canadian Cities*. Waterloo, ON: Wilfrid Laurier Press.

Teelucksingh, Cheryl, and Grace-Edward Galabuzi. 2005. *Working Precariously: The Impact of Race and Immigrant Status on Employment Opportunities and Outcomes in Canada*. Toronto: Canadian Race Relations Foundation.

Temelini, Michael. 2007. "Multicultural Rights, Multicultural Virtues: A History of Multicultur-alism in Canada," in *Multiculturalism and the Canadian Constitution*. S. Tierney (ed.). Vancouver: UBC Press.

Tepper, Elliot L. 1988. *Changing Canada: The Institutional Response to Polyethnicity: The Review of Demography and Its Implications for Economic and Social Policy*. Ottawa: Carleton University.

ter Wal, Jessika, Leen d' Haenans, and Joyce Koe-man. 2005. "(Re)presentation of Ethnicity in EU and Dutch Domestic Views: A Quantitive Analysis." *Media, Culture, and Society, 27*(6), 937–950.

Thobani, Sunera. 1995. "Multiculturalism: The Poli-tics of Containment," in *Social Problems in Canada Reader*. E. Nelson and A. Fleras (eds.). Pp. 213–216. Toronto: Prentice-Hall.

Thobani, Sunera. 2000a. "Closing Ranks: Racism and Sexism in Canada's Immigration Policy." *Race & Class, 42*(1), 35–55.

Thobani, Sunera. 2000b. "Closing the Nation's Doors to Immigrant Women: The Restructuring of Canadian Immigration Policy." *Atlantis, 24*(2), 16–29.

Thobani, Sunera. 2007. *Exalted Subjects: Studies in the Making of Race and Nation in Canada*. Toronto: University of Toronto Press.

Thomas, Derrick. 2001. "Evolving Family Arrange-ments of Canada's Immigrants." *Canadian Social Trends* (Summer), 16–19.

Thomas, Derrick. 2010. *Foreign Nationals Working Temporarily in Canada*. Ottawa: Statistics Canada.

Thomas, James M. 2007. "Re-Upping the Contract with Sociology: Charles Mill's Racial Contract Revisited a Decade Later." *Sociology Compass, 1*(1), 255–264.

Thomas, Robyn, Albert J. Mills, and Jean Helms Mills. 2004. *Identity Politics at Work: Resisting Gender, Gendering Resistance*. New York: Routledge.

Thompson, Allan. 2001. "Minister Defends Refugee System." *Toronto Star*, 15 September.

Thompson, Allan. 2005. "Immigration in Dire Need of Overhaul." *Toronto Star*, 22 January.

Thompson, Allan. 2006. "Time to Take a Look at Selection Process Flaws." *Toronto Star*, 11 March.

Thompson, Allan, John Herd, and Morton Weinfeld. 1995. "Entry and Exit: Canadian Immigration Policy in Context." *Annals of the American Academy AAPSS, 538* (March), 185–198.

Tierney, Stephen (ed.). 2007. *Multiculturalism and the Canadian Constitution*. Vancouver: UBC Press.

Tishkov, Valery. 2004. *Chechnya: Life in a War Torn Society*. Berkeley: University of California Press.

Toronto Board of Trade. 2010. *Lifting All Boats. Promoting Social Cohesion and Economic Inclusion in the Toronto Region*. Toronto: Author.

Tran, Kelly, Stan Kustec, and Tina Chui. 2005. "Becoming Canadian: Intent, Process, and Out-come." *Canadian Social Trends* (Spring), 8–10.

Transatlantic Trends. 2010. *Immigration 2010: Key Findings*. Washington, DC: Author.

Travers, James. 2005. "Her Story Not Today's Story." *Toronto Star*, 6 August.

Treasury Board of Canada Secretariat. 2010. *Employment Equity in the Public Service of Canada, 2008–09*. Available online at **http://www.tbs.sct.gc.ca**

Trepagnier, Barbara. 2007. *Silent Racism*. Boulder, CO: Paradigm.

Tully, James. 1995. *Strange Multiplicity: Constitu-tionalism in an Age of Diversity*. Cambridge: Cambridge University Press.

Turner, Bryan S. 2006. "Citizenship and the Crisis of Multiculturalism: Review Article." *Citizenship Studies, 10*(5), 607–618.

Turner, Dale. 2006. *This Is Not a Peace Pipe*. Toronto: University of Toronto Press.

Turton, Anthony R. 2007. *Governance as a Trialogue: Government-Society-Science in Transition*. New York: Springer.

Tushnet, Mark. 2003. *The New Constitutional Order.* Princeton, NJ: Princeton University Press.

Tyyska, Vappu. 2008. *Youth and Society. The Long and Winding Road* (2nd ed.). Toronto: Canadian Scholars' Press.

Ubelacker Sheryl. 2010. "Accessing Care a Challenge for Minority Women." *The Globe and Mail*, 30 March.

Ucarer, Emek M. 1997. "Introduction: The Coming of an Era of Human Uprootedness: A Global Challenge," in *Immigration into Western Societies: Problems and Policies.* E.M. Ucarer and D.J. Puchala (eds.). Pp. 1–16. London: Cassells.

Uitermark, J., U. Rossi, and H. van Houtum. 2005. "Multiculturalism, Urbanization, and Citizenship: Negotiation of Ethnic Diversity in Amsterdam." *International Journal of Urban and Regional Research, 29*(3), 622–640.

Ujimoto, K. Victor. 2000. "Multiculturalism, Ethnic Identity, and Inequality," in *Social Issues and Contradictions in Canadian Society.* B. Singh Bolaria (ed.). Pp. 228–247. Toronto: Harcourt Brace.

United Nations. 2006. *The Concept of Reasonable Accommodation in Selected National Disability Legislation.* Prepared by the Ad Hoc Committee on a Comprehensive and Integral International Convention on the Protection and Promotion of the Rights and Dignities of Persons with Disabilities. Available online at **http://www.un.org/esa/socdev/enable/rights/ahc7bkgrndra.htm**

United Nations. 2007. *Concluding Observations of the Committee on the Elimination of Racial Discrimination: Canada.* CERD. Convention for the Elimination of all Forms of Racial Discrimination.

United Nations. 2010. *15 Years of the United Nations Special Rapporteur on Violence Against Women (1994–2009). A Critical Review.* Available online at **http://www2.ohchr.org/english/issues/women/rapporteur/docs/15YearReviewofVAWMandate.pdf**

United Nations Development Programme. 2004. *Cultural Liberty in Today's Diverse World.* Summary: Human Development Report.

United Nations Development Programme. 2009. *Human Development Index.* New York: United Nations Development Programme.

United Nations High Commission for Refugees. 2008. *2007 Global Trends.* Paris: Author.

Valaskakis, Gail, Madeleine Dion Stout, and Eric Guimond (eds). 2009. *Restoring the Balance: First Nations Women, Community and Culture.* University of Manitoba Press.

Valpy, Michael. 2007. "Diversity Heading Down a Rough Road, Conference Told." *The Globe and Mail*, 13 August.

van den Berghe, Pierre. 1967. *Race and Racism.* New York: John Wiley & Sons.

van den Berghe, Pierre. 1981. *The Ethnic Phenomenon.* New York: Elsevier.

van Dijk Teun. 1991. *Racism and the Press.* New York: Routledge.

van Dijk, Teun. 1998. *Ideology: A Multidisciplinary Approach.* London, UK: Sage.

van Kerckhove, Carmen. 2009. *How to Respond to a Racist Joke.* Available online at **http://www.carmenvankerckhove.com**

Vasta, Ellie, and Stephen Castles. 1996. *The Teeth Are Smiling: The Persistence of Racism in a Multicultural Australia.* Sydney: Allen & Unwin.

Velez, William (ed.). 1998. *Race and Ethnicity in the United States: An Institutional Approach.* Dix Hills, NY: General Hall, Inc.

Venne, Michel (ed.). 2001. *Vive Quebec! New Thinking and New Approaches to the Quebec Nation.* Toronto: James Lorimer & Sons.

Venne, Sharon. 1998. "Analysis of Delgamuukw." *Internet*, 3 March.

Verkuyten, Maykel. 2007. "Social Psychology and Multiculturalism." *Social and Personality Psychology Compass, 1*(1), 280–297.

Vertovec, Steven. 2006. "Diasporas Good? Diasporas Bad?" *Metropolis World Bulletin, 6*, 5–8.

Vickers, Jill. 2002. *The Politics of "Race": Canada, Australia, the United States.* Ottawa: The Golden Dog Press.

Vickers, Jill, and Micheline de Seve. 2000. "Introduction." *Journal of Canadian Studies.* [Special edition devoted to nationalism and gender.]

Volpe, Joe. 2005. "Canada Needs More Skilled Immigrants, Minister Says." *Workpermit.com.* 29 April. Available online at **http://www.workpermit.com/news/2005_04_29/canada/canada_needs_recruiting_drive.htm**

Vukow, Tamara. 2003. "Imagining Communities through Immigration Policies. Government Regulation, Media Spectacles, and the Affective Politics of National Borders." International Journal of Cultural Studies, 6(3), 335–353.

Waldie, Paul. 1998. "More Refugees Sheltered in Canada by New Rules." *The Globe and Mail*, 14 November.

Waldron, Jeremy. 2002. *Indigeneity? First Peoples and Last Occupancy?* Paper presented to the Quentin-Baxter Memorial Lecture. Victoria University of Wellington NZ, 5 December.

Walker, James W. St. G. 1997. *"Race," Rights and the Law in the Supreme Court of Canada*. Waterloo, ON: Wilfred Laurier Press.

Walker, James. W. St. G. 2001a. "'Race' and Resistance in Nova Scotia, 1945–1970," in *Canada: Confederation to the Present*. R. Hesketh et al. (eds.). Edmonton: Chinook Multimedia.

Walker, James W. St. G. 2001b. *Routes of Diversity: Strategies for Change, 1945–1970*. A background paper prepared for the Multiculturalism Program, Department of Canadian Heritage.

Walkom, Thomas. 1998. "The Big Power Shift." *Toronto Star*, 5 December.

Walkom, Thomas. 2001. "Conflict at the Core." *Toronto Star*, 13 January.

Wallis, Maria, and Augie Fleras. 2008. *The Politics of Race in Canada*. Toronto: Oxford University Press.

Wallis, Maria, and Siu-Ming Kwok. 2008. *Daily Struggles: The Deepening Racialization and Feminization of Poverty in Canada*. Toronto: Canadian Scholars' Press.

Walters, David, Kelli Phythian, and Paul Anisef. 2006. *Understanding the Economic Integration of Immigrants: A Wage Decomposition of the Earnings Disparities between Native-born Canadians and Immigrants of Recent Cohorts*. CERIS Working Paper No. 42. Toronto: Joint Centre of Excellence for Research and Immigration and Settlement.

Walton-Roberts, Margaret W. 2011. "Immigration, the University, and the Welcoming Second Tier City." *Journal of International Migration & Integration* (19 April).

Ward, Olivia. 2004. "Battling to Understand Our Genocidal Instincts." *Toronto Star*, 5 June.

Warry, Wayne. 2007. *Ending Denial: Understanding Aboriginal Issues*. Peterborough, ON: Broadview Press.

Watson, William. 2008. "Still Speaking with Forked Tongues." *The Globe and Mail*, 20 August.

Wayland, Sarah V. 2006. *Unsettled: Legal and Policy Barriers for Newcomers to Canada: Literature Review*. Ottawa: Law Commission of Canada/Community Foundations of Canada.

We Interrupt the News/Youth Force. 2001. *How the New York Times Frames the News*. New York: Between the Lines.

Weaver, Sally M. 1981. *Making Canadian Indian Policy: The Hidden Agenda, 1968–1970*. Toronto: University of Toronto Press.

Weaver, Sally M. 1984. "Struggles of the Nation-State to Define Aboriginal Ethnicity: Canada and Australia," in *Minorities & Mother Country Imagery*. G. Gold (ed.). Pp. 182–210. Institute of Social and Economic Research No. 13. St. John's: Memorial University Press.

Weaver, Sally M. 1993a. "First Nations Women and Government Policy 1970–1992: Discrimination and Conflict," in *Changing Patterns: Women in Canada* (2nd ed.). Sandra Burt et al. (eds.). Toronto: McClelland & Stewart.

Weaver, Sally M. 1993b. "Self-Determination, National Pressure Groups, and Australian Aborigines: The National Aboriginal Conference 1983–1985," in *Ethnicity and Aboriginality: Case Studies in Ethnonationalism*. Michael D. Levin (ed.). Pp. 3–74. Toronto: University of Toronto Press.

Webb, Jim. 2010. "Diversity and the Myth of White Privilege." *Wall Street Journal*, 22 July.

Webber, Jeremy. 1994. *Reimaging Canada: Language, Culture, Community, and the Canadian Constitution*. Montreal/Kingston: McGill-Queen's University Press.

Weber, T. 2005. "Ottawa Targets Immigration." *The Globe and Mail*, 18 April.

Weinfeld, Morton. 2001. *Like Everyone Else but Different: The Paradoxical Success of Canadian Jews*. Toronto: McClelland & Stewart.

Weinfeld, Morton. 2005. "The Changing Dimensions of Contemporary Canadian Antisemitism," in *Contemporary Antisemitism: Canada and the World*. D.J. Penslar (ed.). Toronto: University of Toronto Press.

Weinfeld, Morton, and Lori A. Wilkinson. 1999. "Immigration, Diversity, and Minority Communities," in *Race and Ethnic Relations in Canada* (2nd ed.). Peter Li (ed.). Pp. 55–87. Toronto: Oxford University Press.

Weisberger, Bernard A. 1999. "Natives and Other Americans." *American Heritage* (May/June), 14–19.

Wente, Margaret. 2007a. "The Culture Gap in Immigrant Homes." *The Globe and Mail*, 13 December.

Wente, Margaret. 2007b. "Immigration and Identity: A Taste of Things to Come." *The Globe and Mail*, 11 October.

Wente, Margaret. 2008. "On the Case for Black Schools." *The Globe and Mail*, 15 January.

Wesley-Esquimaux, C., 2009. "Trauma to Resilience: Notes on Decolonization," in *Restoring the Balance*. G. Valaskakis et al. (eds.). Pp. 13–34. Winnipeg: University of Manitoba Press.

Weston, Mary Ann. 2003. *Journalists and Indians: The Clash of Cultures*. Keynote speech on Symposium on American Indian Issues in the California Press, 21 February. Available online at **http://www.bluecorncomics.com/ weston.htm**

Wetherell, M., and J. Potter. 1993. *Mapping the Language of Racism: Discourse and the Legitimation of Exploitation*. New York: Columbia University Press.

Whitaker, Reginald A. 1991. *Double Standard: The Secret Story of Canadian Immigration*. Toronto: Lester and Orpen Dennys.

White, Ismail K. 2007. "When Race Matters and When It Doesn't: Racial Group Differences in Response to Racial Cues." *American Political Science Review, 101*(2), 339–350.

White, N J. 1999. "Beyond 2000: Home to the World." *Toronto Star*, 23 April.

White, Patrick. 2010. A Native Group Home and a Town's "Lynch Mob Mentality." *The Globe and Mail*, 15 July.

Whittington, Les. 1998. "Canada Hailed as a Model for the 21st Century." *Toronto Star*, 10 August.

Whyte, John D. 2007. "Multiculturalism Meets 'Reasonable Accommodation.'" *SIPP Policy Dialogue* (Fall), 4–5.

Widdowson, Frances. 2003. *Separate but Unequal: The Political Economy of Aboriginal Dependency*. Paper presented to the Annual Conference of the Canadian Political Sciences Association.

Widdowson, Frances, and Albert Howard. 2002. "The Aboriginal Industry's New Clothes." *Policy Options* (March), 30–35.

Widdowson, Frances, and Albert Howard. 2008. *Disrobing the Aboriginal Industry*. Montreal/ Kingston: McGill Queen's University Press.

Wilkins, Kerry (ed.). 2004. *Advancing Aboriginal Claims: Visions, Strategies, Directions*. Saskatoon: Purich Publishing.

Wilkinson, Richard G. 2005. *The Impact of Inequality— How to Make Sick Societies Healthier*. London: Routledge.

Willett, Cynthia. 1998. *Theorizing Multiculturalism: A Guide to the Current Debate*. Malden, MA: Blackwell.

Willis, Katie, and Brenda Yeoh (eds.). 2000. *Gender and Migration*. Northampton, MA: Edward Elgar Publishing.

Wilson, Clint C., Felix Gutierrez, and Lena M. Chao. 2003. *Racism, Sexism, and the Media. The Rise of Class Communication in Multicultural America* (3rd ed.). Thousand Oaks, CA: Sage.

Wilson, Daniel, and David Macdonald. 2010. *The Income Gap between Aboriginal Peoples and the Rest of Canada*. Ottawa: Canadian Centre for Policy Alternatives.

Wilson, Gary N. 2008. "Nested Federalism in Arctic Quebec: A Comparative Perspective." *Canadian Journal of Political Science, 41*(1), 71–92.

Winant, Howard. 1998. "Racism Today: Continuity and Change in the Post–Civil Rights Era." *Ethnic and Racial Studies, 21*(4), 89–97.

Winsor, Hugh. 2001. "The Medicine Man at Indian Affairs." *The Globe and Mail*, 27 August.

Winter, Elke. 2001. "National Unity versus Multiculturalism? Rethinking the Logic of Inclusion in Germany and Canada." *International Journal of Canadian Studies, 24*, 169–182.

Winter, Elke. 2007. "How Does the Nation Become Pluralist?" *Ethnicities, 7*(4), 483–518.

Winter, Elke. 2009. "The Dialectics of Multicultural Identity." *World Political Science Review, 5*(1).

Wise, Amanda, and S. Velayutham (eds.). 2009. *Everyday Multiculturalism*. London, UK: Palgrave.

Wise, Tim. 1999. "Exploring the Depths of Racist Socialization." *Z Magazine* (July/August), 17–18.

Wise, Tim. 2005. "Race to Our Credit: Denial, Privilege and Life as a Majority." Available online at **http://www.lipmagazine.org/~timwise/ RaceToOurCredit. html**

Wise, Tim. 2008. *Explaining White Privilege to the Deniers and Haters*. Available online at **http://www.redroom.com**

Wise, Tim. 2009. "Racism and Implicit Bias in Cambridge." *Racism Review*. Available online at **http://www.racismreview.com**

Wise, Tim. 2010. *Color-Blind. The Rise of Post-Racial Politics and the Retreat from Racial Equity*. San Francisco, CA: City Lights Publishing.

Witt, Shirley Hill. 1984. "Native Women Today: Sexism and the Indian Woman," in *Feminist Frameworks*. A. Jaggar and P. Rothenberg (eds.). Pp. 23–31. Toronto: McGraw-Hill.

Wiwa, Ken. 2001. "Black, White, and Colourful." *The Globe and Mail*, 15 September.

Wiwa, Ken. 2003. "The Fusion Generation." *The Globe and Mail*, 12 June.

Wong, Jan. 1998. "Why Should I? This Is My Home." *The Globe and Mail*, 26 November.

Wong, Lloyd. 2008. "Multiculturalism and Ethnic Pluralism in Sociology. An Analysis of the Fragmentation Position Discourse." *Canadian Ethnic Studies* (Spring).

Wood, Patricia, and Liette Gilbert. 2005. "Multiculturalism in Canada: Accidental Discourse, Alternative Vision, Urban Practice." *International Journal of Urban and Regional Research, 29*(3), 679–691.

Woodward, Jonathan. 2005. "B.C. Farms Face Crackdown Over Migrants." *The Globe and Mail*, 6 October.

Wortley, Scot. 2005. *Bias-free Policing: The Kingston Data Collection Project: Preliminary Results*. Toronto: University of Toronto and the Centre for Excellence for Research on Immigration and Settlement.

Wrench, John. 2007. *Diversity Management and Discrimination: Immigrants and Ethnic Minorities in the EU*. Burlington, VT: Ashgate Publishers.

Wright, Pike. 2007. "Essay of Borat and Sarah Silverman for Make Benefit of Cultural Learnings About Racism." *This Magazine* (January/February), 42–43.

Wrzesnewskyj, Borys. 2005. "Hell Is Still Darfur." *The Globe and Mail*, 31 October.

Xu, Kathy. 2009. "Public Service Remains Short on Visible Minorities' Proportional Representation." *Epoch Times*, 16 September.

Yamato, Gloria. 2001. "Racism: Something about the Subject That Makes It Hard to Name," in *Race, Class, and Gender: An Anthology*. Margaret L. Andersen and Patricia Hill Collins (eds.). Pp. 150–158. Scarborough, ON: Wadsworth/Nelson.

Yelaja, Prithi, and Nicholas Keung. 2005. "Living Is Where It's Like Home." *Toronto Star*, June.

Yinger, J. Milton. 1994. *Ethnicity: Source of Strength? Source of Conflict?* Albany, NY: SUNY Press.

Yoshino, Kenji. 2006. "The Pressure to Cover." *New York Times Magazine*, 15 January.

Young, Iris Marion. 1990. *Justice and the Politics of Difference*. Princeton: Princeton University Press.

Young, Iris Marion. 2005. "Self-Determination as Non-Domination." *Ethnicities, 5*(2), 139–159.

Yu, Soojin, and Anthony Heath. 2007. "Inclusion for All but Aboriginals in Canada," in *Unequal Chances: Ethnic Minorities in Western Labour Markets*. A. Heath and S.Y. Cheung (eds.). Pp. 181–220. New York: Oxford University Press.

Yuval-Davis, Nira. 2007. "Intersectionality, Citizenship and Contemporary Politics of Belonging." *Critical Review of International Social and Political Philosophy, 10*(4), 561–574.

Zachariah, Mathew, Allan Sheppard, and Leona Barrett (eds.). 2004. *Canadian Multiculturalism: Dreams, Realities, and Expectations*. Edmonton: Canadian Multicultural Education Foundation.

Zaman, Habiba. 2006. *Breaking the Iron Wall: Decommodification and Immigrant Women's Labor in Canada*. Lanham, MD: Lexington Books.

Zaman, Habiba. 2007. "Neo-Liberal Policies and Immigrant Women in Canada." *Neo-Liberalism, State Power, and Global Governance, 3*, 145–153.

Zaman, Habiba. 2010. "Asian Immigrants' Vision of an Alternative Society in Australia and Canada: Impossibly Utopian or Simply Social Justice?" *Journal of Identity and Migration Studies, 4*(1), 2–23.

Zawilski, Valerie (ed.). 2010. *Social Inequality in Canada: A Reader on the Intersections of Gender, Race, and Class*. Toronto: Oxford University Press.

Zerbisias, Antonia. 2008. "Men Hardwired to Be Extreme," *Toronto Star*, 5 March.

Zhou, Min. 1997. "Segmented Assimilation: Issues, Controversies, and Recent Research on the New Second Generation." *International Migration Review, 31*(4), 975–1008.

Zick, A., T.F. Pettigrew, and U. Wagner. 2008. "Ethnic Prejudice and Discrimination in Europe." *Journal of Social Issues, 64*(2), 233–251.

Zine, Jasmin. 2002. "Inclusive Schooling in a Pluralistic Society." *Education Canada, 42*(3).

Zinn, Maxine Baca, Pierette Hondagneu-Sotelo, and Michael A. Messner (eds.). 2011. *Gender through the Prism of Difference*. New York: Oxford University Press.

Index